# Learning and Literature in Anglo-Saxon England

Peter Clemoes

# LEARNING AND LITERATURE IN ANGLO-SAXON ENGLAND

STUDIES PRESENTED TO PETER CLEMOES
ON THE OCCASION OF HIS
SIXTY-FIFTH BIRTHDAY

EDITED BY
MICHAEL LAPIDGE
AND
HELMUT GNEUSS

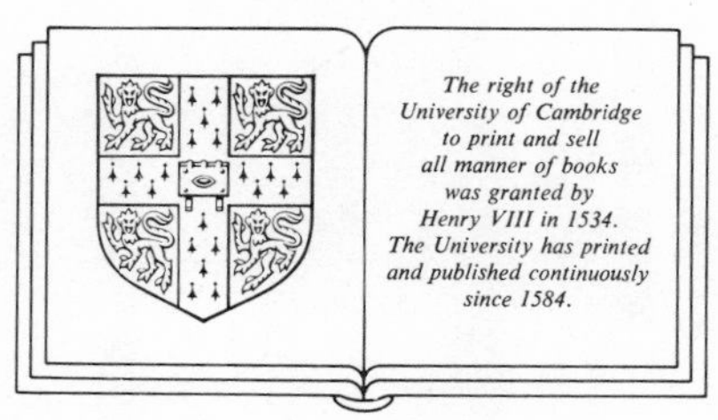
The right of the
University of Cambridge
to print and sell
all manner of books
was granted by
Henry VIII in 1534.
The University has printed
and published continuously
since 1584.

CAMBRIDGE UNIVERSITY PRESS

CAMBRIDGE
LONDON NEW YORK NEW ROCHELLE
MELBOURNE SYDNEY

Published by the Press Syndicate of the University of Cambridge
The Pitt Building, Trumpington Street, Cambridge CB2 1RP
32 East 57th Street, New York, NY 10022, USA
10 Stamford Road, Oakleigh, Melbourne 3166, Australia



First published 1985

Printed in Great Britain at
the University Press, Cambridge

Library of Congress catalogue card number: 84-23806

*British Library Cataloguing in Publication Data*

Learning and literature in Anglo-Saxon England:
studies presented to Peter Clemoes on the
occasion of his sixty-fifth birthday.
1. Civilization, Anglo-Saxon 2. Great Britain
Civilization—To 1066
I. Clemoes, Peter II. Lapidge, Michael
III. Gneuss, Helmut
942.01 DA152.2

ISBN 0 521 25902 9



SE

# Contents

# Illustrations

PLATES



FIGURES

## ACKNOWLEDGEMENTS

Permission to publish a photograph or photographs has been granted by: the Bodleian Library, Oxford (pl. I); the British Library Board (pls. II–IV, VI–VIII and XI); His Grace the Archbishop of Canterbury and the Trustees of Lambeth Palace Library, London (pl. V); the Master and Fellows of Corpus Christi College, Cambridge (pls. IX and X); the Director of the Kunstsammlungen, Veste Coburg (pl. XII); the Director of the Stiftsbibliothek, St Gallen (pl. XIII); the Director of the Stiftsarchiv, St Gallen (pls. XIV and XVI); the Director of the Zentralbibliothek, Zürich (pl. XV); and to Mr J. E. Leigh, Cambridge (frontispiece). A grant from Trinity College, Cambridge towards the cost of printing the plates is also gratefully acknowledged.

The Editors wish to express their gratitude to Miss Rosemary Graham for meticulous and unstinting help with sub-editorial work; to Dr Peter Richards of the Cambridge University Press for his creative interest in the volume; and to Dr Karl Toth and Mr Alfred Wollmann for help with the indexing.

# Preface

When Peter Clemoes recently retired from his post as Elrington and Bosworth Professor of Anglo-Saxon in the University of Cambridge, he could look back with satisfaction on a very successful scholarly career. The years of his tenure of that Chair, from 1969 to 1982, coincided with a period of severe financial difficulties for British universities, and it is a tribute to his remarkable administrative skill and vision that he was able to maintain the Department of Anglo-Saxon, Norse, and Celtic in Cambridge as an internationally recognized centre of excellence in the field, and even to extend the range of its teaching programme into such fields as Insular Latin and palaeography so that it more nearly reflected his own interdisciplinary conception of Anglo-Saxon studies. These same years also saw many significant developments in the field of Anglo-Saxon studies at large, and he was directly involved in many of them. For a number of years, for example, he was general editor of the series Early English Manuscripts in Facsimile. More important, he was chief editor of *Anglo-Saxon England* from its inception in 1972 until 1982 (and continues his involvement with the journal as one of three executive editors). Here too his enthusiasm for interdisciplinary approaches to Anglo-Saxon studies and his meticulous concern with the accurate presentation of scholarly argument and evidence have secured *Anglo-Saxon England*'s reputation as the principal periodical publication in the field. But he has also been active in his own scholarly right. His early work on Ælfric – and particularly on the chronology of Ælfric's writings – laid the foundation for all subsequent study of that author. His work on the authorship of the Old English Hexateuch inaugurated a new era of Byrhtferth studies. His various articles on Old English poetry have been seminal, and it is welcome news that his abiding interest in the style of Old English poetry is about to issue in a book on that subject.

In appreciation of his enduring contributions to the field of Anglo-Saxon studies we, his friends and colleagues, have written the present collection of essays – all, we hope, on aspects of the subject close to his own heart – to mark the occasion of his sixty-fifth birthday, which falls in 1985. It is particularly gratifying to note that this same year is to see him preside in Cambridge at the second meeting of the International Society of Anglo-Saxonists as that Society's President. In this auspicious year, therefore, we offer the present book to Peter with our very best wishes for his present and future work in Anglo-Saxon studies.

MICHAEL LAPIDGE
HELMUT GNEUSS

# Abbreviations

| | |
|---|---|
| *AAe* | *Archaeologia Aeliana* |
| *AB* | *Analecta Bollandiana* |
| *AntJ* | *Antiquaries Journal* |
| *ArchJ* | *Archaeological Journal* |
| ASC | Anglo-Saxon Chronicle |
| *ASE* | *Anglo-Saxon England* |
| *ASNSL* | *Archiv für das Studium der neueren Sprachen und Literaturen* |
| ASPR | The Anglo-Saxon Poetic Records, ed. G. P. Krapp and E. V. K. Dobbie, 6 vols. (New York, 1931–42) |
| BAR | British Archaeological Reports, British series (Oxford) |
| *BGDSL* | *Beiträge zur Geschichte der deutschen Sprache und Literatur* |
| *BHL* | [Bollandists], *Bibliotheca Hagiographica Latina*, 2 vols. (Brussels, 1899–1901) |
| BL | British Library manuscript |
| BN | Bibliothèque Nationale |
| *CA* | *Current Archaeology* |
| CCSL | Corpus Christianorum, Series Latina (Turnhout) |
| CM | Continuatio Mediaevalis |
| CSEL | Corpus Scriptorum Ecclesiasticorum Latinorum (Vienna) |
| EEMF | Early English Manuscripts in Facsimile (Copenhagen) |
| EETS | Early English Text Society |
| e.s. | extra series |
| o.s. | original series |
| s.s. | supplementary series |
| *EHD* | D. Whitelock, *English Historical Documents c. 500–1042*, 2nd ed. (London, 1979) |
| *EHR* | *English Historical Review* |
| *ELN* | *English Language Notes* |
| EPNS | English Place-Name Society |
| *ES* | *English Studies* |

| | |
|---|---|
| *FS* | *Frühmittelalterliche Studien* |
| HBS | Henry Bradshaw Society Publications |
| *HE* | Bede's *Historia ecclesiastica gentis Anglorum* |
| *JBAA* | *Journal of the British Archaeological Association* |
| *JEGP* | *Journal of English and Germanic Philology* |
| *JEH* | *Journal of Ecclesiastical History* |
| *JTS* | *Journal of Theological Studies* |
| *MÆ* | *Medium Ævum* |
| MGH | Monumenta Germaniae Historica |
| Auct. antiq. | Auctores antiquissimi |
| Epist. | Epistolae Aevi Carolini |
| Epist. select. | Epistolae selectae |
| PLAC | Poetae Latini Aevi Carolini |
| Script. | Scriptores |
| Script. rer. Meroving. | Scriptores rerum Merovingicarum |
| *MLR* | *Modern Language Review* |
| *MP* | *Modern Philology* |
| *MS* | *Mediaeval Studies* |
| *NM* | *Neuphilologische Mitteilungen* |
| *N&Q* | *Notes & Queries* |
| *OED* | *Oxford English Dictionary* |
| *OEN* | *Old English Newsletter* |
| *PBA* | *Proceedings of the British Academy* |
| PL | Patrologia Latina, ed. J. P. Migne (Paris, 1841–64) |
| *PMLA* | *Publications of the Modern Language Association of America* |
| *RB* | *Revue bénédictine* |
| *RHE* | *Revue d'histoire ecclésiastique* |
| *SM* | *Studi medievali* |
| *SN* | *Studia Neophilologica* |
| *TPS* | *Transactions of the Philological Society* |
| *YAJ* | *Yorkshire Archaeological Journal* |
| *ZDA* | *Zeitschrift für deutsches Altertum* |

# The writings of Peter Clemoes

*Liturgical Influence on Punctuation in Late Old English and Early Middle English Manuscripts*, Department of Anglo-Saxon Occasional Papers 1 (Cambridge, 1952) [repr. *OEN* Subsidia 4 (Binghamton, NY: CEMERS, SUNY, 1980)].

'The Chronology of Ælfric's Works', *The Anglo-Saxons: Studies in some Aspects of their History and Culture presented to Bruce Dickins*, ed. P. Clemoes (London: Bowes and Bowes, 1959), pp. 212–47 [repr. *OEN* Subsidia 5 (Binghamton, NY: CEMERS, SUNY, 1980)].

'The Old English Benedictine Office, Corpus Christi College, Cambridge, MS 190, and the Relations between Ælfric and Wulfstan: a Reconsideration', *Anglia* 78 (1960), 265–83.

'Supplementary Introduction', *Angelsächsische Homilien und Heiligenleben*, ed. B. Assmann, Bibliothek der angelsächsischen Prosa 3 (Kassel, 1889) [repr. Darmstadt: Wissenschaftliche Buchgesellschaft, 1964], pp. xi–xxxv.

*Ælfric's First Series of Catholic Homilies: B. M. Royal 7 C. XII, fols. 4–218*, EEMF 13 (Copenhagen: Rosenkilde and Bagger, 1966) [with N. Eliason].

'Supplement to the Introduction', *Die Hirtenbriefe Ælfrics*, ed. B. Fehr, Bibliothek der angelsächsischen Prosa 9 (Hamburg, 1914) [repr. Darmstadt: Wissenschaftliche Buchgesellschaft, 1966], pp. cxxvii–cxlviii.

'Ælfric', *Continuations and Beginnings*, ed. E. G. Stanley (London: Nelson, 1966), pp. 176–209.

'*Mens absentia cogitans* in *The Seafarer* and *The Wanderer*', *Medieval Literature and Civilisation: Studies in Memory of G. N. Garmonsway*, ed. D. A. Pearsall and R. A. Waldron (London: Athlone Press, 1969), pp. 62–77.

*Rhythm and Cosmic Order in Old English Christian Literature: an Inaugural Lecture* (Cambridge: Cambridge University Press, 1970).

'Cynewulf's Image of the Ascension', *England before the Norman Conquest: Studies in Primary Sources presented to Dorothy Whitelock*, ed. P. Clemoes and K. Hughes (Cambridge: Cambridge University Press, 1971), pp. 293–304.

'The Common Origin of Ælfric Fragments at New Haven, Oxford, Cambridge and Bloomington', *Old English Studies in Honor of John C. Pope*, ed. R. B. Burlin and E. C. Irving, Jr (Toronto and Buffalo: University of Toronto Press, 1974), pp. 285–326 [with R. L. Collins].

*The Old English Illustrated Hexateuch: B. M. Cotton Claudius B. iv*, EEMF 18 (Copenhagen: Rosenkilde and Bagger, 1974) [with C. R. Dodwell].

'De quelques articulations entre présent et passé dans la technique narrative vieil-anglaise', *Actes du Colloque de l'Association des médiévistes de l'enseignement supérieur sur les techniques narratives au moyen âge*, ed. A. Crépin (Amiens, 1974), pp. 5–21.

'Late Old English Literature', *Tenth Century Studies: Essays in Commemoration of the Millennium of the Council of Winchester and 'Regularis Concordia'*, ed. D. Parsons (London and Chichester: Phillimore, 1975), pp. 103–14 and 230–3.

'Action in *Beowulf* and our Perception of it', *Old English Poetry: Essays on Style*, ed. D. G. Calder (Berkeley, Los Angeles and London: University of California Press, 1979), pp. 147–68.

'Style as the Criterion for Dating the Composition of *Beowulf*', *The Dating of Beowulf*, ed. C. Chase (Toronto, Buffalo and London: University of Toronto Press, 1981), pp. 173–85.

'A Memorial Address [on Dorothy Whitelock]', *OEN* 16.1 (1982), 15–17.

*The Cult of St Oswald on the Continent*, Jarrow Lecture 1983 (Jarrow, 1984).

'"Symbolic" Language in Old English Poetry' (forthcoming).

'Language in Context: "Her" in the 890 *Anglo-Saxon Chronicle*', *Leeds Stud. in Eng.* 16 (1985), forthcoming.

# I

# The Background

## Books, Libraries and Learning in Anglo-Saxon England

# Whitby as a centre of learning in the seventh century

PETER HUNTER BLAIR (†)

[In the middle years of the seventh century, particularly the 650s and 660s, the fortunes of the English church were at their nadir. The impetus of the Gregorian mission had all but petered out, and many parts of the country which had early been converted lapsed into paganism. It had proved impossible as yet to implement Gregory's far-sighted design for the establishment of English dioceses, and many bishoprics were vacant. We know from hindsight that regeneration was to begin with the arrival in Canterbury of Archbishop Theodore in 669, but contemporaries during those decades could have had little reason for optimism. Nevertheless, during those dark decades of the mid-seventh century there was one ecclesiastical centre in England which shone uniquely, a metaphorical lighthouse as it were, and illuminated the entire country: Hild's monastic foundation at Whitby. From Whitby came a number of important bishops of late-seventh-century England. At Whitby the untutored peasant Cædmon first turned biblical themes into English verse. It was not by accident that one of the earliest and most famous ecclesiastical gatherings was held at Whitby in 664. The following pages are an attempt to illustrate and estimate the unique contribution made by Whitby to the life of the seventh-century English church.][1]

## ABBESS HILD AND THE FOUNDATION OF WHITBY

We cannot think of Whitby without immediately thinking of Hild.[2] Indeed the early chronology of the monastery depends upon one well-established date,

1 [Peter Hunter Blair, formerly Reader in the Department of Anglo-Saxon, Norse, and Celtic in the University of Cambridge, died in September 1982. Shortly before his death he had discussed with members of the Department the possibility of assembling a collection of essays in honour of Peter Clemoes (his colleague at Emmanuel College), and it is through the kindness of his widow, Pauline Hunter Blair, that the present essay is included here. The essay had been delivered as a public lecture in Cambridge in the Michaelmas Term 1981, and he was actively engaged in preparing it for publication. At the time of his death he had thoroughly revised the sections on Hild and the synod of Whitby, and had drafted the Appendix; the remainder was in preliminary draft. Additions made by the editors to his incomplete typescript are given within square brackets.]

2 [A valuable recent study of Hild is C. E. Fell, 'Hild, Abbess of Streonaeshalch', *Hagiography and Medieval Literature: a Symposium*, ed. H. Bekker-Nielsen *et al.* (Odense, 1981), pp. 76–99.

that of Hild's death, which is recorded in two reliable sources,[3] Bede's *Historia ecclesiastica* and Willibrord's Calendar. Bede specifies not only the year, 680, but also the day of the month, 17 November, as well as Hild's age, 'cum esset LXVI annorum'.[4] In Willibrord's Calendar the entry *Hildae abbatissae* occurs at *.xv. kl. Dec.* (= 17 November); the entry is not in the primary hand, but it is unlikely to be later than the eighth century.[5] Since we do not know the day of her birth, we can say only that she is likely to have been born in 614. Her father, Hereric, is described by Bede as 'nepos Eduini regis', and if we translate *nepos* as 'nephew', Hereric's father, and so Hild's grandfather, will have been a brother of Edwin.[6] Her mother was called Breguswith,[7] but nothing is known of her origin, and she had a sister, Hereswith, who became the mother of an East Anglian king, Ealdwulf.[8] Hereric, Bede tells us, was poisoned while living in exile under a British king, Cerdic.[9] Hild,[10] then, of noble or even royal

Earlier studies (of dubious value) include D. Haigh, 'The Monasteries of St Heiu and St Hild', *Yorkshire Archaeol. Jnl* 3 (1875), 349–91; G. Buchannan, 'The Feast Days of St Hilda', *ibid.* 17 (1903), 249–53; and I. G. Sieveking, 'St Hild and her Abbey at Whitby', *The Antiquary* 40 (1904), 327–40.]

3 [The possibility of another early source for Hild's life has recently been mooted by J. E. Cross, 'A Lost Life of Hilda of Whitby: the Evidence of the *Old English Martyrology*', *Acta* 6 (1979), 21–43; see also below, p. 248. Cross's argument for a lost *uita*, which is based on the occurrence of a few tiny details in the Old English Martyrology which are not found in Bede, is suggestive but not utterly convincing.]

4 *Bede's Ecclesiastical History of the English People*, ed. B. Colgrave and R. A. B. Mynors (Oxford, 1969) (hereafter abbreviated *HE*); the quotation is found at *HE* IV.23 (21). Note that elsewhere Colgrave errs in dating Hild's death to 17 May (*The Earliest Life of Gregory the Great*, ed. B. Colgrave (Lawrence, Kan., 1968), p. 38).

5 *The Calendar of St Willibrord*, ed. H. A. Wilson, HBS 55 (London, 1918), p. xxii and pl. XI.

6 Edwin was killed in 633 at the age of 48 (*HE* II.20) and so born in 585. If Hild was born in 614, the gap between her birth and that of Edwin (her great-uncle) was only twenty-nine years: short, but not impossibly so. It may suggest either that her grandfather was considerably older than Edwin, or that *nepos* is used here in the looser sense of 'cousin'. Bede might not have known the exact relationship, since he evidently did not know the name of Hild's grandfather.

7 *HE* IV.23 (21). The first element of the name (meaning 'prince' or 'ruler') is uncommon, but would be appropriate to one of royal or noble birth; see H. Ström, *Old English Personal Names in Bede's History*, Lund Stud. in Eng. 8 (Lund, 1939), 9–10.

8 *Ibid.*

9 *Ibid.* It has been conjectured that the Cerdic in question was ruler of Elmet, a British kingdom, and that Edwin's subsequent expulsion of Cerdic was part of a campaign of vengeance for the death of Hereric; see F. M. Stenton, *Anglo-Saxon England*, 3rd ed. (Oxford, 1971), p. 80, and *EHD*, p. 262.

10 This is the form regularly used by Bede in the nominative, with appropriate inflexions for the oblique cases. The name, meaning 'war' or 'battle', is a common theme in Germanic personal names, but we do not know whether it is an original appellative or a hypocoristic form shortened from a compound; see Ström, *Old English Personal Names*, pp. 23 and 83. [Note that Fell ('Hild, Abbess of Streonaeshalch', p. 78) argues persuasively that Hild *is* a hypocoristic form of either Hildigyth, Hildithryth or Hildeburg.]

parentage, was born in a part of the country which had not yet been visited by any member of the Augustinian mission in Kent or of the Columban mission in Iona, and which was dominated by the pagan ruler Æthelfrith. It is probable that her parents, like Edwin himself, had been living in exile to escape the murderous feuding which characterized the rivalry of different royal families in this period.

Between the ages of two and nineteen, Hild will have been closely touched by three major events in Northumbrian history – the accession of Edwin after 12 April 616 (following the death of Æthelfrith), his baptism on 12 April 627 and his death on 12 October 633.[11] The conjecture that Edwin's expedition was to avenge the death of her father, and the reverence later paid to Edwin's relics at Whitby, may suggest that Edwin had taken the infant Hild under his protection, but if this can be no more than surmise, Hild's direct involvement in the second event is not open to question. Edwin was baptized 'cum cunctis gentis suae nobilibus ac plebe perplurima'.[12] No names are mentioned in this passage, but in a later passage Bede associates Hild's baptism directly with Edwin's. He writes (with Hild as the subject of the sentence) 'cum quo etiam rege [*sc.* Edwin] ad praedicationem beatae memoriae Paulini primi Nordanhymbrorum episcopi fidem et sacramenta Christi suscepit'.[13] The passage can only mean that Hild was baptized by Paulinus on the same day as Edwin and others of the nobility and common people, that is to say in York at Easter 627. She was then aged about fourteen and the occasion will have remained vividly in her memory, one to be recalled in her later years at Whitby. We must surely be right in assuming the presence also of Edwin's wife, Æthelburg, herself the Christian daughter of a Frankish Christian princess, Bertha, and the granddaughter of Charibert, Christian Frankish ruler of Paris. We do not know the date of Æthelburg's marriage to Edwin[14] and we have no evidence touching her relationship with Hild.

The year following Edwin's death on 12 October 633 was characterized by Bede as 'infaustus ille annus', marked by the apostasy of the English kings and the savagery of the Welsh invaders.[15] The widowed Æthelburg, her infant Eanflæd, and other children of the royal family, went to Kent under the protection of Paulinus, but there had been a change of ruler there and in order to find greater security Æthelburg sent two of the royal children, a son and a

11 On the complex problems of Northumbrian chronology in this period, see K. Harrison, *The Framework of Anglo-Saxon History to A.D. 900* (Cambridge, 1976), pp. 76–98, and M. Miller, 'The Dates of Deira', *ASE* 8 (1979), 35–61.

12 *HE* II.14.

13 *Ibid.* IV.23 (21).

14 See P. Hunter Blair, 'The Letters of Pope Boniface V and the Mission of Paulinus to Northumbria', *England before the Conquest*, ed. P. Clemoes and K. Hughes (Cambridge, 1971), pp. 5–13 [repr. P. Hunter Blair, *Anglo-Saxon Northumbria*, ed. M. Lapidge and Pauline Hunter Blair (London, 1984), no. XI].

15 *HE* III.1.

grandson of Edwin, to Gaul to be cared for by Dagobert, who was her friend.[16] The children were sent to Gaul because Æthelburg feared for their safety from the new kings in Kent (Eadbald) and Northumbria (Oswald), but both children died in Gaul in infancy and were buried there in a church with the honour due to royal children and innocents of Christ.[17] Nothing more is known of Æthelburg.

What happened to Hild? Bede goes directly from her baptism to her decision to abandon secular life, a decision which was followed by her withdrawal to East Anglia: 'erat namque propinqua regis illius'.[18] Bede believed that Hild was thirty-three when she decided to enter religious life, an event which should belong to 647, if she was born in 614. We are left with a gap of twenty years from her baptism and of fourteen from the death of Edwin. At some unknown date in this period Hild's sister, Hereswith, married into the East Anglian royal family.[19] Bede does not name Hereswith's husband and may not have known his name, but he does say that Hereswith became the mother of Ealdwulf who was later to become king of the East Angles. When Hild reached East Anglia she found that her sister had already left the country and was living as a nun in a Gaulish monastery. Of Hereswith's earlier life we know nothing, but, despite the difficulties of establishing the chronology of the East Anglian kings,[20] we do know that by 647 the saintly King Anna had been reigning for more than ten years, we believe that Hereswith's relationship to him was that of sister-in-law, and we know that in the 640s and later there was a remarkable movement of women of royal birth to the monasteries of northern Gaul. They went mostly, says Bede, to the houses of Faremoutiers-en-Brie, Chelles and Andelys-sur-Seine. Among them were a daughter of Anna (Æthelburg) and a stepdaughter (Sæthryth), both of whom became abbesses at Faremoutiers. Their aunt, Hereswith, went to Chelles which had itself been refounded by an Englishwoman.[21]

It would be wrong to speculate on Hild's whereabouts during the years 633–47,[22] but it would be equally wrong to ignore the fact of Hereswith's marriage and the likelihood that Hild will have been well informed about at least some of the events of her sister's married life in East Anglia. When Hild had determined to enter the religious life she went to East Anglia with the firm intention

[16] *Ibid.* II.20: 'qui erat amicus illius', an interesting pointer to continuing contact between Northumbria and Gaul. [17] *Ibid.* [18] *HE* IV.23 (21). [19] *Ibid.*

[20] See F. M. Stenton, 'The East Anglian Kings of the Seventh Century', *The Anglo-Saxons*, ed. P. Clemoes (London, 1959), pp. 43–52, and D. Whitelock, 'The Pre-Viking Age Church in East Anglia', *ASE* 1 (1972), 1–22.

[21] *HE* III.8. Both Chelles (near Paris) and Corbie (in Picardy) were founded by Balthild, who was sold overseas as a slave and became the wife of King Clovis II; see W. Levison, *England and the Continent in the Eighth Century* (Oxford, 1946), pp. 9–10.

[22] [Fell ('Hild, Abbess of Streonaeshalch', p. 80) speculates with some plausibility that Hild was married to a pagan during this period.]

of going thence to Gaul and ending her days in the monastery at Chelles to which her sister had already gone. In the mean while Aidan and his companions from Iona had reached Lindisfarne; they had been established there for some twelve years at the time of Hild's decision to go to Gaul. We have no evidence of a previous meeting between Hild and Aidan but such a meeting seems to be demanded, for it was at the summons of Aidan that Hild, against her own will, returned to Northumbria. Bede's account[23] clearly expresses the conflict felt by Hild between the attractions of life in northern Gaul (where several monasteries were recognized as centres of education for English women) and the more arduous task of establishing that kind of life in her native Northumbria, as yet scarcely removed from paganism.

Returning to Northumbria after her year in East Anglia, Hild was given a small estate on the north bank of the river Wear and there she lived a monastic life for a further year with a very small number of companions. We may presume, even if we are not told, that they were women. The site of the settlement is not known, but it was not the first women's house in Northumbria, nor was Hild herself the first Northumbrian woman to take monastic vows. This claim was made for Heiu, who had been consecrated by Aidan and became the abbess of a monastery at Hartlepool, founded not long before the house on the north bank of the Wear.[24] Soon after the establishment of Hartlepool, Heiu went 'ad ciuitatem Calcariam quae a gente Anglorum Kaelcacaestir appellatur', thought to be Tadcaster,[25] and Hild became abbess at Hartlepool, where she proceeded to organize a life regular in all respects, and where she was frequently visited by Aidan and other religious men who instructed her in the religious way of life. She remained at Hartlepool *aliquot annos*.[26] Hartlepool is generally said to have been a double house for both men and women, but we may doubt whether this will have been true of Heiu's own

23 *HE* IV.23 (21).

24 The name Heiu is of obscure origin; see T. J. M. van Els, *The Kassel Manuscript of Bede's 'Historia Ecclesiastica Gentis Anglorum' and its Old English Material* (Assen, 1972), p. 147. She is not found in the Lindisfarne *Liber uitae*, nor is anything known about her save her association with Hartlepool and *Kaelcacaestir*. There is no ground for the belief (noted by C. Plummer, *Venerabilis Baedae Opera Historica*, 2 vols. (Oxford, 1896) (hereafter Plummer) II, 245) that her name is preserved in the place-name Healaugh; see A. H. Smith, *The Place-Names of the West Riding of Yorkshire*, 8 vols., EPNS 30–7 (Cambridge, 1961–3) IV, 240–1. Nor should we credit the belief of D. H. Haigh (cited by Plummer, II, 245) that her name was to be seen on a gravestone from Hartlepool: no such stone now survives and some antiquaries tended to read what they wanted to see.

25 Smith, *The Place-Names of the West Riding of Yorkshire* IV, 76–7, and van Els, *The Kassel Manuscript*, pp. 154–5. *Kaelcacaestir* is attested only in this passage in Bede. The name Tadcaster does not occur before the eleventh century and we do not know when – provided the identification is correct – the one name replaced the other.

26 *HE* IV.23 (21). For remains of what seems to have been the monastic cemetery and of some timber buildings, see R. Cramp, 'Monastic Sites', *The Archaeology of Anglo-Saxon England*, ed. D. M. Wilson (London, 1976), pp. 201–52, at 220–3.

foundation, since it was Aidan who consecrated Heiu to the religious life and at this date the double house was not known in the Columban church. Two arguments have been advanced for thinking that Hartlepool was a double house in Hild's time. Bede tells us that Oftfor, later bishop among the Hwicce, studied 'in utroque Hildae abbatissae monasterio',[27] seeming thus to refer to Hartlepool and Whitby; but in the year of her death Hild founded a monastery at Hackness, and since Oftfor was not consecrated bishop until after Theodore's death in 690,[28] it is possible that he might have gone from Whitby to Hackness rather than from Hartlepool to Whitby. The second argument derives from the occurrence of both male and female names on inscribed memorial slabs from the cemetery at Hartlepool; but we do not know the date of these stones, and they cannot establish the point in themselves, since laymen might have been buried in the cemetery. Indeed one stone which bears both a male and a female name seems to point to lay burial.[29]

We cannot establish the chronology of Hild's movements exactly, but the year in East Anglia, the year north of the Wear and the move to Hartlepool will have fallen between 647, the year of her decision to enter religious life, and 31 August 651, when Aidan died. Her stay at Hartlepool extended beyond Aidan's death, for she was still there as abbess late in 655 when Osuiu sent her his infant daughter Ælfflæd after his victory over Penda in the battle at the *Uinued*. Two years later Hild acquired the estate which grew into what we know as the monastery of Whitby.[30] Bede does not give the date of its foundation and we can only infer that it was 657 by reference to the battle at the river *Uinued*.

Bede's first reference to the foundation of the monastery is in simple terms – 'ibi monasterium construxit'[31] – but his second reference is more elaborate. Part of this second passage has been translated as 'she undertook either to found or to set in order a monastery',[32] a translation which has given rise to a question whether Hild's foundation was *de novo* or merely the taking over of an existing monastic establishment such as might have been founded by some of the Irish monks who came to Northumbria with Aidan.[33] This doubt, however, seems to rest on a misunderstanding of Bede's Latin. The relevant passage reads in full: 'Cum ergo aliquot annos huic monasterio [*sc.* Hartlepool] regularis uitae institutioni multum intenta praeesset, contigit eam suscipere etiam construendum siue ordinandum monasterium in loco qui uocatur Streanaeshalch.'[34] To render *etiam . . . siue* as 'either . . . or' seems wrong in the

[27] *Ibid.* [28] See below, p. 28.

[29] For the inscribed stones from Hartlepool, see E. Okasha, *Hand-List of Anglo-Saxon Non-Runic Inscriptions* (Cambridge, 1971), pp. 76–9. Hartlepool IV (no. 46) has both the male name Uermund and the female name Torhtsuid.

[30] *HE* III.24. [31] *Ibid.* [32] *Ibid.* IV.23 (21) (the translation is Colgrave's).

[33] See Cramp, 'Monastic Sites', p. 223. [34] *HE* IV.23 (21).

context, the more so since *siue* is regularly used in post-classical Latin as the conjunctive 'and'. Moreover *ordinare* does not mean 'to set in order' in the sense of 'repair', but rather takes its meaning from 'regularis uitae institutioni' in the earlier part of the sentence. I would translate the passage: 'and so when she had governed this monastery (Hartlepool) for some years, closely occupied with the establishment of a life according to rule, it came about that she undertook also the building of, and the establishment of regular life in, a monastery in a place which is called *Streanaeshalch*'. Bede's emphasis throughout this passage is on Hild's concern for the establishment of life according to a rule both at Hartlepool and at Whitby.

The place-name Whitby is first recorded in Domesday Book, and being of Scandinavian origin it is not likely to be older than the tenth century.[35] Bede refers five times in the *Historia ecclesiastica* to the name by which it was known to him, and presumably also to Hild.[36] The best authenticated form of this name is *Strēanæshalch*.[37] On four of these five occasions he introduces the name with some such general term as 'locus qui dicitur' or 'monasterium quod uocatur', but on his second reference, and not as we might have expected on his first, he writes 'in monasterio quod dicitur Streaneshalch, quod interpretatur sinus fari'.[38] This passage raises three problems: the etymology of OE *Strēanæshalch*, the meaning of Bede's *sinus fari* and the relationship between the English name and the Latin gloss. *Halch* (*halh*, *healh*) is a common element in English place-names, occurring sometimes as a simplex, but usually as the second element in a compound, and rather less frequently in northern than in midland or southern counties.[39] Equated in glosses with Latin *angulus*, in place-names it usually takes its particular meaning from topographical features indicating a nook, a secluded hollow or a piece of land in some way cut off from its surroundings. Despite much discussion no agreement has been reached about the element *Strēanæs-*.[40] Some have taken it as an unrecorded personal name **Strēona*, seen as a hypocoristic form related to the compound names *Strēonberct* and *Strēonuulf* found in the Lindisfarne *Liber uitae*.[41] *Strēona* is

35 See A. H. Smith, *The Place-Names of the North Riding of Yorkshire*, EPNS 5 (Cambridge, 1928), 126.

36 *HE* III.24 and 25, IV.23 (21) (twice) and IV.26 (24).

37 *Strean-* is found invariably in MSS K and L, and normally in M and C (though in one passage the latter has *stren-*); B has *Strean-* once, but is defective in the other passages. Minor variations between *-æs* and *-es* and between *-halch* and *-halh* are of no significance for the present purpose. See van Els, *The Kassel Manuscript*, pp. 105 and 168, for references to earlier discussions of the place-name *Streanæshalch*.

38 *HE* III.25.

39 See A. H. Smith, *English Place-Name Elements*, 2 vols., EPNS 25–6 (Cambridge, 1956) I, 223–4.

40 See van Els, *The Kassel Manuscript*, pp. 168–9, and the references there cited.

41 *The Oldest English Texts*, ed. H. Sweet, EETS o.s. 83 (London, 1885), 157, line 109, and 162, line 302. On *eo/ea* in Northumbrian texts, see A. Campbell, *Old English Grammar* (Oxford, 1959), §278, and Ström, *Old English Personal Names*, pp. 98–9.

familiar as the by-name applied to Eadric, the notorious ealdorman of Mercia in the reign of Æthelred the Unready. Others take the element as related to OE *gestrēon*, meaning 'gain', 'treasure', and also 'progeny', 'generation', from which indeed a personal name might have evolved. Both elements occur in the Yorkshire place-name Strensall[42] and in a lost Worcestershire field-name *Streonenhalh*.[43] If the first element is taken as a personal name then 'Streon's nook of land'[44] is a possible meaning, but if it is taken as an abstract noun the choice is widened to variants such as 'nook of treasure' or 'corner of generation'.[45]

Bede's gloss *sinus fari* has commonly been translated 'the bay of the lighthouse',[46] but there are objections to such a translation. There is no evidence for any Anglo-Saxon lighthouse either at Whitby or anywhere else in Anglo-Saxon England. Only two lighthouses are known from Roman Britain, and they stood one on each side of Dover harbour.[47] Since the Roman work at one of them still rises to a height of 43 feet, both are likely to have been standing in the seventh century, and it may be that Bede had heard of them. Moreover, it is very difficult to see how 'the bay of the lighthouse' can be equated with any of the possible meanings of *Strēonæshalh*. To overcome this difficulty it has been suggested that Bede's *fari* is a mistake for *fare* or *farae* (from medieval Latin *fara*, meaning 'strain', 'descent'), so providing a possible equation with *strēon-*,[48] but Bede did not make mistakes of this kind. Nor can we easily invoke scribal error or textual corruption. The text of the *Historia ecclesiastica* has been transmitted with great accuracy, and it is only on the rarest of occasions that emendation seems necessary or permissible.[49] We must accept *fari* as what Bede wrote, but what did he mean? He does not use the word again in the *Historia ecclesiastica*; but in *De temporum ratione*, in a passage in which he seeks to explain how it comes about that the moon sometimes seems to be higher in the sky than the sun, he describes a church illuminated with hanging lamps in honour of some saint's festival in the following terms:

42 See Smith, *The Place-Names of the North Riding of Yorkshire*, p. 13. The remains of the monastery discovered at Whitby rule out any possibility of Bede's *Streonæshalh* being identified with the modern Strensall.

43 A. Mawer and F. M. Stenton, *The Place-Names of Worcestershire*, EPNS 4 (Cambridge, 1927), 398.

44 As, for example, by K. Cameron, *English Place-Names* (London, 1961), p. 80.

45 Cf. *EHD*, p. 696, where Bede's *sinus fari* is so rendered.

46 So Colgrave in *Bede's Ecclesiastical History*, p. 299.

47 R. G. Collingwood and I. Richmond, *The Archaeology of Roman Britain*, 2nd ed. (London, 1969), pp. 66–7.

48 Smith, *The Place-Names of the North Riding of Yorkshire*, p. 126, and accepted by Whitelock, *EHD*, p. 696.

49 See R. A. B. Mynors in *Bede's Ecclesiastical History*, pp. xxxix–xl.

Inter quas duae maximae ac mirandi operis fari suis quaeque suspensae ad laquearia catenis, sed quae tibi ex his intranti uicinior ipsa quoque est subiacenti pauimento uicinior; tanta autem uastitas domus, tanta est longe distantium celsitudo farorum, ut magis nocturno uiso lucem comasque flammarum quam ipsa ignium ualeas uasa dignoscere. Nimirum ubi faribus appropinquare incipiens recto intuitu oculos ad faros et per faros ad contraposita laneariorum uel parietis loca sustuleris, illa tibi altior quae uicinior est farus apparebit.[50]

The context indicates a meaning of 'lamp' or 'chandelier', a meaning which is common in other medieval sources. Gregory of Tours uses the word more than once in an abstract sense as meaning 'a blaze of light' ('pharus magna per caelum discurrens').[51] This usage suggests that Bede's *sinus fari* could be translated 'the bay of (the) light', but the word *sinus* itself invites further attention. Bede uses *sinus* in its geographical sense,[52] 'a bay of the sea', but he was well aware that its primary meaning referred to a fold in a garment, and hence (though not in a strictly physical sense) to the bosom. He had met it in this sense in both the Old and the New Testaments, notably in the account of Lazarus and Dives: 'Factum est autem, ut moreretur et portaretur ab angelis in sinum Abrahae. Mortuus est autem et diues, et sepultus est in inferno. Eleuans autem oculos suos, cum esset in tormentis, uidit Abraham a longe, et Lazarum in sinu eius' (Luke XVI. 22–3). In his commentary on this passage Bede writes, in words borrowed from Gregory the Great, 'sinus Abraham requies est beatorum pauperum'.[53]

Let us now look again at Bede's words 'in monasterio quod dicitur Streaneshalch quod interpretatur sinus fari'. There are more than twenty passages in the *Historia ecclesiastica* in which Bede glosses or interprets a name. In more than half of these he uses the simple formula *id est*, as for example 'Heruteu id est Insula Cerui' (*HE* III.24). In other passages he uses such phrases as 'Alcluith quod lingua eorum significat' (I.2), 'ad Ciuitatem Legionum quae a gente Anglorum Legacaestir . . . appellatur' (II.2), and other similar phrases. In no case other than that of *Streaneshalch* does he use the phrase 'quod interpretatur'. Recalling the Vulgate usage of *sinus* we can now see that Bede is not here translating an English name into a Latin equivalent. He did not write 'Streaneshalch id est Sinus Fari'. He is rather interpreting or expounding the name in an exegetical manner, not engaging in an etymological exercise. But why then 'the bay of (the) light'? We find the answer later in the *Historia ecclesiastica* in the chapter which Bede devotes entirely to Hild.[54]

[50] *Bedae Opera de Temporibus*, ed. C. W. Jones (Cambridge, Mass., 1943), pp. 229–30 (ch. 26).

[51] *Historiae* VII.11 [52] *HE* I.1.

[53] *In Lucae Evangelium Expositio*, ed. D. Hurst, CCSL 120 (Turnhout, 1960), 303.

[54] *HE* IV.23 (21).

He tells here of her mother Breguswith and of the dream she had when Hild was still an infant and when Hild's father, Hereric, was in exile later to be poisoned. In her dream, as Breguswith looked for her husband, she found a most precious necklace under her garment and, as she gazed at it, it seemed to spread such a blaze of light that it filled all Britain with its splendour. This dream (Bede writes) was fulfilled in her daughter Hild, for Hild's life was an example of the works of light. The metaphor seems clear: *sinus fari* is both 'the bay of light' and 'the bosom of light', the necklace in the folds of Breguswith's garment, the infant Hild herself and the monastery at Whitby where the Celtic ways were rejected in favour of the Roman.

Hild was aged about forty-three when she founded the monastery at Whitby, ten years having passed since her decision to enter the religious life and a further twenty-three remaining before her death in 680, but of these she was ill for the last six. No contemporary written records of Whitby origin have survived from this period (see below, p. 29). Excavation has yielded the location of the monastic cemetery and the plans of some buildings, but not in such detail as to show the general layout of the monastery.[55] The original foundation is said to have comprised ten households, a nucleus which is likely to have been enlarged by later endowments, but no record of any such gifts has survived. We know that there was a church dedicated to St Peter and that within it there was an altar dedicated to St Gregory,[56] but we do not know where it lay, nor do we know whether these strongly Roman dedications date from the earliest days of the foundation or from a later period. The rule observed at Whitby was the same as that observed at Hartlepool, and since Hild's instruction is said to have been mainly at the hands of Aidan we may surmise that the earliest Whitby rule will have resembled the rule observed in the early days at Lindisfarne.[57] The community undoubtedly housed both men and women, a fact which may point to some Gaulish influences, perhaps mediated through East Anglia.[58]

Because Hild died before the writing of the earliest Northumbrian

[55] For the archaeological remains at Whitby, see C. Peers and C. A. R. Radford, 'The Saxon Monastery at Whitby', *Archaeologia* 89 (1943), 27–88, as well as Cramp, 'Monastic Sites', pp. 223–9; see also Cramp's 'Analysis of the Finds of Whitby Abbey', *The Archaeology of Anglo-Saxon England*, ed. Wilson, pp. 453–7, and P. Rahtz, 'The Building Plan of the Anglo-Saxon Monastery of Whitby Abbey', *ibid.*, pp. 459–62. The plan redrawn by Rahtz and used by Cramp as fig. 5.7 (*ibid.* p. 224) does not show the location of the monastic cemetery, but this can be seen in Peers and Radford, 'The Saxon Monastery', pl. XXI.

[56] *HE* III.24; cf. also *The Earliest Life of Gregory the Great*, ed. Colgrave, p. 104.

[57] *Ibid.* IV.23 (21).

[58] For the Gaulish antecedents of double houses, see S. Hilpisch, *Die Doppelklöster. Entstehung und Organisation*, Beiträge zur Geschichte des alten Mönchtums und des Benediktinerordens 15 (Münster, 1928), and P. Hunter Blair, *The World of Bede* (London, 1970), pp. 144–6. For a possible link between Whitby and the Gaulish double houses, see the Appendix, below, pp. 30–2.

hagiographies, we can only see her as a later generation saw her. Bede's account, written fifty years after her death, is of a saintly but commanding figure whose royal background gave strength to her foundation at a time when success depended upon royal patronage and peace upon warrior kings. If we lack the details of particular incidents in her life, we know something of the direction in which, according to Bede, she wished her monastery to go. She laid stress upon the virtues of righteousness, devotion and chastity, striving to follow the ways of the primitive church when all men had all things in common and none had any private property.[59] Bede's reference to the apostolic tradition seems to be echoing his account of the primitive community at Lindisfarne and expressing his own anxiety at the corrupting power of the wealth enjoyed by many of the monasteries of his own day. We know that Hild's advice was sometimes sought by kings and princes in times of difficulty and we may guess that some among them were her own kinsmen. She insisted that those who lived under her direction should devote time to study so that there might be an ample supply of those who were properly educated for holy orders.

Hild died at cock-crow on 17 November 680. Visions of her death were seen by two of the nuns at Hackness, a monastery founded by Hild herself within the year of her death and lying some 13 miles from Whitby. At the time of Hild's death a nun called Frigyth was presiding over Hackness in the absence of the abbess, whose name is not known. One of those to whom visions were vouchsafed was called Begu, said to have been dedicated to God for more than thirty years, but the other is not named.[60] Nothing has been recorded about Hild's burial-place. It is more than likely that she will have been buried within the church at Whitby, but we hear nothing of any shrine; there is no record of any posthumous miracles, no hint of the growth of any cult.[61] Her name was entered in Willibrord's Calendar, but apparently not in the Lindisfarne *Liber uitae*[62] nor in the Anglo-Saxon lists of saints' resting-places.[63] All this is in

59 [See now G. Olsen, 'Bede as Historian: the Evidence from his Observations on the Life of the First Christian Community at Jerusalem', *JEH* 33 (1982), 519–30.]

60 *HE* IV.23 (21). Two Latin inscriptions from Hackness refer to one Oedilburga in such a way as to suggest that she was abbess at Hackness; see Okasha, *Hand-List of Non-Runic Inscriptions*, pp. 73–4 (no. 42), as well as R. I. Page, *An Introduction to English Runes* (London, 1973), pp. 65–6 and pl. XV, for a cryptic runic inscription which as yet cannot be read. For architectural features of Anglo-Saxon date in St Peter's Church at Hackness, see H. M. and J. Taylor, *Anglo-Saxon Architecture*, 3 vols. (Cambridge, 1965–78) I, 268–9.

61 [The situation would be slightly altered if arguments for the existence of an early but now lost *Vita S. Hildae* could be accepted; see above, n. 3.]

62 [Unless the name Hild is a hypocoristic form, and her real name was (say) Hildigyth, Hildithryth or Hildeburg, all of which occur in the Lindisfarne *Liber uitae* (as pointed out by Fell, 'Hild, Abbess of Streonaeshalch', p. 78). Given that Hild's successors Ælfflæd and Eanflæd *do* occur in the *Liber uitae*, the omission of the foundress's name is all the more surprising.]

63 See D. W. Rollason, 'Lists of Saints' Resting-Places in Anglo-Saxon England', *ASE* 7 (1978), 61–93.

strong contrast to the posthumous lives of both Cuthbert and Æthelthryth.

Hild was succeeded by Ælfflæd who, when scarcely a year old, had been dedicated to God by her father, King Osuiu, in thanksgiving for his victory at the battle of *Uinued* in 655. She was put in Hild's charge at Hartlepool and taken thence to the newly founded Whitby. In later years she was helped in the government of the community by her mother, Eanflæd. We may conjecture that Eanflæd went to Whitby upon the death of her husband in 670, and we know that she was still there in 685,[64] but the date of her death is not known. The influence of Whitby not only in Northumbria but also more widely through England will have been greatly strengthened by the presence there for a decade (670–80) of these three royal ladies, whose joint experiences and relationships embraced directly or indirectly the later stages of the Gregorian mission and the royal families of East Anglia, Kent and northern Gaul, and who were in contact with churchmen and monasteries both in Gaul and in Germany. Ælfflæd, moreover, was sister of the reigning king of Northumbria, Ecgfrith, he who made the first endowments for the new foundations at Wearmouth (673) and Jarrow (681). Since she was approaching sixty when she died, her death will have occurred *c.* 714. She and her mother were both commemorated in the Lindisfarne *Liber uitae*,[65] and it is possible that one of the commemorative inscriptions found at Whitby may refer to Eanflæd; but the identification is by no means certain.[66] The death of Ælfflæd is the last recorded incident in the history of the monastery at Whitby. Even the name of her successor is not known. Since we have no reason to suppose that the monastery did not continue to prosper during the remainder of the eighth century and into the ninth, we can only account for the absence of any further details in its history by the later destruction of its records. Archaeological evidence, and particularly finds of coins ranging in date from *c.* 700 to *c.* 850, testify to the continuing occupation of the site down to the beginning of the Viking age.[67]

## THE SYNOD OF WHITBY: THE HISTORICAL CONTEXT

The community at Whitby was ruled by only two abbesses from its foundation in 657 until *c.* 714, so enjoying a measure of stability and continuity which will seem all the more pronounced when we recall that the second of the two, Ælfflæd, had been a member of the community throughout this period of nearly sixty years. If we are to understand the significance of Whitby at the time

[64] *HE* IV.26 (24). [65] *The Oldest English Texts*, ed. Sweet, p. 154, line 18.

[66] See Peers and Radford, 'The Saxon Monastery', pp. 41–2, and, for a more cautious view, Okasha, *Hand-List of Non-Runic Inscriptions*, p. 125 (no. 133).

[67] Peers and Radford, 'The Saxon Monastery'.

of the famous synod which bears its name, we must briefly explore the wider historical context. What, in the years *c.* 660 × 669, had become of Gregory's vision of two metropolitans each with twelve diocesan bishops? Deusdedit, archbishop of Canterbury, died on 14 July 664. Wigheard, chosen as his successor, died in Rome whither he had gone for consecration, and the archbishopric remained vacant until 669.[68] At Rochester the see had been vacant for a long time when Theodore reached England.[69] There was no bishop among the South Saxons, who were still largely pagan. In Wessex Cenwalh had given an episcopal seat to Agilbert, a Gaulish bishop (on whom see the Appendix, below, pp. 30–2), *c.* 650. Some years later the king tried to establish a second bishopric, giving it to Wine, who was of English origin but had been consecrated in Gaul. Agilbert took offence and returned to Gaul. A few years later the king himself expelled Wine, and the West Saxons were without a bishop for a considerable time.[70] The London see established by Augustine lapsed after its first holder became archbishop of Canterbury (*c.* 619), and there is no trace of any further bishop in London for nearly fifty years until, after his expulsion from Wessex, Wine bought the see from the king of Mercia. He remained there until his death.[71] Among the East Saxons Cedd was bishop for several years, but he had no established seat and he died of the plague in 664.[72] In East Anglia there seems to have been a regular succession from Felix (*c.* 630) to Berhtgils (also called Boniface), who died *c.* 669 after holding the see for seventeen years.[73] For much of the seventh century the general shortage of bishops had made it necessary, as Bede writes,[74] that there should only be one bishop for the whole of the midland area embraced by Middle Anglia and Mercia. Lindsey may also have been included since there is no evidence of any separate bishopric in that kingdom. Jaruman, who died shortly before Theodore's arrival, was followed as bishop in the midlands by Chad, a Northumbrian who had been consecrated in Wessex by Wine, assisted by two British bishops.[75] In Northumbria there was not and never had been an archbishop at York, nor can we find any trace of diocesan organization. At Lindisfarne, where the bishops had also been abbots, Tuda died of the plague in 664[76] and thereafter there seems not to have been any

[68] *HE* IV.1.

[69] *Ibid.* II.2 ('defuncto Damiano episcopatus iam diu cessauerat'). The exact date of Damian's death is not known.

[70] *Ibid.* III.7 ('sicque prouincia Occidentalium Saxonum tempore non pauco absque praesule fuit').

[71] *Ibid.* We do not know when Wine died, but he was not present at the Council of Hertford in 672.

[72] *Ibid.* III.22–3.

[73] Whitelock, 'The Pre-Viking Age Church in East Anglia', p. 20.

[74] *HE* III.21.

[75] *Ibid.* III.28.

[76] *Ibid.* III.27.

bishop for several years. Wilfrid was consecrated in Gaul *c.* 664, but several years passed before he returned to Northumbria.

In summary we find a simoniacal bishop in London, but we do not know whether he was still alive when Theodore arrived in 669; Chad in the midlands with orders of doubtful validity in Roman eyes; Berhtgils in East Anglia, but again we do not know if he was still alive in 669; and Wilfrid, consecrated in Gaul but absent from England for several years.[77] There was no archbishop either at Canterbury or at York and no diocesan organization, and from this it follows that there was no body either in the north or in the south, let alone the whole country, which could meet in council or synod: and if these are valid criteria, there was no Anglo-Saxon church at this date.

Add to all this a particularly severe outbreak of *pestilentia* in the summer of 664. Parts of southern Britain were depopulated, a great number of people were carried off in Northumbria and there was similar destruction in Ireland.[78] Particular incidents – apostasy and the repair of heathen temples among the East Saxons,[79] the death of Tuda,[80] the death of Cedd and of some thirty monks who had gone from Essex to be near Cedd's body at Lastingham,[81] the death of Wigheard, archbishop elect, and of his companions[82] – are enough to suggest that Bede was not exaggerating the effects of what seems to have been the most severe of several visitations of pestilence from which Britain suffered in the seventh century. The year 664 was likely to be long remembered, for it was marked not only by the pestilence but also by an eclipse of the sun on 1 May, seen as total in Northumbria,[83] as well as by the death of the archbishop of Canterbury and the king of Kent on one and the same day.[84]

With the benefit of hindsight we may see the seventh century as the age of conversion, of the spread of Christianity to all the kingdoms of the English and of the growth of an organized diocesan church, and, in retrospect, it was indeed all of these things. But it will hardly have seemed so to Hild, who had wanted to follow her sister and other English women to the monasteries of Gaul in search of the religious life which was not then to be found in England.

77 *The Life of Bishop Wilfrid by Eddius Stephanus*, ed. B. Colgrave (Cambridge, 1927), pp. 24–6 (ch. 12). [It has recently been argued convincingly that the attribution of the *Vita S. Wilfridi* to the Eddius mentioned in the work is extremely improbable and rests on no more secure foundation than the fact that it has been attributed to 'Eddius' since the seventeenth century: see D. P. Kirby, 'Bede, Eddius Stephanus and the Life of Wilfrid', *EHR* 98 (1983), 101–14. For that reason the name Eddius has been placed in inverted commas when it occurs in the present article.]

78 *HE* III.27. 79 *Ibid.* III.30. 80 *Ibid.* III.27. 81 *Ibid.* III.23. 82 *Ibid.* IV.1.

83 For outbreaks of *pestilentia*, see Plummer II, 194–6. Bede errs (*HE* III.27) in dating the eclipse to 3 May. For the occasion of his error, see P. Grosjean, 'La Date du colloque de Whitby', *AB* 78 (1960), 233–55, at 239–41. The eclipse, coinciding with the Office of Nones, will have been at its most marked phase at Whitby at about 16.00 hours (Plummer II, 239, n. 1). 84 *HE* IV.1

With hindsight, too, we can appreciate the achievements of the Gregorian mission. But by the middle of the seventh century how many were there in England who were even aware of that mission? Adomnan claimed that the English were all heathen until the conversion of Oswald, and he was a learned man who had visited Northumbria twice and Jarrow once.[85] So completely had the work of the Roman mission been forgotten that no one remembered that Christmas Day in 597 when a great mass of the people of Kent was converted; and even Bede never learned of that occasion.[86] Moreover, nobody knew the year of Augustine's death, not even in Canterbury.[87] But there were two or three who knew a little. First and most important was Hild herself, baptized by Paulinus at an age when she was old enough to remember. Second, though less certainly, was Eanflæd. She too was baptized by Paulinus, but as an infant and certainly with no memory of the event. Yet Paulinus took her to Kent, where she remained until she returned to Northumbria to marry Osuiu at some date after 642. Since Paulinus did not die till 644,[88] there was a period of some ten years or so when she and Paulinus were both in Kent. I know of no evidence that they kept in touch, but I find it scarcely credible to suppose that Paulinus had no further contact with this daughter of Edwin, first Christian king of Northumbria. And what of her mother, the Kentish-born Æthelburg? How long did she live? The third link was one of Paulinus's own companions, James the Deacon, who remained in Northumbria after Edwin's death and who lived till Bede's own days.[89] We know that James had contacts with Whitby because he was one of those present at the synod in 664. With this background in mind, and remembering that Eanflæd and her husband, King Osuiu, were the couple of whom one celebrated Easter while the other was still keeping Lent – with the consequence that Easter was sometimes celebrated twice in one year – we can begin to understand why it was that Whitby, founded at the instigation of Aidan and so looking back beyond Lindisfarne to Iona, was yet so inevitably involved with the Easter problem and also with the life and works of Gregory the Great.

### THE SYNOD OF WHITBY: THE PERSONNEL AND THE ISSUES

There are two accounts of the synod and both are retrospective – that of 'Eddius' some fifty years after the event and Bede's some eighty.[90] Both writers

85 Adomnán, *Vita S. Columbae* II.46 (*Adomnan's Life of Columba*, ed. A. O. and M. O. Anderson (Edinburgh, 1961), pp. 460–2; for the dates of these visits, see *ibid.* p. 94).

86 Gregory, *Registrum epistolarum* VIII.29.

87 *HE* II.3; and cf. Plummer II, 81.

88 *Ibid.* III.23.

89 *Ibid.* II.6: 'qui [*sc.* Iacobus] ad nostra usque tempora permansit'.

90 *The Life of Bishop Wilfrid*, ed. Colgrave, pp. 20–2 (ch. 10), and Bede, *HE* III.25. Both writers use the term *synodus*. Formal ecclesiastical gatherings had become well established by Bede's time, but the earliest of them was the Council of Hertford in 672. In the context of 664, the term *synodus* was something of an anachronism.

would have had access to good sources of information, particularly 'Eddius', who could have drawn directly upon Wilfrid's own memories; but both, and more particularly Bede, are likely to have been influenced by the view of events extending more than half a century after the holding of the synod. 'Eddius' gives no date, but he makes very few time references in the *Vita S. Wilfridi*. Like Bede, he locates the meeting at Whitby, and he sees it primarily as a meeting of abbots, priests and men of all other ecclesiastical ranks. In particular he names as present Hild, the Northumbrian kings Osuiu and Alhfrith, the bishops Colman and Agilbert, the latter's priest Agatho, and Wilfrid who had recently been ordained priest by Agilbert. Three of these seven are made to take part in the debate. Colman put his case first, basing it upon the apostle John's practice. Agilbert bade Wilfrid reply 'in sua lingua' and he put the case for the apostolic see 'et paene totius mundi'. King Osuiu, judging between St Columba and St Peter, thought it wise to follow the keeper of the keys of heaven. Colman was told that he must withdraw from his see; 'et sic fecit'. Bede adds to the account of 'Eddius' the names of James the Deacon, of Romanus (a priest from Kent) and of Bishop Cedd. He supports 'Eddius' in presenting Wilfrid as speaking on behalf of Agilbert because he could explain the problem more clearly in his own tongue than could Agilbert (a Gaul) speaking through an interpreter. Though he adds little of factual detail his account is some five times as long as that in 'Eddius'. This extra length is mainly due to the long speeches attributed to Colman and Wilfrid, both of whom are made to speak three times.

That the synod took place in 664, as Bede states, seems all but certain. The synod, the eclipse, the outbreak of pestilence and the death of Archbishop Deusdedit on 14 July are all ascribed by Bede to this same year.[91] A difficulty has arisen because Bede states that Honorius, Deusdedit's predecessor, died on 30 September 653, that the see was then vacant for eighteen months, and that Deusdedit was consecrated on 26 March and held the bishopric for nine years, four months and two days.[92] Such exactness indicates that Bede probably derived his figures from a Canterbury list of the archbishops. If Deusdedit was consecrated on 26 March 655 and if Bede was right about the length of his tenure, he should have died on 28 July 664 (and not 14 July, as Bede states), but 26 March in 655 was the Thursday before Easter and this is an unlikely date for the consecration of an archbishop. Grosjean,[93] arguing back from 14 July (the day of Deusdedit's death), arrives at 14 March 655 for the consecration; and this date, although a Thursday in Lent, was the feast of St Gregory the Great,

[91] *HE* III.26–7 and IV.1.

[92] *Ibid.* III.20. MS M originally read *.vii. menses*, but this was altered to *.iv. menses*, and this reading is preferred by Plummer as well as by Colgrave and Mynors.

[93] 'La Date du colloque de Whitby', p. 233–4.

whose memory was greatly venerated by the Anglo-Saxons. Grosjean further argues,[94] convincingly, that Bede's seeming error in writing *.vii. kl. Apr.* (= 26 March) instead of *.iv. id. Mart.* (= 12 March) arose from the fact that the former was the date on which Theodore, the next archbishop of Canterbury, was consecrated. If, as seems likely, Bede's information was derived from a Canterbury list, it is easy to see how error could have arisen by the wrong alignment of a name and a date either at Canterbury or at Jarrow. A further difficulty has arisen from the belief that Bede began the *annus Domini* in September at the change of the indiction, with the consequence that when he dates the death of Honorius to 30 September 653 we must correct the year to 652 and so throw back the synod to 663.[95] This belief is erroneous. Bede began the *annus Domini* on 1 January without any reference to the indictional change in September.[96] The dates which he gives for the death of Honorius and the holding of the synod are not indictional dates but dates reckoned according to the *annus Domini*. We should accordingly accept 664 as the year of the synod, and probably its earlier part, since Bede seems to imply that the eclipse of 1 May and the outbreak of pestilence both occurred subsequently.

It is common knowledge that the main issue discussed at the synod was how to determine the proper date for the celebration of Easter, that all solutions depended upon the use of cycles which sought to reconcile the different lengths of lunar and solar years, that the problem was one which had vexed Christendom for several centuries, and that the reaching of any solution involved a far from elementary knowledge of computus. It is commonly, but mistakenly, believed that the issue was a simple, straightforward clash between a Roman church and a Celtic church, concepts which for this date seem to have as little validity as that of an Anglo-Saxon church. What *was* the historical background to the Whitby argument?[97] So far as the western church is concerned, we need to be aware of three cyclical tables (even if we do not know how to use them, let alone compile them): an eighty-four-year cycle whose origin is obscure but may date from the third century, a nineteen-year cycle compiled by Victorius of Aquitaine in 457 (lunar limits, sixteen to twenty-two) and another nineteen-year cycle compiled by Dionysius Exiguus early in the sixth century, but with different lunar limits (fifteen to twenty-two). These three tables might all give different dates for Easter; they might all give the

[94] *Ibid.* p. 238. [95] This argument is advanced in Stenton, *Anglo-Saxon England*, p. 129.

[96] Much confusion and consequent error about Bede's chronology have recently been eradicated by K. Harrison, notably in 'The Beginning of the Year in England, *c.* 500–900', *ASE* 2 (1973), 51–70; 'The Synod of Whitby and the Beginning of the Christian Era in England', *YAJ* 45 (1973), 108–14; and *The Framework of Anglo-Saxon History*, pp. 76–98.

[97] For what follows I am heavily indebted to *Bedae Opera de Temporibus* (ed. Jones, pp. 6–104), and to two recent studies by Harrison (cited above, n. 96): 'The Synod of Whitby', and *The Framework of Anglo-Saxon History*, esp. pp. 30–75.

same date; or any two of them might agree against the third. The same table might even give two choices. Moreover, we can very seldom know whether Easter was actually celebrated in a particular place on the day theoretically indicated by the table there in use.[98]

When Augustine came to England in 597, and Paulinus to York some thirty years later, Rome was using the Victorian tables; but during the period 630 × 640 Rome gradually changed to the more accurate Dionysiac tables. In Gaul the Victorian tables were formally accepted in a synod at Orléans in 541[99] and seem to have been in use side by side with the Dionysiac tables as late as 743.[100] In parts of Ireland the Victorian tables began to be adopted *c.* 628 and the Dionysiac tables were known there *c.* 630[101] – and that was before Paulinus had left York. But from northern Ireland Columba had taken the eighty-four-year cycle to Iona, whence it spread to the Pictish church and through the person of Aidan to Lindisfarne. So by *c.* 650 Rome had moved to the Dionysiac tables, and so had southern Ireland. Canterbury was still using the Victorian tables – now abandoned by Rome – but Lindisfarne and its offshoots used the eighty-four-year cycle.

So let us now turn from the broad view of the churches of western Europe trying to solve a computistical problem (remembering that it could take many years to gain practical experience of a theoretical solution calculated in advance of the event) and look in more detail at a key figure – Wilfrid. He was born *c.* 634, the year after the death of Edwin and the withdrawal of Paulinus to Kent. About fourteen years later he went to Lindisfarne[102] where Aidan was bishop, and he will very soon have become aware of the differing practices which arose from the marriage of Osuiu to Eanflæd, for Osuiu had been educated and baptized by the Irish,[103] while Eanflæd, baptized by Paulinus, is likely to have been further instructed by him while they were both in Kent. But there is no hint of any bitterness or hostility. It was Eanflæd herself who entrusted Wilfrid to Aidan at Lindisfarne. Because of the affection which all men felt for Aidan the differences were tolerated, even though this meant that king and queen might celebrate Easter at different times.[104] Aidan died in 651,[105] and perhaps it is significant that in the next year, so far as we can tell, Eanflæd sent Wilfrid to Canterbury.[106]

98 Bede states that the Easter of 627, when Edwin was converted, was 12 April. The Victorian and Dionysiac tables agree upon 12 April for 627, whereas the eighty-four-year cycle gives 5 April; but we may suspect that Bede will have identified the day of the month from his own Easter tables. For the Easter dates, see the table compiled by D. J. O'Connell, 'Easter Cycles in the Early Irish Church', *Jnl of the R. Soc. of Antiquaries of Ireland* 66 (1936), 67–106, at 97–105. This table shows the agreements and differences of the three cycles during the years 432–720, but it should be remembered that they are theoretical rather than actual.

99 *Bedae Opera de Temporibus*, ed. Jones, p. 65.

100 *Ibid.* p. 104, n. 1.

101 Harrison, *The Framework of Anglo-Saxon History*, p. 59.

102 'Eddius', *Vita S. Wilfridi*, ch. 2 (ed. Colgrave, pp. 4–6).

103 *HE* III.25.

104 *Ibid.*

105 *Ibid.* III.14 and V.24.

106 'Eddius', *Vita S. Wilfridi*, ch. 3 (ed. Colgrave, p. 8).

While Wilfrid was travelling to Canterbury, as a stopping-place on a longer journey to Rome, there was a great change at Lindisfarne. The new bishop, Finan, showed none of the qualities which had endeared Aidan to all men, and while he was in office a great controversy arose, but it was not a dispute between the English and the Irish. What Bede defined as the true Easter[107] was vigorously defended by Ronan, an Irishman who had been taught in Gaul and Italy; he was, Bede writes, *acerrimus defensor*, 'a most passionate defender', and in the same sentence Bede writes also of *homo ferocis animi*, 'a man of fierce temper', referring, I think, to Finan.[108] So the spectacle we watch is that of two hot-tempered Irishmen going for each other hammer and tongs. The more Ronan argued, the more stubborn did Finan become. The argument presumably concerned the eighty-four-year cycle followed by Finan and the Victorian nineteen-year cycle which Ronan will have found in Gaul and probably in Italy as well. Leaving the two Irishmen to argue, let us return to the fortunes of Wilfrid.

Wilfrid spent a year in Canterbury. We know that the version of the psalter which he found in use there was different from that in use at Lindisfarne[109] and we may suppose that he would also find the Victorian tables in use there. Crossing Gaul he is likely to have found similar practices, but when he got to Rome (*c.* 653) he will have met something new to him – the Dionysiac tables. While he was there he was fully instructed by Archdeacon Boniface not only in the four gospels, which he learned by heart (presumably in the Vulgate text), but also in the correct method of calculating Easter. Wilfrid spent three years in Gaul after leaving Rome[110] (*c.* 655–8) and finally reached England *c.* 658/9, having been absent from Northumbria for more than four years. He will have brought back with him knowledge, and probably copies, of the Dionysiac Easter tables. During his absence there had been no change at Lindisfarne. The obstinate Finan was still in office – and from what we know of these two men it would surely be difficult to find two individuals of more determined and uncompromising character than Finan and Wilfrid. Osuiu was still reigning with his wife Eanflæd, but when Wilfrid reached Northumbria he was welcomed by Osuiu's son, Alhfrith, who was reigning in Deira. After being instructed by Wilfrid in all that he had learned at Rome, Alhfrith was persuaded to the Roman point of view and gave Wilfrid two estates of which one lay at Ripon.[111] We do not know the exact date, but the year was probably 660; and in the next year Finan died, to be succeeded by Colman who, as his later behaviour shows, seems to have been no less determined in the rightness of his own ways than was Finan. At this point, says Bede,[112] the controversy became still more acute and, because so many people found themselves greatly

[107] *HE* III.25. [108] *Ibid.* [109] 'Eddius', *Vita S. Wilfridi*, ch. 3 (ed. Colgrave, p. 8).
[110] *Ibid.* chs. 5–6 (ed. Colgrave, pp. 10–14). [111] *Ibid.* chs. 7–8 (ed. Colgrave, pp. 14–18).
[112] *HE* III.25.

troubled by it, it was agreed that the whole matter should be discussed in a synod which was to be held in Hild's monastery at Whitby.

Whether or not particular significance should be attached to the year 664 for the holding of the synod seems now difficult to determine. It is a fact that from 646 to 664 the Victorian and Dionysiac tables agreed with one another, although they several times clashed with the eighty-four-year cycle; but in 665 the Victorian table offered a choice of dates, of which one differed by a week from the Dionysiac date.[113] There may, then, have been those who thought it appropriate to hold the synod in 664 with the hope that unity might be achieved for 665; yet the argument even within Northumbria alone had been growing in intensity ever since the death of Aidan in 651. We know too little of the background, and in particular of the movements of those involved to be well informed of all the circumstances. We have seen that ten of those present at the synod are known to us by name, and, if to these we add the unnamed abbots, priests and men of all ecclesiastical ranks to whom 'Eddius' refers,[114] we shall envisage a large gathering whose members embodied a wide range of experience. James the Deacon had known Paulinus and so could speak of the Gregorian mission, as could Hild herself. Romanus had recent experience of Kent. Hild and Colman had known Aidan through whom they could look beyond Lindisfarne to Iona. Wilfrid not only knew Lindisfarne and Canterbury, but also had experience of Gaul and Italy extending over some years. Another important participant who possessed wide experience of ecclesiastical affairs in England and Gaul was Agilbert, sometime bishop of the West Saxons (on the career of Agilbert and his possible links with Whitby, see the Appendix, below, pp. 30–2). Even if the gathering was of mainly Northumbrian interest and could not be representative of an Anglo-Saxon church which had no organized existence, it would be hard to find anywhere in Britain a group of men and women who were better qualified to discuss the issue before them. Although the outcome of the synod of Whitby is well known and has frequently been the subject of scholarly discussion, the significance of the choice of Whitby as the venue for the synod has not hitherto been sufficiently appreciated. This significance, as I hope to have shown, is best understood by viewing Whitby from the wider perspective of seventh-century Christendom.

## THE SIGNIFICANCE OF CÆDMON

Our approach to the synod of Whitby demanded the taking of a view wide enough to embrace most of seventh-century Christendom. Turning now to

[113] O'Connell, 'Easter Cycles', pp. 103–5. For 664 all three tables gave 21 April, but the eighty-four-year cycle gave 14 April as an alternative; for 665 all three gave 6 April, but the Victorian gave 13 April as an alternative.

[114] 'Eddius', *Vita S. Wilfridi*, ch. 10 (ed. Colgrave, pp. 20–2).

Cædmon we may become more insular in our outlook. We can learn from almost any reference book that Cædmon was the first English poet – a statement which seems a little unhelpful to those who go on to discover that the surviving corpus of his poetry amounts to one rather tedious hymn of no more than nine lines. Historians will conclude that there is a limit to what can usefully be said about a source of such minimal length, and as they read the multitudinous scholarly articles that have been written about it they will further conclude that the limit has long since been passed.[115] But then historians will not see Cædmon as the first of the long and illustrious line that once made the English a nation of poets; they will rather see him as a character set firmly in the seventh century when missionaries from several countries were seeking to convert the English from paganism to Christianity.

Cædmon's story is familiar to all, but let us remind ourselves briefly of what we know, and of what we do not know. First, it should be noted that there is no contemporary evidence about him; our only source is Bede's account,[116] written many years later. Nothing of Whitby origin has survived. We do not know when he was born or when he died; our only chronological evidence is that he flourished when Hild was abbess and those dates were, as we have seen, *c.* 657 x 680. We do not know whether he died before or after Hild, and if we place his activities within a decade on either side of 670 perhaps that is as near as we can get. Summarizing Bede's account we see Cædmon as a man, possibly of British rather than English descent,[117] who worked on an estate near Whitby and who continued to live in the secular world until late in life. In telling of his embarrassment when his turn came to entertain the company on occasions of merrymaking, Bede emphasizes Cædmon's lack of skill in versifying until the night-time visitation when he received that divine inspiration which led him to compose his hymn in praise of creation. Cædmon went first to his master to tell of the gift he had received; he was then taken to Hild and was finally questioned by many of the more learned men in the monastery. He submitted himself to regular monastic discipline and after learning from the scriptures through interpreters – the implication seems to be that Cædmon never learned

[115] [For the ample bibliography on Cædmon and his hymn, see S. B. Greenfield and F. C. Robinson, *A Bibliography of Publications on Old English Literature to the End of 1972* (Toronto and Manchester, 1980), nos. 3202–622; particular mention may be made of C. L. Wrenn, 'The Poetry of Cædmon', *PBA* 32 (1946), 277–95, and F. P. Magoun, 'Bede's Story of Cædmon: the Case History of an Anglo-Saxon Oral Singer', *Speculum* 30 (1955), 49–63. For work on Cædmon published since 1972, see the annual bibliographies in *ASE*.]

[116] *HE* IV.24 (22).

[117] Philologists think that the name *Cædmon* is British and not English; see K. H. Jackson, *Language and History in Early Britain* (Edinburgh, 1953), pp. 244, 488 and 554; O. S. Anderson, *Old English Material in the Leningrad Manuscript of Bede's Ecclesiastical History*, Skrifter utg. av Kungl. Humanistiska Vetenskapssamfundet i Lund 31 (Lund, 1941), 70 and 91; van Els, *The Kassel Manuscript*, p. 130; and Campbell, *Old English Grammar*, p. 252, n. 1.

to read, nor indeed would we expect him to have done so – he composed a large number of songs on topics which were derived in part from the Old Testament and in part from the New – Genesis and Exodus, the incarnation, the passion, the resurrection, the ascension, the coming of the Holy Spirit and the teaching of the apostles. He also composed songs about the Day of Judgement, the pains of hell and the joys of heaven.

Whether we think that Cædmon was the sole author of what was evidently a considerable bulk of religious poetry or whether he was merely the inspiration to others who shared in the work, what was the historical setting to which it belonged? It was, so far as the chronological evidence allows us to see, the same setting into which Theodore entered when he reached Canterbury in 669 – parts of the country still pagan, scarcely any bishops or dioceses, few churches, no system of ecclesiastical government, all this the aftermath of the devastation caused by the plague. Some kings had been baptized, some kingdoms were reverting to paganism. Some of the nobles had been baptized, perhaps moved more by a sense of loyalty than by well-grounded faith. Are we, I wonder, a little over-persuaded by Bede's *Historia ecclesiastica* about the extent to which England had become a Christian country half a century or so before he wrote that work?[118] Yet Bede himself seems to give the clue to the importance of Cædmon's poetry – in his view it has nothing to do with English literature, but a great deal to do with the conversion of pagans. 'By his songs [Bede writes] the minds of many were inspired to despise the world and to long for the heavenly life.'[119]

How, in the seventh century, did one teach Christianity to a pagan people who could not read? The scriptures were in Latin, a language understood only by a small number of scholars. The number of copies of the gospels, even in Latin, is not likely to have been very large by *c.* 660; they could not easily be multiplied. There is no evidence of any vernacular translations from the seventh century. Bede himself was the author of the earliest surviving collections of homilies, but they were in Latin and they imply both a developed liturgy and an educated audience. How, then, did one teach even the nobility, let alone those yokels who jeered at Cuthbert saying that thay had been robbed of their old ways of worship and no one knew how the new worship was to be conducted?[120] We know that Bede used to give English translations of the *Credo* and the *Pater noster* to those priests who had no Latin.[121] We know also

118 For two discussions of aspects of the conversion, see R. Hill, 'Bede and the Boors', *Famulus Christi*, ed. G. Bonner (London, 1976), pp. 93–105, and P. Wormald, 'Bede, *Beowulf* and the Conversion of the Anglo-Saxon Aristocracy', *Bede and Anglo-Saxon England*, ed. R. T. Farrell, BAR 46 (Oxford, 1978), 32–95.

119 *HE* IV.24 (22).

120 See Bede's prose *Vita S. Cuthberti*, ch. 3 (*Two Lives of St Cuthbert*, ed. B. Colgrave (Cambridge, 1940), pp. 160–5).

121 *Epistola Bede ad Ecgbertum episcopum* (Plummer I, 409).

that paintings illustrating scenes from both the Old and the New Testaments were hung in the churches at Jarrow and Wearmouth[122] and that Christian figures were portrayed on stone crosses, but both paintings and crosses seem to belong to a slightly later age than the times of Hild and Cædmon.

If Cædmon seems to cut a poor figure as the first English poet, his historical significance for the conversion of the English is of quite a different order, for it was he, as Bede would have us believe, who solved the problem which faced those men of learning at Whitby who examined and then taught him – the problem of communicating the fundamentals of Christian teaching to a society (nobles and peasants alike) which knew nothing of books.[123] Poetry was part of their age-old inheritance: passed by word of mouth, it needed no books outside the monastery where it was composed nor any knowledge of reading. We cannot tell how widely Cædmon's poetry spread, but Hild's monastery, and the men of learning who saw how it could be put to use, made a great contribution to the spreading of Christianity among the Anglo-Saxons.

## WHITBY AS A NURSERY OF BISHOPS

Cædmon, Bede tells us, was questioned about his dream 'in the presence of many of the more learned men in the monastery'[124] and he tells us elsewhere that Hild required those in her care to devote part of their time to the study of the holy scriptures and part of it to the performance of good works so that 'there might very easily be found there many men who were fitted for holy orders and for the service of the altar'.[125] Religious poetry offered a means of teaching the laity the elements of Christianity, but it did not meet the other great need of the seventh century, the need for men of English race who were adequately trained to hold office as priests and bishops. Wherever we look in the years before *c.* 650 – whether to Northumbria or to Canterbury, to the midlands, East Anglia or Wessex – the bishops or archbishops are Italian, Gaulish or Irish. We know nothing of the lower orders at this time. The only

122 Bede, *Historia abbatum* (Plummer I, 369 and 373). [See now P. Meyvaert, 'Bede and the Church Paintings at Wearmouth–Jarrow', *ASE* 8 (1979), 63–77.]

123 [Cædmon's discovery, as recounted by Bede, was undoubtedly important for the propagation of Christian faith in Northumbria. But it should not be forgotten that Cædmon's approximate contemporary, the poet and scholar Aldhelm (*ob.* 709 or 710) similarly devised a technique of expounding Christian doctrine orally in the form of Old English verse, and that – according to William of Malmesbury – he was an Old English poet of distinction and was King Alfred's favourite vernacular poet; see M. Lapidge, 'Aldhelm's Latin Poetry and Old English Verse', *Comparative Lit.* 31 (1979), 209–31. Unfortunately, none of Aldhelm's Old English verse has survived or has been identified among the surviving corpus.]

124 *HE* IV.24 (22).

125 *Ibid.* IV.23 (21).

exception is, as we might have expected, in Kent. When Paulinus died in 644 he was succeeded at Rochester by Ithamar, a man of Kentish race. Ithamar's successor (Damian) was a South Saxon, and it was Ithamar who in 655 consecrated the first English holder to the see of Canterbury – Deusdedit, a West Saxon by origin.[126]

So in south-eastern England the change from foreign to native bishops begins about the middle of the seventh century. It was a great part of Hild's vision that she saw Whitby not as a community of men and women withdrawn from the world, but as a place where men were to be trained for the minor and for the major orders of the clergy. Bede was able to look back over the years and to see how Hild's vision had been fulfilled. From this one monastery, he could write, there had come five bishops, and a sixth who had been appointed to his see but died before his consecration. We cannot even guess at the number of priests who were trained at Whitby.

Who were the six bishops? Three of them held episcopal office in Northumbria. There was Bosa who was consecrated by Archbishop Theodore in 678 and had his seat in York, following the dissensions which led to Wilfrid's expulsion.[127] Among those who were educated from childhood with Bosa's clergy in York was Acca, remembered as the scholarly bishop of Hexham who assembled there a very splendid library and to whom Bede dedicated many of his theological commentaries.[128] There was John who became bishop first of Hexham and then, after Bosa's death, of York. John died at Beverley in 721 after holding episcopal office for thirty-three years.[129] It was this John who ordained Bede as deacon and priest.[130] Bede devotes no fewer than five consecutive chapters to John's achievements in curing the sick.[131] Among other things we learn from these chapters that John had received medical teaching from Archbishop Theodore[132] and that his standards were sufficiently demanding for him to have forbidden a priest to baptize others because he was too slow-witted to learn the office of catechism or baptism.[133] And then there was the so-called 'other' Wilfrid (*not* the more famous Wilfrid of whom 'Eddius' wrote). This second Wilfrid was consecrat-

126 For Ithamar, see *ibid.* III.14; for Damian and Deusdedit, see *ibid.* III.20.

127 *Ibid.* IV.12 and 23 (21), V.3 and 24.

128 *Ibid.* V.20. For those of Bede's works which mention Acca, see Plummer I, xlix and cxlvii–cxlix; see also D. Whitelock, 'Bede and his Teachers and Friends', *Famulus Christi*, ed. Bonner, pp. 19–39, at 26–7.

129 *HE* IV.23 (21), V.2 and 6. *HE* V.6 records John's death in 721 after holding episcopal office for thirty-three years. ASC 721 D and E state more precisely that he held office for thirty-three years, eight months and thirteen days. His festival was observed at Beverley on 7 May (see Plummer II, 273). These figures would put his consecration on 26 August 687. In the year 687, 25 August was a Sunday; the coincidence seems accurate enough if we allow for uncertainty about whether or not the day of his death was included in the total length.

130 *Ibid.* V.24. 131 *Ibid.* V.2–6. 132 *Ibid.* V.3. 133 *Ibid.* V.6.

ed to the see of York by John, who in his old age felt himself unable to fulfil his duties. Wilfrid in turn resigned his office in 732, but lived until *c.* 745.[134] He was remembered by Alcuin as a man who had richly endowed the church at York with great wealth of precious plate, both gold and silver, and also as a man who fed the ignorant with instructive speech, giving generously with both hand and word.[135] Bosa, John and the second Wilfrid – all were trained at Whitby and all were bishops of note in the Northumbrian church of the late seventh century and the early eighth.

The other three bishops trained at Whitby lead us outside Northumbria to southern England and to the west midlands. Their names, as Bede gives them, were Ætla, Tatfrith and Oftfor. Of Ætla Bede writes that 'it may briefly be said that he was bishop of Dorchester',[136] and it is believed that the place to which he was referring was Dorchester-on-Thames and not Dorchester in Dorset. Bede was not well informed about either the political or the ecclesiastical history of Wessex, and it seems that he knew nothing about Ætla's dates or about his relationship to other seventh-century bishops among the West Saxons, of whom two, and possibly a third, were of Gaulish origin.[137] Yet there are Northumbrian connections which might have led Hild and her successor, Ælfflæd, to take an interest in the conversion of the West Saxons. The first recorded bishop there was Birinus, who converted King Cynegils. Bede tells us that Oswald, king of Northumbria, was present on the occasion, that the Northumbrian Oswald stood as godfather to the West Saxon Cynegils and that both kings jointly gave Dorchester to the bishop as an episcopal seat. This will have been about 635,[138] long before Whitby was founded, yet King

134 *Ibid.* IV.23 (21), V.6 and 23; see also the entry *s.a.* 732 in the eighth-century annals found in the Moore manuscript of Bede's *Historia ecclesiastica* (*Bede's Ecclesiastical History*, ed. Colgrave and Mynors, p. 572). Symeon of Durham in the *Historia regum* (*Symeonis Monachi Opera Omnia*, ed. T. Arnold, 2 vols., Rolls Ser. (London, 1882–5) II, 39) places Wilfrid's death on 29 April 745; the anonymous *Baedae continuatio* (ed. Plummer I, 362) also gives 745, but without the day of the month. ASC 744 D and E give 29 April, after thirty years of episcopal office, but this last figure is certainly wrong since Wilfrid cannot have been consecrated much before 721, the year of John's death.

135 [*Alcuin: the Bishops, Kings and Saints of York*, ed. P. Godman (Oxford, 1982), pp. 94–8 (lines 1216–47).]

136 *HE* IV.23 (21).

137 *Ibid.* IV.12, where the first four bishops of the West Saxons are listed as Birinus, Agilbert, Wine and Leuthere; but we should not infer such regularity of succession as the list seems to imply. Of these four Agilbert and Leuthere were both Gaulish, the latter being nephew of the former (*HE* III.7). I have not found any evidence to support the claim made by M. Deanesly (*The Pre-Conquest Church in England* (London, 1961), p. 77) that Birinus was 'another missionary from Gaul' or that he landed at 'Southampton or further west'.

138 *Ibid.* III.7. Birinus came to Britain after consulting with Pope Honorius, who held office 625–38. King Oswald was fighting Cadwallon at Heavenfield in 634 and can hardly have gone to Wessex before 635. ASC A, B and C record that Birinus preached among the West Saxons in 634 and baptized Cynegils with Oswald as sponsor in 635, but these dates may be no more than an inference from Bede's narrative.

Oswald was uncle to Abbess Ælfflæd and she may well have known of the part that he had played. The next West Saxon bishop of whom we have record was Agilbert, a Gaul who had studied in Ireland before going to Wessex and who in later years became bishop of Paris (see Appendix, below, pp. 30–2). Before going back to Gaul, Agilbert visited Northumbria, where he attended the synod of Whitby and will have been able to tell Hild about conditions in Wessex. But perhaps this is as far as we can go.[139] Ætla's name is not found in any of the episcopal lists, nor are there any charters which include his name in the witness-list.[140] We can only guess that he worked among the West Saxons in the latter part of the seventh century.

Tatfrith and Oftfor, the remaining two of the Whitby bishops named by Bede, take us to the west midlands, to the small kingdom of the Hwicce which was in all probability a Mercian creation of the seventh century.[141] The kingdom lay on the western borders of Mercia and its lands were largely in the Severn valley. We know the names of several of its rulers, who seem to have been subject to Mercian overlords, and in the later years Hwiccean bishops were established in Worcester.[142] Of Tatfrith Bede tells us that he was a man of very great energy and learning, that he was appointed bishop among the Hwicce shortly before Bosel became bishop, but that he died an untimely death before his consecration.[143] Of Oftfor Bede tells us rather more. He had studied in both of Hild's monasteries – that is in Hartlepool as well as in Whitby – and subsequently went to Kent to join Archbishop Theodore; and after studying there for some time he went to Rome. Coming back to Britain he went to the kingdom of the Hwicce and there he remained for a long time. At that time – the phrase (*quo tempore*) is characteristic of Bede when he lacks precise chronological information – Bosel was too ill to perform his duties and Oftfor was appointed in his place, being consecrated bishop by Wilfrid, who was then acting as bishop among the Middle Angles.[144]

So here we have a succession of three names – Tatfrith, Bosel and Oftfor – two of them from Whitby and those two both men of learning. We know nothing of Bosel; and if the name recalls Boisil, prior of Melrose, and Bosa, bishop of York, any suggestion that Bosel too was a Northumbrian would be

139 For Agilbert, see *HE* III.7, 25, 26 and 28, IV.1 and 12, and V.19, as well as 'Eddius', *Vita S. Wilfridi*, chs. 9, 10 and 12; see also the Appendix, below, pp. 30–2.

140 The name *etla* occurs in the Lindisfarne *Liber uitae* (*The Oldest English Texts*, ed. Sweet, p. 160, line 229) among the *nomina clericorum* (there is no separate list of bishops). [It is also possible that Ætla's name does not occur among bishops' lists and witness-lists because it was a hypocoristic form.]

141 See Stenton, *Anglo-Saxon England*, pp. 45–6.

142 It has been argued that the princes of the Hwicce were related to the Northumbrian royal family; see, e.g., H. P. R. Finberg, *The Early Charters of the West Midlands* (Leicester, 1961), pp. 167–80.

143 *HE* IV.23 (21).

144 *Ibid.*

speculation without evidence. And what of the chronology of these three? Bede tells us that when Oftfor was consecrated by Wilfrid, Archbishop Theodore was dead and no successor had yet been appointed,[145] information which enables us to date Oftfor's consecration to between 19 September 690 and 30 June 692. There is no early evidence to show us when he died, nor how long he had been among the Hwicce before becoming their bishop.[146] For the earlier limit there is some negative evidence deriving from the so-called foundation charter of the abbey of Bath which is dated 6 November 675 and has no bishop of the Hwicce among its witnesses.[147] So it would seem that during the last twenty-five or so years of the seventh century, the monastery of Whitby was actively engaged in the furtherance of Christianity among the Hwicce, sending there two men whose energy and intellectual ability were stressed by Bede. There cannot have been many men at this date who had been trained at Whitby, at Canterbury under that great scholar Archbishop Theodore, and at Rome.

## CONCLUSIONS

[The importance of Whitby as a centre of learning in seventh-century England is sufficiently clear from its achievements: from the number of bishops it trained for service in Northumbria, the midlands and Wessex, from the accomplishments of Cædmon and from the fact that Whitby hosted the synod on Easter-dating which took place in 664. Unfortunately, it is not possible to form any precise notion as to the books which must have been assembled and copied at Whitby, or as to the teaching which undoubtedly took place there. Only two Latin works are certainly attributable to pre-Conquest Whitby, and both of them fall (just) outside the chronological scope of this essay. First, there is a brief letter of introduction written by Abbess Ælfflæd, probably in the early eighth century (Ælfflæd died *c.* 714), intended for the use of an unnamed Anglo-Saxon abbess on pilgrimage and addressed to Abbess Adola

145 *Ibid.* For Theodore's death, see *ibid.* IV.2 and V.8, and for the appointment of his successor, see *ibid.* V.8.

146 See Finberg, *The Early Charters of the West Midlands*, p. 32.

147 The charter is listed by P. H. Sawyer, *Anglo-Saxon Charters: an Annotated List and Bibliography* (London, 1968), no. 51, and ptd W. deG. Birch, *Cartularium Saxonicum*, 3 vols. and index (London, 1885–99), no. 43. The date 6 November 675 is defended by K. Harrison, 'The *Annus Domini* in some Early Charters', *Jnl of the Soc. of Archivists* 4 (1973), 551–7, at 553, and parts of the charter's content by P. Sims-Williams, 'Continental Influence at Bath Monastery in the Seventh Century', *ASE* 4 (1975), 1–10, at 1–3.

of Pfalzel (near Trier);[148] the letter has been preserved in one of the manuscripts of the Bonifatian correspondence (now Vienna, Nationalbibliothek, 751, 32r), presumably because it was carried to Pfalzel, where it perhaps came into the hands of Boniface himself, who stayed there in 721. Secondly, there is the *Vita S. Gregorii*[149] by an anonymous monastic[150] of Whitby, a fascinating and idiosyncratic work whose composition is to be placed in the early eighth century (probably the decade 704 × 714); its very idiosyncrasy makes any deductions about the learning and library drawn on by its author a hazardous business.[151] Similarly, although we may deduce from the styluses and book-clasps which have been excavated at Whitby[152] that it must surely have housed a scriptorium, no surviving manuscript has ever been identified as a product of seventh-century Whitby. Nevertheless, during the middle years of the seventh century, Whitby was unquestionably the pre-eminent centre of learning in Anglo-Saxon England, and we are justified in regarding it – to use Bede's metaphor – as 'the blaze of light which filled all Britain with its splendour'.]

APPENDIX

## The Career of Agilbert

The chief source about Agilbert's family background is the so-called 'Genealogy of the Founders', a document which is thought to have been compiled not earlier than the twelfth century from the *Liber uitae* of Jouarre Abbey, but which is now known only from seventeenth-century copies.[1] Although questionable in some of its details, the

148 [*S. Bonifatii et Lullii Epistolae*, ed. M. Tangl, MGH, Epist. select. 1 (Berlin, 1916), 3–4 (no. 8).]

149 [*The Earliest Life of Gregory*, ed. Colgrave. See also C. W. Jones, *Saints' Lives and Chronicles in Early England* (Ithaca, NY, 1947), pp. 64–7 and 94–121 (English translation of the *uita*); B. Colgrave, 'The Earliest Life of St Gregory the Great, Written by a Whitby Monk', *Celt and Saxon: Studies in the Early British Border*, ed. N. K. Chadwick (Cambridge, 1963), pp. 119–37; and O. Limone, 'La vita di Gregorio Magno dell'Anonimo di Whitby', *SM* 3rd ser. 19 (1978), 37–67.]

150 [It is customarily stated that the work was composed by a 'monk' of Whitby, but there is nothing in the text to exclude the possibility that its author was a nun.]

151 [Compare the remarks by Colgrave (*The Earliest Life of Gregory*, pp. 53–4) with those of Jones (*Saints' Lives and Chronicles*, pp. 66–7).]

152 [See Cramp, 'Monastic Sites', p. 228.]

1 See J. Guerout, 'Les Origines et le premier siècle de l'abbaye', *L'Abbaye royale de Notre Dame de Jouarre*, ed. Y. Chaussy *et al.* (Paris, 1961), 1–67, at 11 and 61; see also Sims-Williams, 'Continental Influence', pp. 3–7.

evidence of this document seems adequate to establish Agilbert's background as that of a noble Frankish family from the neighbourhood of Soissons, and to establish further that some of his relatives were closely associated with the development of monasticism in northern Francia in the first half of the seventh century, a movement which had its roots in the earlier foundations of Columbanus. Agilbert's sister, Telchildis, became the first abbess of the monastery founded at Jouarre by his cousin Adon, and Adon's brother, bishop of Rouen and the future St Ouen (Audoenus), was one of the great ecclesiastical personalities of the seventh century.

Bede's first reference to Agilbert is in his account of the conversion of the West Saxons (*HE* III.7). Cynegils, baptized by Birinus, was succeeded as king of the West Saxons by Cenwalh, a pagan who had married and subsequently put away a sister of Penda, king of Mercia. Penda, seeking to avenge his sister, expelled Cenwalh who took refuge with Anna, king of the East Angles. After spending three years in exile in East Anglia, during which time he was baptized, he was restored to his kingdom in Wessex. After his restoration there came into his kingdom – 'uenit in prouinciam' – a bishop called Agilbert who was of Gaulish birth but had lived for no little time in Ireland for the sake of scriptural study. Cenwalh, greatly impressed by his learning and industry, asked him to remain as bishop. After a while Cenwalh grew weary of his barbarous speech and secretly introduced another bishop into his kingdom, whereupon Agilbert, deeply offended, went back to Francia and after becoming bishop of Paris died there 'senex ac plenus dierum'. Cenwalh tried to persuade him to return, but he excused himself by saying that he could not leave his Parisian diocese, and instead sent his nephew (Leuthere), who was consecrated by Theodore (*HE* III.7). There are no dates in this narrative, which Bede presumably derived from Daniel, bishop of Winchester. According to the Anglo-Saxon Chronicle, Cenwalh succeeded to his kingdom in 641, was driven out by Penda in 645, was baptized in 646 and was back in Wessex in 648. Agilbert's arrival is dated 650 and his return to Gaul 660.

Nothing is known about either the date or the place of Agilbert's birth. He is believed to have died between *c.* 680 and 691, and Bede, though not knowing the date, describes him as being at the time of his death 'senex ac plenus dierum' (*HE* III.7), a phrase which he borrowed from the biblical book of Job (XLII.16) and which he also used of the long-lived James the Deacon (*HE* II.20). Slight though it is, the evidence suggests that his birth may have fallen in the decade 610 x 620. We do not know when or where he first entered upon the religious life, but there is a little evidence to suggest that he was in some way involved in the beginnings of the monastery at Jouarre which was founded *c.* 635 and of which his sister, Telchildis, became the first abbess.[2] Whatever may have been the precise contributions of Agilbert, of his cousin Adon and of his sister Telchildis to the early history of Jouarre, there is no doubt of Agilbert's lasting interest in Jouarre, for he built there the family mausoleum in which he was buried himself and where his sculptured sarcophagus may still be seen.

Although neither Gaulish nor English sources yield any additional details about Agilbert's early life, we ought to take into account contemporary circumstances which are likely to have played their part in those decisions which took him subsequently to

[2] *Ibid.* pp. 15, 18 and 34–48.

Ireland, to England and finally to the bishopric of Paris. Jouarre, some 40 km east of Paris, had close links with two other religious foundations: Faremoutiers, some 17 km to the south-west of Jouarre, and Chelles, on the eastern outskirts of Paris itself. Faremoutiers, a daughter-house of Luxeuil, was founded *c.* 617–20 by Burgundofara (better known as St Fare), who had been dedicated to God by Columbanus himself. It was at Faremoutiers that Telchildis, first abbess of Jouarre, received her earliest instruction in the religious life. Chelles was originally founded in the sixth century by Clotild, wife of King Clovis I. Between 657 and 664 it was either refounded or enlarged by Balthild, an Englishwoman who had been brought to Gaul as a slave and subsequently rose to eminence as the wife of Clovis II. At Balthild's instigation a group of nuns went from Jouarre to Chelles under the leadership of Bertila, who, at the request of Anglo-Saxon rulers, later sent men, women and books to England to help in founding monasteries. Jouarre, Faremoutiers and Chelles were all double houses governed by abbesses. When we reflect that the greatest geographical distance between any two of them was less than that between Hartlepool and Whitby, we shall surely conclude that each is likely to have been well informed about the activities of the others. From the English side we know that after the death of King Edwin in 633, his widow Æthelburg, herself the granddaughter of Charibert, king of Paris, sent two of the royal children to Gaul to be brought up by her friend King Dagobert. And we have remarkable evidence from Bede testifying to close links between English royal families and these Frankish monasteries (*HE* III.8). Referring to about (or a little before) the middle of the seventh century, Bede remarks that at that time, when there were few monasteries among the English, many used to go from Britain to the Frankish monasteries in search of the monastic life which they could not find at home, and they also sent their daughters there for instruction in the religious life. He names three monasteries as being particularly favoured by the English. One of them, Andelys-sur-Seine, lies north-west of Paris; the other two were Chelles and Faremoutiers. Two daughters of the East Anglian royal family eventually became abbesses of Faremoutiers, and a daughter of a Kentish king married to an East Anglian was at the same monastery. It will be recalled that it was to Chelles that Hereswith, Hild's sister, had gone and that Hild herself would have gone to the same monastery had she not been dissuaded by Aidan (see above, p. 7). Hereswith had gone to Chelles before 651 and probably before 647, so it will have been to the old foundation that she originally went (that is, before the enlargement undertaken by Balthild between 657 and 664). We do not know how long Hereswith lived, but her sister Hild did not die until 680. We cannot make any direct link between Hereswith and Agilbert, but the link between Chelles and Faremoutiers on the one hand and the East Anglian royal family on the other is beyond all doubt. Through Hereswith that link is extended to her sister at Whitby.

# Surviving booklists from Anglo-Saxon England

MICHAEL LAPIDGE

In our attempts to understand the mental world of the Anglo-Saxons, and to interpret the literature which they have bequeathed to us, there is one tool of interpretation which allows perhaps a surer estimation than any other, and that is knowledge of the books which the Anglo-Saxons themselves knew and studied. But the attempt to acquire an overall understanding of what books were known to the Anglo-Saxons is no easy matter,[1] for it requires the judicious assessment of information gleaned from a variety of sources, none of them easily controlled. It must begin, obviously, with comprehensive knowledge of the contents of the surviving manuscripts known to have been written or owned in Anglo-Saxon England.[2] This knowledge must then be augmented in various ways, but principally by the identification of sources used by Anglo-Saxon authors writing either in Latin or in English. Such identification may be relatively straightforward in the case of Latin authors such as Aldhelm and Bede who frequently name their sources, but it can be a lengthy and painstaking business in the case of a widely read English author such as the (so-called) Old English Martyrologist,[3] who seldom specifies his sources. Until the sources used by Anglo-Saxon authors have all been identified, and the surviving Anglo-Saxon manuscripts catalogued, it is not possible to form a complete or accurate notion of what books were known and studied in Anglo-Saxon England; but it is welcome news that a number of scholars in different countries have begun to collaborate in the effort to achieve this distant but important goal.[4]

[1] There is a preliminary essay by J. D. A. Ogilvy, *Books known to the English, 597–1066* (Cambridge, Mass., 1967). This work, however, is slovenly and unreliable (particularly where the author refers to manuscript evidence), and cannot be consulted with confidence on any point; cf. the review by H. Gneuss, *Anglia* 89 (1971), 129–34.

[2] An excellent (and indispensable) beginning in this direction is H. Gneuss, 'A Preliminary List of Manuscripts written or owned in England up to 1100', *ASE* 9 (1981), 1–60. It is much to be hoped that Gneuss's preliminary list will serve as the basis for an eventual catalogue of the contents of all surviving Anglo-Saxon manuscripts.

[3] See J. E. Cross, 'On the Library of the Old English Martyrologist', below, pp. 227–49.

[4] See the reports in *OEN* 16.2 (1983), 58–69, and 17.1 (1983), 20–2. At a conference held at the University of Leeds on 24 March 1984 a committee (under the chairmanship of J. E. Cross) was formed to co-ordinate work on the sources used by Anglo-Saxon authors and to supervise the collection and eventual publication of such material.

In the meantime there is one source – hitherto insufficiently explored - which can provide a valuable index of what books were available in Anglo-Saxon England: namely the various booklists and inventories which record the contents of Anglo-Saxon libraries or the gifts of donors to these libraries. Although these booklists – some thirteen in number – have all previously been printed, they have never been collected and have not been studied systematically in the attempt to identify their contents. I have re-edited these various booklists below, and have provided each booklist with detailed commentary, establishing where possible the identity of each item; in a separate Appendix (below, pp. 82–9) I provide an alphabetical list of those identifications which may be regarded as certain. This list will provide some indication of what books and authors were known in Anglo-Saxon England, but I should stress that its evidence must always be used in combination with information derived from the contents of surviving Anglo-Saxon manuscripts and from identifiable sources of Anglo-Latin and Old English texts.

The booklists edited here are of various kinds: some are wills, some are lists of donations. Some, however, are inventories of libraries. Study of the contents of early medieval libraries necessitates some awareness of their physical arrangement and furniture. The library as we know it today – a capacious room with bookstacks or standing presses, readers' tables and lecterns – simply did not exist in the early Middle Ages.[5] Books were normally housed in a book-chest or book-cupboard (*armarium*[6] or *arca libraria*[7]). Books would have been kept in *armaria* whether they were owned privately by (say) kings,[8] wealthy aristocrats[9] or secular clerics, or corporately, as by a monas-

[5] See J. W. Clark, *The Care of Books*, 2nd ed. (Cambridge, 1902), pp. 51–94, and E. Lehmann, *Die Bibliotheksräume der deutschen Klöster im Mittelalter* (Berlin, 1957), pp. 2–7.

[6] *Ibid.* pp. 72–7.

[7] As evidence for the early Anglo-Saxon period, note Aldhelm's *enigma* on the *arca libraria* (no. lxxxix): *Aldhelmi Opera*, ed. R. Ehwald, MGH, Auct. antiq. 15 (Berlin, 1919), 138.

[8] There is little evidence for libraries owned by Anglo-Saxon kings. King Aldfrith of Northumbria (685–705) had a distinguished reputation for learning, was the dedicatee of Aldhelm's massive *Epistola ad Acircium*, and on one occasion sold eight hides of land in return for a magnificent manuscript of cosmographical writings (*cosmographiorum codice*) which Benedict Biscop had acquired in Rome (see below, n. 39); but we know nothing of Aldfrith's personal library. In the latter part of his reign King Alfred (871–99) was actively engaged in translating various Latin works into English, and must presumably have assembled a royal library of some size; but as to its contents we have no certain information (see S. Keynes and M. Lapidge, *Alfred the Great* (Harmondsworth, 1983), p. 214, n. 26). King Athelstan is well known as a donor of books to various churches (see S. Keynes, 'King Athelstan's Books', below, pp. 143–201), but, again, there is no evidence for a royal library in Athelstan's reign. A twelfth-century writer, Adelard of Bath, refers at one point to a book on hunting owned by Harold Godwinson (see C. H. Haskins, 'King Harold's Books', *EHR* 37 (1922), 398–400), but the book cannot be identified, and a single book does not in any case make a library. By contrast, there is abundant evidence for the royal libraries of Charle-

tery.[10] In the case of a monastery, however, books were needed for various purposes: school-books for the monastic classroom, service-books for the liturgical performance of mass and Office, legendaries for reading aloud in the refectory,[11] monastic rules and martyrologies for reading at chapter,[12] and reading-books for the private meditation and study of the monks.[13] There may often have been a separate *armarium* at each of these locations;[14] and the total contents of all *armaria* could be thought to constitute a monastic library's holdings. An inventory or booklist, therefore, might be an account of a monastery's entire holdings; on the other hand, it might simply be a record of the contents of one particular *armarium*. Thus, of the booklists edited below it is clear that nos. VI and VII are simple lists of service-books; nos. IV and IX

magne, his son Louis the Pious, and his grandson Louis the German: evidence brought to light by Bernhard Bischoff, *Mittelalterliche Studien*, 3 vols. (Stuttgart, 1966–81) III, 149–69 ('Die Hofbibliothek Karls des Grossen'), 170–86 ('Die Hofbibliothek unter Ludwig dem Frommen') and 187–212 ('Bücher am Hofe Ludwigs des Deutschen und die Privatbibliothek des Kanzlers Grimalt'); see also R. McKitterick, 'Charles the Bald (823–877) and his Library: the Patronage of Learning', *EHR* 95 (1980), 28–47.

9 I know of no evidence for libraries owned by Anglo-Saxon noblemen, although some, such as Ælfric's patron the ealdorman Æthelweard, must surely have possessed some number of books. By contrast, there is abundant evidence for libraries of continental, Carolingian noblemen; see P. Riché, 'Les Bibliothèques de trois aristocrates laïcs carolingiens', *Le moyen âge* 69 (1963), 87–104.

10 In the case of Benedictine monks all property (including books) was owned corporately; no monk was permitted to own so much as a book or pen: 'Ne quis praesumat aliquid dare aut accipere sine iussione abbatis neque aliquid habere proprium: nullam omnino rem, neque codicem, neque tabulas, neque graphium, sed nihil omnino' (*Regula S. Benedicti*, ch. 33). Bear in mind, however, that this stipulation would not pertain to colleges of secular canons and the like; cf. my remarks concerning Ælberht and Alcuin, below, p. 45.

11 Some idea of what books were read at mealtimes in the refectory may be gleaned from a twelfth-century list from Durham: 'Hii sunt libri qui leguntur ad collationem: Vitae patrum; Diadema monachorum; Effrem cum vitis Egiptiorum; Paradisus; Speculum; Dialogus; Pastoralis eximius liber; Ysidorus de summo bono; Prosper de contemplatiua uita; liber Odonis; Iohannes Cassianus decem Collationes' (*Catalogi Bibliothecarum Antiqui*, ed. G. Becker (Bonn, 1885), p. 245). When we encounter some of these titles in pre-Conquest booklists – especially the *Vitas patrum*, Gregory the Great's *Dialogi* and *Regula pastoralis*, Julianus Pomerius's *De uita contemplatiua*, Isidore's *Sententiae* and Cassian's *Collationes* – there is some presumption that they may have been used for refectory reading.

12 See the remarks of H. Gneuss, below, pp. 128–31.

13 The *Regula S. Benedicti* (ch. 48) required each monk to read one book of the bible during Lent. Carolingian commentators reinterpreted this provision to mean that each monk was required to read one entire book (not merely a book of the bible) during the course of each year; see K. Christ, 'In caput quadragesimae', *Zentralblatt für Bibliothekswesen* 60 (1944), 33–59, and A. Mundó, '"Bibliotheca": Bible et lecture du Carême d'après Saint Benoît', *RB* 60 (1950), 65–92. A large part of any monastic library's holdings will have been earmarked for private reading of this sort.

14 For examples from a later period, see Clark, *The Care of Books*, pp. 98–100; see, further, the discussion by F. Wormald: *The English Library before 1700*, ed. F. Wormald and C. E. Wright (London, 1958), pp. 15–20.

lists of books used in the classroom; and no. XII an inventory of an *armarium commune* containing books for the monks' private study and meditation.

As long as libraries were relatively small, it was possible merely to list the contents of the separately located *armaria*, if indeed any record were needed; in such cases the record need only have been a simple list or inventory. Such inventories as survive are sometimes organized (in the sequence bibles, Church Fathers, theology, classical authors, and so on); more often the books are listed randomly, as they came to hand. From the late eleventh century onwards, however, libraries grew considerably in size, so that the common store of books was typically numbered in the hundreds and housed in many *armaria*. At this point it became necessary to develop a system of recording the contents of the various *armaria* so that books could be located and retrieved. Thus developed the true 'library catalogue' with its corresponding system of shelf-marks: henceforth each entry in a booklist or catalogue was provided with a shelf-mark which directed the enquirer to a particular *armarium* (and, in the case of more sophisticated systems, to a particular shelf of the *armarium*); the shelf-mark was entered in the book as well so that it could be relocated.[15] And in order further to facilitate the search for individual books, lengthy catalogues were often provided with what we would call an 'index' – an alphabetical list of authors and works (such catalogues are referred to as 'double lists').[16] But the complex methods of catalography which were evolved to record the contents of large monastic libraries pertain to the later Middle Ages. In the Anglo-Saxon period, booklists were no more than simple inventories.

Although the inventories of the earlier period are never as extensive or complex as the later medieval catalogues, they are none the less the principal source of information about the nature and contents of early medieval libraries.[17] Numerous inventories or booklists of various origin and date survive from early medieval Europe, and many of these have been listed by

[15] On the development of techniques of catalography, see the general remarks of D. M. Norris, *A History of Cataloguing and Cataloguing Methods 1100–1850* (London, 1939), esp. pp. 7–25, and the excellent discussion by A. Derolez, *Les Catalogues des bibliothèques*, Typologie des sources du moyen âge occidental 31 (Turnhout, 1979).

[16] See Derolez, *Les Catalogues*, pp. 40–2. A good example of a double list from Dover is ptd M. R. James, *Ancient Libraries of Canterbury and Dover* (Cambridge, 1903), pp. 407–95.

[17] On medieval libraries in general, see discussion by K. Christ in *Handbuch der Bibliotheks-wissenschaft*, ed. F. Milkau, 2nd ed., rev. G. Leyh, 3 vols. in 5 (Wiesbaden, 1952–65) III, 243–498; see also K. Christ, 'Bibliotheksgeschichte des Mittelalters. Zur Methode und zur neuesten Literatur', *Zentralblatt für Bibliothekswesen* 61 (1947), 38–56, 149–66 and 233–52, as well as J. W. Thompson, *The Medieval Library* (New York, 1939), repr. with suppl. by B. Boyer (1957), a book impressive in scope but unreliable in detail. There is also a brief introduction to the subject by K. W. Humphreys, 'The Early Medieval Library', *Paläographie 1981*, ed. G. Silagi (Munich, 1982), pp. 59–70. These general accounts must be supplemented by individual studies. On the relationship of library to scriptorium there is an

Theodor Gottlieb.[18] Gottlieb's catalogue covers the entire medieval period up to the fifteenth century, and is arranged according to the various countries of Europe. Not all the booklists catalogued by Gottlieb have been printed, but for the early period (up to the twelfth century) there is a serviceable edition of some 136 lists by Gustav Becker.[19] However, because of the incompleteness and the limited chronological scope of Becker's book, the full scholarly edition of surviving booklists and catalogues has long been a desideratum of students of medieval books and libraries. As a result of large-scale projects mounted in several European countries earlier this century, we now have reliable and scholarly editions of booklists and catalogues from Austria[20] and from most of Germany and Switzerland;[21] an edition of catalogues from Belgium is in progress,[22] and work has begun on the edition of catalogues from France.[23]

excellent study by B. Bischoff, 'Die Bibliothek im Dienste der Schule', *Mittelalterliche Studien* III, 213–33. On monastic libraries in general, see D. Leistle, 'Über Klosterbibliotheken des Mittelalters', *Studien und Mitteilungen zur Geschichte des Benediktiner-Ordens und seiner Zweige* 36 (1915), 197–228 and 357–77; for monastic libraries of the Lotharingian and Cluniac reform movements (a topic which has some relevance to Anglo-Saxon England), see R. Kottje, 'Klosterbibliotheken und monastische Kultur in der zweiten Hälfte des 11. Jahrhunderts', *Zeitschrift für Kirchengeschichte* 80 (1969), 145–62. Finally, there are some particular studies of monastic libraries in various countries. For Germany, see K. Löffler, *Deutsche Klosterbibliotheken*, 2nd ed. (Bonn and Leipzig, 1922); B. Bischoff, *Die südostdeutschen Schreibschulen und Bibliotheken in der Karolingerzeit*, 2 vols. (Wiesbaden, 1960–80); and L. Buzas, *Deutsche Bibliotheksgeschichte des Mittelalters* (Wiesbaden, 1975). For France, see E. Lesne, *Les Livres, scriptoria et bibliothèques du commencement du VIIIe à la fin du XIe siècle*, Histoire de la propriété ecclésiastique en France, 6 vols. (Lille and Paris, 1910–43) IV (1938). For Spain, see M. C. Díaz y Díaz, *Libros y librerías en la Rioja altomedieval* (Logroño, 1979). For England, see below, n. 26.

18 *Über mittelalterliche Bibliotheken* (Leipzig, 1890). Gottlieb's catalogue is indispensable, but is now much in need of revision; see P. G. Meier, 'Nachträge zu Gottlieb, ueber mittelalterliche Bibliotheken', *Zentralblatt für Bibliothekswesen* 20 (1903), 16–32, and J. S. Beddie ('The Ancient Classics in Mediaeval Libraries', *Speculum* 5 (1930), 3–20), who adds seventy-one catalogues to Gottlieb's list.

19 G. Becker, *Catalogi Bibliothecarum Antiqui* (Bonn, 1885). This work has been superseded in many respects: by more recent editions of catalogues, by more accurate attribution of manuscripts containing booklists. It contains no commentary, and no attempt is made to identify any of the items in the list; the index is virtually useless. Nevertheless, for the early medieval period the book is (as yet) indispensable.

20 *Mittelalterliche Bibliothekskataloge Österreichs*, 5 vols. and suppl. (Vienna, 1915–71).

21 *Mittelalterliche Bibliothekskataloge Deutschlands und der Schweiz*, 4 vols. in 6 (Munich, 1918–79) (hereafter *MBKDS*).

22 *Corpus Catalogorum Belgii I*, ed. A. Derolez (Brussels, 1966); see also *Contributions à l'histoire des bibliothèques et de la lecture aux Pays-Bas avant 1600* (Brussels, 1974).

23 The *Index systematique des bibliothèques anciennes* (*ISBA*) is in preparation, under the direction of André Vernet, at the Institut de recherche et d'histoire des textes in Paris; see 'Pour un traitement automatique des inventaires anciens de manuscrits', *Revue d'histoire des textes* 3 (1973), 313–14, and 4 (1974), 436–7. In the meantime, editions of a large number of medieval French library catalogues are to be found in L. Delisle, *Le Cabinet des manuscrits de la Bibliothèque impériale*, 3 vols. (Paris, 1868–81).

Unfortunately, for the British Isles, and for England in particular, we are less well served: no complete list of surviving booklists and catalogues of English medieval libraries has ever been published,[24] and the booklists themselves have yet to be collected and edited,[25] with the result that we are poorly placed to form an accurate impression of the extent and holdings of medieval English libraries.[26] The British Academy has recently appointed a committee to plan and oversee the publication of medieval English booklists and catalogues; the appearance of the first volumes is said to be imminent. However, the committee's principal concern is with catalogues of individual houses from the period after 1100. The present edition of surviving booklists from Anglo-Saxon England is complementary to that larger project, therefore, and may be seen as a prolegomenon to the history of Anglo-Saxon libraries.[27]

In determining which Anglo-Saxon booklists to print I have been guided by several criteria. I have excluded, for example, statements by churchmen concerning what liturgical books priests were expected to own. Such statements occur in the penitential attributed to Archbishop Egbert of York (732–66),[28] and on several occasions in the pastoral writings of Ælfric;[29] but these

24 See Gottlieb, *Über mittelalterliche Bibliotheken*, nos. 435–512. There is a useful (but incomplete) list in E. A. Savage, *Old English Libraries* (London, 1911), pp. 263–85; see also L. Gougaud, 'Inventaires de manuscrits provenants d'anciennes bibliothèques monastiques de Grande Bretagne', *RHE* 33 (1937), 789–91 (a brief list of some thirty catalogues). The indispensable tool for the study of medieval English libraries and their catalogues is N. R. Ker, *Medieval Libraries of Great Britain*, 2nd ed. (London, 1964); surviving booklists and catalogues are listed where relevant under individual houses.

25 See H. Omont, 'Anciens Catalogues de bibliothèques anglaises (XIIIe–XIVe siècle)', *Zentralblatt für Bibliothekswesen* 9 (1892), 201–22 (prints four catalogues), as well as the important studies by M. R. James: *On the Abbey of St Edmund at Bury* (Cambridge, 1895), *Ancient Libraries of Canterbury and Dover* (Cambridge, 1903), and *Lists of Manuscripts formerly in Peterborough Abbey* (Oxford, 1926).

26 Surviving books from medieval English libraries are listed by Ker, *Medieval Libraries*; but this information needs always to be collated with the evidence of booklists and catalogues. There is a useful (but outdated) survey by Savage, *Old English Libraries*, and valuable introductions to the subject in *The English Library before 1700*, ed. Wormald and Wright, and especially in H. Gneuss, 'Englands Bibliotheken im Mittelalter und ihr Untergang', *Festschrift für Walter Hübner*, ed. D. Riesner and H. Gneuss (Berlin, 1964), pp. 91–121.

27 The history of Anglo-Saxon libraries cannot be written in the present state of knowledge. Various essays on the subject are in print, but none are satisfactory: R. B. Hepple, 'Early Northumbrian Libraries', *AAe* 3rd ser. 14 (1917), 92–106; R. Bressie, 'Libraries of the British Isles in the Anglo-Saxon Period', *The Medieval Library*, ed. Thompson, pp. 102–25; and R. Irwin, 'In Saxon England: Studies in the History of Libraries', *Lib. Assoc. Record* 57 (1955), 290–6. See instead the judicious remarks by Gneuss, 'Englands Bibliotheken', pp. 94–9.

28 A. W. Haddan and W. Stubbs, *Councils and Ecclesiastical Documents relating to Great Britain and Ireland*, 3 vols. (Oxford, 1869) III, 417.

29 *Die Hirtenbriefe Ælfrics in altenglischer und lateinischer Fassung*, ed. B. Fehr, Bibliothek der angelsächsischen Prosa 9 (Hamburg, 1914), repr. with suppl. by P. Clemoes (Darmstadt, 1966), 13, 51 and 126–7.

lists are desiderata, not actual records of existing books. Also, I have assumed that a 'list' must include at least two specific items. I therefore omit the various references to books (specified and unspecified) which often occur in Anglo-Saxon wills.[30] By the same token I omit the reference to two gospel-books and a lavishly decorated collectary which, according to William of Malmesbury, were bequeathed to Glastonbury by Brihtwold, bishop of Ramsbury, on his death in 1045.[31] I also omit reference to Gunhild (sister of Harold Godwinson) who on her death in 1087 bequeathed to Saint-Donatien in Bruges a psalter which, since it contained glosses in Old English, must have been of English origin (see below, n. 93). Similarly, at a later period, Judith of Flanders, sometime wife of Earl Tostig of Northumbria (*ob.* 1066), was well known as a collector of manuscripts, particularly of lavishly decorated gospel-books.[32] After Tostig's death she married a Bavarian duke, and on her death in 1094 she bequeathed her collection of manuscripts to the abbey of Weingarten (in Württemberg).[33] Two at least of these books (both of them gospel-books) were written in Anglo-Saxon England.[34] Another important source of evidence for books and libraries is the various collections of correspondence which have survived from the Anglo-Saxon period. Books are frequently mentioned in the letters of Boniface and his circle of English correspondents,[35]

30 See D. Whitelock, *Anglo-Saxon Wills* (Cambridge, 1930), pp. 2 and 4 (sacramentaries), 14 and 52 (unspecified books) and 54 (a psalter).

31 William of Malmesbury, *De Antiquitate Glastonie Ecclesie*, ed. J. Scott (Ipswich, 1981), p. 138: 'Hic misit . . . textus euangeliorum .ii. . . . Dedit eciam collectaneum auro illuminatum.'

32 On Judith as book-collector, see M. Harrsen, 'The Countess Judith of Flanders and the Library of Weingarten Abbey', *Papers of the Bibliographical Soc. of America* 24 (1930), 1–13.

33 The record of her donation is preserved as an addition to Fulda, Landesbibliothek, Aa 21 (Saint-Omer, s. xi$^{med}$), 89v: '. . . tria plenaria cum uno textu euangelii'; see Gottlieb, *Über mittelalterliche Bibliotheken*, no. 938, and *MBKDS* 1, 399.

34 They survive as New York, Pierpont Morgan Library, 708 and 709.

35 *S. Bonifatii et Lullii Epistolae*, ed. M. Tangl, MGH, Epist. select. 1 (Berlin, 1916), 27 ('passiones martyrum'; 'congregationes aliquas sanctarum scripturarum'), 54 ('sanctorum librorum munera'), 57 ('interrogationes Augustini pontificis . . . et responsiones sancti Gregorii pape'), 59 ('tractatus super apostolum Paulum . . . super duas epistolas tractatus, id est ad Romanos et ad Corintheos primam'), 60 ('epistolae . . . sancti Petri apostoli'), 131 ('liber [sex] prophetarum'), 144 ('Aldhelmi . . . aliqua opuscula'), 158 ('de opusculis Bedan lectoris aliquos tractatus' and 'exemplaria epistolarum sancti Gregorii'), 159 ('de opusculis . . . Bedan'), 207 ('Beda . . . super lectionarium anniuersarium et prouerbia Salomonis'), 245 ('librum pyrpyri metri' [=Optatianus Porphyrius, *Carmina*?]), 247 ('saecularis scientiae libros . . . de medicinalibus'), 251 ('libellos de uiro Dei Cudbercto metro et prosa conpositos'), 261 ('libros cosmografiorum'), 263 ('Beda . . . in primam partem Samuelis usque ad mortem Saulis libros quattuor, siue in Esdram et Nehemiam libros tres, uel in euangelium Marci libros quattuor'), 264 ('Beda . . . de edificatione templi, uel in cantica canticorum, siue epigrammatum heroico metro siue elegiaco conpositorum') and 265 ('Baeda de aedificio templi').

in the letters of Alcuin,[36] in a famous letter of Lupus of Ferrières addressed to Abbot Ealdsige of York[37] and in the various letters of the later Anglo-Saxon period which have been preserved as a collection in London, BL Cotton Tiberius A. xv.[38] Such isolated references deserve to be collected and studied in their own right, but they can scarcely qualify as booklists. The same is true of incidental references to books in various historical and hagiographical writings of the period; these too deserve to be collected.[39]

[36] In his correspondence Alcuin seldom mentions books (as physical objects, that is, rather than as sources of quotations). Only in letters to very intimate friends are books a subject of discussion: thus, for example, in letters to Hrabanus Maurus (*Ep.* cxlii), Ricbod (*Ep.* cxci) and Arno (*Ep.* cxciii) (MGH, Epist. 4, ed. E. Dümmler *et al.* (Berlin, 1895), 223–4, 318 and 319–21 respectively). By the same token, books are seldom mentioned in his letters to colleagues in England. An interesting exception is a letter of 801 addressed to Archbishop Eanbald II of York (*Ep.* ccxxvi): 'De ordinatione et dispositione missalis libelli nescio cur demandasti. Numquid non habes Romano more ordinatos libellos sacratarios abundanter? Habes quoque et ueteris consuetudinis sufficienter sacramentaria maiora' (MGH, Epist. 4, 370).

[37] MGH, Epist. 6 (Berlin, 1925), 62: 'Atque ut, quod polliceor, uos exequamini priores, obnixe flagito, ut quaestiones beati Ieronimi, quas, teste Cassiodoro, in uetus et nouum testamentum elaborauit, Bedae quoque uestri similiter quaestiones in utrumque testamentum itemque memorati Ieronimi libros explanationum in Hieremiam, praeter sex primos, qui apud nos reperiuntur, ceteros qui secuntur; preterea Quintiliani Institutionum oratoriarum libros XII per certissimos nuntios mihi ad cellam sancti Iudoci, quae tandem aliquando nobis reddita est, dirigatis tradendos Lantrammo, qui bene uobis notus est, ibique exscribendos uobisque, quam poterit fieri celerius, remittendos.' The letter is datable to 852, and has been translated by D. Whitelock, *EHD*, pp. 877–8. Nothing further is known of this Abbot Ealdsige (or *Altsig*, as his name is given in Lupus's letter), and I must confess to some suspicions about his rôle as 'abbot' at York in the mid-ninth century, since, as far as we can tell from other sources, York was a house of secular clerics.

[38] *Memorials of St Dunstan*, ed. W. Stubbs, Rolls Ser. (London, 1874), pp. 354–404. Books are mentioned on pp. 362 ('quendam nostri coenobii librum scilicet euangeliorum'), 376 ('commentum Flori . . . et alios libellos qui habentur Wintonie') and 388 ('Ealdelmi . . . de parthenali laude libellum').

[39] For example, the well-known references in Bede's *Historia abbatum* to the books collected by Benedict Biscop (*Venerabilis Baedae Opera Historica*, ed. C. Plummer, 2 vols. (Oxford, 1896) I, 369: 'innumerabilem librorum omnis generis copiam adportauit') and by Ceolfrith (*ibid.* pp. 379–80: 'bibliothecam utriusque monasterii, quam Benedictus abbas magna caepit instantia, ipse non minori geminauit industria; ita ut tres pandectes nouae translationis, ad unum uetustae translationis quem de Roma adtulerat, ipse super adiungeret; quorum unum senex Romam rediens secum inter alia pro munere sumpsit, duos utrique monasterio reliquit; dato quoque Cosmographiorum codice mirandi operis, quem Romae Benedictus emerat, terram octo familiarum iuxta fluuium Fresca ab Aldfrido rege in scripturis doctissimo in possessionem monasterii beati Pauli apostoli comparuit'); or the lavish gospel-books commissioned by Wilfrid and described in the *Vita S. Wilfridi* (*The Life of Bishop Wilfrid by Eddius Stephanus*, ed. B. Colgrave (Cambridge, 1927), p. 36: 'Nam quattuor euangelia de auro purissimo in membranis depurpuratis, coloratis, pro animae suae remedio scribere iussit'). From the later period we learn of a collection of religious and grammatical books taken from London to Evesham by Bishop Ælfweard (*Chronicon Abbatiae de Evesham*, ed. W. D. Macray,

Indirect light may also be thrown on the nature and contents of Anglo-Saxon libraries in the early period by consideration of the monastic libraries in monasteries founded by Anglo-Saxon missionaries,[40] for it is a reasonable assumption that these would in the first instance have been stocked with books sent over from England.[41] It is not possible to trace the early holdings of all the Anglo-Saxon foundations on the continent, but it is especially interesting that early booklists survive from two of these foundations – Fulda (founded 744) and Würzburg (Burghard appointed bishop by Boniface 742) – and that these two booklists are among the earliest such documents to survive. First, the Fulda list. In a copy of Isidore's *De natura rerum* now in Basle (Universitätsbibliothek, F. III. 15a),[42] a scribe writing Anglo-Saxon minuscule (datable on palaeographical grounds to the late eighth century) copied on 17v–18r a list of some twenty books. Paul Lehmann, who first recognized the importance of this list, demonstrated that it (like the manuscript) originated at Fulda and was thus the earliest record of the Fulda library.[43] Secondly, the Würzburg list. On a page originally blank (260r) of a copy of Augustine's *De trinitate* now in Oxford (Bodleian Library, Laud Misc. 126)[44] a scribe writing Anglo-Saxon minuscule datable to s. viii$^{ex}$ copied a list of some thirty-six books. E. A. Lowe, who first identified the list, argued that it was a record of the episcopal library of Würzburg,[45] and his conclusions have been followed by subsequent scholars.[46] Each of these booklists, therefore, was copied in Anglo-Saxon minuscule at an important Anglo-Saxon foundation within a half-century of that foundation's establishment, and hence has direct relevance to the question of what books were thought essential to the Anglo-Saxon mission. But they

Rolls Ser. (London, 1863), p. 83: 'Libros etiam plurimos tam diuinos quam grammaticos de Londonia transmisit'). And shortly after the Conquest Abbot Frederick of St Albans, being obliged to flee to Ely, took a number of books with him (Thomas Walsingham, *Gesta Abbatum Monasterii S. Albani*, ed. H. T. Riley, 3 vols., Rolls Ser. (London, 1867–9) I, 51: 'assumptis secum quibusdam libris'). Many similar references no doubt await detection and collection.

40 In general see W. Levison, *England and the Continent in the Eighth Century* (Oxford, 1946), pp. 139–48.

41 This assumption is confirmed by the repeated requests for books which are found in the letters of Boniface and his colleagues; see above, n. 35.

42 See E. A. Lowe, *Codices Latini Antiquiores* I–XI and Suppl. (Oxford, 1934–71), and II, 2nd ed. (1972) (hereafter abbreviated *CLA*), VII, no. 842.

43 P. Lehmann, *Fuldaer Studien*, Sitzungsberichte der bayerischen Akademie der Wissenschaften 1925 (Munich, 1925), pp. 4–6; the list is ed. *ibid.* pp. 48–50.

44 *CLA* II, no. 252.

45 E. A. Lowe, 'An Eighth-Century List of Books in a Bodleian Manuscript from Würzburg and its Probable Relationship to the Laudian Acts', *Speculum* 3 (1928), 3–15, repr. in his *Palaeographical Papers 1907–1965*, ed. L. Bieler, 2 vols. (Oxford, 1972) II, 239–50.

46 See B. Bischoff and J. B. Hofmann, *Libri Sancti Kyliani* (Würzburg, 1952), pp. 142–8 (which includes an edition and full commentary on the booklist), and *MBKDS* IV.2, 977–9 (no. 126).

have only indirect relevance to the question of library-holdings in England itself, and have therefore been omitted here.

In determining which booklists to include I have adopted a date of *c.* 1100 as an outer chronological limit; but I have included a list from the period *c.* 1070 × *c.* 1100 only when there is evidence that it pertains to a house which was in existence in the pre-Conquest period and that the books in question were the products of Anglo-Saxon rather than Norman scriptoria. I have therefore omitted lists of donations made by Norman churchmen to English libraries. Thus I omit the substantial list of some fifty books donated by William of Saint-Carilef (*ob.* 1096) to Durham,[47] since there is no means of establishing that any of the books in question was in the possession of an English library before 1066; indeed, of those books in William's list which survive and can be identified, nearly all are of Norman, not Anglo-Saxon, manufacture.[48] By the same token, I omit the substantial list of books which were donated by Paul of Caen, abbot of St Albans (1077–93), to the abbey of St Albans.[49] The question of the Norman contribution to English book-production and libraries is a fundamental one, but it is too vast to be broached here.[50]

In treating booklists and inventories as evidence for early medieval libraries, the principal problem is that of identifying the items listed. Although numerous booklists have been printed, they have only rarely been supplied with a sufficient amount of commentary to permit reasonable inferences to be

47 C. H. Turner, 'The Earliest List of Durham Manuscripts', *JTS* 19 (1918), 121–32.

48 See R. A. B. Mynors, *Durham Cathedral Manuscripts to the End of the Twelfth Century* (Oxford, 1939), pp. 32–45 and pls. 16–31. Of the manuscripts listed by Mynors only one is written in a hand which (in my opinion) is more characteristic of Anglo-Saxon than Norman scribal practice (Mynors described it as being in a hand 'unlike any other Durham book', p. 36). This is a copy of Augustine, *Tractatus in euangelium Ioannis*, now Durham, Cathedral Library, B. II. 16, which is written in the characteristic spindly late Anglo-Caroline script seen in the work of Eadui Basan (T. A. M. Bishop, *English Caroline Minuscule* (Oxford, 1971), pp. xxiii and 22–4); see Mynors, *ibid.* pl. 24. But it is not certain that Durham B. II. 16 was one of William's books, and it may have reached Durham by a different route.

49 *Gesta Abbatum Monasterii S. Albani* I, 58: 'Dedit igitur huic ecclesie uiginti octo uolumina notabilia, et octo psalteria, collectarium, epistolarium, et librum in quo continentur euangelia legenda per annum; duos textus, auro et argento et gemmis ornatos, sine ordinalibus, consuetudinariis, missalibus, tropariis, collectariis et aliis libris qui in armariolis habentur.'

50 In general see D. Knowles, *The Monastic Order in England*, 2nd ed. (Cambridge, 1963), pp. 522–7, and N. R. Ker, *English Manuscripts in the Century after the Norman Conquest* (Oxford, 1960), pp. 7–8. On the holdings of twelfth-century libraries in general, see J. S. Beddie, 'Libraries in the Twelfth Century: their Catalogues and Contents', *Anniversary Essays in Mediaeval History by Students of Charles Homer Haskins*, ed. C. H. Taylor (Boston and New York, 1929), pp. 1–23; on the holdings of Norman libraries in Normandy, see G. Nortier-Marchand, *Les Bibliothèques médiévales des abbayes bénédictines de Normandie*, 2nd ed. (Paris, 1971).

drawn about what books were in question.[51] It is to be hoped that future editors of early medieval booklists will turn their attention to the need for commentary and identification of items listed. In some cases identification is simple and straightforward; in others, it can be extremely problematic. In the case of classical authors, for example, identification is usually unproblematic:[52] as tools of research we have Manitius's detailed study of entries pertaining to classical authors in medieval library catalogues,[53] as well as Munk Olsen's recent and comprehensive catalogue of pre-twelfth-century manuscripts of classical authors.[54] For Latin patristic authors there is the indispensable *Clavis Patrum Latinorum*,[55] which provides convenient bibliographical guidance to the manuscript transmission of patristic texts. There are problems here, however, in that a single patristic work may have travelled under many different titles, and that many pseudonymous works travelled undetected under the name(s) of the great Latin Fathers. Furthermore, references to patristic texts in medieval booklists and catalogues have not been systematically collected or studied in the way that Manitius, for example, has treated references to classical texts. Identification of patristic texts, therefore, is often a matter of guesswork. For works composed later than *c*. 800, when the *Clavis* ceases to be a guide, we have Manitius's compendious *Geschichte der lateinischen Literatur des Mittelalters*,[56] but even this great work has now been superseded in some respects.[57] For the transmission and circulation in the Latin west of Greek patristic authors in Latin translation there is reliable guidance avail-

[51] For example, there is no commentary whatsoever in Becker, *Catalogi*, and only occasional annotation in *MBKDS*.

[52] The classical holdings of medieval libraries have been a perennial subject of interest; in general see Beddie, 'The Ancient Classics', pp. 3–17, and D. Knowles, 'The Preservation of the Classics', *The English Library before 1700*, ed. Wormald and Wright, pp. 136–47.

[53] M. Manitius, *Handschriften antiker Autoren in mittelalterlichen Bibliothekskatalogen*, ed. K. Manitius (Leipzig, 1935). This work (published posthumously) is a revised and much-amplified version of Manitius's earlier *Philologisches aus alten Bibliothekskatalogen (bis 1300)*, Rheinisches Museum 47, Ergänzungsheft (Frankfurt a.M., 1892).

[54] B. Munk Olsen, *L'Étude des auteurs classiques latins aux XIe et XIIe siècles: I, Catalogue des manuscrits classiques latins copiés du IXe au XIIe siècle, Apicius–Juvenal* (Paris, 1982) (work in progress). An excellent handbook, which presents a brief sketch of the manuscript transmission of each classical Latin author, is *Texts and Transmission: a Survey of the Latin Classics*, ed. L. D. Reynolds (Oxford, 1983).

[55] E. Dekkers and A. Gaar, *Clavis Patrum Latinorum*, 2nd ed. (Steenbrugge, 1961), a work which is now in some need of revision.

[56] M. Manitius, *Geschichte der lateinischen Literatur des Mittelalters*, 3 vols. (Munich, 1911–31). As a matter of course Manitius discusses (with reference to each author) the manuscript transmission and references in medieval catalogues; inevitably, in a work of such enormous scope, the references are not always complete.

[57] For example, Haimo of Auxerre is now recognized as an important and influential biblical commentator and homiliarist (see *Deutschlands Geschichtsquellen im Mittelalter* v, ed. H. Löwe (Weimar, 1973), 564–5), but he is barely mentioned by Manitius (*Geschichte* I, 516–17).

able.[58] But many problematical areas remain.[59] In proposing identifications of items in the following booklists, I have always attempted to indicate where an identification is reasonably certain, and where it is no more than a guess. It is to be hoped that, as work proceeds on cataloguing manuscripts of Anglo-Saxon origin or provenance, and on the literary sources used by Anglo-Saxon authors, hesitant identifications may be tested more thoroughly.

In the Commentary which accompanies each booklist, I use the following abbreviations (other abbreviations, used throughout this volume, are listed above, pp. xi–xii):

| | |
|---|---|
| Becker, *Catalogi* | G. Becker, *Catalogi Bibliothecarum Antiqui* (Bonn, 1885) |
| *CLA* | E. A. Lowe, *Codices Latini Antiquiores* I–XI and Suppl. (Oxford, 1934–71) and II, 2nd ed. (1972) |
| *Clavis* | E. Dekkers and A. Gaar, *Clavis Patrum Latinorum*, 2nd ed. (Steenbrugge, 1961) |
| Gneuss, 'Liturgical Books' | H. Gneuss, 'Liturgical Books in Anglo-Saxon England and their Old English Terminology', below, pp. 91–141 |
| Gottlieb | T. Gottlieb, *Über mittelalterliche Bibliotheken* (Leipzig, 1890) |
| *GL* | H. Keil, *Grammatici Latini*, ed. H. Keil, 8 vols. (Leipzig, 1857–80) |
| *ICL* | D. Schaller and E. Könsgen, *Initia Carminum Latinorum saeculo undecimo Antiquiorum* (Göttingen, 1977) |
| Manitius, *Geschichte* | M. Manitius, *Geschichte der lateinischen Literatur des Mittelalters*, 3 vols. (Munich, 1911–31) |
| Manitius, *Handschriften* | M. Manitius, *Handschriften antiker Autoren in mittelalterlichen Bibliothekskatalogen*, ed. K. Manitius (Leipzig, 1935) |

Note, finally, that in the booklists edited below the numbers in the left-hand margin refer to individual items, not to line-numbers of text (accordingly material in the texts other than references to books does not figure in the numbering).

58 See A. Siegmund (*Die Überlieferung der griechischen christlichen Literatur* (Munich and Pasing, 1949)), who provides a convenient conspectus of pre-twelfth-century manuscripts of Latin translations of Greek patristic texts, arranged by author (pp. 49–138); see also the valuable introduction by W. Berschin, *Griechisch–lateinisches Mittelalter* (Bern and Munich, 1980).

59 Liturgical books, for example. As far as I am aware there exists no comprehensive treatment of the Latin terminology for liturgical books of the early medieval period; cf. the remarks of Helmut Gneuss, 'Liturgical Books in Anglo-Saxon England and their Old English Terminology', below, pp. 91–141, at 95.

## *I. Books owned by Ælberht, archbishop of York, and bequeathed to Alcuin (c. 778)*

In 778 Ælberht, archbishop of York, determined to relinquish his worldly and ecclesiastical authority, and to spend the remainder of his life in seclusion. Before retiring from the world he distributed his earthly possessions to his two closest followers. To Eanbald, who succeeded him as archbishop, he bequeathed his treasures, estates and money; to Alcuin he bequeathed his books. Our principal source for this distribution of Ælberht's wealth is Alcuin's long poem on the saints of York, called by its editors *Versus de patribus, regibus et sanctis Euboricensis ecclesiae*.[60] Alcuin had been deeply devoted to Ælberht, and he was concerned in his poem to stress the munificence of Ælberht's legacy to him. Hence Alcuin included an extensive account of the library which Ælberht had amassed, and this account has customarily been regarded as one of the earliest surviving medieval booklists.[61]

It is important to stress that Ælberht's books were *bequeathed* to Alcuin, and that he henceforth took ownership of them. Although the books were housed at York, they were not the property of the York *familia*; Ælberht and Alcuin were secular clerics, not monks, and their books accordingly were private property, not owned corporately by the cathedral *familia*. The books mentioned in Alcuin's poem are often referred to as 'the York Cathedral library' (or whatever); but such designations are misleading. When Alcuin left York for the continent in 782 to take up duties as master of Charlemagne's palace school, he left his collection of books behind in York, no doubt as a matter of convenience. However, he did not forget about them. Thus he wrote to Eanbald II on his election to the archbishopric of York in 796 to remind Eanbald that he (Alcuin) had inherited – and hence was owner of – the books that were housed at York: '. . . et praesse [*sc.* Eanbald II] thesauris sapientiae, in quibus me magister meus dilectus Aelberhtus archiepiscopus *heredem reliquit*' (my italics).[62] Shortly thereafter Alcuin was appointed abbot of Tours; and he then wrote to Charlemagne stating that he greatly missed his 'exquisitiores . . . libelli' and reporting to the king that he was making arrangements to have the library transported from York (to Tours, presumably), so that the 'flowers of Britain' might be brought to France: 'Sed ex parte desunt mihi, seruulo uestro, exquisitiores eruditionis scolasticae libelli . . .

[60] Ed. E. Dümmler, MGH, PLAC 1 (Berlin, 1881), 169–206; P. Godman, *Alcuin: the Bishops, Kings, and Saints of York* (Oxford, 1982).

[61] Alcuin's description is ptd Becker, *Catalogi*, no. 3. In reprinting Alcuin's list I have renumbered the lines (which are lines 1540–56 in Dümmler's edition and 1541–57 in Godman's).

[62] *Ep.* cxiv (MGH, Epist. 4, 167).

Ideo haec uestrae excellentiae dico . . . ut aliquos ex pueris nostris remittam, qui excipiant inde nobis necessaria quaeque et reuehant in Franciam flores Brittaniae.'[63] Unfortunately we do not know whether the students were indeed dispatched to collect the books, and whether Alcuin was ever united with his library in the last years of his life; but we should be cautious in assuming (without evidence) that any of the books remained in England.[64]

Alcuin's booklist has been discussed on many occasions.[65] But because Alcuin did not give specific titles it is impossible in most cases to be certain of what books were in question. In the commentary which accompanies the text I rely frequently on the detailed discussion of this list by Peter Godman.[66]

quod pater Hieronymus, quod sensit Hilarius atque
Ambrosius praesul, simul Augustinus et ipse
sanctus Athanasius, quod Orosius edit acutus,
quicquid Gregorius summus docet et Leo papa,
Basilius quicquid Fulgentius atque coruscant,
Cassiodorus item, Chrysostomus atque Iohannes;
quicquid et Althelmus docuit, quid Beda magister;
quae Victorinus scripsere Boethius atque;
historici ueteres, Pompeius, Plinius ipse,
acer Aristoteles, rhetor quoque Tullius ingens;
quid quoque Sedulius uel quid canit ipse Iuuencus,
Alcimus et Clemens, Prosper, Paulinus, Arator,
quid Fortunatus uel quid Lactantius edunt,
quae Maro Virgilius, Statius, Lucanus et auctor,
artis grammaticae uel quid scripsere magistri
quid Probus atque Focas, Donatus Priscianusue,
Seruius, Euticius, Pompeius, Cominianus.

COMMENTARY **1** *Hieronymus*: *Clavis*, nos. 580–642. **1** *Hilarius*: *Clavis*, nos. 427–72. **2** *Ambrosius*: *Clavis*, nos. 123–68. **2** *Augustinus*: *Clavis*, nos. 250–386. **3** *Athanasius*: presumably Evagrius's Latin translation of Athanasius's Greek *Vita S. Antonii* (*BHL*,

[63] *Ep.* cxxi (*ibid.* p. 177).

[64] Cf. P. Hunter Blair ('From Bede to Alcuin', *Famulus Christi*, ed. G. Bonner (London, 1976), pp. 239–60), who suggests (p. 252) that copies of Vergil and Statius that were available at Worcester in the second half of the tenth century may have come directly from York via Wulfstan (*ob.* 1023), who held the sees of Worcester and York in plurality. This is to assume that Alcuin's books remained in York despite his efforts to retrieve them, and that they survived the (presumed) Viking depredations of the York library in the 860s.

[65] See *inter alia* R. F. West, *Alcuin and the Rise of the Christian Schools* (New York, 1892), pp. 33–7; A. F. Leach, *The Schools of Medieval England* (London, 1915), pp. 60–3; Hepple, 'Early Northumbrian Libraries'; V. R. Stallbaumer, 'The York Cathedral School', *ABR* 22 (1971), 286–97; and C. B. L. Barr, 'The Minster Library', *A History of York Minster*, ed. G. E. Aylmer and R. Cant (Oxford, 1977), pp. 487–538.

[66] Godman, *Alcuin*, pp. 122–7.

no. 609). **3** *Orosius*: presumably the *Historiae aduersum paganos* (*Clavis*, no. 571). **4** *Gregorius*: *Clavis*, nos. 1708–14. **4** *Leo papa*: a reference either to the collection of Leo's *Epistolae* (*Clavis*, no. 1656), or, perhaps more likely, his *Sermones* (*Clavis*, no. 1657). **5** *Basilius*: possibly Rufinus's Latin translation of St Basil's monastic Rules (see J. Gribomont, *Histoire du texte des ascétiques de Saint Basile* (Louvain, 1953), pp. 95–107), a work apparently known to Aldhelm, or possibly Basil's nine Homilies on the Hexameron, a work translated into Latin by the obscure Eusthathius and used by Bede in several of his writings (notably the commentary *In Genesim*). **5** *Fulgentius*: presumably a reference to the writings of Fulgentius of Ruspe (*ob.* 533), an eloquent defender of Augustine's doctrine of grace, some of whose writings – notably the three-book treatise *Ad Thrasamundum* (*Clavis*, no. 816) and the *De fide ad Petrum* (*Clavis*, no. 826) – were known to Bede and Alcuin; but certainty is not possible, for in the early Middle Ages the writings of Fulgentius 'the Mythographer', author of the *Mitologiae* and the *Sermones antiqui*, were in wide circulation (see M. L. W. Laistner, 'Fulgentius in the Carolingian Age', *The Intellectual Heritage of the Early Middle Ages*, ed. C. G. Starr (Ithaca, NY, 1957), pp. 202–15). **6** *Cassiodorus*: an important and voluminous author, many of whose works (*Clavis*, nos. 896–908) might here be in question; it is interesting to note, nevertheless, that an abbreviated version of Cassiodorus's *Expositio psalmorum* was used by Alcuin and is preserved in an early manuscript possibly from York (see D. A. Bullough, 'Alcuin and the Kingdom of Heaven: Liturgy, Theology and the Carolingian Age', *Carolingian Essays*, ed. U.-R. Blumenthal (Washington, DC, 1983), pp. 1–69, at 18–19, and n. 39). **6** *Iohannes Chrysostomus*: Greek Father (patriarch of Constantinople, 397–407) whose twenty-five Homilies on Matthew and seven Homilies on St Paul were translated into Latin by one Anianus (cf. *Clavis*, nos. 771–2, and C. Baur, 'L'Entrée de Saint Chrysostome dans le monde littéraire', *RHE* 8 (1906), 249–65), as were various other homilies such as the *De compunctione* and *De reparatione lapsi* (fragments of a mid-eighth-century Northumbrian manuscript of the last two items survive: see *CLA* VIII, no. 1187); see also below, no. XIII, line 18. **7** *Althelmus*: Aldhelm (*Clavis*, nos. 1331–5). **7** *Beda*: *Clavis*, nos. 1343–82. **8** *Victorinus*: possibly a reference to Marius Victorinus's theological writings (*Clavis*, nos. 95–8); the coupling with Boethius suggests, however, that the work here in question was the *De definitionibus* (*Clavis*, no. 94), which was frequently transmitted with the logical writings of Boethius (see H. Chadwick, *Boethius* (Oxford, 1981), pp. 115–18). **8** *Boethius*: as Godman observes (*Alcuin*, p. 124), it has yet to be demonstrated that the *De consolatione Philosophiae* was known in England before the late ninth century; the works in question here are probably Boethius's logical writings (see Chadwick, *Boethius*, pp. 108–73). **9** *Pompeius*: the work in question is Justinus's *Epitome* of the *Historiae Philippicae* of Pompeius Trogus; a single leaf of this *Epitome* of Northumbrian origin and mid-eighth-century date survived till recent times (see *CLA* IX, no. 1370, and *Texts and Transmission*, ed. Reynolds, pp. 197–9). **9** *Plinius*: the Elder Pliny, a natural historian rather than a historian proper, parts at least of whose *Historia naturalis* were known to Aldhelm and Bede; an important early-eighth-century Northumbrian manuscript of bks II–VI of this text survives (*CLA* X, no. 1578; see *Texts and Transmission*, ed. Reynolds, p. 309). **10** *Aristoteles*: presumably the Latin translations by Boethius of two logical treatises, the Categories and the *Peri hermeneias* (=*De interpretatione*), both of which were widely known in the early Middle Ages. **10** *Tullius*: Cicero (M. Tullius Cicero), two of whose works – the *De inuentione* and *De oratore* – were known to Alcuin; see Godman, *Alcuin*, p. 125. **11–13**: The Christian–Latin poets listed here formed the staple of the medieval school curriculum (see G. Glauche, *Schullektüre im Mittelalter. Entstehung und Wandlungen des Lektürekanons bis 1200* (Munich, 1970), esp. pp. 10–11); for the study of these authors in Anglo-Saxon England, see M. Lapidge, 'The Study of Latin Texts in Late Anglo-Saxon England: I. The Evidence of Latin Glosses', *Latin and the Vernacular Languages in Early Medieval Britain*, ed. N. Brooks (Leicester, 1982), pp. 99–140. **11** *Sedulius*: the *Carmen Paschale* of Caelius Sedulius (*Clavis*, no. 1447). **11** *Iuuencus*: the hexametrical *Euangelia quattuor* of the Spanish priest Juvencus (*Clavis*, no. 1385). **12** *Alcimus*: Alcimus Avitus, *De spiritalis historiae gestis* (*Clavis*, no. 995). **12** *Clemens*: Aurelius Prudentius Clemens (best known as Prudentius), whose various poems – *Cathemerinon*, *Apotheosis*, *Hamartigenia*, *Psychomachia*, *Contra Symmachum*, *Peristephanon* and *Dittochaeon* (*Clavis*, nos. 1438–44) – were widely studied in the early Middle Ages; for an example of the study of the *Psychomachia* at late Anglo-Saxon Canterbury, see G. R. Wieland, *The Latin Glosses on Arator and Prudentius in Cambridge University Library MS Gg.5.35* (Toronto, 1983). **12** *Prosper*: Prosper of Aquitaine, whose *Epigrammata* (*Clavis*, no. 518), metrical versions of various apophthegms by Augustine, were also widely studied in early medieval schools. **12** *Paulinus*: Paulinus of Nola, whose *Carmina* (*Clavis*, no. 203), for the most part concerning the local patron saint of Nola, St Felix, were known early in Northumbria and are preserved in two early-eighth-century Northumbrian manuscripts (*CLA* I, no. 87, and XI, no. 1622); see T. W. Mackay, 'Bede's Hagiographical Method: his Knowledge and Use of Paulinus of Nola', *Famulus Christi*, ed. Bonner, pp. 77–92. **12** *Arator*: Arator, *De actibus apostolorum* (*Clavis*, no. 1504); on the study of Arator at late Anglo-Saxon Canterbury, see Wieland, *The Latin Glosses on Arator and Prudentius* (note, however, that Wieland's statements (p. 4) on the dating and origin of Arator manuscripts need correction). **13** *Fortunatus*: Venantius Fortunatus, whose *Carmina* (*Clavis*, no. 1033) were well known in early Anglo-Saxon England (see my remarks in *ASE* 8 (1979), 287–95). **13** *Lactantius*: since Lactantius is here listed among the Christian–Latin poets, Alcuin's reference is presumably to the poem *De aue phoenice* (*Clavis*, no. 90) which is possibly but not certainly by Lactantius. **14** *Maro Virgilius*: see Manitius, *Handschriften*, pp. 47–55, and *Texts and Transmission*, ed. Reynolds, pp. 433–6. **14** *Statius*: see Manitius, *Handschriften*, pp. 125–9, and *Texts and Transmission*, ed. Reynolds, pp. 394–9. **14** *Lucanus*: see Manitius, *Handschriften*, pp. 115–20, and *Texts and Transmission*, ed. Reynolds, pp. 215–18. **15–17**: on the knowledge of these various grammatical texts in Anglo-Saxon England, see V. Law, *The Insular Latin Grammarians* (Ipswich, 1982), pp. 11–29, and 'The Study of Latin Grammar in Eighth-Century Southumbria', *ASE* 12 (1983), 43–71. **16** *Probus*: Law (*The Insular Latin Grammarians*, pp. 26–7) argues convincingly that the grammatical writings of Probus did not cross the Alps until the end of the eighth century, and that Insular authors of the seventh and eighth centuries knew them only at second hand from other grammarians; one must wonder how many other authors mentioned by Alcuin were known to him only at second hand (see the note on

Cominianus, below). **16** *Focas*: Phocas, *Ars de nomine et uerbo*; see C. Jeudy, 'L'*Ars de nomine et uerbo* de Phocas: Manuscrits et commentaires médiévaux', *Viator* 5 (1974), 61–156. **16** *Donatus*: the *Ars maior* and *Ars minor* of Donatus were the introductory grammars *par excellence* of the early Middle Ages; see L. Holtz, *Donat et la tradition de l'enseignement grammatical* (Paris, 1981). **16** *Priscianus*: either the lengthy *Institutiones grammaticae* (see J. R. O'Donnell, 'Alcuin's Priscian', *Latin Script and Letters A.D. 400–900*, ed. J. J. O'Meara and B. Naumann (Leiden, 1976), pp. 222–35, together with M. Gibson, 'Priscian, *Institutiones Grammaticae*: a Handlist of Manuscripts', *Scriptorium* 26 (1972), 105–24), or the shorter *Institutio de nomine et pronomine et uerbo* (see C. Jeudy, 'L'*Institutio de nomine, pronomine et uerbo* de Priscien: Manuscrits et commentaires médiévaux', *Revue d'histoire des textes* 2 (1972), 73–144) – or both. **17** *Seruius*: possibly either the commentaries on Vergil or the *De finalibus* (a metrical treatise) of Seruius, or, more likely perhaps, the *De littera* of Sergius (a commentary on Donatus, *Ars maior*), a work which frequently travelled under the name of Servius (see Law, *The Insular Latin Grammarians*, p. 17). **17** *Euticius*: Eutyches, *Ars de uerbo* (see C. Jeudy, 'Les Manuscrits de l'*Ars de uerbo* d'Eutychès et le commentaire de Remi d'Auxerre', *Études de civilisation médiévale (IXe–XIIe s.): Mélanges offerts à E.-R. Labande* (Poitiers, 1974), pp. 421–36). **17** *Pompeius*: the author of a commentary on the *Ars maior* of Donatus; see L. Holtz, 'Tradition et diffusion de l'oeuvre grammaticale de Pompée, commentateur de Donat', *Revue de philologie* 45 (1971), 48–83. **17** *Cominianus*: a Late Latin grammarian whose writings are not extant and do not appear to have been transmitted intact to the Middle Ages, but are known only through the grammatical compilation of Charisius (see Law, *The Insular Latin Grammarians*, pp. 19 and 75, n. 108); it is most unlikely, therefore, that Alcuin knew the work at first hand.

## *II. Books donated by King Athelstan (924–39) to the congregation of St Cuthbert at Chester-le-Street*

The *Historia de S. Cuthberto*[67] is a text, probably composed in the eleventh century,[68] which purports to record the early history of the congregation or *familia* of St Cuthbert, housed at Lindisfarne and later at Chester-le-Street, from its foundation to 945. It records various grants and bequests to the congregation, and among these is the record of a grant by King Athelstan of various lands, liturgical books and ecclesiastical furnishings.[69] The *Historia* is best preserved in Cambridge, University Library, Ff. 1. 27 (Sawley, s. xiii$^{in}$),[70]

67 *Symeonis Monachi Opera Omnia*, ed. T. Arnold, 2 vols., Rolls Ser. (London, 1882–5) I, 196–214.

68 See H. E. Craster, 'The Patrimony of St Cuthbert', *EHR* 69 (1954), 177–99.

69 *Symeonis Monachi Opera Omnia*, ed. Arnold, I, 211; it is also ptd J. M. Kemble, *Codex Diplomaticus Aevi Saxonici*, 6 vols. (London, 1839–48), no. 1125, and W. deG. Birch, *Cartularium Saxonicum*, 3 vols. and index (London, 1885–99), no. 685.

70 On the manuscript, see D. N. Dumville, 'The Sixteenth-Century History of Two Cambridge Books from Sawley', *Trans. of the Cambridge Bibliographical Soc.* 7 (1977–80), 427–44.

pp. 195–202; the text printed below is found on pp. 201–2. Athelstan's donation has been discussed on several occasions.[71]

In nomine Domini nostri Iesu Christi. Ego Æþelstanus rex do sancto Cuthberto

hunc textum euuangeliorum . . .
et .i. missalem
et .ii. euangeliorum textus, auro et argento ornatos
[4] et .i. sancti Cuthberti uitam, metrice et prosaice scriptam.

COMMENTARY 1 *hunc textum euuangeliorum*: these words imply that the list of Athelstan's donations was once copied in a gospel-book, but, as Simon Keynes suggests (below, p. 177), it was more likely concocted by the author of the *Historia de S. Cuthberto* from information contained in a note entered in London, BL Cotton Otho B. ix, which would accordingly be the gospel-book in question here. **2** *missalem*: at this date the book in question was presumably a sacramentary, not a plenary missal (see Gneuss, below, p. 99). **3** *.ii. euangeliorum textus*: it is not possible to identify these two gospel-books; see Keynes, below, p. 178. **4** *.i. sancti Cuthberti uitam*: apparently a book containing both Bede's verse and his prose *Vitae S. Cuthberti* (*BHL*, nos. 2020–1), which almost certainly survives as Cambridge, Corpus Christi College 183 (see Keynes, below, p. 182); Mynors (*Durham Cathedral Manuscripts*, p. 26) noted in discussing the Athelstan donation that 'the volume does not appear in the medieval catalogues, and was no doubt kept among the treasures of the Cathedral church'; but note the entry in a twelfth-century Durham catalogue: 'duae uitae sancti Cuthberti' (Becker, *Catalogi*, no. 117).

## *III. Books owned by a grammarian named Athelstan (s. x²)*

To an English copy of Isidore's *De natura rerum*, now London, BL Cotton Domitian i (written in Anglo-Caroline minuscule of mid-tenth-century date) was added on 55v a list of books belonging to one Athelstan in a late form of Anglo-Saxon square minuscule, datable perhaps to the second half of the tenth century.[72] The manuscript is from St Augustine's, Canterbury, and was apparently written there.[73] The booklist has been variously attributed to King

[71] See J. A. Robinson, *The Times of St Dunstan* (Oxford, 1923), p. 53, and discussion by Battiscombe in *The Relics of St Cuthbert*, ed. C. F. Battiscombe (Oxford, 1956), pp. 7, n. 2, and 31–3, as well as discussion by Simon Keynes, 'King Athelstan's Books', below, pp. 177–8.

[72] Cf. N. R. Ker (*Catalogue of Manuscripts containing Anglo-Saxon* (Oxford, 1957), pp. 185–6 (no. 146)), who dates the entry s. x/xi. The square minuscule script has several Caroline features, which suggest a date late in the career of square minuscule script; but the chronology of that career is as yet improperly understood.

[73] T. A. M. Bishop, 'Notes on Cambridge Manuscripts, Part IV: MSS. connected with St Augustine's, Canterbury', *Trans. of the Cambridge Bibliographical Soc.* 2 (1954–8), 323–36, at 334–5; a plate showing the booklist is included by Bishop as pl. XIV (b). Bishop avoids assigning a date to the square minuscule additions on 55v.

Athelstan[74] and to Ealdorman Athelstan the 'Half-King',[75] but the date of the script rules out the king, and the subject-matter of the list rules out the ealdorman, and indicates rather that an otherwise unknown schoolmaster or grammarian was the owner of the books.[76] The booklist has been printed and discussed several times.[77]

Þis syndon ða bec þe Æþestanes wæran:
De natura rerum
Persius
De arte metrica
Donatum minorem
[5] Excerptiones de metrica arte
Apocalipsin
Donatum maiorem
Alchuinum
Glossam super Catonem
[10] Libellum de grammatica arte que sic incipit 'Terra que pars'
Sedulium[78]
7 .i. gerim wæs Alfwoldes preostes
Glossa super Donatum
Dialogorum

COMMENTARY **1** *De natura rerum*: Isidore, *De natura rerum* (*Clavis*, no. 1188), the work which constitutes the major part of the manuscript to which this booklist is appended; on the work itself and its transmission, see J. Fontaine, *Isidore de Séville, Traité de la nature* (Bordeaux, 1960). **2** Persius: see Manitius, *Handschriften*, pp. 112–15, and *Texts and Transmission*, ed. Reynolds, pp. 293–5. **3** *De arte metrica*: possibly Bede's treatise of that name (*Clavis*, no. 1565), but without further specification certainty is impossible. **4** *Donatum minorem*: Donatus, *Ars minor*; on the manuscript tradition of Donatus, see Holtz, *Donat et la tradition de l'enseignement grammatical*, pp. 445–97. **5** *Excerptiones de metrica arte*: without further specification it is impossible to guess what this might be. **6** *Apocalipsin*: presumably the biblical Apocalypse (Revelations), but why such a biblical text should be included amongst a grammarian's books is not clear. **7** *Donatum maiorem*: Donatus, *Ars maior*; on the manuscript tradition of Donatus, see

74 Gottlieb, no. 436.

75 F. J. Haverfield, 'The Library of Æthelstan, the Half-King', *The Academy* 26 (1884), 32.

76 It is interesting to note that the names of Æthelstan and Ælfwold mentioned in this list recur in the document recording Bishop Æthelwold's donations to Peterborough (Birch, *Cartularium Saxonicum*, no. 1128), part of which is ptd below as no. IV; but the combination of names (which are not rare) may be merely coincidental.

77 M. R. James, *Ancient Libraries of Canterbury and Dover*, p. lxix; R. M. Wilson, 'More Lost Literature II', *Leeds Stud. in Eng.* 6 (1937), 30–49, at 49; and A. J. Robertson, *Anglo-Saxon Charters* (Cambridge, 1939), p. 250.

78 There is an erasure of one entry here in the manuscript.

Holtz, *Donat et la tradition de l'enseignement grammatical*, pp. 445–97. **8** *Alchuinum*: given the context, the work in question was presumably either Alcuin's *De orthographia* (PL 101, cols. 901–20) or his *De grammatica* (PL 101, cols. 849–902) – or both. **9** *Glossam super Catonem*: a commentary on the *Disticha Catonis* (a favourite school-text in the early Middle Ages), presumably that of Remigius of Auxerre; a fragmentary copy of Remigius's commentary that was later owned by St Augustine's survives as Cambridge, Gonville and Caius College 144/194, and may be the book in question here (see Lapidge, 'The Study of Latin Texts', p. 104 and n. 36). **10** *Libellum . . . 'Terra que pars'*: apparently a copy of what may be called a 'parsing grammar', a type of grammar which appears from the mid-ninth century onwards, and which is characterized by an opening question – 'what part of speech is X?' – with examples varying from text to text and including *anima*, *codex*, *columna*, *iustus*, *terra* etc.; a copy of such a work beginning 'Terra quae pars' is found in Bern, Burgerbibliothek, A.92 (34) (s. xi/xii), 7r–8v, but no copy of the work from Anglo-Saxon England has yet come to light (I am extremely grateful to Vivien Law for this information); the only copy of a 'parsing' grammar yet known from Anglo-Saxon England, as Helmut Gneuss points out to me, is one beginning 'Iustus quae pars' in London, BL Cotton Cleopatra A. vi, 31v–47r. **11** *Sedulium*: Caelius Sedulius, *Carmen Paschale* (*Clavis*, no. 1447). **12** *gerim*: a manuscript of computistical materials; on the OE term *gerim*, see Gneuss, 'Liturgical Books', below, p. 139. **13** *Glossa super Donatum*: presumably a copy of one of the Late Latin commentaries on Donatus – Pompeius, Consentius, Cledonius or Sergius (see Law, *The Insular Latin Grammarians*, pp. 16–17 and 30). **14** *Dialogorum*: the title may suggest Gregory the Great's *Dialogi* (*Clavis*, no. 1713), but it is not clear what such a text would be doing in the hands of a grammarian; one might suspect, therefore, that the book in question was a manuscript of scholastic colloquies (*dialogi*) such as we know to have been used in Anglo-Saxon England for elementary instruction in Latin (see G. N. Garmonsway, 'The Development of the Colloquy', *The Anglo-Saxons*, ed. P. Clemoes (London, 1959), pp. 248–61).

## *IV. Books donated by Æthelwold, bishop of Winchester (963–84), to the monastery at Peterborough*

In 963 Æthelwold was consecrated bishop of Winchester. Shortly thereafter, according to a lengthy entry in the E- (or Peterborough-) version of the Anglo-Saxon Chronicle, Æthelwold determined to restore all the minsters in Edgar's kingdom which had fallen into desuetude through Viking attacks; among these was the minster at *Medeshamstede* or Peterborough which, according to the E-version, then consisted of nothing more than 'old walls and wild woods'.[79] Æthelwold's biographer, Wulfstan of Winchester, reports in his

[79] *The Anglo-Saxon Chronicle*, ed. B. Thorpe, 2 vols., Rolls Ser. (London, 1861) I, 220: 'Syððon com se biscop Aðelwold to þære mynstre þe wæs gehaten Medeshamstede . þe hwilon wæs fordon fra heðene folce . ne fand þær nan þing buton ealde weallas 7 wilde wuda.'

*Vita S. Æthelwoldi* that the bishop subsequently consecrated to St Peter 'the church adorned with appropriate structures of buildings and abundantly enriched with adjacent lands'.[80] A record of Æthelwold's endowment of Peterborough survives in the Peterborough *Liber niger*, a mid-twelfth-century cartulary now preserved as London, Society of Antiquaries 60; the charter in question is on 39v–40v.[81] Part of Æthelwold's donation was some twenty-one books, and these have been discussed on various occasions.[82] The donation cannot be dated exactly; the outer limits are the dates of Æthelwold's bishopric (963 × 984); to judge from the account in the E-version of the *Chronicle*, the grant may have occurred within a few years of Æthelwold's elevation to Winchester.

Þis synd þa madmas þe Adeluuold bisceop sealde into þam mynstre þe is Medeshamstede gehaten . . . þæt is þonne

an Cristes boc mid sylure berenod . . .

And antwentig is þara boca þe Adeluuold biscop gesealde into Burch . þæt is þonne

Beda in Marcum
Liber miraculorum
Expositio Hebreorum nominum
[5] Prouisio futurarum rerum
Augustinus de achademicis
Vita sancti Felicis metrice
Sinonima Isidori
Vita Eustachii
[10] Descidia Parisiace polis
Medicinalis
De duodecim abusiuis
Sermo super quosdam psalmos
Commentum cantica canticorum

80 *Three Lives of English Saints*, ed. M. Winterbottom (Toronto, 1972), p. 48: 'Cuius loci basilicam congruis domorum structuris ornatam et terris adiacentibus copiose ditatam in honore beati Petri principis apostolorum consecrauit.'

81 The cartulary is listed by G. R. C. Davis, *Medieval Cartularies of Great Britain* (London, 1958), p. 86 (no. 754). The charter is listed by P. H. Sawyer, *Anglo-Saxon Charters: an Annotated List and Bibliography* (London, 1968), no. 1448; it is ed. Birch, *Cartularium Saxonicum*, no. 1128, and Robertson, *Anglo-Saxon Charters*, pp. 72–5.

82 See A. Way, 'The Gifts of Æthelwold, Bishop of Winchester (A.D. 963–984) to the Monastery of Peterborough', *ArchJ* 20 (1863), 355–66, and M. R. James, *Lists of Manuscripts formerly in Peterborough Abbey Library*, pp. 19–20; see also Robertson, *Anglo-Saxon Charters*, pp. 326–7, and D. A. Bullough, 'The Educational Tradition in England from Alfred to Ælfric: Teaching *utriusque linguae*', *Settimane di studio del Centro italiano di studi sull'alto medioevo* 19 (1972), 453–94, at 481–2.

De eucharistia
Commentum Martiani
Alchimi Auiti
Liber differentiarum
Cilicius Ciprianus
De litteris Grecorum
Liber bestiarum

COMMENTARY **1** *an Cristes boc*: a gospel-book (on the terminology, see Gneuss, 'Liturgical Books', below, p. 107). **2** *Beda in Marcum*: Bede's Commentary on Mark (*Clavis*, no. 1355). **3** *Liber miraculorum*: possibly the work of that title by Gregory of Tours (*Clavis*, no. 1024); but the title could equally well refer to any collection of miracle stories (see also below, no. XIII, line 64). **4** *Expositio Hebreorum nominum*: presumably a copy of Jerome, *Liber interpretationis Hebraicorum nominum* (*Clavis*, no. 581). **5** *Prouisio futurarum rerum*: Julian of Toledo, *Prognosticum futuri saeculi* (*Clavis*, no. 1258; see also below, no. XIII, line 40). **6** *Augustinus de achademicis*: Augustine, *Contra Academicos* (*Clavis*, no. 253). **7** *Vita sancti Felicis metrice*: presumably the *Carmina* of Paulinus of Nola (*Clavis*, no. 203), the majority of which concern St Felix, the patron saint of Nola; see also below, no. XIII, line 38. **8** *Sinonima Isidori*: Isidore's *Synonyma de lamentatione animae peccatricis* (*Clavis*, no. 1203). **9** *Vita Eustachii*: without further specification, it is not possible to determine which of the various *uitae* of St Eustace may be in question; it is probable, however, that this book is identical with that listed below, no. XIII, line 60 (on which see the accompanying Commentary, below, p. 82). **10** *Descidia Parisiacae polis*: Abbo of Saint-Germain-des-Prés, *Bella Parisiacae urbis* (MGH, PLAC 4, 72–122); on knowledge of this work in Anglo-Saxon England, see my remarks in *ASE* 4 (1975), 75–6. **11** *Medicinalis*: a particular work cannot be recognized in so general a title; for the range of medical writings known in Anglo-Saxon England, see M. L. Cameron, 'The Sources of Medical Knowledge in Anglo-Saxon England', *ASE* 11 (1982), 135–55. **12** *De duodecim abusiuis*: a work which passed during the Middle Ages under the name of St Cyprian, but which is known to have been composed in seventh-century Ireland (*Clavis*, no. 1106). **13** *Sermo super quosdam psalmos*: not identifiable as such; but note that commentaries on a few selected psalms were composed by Ambrose, Origen as translated by Rufinus, and Prosper of Aquitaine (*Clavis*, nos. 140, 198f and 524). **14** *Commentum cantica canticorum*: a number of commentaries on the Song of Songs circulated in the early Middle Ages, including those of Aponius (*Clavis*, no. 194) and Gregory the Great's *Homiliae .ii. in Canticum Canticorum* (Clavis, no. 1709), but the commentary most likely to be in question is that of Bede (*Clavis*, no. 1353), which survives in a large number of manuscripts (see M. L. W. Laistner and H. H. King, *A Handlist of Bede Manuscripts* (Ithaca, NY, 1943), pp. 66–70); other medieval commentaries on the Song of Songs were compiled by Alcuin (PL 100, cols. 641–64), Angelomus of Luxeuil (PL 115, cols. 551–628) and Haimo of Auxerre (PL 117, cols. 295–358). **15** *De eucharistia*: I have been unable to discover a patristic work – in Greek or Latin – with this title; the reference is possibly to a work of Ambrose, either *De sacramentis* (*Clavis*, no. 154) or *De mysteriis* (*Clavis*, no. 155), or to one of Augustine's letters (*Ep.* liv, addressed 'ad inquisitiones Ianuarii . . . de sacramentis . . . et eucharistia': PL 33, cols. 199–204); or to one of the ninth-century treatises entitled *De corpore et sanguine Domini* by Paschasius Radbertus (PL 120, cols. 1255–1350) or Ratramnus of Corbie (PL 121, cols. 103–70); or just possibly it refers to one of the various *expositiones missae* which circulated widely in the early Middle Ages (see A. Wilmart, *Dictionnaire d'archéologie chrétienne et de liturgie* 5 (Paris, 1922), 1014–27, s.v. 'Expositio missae'), such as is found in Oxford, Bodleian Library, Hatton 93 (*CLA* II, no. 241). **16** *Commentum Martiani*: presumably the Commentary on Martianus Capella by Remigius of Auxerre; for a recently discovered copy of this work from Anglo-Saxon England, see M. B. Parkes, 'A Fragment of an Early-Tenth-Century Anglo-Saxon Manuscript and its Significance', *ASE* 12 (1983), 129–40. **17** *Alchimi Auiti*: the hexametrical poem by Alcimus Avitus, *De spiritalis historiae gestis* (*Clavis*, no. 995). **18** *Liber differentiarum*: Isidore, *De differentiis uerborum* (*Clavis*, no. 1187). **19** *Cilicius Ciprianus*: if the book in Æthelwold's donation is identical with that in the later Peterborough booklist (below, no. XIII, line 56), it was a copy of the *Epistolae* of Caecilius Cyprianus, or St Cyprian (*Clavis*, no. 50). **20** *De litteris Grecorum*: presumably a Greek–Latin glossary. **21** *Liber bestiarum*: the Latin *Physiologus*, a text which survives in various recensions, all of them dependent (directly or indirectly) on various Greek originals. Some redaction of the *Physiologus* was known in early Anglo-Saxon England, for it was used by Aldhelm and the anonymous author of the *Liber monstrorum*; in the late Anglo-Saxon period a redaction of the *Physiologus* was used by the author of the Old English poems 'Panther', 'Whale' and 'Partridge' in the Exeter Book – possibly the redaction known as 'Redaction B' (*Physiologus Latinus. Éditions préliminaires, versio B*, ed. F. J. Carmody (Paris, 1939)); on the transmission of the Latin *Physiologus* in Anglo-Saxon England, see now L. Frank, *Die Physiologus-Literatur des englischen Mittelalters und die Tradition* (Tübingen, 1971), and the concise discussion by G. Orlandi, 'La tradizione del *Physiologus* e la formazione del bestiario latino', *Settimane di studio del Centro italiano di studi sull'alto medioevo* 30 (1984), forthcoming.

## *V. Books mentioned in the will of Ælfwold, bishop of Crediton (c. 997–c. 1016)*

Among the collection of Crawford Charters (now Oxford, Bodleian Library, Eng. hist. a. 2) is an original copy of a will by Ælfwold, bishop of Crediton, who died 1011 × 1016. Ælfwold's will[83] is no. XIII in the Crawford collection, and has been edited by Napier and Stevenson,[84] and translated and discussed on two occasions by Whitelock.[85] Among the list of possessions bequeathed by Ælfwold were the five books listed below.

83 Listed by Sawyer, *Anglo-Saxon Charters*, no. 1492.

84 *The Crawford Collection of Early Charters and Documents now in the Bodleian Library*, ed. A. S. Napier and W. H. Stevenson, Anecdota Oxoniensia (Oxford, 1895), pp. 23–4 (no. 10).

85 *EHD*, pp. 580–1 (no. 122); *Councils and Synods with other Documents relating to the English Church I: A.D. 871–1204*, ed. D. Whitelock, M. Brett and C. N. L. Brooke, 2 vols. (Oxford, 1981) I, 382–6 (no. 51).

+ Þis is Alfwoldes bisceopes cwyde þæt is ðæt he
geann . . . Ordulfe twegra boca
Hrabanum
7 martyrlogium . . .
7 in to Crydian tune þreo þeningbec
mæsseboc
7 bletsungboc
7 pistelboc

COMMENTARY **1–2** *Hrabanum 7 martyrlogium*: a copy of an unspecified work by Hrabanus Maurus (see Manitius, *Geschichte* I, 288–302) and a martyrology; conceivably the martyrology in question was that by Hrabanus ('Rabani Mauri Martyrologium', ed. J. McCulloh, CCSL, CM 44 (Turnhout, 1979), 1–134), but there is no possibility of proof. **3–5** the three service-books (*þeningbec*) in question were probably a sacramentary (*mæsseboc*), a pontifical (*bletsungboc*) and an epistolary (*pistelboc*); on these various Old English terms, see Gneuss, 'Liturgical Books', below, pp. 100, 131 and 110, respectively.

## *VI. Liturgical books belonging to the church of Sherburn-in-Elmet (s. xi$^{\text{med}}$)*

In a lavish Anglo-Saxon gospel-book written in the early eleventh century (possibly at Christ Church, Canterbury) and known generally as the 'York Gospels', now York, Minster Library, Add. 1,[86] there are numerous additions of various date. Among these additions is a list of service-books and other ecclesiastical furniture (161r) belonging to the church of Sherburn-in-Elmet;[87] the list is datable on palaeographical grounds to s. xi$^{\text{med}}$. The books in question are as follows.

Þis syndon þa cyrican madmas on Scirburnan . þæt synd
twa Cristes bec . . .
7 .i. aspiciens
7 .i. adteleuaui
7 .ii. pistolbec
7 .i. mæsseboc
7 .i. ymener
7 .i. salter . . .

[86] See Ker, *Catalogue*, pp. 468–9 (no. 402), and E. Temple, *Anglo-Saxon Manuscripts 900–1066* (London, 1976), pp. 79–80 (no. 61).

[87] Birch, *Cartularium Saxonicum*, no. 1324; W. H. Stevenson, 'Yorkshire Surveys and other Eleventh-Century Documents in the York Gospels', *EHR* 27 (1912), 1–25, at 9; and Robertson, *Anglo-Saxon Charters*, p. 248.

COMMENTARY 1 *twa Cristes bec*: two gospel-books (on the terminology, see Gneuss, 'Liturgical Books', below, p. 107). **2** *aspiciens*: an antiphonary, so named from the first word of the respond following the first lesson in the Night Office of the first Sunday in Advent (see Gneuss, below, p. 117). **3** *adteleuaui*: a gradual, so named from the opening words of the introit for mass on the first Sunday in Advent; see Gneuss, below, p. 103. **4** *pistolbec*: epistolaries; see Gneuss, below, p. 110. **5** *mæsseboc*: a sacramentary; see Gneuss, below, p. 100. **6** *ymener*: a hymnal; see Gneuss, below, p. 119. **7** *salter*: a psalter; see Gneuss, below, p. 114.

## *VII. Liturgical books belonging to Bury St Edmunds in the time of Abbot Leofstan (1044–65)*

Oxford, Corpus Christi College 197 is a copy of the *Regula S. Benedicti* in Latin with accompanying Old English translation.[88] The origin of the manuscript is unknown; its script is datable to the second half of the tenth century. At some point the book came to Bury St Edmunds, for into a quire of four added at the end of the manuscript (fols. 106–9) was copied a lengthy account of the possessions and rents of Bury in the time of abbots Leofstan and Baldwin (106v–108r).[89] The handwriting of this addition is of the second half of the eleventh century. The possessions include a number of books (all listed on 107r–v).[90]

Betæhte nu cincg se goda Eadward 7 se wurðfulla his mæges
mynstere on Bædericeswyrde Leofstan abbode þæt he bewiste
þæt þæt þær wære inne 7 ute . 7 he þa þær þus mycel funde
.x. bec inne ðæra circean
.iiii. Cristes bec
7 .i. mæsseboc
7 .i. pistelboc
7 .i. salter
7 .i. god spellboc
7 .i. capitularia
7 sancte Eadmundes uita . . .
Blakere hæfð .i. winter rædingboc
Brihtric hæfð . . . .i. mæsseboc
7 winter rædingboc
7 sumerboc

[88] See Ker, *Catalogue*, pp. 430–2 (no. 353).

[89] See D. C. Douglas, 'Fragments of an Anglo-Saxon Survey from Bury St Edmunds', *EHR* 43 (1928), 376–83, and Robertson, *Anglo-Saxon Charters*, pp. 192–201.

[90] See also M. R. James, *On the Abbey of St Edmund at Bury*, p. 6.

Siuerð hæfð . . . mæsseboc
7 Leofstan an handboc
Æþeric an mæsseboc
[15] 7 capitularia
Durstan an psalter
Oskytel hæfð . . . mæsseboc
    7 an Ad te leuaui . . .
Her syndon .xxx. boca ealre on Leofstanes abbodes hafona butan mynsterbec.

COMMENTARY **1** *.iiii. Cristes bec*: four gospel-books; see Gneuss, 'Liturgical Books', below, p. 107. **2** *mæsseboc*: a sacramentary or, possibly, at this date, a plenary missal; see Gneuss, below, p. 100. **3** *pistelboc*: an epistolary; see Gneuss, below, p. 110. **4** *salter*: a psalter; see Gneuss, below, p. 114. **5** *god spellboc*: probably a homiliary rather than a gospel-book; see Gneuss, below, p. 123. **6** *capitularia*: a collectar; see Gneuss, below, p. 113. **7** *sancte Eadmundes uita*: a copy of Abbo of Fleury's *Passio S. Eadmundi* (*BHL*, no. 2392; see also *Three Lives of English Saints*, ed. M. Winterbottom (Toronto, 1972), pp. 67–87); although several English manuscripts of the late eleventh century survive (for example, London, BL Cotton Tiberius B. ii, and Lambeth Palace 362, and Copenhagen, Kongelige Bibliotek, G.K.S. 1588 (4°)), none of them appears to have been written by the time of Leofstan's abbacy, and the manuscript mentioned in this list must be presumed lost. **8** *winter rædingboc*: presumably an Office lectionary; see Gneuss, below, p. 121. **9** *mæsseboc*: see above, line 2. **10** *winter rædingboc*: an Office lectionary, as above, line 8. **11** *sumerboc*: also an Office lectionary, as above, line 8. **12** *mæsseboc*: see above, line 2. **13** *handboc*: presumably a ritual or manual, a book containing occasional offices which a priest might have to perform; see Gneuss, below, p. 134. **14** *mæsseboc*: see above, line 2. **15** *capitularia*: a collectar, as above, line 6. **16** *psalter*: see Gneuss, below, p. 114. **17** *mæsseboc*: see above, line 2. **18** *Ad te leuaui*: a gradual, so named from the opening words of the introit for mass on the first Sunday in Advent; see Gneuss, below, p. 103.

## *VIII. Books donated by Sæwold, sometime abbot of Bath, to the church of Saint-Vaast in Arras (*c. *1070)*

At the time of the Norman Conquest, the abbot of the monastery of St Peter, Bath, was one Sæwold, about whom very little is known.[91] In the aftermath of the Conquest, the family of Harold Godwinson first took refuge in Exeter and later were forced to flee to Flanders, probably in 1068 or 1069.[92] Among the

[91] Sæwold attests a charter of Edward the Confessor in favour of Wells, dated 4 May 1065 (Sawyer, *Anglo-Saxon Charters*, no. 1042), and one undated manumission from Bath (Kemble, *Codex Diplomaticus*, no. 1351).

[92] See E. A. Freeman, *The Norman Conquest*, 6 vols. (Oxford, 1867–79) IV, 138–60.

refugees was Gunhild, Harold's sister (and the daughter of King Cnut), and it is interesting to note that she took at least one book with her, for on her death in 1087 she bequeathed to the church of Saint-Donatien in Bruges a psalter which was glossed in Old English.[93] It would appear that Abbot Sæwold fled to Flanders at the same time, for he is next recorded as having made a donation of thirty-three books to the church of Saint-Vaast in Arras where, presumably, he had taken refuge. In an eleventh-century copy of Augustine, *Tractatus in euangelium Ioannis*, now Arras, Bibliothèque Municipale, 849 (539), the main scribe has entered on 159r a list of the books donated by Sæwold to Saint-Vaast.[94] Because a number of Sæwold's books which survive were evidently written in England (see below), there is some presumption that Sæwold, like Harold's sister Gunhild, took his books with him when he left England and subsequently bequeathed them to the house which gave him refuge. Although it is preserved in a continental manuscript, therefore, the Sæwold booklist may be taken as evidence of the personal[95] library of an English ecclesiastic at the time of the Conquest. The booklist has been printed by Becker,[96] and reprinted and furnished with excellent commentary by Philip Grierson.[97] In what follows I am heavily indebted to Grierson, particularly for the identification of surviving books.

Abbas deuotus probus ac uita Seiwoldus
Contulit hos libros Christo dominoque Vedasto.
Textum argenteum
Missalem
Librum heptaticum Moysi
Librum moralium Gregorii .xx.
Librum Haimonis usque in Pascha
Librum Claudii super Matheum
Librum regule sancti Benedicti et Diadema monachorum
Librum dialogorum Gregorii
Librum uitarum patrum
Librum expositionis Ambrosii de psalmo CXVIII
Librum item (Ambrosii) De initiandis (liber I) eiusdem

93 Ker, *Catalogue*, p. 469 (no. 403). Ker gives the date of Gunhild's death erroneously as 1043; the psalter in question, known as 'Gunhild's Psalter', was still at Bruges in the sixteenth century, but is now presumably lost.

94 *Catalogue général des manuscrits des bibliothèques publiques des départements* [quarto ser.] IV (Paris, 1872), 215–16.

95 It is possible, of course, that some of the books donated by Sæwold had been the property of the monks of Bath, and that Sæwold in flight had absconded with them (the book listed above, line 7, for example, would appear to have been a book used for reading at chapter).

96 *Catalogi*, no. 58.

97 'Les Livres de l'Abbé Seiwold de Bath', *RB* 52 (1940), 96–116.

De mysteriis (libri VI), Commonitorium Palladii de Bragmanis (liber I), Ysidori De officiis (libri II) in uno uolumine

Librum pronosticon

Librum enkiridion

Librum exameron Ambrosii

[15] Librum Prosperi ad Iulianum et Ambrosii De officiis

Librum Bede super VII epistolas canonicas

Librum epistolarum Bacharii, Augustini, Eubodii, Macedonii

Librum uite sancti Richarii

Librum uitae sanctorum confessorum Cutberti, Gutlaci, Aichadri, Filiberti, Dunstani

[20] Librum De assumptione sancte Mariae

Librum canonum

Librum hystoriae aecclesiastice gentis Anglie

Librum uite sancti Walerici, Mauri, passionum sanctorum martirum Luciani, Maxiani atque Iuliani, in uno uolumine

Librum medicinalis

[25] Librum Cassiodori De ortographia

Librum uersuum et tractuum totius anni

Librum parabolarum Salomonis

Librum De laude uirginitatis

Librum De professione coniugatorum

[30] Librum Prudentii

Iuuencus, Sedulius in uno uolumine

Librum Rabbani super Iudith et Hester

Librum tripartite historie ecclesiastice

COMMENTARY **1** *Textum argenteum*: a gospel-book, decorated with silver. **2** *Missalem*: a sacramentary or plenary missal; see Gneuss, 'Liturgical Books', below, p. 101. **3** *heptaticum Moysi*: the Old Testament Heptateuch (Genesis, Exodus, Leviticus, Numbers, Deuteronomy, Joshua and Judges), thought in the Middle Ages to have been composed by Moses. **4** *moralium Gregorii .xx.*: Gregory's *Moralia in Iob* (*Clavis*, no. 1708), a work which in fact consists of thirty-five books. **5** *Haimonis usque in Pascha*: the first part of the Homiliary of Haimo of Auxerre, containing homilies from Advent to Easter; see H. Barré, *Les Homéliaires carolingiens de l'école d'Auxerre*, Studi e testi 225 (Rome, 1962), 49–70. **6** *Claudii super Matheum*: the commentary – in fact it is a *catena* of earlier authorities – on Matthew by Claudius of Turin (*ob.* 827), which is as yet unprinted (see PL 104, cols. 833–8, and Manitius, *Geschichte* I, 394). **7** *regule . . . monachorum*: the *Regula* of St Benedict (*Clavis*, no. 1852), together with the *Diadema monachorum* of Smaragdus of Saint-Mihiel (PL 102, 593–690); the collocation of texts is found in other Anglo-Saxon manuscripts (for example, Cambridge, Corpus Christi College 57) and suggests a book intended for reading at chapter. **8** *dialogorum Gregorii*: Gregory the Great, *Dialogi* (*Clavis*, no. 1713). **9** *uitarum patrum*: the so-called *Vitas patrum*, an early title used to describe a massive but heterogeneous collection of lives and sayings principally of the early Egyptian Desert Fathers (see *BHL*, nos. 6524–47); the manuscript in question survives as Brussels, Bibliothèque Royale, 9850–2 (Soissons, s. vii/viii: see *CLA* x, no. 1547a). **10** *expositionis Ambrosii*: Ambrose, *Expositio de psalmo CXVIII* (*Clavis*, no. 141); the manuscript survives as Arras, Bibliothèque Municipale, 899 (590) (s. ix). **11** *Ambrosii De initiandis (liber I)*: Ambrose, *De mysteriis* (*Clavis*, no. 155). **11** *eiusdem De mysteriis (libri VI)*: Ambrose, *De sacramentis* (*Clavis*, no. 154). **11** *Palladii de Bragmanis*: Palladius, *De moribus Brachmanorum* (PL 17, cols. 1131–46); see A. Wilmart, 'Les Textes latins de la lettre de Palladius sur les moeurs des Brahmanes', *RB* 45 (1933), 29–42. **11** *Ysidori De officiis*: Isidore, *De ecclesiasticis officiis* (*Clavis*, no. 1207); the manuscript containing the four items listed in line 11 survives as Arras, Bibliothèque Municipale, 1068 (276) (s. x). **12** *pronosticon*: Julian of Toledo, *Prognosticum futuri saeculi* (*Clavis*, no. 1258). **13** *enkiridion*: Augustine, *Enchiridion ad Laurentium* (*Clavis*, no. 295). **14** *exameron Ambrosii*: Ambrose, *Exameron* (*Clavis*, no. 123); the manuscript survives as Arras, Bibliothèque Municipale, 346 (867) (s. x^ex and xi^med) and is listed by Gneuss, 'A Preliminary List', no. 778. **15** *Prosperi ad Iulianum*: Julianus Pomerius, *De uita contemplatiua* (*Clavis*, no. 998); on the manuscript tradition of this work, see M. L. W. Laistner, 'The Influence during the Middle Ages of the Treatise *De vita contemplativa* and its Surviving Manuscripts', in his *The Intellectual Heritage of the Early Middle Ages*, ed. C. G. Starr (Ithaca, NY, 1957), pp. 40–56; the manuscript in question survives as Arras, Bibliothèque Municipale, 435 (326), fols. 65–122 (s. xi). **15** *Ambrosii De officiis*: Ambrose, *De officiis ministrorum* (*Clavis*, no. 144); note that the copy of Ambrose, which was once cognate with (or bound with) the copy of Julianus Pomerius in Arras 435 (326) is no longer extant. **16** *Bede*: Bede, *Super epistolas catholicas expositio* (*Clavis*, no. 1362). **17** *epistolarum Bacharii*: for the various letters transmitted under the name of Bachiarius, see *Clavis*, nos. 568–70. **17** *Augustini, Eubodii, Macedonii*: apparently a collection of *epistolae* of Augustine (*Clavis*, no. 262) to Evodius (*Epp*. clviii, clx, clxi, clxiii and clxxvii) and Macedonius (*Epp*. clii and cliv). **18** *uite sancti Richarii*: probably Alcuin's *Vita S. Richarii* (*BHL*, nos. 7223–7, ptd PL 101, cols. 681–90), on which see now I. Deug-Su, *L'opera agiografica di Alcuino* (Spoleto, 1983), pp. 115–65; on the possible identity of the manuscript in question, see Grierson, 'Les Livres', p. 109, n. 18. **19** *uitae sanctorum . . . Dunstani*: a manuscript now preserved as Arras, Bibliothèque Municipale, 1029 (812) (? Bath, s. x^ex), which contains the anonymous *Vita S. Cuthberti* (*BHL*, no. 2019), Felix's *Vita S. Guthlaci* (*BHL*, no. 3723), the *Vita S. Aichardi* (*BHL*, no. 181), the *Vita S. Filiberti* (*BHL*, no. 6806), and the anonymous *Vita S. Dunstani* by the English monk .B. (*BHL*, no. 2342). **20** *De assumptione*: the manuscript in question survives as Arras, Bibliothèque Municipale, 732 (684) (s. xi), and contains Jerome's *Epistola ad Paulam et Eustochium de assumptione beate Virginis* (*Ep*. xlvi; see *Clavis*, no. 620), as well as Cassiodorus, *De anima* (*Clavis*, no. 897) and *Institutiones* (*Clavis*, no. 906). **21** *Librum canonum*: the manuscript survives as Arras, Bibliothèque Municipale, 644 (572) (s. viii/ix); its principal content is the collection of canons known as the *Collectio Quesnelliana* (*Clavis*, no. 1770). **22** *Librum hystoriae . . . Anglie*: Bede, *Historia ecclesiastica gentis Anglorum* (*Clavis*, no. 1375); see further the discussion by Grierson ('Les Livres', p. 110, n. 22), who suggests that a fragment of the manuscript in question was preserved as a Phillipps manuscript; the fragment is now New York, Pierpont Morgan Library, M. 826 (Northumbria, s. viii$^{ex}$: *CLA* XI, no. 1662). **23** *Librum uite sancti Walerici . . . uno uolumine*: the manuscript does not appear to survive; for the *uitae* in question, see *BHL*, nos. 8762 (Walaricus), 5783 (Maurus), 5015 (Lucianus and Marcianus) and 4544–5 (Iulianus). **24** *Librum medicinalis*: not identifiable without further specification; but see Grierson's note ('Les Livres', p. 110, n. 24). **25** *Librum Cassiodori*: Cassiodorus, *De orthographia* (*Clavis*, no. 907). **26** *Librum uersuum et tractuum totius anni*: a gradual or responsorial which contained the verses and responds as well as the tracts (that is, the chants which replaced the Alleluia during penitential periods and which were sung without response) for the entire liturgical year; the scribe has added the word *tonos* after *anni*, which may suggest that the manuscript was notated. **27** *Librum parabolarum Salomonis*: the manuscript survives as Arras, Bibliothèque Municipale, 1079 (235), fols. 28–80 (s. ix/x); it contains three apparently unedited commentaries on Proverbs, Ecclesiastes and the Song of Songs, as well as Bede's *In Esdram et Nehemiam prophetas allegorica expositio* (*Clavis*, no. 1329); on the manuscript, see further Grierson, 'Les Livres', pp. 114–16. **28** *De laude uirginitatis*: a copy either of Aldhelm's prose *De uirginitate* (*Clavis*, no. 1332) or his *Carmen de uirginitate* (Clavis, no. 1333), both of which bore the rubric *De laude uirginitatis* on occasion, and which, to judge from surviving manuscripts, do not seem ever to have been combined in one codex. **29** *De professione coniugatorum*: Grierson ('Les Livres', p. 111, n. 29) confessed himself unable to identify this item, and I agree that it is unidentifiable without further specification, although possibly Augustine's *De bono coniugali* (*Clavis*, no. 299) is in question. **30** *Librum Prudentii*: a copy of all or some of Prudentius's *Carmina* (*Clavis*, nos. 1437–45). **31** *Iuuencus, Sedulius*: Juvencus, *Evangelia quattuor* (*Clavis*, no. 1385) together with Caelius Sedulius, *Carmen Paschale* (*Clavis*, no. 1447). **32** *Librum Rabbani . . . Hester*: Hrabanus Maurus, *Expositio in librum Iudith* (PL 109, cols. 539–92) and *Expositio in librum Esther* (PL 109, cols. 635–70); the manuscript survives as Arras, Bibliothèque Municipale, 764 (739), fols. 1–93 (s. x), and is listed by Gneuss, 'A Preliminary List', no. 779. **33** *Tripartite historie ecclesiastice*: Cassiodorus, *Tripartita historia ecclesiastica* (PL 69, cols. 879–1214); on the medieval transmission of this work, see M. L. W. Laistner, 'The Value and Influence of Cassiodorus's Ecclesiastical History', *The Intellectual Heritage of the Early Middle Ages*, ed. Starr, pp. 22–39.

## *IX. Books belonging to Worcester (*c. *1050)*

Cambridge, Corpus Christi College 367 is a composite manuscript, consisting of two parts each separately foliated and each composite in turn. Into a single and separate quire (Part ii, fols. 45–52) containing the conclusion of a *Vita S. Kenelmi*, a scribe has copied a list of books in handwriting datable to the mid-eleventh century (48v).[98] Because some of the books listed can be identified with surviving books from Worcester, and because a Worcester document was later copied into the quire, there are good grounds for thinking that the booklist itself is from Worcester. It has been printed and discussed on several occasions.[99]

Ðeo englissce passionale
7 .ii. englissce dialogas
7 Oddan boc
7 þe englisca martirlogium
7 .ii. englisce salteras
7 .ii. pastorales englisce
7 þe englisca regol
7 Barontus

COMMENTARY **1** *Ðeo englissce passionale*: a legendary in Old English (see Gneuss, 'Liturgical Books', below, p. 126), possibly a copy of Ælfric's *Lives of Saints*. **2** *.ii. englissce dialogas*: two copies of Werferth's Old English translation of Gregory's *Dialogi* (*Bischof Waerferths von Worcester Übersetzung der Dialoge Gregors des Grossen*, ed. H. Hecht, 2 vols. (Hamburg, 1900–7)); the two manuscripts in question are probably London, BL Cotton Otho C. i, vol. 2 (Worcester, s. xi$^{in}$ and xi$^{med}$) and Oxford, Bodleian Library, Hatton 76 (Worcester, s. xi$^{1}$). **3** *Oddan boc*: presumably a book belonging to one *Odda* or *Oda* (hence the genitive) rather than a book *by* Oda; it is interesting to note that a charter of Edward the Confessor dated 1044 × 1051 (listed Sawyer, *Anglo-Saxon Charters*, no. 1058 and ptd Kemble, *Codex Diplomaticus*, no. 797) leasing land at Lench, Worcestershire, to Lyfing, bishop of Worcester, is witnessed by a monk of Worcester named Odda: 'Ego Odda monachus consensi'; this Odda was arguably the owner of the book in question. **4** *þe englisca martirlogium*: apparently a copy of the so-called Old English Martyrology (*Das altenglische Martyrologium*, ed. G. Kotzor, 2 vols., Bayerische Akademie der Wissenschaften, Phil.-hist. Klasse, Abhandlungen n.s. 88 (Munich, 1981); see Gneuss, below, p. 128); but it does not seem possible to identify the entry in this booklist with any surviving manuscript of the work. **5** *.ii. englisce salteras*: two psalters, either in Old English translation or, more likely perhaps, with extensive interlinear glossing in Old English (see Gneuss, below, p. 128). **6** *.ii. pastorales englisce*: two copies of King Alfred's English translation of Gregory's *Regula pastoralis* (*King Alfred's West Saxon Version of Gregory's Pastoral Care*, ed. H. Sweet, EETS o.s. 45 and 50 (London, 1871)); the two manuscripts in question are probably Cambridge, Corpus Christi College 12 (Worcester, s. x$^{2}$) and Oxford, Bodleian Library, Hatton 20 (Worcester, s. ix$^{ex}$). *7 þe englisca regol*: probably a copy of Æthelwold's English translation of the *Regula* of St Benedict (*Die angelsächsischen Prosabearbeitungen der*

[98] Ker, *Catalogue*, p. 110 (no. 64).

[99] Robertson, *Anglo-Saxon Charters*, pp. 250 and 498–9, and R. M. Wilson, *The Lost Literature of Medieval England*, 2nd ed. (London, 1970), pp. 81–2.

*Benediktinerregel*, ed. A. Schröer, rev. H. Gneuss (Darmstadt, 1964)); the manuscript in question is probably Cambridge, Corpus Christi College 178, pp. 287–457 (Worcester, s. xi[1]). **8** *Barontus*: the *Visio S. Baronti monachi* (*Clavis*, no. 1313; *BHL*, no. 997); the occurrence of the work in the present list may suggest that an Old English translation of the *Visio Baronti* is in question, but no such translation has come down to us (the only Latin version known to me in an Anglo-Saxon manuscript is some fragments in London, BL Cotton Otho A. xiii); on the work itself, see M. P. Ciccarese, 'La *Visio Baronti* nella tradizione letteraria delle *uisiones* dell'aldilà', *Romanobarbarica* 6 (1981–2), 25–52; see also below, no. XIII, line 51.

## *X. Inventory of books procured by Bishop Leofric for the church of Exeter (1069 × 1072)*

When Leofric moved his see from Crediton to Exeter in 1050 he found at Exeter no more than a handful of worn-out service-books. During the years of his episcopacy he evidently took great pains to acquire or have copied a full complement not only of necessary service-books, but also of other books, so that on his death in 1072 he was able to bequeath some sixty-six books to his church. Leofric's bequest (of estates and ecclesiastical furnishings as well as of books) is recorded in a document copied in the third quarter of the eleventh century into a preliminary quire (now fols. iv, 1–6) that was prefixed to a gospel-book which Leofric had acquired, now Oxford, Bodleian Library, Auct. D. 2. 16 (Landévennec, Brittany, s. x);[100] the list is found on 1r–2v. It is this copy which serves as the basis for the edition printed below. A second contemporary copy is found in a quire now prefixed to the Exeter Book (Exeter, Cathedral Library, 3501, fols. 0, 1–7; the list is on 1r–2v); this quire was originally part of a copy of the West Saxon gospels, now Cambridge, University Library, Ii. 2. 11.[101] The few minor variants which occur in the Exeter Book-version have also been recorded below. Leofric's booklist has been printed and discussed on many occasions,[102] most thoroughly by Max Förster in his introduction to the facsimile of the Exeter Book.[103] It is possible

[100] See Ker, *Catalogue*, pp. 351–2 (no. 291).

[101] *Ibid.* pp. 28–31 (no. 20).

[102] H. Wanley, *Librorum Veterum Septentrionalium . . . Catalogus* (Oxford, 1705), p. 80 (interesting annotation); T. Wright, 'On Bishop Leofric's Library', *JBAA* 18 (1862), 220–4; F. E. Warren, *The Leofric Missal* (Oxford, 1883), pp. xxii–xxiv; C. Edmonds, 'The Formation and Fortunes of Exeter Cathedral Library', *Report and Trans. of the Devonshire Assoc.* 31 (1899), 25–50; Robertson, *Anglo-Saxon Charters*, pp. 226–30 and 473–80; L. J. Lloyd, 'Leofric as Bibliophile', *Leofric of Exeter*, ed. F. Barlow *et al.* (Exeter, 1972), pp. 32–42; M. McC. Gatch, *Preaching and Theology in Anglo-Saxon England: Ælfric and Wulfstan* (Toronto, 1977), pp. 42–4; E. M. Drage, 'Bishop Leofric and Exeter Cathedral Chapter (1050–1072): a Reassessment of the Manuscript Evidence' (unpubl. D. Phil. dissertation, Oxford Univ., 1978), *passim*.

[103] *The Exeter Book of Old English Poetry*, ed. R. W. Chambers, M. Förster and R. Flower (London, 1933), pp. 10–32, esp. 25–30.

to identify a number of items in Leofric's list because Leofric took care to have *ex libris* inscriptions copied into the books which he donated;[104] I note below those cases where an identification can be confirmed by such evidence.

> Her swutelað on þissere Cristes[105] bec hwæt Leofric bisceop hæfð gedon inn to sancte Petres minstre on Exanceastre þær his bisceopstol is . . .
>
> .ii. mycele Cristes bec gebonede . . .
> 7 .ii. fulle mæssebec
> 7 .i. collectaneum
> 7 .ii. pistelbec
> 7 .ii. fulle sangbec
> 7 .i. nihtsang
> 7 .i. adteleuaui
> 7 .i. tropere
> 7 .ii. salteras
> 7 se þriddan saltere[106] swa man singð on Rome
> 7 .ii. ymneras
> 7 .i. deorwyrðe bletsingboc
> 7 .iii. oðre
> 7 .i. englisc Cristes boc[107]
> 7 .ii. sumerrædingbec
> 7 .i. winterrædingboc
> 7 regula canonicorum
> 7 martyrlogium
> 7 .i. canon on leden
> 7 .i. scriftboc on englisc
> 7 .i. full spelboc wintres 7 sumeres
> 7 Boeties boc on englisc
> 7 .i. mycel englisc boc be gehwilcum þingum on leoðwisan geworht

104 A convenient list of manuscripts with Leofric's inscriptions is found in R. Frank and A. Cameron, *A Plan for the Dictionary of Old English* (Toronto, 1973), p. 193. Note that one manuscript which has a Leofric *ex libris* inscription (Cambridge, Corpus Christi College 41) does not apparently figure in the list of Leofric's donation, unless it is one of the sacramentaries listed in line 2 (though it could hardly be described as a *fulle mæsseboc*; on its liturgical contents, see R. J. S. Grant, *Cambridge, Corpus Christi College 41: the Loricas and the Missal* (Amsterdam, 1979)).

105 The Exeter Book omits the word *Cristes*.

106 The Exeter Book omits the word *saltere*.

107 In lieu of this entry the Exeter Book has 'þeos englisce Cristes boc' (but recall that the quire containing this document was originally prefixed not to the Exeter Book – which is in no way a *Cristes boc* – but to Cambridge, University Library Ii. 2. 11).

7 he ne funde on þam mynstre þa he tofeng boca na ma buton
ane capitularie
7 .i. forealdodne nihtsang
7 .i. pistelboc
7 .ii. forealdode rædingbec swiðe wake . . .
7 þus fela leden boca he beget inn to þam mynstre.
liber pastoralis
7 liber dialogorum
7 libri .iiii. prophetarum
7 liber Boetii De consolatione[108]
7 Isagoge Porphirii[109]
7 .i. passionalis
7 liber Prosperi
7 liber Prudentii psicomachie
7 liber Prudentii ymnorum
7 liber Prudentii de martyribus[110]
7 liber Ezechielis prophete
7 Cantica canticorum
7 liber Isaie prophete on sundron
7 liber Isidori Ethimolagiarum
7 Passiones apostolorum
7 Expositio Bede super euuangelium Luce
7 Expositio Bede super apocalipsin
7 Expositio Bede super .vii. epistolas canonicas
7 Liber Isidori De nouo et ueteri testamento
7 liber Isidori De miraculis Christi
7 liber Oserii
7 liber Machabeorum
7 liber Persii
7 Sedulies boc
7 liber Aratoris
7 Diadema monachorum[111]
7 Glose Statii
7 liber officialis Amalarii

COMMENTARY 1 *.ii. mycele Cristes bęce gebonede*: two large gospel-books, ornamented. 2 *fulle mæssebec*: sacramentaries or missals (see Gneuss, below, p. 100); it is not precisely clear what *fulle* means in this context, and it is possible that the scribe was attempting to

[108] In the Exeter Book this entry is followed by *Liber officialis Amalarii*; see below, line 55.

[109] Following this item there is an erasure of one item in Auct. D. 2. 16.

[110] After *martyribus* the Exeter Book adds 'on anre bec'.

[111] The Exeter Book omits this entry; in its stead a later hand has written 'liber de sanctis patribus'.

distinguish the plenary missal from the sacramentary; one of the books in question is possibly Oxford, Bodleian Library, Bodley 579 (the 'Leofric Missal'), which bears a Leofric *ex libris* inscription. **3** *collectaneum*: a collectary (see Gneuss, below, p. 113); the book probably survives as London, BL Harley 2961 (Exeter, s. xi$^{\text{med}}$) (*The Leofric Collectar*, ed. E. S. Dewick and W. H. Frere, 2 vols., HBS 45–6 (London, 1914–21)); Harley 2961 once bore a Leofric *ex libris* which is no longer preserved (see Ker, *Catalogue*, p. 308). **4** *pistelbec*: epistolaries for the mass; see Gneuss, below, p. 110. **5** *fulle sangbec*: possibly books for the Office, but the precise meaning of *sangbec* (and the qualifying adjective *fulle* in this context) is not clear; see Gneuss, below, p. 103. **6** *nihtsang*: an antiphonary for the nocturnal hours (*antiphonarium nocturnale*); see Gneuss, below, p. 117. **7** *adteleuaui*: a gradual; see Gneuss, below, p. 103. **8** *tropere*: a troper for the mass; see Gneuss, below, p. 104. **9** *salteras*: two psalters, presumably of the Gallican type, since a Roman psalter in the following line is distinguished from them; one of these Gallican psalters may survive as London, BL Harley 863 (Exeter, s. xi$^{2}$). **10** *se þriddan . . . on Rome*: a psalter of 'Roman' type (*psalterium Romanum*). **11** *ymneras*: hymnals for the Office; see Gneuss, below, p. 119. **12** *deorwyrðe bletsingboc*: a valuable pontifical or benedictional – or both combined (see Gneuss, below, p. 131); the manuscript in question is possibly London, BL Add. 28188 (Exeter, s. xi$^{2}$). **13** *.iii. oðre*: three other (less valuable) pontificals or benedictionals – or both combined. **14** *englisc Cristes boc*: the West Saxon version of the gospels, now Cambridge, University Library, Ii. 2. 11 (Exeter, s. xi$^{2}$), a manuscript which bears a Leofric *ex libris* inscription. **15–16** *.ii. sumerrædingbec 7 .i. winterrædingboc*: as Gneuss points out (below, p. 121), the division of the lectionary (*rædingboc*) into winter and summer volumes suggests an Office book rather than a mass lectionary. **17** *regula canonicorum*: a copy of Chrodegang of Metz's *Regula canonicorum* (*Clavis*, no. 1876); Leofric is known to have introduced Chrodegang's *Regula* to his secular clergy at Exeter, and it is possible that the book in question survives as Cambridge, Corpus Christi College 191 (Exeter, s. xi$^{2}$). **18** *martyrlogium*: presumably a copy of the Old English Martyrology, and possibly that which survives as Cambridge, Corpus Christi College 196 (Exeter, s. xi$^{2}$). **19** *canon on leden*: a collection of ecclesiastical canons which (without further specification) cannot be identified. **20** *scriftboc on englisc*: a manuscript containing penitential texts in Old English (see A. J. Frantzen, *The Literature of Penance in Anglo-Saxon England* (New Brunswick, NJ, 1983), pp. 133–41); it is probable that the *scriftboc* in question survives as Cambridge, Corpus Christi College 190 (Exeter, s. xi$^{1}$ and xi$^{\text{med}}$). **21** *full spelboc*: a homiliary in two volumes, for summer and winter; see Gneuss, below, p. 123. **22** *Boeties boc*: apparently a copy of King Alfred's English translation of Boethius, *De consolatione Philosophiae*; the manuscript in question does not survive. **23** *mycel englisc boc*: 'a large book in English on various subjects composed in verse', presumably the Exeter Book itself, now Exeter, Cathedral Library, 3501 (s. x$^{2}$). **24** *ane capitularie*: a collectar, presumably; see Gneuss, below, p. 113. **25** *forealdodne nihtsang*: a worn-out antiphonary; see Gneuss, below, p. 117. **26** *pistelboc*: an epistolary; see Gneuss, below, p. 110. **27** *.ii. forealdode rædingbec swiðe wake*: 'two worn-out (Office) lectionaries in very bad condition'; see Gneuss, below, p. 121. **28** *liber pastoralis*: Gregory's *Regula pastoralis* (*Clavis*, no. 1712); the book in question survives as Oxford, Bodleian Library, Bodley 708 (Christ Church, Canterbury, s. x$^{\text{ex}}$; provenance Exeter), which has a Leofric *ex* *libris* inscription. **29** *liber dialogorum*: Gregory the Great, *Dialogi* (*Clavis*, no. 1713). **30** *libri .iiii. prophetarum*: a copy of the four 'great' biblical prophets (Isaiah, Jeremiah, Ezekiel and Daniel). **31** *Boetii De consolatione*: Boethius, *De consolatione Philosophiae* (*Clavis*, no. 878); the book survives as Oxford, Bodleian Library, Auct. F. 1. 15 (St Augustine's, Canterbury, s. x²; provenance Exeter), and has a Leofric *ex libris* inscription. **32** *Isagoge Porphirii*: Porphyry's *Isagoge* or 'Introduction' to Aristotle's *Categories* was, in the Latin translation of Boethius, the standard account of logic in the early Middle Ages; Boethius also wrote a commentary (*Clavis*, no. 881) on Porphyry's *Isagoge*, which is also conceivably in question here. **33** *passionalis*: a passional or legendary (see Gneuss, below, p. 126); its position here in the list may suggest that it was intended for meditational rather than liturgical reading. **34** *liber Prosperi*: in medieval booklists references to Prosper almost invariably refer to his *Epigrammata* (*Clavis*, no. 518), which were a standard school-text in the early Middle Ages; see Manitius, *Handschriften*, p. 247. **35–7**: three works of Prudentius – the *Psychomachia* (*Clavis*, no. 1441), the *Cathemerinon* (*Clavis*, no. 1438) and *Peristephanon* (*Clavis*, no. 1443); in the Exeter Book-version of this list the three works of Prudentius are said to be *on anre bec*; and indeed all three survive as Oxford, Bodleian Library, Auct. F. 3. 6 (Exeter, s. xi¹), which also has a Leofric *ex libris* inscription. **38** *liber Ezechielis*: another copy of the prophet Ezekiel; see above, line 30. **39** *Cantica canticorum*: the biblical Song of Songs. **40** *liber Isaie*: another copy of the prophet Isaiah, said to be *on sundron* because distinct from that listed above (line 30). **41** *liber Isidori Ethimolagiarum*: Isidore, *Etymologiae* (*Clavis*, no. 1186). **42** *Passiones apostolorum*: any one of a number of works might be in question here: pseudo-Abdias, *Historiae apostolicae*; the anonymous *Breuiarium apostolorum* (*BHL*, no. 652); Isidore, *De ortu et obitu patrum* (*Clavis*, no. 1191); a Hiberno-Latin treatise of the same name (unptd, but cf. PL 83, cols. 1275–94); or a collection of *passiones apostolorum* such as that in Würzburg, Universitätsbibliothek, M. p. th. f. 78 (see *CLA* IX, no. 1425). **43** *Expositio Bede . . . Luce*: Bede, *In Lucae euangelium expositio* (*Clavis*, no. 1356). **44** *Expositio Bede . . . apocalipsin*: Bede, *Explanatio Apocalypsis* (*Clavis*, no. 1363); the book possibly survives as London, Lambeth Palace Library, 149 (s. x²). **45** *Expositio Bede . . . canonicas*: Bede, *Super epistolas catholicas expositio* (*Clavis*, no. 1362); the manuscript possibly survives as Oxford, Bodleian Library, Bodley 849 (Loire region, s. ix¹; provenance Exeter). **46** *Liber Isidori . . . testamento*: it is not clear whether the work in question here is Isidore's *Prooemia* to the books of the Old and New Testaments (*Clavis*, no. 1192; see below, no. XI, line 33), or the pseudo-Isidorian *Quaestiones de ueteri et nouo testamento*, a work of Hiberno-Latin origin (*Clavis*, no. 1194; see R. E. McNally, 'The pseudo-Isidorian *De ueteri et nouo Testamento Quaestiones*', *Traditio* 19 (1963), 37–50). **47** *Isidori De miraculis Christi*: Isidore, *De fide catholica contra Iudaeos* (*Clavis*, no. 1198); the book in question is possibly Oxford, Bodleian Library, Bodley 394 (s. xi; provenance Exeter). **48** *liber Oserii*: a much-discussed entry which has been thought to be a garbled reference either to Asser's Life of King Alfred (*liber Asserii*) or to Orosius's *Historiae aduersum paganos* (*liber Orosii*), or possibly to a work of Isidore (see full discussion by Förster, *The Exeter Book*, p. 29). **49** *liber Machabeorum*: the biblical books of Maccabees. **50** *liber Persii*: see Manitius, *Handschriften*, pp. 112–15, and *Texts and Transmission*, ed. Reynolds, pp. 293–5; the book in question is possibly Oxford, Bodleian Library, Auct. F. 1. 15, fols. 78–93 (St Augustine's, Canterbury, s. x$^2$; provenance Exeter). **51** *Sedulies boc*: Caelius Sedulius, *Carmen Paschale* (*Clavis*, no. 1447). **52** *liber Aratoris*: Arator, *De actibus apostolorum* (*Clavis*, no. 1504). **53** *Diadema monachorum*: Smaragdus of Saint-Mihiel, *Diadema monachorum* (PL 102, cols. 593–690). **54** *Glose Statii*: presumably a glossed copy of Statius, *Thebaid*, such as that in Worcester, Cathedral Library, Q. 8, part II + Add. 7 (English, s. x/xi) (see T. A. M. Bishop, *English Caroline Minuscule* (Oxford, 1971), p. 18); for Statius, see Manitius, *Handschriften*, pp. 125–9, and *Texts and Transmission*, ed. Reynolds, pp. 394–7. **55** *liber . . . Amalarii*: Amalarius of Metz, *De ecclesiasticis officiis* (PL 105, cols. 985–1242, and *Amalarii episcopi Opera Liturgica Omnia*, ed. J. M. Hanssens, 3 vols., Studi e testi 138–40 (Rome, 1948–50) II, 13–543); the manuscript survives as Cambridge, Trinity College B. 11. 2 (St Augustine's, Canterbury, s. x$^2$; provenance Exeter), which has a Leofric *ex libris* inscription.

## *XI. Booklist from an unidentified centre, possibly Worcester (s. xi$^{ex}$)*

Oxford, Bodleian Library, Tanner 3 (S.C. 9823) is an early-eleventh-century copy of Gregory's *Dialogi* written at an unidentified English centre. At some later time, probably in the late eleventh century, a list of books and ecclesiastical vestments was added on blank folios at the end of the manuscript (189v–190r). The manuscript was at Worcester by the second half of the twelfth century, when a letter from Pope Alexander III to Bishop Roger of Worcester (1164–79) was copied onto the front flyleaf; but it is an open question whether the manuscript was at Worcester when the booklist was copied, and therefore whether it can be used as evidence for the library at Worcester in the late eleventh century. In a recent study of Worcester manuscripts it is stressed that the handwriting of the booklist 'does not resemble that of any known Worcester books of a similar date';[112] on the other hand, the later Worcester provenance of the manuscript combined with the fact that Worcester librarians had a pronounced interest in acquiring texts of Gregory the Great,[113] indicates that a Worcester origin for the booklist cannot be ruled out in the present state of our knowledge. The booklist has previously been printed and discussed by Bannister.[114] It is principally a list of books intended for use in a schoolroom (note the multiple copies of some school-texts), with the subsequent addition of a few liturgical books (lines 57–60).

112 E. A. McIntyre, 'Early Twelfth-Century Worcester Cathedral Priory with special Reference to the Manuscripts copied there' (unpubl. D.Phil. dissertation, Oxford Univ., 1978), p. 87.

113 *Ibid.* pp. 94–8.

114 H. M. Bannister, 'Bishop Roger of Worcester and the Church of Keynsham, with a List of Vestments and Books possibly belonging to Worcester', *EHR* 32 (1917), 387–93.

Daniel propheta
Orosius
Sedulius
Dialogus
[5] Glosarius
Martianus
Persius
Prosper
Terrentium
[10] Sedulius
Sychomagia
Boetius
Lucanus
Commentum Remigii super Sedulium
[15] Isidorus De natura rerum
Arator
Glosarius
Priscianus maior
Tractatus grammatice artis
[20] Commentum super Iuuenalem
Bucholica et Georgica Virgilii
Persius
Hystoria anglorum
Vita Kyerrani
[25] Liber pronosticorum Iuliani
.XL. omelia
Arator
Psalterium Hieronimi
Commentum Boetii super Categorias
[30] Liber Luciferi
Epigrammata Prosperi
Beda De temporibus
Liber proemiorum ueteris et noui[115]
Liber dialogorum
[35] Prosper
Seruius De uoce et littera
Apollonius
Ars Sedulii
Boetius Super Perhiermenias

115 The word *testamenti* has been omitted by the scribe.

Ordo Romanus
Liber Albini
Psalterium
Historia anglorum
Glosarius per alfabetum
Textus euangeliorum
Expositio psalterii
Kategorie Aristotili
Aeclesiastica istoria
Liber soliloquiorum
Vita S. Willfridi episcopi
Haimo
Textum .i.
Omelia .i.
Liber magnus de grammatica arte
Troparium .i.
Hymnarium .i. . . .[116]
Missalem .i.[117]
Epistolarem .i.
Ad te leuaui
et Aspiciens

COMMENTARY **1** *Daniel propheta*: the biblical book of Daniel. **2** *Orosius*: presumably the *Historiae aduersum paganos* (*Clavis*, no. 571). **3** *Sedulius*: Caelius Sedulius, *Carmen Paschale* (*Clavis*, no. 1447). **4** *Dialogus*: one thinks inevitably of Gregory's *Dialogi* (*Clavis*, no. 1713), but the context and the nominative singular form of the title may rather suggest that the book in question was a volume of scholastic colloquies (see above, no. III, line 14, and below, line 34). **5** *Glosarius*: an unidentifiable glossary. **6** *Martianus*: Martianus Capella, *De nuptiis Philologiae et Mercurii*; see Manitius, *Handschriften*, pp. 237–42, and *Texts and Transmission*, ed. Reynolds, pp. 245–6. **7** *Persius*: see Manitius, *Handschriften*, pp. 112–15, and *Texts and Transmission*, ed. Reynolds, pp. 293–5. **8** *Prosper*: Prosper of Aquitaine, *Epigrammata* (*Clavis*, no. 518). **9** *Terrentium*: presumably a play (or plays) by Terence; see Manitius, *Handschriften*, pp. 12–16, and *Texts and Transmission*, ed. Reynolds, pp. 412–20. **10** *Sedulius*: another copy of the *Carmen Paschale*; see above, line 3. **11** *Sychomagia*: Prudentius, *Psychomachia* (*Clavis*, no. 1441). **12** *Boetius*: presumably (but not necessarily) the *De consolatione Philosophiae* (*Clavis*, no. 878). **13** *Lucanus*: Lucan, *Pharsalia*; see Manitius, *Handschriften*, pp. 115–20, and *Texts and Transmission*, ed. Reynolds, pp. 215–18. **14** *Commentum Remigii super Sedulium*: Remigius of Auxerre's unptd commentary on the *Carmen Paschale* of Caelius Sedulius (excerpts are ptd J. Huemer, CSEL 10 (Vienna, 1885),

[116] I omit here the list of ecclesiastical vestments.

[117] Lines 57–60 were added by the same scribe, but on the following leaf (190r) and after a break.

319–59; cf. also Huemer's discussion, *Über ein Glossenwerk zum Dichter Sedulius*, Sitzungsberichte der kaiserlichen Akademie der Wissenschaften zu Wien, phil.-hist. Klasse, 96 (Vienna, 1880), 505–51); two manuscripts of Anglo-Saxon origin or provenance survive in Cambridge, Gonville and Caius College 144/194 (s. x; provenance St Augustine's, Canterbury) and Salisbury, Cathedral Library, 134 (English, s. x/xi); the latter manuscript has the rubric *Commentum Remegii super Sedulium* (1r) and may possibly be the book in question here. **15** *Isidorus De natura rerum*: *Clavis*, no. 1188. **16** *Arator*: Arator, *De actibus apostolorum* (*Clavis*, no. 1504). **17** *Glosarius*: another glossary; see above, line 5. **18** *Priscianus maior*: in manuscripts of Priscian the term *maior* usually refers to his *Institutiones grammaticae*, bks I–XVI (*GL* II, 1–597, and III, 1–377). **19** *Tractatus grammatice artis*: unidentifiable as such. **20** *Commentum super Iuuenalem*: possibly the commentary on Juvenal by Remigius of Auxerre, which is not extant but is known from medieval library catalogues; see Manitius, *Geschichte* I, 512–13, and E. M. Sanford, 'Juvenal', *Catalogus Translationum et Commentariorum: Medieval and Renaissance Latin Translations and Commentaries*, ed. P. O. Kristeller *et al.*, 4 vols. so far (Washington, DC, 1960–80) I, 175–238, at 176. **21** *Bucholica . . . Virgilii*: the Eclogues and Georgics of Vergil; see Manitius, *Handschriften*, pp. 47–55, and *Texts and Transmission*, ed. Reynolds, pp. 433–6. **22** *Persius*: another copy; see above, line 7. **23** *Hystoria anglorum*: presumably Bede, *Historia ecclesiastica gentis Anglorum* (*Clavis*, no. 1375). **24** *Vita Kyerrani*: a *uita* of an Irish St Ciaran, either the saint of Clonmacnois (*BHL*, nos. 4654–5; see R. A. S. Macalister, *The Latin and Irish Lives of Ciaran* (London, 1921)) or of Saigir (*BHL*, nos. 4657–8; see P. Grosjean, 'Vita S. Ciarani episcopi de Saighir', *AB* 59 (1941), 217–71). **25** *Liber pronosticorum Iuliani*: Julian of Toledo, *Prognosticum futuri saeculi* (*Clavis*, no. 1258). **26** *.XL. omelia*: the specific number of homilies – forty – suggests that the work in question is Gregory's *Homiliae .xl. in euangelia* (*Clavis*, no. 1711). **27** *Arator*: another copy; see above, line 16. **28** *Psalterium Hieronimi*: the specification of Jerome's authorship probably indicates that a copy of the version *iuxta Hebraeos* is in question here; see below, no. XIII, line 62: 'psalterium Hieronimi secundum Hebreos'. **29** *Commentum Boetii*: Boethius's Commentary on Aristotle's Categories (*Clavis*, no. 882). **30** *Liber Luciferi*: apparently one of the works of Lucifer of Cagliari (*Clavis*, nos. 112–18). **31** *Epigrammata Prosperi*: another copy; see above, line 8. **32** *Beda De temporibus*: *Clavis*, no. 2318. **33** *Liber proemiorum*: Isidore, *In libros ueteris ac noui testamenti prooemia* (*Clavis*, no. 1192). **34** *Liber dialogorum*: presumably Gregory, *Dialogi* (*Clavis*, no. 1713), but see above, line 4; note that the book containing the present booklist is a copy of Gregory's *Dialogi*. **35** *Prosper*: another copy; see above, line 8. **36** *Seruius De uoce et littera*: the title suggests that the work in question was not by Seruius but by Sergius, whose commentary on Donatus's *Ars maior* (bk I) was entitled *De littera* (*GL* IV, 475–85); the names Servius and Sergius were inevitably confused in medieval manuscripts (see Law, *The Insular Latin Grammarians*, p. 17). **37** *Apollonius*: a copy of the Latin romance entitled *Historia Apollonii regis Tyri* (ed. A. Riese (Leipzig, 1893)), a work which was evidently known in Anglo-Saxon England, given that an Old English translation of the work is found in Cambridge, Corpus Christi College 201 (*The Old English Apollonius of Tyre*, ed. P. Goolden (Oxford, 1958)); the Latin original on which this translation was based does not appear to survive (see J. Zupitza,

'Welcher Text liegt der altenglischen Bearbeitung der Erzählung von Apollonius von Tyrus zu Grunde?', *Romanische Forschungen* 3 (1886), 269–79), nor, apparently, does the book listed here. **38** *Ars Sedulii*: one of the grammatical commentaries by Sedulius Scottus (see Manitius, *Geschichte* I, 318–19), who wrote commentaries on Donatus (*Ars maior* and *Ars minor*), Priscian and Eutyches (all of which are ed. B. Löfstedt, CCSL, CM 40B–C (Turnhout, 1977)). **39** *Boetius Super Perhiermenias*: Boethius's commentary on Aristotle's *Peri Hermeneias*, also called *De interpretatione* (*Clavis*, no. 883). **40** *Ordo Romanus*: a copy of one of the many *ordines Romani* (books, that is, which give directions for the performance of liturgical ceremonies), of which Michel Andrieu identified and edited fifty in his monumental *Les Ordines Romani du haut moyen âge*, 5 vols. (Louvain, 1931–61). **41** *Liber Albini*: a work (unspecified) by Alcuin. **42** *Psalterium*: as above, line 28. **43** *Historia anglorum*: as above, line 23. **44** *Glosarius per alfabetum*: a glossary arranged in alphabetical order. **45** *Textus euangeliorum*: a gospel-book. **46** *Expositio psalterii*: to judge from the title, the work in question was Cassiodorus, *Expositio psalmorum* (*Clavis*, no. 900); but a number of commentaries on the psalter were in circulation, in particular those by Augustine (*Clavis*, no. 283), Hilary (*Clavis*, no. 428) and Jerome (*Clavis*, no. 582), as well as various anonymous compilations, any one of which could be in question here. **47** *Kategorie Aristotili*: presumably Boethius's Latin translation of Aristotle's Categories (rather than the *Categoriae decem*, which in the Middle Ages passed under the name of Augustine). **48** *Aeclesiastica istoria*: possibly Bede's *Historia ecclesiastica* (see above, lines 23 and 43), but more likely the *Historia ecclesiastica* of Eusebius in the Latin translation of Rufinus (ed. T. Mommsen, 3 vols., Griechisch–christliche Schriftsteller 9 (Leipzig, 1903–9)); see below, no. XIII, line 7. **49** *Liber soliloquiorum*: Augustine, *Soliloquia* (*Clavis*, no. 252). **50** *Vita S. Willfridi episcopi*: presumably the *Vita S. Wilfridi* attributed to 'Eddius' Stephanus (*BHL*, no. 8889; *The Life of Bishop Wilfrid by Eddius Stephanus*, ed. B. Colgrave (Cambridge, 1927); see also below, no. XIII, line 41). **51** *Haimo*: one of the works of Haimo of Auxerre (on whom see *Deutschlands Geschichtsquellen im Mittelalter*, ed. H. Löwe, V, 564–5), either one of his many biblical commentaries (see below, no. XIII, lines 32–3) or else his Homiliary (see above, no. VIII, line 5). **52** *Textum*: a gospel-book; see above, line 45. **53** *Omelia*: probably a homiliary; see Gneuss, below, p. 122. **54** *Liber magnus . . . arte*: unidentifiable, unfortunately. **55** *Troparium*: a troper; see Gneuss, below, p. 104. **56** *Hymnarium*: a hymnal; see Gneuss, below, p. 118. **57** *Missalem*: a sacramentary or missal; see Gneuss, below, p. 99. **58** *Epistolarem*: an epistolary; see Gneuss, below, p. 110. **59** *Ad te leuaui*: a gradual; see Gneuss, below, p. 102. **60** *Aspiciens*: an antiphonary; see Gneuss, below, p. 116. Although the last two items in the list are linked by *et*, it is perhaps unlikely that the chants for mass and Office would have been bound in one book (certainly no such combination is found in a surviving Anglo-Saxon manuscript), and hence I have listed them separately; note, however, that the combination occurs – but rarely – in continental manuscripts.

### XII. *Various books in the possession of monks of Bury St Edmunds (s. xi^ex)*

Oxford, Bodleian Library, Auct. D. 2. 14 (S.C. 2698) is an uncial gospel-book written probably in Italy (s. vi/vii).[118] The book was in England by the end of the eighth century, when some marginalia were added by Anglo-Saxon scribes. On a flyleaf which was not part of the original volume two scribes have copied a list of some fifteen books (173r); their handwriting is excessively crude and is datable to the late eleventh century. Following the list are several names (copied by yet another scribe) including 'Bealdwine abb.'; if this is Baldwin, abbot of Bury St Edmunds (1065–98), then the booklist was probably copied at Bury. The scribe(s) apparently did a certain amount of tinkering with the list: three items have been erased, leaving only fifteen; but since one scribe wrote *.xv. bocas* at the end of the list, it was clearly he who made the erasures. It is possible that the list is a librarian's record of what books from the monastery's *armarium commune* were on loan to whom – note the wording 'þas bocas haueð Salomon preost' – and that the erasures indicate that books had been returned (and hence the record of the loan was deleted); but the large number of service-books in the list may cast some doubt on this hypothesis. The booklist has been printed and discussed by Robertson.[119]

Þas bocas haueð Salomon preost
þæt is þe codspel traht
7 þe martyrliua
7 þe[120]
7 þe æglisce saltere
7 þe cranc
[5] 7 ðe tropere
7 Wulfmer cild
þe atteleuaui
7 pistelari
7 þe[121]
7 ðe imnere
7 ðe captelari[122]
[10] 7 þe spel boc

118 *CLA* II, no. 230.

119 *Anglo-Saxon Charters*, pp. 250 and 501; see also Ker, *Catalogue*, p. 350 (no. 290).

120 Following *þe* is an erasure of some seven letters, now illegible.

121 Following *þe* is an erasure of four letters; I read the erased letters as *lece* (with ultraviolet light), not *litle*, as Ker suggested (*Catalogue*, p. 350).

122 Following *captelari* is an erasure of six letters, now illegible.

7 Sigar preost
    þe lece boc
    7 blake had boc
7 Æilmer
    ðe grete sater
    7 ðe litle tropere forbeande
[15] 7 ðe donatum
.xv. bocas

COMMENTARY **1** *codspel traht*: a homiliary; see Gneuss, below, p. 122. **2** *martyrliua*: a martyrology; see Gneuss, below, p. 128. **3** *æglisce saltere*: either a psalter in Old English or (more probably) a Latin psalter with continuous Old English interlinear gloss (no manuscript of a prose translation of the psalter has come down to us, whereas some thirteen psalters with continuous Old English gloss survive, of which none, I think, is certainly from Bury St Edmunds). **4** *cranc*: OE *cranc* or *cranic* is a loan-word from *chronicon*, and could refer to a historical work in general, or possibly to a particular text entitled *Chronicon* or *Chronica*, such as those by Sulpicius Severus (*Clavis*, no. 474), Prosper (*Clavis*, no. 2257; cf. below, no. XIII, line 49), Isidore (*Clavis*, no. 1205) or Bede (*Clavis*, no. 2273); but certainty is impossible. **5** *tropere*: a troper; see Gneuss, below, p. 105. **6** *atteleuaui*: a gradual; see Gneuss, below, p. 103. **7** *pistelari*: an epistolary; see Gneuss, below, p. 110. **8** *imnere*: a hymnal; see Gneuss, below, p. 118. **9** *captelari*: a collectar; see Gneuss, below, p. 113. **10** *spel boc*: a homiliary; see Gneuss, below, p. 123. **11** *lece boc*: a book containing medical recipes in Old English; the best known of such books is Bald's *Leechbook* (London, BL Royal 12. D. XVII), but a number of other 'leechbooks' survive from Anglo-Saxon England; see A. L. Meaney, 'Variant Versions of Old English Medical Recipes', *ASE* 13 (1984), 235–68. **12** *blake had boc*: Robertson suggests (*Anglo-Saxon Charters*, p. 501) that the reference is to a copy of the *Regula S. Benedicti*, for the reason that 'Benedictines were called "black monks" from the colour of their dress'. However, this solution is not entirely satisfactory: it is unlikely that 'Black Monks' would have been so designated before there was a need to distinguish them from other orders, in particular from the Cistercians, who wore a white habit and consequently were referred to as 'White Monks'. The first Cistercian houses established in England were Waverley (1128–9) and Rievaulx (*c.* 1131), and I can discover no reference in English sources to 'Nigri Monachi' earlier than the second half of the twelfth century (cf. *OED*, s.v. 'black'). The entry is in need of some other explanation, therefore, and several possibilities may be raised. First, it is just conceivable that *Blake* is a proper name (see W. G. Searle, *Onomasticon Anglo-Saxonicum* (Cambridge, 1897), p. 108; M. Redin, *Studies on Uncompounded Personal Names in Old English* (Uppsala, 1919), pp. 11 and 179; O. von Feilitzen, *The Pre-Conquest Personal Names of Domesday Book* (Uppsala, 1937), p. 203; G. Tengvik, *Old English Bynames* (Uppsala, 1938), pp. 292–3); in this case Blake, like Wulfmer, Sigar, etc., will have had a *had boc* in his possession (though one might accordingly expect a definite article before *had boc*). What the *had boc* was is not clear either: possibly a *handboc* (with a suspension-mark omitted) or (less likely) a *hadboc*, that is, a book on the various ecclesiastical grades, such as Isidore, *De ecclesiasticis officiis* (*Clavis*, no. 1207). Alternatively, *blake* could be acc. sg. fem. of *blæc*, and so refer to the colour of the binding. Finally, given that the other book in Sigar's possession was a *leceboc*, it is worth asking if *blakehad* is a *hapax legomenon* formed from *blæco* (n.), 'pallor', 'leprosy', + *-had*, hence meaning 'the condition of leprosy': in other words, the *blakehad boc* could have been a collection of remedies for leprosy, such as that found in Bald's *Leechbook* I.xxxii ('Læcedomas wiþ blæce') (*Leechdoms, Wortcunning and Starcraft of Early England*, ed. O. Cockayne, 3 vols., Rolls Ser. (London, 1864–6) II, 76–80); but this solution is an improbable one. (I am very grateful to Helmut Gneuss for advice on this problem, which remains insoluble at present.) **13** *grete sater*: a psalter in large format, presumably. **14** *litle tropere forbeande*: a troper in small format. What *forbeande* means is not clear; I suggest a misspelling of *forbearnde* (p.p. of *forbærnan*: one would normally expect *forbærnde*, but the spelling in this booklist is chaotic), and that the book in question was badly damaged by fire. **15** *donatum*: a copy of Donatus, either the *Ars maior* or *Ars minor*, or perhaps simply a miscellaneous grammar-book.

## *XIII. Booklist from Peterborough (?) (s. xi/xii)*

Oxford, Bodleian Library, Bodley 163 (S.C. 2016), is a composite manuscript made up of three separate parts. Of these the first (fols. 1–227) contains Bede's *Historia ecclesiastica gentis Anglorum* and Æthilwulf's so-called *De abbatibus*, in Anglo-Caroline minuscule (s. xi$^{in}$). The second part (fols. 228–49) is a copy of the Gildasian recension of the *Historia Brittonum*, datable to s. xii$^{in}$. The third part, which contains *inter alia* the booklist, is a single bifolium (fols. 250–1). The three parts have been together since the late Middle Ages, for the binding is medieval, probably of fourteenth-century date. A scribble in the third part (250v) records the obit of a monk of Peterborough in 1359.[123] The booklist itself is found on 251r and is datable on palaeographical grounds to *c.* 1100 (s. xi/xii). There may be reason to think that the booklist was written at Peterborough, not only because of the later Peterborough provenance of fols. 250–1, but because several items in the list appear to be identical both with books donated to Peterborough by Æthelwold (see above, no. IV) and with books listed in the abbey's fifteenth-century *Matricularium*.[124] On the other hand, it is worth recalling that Peterborough Abbey was utterly destroyed by fire in 1116 (ASC 1116 E). Few books are likely to have escaped such a conflagration, and this must make one cautious in accepting any book written before 1116 as the erstwhile property of the abbey's library. In any case several items in the list are said to be written in English, and the list can therefore be

123 See Ker, *Catalogue*, p. 358 (no. 304).

124 See M. R. James, *Lists of Manuscripts formerly in Peterborough Abbey*, pp. 30–81.

accepted as the record of a monastic library – arguably Peterborough's – of the late Anglo-Saxon period, in spite of its post-Conquest date. The list has been printed on several occasions.[125]

Augustinus De ciuitate Dei
Augustinus De uerbo Domini
Augustinus De bono coniugii et uirginitatis
Augustinus Super Iohannem
[5] Augustinus Retractionum
Augustinus De uidendo Deum et uera religione
Ecclesiastica historia Eusebii Cesaris
Historia anglorum
Tripartita historia
[10] Hieronimus Super Iosue
Hieronimus Contra Iouinianum
Hieronimus Super Isaiam
Hieronimus Super prophetas
Hieronimus Super Ezechielem (libri duo)
[15] Hieronimus Super Danihelem
Ambrosius De sacramentis et Vita sanctorum Nicolai, Botulfi, Guðlaci
Origenis De singularitate clericorum
Dialogus Basilii et Iohannis
Augustinus De penitentia
[20] Genadius ecclesiasticorum dogmatum
Collatio Nesterotis abbatis de spirituali scientia, Abraham de mortificatione, Cremonis de perfectione
Ambrosius De uirginitate
Hisidorus Super Genesim
Amalarius De diuinis officiis
[25] Fredulfus historiographus
Iosephus Antiquitatum
Isidorus In Hebreis numeris
Gregorius Pastoralis cure
Gregorii Moralia in Iob
[30] Epistole Pauli
Vite patrum

[125] It is listed in Gottlieb, no. 515; it has been ptd Becker, *Catalogi*, no. 96; R. Pauli, 'Aus Oxforder Handschriften', *Neues Archiv* 2 (1886), 432–4, at 433; James, *Lists of Manuscripts*, pp. 27–8.

Haimo Super epistolas Pauli
Haimo In euangeliis
Epistolares Hieronimi .iii. (unus maior, duo minores)
[35] Liber notarum
Questiones in Genesi et diffinitio philosophie et liber differentiarum
Item liber differentiarum
Vita sancti Felicis uersifice
Vita sancti Aðeluuodi
[40] Pronosticon futuri secli
Vita sancti Wilfridi
Vita sancti Giseleni
Diadema monachorum
Lectionarius
[45] Paradisus
Glosa in Genesim
Super Psalterium
Isidorus De summo bono
Cronica Prosperi
[50] Augustinus De diuersis rebus
Vita sancti Fursei et Baronti uisio
Gregorii Nazanzeni apologiticus
Historia Romanorum et Africanorum
Vite sanctorum anglice
[55] Expositio super .l. psalmos
Epistolaris Cipriani
Vita beati Gregorii pape
Exameron Ambrosii
Canones
[60] Passio Eustachii Placide uersifice
Historia Clementis et Vita beati Martini
Psalterium Hieronimi secundum Hebreos
Rabanus De institutione clericorum
Liber miraculorum
[65] Elfredi regis liber anglicus

COMMENTARY **1** *Augustinus De ciuitate Dei*: *Clavis*, no. 313. **2** *Augustinus de uerbo Domini*: Augustine wrote no work with this title (but cf. Becker, *Catalogi*, nos. 36, line 75, and 51, line 34); the work in question is probably the two-book treatise *De sermone Domini in monte* (*Clavis*, no. 274). **3** *Augustinus . . . uirginitatis*: two works are in question here, the *De bono coniugali* (*Clavis*, no. 299) and the *De sancta uirginitate* (*Clavis*, no. 300). **4** *Augustinus Super Iohannem*: the *Tractatus in euangelium Ioannis* (*Clavis*, no. 278). **5**

*Augustinus Retractionum*: the *Retractiones* (*Clavis*, no. 250). **6** *Augustinus . . . religione*: the first of these items is in fact one of Augustine's *epistolae* (*Ep.* cxlvii), although it often circulated separately (see Becker, *Catalogi*, no. 11, line 45); the other is his treatise *De uera religione* (*Clavis*, no. 264). **7** *Ecclesiastica . . . Cesaris*: the *Historia ecclesiastica* of Eusebius, in the Latin translation of Rufinus (see above, no. XI, line 48); for *Cesaris* understand *Cesariensis* (Eusebius was from Caesarea in Palestine). **8** *Historia anglorum*: presumably Bede, *Historia ecclesiastica gentis Anglorum* (*Clavis*, no. 1375); the book in question is possibly Bodley 163 itself, assuming that the part containing Bede (fols. 1–227) was at Peterborough when the booklist was written. **9** *Tripartita historia*: Cassiodorus, *Tripartita historia ecclesiastica* (PL 69, cols. 879–1214; see above, no. VIII, line 33). **10** *Hieronimus Super Iosue*: Jerome did not write a commentary on Joshua; conceivably the work in question is Rufinus's Latin translation of Origen's twenty-six homilies on Joshua, which frequently passed during the Middle Ages under the name of Jerome (see M. Schanz, *Geschichte der römischen Literatur* IV.1 (Munich, 1914), 419); other commentaries on Joshua were composed by Claudius of Turin (unptd) and Hrabanus Maurus (PL 108, cols. 999–1108). **11** *Hieronimus Contra Iouinianum*: Jerome, *Aduersus Iouinianum* (*Clavis*, no. 610). **12** *Hieronimus Super Isaiam*: Jerome, *Commentarii in Isaiam* (*Clavis*, no. 584). **13** *Hieronimus Super prophetas*: presumably Jerome's *Commentarii in prophetas minores* (*Clavis*, no. 589). **14** *Hieronimus Super Ezechielem*: Jerome, *Commentarii in Ezechielem* (*Clavis*, no. 587). **15** *Hieronimus Super Danihelem*: Jerome, *Commentarii in Danielem* (*Clavis*, no. 588). **16** *Ambrosius De sacramentis*: *Clavis*, no. 154. **16** *Vita . . . Guðlaci*: the *uitae* in question are probably Otloh of St Emmeram's *Vita S. Nicholai* (*BHL*, no. 6126), Folcard of Saint-Bertin's *Vita S. Botulfi* (*BHL*, no. 1428), and Felix's *Vita S. Guthlaci* (*BHL*, no. 3723); if so, the manuscript in question survives as London, BL Harley 3097 (note that in addition to the three *uitae* listed here the manuscript also contains Ambrose *De sacramentis*). **17** *Origenis . . . clericorum*: the work of this title (*Clavis*, no. 62) is not by Origen; it was frequently transmitted during the Middle Ages under the name of Cyprian (see P. Schepens, 'L'Épître *De singularitate clericorum* du ps.-Cyprien', *Recherches de science religieuse* 13 (1922), 178–210 and 297–327, and 14 (1923), 47–65; cf. also Becker, *Catalogi*, no. 115, line 161). **18–21**: according to the fifteenth-century Peterborough *Matricularium*, the items listed in lines 18–21 were all one book; see James, *Lists of Manuscripts*, p. 30. **18** *Dialogus Basilii et Iohannis*: the work in question is the Latin translation of John Chrysostom's *De sacerdotio*, a dialogue in six books between John and one Basil; the identity of the Latin translator is unknown, though some have suggested Anianus of Celeda, who translated other of John's works; the translation was available from at least the early ninth century, for it is quoted by Hilduin of Saint-Denis; the Latin translation has not apparently been printed, though it survives in some eight manuscripts (see A. Siegmund, *Die Überlieferung der griechischen christlichen Literatur* (Munich and Pasing, 1949), p. 97). **19** *Augustinus De penitentia*: presumably a copy of Augustine's two *sermones* (nos. cccli–ccclii) which together form a treatise *De utilitate agendae poenitentiae* which often circulated separately; but note also that two of Augustine's *epistolae* (nos. xci and cliii) are concerned with penitence and may be in question here. **20** *Genadius . . . dogmatum*: Gennadius, *Liber siue diffinitio ecclesiasticorum dogmatum* (*Clavis*, no. 958). **21** *Collatio . . . de perfectione*: the three works listed separately here are from Cassian's *Conlationes*

(*Clavis*, no. 512), nos. xiv (*de spirituali scientia*), xxiv (*de mortificatione*) and xi (*de perfectione*) respectively. **22** *Ambrosius De uirginitate*: *Clavis*, no. 147. **23** *Hisidorus Super Genesim*: although Isidore did not devote a separate commentary to Genesis, the work in question is probably his *Mysticorum expositiones sacramentorum seu quaestiones in uetus testamentum* (*Clavis*, no. 1195), an extensive work of exegesis which begins with a long section on Genesis (PL 83, cols. 207–88). **24** *Amalarius . . . officiis*: Amalarius of Metz, *De ecclesiasticis officiis*; see above, no. X, line 55. **25** *Fredulfus historiographus*: presumably Freculf of Lisieux, a ninth-century historian (see Manitius, *Geschichte* I, 663–8), whose *Historia* (PL 106, cols. 917–1258) enjoyed fairly wide circulation during the Middle Ages; several manuscripts of the Anglo-Saxon period survive (see Gneuss, 'Preliminary List', nos. 74, 724 and 725). **26** *Iosephus Antiquitatum*: Cassiodorus's Latin translation of Josephus, *Antiquitates*; see Manitius, *Geschichte* I, 51–2. **27** *Isidorus In Hebreis numeris*: Isidore wrote no work of this title; the work in question is probably the pseudo-Isidorian *Liber de numeris*, a Hiberno-Latin compilation of the eighth century (incomplete ed. in PL 83, cols. 1293–1302; see R. E. McNally, *Der irische Liber de Numeris* (Munich, 1957)); that the work was known in late Anglo-Saxon England is clear from the fact that the names of Noah's wife – Percova – and of his three sons' wives – Olla, Olliva and Ollivana – were interpolated into the Old English poem *Genesis* (lines 1547–8), apparently from this source (see McNally, *Der irische Liber de Numeris*, pp. 127–8). **28** *Gregorius Pastoralis cure*: Gregory, *Regula pastoralis* (*Clavis*, no. 1712). **29** *Gregorii . . . Iob*: Gregory, *Moralia siue expositio in Iob* (*Clavis*, no. 1708). **30** *Epistole Pauli*: the Pauline Epistles, presumably. **31** *Vite patrum*: the so-called *Vitas patrum*, an early title used to describe a massive but heterogeneous collection of lives and sayings principally of the early Egyptian Desert Fathers (*BHL*, nos. 6524–47; see above, no. VIII, line 9). **32** *Haimo . . . Pauli*: Haimo of Auxerre's Commentary on the Pauline Epistles (PL 117, cols. 359–820). **33** *Haimo In euangeliis*: Haimo of Auxerre is not known to have composed a commentary on the gospels (see *Deutschlands Geschichtsquellen im Mittelalter*, ed. H. Löwe, v, 564–5); it is not clear, therefore, what work might be in question. **34** *Epistolares Hieronimi*: three volumes of Jerome's *epistolae* (*Clavis*, no. 620). **35** *Liber notarum*: the scribe apparently misread *Liber rotarum* (which may suggest that the title before him was in some grade of Insular minuscule script), a title which was frequently applied to Isidore's *De natura rerum* (*Clavis*, no. 1188), because it contained a large number of diagrams. **36** *Questiones . . . differentiarum*: assuming that the third of these titles refers to Isidore's treatise *De differentiis uerborum* (*Clavis*, no. 1187), it is possible that the first was a copy of Isidore's *Quaestiones in uetus testamentum* (*Clavis*, no. 1195; cf. above, line 23); on the other hand, the *liber differentiarum* could conceivably be Boethius, *De differentiis topicis* (*Clavis*, no. 889), in which case the *diffinitio philosophie* might be the treatise *De definitionibus* (*Clavis*, no. 85), a work now known to be by Marius Victorinus but which passed under Boethius's name during the Middle Ages; it was intended as an introduction to Cicero's *Topica* and would have combined well with Boethius's *De differentiis topicis*. And if Isidore was not the author of the *liber differentiarum*, there is perhaps no reason to link his name with the *Questiones in Genesim*; recall that Jerome composed a treatise *Quaestiones Hebraicae in Genesim* (*Clavis*, no. 580) and that Alcuin compiled a set of *Questiones in*

*Genesim* (PL 100, cols. 515–66). **37** *Item*: another copy of the (unidentifiable) work mentioned in line 36. **38** *Vita . . . uersifice*: presumably Paulinus of Nola's *Carmina* (*Clavis*, no. 203) on Felix, the patron saint of Nola. **39** *Vita sancti Aðeluuodi*: a *uita* of St Æthelwold of Winchester (*ob.* 984), either that by Wulfstan of Winchester (*BHL*, no. 2647), or the later abbreviation of it by Ælfric (*BHL*, no. 2646); both *uitae* are ed. M. Winterbottom, *Three Lives of English Saints* (Toronto, 1972), pp. 33–63 and 17–29 respectively. **40** *Pronosticon*: Julian of Toledo, *Prognosticum futuri saeculi* (*Clavis*, no. 1258). **41** *Vita sancti Wilfridi*: presumably the *uita* of Wilfrid attributed to 'Eddius' Stephanus (*BHL*, no. 8889; see above, no. XI, line 50). **42** *Vita sancti Giseleni*: one of the several *uitae* of this Flemish saint (*BHL*, nos. 3552–61); it is interesting to note the *uita* of a Flemish saint at Peterborough at this time. **43** *Diadema monachorum*: Smaragdus of Saint-Mihiel, *Diadema monachorum*; see above, nos. VIII, line 7, and X, line 53. **44** *Lectionarius*: a lectionary, but whether intended for mass or Office is not clear without further specification (see Gneuss, below, p. 105). **45** *Paradisus*: presumably the text referred to as *Paradisus Heraclidis* (*BHL*, no. 6532; PL 74, cols. 243–342), which is a Latin translation of part of the *Historia Lausiaca* of Palladius, which in turn circulated as part of the massive collection of *Vitas patrum* (see above, line 31); at least two manuscripts of the *Paradisus Heraclidis* survive from late Anglo-Saxon England (see Gneuss, 'Preliminary List', nos. 10 and 267). **46** *Glosa in Genesim*: unidentifiable as such. **47** *Super Psalterium*: unidentifiable as such; see above, no. XI, line 46. **48** *Isidorus De summo bono*: Isidore, *Sententiae* (*Clavis*, no. 1199); the title *De summo bono* derives from the first sentence of the treatise ('Summum bonum Deus est . . .'). **49** *Cronica Prosperi*: Prosper of Aquitaine, *Epitoma chronicorum* (*Clavis*, no. 2257). **50** *Augustinus De diuersis rebus*: possibly a copy of Augustine's *De diuersis quaestionibus .lxxxiii.* (*Clavis*, no. 289), or perhaps simply a miscellaneous collection of his writings. **51** *Vita sancti Fursei*: presumably the Merovingian *uita* of Fursa (*BHL*, no. 3209). **51** *Baronti uisio*: *Clavis*, no. 1313; see above, no. IX, line 8. **52** *Gregorii . . . apologiticus*: Gregory of Nazianzus, *Oratio* II (*Liber apologeticus de fuga*) in the Latin translation of Rufinus (*Tyranii Rufini Orationum Gregorii Nazianzeni nouem Interpretatio*, ed. A. Engelbrecht, CSEL 46 (Vienna, 1910), 7–84; see also M. M. Wagner, *Rufinus the Translator: a Study of his Theory and Practice as Illustrated in his Version of the Apologetica of St Gregory Nazianzen* (Washington, DC, 1945), and A. C. Way, in *Catalogus Translationum et Commentariorum* II, 127–34); the work is preserved in at least one manuscript of the Anglo-Saxon period (Oxford, Trinity College 4 (St Augustine's, Canterbury, s. xi), 112r–142v). **53** *Historia Romanorum et Africanorum*: probably Victor of Vita, *Historia persecutionis Africanae prouinciae* (*Clavis*, no. 798); on the probable identity, see Manitius, *Handschriften*, p. 261. **54** *Vite sanctorum anglice*: a collection of saints' lives in English, possibly that of Ælfric. **55** *Expositio super .l. psalmos*: either an incomplete copy of a full commentary on the psalms (see above, no. XI, line 46), or possibly the commentary attributed to Prosper of Aquitaine (*Clavis*, no. 524) on Psalms C–CL. **56** *Epistolaris Cipriani*: Cyprian, *Epistolae* (*Clavis*, no. 50); see above, no. IV, line 19. **57** *Vita beati Gregorii pape*: probably not the Anglo-Latin *Vita S. Gregorii* composed at Whitby in the late seventh century (*BHL*, no. 3637), but more likely the later continental *uita* by John the Deacon (*BHL*, no. 3641), which survives in at least one manuscript of the Anglo-Saxon period

(Oxford, Bodleian Library, Bodley 381 (s. x; provenance St Augustine's, Canterbury)). **58** *Examerom Ambrosii*: Ambrose, *Exameron* (*Clavis*, no. 123). **59** *Canones*: an unidentifiable collection of ecclesiastical legislation. **60** *Passio Eustachii Placide uersifice*: a number of metrical versions of the *Vita S. Eustachii* existed in the Middle Ages, but three are perhaps early enough to be in question here: a rhythmical poem preserved in a late-ninth-century manuscript from Verona (*ICL*, no. 12031), a poem in elegiacs preserved only in a late-fourteenth-century manuscript (*ICL*, no. 2175), and a poem in hexameters preserved in an eleventh-century German manuscript (*ICL*, no. 14237). Several factors help us to identify the poem in question: a *Vita Eustachii* was given by Æthelwold to Peterborough (see above, no. IV, line 9); the same book was still at Peterborough *c.* 1100, to judge from the present entry; and the book apparently remained at Peterborough until the Dissolution, for it was seen by John Leland and described by him as *Vita S. Eustachii carmine heroico* (*Collectanea*, ed. T. Hearne, 2nd ed., 6 vols. (London, 1770) IV, 31). Leland's observation that the poem was in hexameters (*carmine heroico*) rules out the poems in rhythmical verse and elegiacs, and indicates that the hexameter poem must be in question here (it is ed. H. Varnhagen, 'Zwei lateinische metrische Versionen der Legende von Placidus–Eustachius II. Eine Version in Hexametern', *ZDA* 25 (1881), 1–25); on the evidence of the Æthelwold donation, the poem must have been in existence by the late tenth century, and its style marks it as a Carolingian product. **61** *Historia Clementis*: the pseudo-Clementine *Recognitiones* in the Latin translation of Rufinus; see B. Rehm, *Die Pseudoklementinen II. Rekognitionen in Rufins Übersetzung*, ed. F. Paschke (Berlin, 1965). **61** *Vita beati Martini*: Sulpicius Severus, *Vita Martini Turonensis* (*Clavis*, no. 475; *BHL*, no. 5610). **62** *Psalterium . . . Hebreos*: Jerome's Latin translation of the psalter *iuxta Hebraeos*. **63** *Rabanus . . . clericorum*: Hrabanus Maurus of Fulda, *De institutione clericorum* (PL 107, cols. 293–420; cf. Manitius, *Geschichte* I, 296–8). **64** *Liber miraculorum*: one of the books earlier given by Æthelwold to Peterborough, possibly the work of this title by Gregory of Tours; see above, no. IV, line 3. **65** *Elfredi . . . anglicus*: a copy of one of the Old English translations by King Alfred – Gregory's *Regula pastoralis*, Boethius's *De consolatione Philosophiae*, Augustine's *Soliloquia*, or possibly the first fifty psalms of the psalter; see Keynes and Lapidge, *Alfred the Great*, pp. 28–34.[126]

APPENDIX

## Books and authors known in Anglo-Saxon England from surviving booklists

Abbo of Fleury
  *Passio S. Eadmundi*: VII.7
Abbo of Saint-Germain-des-Prés
  *Bella Parisiacae urbis*: IV.10

126 I am extremely grateful to David Dumville and Helmut Gneuss for commenting on an earlier draft of this article and saving me from a number of errors, and to Vivien Law for advice on the various grammatical entries in the booklists.

# Liturgical books in Anglo-Saxon England and their Old English terminology

HELMUT GNEUSS

This paper is an attempt to bring together and explain the Old English terms for the various types of liturgical books, and to provide a brief introduction to the contents and preservation of Anglo-Saxon copies of these books, including a preliminary inventory of extant manuscripts.

Bernhard Fehr, Max Förster and Milton McC. Gatch have made valuable contributions to our knowledge of liturgical terminology in Old English,[1] but there is as yet no systematic treatment of the words to be discussed in the present article, and many of the dictionary definitions of these words are unsatisfactory. It is hoped that in what follows most of the pertinent lexicographical problems can be solved; it is also hoped that the documentation of surviving liturgical manuscripts may be of some use to the liturgiologist and to the literary historian at a time when the significance of the liturgy for our understanding of Old English prose and poetry is becoming more widely appreciated and acknowledged. Peter Clemoes, to whom this volume is dedicated, has been foremost among those who have paved the way for this new direction in scholarship.

The main part of this paper consists of an inventory of the various types of liturgical books employed in Anglo-Saxon England. For each type (numbered in a series **A**–**Y**) I give a brief explanation of its use and contents, and some discussion of the Latin term(s) for the book and of its possible combination with other books. Each entry is then normally subdivided into three sections: Old English Terminology, Surviving Manuscripts, and Bibliography.

*Old English Terminology*. Under this heading I discuss the Old English word or words for the book, in most cases with full references to the texts in which they occur; notes on difficult or doubtful points have been added wherever necessary.[2]

[1] See references to their works in the list of abbreviated titles, below, pp. 95–7.

[2] A. diPaolo Healey and R. L. Venezky, *A Microfiche Concordance to Old English* (Toronto, 1980), has been invaluable for verifying and supplementing my references.

*Surviving Manuscripts.* Here I provide a list of extant manuscripts and manuscript fragments written or owned in England up to the end of the eleventh century and containing the particular book. Where more than one liturgical book is found in a manuscript volume, cross-references have always been given to the first entry in this inventory. For complete or fairly complete books, present location and press-mark, origin, date and provenance as well as references to printed editions and facsimiles, have been supplied. Dates are always those of the main part of the manuscript; only in a few cases where substantial additions to a manuscript were made, have dates for such additions been given. As for provenance, only places where a manuscript is known to have been kept before *c.* 1100 – or where this is fairly certain – have been listed. No folio numbers for individual items within a manuscript have been given; these can usually be ascertained from editions, and from the catalogues of manuscript collections.

For fragments, no details are provided; instead, the reader is referred to my previously printed 'List' (see below, under Abbreviations). 'Supplementary items' became known to me after the 'List' was published (1981) and will be included in a forthcoming supplement.

Only complete liturgical books, or parts or fragments of such books, have been listed. A number of masses, Offices, saints' lives and other elements of the liturgy, and groups or parts of such texts, can be found scattered through various liturgical and non-liturgical manuscripts;[3] these have not been included; a complete index to them is needed, as their evidence is a valuable addition to what we know from the regular service-books.

In order to be able to record the later and latest products of the Anglo-Saxon liturgical tradition, the cut-off date has been fixed at 1100; this may have led to the inclusion of books influenced by Norman usage, but it seems impossible to draw a rigid line between the two traditions, and important evidence might be lost if manuscripts written after 1066 or 1070 were to be excluded.

*Bibliography.* Under this heading I supply references to publications dealing specifically with the respective type of liturgical book in Anglo-Saxon England, including editions of texts in more than one manuscript; however, editions (even if considered standard) that do not collate English manuscripts and critical editions of books of the Latin bible have not been recorded. The introductions to the printed editions listed with the surviving manuscripts should also be consulted. It is to be regretted that for most types of Anglo-

[3] For an example see section **N**, below.

Saxon books no comprehensive treatment is available as yet; in the absence of such work, I have had to include studies of particular manuscripts or special aspects.[4]

There is hardly any need to point to the limitations of this article. Definitions have had to be brief, and some simplification was unavoidable. Categories of liturgical books in the early Middle Ages were not yet fully fixed and standardized; there are, for example, intermediate stages in the development from the sacramentary to the missal, or from the collectar to the breviary. Also, categories overlap: certain liturgical texts might appear in a sacramentary, or a pontifical or a manual. Books within the same category may differ greatly from each other; this is particularly so with private prayer-books, but also with books of the 'official' liturgy. It was impossible to describe adequately such complex books as, for example, the Leofric Missal, the Red Book of Darley or the Portiforium of St Wulfstan within the framework of categories I have adopted, although I hope that the essential character of such manuscripts will be clear from my presentation.

There was neither space nor time to go beyond the brief explanation of the use and contents of the Anglo-Saxon liturgical books.[5] Neither have I been able to deal with the history and relationships of the texts and manuscripts, or

[4] More general bibliographical information is now conveniently accessible through R. W. Pfaff, *Medieval Latin Liturgy: a Select Bibliography*, Toronto Med. Bibliographies 9 (Toronto, 1982). For the contents and terminology of liturgical books in medieval England, two older works are still useful: W. Maskell, 'A Dissertation upon the Ancient Service Books of the Church of England', in his *Monumenta Ritualia Ecclesiae Anglicanae*, 2nd ed. (Oxford, 1882) I, iii–ccxxiii, and C. Wordsworth and H. Littlehales, *The Old Service-Books of the English Church* (London, 1904). For more recent treatments, see [S. J. P. van Dijk], *Latin Liturgical Manuscripts and Printed Books: Guide to an Exhibition Held during 1952* (Bodleian Library, Oxford, 1952); V. Fiala and W. Irtenkauf, 'Versuch einer liturgischen Nomenklatur', in *Zur Katalogisierung mittelalterlicher und neuerer Handschriften*, Zeitschrift für Bibliothekswesen und Bibliographie, Sonderheft 1 (1963), 105–37; and A. Hughes, *Medieval Manuscripts for Mass and Office: a Guide to their Organization and Terminology* (Toronto, 1982). See also the pertinent entries in F. Cabrol and H. Leclercq, *Dictionnaire d'archéologie chrétienne et de liturgie*, 15 vols. (Paris, 1907–53), and the catalogues of liturgical manuscripts, especially those by V. Leroquais and P. Salmon, listed by Pfaff.

[5] For a historical introduction to the liturgy of mass and Office and to the pontifical and manual services, see *L'Église en prière: Introduction à la liturgie*, ed. A.-G. Martimort, 3rd ed. (Paris, 1965). Only part of this work has been translated into English: *The Church at Prayer: Introduction to the Liturgy*, trans. R. Fisher *et al.* (New York, 1968–73). There is a complete translation of the first (1961) edition into German: *Handbuch der Liturgiewissenschaft* (Freiburg im Breisgau, 1963–5). An eminently practical introduction to the structure of Roman mass and Office has been provided by K. Young, *The Drama of the Medieval Church*, 2 vols. (Oxford, 1933) I, 15–75. For a thorough study of the Latin liturgy, Hughes, *Medieval Manuscripts*, is invaluable.

to supply any information about their musical notation.[6] Some elements of the liturgy, like litanies[7] and the *laudes regiae*[8] have not been discussed, penitentials – not being liturgical books in the strict sense – have been excluded,[9] and no notice has been taken of the use of lectionaries for pious reading in the refectory. No attempt has been made to deal with the history of the liturgy in Anglo-Saxon England in general; much important work has been done in this field, by scholars like W. Maskell, H. M. Bannister, E. Bishop, E. Dewick, W. H. Frere, J. W. Legg, F. Warren, H. A. Wilson and, more recently, by Francis Wormald, Lilli Gjerløw, Christopher Hohler and D. H. Turner, to mention only a few;[10] but much remains to be done.

As will be seen, most of our knowledge of Anglo-Saxon liturgical books comes from the late period, the tenth and eleventh centuries. There is little evidence for the time before the tenth century: a number of gospel-books remain, a few psalter manuscripts and some fragments from sacramentaries, almost all of these having been written in the eighth century.[11] But even for the late period our information is not as full as we could wish; of some categories of books not a single copy survives (antiphoner, epistolary); copies of other books are rare or mainly very late (gradual, homiliary, legendary), while some types of book are well represented (sacramentary, gospel-book, psalter, pontifical, benedictional). We must also remember that most of the surviving books come from a few cathedral libraries and the monasteries at Bury St Edmunds, Canterbury and Winchester. Other monastic and collegiate communities or parish churches are hardly represented, as a result of the vicissitudes in the history of books and libraries, particularly in the sixteenth century. However, there is abundant evidence for the strong influence exercised by the continental reforms of the ninth and tenth centuries on the liturgy of Anglo-Saxon England since the Benedictine Revival, if not earlier. Thus, in the mass

6 Studies and catalogues of Anglo-Saxon manuscripts with musical notation are (independently) in preparation by Dr K. D. Hartzell, Dr Christopher Page and Dr Susan Rankin.

7 A catalogue and edition of Anglo-Saxon litanies is in preparation by Dr Michael Lapidge.

8 For these, see now H. E. J. Cowdrey, 'The Anglo-Norman Laudes Regiae', *Viator* 12 (1981), 37–78.

9 For penitentials, see now A. J. Frantzen, *The Literature of Penance in Anglo-Saxon England* (New Brunswick, NJ, 1983), and 'The Tradition of Penitentials in Anglo-Saxon England', *ASE* 11 (1983), 23–56.

10 The more important publications of these authors have been recorded in Pfaff, *Medieval Latin Liturgy*.

11 For the liturgy in early Anglo-Saxon England, see G. G. Willis, 'Early English Liturgy from Augustine to Alcuin', *Further Essays in Early Roman Liturgy*, Alcuin Club Collections 50 (London, 1968), 189–242, and H. Mayr-Harting, *The Coming of Christianity to Anglo-Saxon England* (London, 1972), pp. 168–90 and Appendix II. For the early sacramentaries, see below, p. 102; for the eighth-century York antiphoner, see below, pp. 117–18; for the early hymnal, see H. Gneuss, *Hymnar und Hymnen im englischen Mittelalter* (Tübingen, 1968), pp. 13–40.

the new genres of tropes and sequences were introduced from the continent;[12] in the Office, the *Psalterium Gallicanum* and the New Hymnal were adopted, as well as Paul the Deacon's Homiliary, a new legendary of French origin and Usuard's Martyrology; supplementary offices and devotions like the Horae BMV found their way to England, and the *textus receptus* of the Benedictine Rule became the standard version.

In dealing with the Old English terminology for the books, I have concentrated on questions of meaning and interpretation. There is much of interest concerning the word-formation and borrowing process of the various loan-words and loan formations, but I must hope to go into these points on another occasion. Similarly, a study of the Old English terms ought to have been preceded by a comprehensive treatment of the Latin terminology and its historical development; but no such treatment is yet available, and I have not been able to make up for the deficiency, except in referring, wherever it was appropriate, to those Latin words for liturgical books that to my knowledge were known and used in Anglo-Latin texts up to the end of the eleventh century.

It will be seen that I have not been able to solve all the problems involved in the interpretation of the Old English words. Some are clear and unambiguous, like *biblioðeca*, *Cristes boc*, *saltere*, *tropere* and *ymnere*; others are ambiguous, but their double meanings can be specified, like those of *antefnere*, *mæsseboc* and *martirlogium*. For a number of words the meanings suggested below seem fairly certain, as for *bletsingboc*, *capitelarie* and perhaps *nihtsang*, whereas in a few other cases it seems difficult to give a reliable definition, as with *rædingboc* and *sangboc*, as well as *halsungboc* and *onsongboc*. Nevertheless, I hope to have provided a safer foundation than has previously been available for the recording of these words in the new *Dictionary of Old English*.

In subsequent discussion I use the following abbreviations and short titles (note that all references to texts are to page and line, unless otherwise stated).

ÆPast — *Die Hirtenbriefe Ælfrics in altenglischer und lateinischer Fassung*, ed. B. Fehr, Bibliothek der angelsächsischen Prosa 9 (Hamburg, 1914), repr. with suppl. by P. Clemoes (Darmstadt, 1966). See esp. the lists of books that priests are expected to own – based on Egbert's list (see below)? – in the

[12] For links between the liturgy of Corbie and the missal and Office antiphoner of Winchester (Old and New Minsters) and other reformed English monasteries, see C. A. Gordon, 'Manuscript Missals: the English Uses', Cambridge University Sandars Lectures 1936 (unpubl., but accessible in BL Add. 44920 + 44921) 1, 20–6; D. H. Turner, *The Missal of the New Minster Winchester*, HBS 93 (London, 1962), xiii–xxvii; and R.-J. Hesbert, 'Les Antiphonaires monastiques insulaires', *RB* 92 (1982), 358–75.

| | |
|---|---|
| | letter to Bishop Wulfsige (p. 13, section 52); in the first Latin letter to Archbishop Wulfstan (p. 51, section 137); in the first Old English letter to Archbishop Wulfstan (pp. 126–7, section 157); and cf. Fehr's introduction, pp. lxxxvi–xcii. All references are to page and section in this edition. The Pastoral Letters are also ed. D. Whitelock, M. Brett and C. N. L. Brooke, *Councils and Synods with other Documents relating to the English Church I: A.D. 871–1204*, 2 vols. (Oxford, 1981); see I, 206–7 (letter to Wulfsige) and 291–2 (first Old English letter to Wulfstan), for the passages in question. |
| Ælfric, *Catholic Homilies* | *The Sermones Catholici or Homilies of Ælfric*, ed. B. Thorpe, 2 vols. (London, 1844–6). |
| Ælfric, *Glossary* | see Ælfric, *Grammar*. |
| Ælfric, *Grammar* | *Ælfrics Grammatik und Glossar*, ed. J. Zupitza (Berlin, 1880), repr. with preface by H. Gneuss (Darmstadt, 1966). |
| Ælfric, *Lives of Saints* | *Ælfric's Lives of Saints*, ed. W. W. Skeat, 4 vols., EETS o.s. 76, 82, 94 and 114 (London, 1881–1900). |
| Ælfwold | List of books mentioned in the will of Ælfwold, bishop of Crediton 1008 × 1012, ptd Lapidge, 'Booklists', no. V, above pp. 55–6. |
| BuryA | List of books belonging to Bury St Edmunds in the time of Abbot Leofstan 1044 × 1065, ptd Lapidge, 'Booklists', no. VII, above pp. 57–8. |
| BuryB | List of books in the possession of monks of Bury St Edmunds, late eleventh century, ptd Lapidge, 'Booklists', no. XII, above pp. 74–6. |
| Carilef | List of books given by Bishop William of Saint-Carilef (1081–96) to Durham Cathedral, ed. C. H. Turner, 'The Earliest List of Durham MSS', *JTS* 19 (1917–18), 121–32; facsimile in *The New Palaeographical Society: Facsimiles of Ancient Manuscripts*, 2nd ser., ed. E. M. Thompson *et al.* (London, 1913–30) II, pl. 17. The list is in Durham Cathedral Library, A. II. 4, 1r; there is no copy of it in Bishop William's Mortuary (Durham Cathedral, Misc. Charter 2622), as has repeatedly been stated, and as might appear from J. Raine, *Wills and Inventories*, Part 1, Surtees Soc. 2 (Durham, 1835), 1. |
| Egbert | List of books that a priest ought to have, in the prologue to the Penitential ascribed to Egbert, archbishop of York (732–66), ptd A. W. Haddan |

and W. Stubbs, *Councils and Ecclesiastical Documents Relating to Great Britain and Ireland*, 3 vols. (Oxford, 1869–78) III, 417. It has been suggested that this list is a later addition, but it appears at any rate in Anglo-Saxon copies of the Penitential from the tenth century onwards; cf. A. J. Frantzen, *The Literature of Penance in Anglo-Saxon England* (New Brunswick, NJ, 1983), p. 74.

Fehr, *Hirtenbriefe* — see ÆPast.

Förster, 'Donations' — M. Förster, 'The Donations of Leofric to Exeter', R. W. Chambers *et al.*, *Chapters on the Exeter Book* (London, 1933), pp. 10–32.

Funke, *Lehn- und Fremdwörter* — O. Funke, *Die gelehrten lateinischen Lehn- und Fremdwörter in der altenglischen Literatur* (Halle, 1914).

Gamber, *CLLA* — K. Gamber, *Codices Liturgici Latini Antiquiores*, 2nd ed. (Freiburg, 1968).

Gatch, *Preaching* — M. McC. Gatch, *Preaching and Theology in Anglo-Saxon England: Ælfric and Wulfstan* (Toronto, 1977) [discusses booklists in Egbert, ÆPast and Leofric, pp. 42–4].

Gneuss, *Hymnar* — H. Gneuss, *Hymnar und Hymnen im englischen Mittelalter*, Buchreihe der Anglia 12 (Tübingen, 1968).

Hughes, *Medieval Manuscripts* — A. Hughes, *Medieval Manuscripts for Mass and Office: a Guide to their Organization and Terminology* (Toronto, 1982).

Indicia — An Old English text on the use of sign language in a monastery, in an eleventh-century manuscript probably from Christ Church, Canterbury (BL Cotton Tiberius A. iii), ed. F. Kluge, 'Zur Geschichte der Zeichensprache. Angelsächsische Indicia Monasterialia', [Techmers] *Internationale Zeitschrift für allgemeine Sprachwissenschaft* 2 (1885), 116–37. References are to the sections in this edition.

Ker, *Catalogue* — N. R. Ker, *Catalogue of Manuscripts containing Anglo-Saxon* (Oxford, 1957).

Kotzor, *Martyrologium* — *Das altenglische Martyrologium*, ed. G. Kotzor, 2 vols., Bayerische Akademie der Wissenschaften, Phil.-hist. Klasse, Abhandlungen n.s. 88 (Munich, 1981).

Lapidge, 'Booklists' — M. Lapidge, 'Surviving Booklists from Anglo-Saxon England', above, pp. 33–89. All references are to line numbers of the booklists there ed.

| | |
|---|---|
| Leofric | List of books given to Exeter Cathedral by Bishop Leofric, and of books available there at his accession, in the inventory of donations by Leofric (1069 × 1072), ptd Lapidge, 'Booklists', no. X, above, pp. 64–9. |
| 'List' | H. Gneuss, 'A Preliminary List of Manuscripts Written or Owned in England up to 1100', *ASE* 9 (1981), 1–60. |
| Mart. | The Old English Martyrology: see Kotzor, *Martyrologium*, above. |
| Padelford, *Musical Terms* | F. M. Padelford, *Old English Musical Terms*, Bonner Beiträge zur Anglistik 4 (Bonn, 1899). |
| Peterborough | List of books given to Peterborough Abbey by Æthelwold, ptd Lapidge, 'Booklists', no. IV, above, pp. 52–5. |
| RegC | W. S. Logeman, 'De Consuetudine Monachorum', *Anglia* 13 (1891), 365–454 [edition of the continuous Old English interlinear gloss to the *Regularis concordia*]. |
| RegC (Symons) | *Regularis Concordia*, ed. T. Symons (London, 1953). |
| RegC (Zupitza) | J. Zupitza, 'Ein weiteres Bruchstück der Regularis Concordia in altenglischer Sprache', *ASNSL* 84 (1890), 1–24. |
| Sherburn | Books listed in an inventory of church goods at Sherburn-in Elmet, s. xi$^{med}$, ptd Lapidge, 'Booklists', no. VI, above pp. 56–7. |
| Wærferth, *Dialogues* | *Bischof Wærferths von Worcester Übersetzung der Dialoge Gregors des Grossen*, ed. H. Hecht, Bibliothek der angelsächsischen Prosa 5 (Hamburg, 1900–7). |
| *Wills* | *Anglo-Saxon Wills*, ed. D. Whitelock (Cambridge, 1930). |
| Worc.A | List of books belonging to Worcester Cathedral Priory, *c.* 1050, ptd Lapidge, 'Booklists', no. IX, above, pp. 62–4. |
| Worc.B | List of books from an unidentified centre, possibly Worcester, *c.* 1100, ptd Lapidge, 'Booklists' no. XI, above, pp. 69–73. |
| Wulfstan(?), *Eccl. Gr.* | *De ecclesiasticis gradibus*, in *Die 'Institutes of Polity, Civil and Ecclesiastical'. Ein Werk Erzbischof Wulfstans von York*, ed. Karl Jost, Schweizer anglistische Arbeiten 47 (Bern, 1959), 223–41. |

The contents are set out as follows:

BOOKS FOR THE MASS

**A** Missal and Sacramentary
**B** Gradual
**C** Troper
– Mass Lectionaries –
**D** Gospel-Book and Gospel Lectionary
**E** Epistolary

BOOKS FOR THE OFFICE

**F** Breviary
**G** Collectar
**H** Psalter
**J** Antiphoner
**K** Hymnal
– Office Lectionaries –
**L** Bible
**M** Homiliary
**N** Legendary
**O** Books with special offices

BOOKS FOR THE CHAPTER OFFICE

**P** Martyrology
**Q** *Regula S. Benedicti* and Chrodegang's *Regula canonicorum*

EPISCOPAL BOOKS AND RITUALS

**R** Pontifical
**S** Benedictional
**T** Manual

OTHER BOOKS

**U** Consuetudinary
**W** Prayer-Books and Private Prayers
**X** Liturgical Calendar
**Y** Confraternity Book

## BOOKS FOR THE MASS

### **A.** Missal and Sacramentary

Liturgical scholarship distinguishes between the 'missal' (which comprises the complete texts of the mass, that is, the prayers, chants and readings, in the order in which they occur in the services) and the 'sacramentary' (which contains only the prayers to be said by the celebrant, including the Canon of the Mass and, for all days with proper texts, the *Collecta*, *Secreta*, *Praefatio* and *Postcommunio*). Unfortunately, Latin *missale/missalis*, as well as the corresponding OE *mæsseboc* and ModE *missal*, are also used to denote a sacramentary, as can be seen (for example) in the Old English Martyrology (see below) and even earlier in a letter from Alcuin to Archbishop Eanbald of York,[13] where *missalis libellus* is synonymous with *libellus sacramentarius* and *sacramentarium*. Also, it seems probable that Latin *missalis* in several lists of liturgical books (Egbert; ÆPast, 51.137; Worc.B and perhaps Carilef) refers to a sacramentary. In what follows I always use the term 'missal' for the more comprehensive type of book, which appears in Anglo-Saxon England from the second half of the tenth century onwards. Clear-cut distinctions, however, cannot always be made; thus, an intermediate stage is represented by the original part of the so-called Leofric Missal (**A.7**), which is basically a sacramentary, to which the original scribe added the incipits of the mass-chants (introit, gradual or tract, offertory, communion) in the margins, while a later hand supplied the incipits of epistles and gospels and of a few sequences. Another example for a stage in the development towards the plenary missal is the now fragmentary Winchester(?) book (**A.6**), in which a sacramentary is followed by an epistle–gospel lectionary.[14] Sacramentaries might also include texts and services that in the late Anglo-Saxon period would be collected into special service-books, such as the pontifical, the benedictional and the manual; for these, see below, sections **R**, **S** and **T**.

## *Old English terminology*

*sacramentorum*: Mart. 112.5–6 and 183.14–15 (but *sacramentorium* in Mart. 112.5–6, MS B).
*mæsseboc*: Mart. 112.6 and eight further occurrences (see Kotzor, *Martyrologium* I, 258*f.); ÆPast 13.52, 126/127.157 (MS Oz: *messeboc*) and 162/163.42 (MSS N and Oz: *messeboc*); Ælfwold 4; BuryA 2, 9, 12, 14 and 17; Indicia 9; Leofric 2; Sherburn 5; Will of Bishop Theodred (*Wills* 2.14 and 4.27).

The form *sacramentorium* may be an attempt to substitute an independent noun for the elliptical (*liber*) *sacramentorum*. Both forms may not have been in general use as loan-words, as an explanation is added in each of the two instances in Mart.; cf. 'on ðæm ealdan sacramentorium, ðæt is on ðæm ealdan *mæssebocum*' (Mart. 112.5–6).

13 MGH, Epist. 4, ed. E. Dümmler *et al.* (Berlin, 1925), 370 (no. 226).
14 For early continental copies of the same type of book, see Gamber, *CLLA*, pp. 467–9 and 487–91.

It seems fairly certain that *mæsseboc* in most of the instances cited must have referred to a sacramentary. This is clearly the case in Mart., while in ÆPast, Ælfwold, BuryA, Indicia, Leofric and Sherburn the *mæsseboc* (one or more copies) is listed side by side with graduals, tropers, epistolaries and gospelbooks. According to Förster,[15] the volumes called '.ii. fulle mæssebec' (Leofric 2) represent the *missale plenum* (that is, one incorporating chants and lessons), and **A.7** was one of them; but there is a possibility, at least, that OE *full* here refers to books covering the whole church year, as opposed to selections of masses.

## *Surviving manuscripts: missal*

**A.1** Le Havre, Bibliothèque Municipale, 330 (Winchester, New Minster, s. xi²); ed. D. H. Turner, *The Missal of the New Minster Winchester*, HBS 93 (London, 1962).

## *Surviving manuscripts: sacramentaries*[16]

**A.2** Cambridge, Corpus Christi College 41 (s. xi¹; provenance Exeter); ed. R. J. S. Grant, *Cambridge, Corpus Christi College 41: the Loricas and the Missal* (Amsterdam, 1979).

**A.3** Cambridge, Corpus Christi College 270 (St Augustine's, Canterbury, s. xi²); ed. M. Rule, *The Missal of St Augustine's Abbey, Canterbury* (Cambridge, 1896).

**A.4** Cambridge, Corpus Christi College 422 (Winchester and Sherborne, s. xi^med^); see C. Hohler, 'The Red Book of Darley', in *Nordiskt Kollokvium II i latinsk liturgiforskning* (Institutionen för klassiska språk vid Stockholms Universitet, 1972), pp. 39–47.

**A.5** London, BL Cotton Vitellius A. xviii (Wells, s. xi²).

**A.6** London, Society of Antiquaries 154* (? Winchester, s. x^ex^); see F. Wormald, 'Fragments of a Tenth-Century Sacramentary from the Binding of the Winton Domesday', *Winchester in the Early Middle Ages: an Edition and Discussion of the Winton Domesday*, ed. M. Biddle (Oxford, 1976), pp. 541–9.

**A.7** Oxford, Bodleian Library, Bodley 579 (NE France, s. ix², with additions made at Glastonbury, s. x², and Exeter, s. xi^med^); ed. F. E. Warren, *The Leofric Missal* (Oxford, 1883).

**A.8** Worcester, Cathedral Library, F. 173 (Old Minster, Winchester, and

[15] 'Donations', p. 25, n. 77.

[16] **A.4** and **A.8** contain only selections of masses, and **A.4** includes elements of a plenary missal (chants and readings) for several masses. For **A.6** and **A.7**, see above, p. 100.

Worcester, s. xi[med]); see F. E. Warren, 'An Anglo-Saxon Missal at Worcester', *The Academy* 28 (1885), 394–5.

**A.9** Orléans, Bibliothèque Municipale, 105 (127) (? Winchcombe, s. x[2]).

**A.10** Rouen, Bibliothèque Municipale, 274 (Y. 6) (? Christ Church, Canterbury, s. xi[1]); ed. H. A. Wilson, *The Missal of Robert of Jumièges*, HBS 11 (London, 1896).

Fragments of manuscript sacramentaries of eighth-century date: 'List', nos. 292, 757, 791 and 929; fragments of manuscript sacramentaries of tenth- and eleventh-century date: 'List', nos. 547, 567, 636, 650 and 810; fragments of manuscript missals: 'List', nos. 143, 212, 454, 524, 572, 649, 789, 871, 872, 875, 936 and eight supplementary items.

BIBLIOGRAPHY For the early sacramentaries, see K. Gamber, *Sakramentartypen. Versuch einer Gruppierung der Handschriften und Fragmente bis zur Jahrtausendwende*, Texte und Arbeiten 49–50 (Beuron, 1958), 60–4; *CLLA*, pp. 233–7; *Das Bonifatius-Sakramentar und weitere frühe Liturgiebücher aus Regensburg*, Studia Patristica et Liturgica 12 (Regensburg, 1975), 53–69 and 80–2; and *Sakramentarstudien und andere frühe Arbeiten zur Liturgiegeschichte*, Studia Patristica et Liturgica 7 (Regensburg, 1978), 27–30; D. A. Bullough, 'Roman Books and Carolingian Renovatio', *Stud. in Church Hist.* 14 (1977), esp. 30–3, and 'Alcuin and the Kingdom of Heaven: Liturgy, Theology, and the Carolingian Age', *Carolingian Essays*, ed. U.-R. Blumenthal (Washington, DC, 1983), pp. 11–12; Kotzor, *Martyrologium* I, 258*–66*; H. Mayr-Harting, *The Coming of Christianity* (see above, n. 11). For the later manuscripts, see E. Moeller, *Corpus Praefationum*, CCSL 161 and 161A–D (Turnhout, 1980–1) [edits or collates the *praefationes* in **A.3**, **A.7**, **A.9** and **A.10**]; C. A. Gordon, 'Manuscript Missals: the English Uses', Cambridge University Sandars Lectures 1936 (unpublished, but accessible in BL Add. 44920+44921); Turner, *The Missal of the New Minister*, pp. vi–x and xiii–xxv; and C. E. Hohler, 'Some Service Books of the Later Saxon Church', *Tenth-Century Studies*, ed. D. Parsons (London, 1975), pp. 60–83 and 217–27.

## **B.** Gradual

This is the book containing the sung portions of the mass, those that were fixed (*Kyrie*, *Gloria*, *Credo*, *Sanctus* and *Agnus*, together with their variable melodies if the book was noted), and those that varied according to the day or feast (introit, gradual, alleluia and versicle, tract, offertory, communion). Graduals or parts of these could be combined with tropers and collections of sequences.

The Latin terminology for this book is not uniform. Ælfric and the Carilef list have *gradale*, and this word may have been in use since the ninth century. Up to the end of the Anglo-Saxon period, however, we find Latin *antiphonarius* and *antiphonarium* employed for both the gradual (*antiphonarium missae*) and the Office antiphoner (*antiphonarium officii*); cf. *antiphonario* for a gradual in RegC (Symons), p. 33. Such ambiguous usage was clearly unsatisfactory and may even have left its traces in the Old English terminology; see the discussion of OE *sangboc*, below. This may be the reason why we find in English booklists – but not, it seems, on the continent – the incipits of texts at the beginning of the two different books employed as their names. *Ad te leuaui* is the beginning of the introit sung on the first Sunday in Advent and therefore opens the gradual; it is attested five times, once in a Latin list (Worc.B), and four times in Old English lists (see below). For *aspiciens*, the term for the Office antiphoner, see section **J**.

## *Old English terminology*

*sangboc*: ÆPast 13.52, 126/127.137; Ælfric, *Grammar* 291.11; Leofric 5.
*antiphonaria*; *antefnere*: Indicia 8; RegC 405.572.
*ad te leuaui*: BuryA 18; BuryB 6; Leofric 7; Sherburn 3.

The dictionary definitions for *sangboc* are all unsatisfactory, and so is Padelford's explanation, 'the church singing-book containing the hymns and the canticles'.[17] Rather, we have to do with books that did *not* contain the hymns and canticles (see below, sections **H** and **K**). In both Old English lists in ÆPast we find the variant readings *sangboc* and *sangbec*, and it is possible that the latter is the reading intended by Ælfric, as this item in the lists corresponds to *nocturnalem* and *gradalem* in his Latin list (ÆPast 51.137), possibly going back to Egbert's *antiphonarium*. Ælfric's *sangboc* would then be a common term for gradual and Office antiphoner, just like Latin *antiphonarius* in early usage. I doubt if Ælfric meant to include a hymnal among the *sangbec*, as Fehr thinks.[18]

Leofric gave to Exeter Cathedral '.ii. fulle sangbec 7 .i. nihtsang 7 .i. adteleuaui'. For *sangboc* in this series, Förster suggested 'a "complete choral-book" . . . which contained all the texts and melodies for the Eucharistic service as well as for the canonical hours',[19] although he notes that such texts and melodies were usually in two separate books. Another solution has been proposed by Gatch,[20] who interprets *sangboc* as '*perhaps* Antiph. diurnale' and the following *nihtsang* as 'Antiph. nocturnale'. The *sangbec* in the Leofric list would therefore be Office books, and this view is supported by *ad te leuaui*, a

[17] *Musical Terms*, p. 91.
[18] *Hirtenbriefe*, pp. lxxxviii–xci.
[19] 'Donations', p. 25, n. 80.
[20] *Preaching*, p. 43.

gradual in the same list; however, there is no absolute certainty about the meaning of *sangboc*, and all we can gather from the citation in Ælfric's *Grammar* is that it could have been a book with musical notation.

The forms of the Old English loan-word derived from *antiphonarius* clearly refer to a gradual in Indicia and, most probably, in the one passage in the *Regularis concordia*.[21]

The use of *ad te leuaui* for a gradual in four different Old English contexts seems to confirm what has been said above about the Latin terminology (cf. section **J** below).

### *Surviving manuscripts*

**B.1** Durham, University Library, Cosin V. v. 6 (Christ Church, Canterbury, s. $xi^{ex}$; provenance Durham); see K. D. Hartzell, 'An Unknown English Benedictine Gradual of the Eleventh Century', *ASE* 4 (1975), 131–44.

**B.2** Oxford, Bodleian Library, Bodley 775 (Old Minster, Winchester, s. $xi^{med}$); see **C.3**.

Fragments of manuscript graduals: 'List', no. 416 and three supplementary items.

BIBLIOGRAPHY *Le Graduel romain: Édition critique* par les moines de Solesmes, *II. Les sources* (Solesmes, 1957) [lists as Anglo-Saxon sources **A.1**, **A.7**, **B.2**, **C.2** and the missal fragment 'List' no. 572; to these should be added **B.1**, **A.4** and the missal fragments listed above, p. 102].

## **C.** Troper

Tropes are interpolations in liturgical texts and in their music, particularly in the chants of the mass. They were introduced into the liturgy of the Anglo-Saxons in the tenth century. A collection of tropes is referred to as the *troparium* (Worc.B), which is closely related to the gradual; both may be combined in one book, as in **C.3**. A special form of trope is the sequence, a composition placed at the end of the Alleluia of the mass. Liturgiologists often distinguish between the *sequence* (that is, a melody) and the *prose* (that is, the words sung to such a melody), but I am here employing *sequence* in the sense in which it is now generally used, of words and music. A collection of sequences, which may or may not be included in the troper, was known as a *sequentiarius*, but I have not

[21] Cf. Symons, p. 33, n. 1.

found this Latin term, or Old English loan-words or translations for it, in Anglo-Saxon sources.

### *Old English terminology*

*tropere*: BuryB 5 and 14; Indicia 11; Leofric 8.

### *Surviving manuscripts*

**C.1** Cambridge, Corpus Christi College 473 (Old Minster, Winchester, s. xi¹); ed. W. H. Frere, *The Winchester Troper*, HBS 8 (London, 1894) [does not include the sequences].

**C.2** London, BL Cotton Caligula A. xiv, fols. 1–36 (? Christ Church, Canterbury, s. xi^med); ed. Frere, *Winchester Troper*.

**C.3** Oxford, Bodleian Library, Bodley 775: see **B.2**; ed. Frere, *Winchester Troper*; sequences ed. W. G. Henderson, *Missale ad usum insignis ecclesiae Eboracensis*, 2 vols., Surtees Soc. 59–60 (Durham, 1872–4) II, 281–318.

**C.1** and **C.3** include collections of sequences; there is also a small collection of sequences in **G.4**.[22] A number of tropes are also found in **B.1**.

BIBLIOGRAPHY Frere, *The Winchester Troper*, pp. v–xli; C. Blume, *Analecta Hymnica* 53 (1911) [collates the sequences in **C.1** and **C.3**]; A. E. Planchart, *The Repertory of Tropes at Winchester*, 2 vols. (Princeton, NJ, 1977) [catalogue of tropes in the three manuscripts]. The contents of the Anglo-Saxon tropers and the tropes in **B.1** are also recorded and collated in the *Corpus Troporum*, of which four volumes have appeared so far: I. *Tropes du propre de la messe 1: Cycle de Noël*, ed. R. Jonsson; II. *Prosules de la messe 1: Tropes de l'Alleluia*, ed. O. Marcusson; III. *Tropes du propre de la messe 2: Cycle de Pâques*, ed. G. Björkvall, G. Iversen and R. Jonsson; IV. *Tropes de l'Agnus Dei*, ed. G. Iversen, Studia Latina Stockholmiensia 21, 22, 25 and 26 (Stockholm, 1975–82).

## Mass Lectionaries

It would seem that the 'epistle' and the gospel of the mass were normally read from two separate books in Anglo-Saxon churches; for these books, the epistolary and the gospel-book, see the following sections. But evidence for

22 The sequences in **C.2** are a later addition (s. xii).

the existence of combined epistle–gospel lectionaries in the early and late Anglo-Saxon period is provided by fragments from such books: Durham, Cathedral Library, A. IV. 19, fol. 89, from an eighth-century lectionary written in Northumbria; Oslo, Riksarkivet, Lat. fragm. 201 (together with Oslo, Universitetsbiblioteket, Lat. fragm. 9) of the late tenth century; and three leaves from an epistle–gospel lectionary which, together with a sacramentary, had formed part of a late-tenth-century 'primitive' missal **A.6**.[23] See also the discussion of OE *pistolboc*, below, section **E**.

The term *liber comitis* for the combined mass lectionary is found in the heading to the lessons in **A.6**, but no Old English equivalent for Latin *comes* or *liber comitis* sems to have existed.

## **D.** Gospel-Book and Gospel Lectionary

There were two different types of book from which the gospel at mass could be read: the gospel-book, and the gospel lectionary; for the combined epistle–gospel lectionary, see above.

'Gospel-book' is here used in the sense of a complete copy of the four gospels, their texts being arranged in the normal order they had in the New Testament. Fifty-nine copies of such books survive more or less complete from the Anglo-Saxon period; twenty-one of them were written in the eighth century or earlier. To these must be added fragments of nineteen further gospel manuscripts, fifteen of them from the eighth century or earlier. A comprehensive study of all these books is needed in order to establish which and how many of them were used in the liturgy of the mass. The lists printed below should therefore not be considered as definitive.

Gospel-books could be provided with the apparatus necessary for liturgical use in two ways: they could be supplied with notes, mainly marginal, indicating the day on which the pericope beginning opposite the note was to be read (in early manuscripts such notes might be quite unsystematic and fragmentary), or they could be accompanied by a gospel list (*capitulare euangeliorum*), usually at the end of the gospels, which would record the pericopes in the order of the church year, and the days on which they were read.

A complete copy of the West Saxon translation of the gospels (Cambridge, University Library, Ii. 2. 11) and a fragment of the same translation (now New

[23] Cf. T. J. Brown, *The Durham Ritual*, EEMF 16 (Copenhagen, 1969), 37; L. Gjerløw, *Antiphonarium Nidrosiensis Ecclesiae*, Libri Liturgici Provinciae Nidrosiensis Medii Aevi 3 (Oslo, 1979), 265–6; F. Wormald – see **A.6** above – p. 549 and pl. IX; and Gamber, *CLLA*, pp. 470–86.

Haven, Yale University, Beinecke Library, 578) have rubrics giving the day of the pericope in Old English and its incipit in Latin in the appropriate places, but these rubrics are no proof of the use of English texts in the liturgy.[24] One can see from Ælfric's Catholic Homilies how such gospel translations might be utilized for preaching in the vernacular.

A gospel lectionary, also called evangeliary or evangelistary, contains only those parts of the gospels read at mass and is always arranged according to the church year. If one is to go by the number of surviving copies, this type of book was much less common in Anglo-Saxon England than the gospel-book, but this is not certain, as many gospel-books may owe their survival to their beautiful script and illumination, while gospel lectionaries may have become out of date and hence more easily discarded.

I have not been able to find a terminological distinction, either in Latin or in Old English, for the two types of book during the Anglo-Saxon period, unless Latin *lectionarium* could also be used for a gospel lectionary (see below, section **E**). An investigation of the development of the system of pericopes in Anglo-Saxon England, taking into account the evidence from manuscripts of the gospels, liturgical books, Bede's[25] and Ælfric's Homilies, and others, would certainly be a rewarding task.

## *Old English terminology*

*Cristes boc*: BuryA 1; Indicia 10; Leofric 1 and 14; Peterborough 1; RegC (Zupitza) 16.225; Sherburn 1; Wulfstan (?), *Eccl. Gr.* 233.30.
*godspellboc*: ÆPast 13.52.

*Cristes boc* is frequent in Old English; I have found ninety-five instances. In early texts it is always used in the plural form: in Mart. 240.4 (the earliest occurrence), in Alfred's Pastoral Care and the Old English Bede. From Æthelwold's translation of the Benedictine Rule onwards, the word, denoting the book comprising all four gospels, is commonly used in the singular. It is not always easy to distinguish between instances of *Cristes boc* referring to a book as physical object, to the contents of the gospels, or to both. I have listed above the occurrences in the texts from which most of our information about

[24] The rubrics in the Cambridge manuscript are printed as marginal entries by W. W. Skeat, *The Holy Gospels in Anglo-Saxon, Northumbrian and Old Mercian Versions*, 4 vols. (Cambridge, 1871–87); they have been listed and discussed by F. Tupper, 'Anglo-Saxon Dæg-Mæl', *PMLA* 10 (1895), 187–241. Some Latin incipits of gospel pericopes are also in Oxford, Bodleian Library, Bodley 441 (s. xi[1]).

[25] A comparative list of the pericopes represented in Bede's Homilies and those in **D.4** and **D.11** has been ptd D. Hurst, *Bedae Venerabilis Opera III: Opera Homiletica*, CCSL 122 (Turnhout, 1955), ix–xvi.

the Old English terminology for liturgical books can be derived; all these instances refer to actual copies of the gospels; in the Leofric booklist, 14, this is a copy of the West-Saxon translation, '.i. englisc Cristes boc'.

Considering the frequent use of OE *godspel*, it seems remarkable that *Cristes boc*, and not *godspellboc*, is the commonly accepted Old English term. The latter may have been introduced by Ælfric, but even he always uses *Cristes boc*, except in the booklist in ÆPast. However, very early in the Middle English period, *Cristes boc* was displaced by *godspellboc*.[26] Professor Gatch[27] rightly criticizes Fehr's translation 'Homilienbuch' for *godspellboc* in ÆPast; but note that Fehr[28] had expressly withdrawn this interpretation.

In BuryA 5, '.i. god spellboc' certainly refers to a homiliary; see below, section **M**.

### *Surviving manuscripts: gospel-books with liturgical notes*

**D.1** Durham, Cathedral Library, A. II. 16 (Northumbria, s. viii; provenance Durham).

**D.2** Durham, Cathedral Library, A. II. 17 (Northumbria, s. viii; provenance Durham); ed. C. D. Verey *et al.*, *The Durham Gospels*, EEMF 20 (Copenhagen, 1980) [facsimile].

**D.3** London, BL Add. 40000 (Brittany, s. x^in; provenance Thorney).

**D.4** London, BL Cotton Nero D. iv (Lindisfarne, s. vii/viii; provenance Chester-le-Street, Durham); ed. T. D. Kendrick *et al.*, *Codex Lindisfarnensis*, 2 vols. (Olten and Lausanne, 1960) [facsimile].

**D.5** London, BL Royal 1. A. XVIII (Brittany, s. ix/x; provenance St Augustine's, Canterbury).

**D.6** London, BL Royal 1. B. VII (? Northumbria, s. viii¹; provenance Christ Church, Canterbury).

**D.7** Oxford, Bodleian Library, Auct. D. 2. 14 (Italy, s. vii).

**D.8** Florence, Biblioteca Medicea Laurenziana, Amiatino 1 (Jarrow–Wearmouth, s. viii^in) [complete bible].

**D.9** Rheims, Bibliothèque Municipale, 9 (s. xi^med).

**D.10** Vatican City, Biblioteca Apostolica Vaticana, Barberini lat. 570 (Southumbria, s. viii²).

**D.11** Würzburg, Universitätsbibliothek, M. p. th. f. 68 (Italy, s. vi; provenance Northumbria, s. vii/viii).

26 For this process, see H. Käsmann, *Studien zum kirchlichen Wortschatz des Mittelenglischen 1100–1350* (Tübingen, 1961), pp. 86–7. It is interesting to note that the translator of the Middle English version of the Leofric list no longer understood OE *Cristes boc*; cf. Förster, 'Donations', p. 31 and n. 140.

27 *Preaching*, p. 43.

28 *Hirtenbriefe*, p. lxxxvii, n. 2.

### *Surviving manuscripts: gospel-books with gospel lists*

**D.12** Cambridge, St John's College 73 (C.23) (Bury St Edmunds, s. xi/xii).
**D.13** Cambridge, Trinity College B. 10. 4 (? Christ Church, Canterbury, s. $xi^1$).
**D.14** London, BL Add. 9381 (Brittany, s. ix/x).
**D.15** London, BL Add. 34890 (Christ Church, Canterbury, s. $xi^1$; provenance New Minster, Winchester).
**D.16** London, BL Cotton Tiberius A. ii (NE France, s. ix; provenance Christ Church, Canterbury).
**D.17** London, BL Harley 76 (? Christ Church, Canterbury, s. $xi^1$; provenance Bury St Edmunds).
**D.18** London, BL Royal 1. D. IX (Christ Church, Canterbury, s. $xi^{in}$).
**D.19** Oxford, Bodleian Library, Auct. D. 2. 16 (Landévennec, s. x; provenance Exeter).
**D.20** Oxford, Bodleian Library, Bodley 155 (Barking, s. x/xi).
**D.21** Besançon, Bibliothèque Municipale, 14 (Old Minster, Winchester, s. $x^{ex}$).
**D.22** Coburg, Landesbibliothek, 1 (? Metz, s. ix).
**D.23** Paris, BN lat. 272 (s. $x^2$).

### *Surviving manuscripts: gospel lectionaries*

**D.24** Cambridge, Fitzwilliam Museum 88–1972 (St Augustine's, Canterbury, s. xi/xii).
**D.25** Cambridge, Pembroke College 302 (? Canterbury, s. $xi^{med}$; provenance Hereford).
**D.26** London, BL Stowe 944 (New Minster, Winchester, s. $xi^1$) [Christmas to Palm Sunday only; for use in the chapter Office?].
**D.27** Oxford, Bodleian Library, Lat. liturg. f. 5 (Scotland, s. $xi^{med}$; provenance Durham).
**D.28** Florence, Biblioteca Medicea Laurenziana, Plut. xii. 17 (Christ Church, Canterbury, s. $xi^1$).
**D.29** Warsaw, Biblioteka Narodowa, i. 3311 (s. x/xi).

Fragments of manuscript gospel lectionaries: 'List', nos. 502 and 817.

BIBLIOGRAPHY T. Klauser, *Das römische Capitulare Evangeliorum*, Liturgiegeschichtliche Quellen und Forschungen 28 (Münster, 1935); T. J. Brown, 'Part II. The Latin Text', T. D. Kendrick *et al.*, *Codex Lindisfarnensis* II, 31–58, esp. 34–58; C. D. Verey, in C. D. Verey *et al.*, *The Durham Gospels*, pp. 26–8; and Gamber, *CLLA*, pp. 227–30 and 446–69.

## E. Epistolary

The lessons called 'epistle' in the mass were mostly taken from the New Testament epistles, but there were also days and periods for which the respective readings came from the Acts of the Apostles, the Apocalypse, or from books of the Old Testament. Consequently, a copy of the epistles in the New Testament would not serve as an epistolary (Latin *epistolarium* ÆPast; *epistolare* Worc.B) throughout the year; a special book, often called a *lectionarium* had to be available (cf. ÆPast 51.137: 'lectionarium quod quidam uocant epistolarium'). No such book seems to have survived from the Anglo-Saxon period, and later copies seem to be rare, too.[29] A complete bible might have been used as an alternative, but I know of no evidence for such a practice.

### *Old English terminology*

*pistolboc*, *pistelboc*: ÆPast 13.52 and 126/127.157; Ælfwold 6; BuryA 3; Indicia 10; Leofric 4; Sherburn 4.
*pistelari*: BuryB 7.

Terms for a gospel-book are found side by side with that for the epistolary in ÆPast 13.52, BuryA, Leofric and Sherburn. The omission of the gospel-book in Ælfwold and BuryB may not be significant in view of the character of these lists. But it seems remarkable that such a book is not mentioned in the fairly systematic catalogues in ÆPast 126/127.157 and in Indicia. Moreover, Indicia 10 explains that one should ask for the *pistolboc* by means of the sign of the cross, 'forþon þe mon ræt godspel þæron and ealswa on þære Cristes bec'. This may indicate that OE *pistolboc* might have been used in some cases in the sense of 'combined epistle–gospel lectionary', but this is by no means certain. See also below, p. 121, for *rædingboc*.

## BOOKS FOR THE OFFICE

## F. Breviary

A breviary (in the sense in which the word is now regularly used) combines all the texts sung or read in the Office – psalms, antiphons, lessons, responsories, chapters, collects etc. – in the order in which they actually occur in the services. There is no English manuscript of this kind before the twelfth century, and it is

[29] Cf. Wordsworth and Littlehales, *The Old Service Books*, p. 194.

generally believed that the earliest continental breviaries date from the eleventh century.[30]

In the Anglo-Saxon period, the Office texts are normally found in separate books such as the collectar, the psalter and others, all to be discussed below. But in the eleventh century the first example of a 'primitive' breviary appears: that is, a volume in which the various Office-books are bound up together, though they still form separate units. This book, the so-called Portiforium of St Wulfstan, is listed as **F.1** below; it contains a calendar, a psalter, canticles, litany, hymnal, monastic canticles, a collectar (including incipits of antiphons, hymns and other chants for the day hours) private prayers, full Offices for the Commune Sanctorum, for Sundays after Trinity Sunday and for weekdays, as well as some special Offices. It is obvious that here an attempt has been made to provide within one volume a large part of what is needed for performing the Office.

Other manuscripts written in the eleventh century and representing various stages of development of the full breviary are:

The Leofric Collectar (**G.4**), a combination of collectar and hymnal, which in the collectar includes for the day hours antiphons, verses, responds and incipits of hymns, as well as hymn incipits for Nocturns; this book therefore provides most of what is required in a breviary for the day hours, that is, a diurnal; another collectar, the so-called Durham Ritual (**G.2**) has been expanded in a similar way, but much less extensively.

The Red Book of Darley (**A.4**), which contains – besides masses and other liturgical texts – full breviary services for Common of Saints, Holy Week and Easter; this book has even been classed as a 'noted portable breviary' by van Dijk and Walker.[31]

Harley 863 (**H.13**), a psalter with offices of Nocturns, Lauds and Vespers for the week after the octave of Epiphany, followed by Nocturns of the Office of the Dead (now incomplete); in the margins of the psalter, antiphons and invitatories for Nocturns have been added.[32]

The so-called 'Benedictine Office' in Oxford, Bodleian Library, Junius 121 gives the Office texts, except those for Nocturns, and Lauds (apparently for weekdays after Epiphany), together with introductions and translations in Old English. We thus have a section from a diurnal, but obviously intended for teaching purposes.

[30] Professor Bernhard Bischoff has kindly informed me that he has recently discovered several leaves from a breviary written at Reichenau in the first half of the ninth century: Nürnberg, Germanisches Nationalmuseum, Kupferstichkabinett, Kapsel 536/SD 2815.

[31] S. J. P. van Dijk and J. H. Walker, *The Origins of the Modern Roman Liturgy* (London, 1960), no. 101. It seems curious that the authors have not included the Portiforium of St Wulfstan (**F.1**) in their lists of early breviaries (pp. 528–42).

[32] See E. S. Dewick and W. H. Frere, *The Leofric Collectar*, 2 vols., HBS 45–6 (London, 1914–21) I, 433–54, and II, 611–13.

No Old English term for the breviary occurs in the lists of Office-books (ÆPast, Leofric) or elsewhere. Latin *breuiarium* in the Carilef list – where *breuiarium* seems to have been altered to *breuiaria .v.* in the twelfth century – may well refer to early copies of the breviary, perhaps of a type like that in **F.1** or **G.4**, since two antiphoners, a *gradale* and '.ii. libri in quibus ad matutinas legitur' follow immediately in the list.

### *Surviving manuscripts*

**F.1** Cambridge, Corpus Christi College 391 (Worcester, s. xi²); ed. A. Hughes, *The Portiforium of Saint Wulstan*, 2 vols., HBS 89–90 (London, 1959–60) [calendar, psalter, hymnal and canticles are not included in this edition].

Fragment of a manuscript breviary(?): 'List', no. 498.[33]

BIBLIOGRAPHY J. B. L. Tolhurst, 'Introduction to the English Monastic Breviaries', *The Monastic Breviary of Hyde Abbey, Winchester* VI, HBS 80 (London, 1942) [based mainly on manuscripts of the later Middle Ages], and *The Benedictine Office: an Old English Text*, ed. J. M. Ure (Edinburgh, 1957) [cf. my review in *Anglia* 77 (1959), 226–31].

## **G.** Collectar

This service-book contains the chapters (*capitula*), that is, short lessons taken from scripture, and the collects, read at each hour of the divine service except Nocturns. Collectars may be expanded by including other elements of the Office, and they may be bound up with other Office-books. In this way, the breviary was evolved – see above, section **F** – just as the sacramentary developed into the full missal.

The Latin term in late Anglo-Saxon England appears to have been *capitulare*, *capitularium* or – perhaps less common – *collectaneum*; see below for the Old English loan-words. It seems striking that the three lists in Ælfric's Pastoral Letters do not provide for a collectar.

[33] I owe the identification of these six leaves in BL Royal 17. C. XVII, written in the late tenth century, to Dr K. D. Hartzell. The texts are from the two weeks before Easter, and it is uncertain if they formed part of a complete breviary.

### *Old English terminology*

*collectaneum*: Leofric 3.
*capitularia*, *capitelari*, *capitelarie*: BuryA 6 and 15; BuryB 10; Leofric 24.

It seems doubtful if *collectaneum* was in general ecclesiastical use as a loan-word, but it is fairly certain that the word means 'a collectar'. If the entry in the Leofric list refers to **G.4**, as Förster thinks,[34] the word may have been used in order to distinguish this kind of expanded collectar from an older and simpler kind, called *capitelarie* in Leofric 24. Professor Gatch has suggested an equation of *collectaneum* with *rædingboc* in ÆPast, but he makes it clear that he considers this doubtful.

OE *capitelarie* might have referred to several things. It might denote a book for the chapter Office, or a *capitulare euangeliorum* (see above, section **D**), while Förster's[35] second alternative, 'a collection of ecclesiastic ordinances', is also a possibility. His first explanation, however, 'a service-book containing the capitula', is probably correct, although he should have included the collects for the day hours in his definition. We should then have an Old English term and loan-word for the collectar, and this would accord very well with the contexts in which the word appears, and with the use of Latin *capitulare* on the continent.

### *Surviving manuscripts*

**G.1** Cambridge, Corpus Christi College 391: see **F.1**.

**G.2** Durham, Cathedral Library, A. IV. 19 (S. England, s. x$^{in}$; provenance Chester-le-Street, Durham); ed. U. Lindelöf and A. H. Thompson, *Rituale Ecclesiae Dunelmensis: the Durham Collectar*, Surtees Soc. 140 (Durham, 1927), and T. J. Brown *et al.*, *The Durham Ritual*, EEMF 16 (Copenhagen, 1969) [facsimile].

**G.3** London, BL Cotton Titus D. xxvi + xxvii (New Minster, Winchester, s. xi$^{1}$); see Gneuss, *Hymnar*, pp. 112–13.

**G.4** London, BL Harley 2961 (Exeter, s. xi$^{med}$); ed. E. S. Dewick and W. H. Frere, *The Leofric Collectar*, 2 vols., HBS 45–6 (London, 1914–21).

BIBLIOGRAPHY P.-M. Gy, 'Collectaire, rituel, processionnal', *Revue des sciences philosophiques et théologiques* 44 (1960), 441–69.

[34] 'Donations', p. 25, n. 78.

[35] *Ibid.* p. 28, n. 97.

## H. Psalter

The psalms constitute the nucleus of the Office chants; for their distribution over the hours of the secular and the monastic office, see Hughes, *Medieval Manuscripts*, p. 230. Psalter manuscripts (Latin *psalterium*: Egbert, ÆPast, Worc.B) intended for liturgical use show large initials in certain positions (see Hughes, *ibid.*, p. 228) and contain additional Office texts sung daily or on a particular day of every week: the canticles from the Old and New Testaments (for Lauds, Vespers and Compline) and, in manuscripts from the tenth century onwards, *Gloria*, *Credo* and *Quicumque uult*. Whether a psalter manuscript was actually employed in singing the Office seems difficult to determine, as monks (and priests?) had to learn the psalms and canticles by heart; the fact that ten of the surviving Anglo-Saxon psalters[36] have been supplied with a continuous interlinear gloss in Old English seems to indicate that they were used for teaching purposes. I list below all extant psalter manuscripts of Anglo-Saxon origin or provenance that may have been used for teaching or performing the Office liturgy.

The Latin text in the older manuscripts is that of the *Psalterium Romanum*; it was gradually replaced by that of the *Psalterium Gallicanum* after the tenth-century Benedictine reform, but see **H.8** for a remarkably late copy of the *Romanum*. The Leofric list refers expressly to the different texts: '.ii. salteras 7 se þriddan saltere swa man singð on Rome.'

Apart from the canticles, various other liturgical texts could be combined with a psalter so as to form one volume: a calendar (usually preceding the psalms), a litany, private prayers, a hymnal, or other elements of the Office.

### *Old English terminology*

*salter(e)*, *sealtere*, *psalter(e)*: ÆPast 13.52, 126/7. 157; BuryA 4 and 16; BuryB 3 and 13; Indicia 32; Leofric 9; Sherburn 7; Worc.A 5; Will of Archbishop Ælfric, *Wills*, 54.1; Ælfric, *Lives of Saints* II, 236.275; *The Old English Life of Machutus*, ed. D. Yerkes, Toronto OE Ser. 9 (Toronto, 1984), 4.2 and 8. *sealmboc*: Ælfric, *Catholic Homilies* I, 604.24.

Of the 128 occurrences of *(p)s(e)alter(e)* recorded in the *Microfiche Concordance to Old English*, fifteen instances of homonyms have to be eliminated (forms of the adjective *sealt*, 'salt, salty', and the noun *sealtere*, 'salt-worker'). Of the

[36] **H.1**, **H.7**, **H.10**, **H.11**, **H.12**, **H.15**, **H.16**, **H.17**, **H.19** and **H.21**. A considerable part of **H.6** has also been glossed in Old English, and there are a number of glosses in **H.24**. In **H.25**, the Latin text is accompanied by an Old English translation in prose for Psalms I–L, by King Alfred, and an Old English translation in verse for Psalms LI–CL.

remaining citations, nearly sixty translate *psalterium* in the Latin psalter 'a stringed musical instrument', while fifteen denote the psalter as an actual book, particularly that used in the Office. These have all been listed above. The rest of the citations refer almost exclusively to the singing of the psalter, especially as an act of penitence.

Ælfric's *sealmboc* is a *hapax legomenon* without an exactly corresponding Latin word in a passage freely translated from I Cor. XIV.26. It was not used for the Latin liturgical book.

### *Surviving manuscripts (psalters with canticles)*[37]

**H.1** *Cambridge, University Library, Ff. 1. 23 (? Winchcombe, s. xi$^{med}$); ed. K. Wildhagen, *Der Cambridger Psalter*, Bibliothek der angelsächsischen Prosa 7 (Hamburg, 1910).

**H.2** Cambridge, Corpus Christi College 272 (Rheims, s. ix$^{2}$).

**H.3** Cambridge, Corpus Christi College 391: see **F.1**.

**H.4** Cambridge, Corpus Christi College 411 (St Augustine's, Canterbury, s. x$^{ex}$).

**H.5** Cambridge, St John's College 59 (C.9) (Ireland, s. x/xi).

**H.6** *London, BL Add. 37517 (Canterbury, s. x$^{2}$ and x$^{ex}$); see F. A. Gasquet and E. Bishop, *The Bosworth Psalter* (London, 1908), and M. Korhammer, 'The Origin of the Bosworth Psalter', *ASE* 2 (1973), 173–87.

**H.7** London, BL Arundel 60 (New Minster, Winchester, s. xi$^{2}$); ed. G. Oess, *Der altenglische Arundel-Psalter*, Anglistische Forschungen 30 (Heidelberg, 1910).

**H.8** *London, BL Arundel 155 (Christ Church, Canterbury, s. xi$^{1}$).

**H.9** London, BL Cotton Galba A. xviii (NE France, s. ix; ? Winchester, s. x$^{in}$).

**H.10** London, BL Cotton Tiberius C. vi (Old Minster, Winchester, s. xi$^{med}$) [canticles lost]; ed. A. P. Campbell, *The Tiberius Psalter* (Ottawa, 1974).

**H.11** *London, BL Cotton Vespasian A. i (St Augustine's, Canterbury, s. viii$^{1}$); ed. S. M. Kuhn, *The Vespasian Psalter* (Ann Arbor, Mich., 1965), and D. H. Wright and A. Campbell, *The Vespasian Psalter*, EEMF 14 (Copenhagen, 1967) [facsimile].

**H.12** London, BL Cotton Vitellius E. xviii (New Minster, Winchester, s. xi$^{med}$); ed. J. L. Rosier, *The Vitellius Psalter*, Cornell Stud. in Eng. 42 (Ithaca, NY, 1962).

**H.13** London, BL Harley 863 (Exeter, s. xi$^{2}$); see above, p. 111.

**H.14** London, BL Harley 2904 (? Ramsey, ? Winchester, s. x$^{ex}$).

**H.15** *London, BL Royal 2. B. V (? Worcester, ? Winchester, ? Christ Church, Canterbury, s. x$^{med}$); ed. F. Roeder, *Der altenglische Regius-Psalter*, Studien zur englischen Philologie 18 (Halle, 1904).

[37] An asterisk indicates the text of the *Psalterium Romanum*; manuscripts not so marked contain the *Psalterium Gallicanum*.

**H.16** London, BL Stowe 2 (? New Minster, Winchester, s. xi$^{med}$); ed. A. C. Kimmens, *The Stowe Psalter*, Toronto OE Ser. 3 (Toronto, 1979).

**H.17** London, Lambeth Palace Library, 427 (s. xi$^{1}$); ed. U. Lindelöf, *Der Lambeth-Psalter*, 2 vols., Acta Societatis Scientiarum Fennicae 35.1 and 43.3 (Helsinki, 1909–14).

**H.18** Oxford, Bodleian Library, Douce 296 (Crowland, s. xi$^{med}$).

**H.19** *Oxford, Bodleian Library, Junius 27 (? Winchester, s x$^{in}$) [canticles lost]; ed. E. Brenner, *Der altenglische Junius-Psalter*, Anglistische Forschungen 23 (Heidelberg, 1908).

**H.20** Oxford, Bodleian Library, Laud lat. 81 (s.xi$^{2}$).

**H.21** Salisbury, Cathedral Library, 150 (s. x$^{2}$; provenance Salisbury); ed. C. and K. Sisam, *The Salisbury Psalter*, EETS o.s. 242 (London, 1959).

**H.22** Salisbury, Cathedral Library, 180 (Brittany, s. x; provenance Salisbury) [*Psalterium Gallicanum* and *Hebraicum*].

**H.23** *East Berlin, Deutsche Staatsbibliothek, Hamilton 553 (Northumbria, s. viii).

**H.24** *New York, Pierpont Morgan Library, 776 (s. viii$^{med}$) [canticles lost].

**H.25** *Paris, BN lat. 8824 (s. xi$^{med}$); ed. B. Colgrave *et al.*, *The Paris Psalter*, EEMF 8 (Copenhagen, 1958) [facsimile].

**H.26** Vatican City, Biblioteca Apostolica Vaticana, Reg. lat. 12 (? Christ Church, Canterbury, s. xi$^{1}$; provenance Bury St Edmunds).

**H.27** Rouen, Bibliothèque Municipale, 231 (A. 44) (St Augustine's, Canterbury, s. xi$^{ex}$).

For psalter fragments, see 'List', nos. 9, 125, 141, 150, 250, 764 and 788, and one supplementary item; for psalters without canticles, see 'List', nos. 422 and 939.

BIBLIOGRAPHY C. and K. Sisam, *The Salisbury Psalter*, esp. pp. 47–52; K. Wildhagen, 'Studien zum Psalterium Romanum in England und zu seinen Glossierungen', *Festschrift für Lorenz Morsbach*, ed. F. Holthausen and H. Spies, Studien zur englischen Philologie 50 (Halle, 1913), 418–72, and 'Das Psalterium Gallicanum in England und seine altenglischen Glossierungen', *Englische Studien* 54 (1920), 35–45; N. Brooks, *The Early History of the Church of Canterbury* (Leicester, 1984), pp. 261–5; and J. Mearns, *The Canticles of the Christian Church* (Cambridge, 1914).

## J. Antiphoner

An antiphoner in the sense now current is the book containing the Office chants: the antiphons, verses, responsories and invitatories. The Latin term is *antiphonarius* or *antiphonarium* in the *Regularis concordia* and in the Carilef list; for the use of the same word denoting a gradual, see above, section **B**. In order to avoid ambiguity, the term *aspiciens* may have been introduced (Worc.B, and see below for an instance in the Sherburn list). *Aspiciens* is the first word of the responsory following the first lesson in the Night Office of the first Sunday of Advent. Although antiphoners do not begin with this responsory, they give special prominence to its initial, and this has led to the adoption of *aspiciens* as signifying the book. For the use of *nocturnale* for an antiphoner, see below. Apart from the epistolary, and perhaps the Office bible, this is the only category of Anglo-Saxon liturgical book of which not a single complete copy survives, but information on the use of antiphons and responsories can be gathered from other liturgical books, especially **F.1**, **G.4**, **H.13** and **U.2**. We also have a collection of antiphons, in use at York in the eighth century, preserved in bk IV of Alcuin's *De laude Dei*. As its name implies, the contents of the responsoriale are more narrowly limited than those of the antiphoner, but it is not certain if this type of liturgical book was known in Anglo-Saxon England.

## *Old English terminology*

*antefnere*, *antemnere*, *antifonere*, *antifenere*: ÆPast 154/5.23; RegC 409.635, 426.868 (to be emended from *antefne*), and 436.1015 (to be emended from *antefnesse*); RegC (Zupitza) 5.38–9.
*aspiciens*: Sherburn 2.
*nihtsang*: Leofric 6 and 25.

For a discussion of OE *sangboc*, 'Office antiphoner', see above, pp. 103–4; there I also list two occurrences of *antefnere* (or related forms) for 'gradual', while the five given here clearly refer to the Office-book, as does *aspiciens* in the Sherburn list.

OE *nihtsang* appears to correspond to *nocturnale* in ÆPast 51.137[38] and is interpreted convincingly by Förster[39] as *nihtsangboc*, 'an *Antiphonarium nocturnale* for the nocturnal hours of the canonical service'. This leaves us with a gap for an *antiphonarium diurnale* (if there was such a book) in the Leofric list and ÆPast 51.137. But the required texts may have been included in the collectar (see above, section **G**), and I can see no evidence for Fehr's claim[40] that a *gradale* may have included sung portions of the day hours of the Office.

The use of *nihtsang* for a book containing texts of the Night Office seems remarkable, as the same word had been in use as a translation for *completorium*, one of the day hours, at least since the time of Æthelwold's translation of the Benedictine Rule.[41]

[38] Cf. Fehr, *Hirtenbriefe*, pp. lxxxix–xc. [39] 'Donations', p. 25, n. 80.
[40] *Hirtenbriefe*, p. xc. [41] See my note in *Anglia* 77 (1959), 228.

*Surviving manuscripts*

Fragments of antiphoners: 'List' nos. 277 and 437,[42] 610, 663 (from a responsoriale?), 666, 675, 777, 873 and 874 and one supplementary item.

It is uncertain if Durham, Cathedral Library, B. III. 11, fols. 136–59, containing a substantial part of an eleventh-century antiphoner written at Liège, was one of the books on the Carilef list.[43] An antiphoner written on the continent in the ninth century, whose remains are now in Rouen, Bibliothèque Municipale, 292 (A. 12), may have been in England in the late Anglo-Saxon period.[44]

BIBLIOGRAPHY The antiphons in Alcuin's *De laude Dei* have been ptd R. Constantinescu, 'Alcuin et les "Libelli precum" de l'époque carolingienne', *Revue de l'histoire de la spiritualité* 50 (1974), 38–51; see Bullough, 'Alcuin and the Kingdom of Heaven', pp. 5–8. R.-J. Hesbert, 'Les Antiphonaires monastiques insulaires', *RB* 92 (1982), 358–75, is based on manuscript sources of the later Middle Ages, of which some may be linked with Anglo-Saxon usage since the Benedictine reform; see p. 95, n. 12, above, and discussion by S. Rankin, 'The Liturgical Background of the Old English Advent Lyrics: a Reappraisal', below, pp. 317–40.

## **K.** Hymnal

With few exceptions, a hymn – metrical and stanzaic – formed part of each of the hours of the daily Office. The collection of these hymns (Latin *hymnarium*, Worc.B 56) seems to have contained less than twenty hymns in the early Anglo-Saxon period, but in the course of the tenth century a much larger book, the 'New Hymnal', with more than a hundred pieces, was introduced from the continent. In monastic manuscripts, the hymnal was usually followed by a collection of Old Testament canticles which were sung in groups of three at the beginning of the third Nocturn of the monastic Office. As the hymnal in its earlier and in its later form would have been a slim volume, it is often found combined with other liturgical books in one manuscript, particularly with a psalter or collectar.

42 Dr Susan Rankin has kindly told me that these two fragments come from the same manuscript.

43 The contents of this antiphoner have been printed by R.-J. Hesbert in *Corpus Antiphonalium Officii*, Rerum Ecclesiasticarum Documenta, ser. maior: Fontes 7–12, 6 vols. (Rome, 1963–79); a facsimile was published as *Pars Antiphonarii*, ed. W. H. Frere, Plainsong and Med. Music Soc. (London, 1923).

44 See K. D. Hartzell, 'An English Antiphoner of the Ninth Century', *RB* 90 (1980), 234–48.

*Old English terminology*

*imnere*, *(h)ymnere*, *hymener*: BuryB 9; Indicia 33; Leofric 11; Sherburn 6.
*ymenboc*: Old English Bede[45] 484.23.

The first of these words – with its variants – seems to have been the commonly accepted term for the liturgical book. The word in the Old English Bede is a *hapax legomenon*, translating *librum hymnorum* (by means of a plural form in Old English), that is, a collection of hymns composed by Bede and obviously intended by him to supply additional liturgical hymns.

*Surviving manuscripts: hymnals with monastic canticles*

**K.1** Cambridge, Corpus Christi College 391: see **F.1**

**K.2** Durham, Cathedral Library, B. III. 32 (Christ Church, Canterbury, s. xi¹); ed. J. Stevenson, *The Latin Hymns of the Anglo-Saxon Church*, Surtees Soc. 23 (Durham, 1851).

**K.3** London, BL Add. 37517: see **H.6**; the hymnal is ed. G. Wieland, *The Canterbury Hymnal*, Toronto Med. Latin Texts 12 (Toronto, 1982).

**K.4** London, BL Cotton Vespasian D. xii (? Christ Church, Canterbury, s. $xi^{med}$).

**K.5** Rouen, Bibliothèque Municipale, 231 (A. 44) (St Augustine's, Canterbury, s. $xi^{ex}$).

**K.6** London, BL Cotton Julius A. vi (? Christ Church, Canterbury, s. $xi^{med}$) [contains monastic canticles only].

*Surviving manuscripts: hymnals*

**K.7** London, BL Harley 2961: see **G.4**.

**K.8** Vatican City, Biblioteca Apostolica Vaticana, Reg. lat. 338 (? English, s. x).

Fragment of a manuscript hymnal: 'List', no. 696; an incomplete hymnal is found in **H.11**. The *Expositio hymnorum* contained in **K.4** (together with a hymnal) and in **K.6** is a school-book, not a liturgical book.

BIBLIOGRAPHY Gneuss, *Hymnar*, and 'Latin Hymns in Medieval England', *Chaucer and Middle English Studies in Honour of Rossell Hope Robbins*, ed. B. Rowland (London, 1974), pp. 407–24; and M. Korhammer, *Die monastischen Cantica im Mittelalter*, Texte und Untersuchungen zur englischen Philologie 6 (Munich, 1976) [edits and collates the monastic canticles from **K.1–4** and **K.6**].

45 *The Old English Version of Bede's Ecclesiastical History of the English People*, ed. T. Miller, 4 vols., EETS o.s. 95, 96, 110 and 111 (London, 1890–8).

## *Office lectionaries*

A central part of Nocturns were the readings, taken from various sources. On weekdays and some saints' days, the Night Office had three such lessons, except for the weekdays in summer, when there was only one. On Sundays and feast-days (including certain saints' days) there were nine lessons in the Office of the secular clergy, but twelve lessons in the monastic Office, arranged in three groups of three (monastic Office: four). The lessons could be of four different kinds: passages from the bible, from sermons (dealing with the respective feast-day, or with a general theme), from homilies (expounding the gospel pericope of the day) and from saints' lives. The distribution of the various texts over the lessons differs, but the groups of three (four) lessons usually form a continuous reading from the same source. The normal arrangement was that on days with three lessons (or only one) a text from the bible was read, on days with nine (twelve) lessons the first group of three (four) was taken from the bible, the second from a sermon, the third from a homily. But there were also days with three lessons only, with a text from a homily, while on days with nine (twelve) lessons the first and second group could be taken from the bible or from a sermon. For further details, see Hughes, *Medieval Manuscripts*, pp. 61–2, and the medieval books themselves. On saints' days, there could either be three readings, all from the life of a saint, or nine (twelve) lessons: the first six (eight) of these, or all nine (twelve) taken from a saint's life, while the last three (four) might be reserved for a homily. Other arrangements were possible.

Until the end of the Anglo-Saxon period, the texts needed for these lessons would usually be found in a number of separate books, which are treated below in sections **L**, **M** and **N**. The Latin and Old English terminology for these is, unfortunately, not always as precise as one could wish, cf. 'librum cum lectionibus ad nocturnas', ÆPast 51.137, and 'libri in quibus ad matutinas legitur', in the Carilef list. I record below those Old English terms that might refer to more than one of categories **L**, **M** and **N**. However, this is not only a problem caused by an imprecise terminology; the contents of the manuscripts may be another reason. Until recently, it was thought that, before the days of the breviary, the different types of lessons would always appear in different liturgical books. But this has become doubtful at least for the late Anglo-Saxon period, since the recent discovery of fragments of a combined homiliary–legendary of the second half of the eleventh century, probably from St Albans, used as wrappers for MSS Gorhambury X.D.4.B and X.D.4.C at the Hertfordshire Record Office.[46]

[46] The fragments were discovered by N. R. Ker; their contents are listed by R. M. Thomson (*Manuscripts from St Albans Abbey 1066–1235*, 2 vols. (Cambridge, 1982) I, 77), who kindly

*Old English terminology*

*rædingboc*: ÆPast 13.52, 126/127.157; Leofric 27.
*sumerrædingboc*: Leofric 15.
*sumerboc*: BuryA 11.
*winterrædingboc*: BuryA 8 and 10; Leofric 16.
*rædingboc*: Wulfstan (?), *Eccl. Gr.* 230.22.
*redeboc*: marginal note in **R.4**; ed. Ker, *Catalogue*, p. 128.

OE *ræding* could refer to the lessons of Nocturns, but also to the gospel recited at mass as well as to texts read in the refectory. In order to determine the meaning of *rædingboc*, we have to rely on the contexts in which the word occurs. In ÆPast 13.52 the list of books includes a gospel-book and a *passionalis*, so that the *rædingboc* must have contained the bible lessons for Nocturns or, more probably, the sermons and homilies. Here and in ÆPast 126/127.157 the Old English word corresponds to 'librum cum lectionibus ad nocturnas' of ÆPast 51.137, which would seem to exclude the meaning 'gospel-book' in 126/127.157, considered a possibility by both Fehr and Gatch. But the omission of the *passionalis* in ÆPast 126/127.157 makes things more difficult.

The division of the *rædingboc* into a winter and a summer volume seems to point to an Office-book, too; beyond this it is difficult to be certain. Förster[47] was sure that the term in the Leofric list must denote a book with the scripture lessons for the Office, and since this list also records homiliaries (*spelboc*) separately, this is not unlikely. However, the same list does not mention a legendary, while the scripture lessons may have been read from a bible, as is suggested by Indicia (see below, section **L**).

The *rædingboc* in *De ecclesiasticis gradibus* and the *redeboc* (a corrupt form?) in a manuscript pontifical (**R.4**) stand for the same thing: for the book that was handed to the *lector* at his ordination. But what was it? Professor Roger E. Reynolds of the Pontifical Institute of Mediaeval Studies, whom I asked for advice on this point, has kindly pointed out to me that books – and other *instrumenta* – handed over at western ordination rites were symbols. Accordingly, at the ordination rite of a lector, the *rædingboc* may have been of a symbolic kind (rather than an epistolary, from which the subdeacon would read,[48] or a book containing prophetic lections for days with three readings at mass).

drew my attention to them before the publication of his book. Lives of local saints are included in the homiliary **M.5**.

47 'Donations', p. 26, n. 89.

48 Note that *subdiaconus* is consistently translated by OE *pistolrædere* in RegC.

## L. Bible

Scripture readings in the Night Office were mainly from the Old Testament, but during certain times of the church year they were taken from the gospels, the New Testament epistles and the Apocalypse. What was needed, therefore, before the days of the breviary was a book that contained all the biblical lessons for Nocturns, or a complete bible. Among extant Anglo-Saxon manuscripts and fragments, a bible lectionary of the kind required for the Office does not seem to exist, while I do not know of an indication that any of the few surviving complete bibles ('List', nos. 169, 270, 449, 825 and 934) were used at Nocturns. But the inclusion of a bible among the books 'þe man æt uhtsange notian sceal' in Indicia, as well as the interpretation of *rædingboc* in ÆPast and the Leofric list (see above), would appear to show that both types of book must have been used; neither Ælfric nor the author of the Leofric list mentions a full bible in their fairly complete catalogues of Office-books.

### *Old English terminology*

*biblioðeca*: Indicia 29.

This Old English loan-word denoting the bible is fairly frequent, but it does not occur in our texts before the end of the tenth century, and it refers to an actual book – and at the same time an Office-book – only in Indicia. Three earlier instances of the word, in the Old English Orosius and in Æthelwold's translation of the Benedictine Rule (and a fourth in the Old English Apollonius) have the signification 'library'.[49]

BIBLIOGRAPHY M. McC. Gatch, 'The Office in Late Anglo-Saxon Monasticism', below, pp. 352–62 [on the outline of the bible lessons during Nocturns in **U.2**].

## M. Homiliary

It is not now possible to ascertain what homilies and sermons were read in the early Anglo-Saxon church during the Night Office; texts by Gregory the Great and Bede must have been among them. Towards the end of the eighth century, Charlemagne commissioned Paul the Deacon to compile a new homiliary, which was then introduced as an official service-book in the Carolingian empire, and which found its way to Anglo-Saxon England in the

[49] Cf. Funke, *Lehn- und Fremdwörter*, p. 151.

course of the ecclesiastical reforms of the tenth century, or even earlier.[50] Here as elsewhere in the western church Paul the Deacon's book became the basis of the Office homiliary. In its original form, it consisted of nearly 250 sermons and homilies selected from patristic writings, almost three quarters coming from the works of Maximus of Turin, Leo the Great, Gregory the Great and Bede. But it must be emphasized that this original homiliary was soon subject to considerable expansion and revision, and it should be one of the foremost tasks of future research to establish the version or versions of Paul's Homiliary employed in the late Anglo-Saxon period, taking into account not only the evidence of the homiliary manuscripts but also of other liturgical manuscripts like **F.1**, and of Ælfric's Homilies, which are largely based on Paul's collection.

Some liturgical handbooks distinguish between two types of Office-books with patristic lessons, the homiliary and the *sermologus*, but no such distinction is to be found in Anglo-Saxon manuscripts, and it is not to be expected, as Paul the Deacon's book provides both sermons and homilies. The '.ii.libri sermonum et omeliarum' in the Carilef list (cf. below, **M.3**) are examples of the composite book that is now usually called a homiliary. For homilies in legendaries, see below, section **N**.

Although there are no unequivocal references to a homiliary in the booklists in ÆPast, I am doubtful about Professor Gatch's claim that 'homiliaries are apparently not among the books Ælfric expects priests to own'.[51] Cf. above (p. 121), concerning the *rædingboc*.

## *Old English terminology*

*spel(l)boc*: BuryA 5; BuryB 10; Leofric 21.
*godspeltraht*: BuryB 1 (MS spelling: *codspel traht*).
*godspelles traht*: Indicia 31.

While it is difficult to say what a *rædingboc* may have been, there can be no doubt about the *spelboc*; cf. Ælfric's reference in his Grammar (2.15) to 'ða twa bec . . . on hundeahtatigum spellum', that is, the Catholic Homilies. The entry in the Leofric list may indicate that the homiliary was often arranged in two volumes: '.i. full spelboc wintres and sumeres'. Förster[52] rightly rejects the identification of this Exeter book with Cambridge, University Library, Gg. 3. 28, as we should expect a homiliary in Latin, while Kotzor[53] notes the erroneous association of the entry with the Old English Martyrology in CCCC 196. The entry in BuryA reads '.i. god spellboc', and this might be taken to

50 For early knowledge of Paul's collection in England, see J. E. Cross, 'The Literate Anglo-Saxon – on Sources and Disseminations', *PBA* 58 (1972), 84–5.

51 *Preaching*, p. 42.

52 'Donations', p. 27, n. 94.

53 *Martyrologium* I, 87*–8*.

point to a gospel-book, word-division in Anglo-Saxon manuscripts being rather inconsistent; but the preceding '.iiii. Cristes bec' in the same booklist clearly speaks against such an interpretation.

In Indicia, *godspelles traht* follows immediately after passages dealing with the other books containing lessons for Nocturns. Kluge's translation, 'ein anderes Buch . . . in dem Religiöses steht' is certainly mistaken. OE *godspelltraht* and *godspelles traht* are also used for Gregory the Great's *Homiliae in euangelia* in Wærferth's translation of Gregory's *Dialogi* (281.9 and 283.1f.), while Ælfric's *godspeltrahtas* (*Catholic Homilies* I, 594.16) may refer to homilies or collections of homilies. Ælfric's *trahtboc*, four times in the Catholic Homilies, more generally signifies writings by the Fathers, but OE *traht*, frequent in Ælfric's homiletic works, means a homily by a Latin writer or by Ælfric himself. In the Old English Benedictine Rule[54] the word is even employed for a sermon or homily read as a lesson in the Night Office. The rare meaning 'gospel, a passage from the gospels', in RegC 416.722 and in Ælfric's *Catholic Homilies* I, 166.7, may have come about by a metonymic shift, while the sense 'exposition, commentary', to be found in glosses and glossaries, appears to be secondary. Förster[55] explains *traht* as an instance of back-derivation from *trahtian*, as opposed to the homonymous loan-word *traht* 'tractus' (in the mass). OE *trahtnian* and *trahtnung* are frequently used by Ælfric with reference to the exposition of gospel texts in homilies by the Fathers and by Haymo of Auxerre; cf. also *trahtnere*.

### *Surviving manuscripts*[56]

**M.1** Cambridge, University Library, Ii. 2. 19 + Kk. 4.13 (Norwich, s. xi$^{ex}$).
**M.2** Cambridge, Pembroke College 23 + 24 (s. xi$^{2}$; provenance Bury St Edmunds).
**M.3** Durham, Cathedral Library, A. III. 29 + B. II. 2 (Durham, s. xi$^{ex}$).
**M.4** Lincoln, Cathedral Library, 158 (C. 2. 2) (s. xi$^{ex}$).
**M.5** London, BL Harley 652 (St Augustine's, Canterbury, s. xi/xii).
**M.6** London, BL Royal 2. C. III (Rochester, s. xi$^{ex}$).
**M.7** Salisbury, Cathedral Library, 179 (Salisbury, s. xi$^{ex}$).
**M.8** Worcester, Cathedral Library, F. 92 (s. xi$^{2}$).

Fragment of a homiliary manuscript: 'List', no. 209.

[54] *Die angelsächsischen Prosabearbeitungen der Benediktinerregel*, ed. A. Schröer, Bibliothek der angelsächsichen Prosa 2 (Kassel, 1885–8), repr. with appendix by H. Gneuss (Darmstadt, 1964), p. 33, line 20.

[55] 'Die liturgische Bedeutung von ae. *traht*', *Beiblatt zur Anglia* 53 (1942), 181.

[56] **M.1** and **M.3** are complete for the church year. All manuscripts divide the homilies into lessons.

BIBLIOGRAPHY R. Grégoire, *Homéliaires liturgiques médiévaux: Analyse de manuscrits*, Biblioteca degli 'Studi medievali' 12 (Spoleto, 1980); C. L. Smetana 'Ælfric and the Early Medieval Homiliary', *Traditio* 15 (1959), 163–204, and 'Paul the Deacon's Patristic Anthology', *The Old English Homily and its Backgrounds*, ed. P. E. Szarmach and B. F. Huppé (Albany, NY, 1978), pp. 75–97; and J. C. Pope, *Homilies of Ælfric: a Supplementary Collection*, 2 vols., EETS o.s. 259–60 (London, 1967–8) I, 157–71.

## N. Legendary

I prefer this term for the collection of saints' lives used throughout the church year in the Night Office, although liturgiologists often make a distinction between passionals (containing only the lives of martyrs) and legendaries (including confessors' lives): our manuscript evidence for the late Anglo-Saxon period consists solely of books that combine martyrs' and confessors' lives, while the only Latin term for such books seems to have been *passionalis* (ÆPast, and see below for Old English terms), apart from names possibly used for books containing both saints' lives and other types of Office lessons (see above, p. 120). The manuscript legendaries which survive from the late Anglo-Saxon period seem to go back to a collection originally compiled in the north of France, which may have been adopted as the standard legendary of the English church in the course of the tenth century. A legendary of this type has been used by Ælfric as the source on which the Old English translations of his Lives of Saints and of the pieces for saints' days in his Catholic Homilies are based.

Individual lives of saints or small groups of such lives are often found either in separate manuscripts or together with other liturgical or non-liturgical matter; these books cannot be classed as legendaries and have not been listed below. Extant Anglo-Saxon examples are numerous, and there is no doubt that such books or parts of books could be employed for reading at the Office; they are often marked for reading, texts having been divided into *lectiones*, and they may also include the Office and mass for the particular saint's day, as can be seen, for instance, in CCCC 183, a copy of Bede's prose and verse *uitae* of St Cuthbert. Future editors of saints' lives would do well to record whenever a life or part of it is marked for reading in the Office.

Homilies read on individual saints' days in the Night Office may be included in a legendary; this is the case in **N.1**. In the legendaries listed below, division of saints' lives into lessons is only found in a few cases in **N.3**.

### *Old English terminology*

*passionalis, passionale*: ÆPast 13.52 (MSS X and Gg; but MS O reads *pastoralem*), corresponding to Latin *passionalem* in ÆPast 51.137; cf. Worc.A 1: 'Đeo englissce passionale.'
*martirlogium*: Indicia 30.

*Passionalis, passionale* is recorded neither in the dictionaries of Old English nor by Funke, *Lehn- und Fremdwörter*, but as it appears in Old English contexts, we shall have to consider it as a loan-word. Fehr's translation 'Heiligenleben' in ÆPast is acceptable, but his equation with *martyrologium*[57] is misleading; cf. also Gatch's equation of *martyrologium* in Egbert with *passionalem* in ÆPast[58] (but see below). The word – and the book – are missing in Ælfric's list in ÆPast 126/127.157.

Although the instance of *martirlogium* in Indicia 30 is translated 'ein Martyrologium' in Kluge's edition, the word certainly refers to a legendary: it occurs in Indicia among the books of the Office, between the bible and the homiliary, and it is clearly distinguished from the martyrology used in the chapter Office, which comes in its proper place (section 45) in Indicia and is there called 'the small martyrology': 'Đonne þu gehwædne martirlogium habban wille . . .' This use of OE *martirlogium* for a legendary seems exceptional; see below, section **P**.

### *Surviving manuscripts*

**N.1** London, BL Cotton Nero E. i + Cambridge, Corpus Christi College 9 (Worcester, s. xi^med) [complete for the church year].

**N.2** London, BL Arundel 91 (St Augustine's, Canterbury, s. xi/xii) [September–November]; see N. R. Ker, *Medieval Manuscripts in British Libraries* II (Oxford, 1977), 289.

**N.3** Oxford, Bodleian Library, Fell 1 + Fell 4 (Salisbury, s. xi^ex) [January–October].

**N.4** Oxford, Bodleian Library, Fell 3 (Salisbury, s. xi/xii) [January–June].

BIBLIOGRAPHY G. Phillippart, *Les Légendiers latins et autres manuscrits hagiographiques*, Typologie des sources du moyen âge occidental 24–5 (Turnhout, 1977); W. Levison, 'Conspectus Codicum Hagiographicorum', MGH, Script. rer. Meroving. 7 (Hanover, 1919–20), 545–6; P. H. Zettel, 'Ælfric's Hagiographic Sources and the Latin Legendary preserved in BL MS

57 *Hirtenbriefe*, p. lxxxvi. 58 *Preaching*, p. 43.

Cotton Nero E. i + CCCC MS 9 and other Manuscripts' (unpubl. D.Phil. dissertation, Oxford Univ., 1979), and 'Saints' Lives in Old English: Latin Manuscripts and Vernacular Accounts: Ælfric', *Peritia* 1 (1982), 17–37; and Kotzor, *Martyrologium* 1, 275*–8*.

## **O.** Books with Special Offices

One of the results of the continental reforms of the liturgy in the eighth and ninth centuries was the considerable accretions in the monastic Office, including the Office of the Dead, the Office of All Saints, the Office of the Blessed Virgin Mary, the Office of the Holy Trinity, and the Office of the Holy Cross. In the course of the tenth and eleventh centuries, these offices found their way to England, where they became part of the monastic horarium. Such supplementary, or votive, offices do not seem to have been collected into independent books; one or more of them is found in other Office-books like the 'primitive' breviary (**O.1**), the collectar (**O.3**), the psalter (**O.4** and **O.5**) or other volumes with miscellaneous contents. This explains why there is no specific Old English term. Later in the Middle Ages, some of these accretions, especially the Horae BMV, formed the basis for the book of private devotions then widely in use, the Book of Hours or Prymer. But it is possible that some or all of the special offices may also have served for private devotions even in Anglo-Saxon times; those in **O.2** and **O.3** could have been employed in this way.

### *Surviving manuscripts*

**O.1** Cambridge, Corpus Christi College 391: see **F.1**.
**O.2** London, BL Cotton Tiberius A. iii (? Christ Church, Canterbury, s. xi$^{med}$).
**O.3** London, BL Cotton Titus D. xxvi + xxvii: see **G.3**.
**O.4** London, BL Royal 2. B. V (addition of s. xi$^{2}$): see **H.15**.
**O.5** Oxford, Bodleian Library, Douce 296: see **H.18**.

A fragment of the Office of the Dead is in **H.13**.

BIBLIOGRAPHY E. S. Dewick, *Facsimiles of Horae de Beata Maria Virgine*, HBS 21 (London, 1902) [edits offices from **O.2** and **O.4**]; E. Bishop, 'On the Origin of the Prymer', *Liturgica Historica* (Oxford, 1918), pp. 211–37; and Gneuss, *Hymnar*, pp. 109–13.

## BOOKS FOR THE CHAPTER OFFICE

Daily, after Prime or after the morning mass, monks or canons assembled in the chapter-house for the chapter Office. This is described in the *Regularis concordia*, ch. 21, in the so-called 'Benedictine Office'[59] and in the Rule of Chrodegang, ch. 16. Among the texts sung or read at this service was the entry in the Martyrology (see below, section **P**) for the coming day, followed by the announcement of obits and anniversaries of that day, and a chapter from the Rule of St Benedict (for monks) or the Rule of Chrodegang (for canons). On feast-days (and Sundays?), however, the gospel for the day was read (possibly followed by a homily), instead of the chapter from one of the Rules.

### **P.** Martyrology

This book contains brief notices of the lives and passions of the saints (that is, martyrs *and* confessors – despite the title of the book), arranged in the order of the year; each day may have notices of one or more saints, according to the dates of their festivals. Following earlier forerunners, several Latin martyrologies were composed during the ninth century, but that written *c.* 850 × 865 by Usuard, a monk of Saint-Germain-des-Prés became the text generally accepted for use in the chapter Office and must have been introduced in England in the tenth century. All the manuscripts listed below contain the work of Usuard. There is no doubt that **P.1** and **P.2** were actually used for reading in chapter, as they also contain the Rule of St Benedict; the Durham manuscript (**P.2**) is most probably the 'Martyrologium et regula' in the Carilef list. It includes further texts for use in the chapter Office: a calender with obit entries and a list of the gospels to be read in chapter, and thus corresponds almost exactly to the type of book described by Fiala and Irtenkauf.[60] For Latin *martyrologium*, see below, on Old English terms.

The Old English Martyrology must have been composed in the ninth century; no Latin martyrology has as yet been found that could have served as its model. There is no evidence for the use of this Old English text in the capitular Office.

#### *Old English terminology*

*martyrologium*, *martirlogium*: Ælfwold 2; Indicia 45; Leofric 18; RegC 400.497 ('on martirlogian'); Worc.A 4.
*martyrliua*: BuryB 2.

59 *The Benedictine Office*, ed. J. M. Ure, pp. 94–5.
60 'Versuch einer liturgischen Nomenklatur', pp. 129–30.

The loan-word *martyr(o)logium* clearly refers to a Latin martyrology in Indicia 45 and RegC, and to a copy of the Old English Martyrology in Worc.A ('þe englisca martirlogium'). The remaining instances probably also denote the Latin book for the chapter Office. But see section **N** above for the use of *martirlogium* (denoting a legendary) in Indicia 30, and for the attempt to distinguish this from the *gehwæde martirlogium* in Indicia 45.

Professor Gatch[61] equates Latin *martyrologium* in the Egbert list and OE *martyrlogium* in the Leofric list with the *passionalis* in ÆPast 13.52 and 51.137, but at least for the item in the Leofric list this seems an unlikely explanation.[62]

OE *martyrliua* may be a corrupt form of the loan-word or, more probably, an interesting loan-formation based on semantic and phonetic associations. The inflexional ending, however, is difficult to explain. In RegC 385.287, Latin *martyrologium* is glossed by *þrowungræding*, which refers to a passage read from the book.

### *Surviving manuscripts*

**P.1** Cambridge, Corpus Christi College 57 (Abingdon, s. x/xi).
**P.2** Durham, Cathedral Library, B. IV. 24 (Durham, s. xi/xii).
**P.3** London, BL Cotton Vitellius C. xii, fols. 114–57 (St Augustine's, Canterbury, s. xi/xii).

Fragment: 'List', no. 66.

BIBLIOGRAPHY J. Dubois, *Les Martyrologes du moyen âge latin*, Typologie des sources du moyen âge occidental 26 (Turnhout, 1978), and Kotzor, *Martyrologium*.

## Q. *Regula S. Benedicti* and Chrodegang's *Regula canonicorum*

Of the Anglo-Saxon copies of the Rule of St Benedict, Oxford, Bodleian Library, Hatton 48 ('List', no. 631) represents the early, interpolated text; all others exhibit the *textus receptus*. 'List', nos. 41 (**P.1**) and 248 (**P.2**) are certainly books for the chapter Office, while the others may or may not have been used for the same purpose. 'List', nos. 55, 248, 379 and 672 are bilingual, with texts in Latin and Old English, but it seems unlikely that the English text was intended for reading in chapter.

All Anglo-Saxon manuscripts of the Rule of Chrodegang have the expanded

[61] *Preaching*, p. 43. [62] Cf. Förster, 'Donations', p. 29, n. 91.

version of the Latin text, and three of them ('List', nos. 60, 206 and 288) are bilingual.

### *Old English terminology*

*regol*: Indicia 46; Worc.A 7.

OE *regol* is frequently used in various senses, including that of an ecclesiastical Rule, especially the Rule of St Benedict. Only the two instances cited above clearly refer to a book containing the Benedictine Rule; as a third instance, Ælfric's *Lives of Saints* I, 152.66 might be added (St Benedict hands his Rule to Maurus and his companions).

In Worc.A we have a reference to a copy of the Old English translation of the Rule, 'þe englisca regol' – or a bilingual copy? In Indicia 46, the word *regol* has so far been consistently misinterpreted. It appears in the following context: '*Regoles* tacen is þæt þu wecge þine hand and stryce mid þinum scytefingre andlang þinre wynstran handa, swylce þu regollige.' Both Kluge (in his edition of Indicia) and Napier[63] interpreted this instance of *regol* as 'Lineal', 'ruler', and the dictionaries followed them. But there cannot be any doubt that a copy of St Benedict's Rule is meant; section 46 in Indicia follows immediately upon two sections concerning the chapter-house and the martyrology, the word for 'ruler' in Indicia (115) and elsewhere is *regolsticca*, whereas OE *regol* is never so used. Obviously, the sign to be made for the book was chosen because of the linguistic association of *regol* and *regolian*.

### *Surviving manuscripts*

For manuscripts of the Rule of St Benedict that include a martyrology, see above, **P.1** and **P.2**. Other manuscripts of the Rule of St Benedict: 'List', nos. 29, 55, 101, 189, 363, 379, 440, 631 and 672.
Manuscripts of the Rule of Chrodegang (including fragments): 'List', nos. 60, 206, 288 and 808.

BIBLIOGRAPHY M. Gretsch, *Die Regula Sancti Benedicti in England und ihre altenglische Übersetzung*, Texte und Untersuchungen zur englischen Philologie 2 (Munich, 1973), and 'Æthelwold's Translation of the *Regula Sancti Benedicti* and

[63] A. S. Napier, 'Contributions to Old English Lexicography', *TPS* (1903–6), 316–17.

its Latin Exemplar', *ASE* 3 (1974), 125–51; and B. Langefeld, 'Die lateinische Vorlage der altenglischen Chrodegang-Regel', *Anglia* 98 (1980), 403–16.

## EPISCOPAL BOOKS AND RITUALS

### R. Pontifical

The pontifical, as its name implies, is a bishop's book, containing the services to be performed by him: the consecration of a church, the ordination of the various orders of the clergy, the blessing of abbots, the consecration of virgins, the coronation of a king, orders for the different kinds of ordeals (not after the twelfth century), and so on. Services that could be performed by a priest might also be found (baptism, marriage and others). Originally, pontifical services were included in sacramentaries (cf. especially **R.12**), but in England they form a separate book from the tenth century onwards, and this is then often combined with a benedictional (see below, section **S**). The texts in **R.3**, **R.9** and **R.11** represent a collection of pontifical *ordines* widely current in Europe in the eleventh century, the so-called Romano-German Pontifical.[64]

#### *Old English terminology*

*bletsingboc*: Leofric 12; *bletsungboc*: Ælfwold 5.
*halgungboc*: Thureth, line 1.[65]

It would be tempting to assume that the Anglo-Saxons meant to distinguish clearly between the pontifical (= *halgungboc*) and the benedictional (= *bletsungboc*), particularly as the verbal elements in the two compounds, OE *halgian* and *bletsian*, seem to suggest a corresponding semantic distinction. However, as pontificals and benedictionals were so often combined, such a distinction seems unlikely; *halgungboc* is in fact used in and for such a combined manuscript, that is, **R.8** and **S.5**, while Förster pointed out that '.i. deorwyrðe bletsingboc 7 .iii. oðre' in the Leofric list must include at least one pontifical.[66] Dobbie thought that *halgung* (in *halgungboc*) refers to the coronation liturgy beginning on 9v of Claudius A. iii,[67] while Napier suggested the interpretation 'a benedictional' for *halgungboc*;[68] it is clear from the manuscript, however, that both were mistaken.

64 Cf. the articles by M. Lapidge, quoted under **R.3** and **R.11**.

65 Ed. E. V. K. Dobbie, *The Anglo-Saxon Minor Poems*, ASPR 6 (New York, 1942), 97; cf. *ibid.* pp. lxxxviii–xc, and D. H. Turner, *The Claudius Pontificals*, HBS 97 (London, 1971), vi–vii.

66 'Donations', p. 26, n. 87.

67 *Anglo-Saxon Minor Poems*, p. lxxxix.

68 'Contributions to Old English Lexicography', p. 299.

*Surviving manuscripts*

**R.1** Cambridge, Corpus Christi College 44 (? St Augustine's, Canterbury, s. xi$^{1}$).

**R.2** Cambridge, Corpus Christi College 146 (Old Minster, Winchester, s. xi$^{in}$; additions made at Worcester, s. xi/xii).

**R.3** Cambridge, Corpus Christi College 163 (s. xi$^{med}$); see M. Lapidge, 'The Origin of CCCC 163', *Trans. of the Cambridge Bibliographical Soc.* 8 (1981), 18–28.

**R.4** Cambridge, Sidney Sussex College △. 5. 15 (100) (Winchester, s. x$^{ex}$; provenance Durham).

**R.5** London, BL Add. 28188 (Exeter, s. xi$^{2}$).

**R.6** London, BL Add. 57337 (? Christ Church, Canterbury, s. x/xi).

**R.7** London, BL Cotton Claudius A. iii, fols. 9–18 and 87–105 (? Christ Church, Canterbury, ? Worcester, s. xi$^{2}$); ed. D. H. Turner, *The Claudius Pontificals*, HBS 97 (London, 1971).

**R.8** London, BL Cotton Claudius A. iii, fols. 31–86 and 106–50 (Worcester or York, s. x/xi, xi$^{1}$); ed. Turner, *The Claudius Pontificals.*

**R.9** London, BL Cotton Tiberius C. i, fols. 43–203 (Germany, s. xi$^{med}$; provenance Sherborne and Salisbury).

**R.10** London, BL Cotton Vitellius A. vii (Exeter, s.xi$^{med}$).

**R.11** London, BL Cotton Vitellius E. xii, fols. 116–60 (Germany, s. xi$^{1}$; additions made at York and Exeter, s. xi$^{2}$); see M. Lapidge, 'Ealdred of York and MS Cotton Vitellus E. xii', *YAJ* 55 (1983), 11–25.

**R.12** Oxford, Bodleian Library, Bodley 579: see **A.7**.

**R.13** Paris, BN lat. 943 (? Christ Church, Canterbury, s. x$^{2}$; provenance Sherborne).

**R.14** Paris, BN lat. 10575 (s. x$^{med}$); ed. W. Greenwell, *The Pontifical of Egbert, Archbishop of York, A.D. 732–766*, Surtees Soc. 27 (Durham, 1853) [the attribution to Egbert is unfounded].

**R.15** Rouen, Bibliothèque Municipale, 368 (A. 27) (Crediton, s. xi$^{in}$); ed. G. H. Doble, *Pontificale Lanaletense*, HBS 74 (London, 1937).

**R.16** Rouen, Bibliothèque Municipale, 369 (Y. 7) (New Minster, Winchester, s. x$^{2}$); ed. H. A. Wilson, *The Benedictional of Archbishop Robert*, HBS 24 (London, 1903) [in the title, 'Benedictional' is misleading].

Fragments of manuscript pontificals: 'List', nos. 157 and 525, and one supplementary item. Some pontifical texts are also included in **A.5** and **A.10** and in Cotton Tiberius A. iii (cf. **O.2**).

BIBLIOGRAPHY J. Brückmann, 'Latin Manuscript Pontificals and Benedictionals in England and Wales', *Traditio* 29 (1973), 391–458; Turner, *The Claudius Pontificals*, pp. v–xlii; J. W. Legg, *Three Coronation Orders*, HBS 19 (London, 1900) [edits coronation text from **R.1**]; P. E. Schramm, 'Die Krönung bei den Westfranken und Angelsachsen von 878 bis um 1000',

*Zeitschrift der Savigny-Stiftung für Rechtsgeschichte* 54, Kanonistische Abteilung 23 (1934), 117–242 [includes editions of coronation texts (1) from **R.12**, **R.14**, **R.15**, (2) from **R.2**], and 'Ordines-Studien III. Die Krönung in England', *Archiv für Urkundenforschung* 15 (1937–8), 305–91, at 310–19 [lists manuscripts; add **R.6** to 'Edgar-Ordo']; and 'Iudicium Dei', ed. F. Liebermann, *Die Gesetze der Angelsachsen*, 3 vols. (Halle, 1903–16) I, 401–29 [edits or collates texts from **R.1**, **R.2**, **R.10**, **R.13**, **R.15**, **A.4** and **G.2**].

## S. Benedictional

This book contains the episcopal benedictions to be said during the Canon of the Mass, after the *Pater noster*, on Sundays and feast-days. It might have been classed as one of the books for the mass, and collections of benedictions do in fact occur in sacramentaries, either as a separate section, as in **S.6**, or incorporated in the individual masses, as in **S.8**.[69] But since the benedictional is a book reserved for the use of bishops (and possibly certain abbots), and since it is very often combined with a pontifical, I have preferred to place it here.

### *Old English terminology*

See above, section **R**.

### *Surviving manuscripts*

**S.1** Cambridge, Corpus Christi College 146: see **R.2**.

**S.2** London, BL Add. 28188: see **R.5**.

**S.3** London, BL Add. 49598 (Old Minster, Winchester, s. x²); ed. G. F. Warner and H. A. Wilson, *The Benedictional of St Ethelwold* (Oxford, 1910) [includes facsimile].

**S.4** London, BL Add. 57337: see **R.6**.

**S.5** London, BL Cotton Claudius A. iii, fols. 31–86 and 106–50: see **R.8**.

**S.6** London, BL Cotton Vitellius A. xviii: see **A.5**.

**S.7** London, BL Harley 2892 (Christ Church, Canterbury, s. xi¹); ed. R. M. Woolley, *The Canterbury Benedictional*, HBS 51 (London, 1917).

**S.8** Oxford, Bodleian Library, Bodley 579: see **A.7**.

**S.9** Paris, BN lat. 943: see **R.13**.

**S.10** Paris, BN lat 987 (Winchester, s. x²; Christ Church, Canterbury, s. xi¹).

**S.11** Paris, BN lat. 10575: see **R.14**.

[69] **S.8** also has a separate section containing benedictions 'in cotidianis diebus'.

**S.12** Vatican City, Biblioteca Apostolica Vaticana, Reg. lat. 338: see **K.8**.
**S.13** Rouen, Bibliothèque Municipale, 368 (A. 27): see **R.15**.
**S.14** Rouen, Bibliothèque Municipale, 369 (Y. 7): see **R.16**.

Fragments of manuscript benedictionals: 'List', nos. 202, 259 and 468, and one supplementary item.

BIBLIOGRAPHY E. Moeller, *Corpus Benedictionum Pontificalium*, 4 vols., CCSL 162 and 162A–C (Turnhout, 1971–9) [edits or collates texts in **S.2**, **S.3**, **S.5**, **S.7**, **S.8**, **S.9**, **S.10**, **S.11**, **S.13** and **S.14**]; Brückmann, 'Latin Manuscript Pontificals and Benedictionals'; and Turner, *The Claudius Pontificals*, pp. xi–xx.

## **T.** Manual

This book, now often called a 'ritual', contains the occasional offices that every priest may have to perform, that is, the services for baptism, marriage, visitation of the sick, extreme unction and burial of the dead. Ælfric lists the manual among the books that priests ought to have (ÆPast, see below), and Egbert similarly has a *baptisterium* in his list of required books. However, no Anglo-Saxon manual survives, but one or more of the services mentioned above are found in most of the sacramentaries and pontificals, although not as a continuous sequence of texts. A full inventory of the manual texts in Anglo-Saxon service-books is needed. I have listed below those liturgical manuscripts – and a penitential (**T.4**) – which include several occasional Offices.

Ælfric's mention of a *manualis*, or *handboc*, makes it appear fairly certain that such books must have existed in his day, but, as they would have consisted of not more than one or two quires, they would have been bound up with other books or kept as unbound booklets, and so were easily lost or destroyed in later times. It is difficult to say what exactly Egbert's *baptisterium* contained.

### *Old English terminology*

*handboc*: ÆPast 13.52, 126/7.157; BuryA 13.

In ÆPast, the Old English word corresponds to *manualem* in Ælfric's Latin list of liturgical books (ÆPast 51.137). Here and in BuryA it seems fairly certain that a manual for the occasional offices is meant.[70] Ælfric may be

[70] Cf. Fehr, *Hirtenbriefe*, pp. xci–xcii, and Gatch (*Preaching*, pp. 42–3), who compares *baptisterium* in the Egbert list.

referring to the same kind of book in his Glossary 314.13: 'Manualis: handlin oðþe handboc', while the only certain instance of OE *handboc* with a different meaning is in Byrhtferth's *Manual*,[71] 132.17–19, where the word translates *enchiridion* and *manualis*, a book in which Byrhtferth has written about 'manega þing ymbe gerimcræft'; cf. section **X** below. For another, doubtful reference to a *handboc*, see Lapidge, 'Booklists', above, p. 75.

OE *halsungboc* ((?), *Eccl. Gr.* 231.25) and OE *onsongboc* (marginal note in the pontifical **R.4**, ptd Ker, *Catalogue*, p. 128) denote the same thing: the book handed by the bishop to the exorcist at his ordination, that is, according to the pontificals, 'libellum in quo (con)scripti sunt exorcismi'. Cf. ÆPast 109.103 ('Exorcista is halsigend') and 9.31; *Bussbuch*[72] 190.410 MS O ('Exorcista þæt is halsere'); Wærferth, Dialogues 73.26, *onsang* (a *hapax legomenon* in MSS C and O, but *galder* in MS H). Professor Reynolds tells me that this *halsungboc* or *onsongboc* was probably a symbolic rotulus, or a codex of only a few quires on which exorcisms (either baptismal or non-baptismal or both) were written.

## *Surviving manuscripts*

**T.1** Cambridge, Corpus Christi College 422: see **A.4**.
**T.2** London, BL Cotton Vitellius A. vii: see **R.10**.
**T.3** Oxford, Bodleian Library, Bodley 579: see **A.7**.
**T.4** Oxford, Bodleian Library, Laud Misc. 482 (Worcester, s. xi$^{med}$).
**T.5** Worcester, Cathedral Library, F. 173: see **A.8**.
**T.6** Orléans, Bibliothèque Municipale, 105 (127): see **A.9**.
**T.7** Vatican City, Biblioteca Apostolica Vaticana, Reg. lat. 338: see **S.12**.
**T.8** Rouen, Bibliothèque Municipale, 274 (Y. 6): see **A.10**.
**T.9** Rouen, Bibliothèque Municipale, 368 (A. 27): see **R.15**.

The *Missa ad sponsas benedicendas* is also in **G.2**, **R.8** and **R.16**.

BIBLIOGRAPHY B. Fehr, 'Altenglische Ritualtexte für Krankenbesuch, heilige Ölung und Begräbnis', *Texte und Forschungen zur englischen Kulturgeschichte. Festgabe für Felix Liebermann* (Halle, 1921), pp. 20–67 [prints texts from **T.1** and **T.4**] (this is supplemented for **T.1** by R. I. Page, 'Old English Liturgical Rubrics in Corpus Christi College, Cambridge, MS 422', *Anglia* 96 (1978), 149–58); and P.-M. Gy, 'Collectaire, rituel, processionnal'.

[71] *Byrhtferth's Manual*, ed. S. J. Crawford, EETS o.s. 177 (London, 1929), 132, lines 17–19.
[72] R. Spindler, *Das altenglische Bussbuch (sog. Confessionale Pseudo-Egberti). Ein Beitrag zu den kirchlichen Gesetzen der Angelsachsen* (Leipzig, 1934).

OTHER BOOKS

## U. Consuetudinary

The ordinal contains instructions concerning the texts and performance of the liturgy of mass and Office, either for the whole church year or for certain parts of it. In the consuetudinary (or customary) such liturgical instructions or *ordines* are combined with rules relating to the life and customs of a monastic community or a collegiate church. Such ordinals and consuetudinaries may vary considerably, according to the time and place of their composition and use. I have chosen the heading 'consuetudinary' because the pertinent Anglo-Saxon (and early Anglo-Norman) texts whose editions are listed below do not deal exclusively with liturgical matters. As will be seen, all these texts were intended for use in English monasteries and cathedral priories in the tenth and eleventh centuries. No specific Old English term seems to exist; none of the texts is found as a separate volume.

### *Surviving manuscripts*

**U.1** London, BL Cotton Faustina B. iii, fols. 159–98 (Christ Church, Canterbury, s. $xi^{med}$); London, BL Cotton Tiberius A. iii (? Christ Church, Canterbury, s. $xi^{med}$): see **O.2**; ed. T. Symons, *Regularis Concordia* (London, 1953).

**U.2** Cambridge, Corpus Christi College 265 (Worcester, s. $xi^{med}$); ed. M. Bateson, 'Excerpta ex Institutionibus Monasticis Aethelwoldi', G. W. Kitchin, *Compotus Rolls of the Obedientiaries of St Swithun's Priory, Winchester*, Hampshire Record Soc. (London, 1892), pp. 171–98 [commonly known as Ælfric's Letter to the Monks of Eynsham; a new edition is in preparation by M. McC. Gatch]. See also J. R. Hall, 'Some Liturgical Notes on Ælfric's *Letter to the Monks of Eynsham*', *Downside Rev.* 93 (1975), 297–303.

**U.3** Cambridge, Corpus Christi College 190 (s. $xi^1$; provenance Exeter); ed. in part as 'Teile aus Ælfrics Priesterauszug' by Fehr, *Hirtenbriefe*, pp. 234–49. Erroneously ascribed to Ælfric; see P. Clemoes, 'The Old English Benedictine Office, Corpus Christi College, Cambridge, MS 190, and the Relations between Ælfric and Wulfstan: a Reconsideration', *Anglia* 78 (1960), 275–7, and Symons, *Regularis Concordia*, p. lvii.

**U.4** Durham, Cathedral Library, B. IV. 24 (s. $xi^{ex}$; provenance Durham); see **P.2** and **Y.1**; ed. [from this and five later manuscripts] D. Knowles, *Decreta Lanfranci* (London, 1951); rev. ed. in *Corpus Consuetudinum Monasticarum* III (Siegburg, 1967).

## W. Prayer-Books and Private Prayers

Books of private devotion and private prayers are not part of the official liturgy, but they have been included here because of their general liturgical interest: songs and prayers intended as devotional texts are often taken from the liturgy of mass and Office.

Four of the five surviving Anglo-Saxon prayer-books were written in the eighth or the early ninth century. They do not seem to have continental models, as opposed to other books of the liturgy, and their contents differ considerably. Complete copies of this type of book would include passages from the gospels (particularly those recounting the Passion), psalms and various other liturgical pieces like antiphons and hymns, and, particularly, long series of prayers. A similar kind of devotional book was composed by Alcuin, *De laude Dei et de confessione orationibusque sanctorum*, believed to be based on Insular sources, but preserved only in two continental copies.[73] It has recently been suggested that King Alfred's *enchiridion*, an early kind of commonplace book, may have included what looks like the basic elements of a private prayer-book.[74] A later prayer-book, with a number of its texts in Old English (**W.2**), can also be linked with the earlier books; but it is not, as the editor of the Old English texts has claimed, a 'livre d'heures'; the terms 'Book of Hours', 'Horae', should be reserved for the essentially different kind of devotional book that was widely used in the later Middle Ages.

The genre of the prayer-book may not have been common in the late Anglo-Saxon period, but we find a large number of private prayers, sometimes grouped together, also in combination with a preceding litany, in liturgical manuscripts; some of these texts go back to the old prayer-books. One of the most comprehensive collections, with more than forty prayers, in Arundel 155 (**H.8**), has an Old English interlinear gloss.[75] There is also a series of such prayers in Old English, evidently translated by Ælfric and preserved in Cambridge, University Library, Gg. 3. 28.[76]

A special kind of private prayer is represented by the psalter collects, that is, collects following the individual psalms in a number of Anglo-Saxon (and continental) psalters. For the use of certain supplementary Offices of the

[73] This book has never been edited in full; an edition is now in preparation by Professor Donald A. Bullough. Cf. R. Constantinescu, 'Alcuin et les "Libelli precum"', and D. A. Bullough, 'Alcuin and the Kingdom of Heaven'.

[74] See S. Keynes and M. Lapidge, *Alfred the Great* (Harmondsworth, 1983), p. 268, n. 208.

[75] Ed. F. Holthausen, 'Altenglische Interlinearversionen lateinischer Gebete und Beichten', *Anglia* 65 (1941), 230–54, and J. J. Campbell, 'Prayers from MS Arundel 155', *Anglia* 81 (1963), 82–117.

[76] Cf. D. G. Bzdyl, 'The Sources of Ælfric's Prayers in Cambridge University Library MS. Gg. 3. 28', *N&Q* 222 (1977), 98–102.

monastic liturgy for private devotions in the late Anglo-Saxon period, see section **O** above.

An Old English term for 'prayer-book' does not seem to exist, and I have not found a special Latin expression in Anglo-Saxon sources.

*Surviving manuscripts: prayer-books*

**W.1** Cambridge, University Library, Ll. 1. 10 (? Mercia, s. ix$^{in}$; provenance Cerne); ed. A. B. Kuypers, *The Prayer Book of Aedeluald the Bishop, commonly called the Book of Cerne* (Cambridge, 1902).

**W.2** London, BL Cotton Galba A. xiv (Nunnaminster, Winchester, s. xi$^{in}$ and xi$^{1}$); see E. Bishop, *Liturgica Historica* (Oxford, 1918), pp. 384–91; R. A. Banks, 'Some Anglo-Saxon Prayers from British Museum MS Cotton Galba A. XIV', *N&Q* 210 (1965), 207–13; and B. Muir, 'An Edition of British Library Manuscripts Cotton Galba A. xiv and Cotton Nero A. ii (fols. 3r–13v)' (unpubl. Ph.D. dissertation, Toronto Univ., 1981).

**W.3** London, BL Harley 2965 (Nunnaminster, Winchester, s. viii/ix); ed. W. deG. Birch, *An Ancient Manuscript of the Eighth or Ninth Century* (London, 1889).

**W.4** London, BL Harley 7653 (? Mercia, s. viii/ix) [incomplete]; ed. F. E. Warren, *The Antiphonary of Bangor*, 2 vols., HBS 4 and 10 (London, 1892–5) II, 83–6.

**W.5** London, BL Royal 2. A. XX (Worcester, s. viii$^{2}$); ed. Kuypers, *The Prayer Book of Aedeluald*, pp. 200–25.

*Surviving manuscripts containing private prayers*

**A.3**, **F.1**, **G.3**, **H.1**, **H.7**, **H.8**, **H.9**, **H.13**, **H.18**, **H.20**, **H.22**, **H.25**, **H.26**, **H.27**, **O.1** and **O.2**.

*Surviving manuscripts containing psalter collects*

**H.2**, **H.9**, **H.10** and **H.16**; ed. L. Brou and A. Wilmart, *The Psalter Collects*, HBS 83 (London, 1949).

BIBLIOGRAPHY Gamber, *CLLA*, pp. 150–2; A. Wilmart, 'Le Manuel de prières de Saint Jean Gualbert', *RB* 48 (1936), 259–99; L. Gjerløw, *Adoratio Crucis* (Oslo, 1961) [edits prayers in **H.27** and other texts]; H. Barré, *Prières anciennes de l'Occident à la mère du Sauveur: Des origines à saint Anselme* (Paris, 1963); K. Hughes, 'Some Aspects of Irish Influence on Early English Private Prayer', *Studia Celtica* 5 (1970), 48–61; and B. Raw, 'The Prayers and Devotions in the *Ancrene Wisse*', *Chaucer and Middle English Studies in Honour of Rossell Hope Robbins*, ed. B. Rowland (London, 1974), pp. 260–71.

## X. Liturgical Calendar

Calendars, like consuetudinaries, are not books or texts of the liturgy, but they are very often bound up with such books. They were important tools for organizing the services of a church throughout the year, listing in particular, within the framework of a complicated system of grading, the saints who were to be commemorated. Calendars thus provide extremely useful evidence for the student of the medieval liturgy.[77]

### *Old English terminology*

*gerim*: ÆPast 13.52, 126/127.157; booklist from St Augustine's, Canterbury, ed. Lapidge, 'Booklists' no. III, line 12; gloss in prologue to Egbert's Penitential (in CCCC 265), ed. Ker, *Catalogue*, p. 93.
*gerimboc*: Ælfric, *Catholic Homilies* I, 98.28.

A *computus* serves for calculating the date of Easter and other movable feasts. Computus materials are often found combined with, and partly incorporated into, both 'practical' and metrical calendars. This explains the use of OE *gerim*, which in ÆPast corresponds to *compotum* in ÆPast 51.137, while the Old English gloss in Egbert interprets the same Latin form. Henel[78] has rightly criticized Fehr[79] for translating *gerim* by 'Kalender'; the Old English term, and also *gerimboc*, were probably meant to refer to a *computus* including a calendar; they may possibly have denoted a calendar only, as well as a *computus* without a calendar. In Oxford, Bodleian Library, Junius 121, the Worcester scribe known as the 'tremulous hand' has actually glossed *gerim* (in ÆPast 13.52) by *Kalendarium*, but Henel suggests that this Latin term would also refer to a *computus*.[80] The use of *gerim* as a technical term is probably due to semantic borrowing; for other meanings of the word, see the dictionaries.

[77] Besides such 'practical' liturgical calendars, various versions of a metrical calendar (with one hexameter verse for each day) were known in Anglo-Saxon England and are still extant. This metrical composition was probably meant for teaching purposes; its value as a guide to liturgical usage is limited. A comprehensive study of metrical calendars by Dr Michael Lapidge is *RB* 94 (1984), 326–69. Cf. P. McGurk, 'The Metrical Calendar', *An Eleventh-Century Anglo-Saxon Illustrated Miscellany*, ed. P. McGurk *et al.*, EEMF 21 (Copenhagen, 1983), 44–50, and Gneuss, *Hymnar*, pp. 95–6. I do not list copies of the metrical calendar in section **X**.

[78] H. Henel, *Studien zum altenglischen Computus*, Beiträge zur englischen Philologie 26 (Leipzig, 1934), 1.

[79] *Hirtenbriefe*, p. lxxxvi.

[80] *Studien*, pp. 3 and 9.

*Surviving manuscripts: calendars in liturgical books*

**A.5**, **A.7**, **A.10**, **F.1**, **G.3**, **H.6**, **H.7**, **H.8**, **H.12**, **H.18**, **H.19**, **H.21**, **H.26** and **N.1**.

*Surviving manuscripts: calendars in other books*

**X.15** Cambridge, University Library, Kk. 5. 32 (Glastonbury, s. xi$^{1}$).
**X.16** Cambridge, Trinity College R. 15. 32 (New Minster, Winchester, s. xi$^{in}$; provenance St Augustine's, Canterbury).
**X.17** London, BL Cotton Nero A. ii, fols. 3–13 (West Country, s. x$^{ex}$).
**X.18** London, BL Cotton Vitellius A. xii (Salisbury, s. xi$^{ex}$).
**X.19** Oxford, Bodleian Library, Digby 63 (North Country, s. ix$^{2}$).
**X.20** Oxford, Bodleian Library, Hatton 113 (Worcester, s. xi$^{2}$).
**X.21** Paris, BN lat. 7299, fols. 3–12 (s. x/xi).
**X.22** Paris, BN lat. 10837 (? Northumbria, s. viii$^{in}$); ed. H. A. Wilson, *St Willibrord's Calendar*, HBS 55 (London, 1918).

Fragments of manuscript calendars: 'List', nos. 791 and 895.

BIBLIOGRAPHY F. Wormald, *English Calendars before A.D. 1100*, HBS 72 (London, 1934) [prints all calendars except **X.21** and **X.22**, except that in **A.10** and the fragments]; Kotzor, *Martyrologium* I, 302*–11*. For early Anglo-Saxon calendars, see W. Levison, *England and the Continent in the Eighth Century* (Oxford, 1946), p. 146 and n.5.

## **Y.** Confraternity Book

A confraternity book, or *Liber uitae*, is a record kept by a monastic community, consisting of lists of names of the members of this community, of its benefactors – kings and other royal personages, bishops, landowners and local layfolk – and of the members of other religious bodies with which an agreement of 'confraternity' had been concluded; the texts of these agreements would also be entered in the book. It was the purpose of such confraternities that the community should pray for all those inscribed in their book, the *familiares*, whether living or dead. Detailed accounts of this practice in the late Anglo-Saxon period can be found in ch. 68 of the *Regularis concordia* (services after the death of a brother of another monastery) and in the preface to the *Liber uitae* of New Minster, Winchester (commemoration of the *familiares* during the celebration of mass). In England, the practice is very old; it was already known in the days of the Venerable Bede. I have not found a special Old English term for the confraternity book.

### *Surviving manuscripts*

**Y.1** Durham, Cathedral Library, B. IV. 24 (Durham, s. xi/xii, with additions s. xii and xiii); see **P.2** and **U.4**.

**Y.2** London, BL Add. 40000 (Thorney, s. xi/xii, with later additions); see **D.3**.

**Y.3** London, BL Cotton Domitian vii (Lindisfarne, s. ix$^1$; continued at Chester-le-Street and Durham); ed. A. H. Thompson, *Liber Vitae Ecclesiae Dunelmensis*, Surtees Soc. 136 (Durham, 1923) [facsimile].

**Y.4** London, BL Stowe 944 (New Minster, Winchester, s. xi$^1$, with later additions); see **D.26**; ed. W. deG. Birch, *Liber Vitae: Register and Martyrology of New Minster and Hyde Abbey Winchester*, Hampshire Record Soc. (London, 1892).

A notice of confraternity is in **D.18**; see Ker, *Catalogue*, no. 247.

BIBLIOGRAPHY W. Levison, *England and the Continent in the Eighth Century* (Oxford, 1946), pp. 101–2; E. Bishop, *Liturgica Historica*, pp. 349–61; and D. Knowles, *The Monastic Order in England*, 2nd ed. (Cambridge, 1963), pp. 472–9.[81]

[81] I am greatly indebted to Dr Michael Lapidge, who read an earlier version of this article and made numerous valuable suggestions for its improvement. For information on individual manuscripts, I am grateful to Professor Bernhard Bischoff, Dr Lilli Gjerløw, Dr K. D. Hartzell, Mr Christopher Hohler, Dr Simon Keynes, Dr Günter Kotzor, Dr Alan Piper and Dr Susan Rankin. For a discussion of linguistic and lexicographical aspects of the Old English terms recorded in this article, see H. Gneuss, 'Linguistic Borrowing and Old English Lexicography: Old English Terms for the Books of the Liturgy', *Problems of Old English Lexicography*, ed. A. Bammesberger (Regensburg, 1985), pp. 107–29.

# King Athelstan's books

SIMON KEYNES

In the tenth century, King Athelstan was probably renowned more as a relic-collector than as a bibliophile.[1] By the time of his accession in 924 he had already amassed a collection of holy relics in England,[2] and his mania for relics soon became known on the continent: in 926 messengers from Hugh, duke of the Franks, brought Athelstan a rich variety of gifts, including the standard of St Maurice, a splinter of the cross and a sprig of the crown of thorns, and the duke received in return the hand of King Athelstan's half-sister Eadhild, and many presents besides;[3] at about the same time, a Breton ecclesiastic sent Athelstan some choice holy bones, 'which we know to be dearer to you than all earthly substance'.[4] According to an English source Athelstan employed 'true and wise men' to gather relics for him on the continent,[5] though continental sources suggest that his agents may sometimes have resorted to theft in their eagerness to satisfy the king's appetite.[6] Athelstan's passion for acquiring relics was, however, matched by his generosity in giving them away: many

1 For Athelstan as a collector of relics, see J. A. Robinson, *The Times of St Dunstan* (Oxford, 1923) (hereafter *TSD*), pp. 71–80, and C. Brooke, *The Saxon and Norman Kings* (London, 1963), pp. 132–9.

2 *Select English Historical Documents of the Ninth and Tenth Centuries*, ed. F. E. Harmer (Cambridge, 1914) (hereafter *SEHD*), no. 19 (*EHD*, no. 140); see, further, below, pp. 185–9.

3 *Willelmi Malmesbiriensis Monachi De Gestis Regum Anglorum Libri Quinque*, ed. W. Stubbs, 2 vols., Rolls Ser. (London, 1887–9) (hereafter *GR*) I, 149–51 (*EHD*, no. 8, pp. 308–9). For the date, see P. Lauer, *Les Annales de Flodoard* (Paris, 1905), p. 36 (*EHD*, no. 24, p. 344). On the significance of the relics received from Hugh, see below, p. 194 and n. 245.

4 *Willelmi Malmesbiriensis Monachi De Gestis Pontificum Anglorum Libri Quinque*, ed. N. E. S. A. Hamilton, Rolls Ser. (London, 1870) (hereafter *GP*), pp. 399–400 (*EHD*, no. 228); see, further, below, p. 167.

5 See the Old English text cited below, n. 7; see also *GR* I, 157, and *GP*, p. 398. Theodred, bishop of London, bought some chasubles in Pavia (*Anglo-Saxon Wills*, ed. D. Whitelock (Cambridge, 1930), no. 1); perhaps he bought some relics at the same time.

6 See P. J. Geary, *Furta Sacra: Thefts of Relics in the Central Middle Ages* (Princeton, NJ, 1978), pp. 59–63, citing the *Vita Sancti Bertulfi* ('Ex Vita Bertulfi Renticensis', ed. O. Holder-Egger, MGH, Script. 15 (Hanover, 1887), 631–41, at 635).

churches claimed to have benefited from his munificence, including Exeter,[7] Abingdon,[8] Glastonbury[9] and Malmesbury.[10]

Athelstan's particular enthusiasm for collecting relics may be attributable to the example of his grandfather Alfred, who had received a piece of the cross from Pope Marinus,[11] and who is said always to have kept his relics of the saints with him.[12] It may also have been Alfred's example that lay behind Athelstan's cultivation of learning. In an acrostic poem addressed to Athelstan (see pl. I), the poet 'John' (probably John the Old Saxon) refers to him as one 'more abundantly endowed with the holy eminence of learning';[13] if, as Michael Lapidge suggests, the poem was composed in the late 890s, Athelstan can have been no more than five years old, so it is perhaps advisable to treat the remark not so much as a statement of his actual ability at the time as a prediction of future distinction (which would accord with the spirit of the poem as a whole). Athelstan perhaps received a basic education in the school established by his grandfather,[14] and by the time he became king he may well have fulfilled what the poet had foretold. William of Malmesbury discovered that Athelstan was literate from a contemporary encomium written in 'a certain very old book', and he also reported a belief current in his own day that 'no one more just or learned administered the state';[15] while more recently it has become clear that

[7] An Old English text listing the relics allegedly given by King Athelstan to Exeter occurs in the Leofric Gospels (Oxford, Bodleian Library, Auct. D. 2. 16); the text is ptd M. Förster, *Zur Geschichte des Reliquienkultus in Altengland* (Munich, 1943), pp. 63–114, and trans. *Anglo-Saxon Prose*, ed. M. Swanton (London, 1975), pp. 15–19. A Latin version of the text occurs in the Leofric Missal (Oxford, Bodleian Library, Bodley 579), and is ptd *The Leofric Missal*, ed. F. E. Warren (Oxford, 1883), pp. 3–5.

[8] *Chronicon Monasterii de Abingdon*, ed. J. Stevenson, 2 vols., Rolls Ser. (London, 1858) I, 88 (cf. *ibid.* II, 276–7), and *TSD*, p. 80.

[9] J. Scott, *The Early History of Glastonbury: an Edition, Translation and Study of William of Malmesbury's 'De Antiquitate Glastonie Ecclesie'* (Woodbridge, 1981), pp. 114–15; J. P. Carley, *John of Glastonbury: 'Chronica sive Antiquitates Glastoniensis Ecclesie'*, BAR 47 (Oxford, 1978), 138–9; and *TSD*, pp. 77–8.

[10] *GR* I, 151 (*EHD*, no. 8, p. 309), and *GP*, pp. 397 and 398–9.

[11] Anglo-Saxon Chronicle 886 (for 885) BC, 885 ADEF, and Asser, *Vita Alfredi*, ch. 71. A reference to Marinus's gift also appears in ASC 884 (for 883) BC, 883 DEF. See, further, S. Keynes and M. Lapidge, *Alfred the Great* (Harmondsworth, 1983), p. 254, n. 137.

[12] Asser, *Vita Alfredi*, ch. 104.

[13] See M. Lapidge, 'Some Latin Poems as Evidence for the Reign of Athelstan', *ASE* 9 (1981), 61–98, at 72–83. The poem occurs in Oxford, Bodleian Library, Rawlinson C. 697, 78v; on this manuscript, see *Manuscripts at Oxford: an Exhibition in Memory of Richard William Hunt (1908–1979)*, ed. A. C. de la Mare and B. C. Barker-Benfield (Oxford, 1980), p. 20.

[14] For this school, see Asser, *Vita Alfredi*, chs. 75, 76 and 102 (cf. Keynes and Lapidge, *Alfred the Great*, p. 257, n. 148). William of Malmesbury says that Athelstan was brought up at the Mercian court, but the early-twelfth-century poem he used (see next note) refers generally to Athelstan's early education in schools; see *GR* I, 145 (*EHD*, no. 8, pp. 305–6).

[15] *GR* I, 144 (*EHD*, no. 8, p. 305). Lapidge ('Some Latin Poems', pp. 62–71) has shown that the contemporary encomium, which was evidently in hermeneutic Latin, cannot have been the

Athelstan's court was the meeting-place for a veritable profusion of learned men from different parts of the British Isles and from the continent.[16]

The agents who collected relics for King Athelstan on the continent may on occasion have acquired manuscripts as well, in order to provide more seeds for the king's cultivation of learning; but of course there would have been many other opportunities for the importation of manuscripts into England during the first half of the tenth century.[17] The close political links between the West Saxon royal family and different ruling houses on the continent, cemented by the marriages of no fewer than four (or five) of Athelstan's half-sisters to continental rulers,[18] must have involved among other things the frequent

poem in rhyming hexameters from which William quotes two long extracts (and which probably dates from the early twelfth century), and he raises the possibility that it was none other than the acrostic addressed by John (the Old Saxon) to Athelstan. If this identification is right, we would be left with no good evidence for Athelstan's literacy, beyond a prediction in the acrostic and opinion current in the early twelfth century. According to William (*GR* I, 151: *EHD*, no. 8, p. 309), all of his material on Athelstan (in prose as well as verse, up to the end of the second verse extract) was apparently derived from the poem in rhyming hexameters; and M. Wood ('The Making of King Æthelstan's Empire: an English Charlemagne?', *Ideal and Reality in Frankish and Anglo-Saxon Society*, ed. P. Wormald (Oxford, 1983), pp. 250–72, at 265–6) suggests that this poem was itself a 'translation' into more palatable Latin of the contemporary hermeneutic encomium. This would rule out the acrostic as William's source, and might give historians cause to hope that the bulk of his information on Athelstan was based ultimately on some good authority. It must be admitted, however, that William gives us no reason to believe that the poem in hexameters was closely related to the contemporary encomium; that, indeed, he implies that the encomium was short, and that he preferred the hexameters not only for stylistic reasons but also because they 'augmented' the record of Athelstan's greatness; and that a fair amount of the information given by William would not seem appropriate to an encomium or poem of any date. At best, therefore, we may only hope that the contemporary encomium which told William that Athelstan was literate was not the acrostic (which seems simply to predict that he would become learned), and that the poem in hexameters (and hence William's main account of the king) was based on earlier sources or genuine tradition; and it should be noted in this connection that William himself distinguishes between his main account, said to have been drawn from reliable sources, and some further material on Athelstan, said to have been drawn from popular legend (*GR* I, 155). The *bella Etheltani regis* recorded as present in a manuscript at Glastonbury in 1247 (Cambridge, Trinity College, R. 5. 33, 103v; see Lapidge, 'Some Latin Poems', p. 61, n. 6) would perhaps not have been the contemporary encomium, but it may have been a source used by the later poet and by William, or the later poem itself.

16 See F. M. Stenton, *Anglo-Saxon England*, 3rd ed. (Oxford, 1971), p. 444, and Wood, 'King Æthelstan's Empire', pp. 256–9. Wood includes Egill Skallagrímsson among the learned men who visited Athelstan's court, but I dare say Egill was more at home with Eric Bloodaxe.

17 For lists of the manuscripts themselves, see F. A. Rella, 'Continental Manuscripts Acquired for English Centers in the Tenth and Eleventh Centuries: a Preliminary Checklist', *Anglia* 98 (1980), 107–16, and H. Gneuss, 'A Preliminary List of Manuscripts written or owned in England up to 1100', *ASE* 9 (1981), 1–60.

18 The main sources for the marriages are *The Chronicle of Æthelweard*, ed. A. Campbell (London, 1962), p. 2, and *GR* I, 116–17, 136–7 and 149–51. See R. L. Poole, 'Burgundian

exchange of gifts; moreover, the kings of Wessex were certainly in contact with religious houses elsewhere, foreign dignitaries visited England, and English ecclesiastics were sent on official business to the continent.[19] It is hardly surprising under such circumstances that a quantity of the imported manuscripts ended up in the hands of King Athelstan. Fortunately, he was as generous with his books as he was with his relics. William of Malmesbury wrote that 'there can scarcely have been an old monastery in the whole of England which he did not embellish either with buildings or ornaments or books or estates',[20] and some of the books given by the king to at least a few of the churches survive to this day. The inscriptions which attest Athelstan's former ownership of the manuscripts in question were discussed by Armitage Robinson over sixty years ago;[21] the purpose of the present article is simply to assemble them again, to reproduce them, and to reconsider their interest in the light of more recent scholarship. It cannot be claimed that they afford much insight into the quality of learning available at the court of King Athelstan, not least because they occur in books that the king chose to give away; moreover, all but one of the books in question were written outside Wessex, and a high proportion of them were copies of the gospels.[22] Nevertheless, the inscriptions enable us to identify a group of manuscripts which came into King Athelstan's possession, throwing valuable light on the range of the king's political and ecclesiastical contacts; they reveal how the manuscripts were given to religious

Notes, I: the Alpine Son-in-Law of Edward the Elder', *EHR* 26 (1911), 310–17; Stenton, *Anglo-Saxon England*, pp. 344–7; D. A. Bullough, 'The Continental Background of the Reform', *Tenth-Century Studies*, ed. D. Parsons (Chichester, 1975), pp. 20–36, at 33–4; and below, nn. 27 and 232.

19 For contacts between West Saxon kings and religious houses elsewhere, see Asser, *Vita Alfredi*, ch. 102, and *EHD*, nos. 26 and 228; for foreign dignitaries in England, see *GR* I, 149–50 (*EHD*, no. 8, p. 308), and K. J. Leyser, *Rule and Conflict in an Early Medieval Society: Ottonian Saxony* (London, 1979), p. 88; for Bishop Cenwald's visit to the continent, see below, pp. 198–201, and for Bishop Oda's, see *Richer: Histoire de France (888–995)*, ed. R. Latouche, Les Classiques de l'histoire de France au moyen âge, 2 vols. (Paris, 1930–7) I, 130.

20 *GR* I, 142 (*EHD*, no. 8, p. 304).

21 *TSD*, pp. 51–67. The manuscripts had previously been discussed as a group by S. Turner, *The History of the Anglo-Saxons from the Earliest Period to the Norman Conquest*, 7th ed., 3 vols. (London, 1852) II, 176, n. 101. Rella ('Continental Manuscripts', p. 109) states that 'most of the inscriptions noted by J. A. Robinson are now believed to be forgeries', but does not say which he has in mind.

22 The Athelstan whose books are listed in a short text entered in a manuscript from St Augustine's, Canterbury (BL Cotton Domitian i, 55v; see above, pp. 50–2), has sometimes been regarded as King Athelstan; but if Ker's suggestion (*Catalogue of Manuscripts containing Anglo-Saxon* (Oxford, 1957), p. 186) that the first entry, *de natura rerum*, refers to Domitian i itself is right, the identification would be impossible, since the relevant part of the manuscript was written in the second half of the tenth century. See also *Anglo-Saxon Charters*, ed. A. J. Robertson, 2nd ed. (Cambridge, 1956), Appendix II, no. 6, and pp. 499–500.

houses throughout England, reflecting the king's desire to secure the goodwill and prayers of the church; and in their own way they demonstrate the importance of Athelstan's reign in the continuing process of the revival of religion and learning initiated by King Alfred and brought to fruition by King Edgar.[23]

## MANUSCRIPTS GIVEN TO CHRIST CHURCH, CANTERBURY

### BL Cotton Tiberius A. ii

BL Cotton Tiberius A. ii is a gospel-book, written on the continent, perhaps at Lobbes in Belgium, in the late ninth or early tenth century.[24] After the usual preliminaries on fols. 3–23 (excluding fol. 15), the text of St Matthew's Gospel begins on 24r. Near the bottom of this folio, a scribe has entered a simple inscription in square capitals (see pl. II):

+ODDA REX
+MIHTHILD MATER REGIS

'Odda' is evidently Otto I, who became king of Germany in 936 (and emperor in 962), and who died in 973; 'Mihthild' is his mother Matilda, who was the second wife of Henry the Fowler, and who died in 968. The inscription would thus seem to have been added at some point between 936 and 968 (or possibly 962); the forms of the personal names show that the inscription was added by an English scribe,[25] and so presumably in England, and the script is certainly compatible with the apparent date.[26] Two other inscriptions (discussed further, below) show that Tiberius A. ii came into the possession of King Athelstan and was given by him to Christ Church, Canterbury.

23 I am most grateful to my colleagues David Dumville and Michael Lapidge for much helpful discussion, and to Nicholas Brooks, Mildred Budny, Christopher Hohler, Susan Kelly, Karl Leyser, Patrick McGurk, Rosamond McKitterick, Professor H. S. Offler, Dagmar Schneider, Richard Sharpe and Patrick Wormald for their advice on particular points. I should also like to thank Professor Raymond Page for allowing new photography of Cambridge, Corpus Christi College 183; the photographs were taken by Mildred Budny. The cost of producing the plates which accompany this article has been met in part by a generous grant from the Master and Fellows of Trinity College, Cambridge.

24 See E. M. Thompson and G. F. Warner, *Catalogue of Ancient Manuscripts in the British Museum, Part II: Latin* (London, 1884), pp. 35–7; A. G. Watson, *Catalogue of Dated and Datable Manuscripts c. 700–1600 in the Department of Manuscripts, the British Library*, 2 vols. (London, 1979) I, 105 (no. 548); and P. E. Schramm and F. Mütherich, *Denkmale der deutschen Könige und Kaiser* (Munich, 1962), p. 140 (no. 64). For the manuscript's origin at Lobbes, see E. Bishop, *Liturgica Historica* (Oxford, 1918), p. 141, n. 1, and *TSD*, p. 60.

25 See Lapidge, 'Some Latin Poems', p. 93 and n. 147.

26 For the use of similar capitals in the first half of the tenth century, see below, p. 155.

Nothing is known of the early history of the manuscript on the continent, but the inscription naming Otto and Matilda suggests that it may have had some connection with the Saxon court of Germany, and that its arrival in England should probably be understood in the context of the relations between this court and King Athelstan. In the *Gesta Ottonis* (written in the 960s), Hrotsvitha of Gandersheim describes how Henry the Fowler (919–36) set about finding a suitable wife for his son Otto I: he sent his representatives to the court of King Athelstan, apparently with the specific intention that they should bring back Edith, daughter of the late king, Edward the Elder; Athelstan's generous response, however, was to give Otto a choice between two of his half-sisters, Edith and *Adiva*, both of whom he duly dispatched to Germany with countless treasures, though in the event it was Edith who was chosen as Otto's bride.[27] The marriage seems to have taken place towards the end of 929 or early in 930;[28] it is quite likely that the visit of Cenwald, bishop of Worcester, to the continent in October 929 was in some way connected with the celebrations, though our only source for this visit creates the impression that the bishop's purpose was simply to tour the monasteries of Germany.[29] Otto's marriage to Edith established a direct link between the Liudolfing and West Saxon dynasties, and if we may assume that they remained in touch there would have been many occasions in the years from 929 onwards for the

27 *Hrotsvit Opera*, ed. H. Homeyer (Munich, 1970), pp. 408–10 (lines 66–124); trans. B. H. Hill, *Medieval Monarchy in Action: the German Empire from Henry I to Henry IV* (London, 1972), pp. 122–3. According to Æthelweard (*Chronicle of Æthelweard*, ed. Campbell, p. 2), the second sister (whom he does not name) was married to a 'certain king near the Alps'; this is developed by William of Malmesbury, who names her as *Aldgitha* (*GR* I, 117) or *Elfgiva* (*ibid.* p. 137). Given the variety of forms, it is uncertain whether the second sister was called Eadgifu, Ealdgyth or Ælfgifu. Poole, 'Alpine Son-in-Law', pp. 313–15, suggested that her husband was Conrad, king of Burgundy; but E. Hlawitschka, 'Die verwandtschaftlichen Verbindungen zwischen dem hochburgundischen und dem niederburgundischen Königshaus. Zugleich ein Beitrag zur Geschichte Burgunds in der 1. Hälfte des 10. Jahrhunderts', *Grundwissenschaften und Geschichte. Festschrift für Peter Acht*, ed. W. Schlögl and P. Herde, Münchener historische Studien, Abteilung geschichtliche Hilfswissenschaften 15 (Kallmünz, 1976), 28–57, at 52–6, argues that the sister who married a 'certain king near the Alps' is the same person as the Eadgifu who married Louis, 'prince of the Aquitainians' (below, p. 191 and n. 232), whom he identifies as Louis, brother of Rudolf II, king of upper Burgundy.

28 *Die Sachsengeschichte des Widukind von Korvei*, ed. P. Hirsch and H.-E. Lohmann, 5th ed., MGH, Script. rer. Germanicarum (Hanover, 1935), p. 54 (I. 37). For discussion of the date, see K. Schmid, 'Neue Quellen zum Verständnis des Adels im 10. Jahrhundert', *Zeitschrift für die Geschichte des Oberrheins* n.s. 69 (1960), 184–232, at 186–203, and 'Die Thronfolge Ottos des Grossen', *Zeitschrift der Savigny-Stiftung für Rechtsgeschichte*, Germanistische Abteilung 81 (1964), 80–163, at 101–25 (both repr. in *Königswahl und Thronfolge in ottonisch–frühdeutscher Zeit*, ed. E. Hlawitschka, Wege der Forschung 178 (Darmstadt, 1971), 389–416 and 417–508). See also K. Leyser, 'Die Ottonen und Wessex', *FS* 17 (1983) 73–97, at 75–8.

29 See below, pp. 198–201.

exchange of gifts between them; Edith herself died in 946,[30] but the fact that Ealdorman Æthelweard presented his Latin translation of the Anglo-Saxon Chronicle to Matilda of Essen,[31] granddaughter of Otto and Edith, shows that contacts were maintained for some time thereafter.

The inscription naming Otto and Matilda could have been made on receipt of the book or some time after its arrival, and its purpose may have been to commemorate the donors or to record its former association with the Liudolfing royal family. It remains uncertain, therefore, whether Tiberius A. ii was given to Athelstan at the time of Otto's marriage to Edith in 929/30 or on a subsequent occasion in the 930s; and since there is always a possibility that the names were simply inserted in the gospel-book for the sake of remembering Otto and Matilda in the owner's prayers, one cannot even be sure that the manuscript itself was actually a gift from the Saxon court. It is accordingly no more than a reasonable guess to conclude that Tiberius A. ii may have been given to Athelstan by Otto and Matilda as part of an exchange of presents between the two families on the occasion of Otto's accession to the throne in 936, and that the inscription naming the donors was entered soon after the manuscript's arrival in England.

The two inscriptions which demonstrate that the manuscript was given by King Athelstan to Christ Church, Canterbury, occur on what is now fol. 15; this folio must originally have preceded fol. 3 (the beginning of the preliminaries in the gospel-book), since there are traces of offset from 3r on 15v (and from 16r on 14v), and it was probably added to the manuscript at the time of the donation.[32] The primary inscription of the two is doubtless that in square minuscule on 15v (see pl. III):

Volumen hoc euuangelii . ÆÐELSTAN . Anglorum basyleos . et curagulus totius Bryttannie . deuota mente . Dorobernensis cathedre primatui . tribuit ecclesie Christo dicatæ . quod etiam archiepiscopus . huius ac ministri ecclesie . presentes successoresque . curiosis affectibus perenniter agnoscant . scilicet et custodire studeant . prout Deo rationem sunt reddituri . ne quis in æternum furua fruade deceptus . hinc illud arripere conetur . Sed manens hic maneat . honoris exemplumque cernentibus . perpetue sibi demonstret . Vos etenim obsecrando postulo . memores ut uestris mei mellifluis oraminibus . consonaque uoce fieri prout confido . non desistatis . ,[33]

[30] *Widukind*, ed. Hirsch and Lohmann, pp. 99–100 (II.41).

[31] *Chronicle of Æthelweard*, ed. Campbell, pp. xii–xiii and 1–2.

[32] The manuscript is difficult to collate, since all the leaves are now mounted separately. Fol. 15 was still at the beginning of the manuscript in the early seventeenth century, to judge from the Cottonian list of contents on 2v (cf. the Cotton catalogue of 1621, BL Harley 6018, 5r and 6r); see also below, n. 47.

[33] 'Athelstan, king of the English and ruler of the whole of Britain, with a devout mind gave this gospel-book to the primatial see of Canterbury, to the church dedicated to Christ. And may the archbishop and the community of this church, present and future, for ever regard

The scribe who wrote this inscription has been identified by Pierre Chaplais as one who between 944 and 949 wrote several charters issued in the names of King Edmund and King Eadred.[34] Chaplais located this scribe, in his capacity as a writer of charters, in the scriptorium of the Old Minster at Winchester, and so regarded the identification as 'one further proof of the activity of the Winchester scriptorium as a centre for the writing of royal documents during Athelstan's reign'; but it can be argued on various grounds that the scribe is more likely to have been one in the personal service of the king himself.[35] Whatever the case, Chaplais's identification is of the utmost importance because it suggests that the scribe's career as a writer of royal documents spanned at least ten years, from 939 (or some time before) until 949 (or some time after). In the inscription in Tiberius A. ii, he employs language which shows that he was already familiar with the conventions of charters, notably in his use of the royal style 'Anglorum basyleos et curagulus totius Bryttannie': a very similar style, 'basileus Anglorum et eque totius Bryttannie orbis curagulus', occurs in charters dated between 935 and 939,[36] and its use within this period suggests that the inscription dates from the closing years of Athelstan's reign.

The inscription on 15r has been examined in detail by Michael Lapidge.[37] It is the poem *Rex pius Æðelstan*, written in Caroline minuscule evidently by a scribe of continental origin (see pl. IV). To judge from the present tenses in the second line, the poem was composed during Athelstan's lifetime, and the reference to him as one whom God set as king over the English so that he 'might be able to conquer other fierce kings, treading down their proud necks', if not mere hyperbole, would seem to place its composition more

the donation with diligent feelings, and in particular may they take pains to safeguard it, in as much as they are to render account to God, lest anyone hereafter, misled by dark deception, should try to steal the book from this place. But may it remain here in safe custody, and may it in perpetuity provide an example of glory for those looking at it. For I beseech you in prayer that you will not cease to be mindful of me in your mellifluous orations, as I trust will take place with harmonious voice.' Ptd W. deG. Birch, *Cartularium Saxonicum*, 3 vols. and index (London, 1885–99) (cited hereafter as *BCS* and number) 711; MS *fruade* is evidently an error for *fraude*.

[34] P. Chaplais, 'The Anglo-Saxon Chancery: from the Diploma to the Writ', repr. *Prisca Munimenta*, ed. F. Ranger (London, 1973), pp. 43–62, at 46–7, and 'The Origin and Authenticity of the Royal Anglo-Saxon Diploma', repr. *ibid.* pp. 28–42, at 41. The charters in question are S (= P. H. Sawyer, *Anglo-Saxon Charters: an Annotated List and Bibliography*, R. Hist. Soc. Guides and Handbooks 8 (London, 1968)) 497, 510, 528, 535 and 552 (*BCS* 791, 813, 820, 869 and 877).

[35] See S. Keynes, *The Diplomas of King Æthelred 'the Unready' 978–1016: a Study in their Use as Historical Evidence* (Cambridge, 1980), pp. 14–83, esp. 26.

[36] S 430, 438 and 446 (*BCS* 707, 714 and 742); variant styles, e.g. with *rex* for *basileus*, occur in several other charters issued during the same period.

[37] Lapidge, 'Some Latin Poems', pp. 93–7.

precisely after Athelstan's victory at the battle of *Brunanburh* in 937.[38] Following his praise of Athelstan in general terms, the poet describes how the king adorned (*ornauit*) the book 'with golden headings and places set with jewels' ('aureolis . . . titulis gemmigerisque locis'), and how he 'embellished it by having its covers adorned with patterned jewels' ('hoc . . . scematicis ornarier ora lapillis auxit');[39] he also states that the king gave the book to Christ Church, urges the community and the archbishop to look after it, and wishes dire punishment on anyone who should take it away. In short, the poem *Rex pius Æðelstan* is a celebration of the king and his munificence, complementing the actual record of donation on 15v, and it seems most likely that it was added to the manuscript at Christ Church, Canterbury; quite apart from its own intrinsic interest, it thus provides valuable evidence for the presence of a continental scribe at Canterbury in the late 930s.[40]

Tiberius A. ii was certainly still at Christ Church in the eleventh and twelfth centuries, when a number of documents in Latin and Old English relating to the community's property were entered in available spaces,[41] but by the early seventeenth century it had come into the possession of Sir Robert Cotton. It was he who provided an elaborate title-page for the manuscript (now 1r), probably in about 1612, using a leaf taken from a late-fifteenth-century Flemish manuscript[42] and incorporating a poem written in gold letters on a blue panel:

Saxonidum dux atque decus primumque monarcham
inclitus Ælfredum qui numerauit auum,

38 *Ibid.* p. 97, n. 158.

39 It is uncertain what the poet meant by all this (*ibid.* p. 96, nn. 155–6), but the simplest explanation is that Athelstan provided the gospel-book with a jewel-encrusted binding.

40 See N. Brooks, *The Early History of the Church of Canterbury: Christ Church from 597 to 1066* (Leicester, 1984), pp. 219–20. Dr Lapidge kindly informs me that lines 15–16 of *Rex pius Æðelstan* are taken from an epigram by Pope Damasus with the incipit 'Psallere qui docuit' (listed D. Schaller and E. Könsgen, *Initia carminum Latinorum saeculo undecimo antiquiorum* (Göttingen, 1977), no. 12730, and ptd A. Ferrua, *Epigrammata Damasiana* (Rome, 1942), p. 228). A copy of the epigram occurs in the Vespasian Psalter (BL Cotton Vespasian A. i, 4v), ptd *The Vespasian Psalter*, ed. S. M. Kuhn (Ann Arbor, Mich., 1965), p. 300. The Vespasian Psalter was at St Augustine's, Canterbury, in the Middle Ages; so it is tempting to speculate that the poet knew the epigram from this manuscript, which he had seen in the neighbouring house. *Rex pius Æðelstan* should be compared generally with the poems written in praise of Carolingian rulers (such as Lothar and Charles the Bald) and entered in manuscripts commissioned by or presented to the rulers in question; see, e.g., Schramm and Mütherich, *Denkmale*, pp. 123 (no. 25), 129–30 (no. 42), 134–5 (no. 52), 135 (no. 54) and 136–7 (no. 56).

41 For details, see Ker, *Catalogue*, no. 185.

42 See F. Wormald, 'The So-Called Coronation Oath-Books of the Kings of England', *Essays in Honor of Georg Swarzenski*, ed. O. Goetz (Chicago, Ill., and Berlin, 1951), pp. 233–7, at 234. Wormald observes that a leaf from the same Flemish manuscript was used in the making of a similar title-page for the 'Athelstan Psalter' (BL Cotton Galba A. xviii), which was in Cotton's possession by 1612.

imperii primas quoties meditantur habenas
me uoluit sacrum regibus esse librum.[43]

This poem was clearly composed at a time when Alfred's reputation had come to surpass that of Athelstan himself, and this alone would be enough to preclude the possibility that it is of pre-Conquest origin.[44] Indeed, it is likely that it is no older than Cotton's time and that it was composed especially for the title-page. Cotton may simply have assumed that a gospel-book given by the king to Christ Church, Canterbury, must have been intended for a special purpose, namely to serve as the book on which future kings would swear their coronation oath, and the poem may therefore be no more than a manifestation of a collector's natural tendency to enhance (or to exaggerate) the interest of his own possessions.[45] Certainly there is no evidence that Tiberius A. ii was ever used for such a purpose in the Middle Ages,[46] but it is interesting that on the occasion of the coronation of Charles I in 1626 Sir Robert Cotton seems to have been determined to ensure that his precious book would live up to its reputation:

About eight of the clocke his Majestie was expected to have landed at Sir Robart Cottons staires, my Lord Marshall having himselfe given order for carpets to be laied. Sir Robart stood readie ther to receave him with a booke of Athelstans being the fower Evangelists in Lattin, that Kings Saxon epistle praefixed, upon which for divers hundred yeares together the Kings of England had solemnlie taken ther coronation oath. But the roiall barge bawked those stepps soe fitlie accommodated, and being put forward was run on ground at the Parliament staires . . . yet I thinke a little after, the booke was delivered.[47]

43 'The renowned leader and ornament of the Saxons [*sc.* Athelstan], who counted Alfred as his grandfather and first monarch, wanted me to be a book sacred to kings [? an oath-book for kings], whenever they were contemplating the initial responsibilities [lit. bonds] of rule.'

44 For this ('remote') possibility, see Lapidge, 'Some Latin Poems', p. 94. On the cult of Alfred, see Keynes and Lapidge, *Alfred the Great*, pp. 44–8; it is the reference to Alfred as 'first monarch' that seems particularly to reflect post-Conquest developments in the cult.

45 In the Cottonian list of contents on 2v, and in the Cotton catalogue of 1621 (no. 6 in BL Harley 6018, 5r and 6r), the manuscript is described explicitly as one sacred to the kings of England, 'in as much as they who formerly touched it when they were to be crowned were wont to take a solemn oath' ('sacer hic regibus Angliae codex, quippe qui olim eo tacto, cum regio diademate cingerentur, iuramentum solemne praestare soliti'). This should presumably be regarded as a clarification of the tradition represented by the poem on the title-page.

46 Robinson (*TSD*, p. 67) suggested that Athelstan himself may have taken his coronation oath on BL Royal 1. B. VII; but see below, pp. 185–9. The Anglo-Saxon coronation *ordines* show that the oath was taken at the altar, but there is no explicit reference to any sacred book on which it was sworn.

47 From a letter of Sir Symonds D'Ewes to Sir Martin Stuteville (BL Harley 383, fol. 24), ptd H. Ellis, *Original Letters Illustrative of English History*, 3 vols. (London, 1824) III, 213–19; for the politics behind this incident, see C. E. Wright, 'The Elizabethan Society of Antiquaries and the Formation of the Cottonian Library', *The English Library Before 1700*, ed. F. Wormald and

In the event it would appear that King Charles actually took his oath on a bible which usually stood on the altar at Whitehall.[48] There is some possibility that Tiberius A. ii was used for the coronation of James II in 1685, so it may be that Sir Robert Cotton's efforts were not entirely in vain.[49]

## London, Lambeth Palace 1370

London, Lambeth Palace 1370 is a 'pocket' gospel-book, generally known as the MacDurnan Gospels; it was written in Ireland, probably at Armagh, in the second half of the ninth century.[50] The recto of fol. 1 was originally left blank, and the book opens with a frontispiece depicting the four evangelist symbols (1v) followed by the text of Matthew I.1–17 (2r–3r), here serving as a preface to the whole; 3v and 4*r were originally left blank, and the Gospel of St Matthew begins, after a portrait of the evangelist (4*v), on 5r.[51] At a later date, apparently in the second quarter of the tenth century, the following inscription in display capitals was entered on 3v (see pl. V):

+MÆIELBRIÐVS·MAC<br>
DVRNANI·ISTV̄·TEXTV̄<br>
PER·TRIQVADRV̄·D̄O·<br>
DIGNE·DOGMATIZAT·<br>
+AST·AETHELSTANVS·<br>
ANGLOSÆXA͡N̄A·REX·ET·<br>
RECTOR·DORVERNENSI·<br>
METROPOLI·DAT·Ꝑ ÆVV̄:.[52]

C. E. Wright (London, 1958), pp. 176–212, at 207, and K. Sharpe, *Sir Robert Cotton 1586–1631: History and Politics in Early Modern England* (Oxford, 1979), p. 140. The 'Saxon epistle' prefixed to the gospel-book presumably refers to the prose inscription in Athelstan's name, which would at this time have been in its original place.

48 See *The Manner of the Coronation of King Charles the First of England*, ed. C. Wordsworth, HBS 2 (London, 1892), 24.

49 *Ibid.*, and Wormald, 'The So-Called Coronation Oath-Books', p. 235; Wormald rightly concluded that the whole story about Tiberius A. ii was probably 'a romantic "invention" of Sir Robert Cotton'.

50 M. R. James and C. Jenkins, *A Descriptive Catalogue of the Manuscripts in the Library of Lambeth Palace* (Cambridge, 1930–2), pp. 843–5; F. Henry, *Irish Art During the Viking Invasions (800–1020 A.D.)* (London, 1967), pp. 102–5; J. J. G. Alexander, *Insular Manuscripts: 6th to the 9th Century*, Survey of Manuscripts Illuminated in the Brit. Isles 1 (London, 1978), 86–7 (no. 70); and Ker, *Catalogue*, no. 284.

51 The collation of the first quire (fols. 1–15) of the manuscript is as follows: I$^{18}$, plus 1 (fol. 4) before 4; 14, 15 and 18 cancelled. The present 4r is a later medieval illumination (depicting the crucifixion); it was formerly pasted down on 4*r, but the leaves are now separated, and fol. 4* is actually unnumbered.

52 'Mael Brigte mac Tornain propounds this gospel-book throughout the world, in a manner worthy of God; but Athelstan, king and ruler of the Anglo-Saxons, gives it for ever to the metropolitan see of Canterbury.'

The 'Mæielbriðus mac Durnani' named in the first part of the inscription can be identified as Mael Brigte mac Tornain, a prominent Irish ecclesiastic in the late ninth and early tenth centuries: he was coarb of Patrick (in effect, abbot of Armagh) from about 888, coarb of Colum Cille (in effect, abbot of Iona and head of all the Columban churches) from 891,[53] and he is also said to have been coarb of Adomnan (in effect, abbot of Raphoe);[54] he died 'in happy old age' in 927, and is described in one source as 'head of the piety of all Ireland and of the greater part of Europe'.[55] The inscription appears to signify that there was some connection between Mael Brigte and the gospel-book: we need not suppose that the book was actually written by him, but the statement that he 'propounds' *istum textum* throughout the world at least implies that he once owned it. There is no means of telling when the manuscript left Ireland, or how it came into Athelstan's possession: it is possible, for example, that the manuscript was brought to England as early as the reign of Alfred the Great[56] (reaching the West Saxon court then or some years later), but if the juxtaposition of Mael Brigte and Athelstan in the inscription implies a direct link between them it is perhaps more likely that the manuscript was given to Athelstan by Mael Brigte himself (so probably between 924 and 927), or that it was given to Athelstan in Mael Brigte's memory after his death (so between

[53] The death of Mael Coba, who would appear to have been Mael Brigte's immediate predecessor as coarb of Patrick, is entered in AU (= *The Annals of Ulster (to A.D. 1131)*, pt I, ed. S. Mac Airt and G. Mac Niocaill (Dublin, 1983)) 888.1; and the death of Flann, apparently his predecessor as coarb of Colum Cille, is entered in AU 891.1.

[54] The only explicit statement to this effect occurs in AFM (= *Annals of the Kingdom of Ireland, by the Four Masters, from the Earliest Period to the Year 1616*, ed. J. O'Donovan, 7 vols., 2nd ed. (Dublin, 1856)), *s.a.* 925 [for 927]; the statement is supported by a pedigree for Mael Brigte found in the 'Genealogies of Irish Saints' (*Corpus Genealogiarum Sanctorum Hiberniae*, ed. P. Ó Riain (Dublin, 1984), §347; I am indebted to Professor Ó Riain for allowing me access to the text before publication), which shows that Mael Brigte was a member of Cenél mBóguine, a population group which inhabited the area around Raphoe, Co. Donegal; Raphoe was the principal church of St Adomnán. I am most grateful to David Dumville for guidance on this point, which he develops at length in 'Mael Brigte Mac Tornáin, Pluralist Coarb (†927)', *Jnl of Celtic Stud.* 4 (1985).

[55] AU 927.1 ('Mael Brigte son of Tornán, successor of Patrick and Colum Cille, rested in happy old age'); AFM 925 [for 927] ('Maelbrighde, son of Tornan, successor of Patrick, Colum Cille and Adamnan, head of the piety of all Ireland, and of the greater part of Europe, died at a good old age, on the 22nd of February'); see also AI (= *The Annals of Inisfallen*, ed. S. Mac Airt (Dublin, 1951)) 927 ('Repose of Mael Brigte son of Tornán, abbot of Ard Macha and abbot of I Coluim Chille'). For Mael Brigte, see, further, A. O. Anderson, *Early Sources of Scottish History A.D. 500 to 1286* (Edinburgh, 1922) I, 425, and J. F. Kenney, *The Sources for the Early History of Ireland: Ecclesiastical* (New York, 1929), rev. imp. L. Bieler (Shannon, 1966), p. 645.

[56] For contacts between England and Ireland in the late ninth century, see Asser, *Vita Alfredi*, chs. 76, 91 and 102, and ASC 891 A. According to the *Vita Dunstani*, Dunstan had studied books of Irish pilgrims at Glastonbury (*EHD*, no. 234, p. 898).

927 and 939). The present tense *dogmatizat* in the inscription seems to suggest that Mael Brigte was still alive when Athelstan gave the book to Canterbury,[57] but it would be dangerous to press the point: after all, Mael Brigte could hardly be propounding *istum textum* at the same time as Athelstan 'gives' it to Canterbury, precluding a too literal interpretation of the inscription, and the author's use of the present tense *dat* might anyway suggest that he was thinking generally in terms of the historic present.

The capitals used for the inscription are compatible with an assumption that the inscription was written some time during the reign of King Athelstan, but one should ask whether they can serve as a criterion to limit the date of the writing more precisely within this period, or even to point in the direction of a particular scriptorium. Capitals of much the same type occur in the display script used in several manuscripts written in the late ninth and early tenth centuries: for example, Oxford, Bodleian Library, Hatton 20 (the copy of Alfred's translation of the *Regula pastoralis* sent to Worcester); Cambridge, Corpus Christi College 173 (the Parker Chronicle); and Cambridge, Trinity College B. 15. 33 (the Trinity Isidore); one might also compare the lettering of the inscriptions on the Cuthbert stole and maniple.[58] Such capitals continued in use during the reign of Athelstan and beyond.[59] Malcolm Parkes has pointed out that the use of square capitals as a display script in these manuscripts of the late ninth and early tenth centuries may be a practice inspired by Carolingian manuscripts of the ninth century;[60] but of course the forms of the letters themselves derive from the Insular tradition of capitals stretching back to the display scripts found in the finest manuscripts of the late seventh and early eighth centuries.[61] One is forced, therefore, to conclude that the capitals in the

57 Wood, 'King Æthelstan's Empire', p. 257, n. 32.

58 See M. B. Parkes, 'The Palaeography of the Parker Manuscript of the *Chronicle*, Laws and Sedulius, and Historiography at Winchester in the Late Ninth and Tenth Centuries', *ASE* 5 (1976), 149–71, at 159–61. For the Cuthbert stole and maniple, see *The Relics of Saint Cuthbert*, ed. C. F. Battiscombe (Oxford, 1956), pls. XXIV, XXV, XXXIII and XXXIV.

59 E.g. BL Cotton Tiberius A. ii, 24r (pl. II), and Cambridge, Corpus Christi College 183, 2r; and note that the inscription placed above the portrait of Athelstan and Cuthbert in BL Cotton Otho B. ix appears to have been in capitals (see below, p. 174). For their use later on, see, e.g., Oxford, Bodleian Library, Junius 11, 1r (N. Denholm-Young, *Handwriting in England and Wales* (Cardiff, 1964), pl. 6).

60 Parkes, 'Parker Manuscript', pp. 159–61.

61 On the use of capitals in early Insular manuscripts, see T. J. Brown, 'The Palaeography of the Latin Text', T. D. Kendrick *et al.*, *Evangeliorum Quattuor Codex Lindisfarnensis*, 2 vols. (Olten and Lausanne, 1956–60) II, 61–106, esp. 75–80, and P. McGurk, 'An Anglo-Saxon Bible Fragment of the Late Eighth Century: Royal 1 E. VI', *Jnl of the Warburg and Courtauld Institutes* 25 (1962), 18–34, at 29–31. The distinctive features of the inscription in the MacDurnan Gospels (full-page; unframed; in mixed capitals, with many angular forms) are paralleled most closely in surviving manuscripts by the monumental inscriptions in BL Royal 1. E. VI (1v, 30r and 44r), written at St Augustine's, Canterbury, in the early ninth

MacDurnan Gospels are of a type so widespread, and used over so long a period, that they cannot be made to serve any useful purpose in the dating or localization of the inscription.

The most remarkable aspect of the inscription in the MacDurnan Gospels is that it is cast in a metrical form and in language which anticipate in certain respects the group of 'alliterative' charters issued in the names of Anglo-Saxon kings in the 940s and 950s.[62] The inscription may be rearranged as two verses separated by the word *ast* (which lies outside the metre); each verse comprises three lines of 4p + 4p (that is, in each half-line the stress falls on the penultimate syllable of four),[63] and there is irregular alliteration within each line.

Mæielbriðus MacDurnani
istum textum per triquadrum
Deo digne dogmatizat
ast
Æthelstanus Anglosæxna
rex et rector Doruernensi
metropoli dat per æuum

These simple verses are replete with interesting words and phrases. *Triquadrus* is here a synonym for *orbis*, and derives ultimately from a usage mentioned by Orosius, whereby the world was called 'tripartite' after its three parts: Asia, Europe and Africa.[64] The word occurs as an adjective in the seventh-century *Hisperica famina*,[65] and was employed several times by Aldhelm in his prose and verse *De uirginitate*;[66] it is also found in eighth-century Anglo-Saxon glossaries.[67] In the reign of Athelstan the draftsmen of charters quarried the works of Aldhelm, and glossaries, for grandiloquent phrases and recondite words, and in fact the adjective *triquadrus* is used in a proem found in two charters issued

century (see M. Budny, 'The Script and Decoration of British Library Manuscript Royal 1 E. vi' (unpubl. Ph.D. dissertation, London Univ., 1984)); the person who wrote the inscription in the MacDurnan Gospels may well have seen the inscriptions in Royal 1. E. VI, but it would be dangerous to assume that they were the only models available in the tenth century.

62 The point was made by Robinson (*TSD*, p. 57), before the alliterative charters had been clearly identified as a group. The charters in question are S 472–3, 479, 484, 520, 544, 548–50, 556–7, 566, 569, 572, 633 and 1606; cf. S 392, 404, 574 and 1497.

63 The terminology is that of D. Norberg, *Introduction à l'étude de la versification latine médiévale*, Studia Latina Stockholmiensia 5 (Stockholm, 1958). Note that the first element of Mael Brigte's name has been split into two syllables, by the intrusive **i**, in order to achieve four syllables in the half-line; for the same reason, *mac* governs a Latin genitive, *Durnani*. The second **a** in *Anglosæxana* and the **v** within the **v** of *Dorvernensi* (if meant for *Doruuernensi*) upset the metre, but both seem to have been inserted as an afterthought.

64 See *Aldhelmi Opera*, ed. R. Ehwald, MGH, Auct. antiq. 15 (Berlin, 1919), 247, n. 3.

65 M. W. Herren, *The Hisperica Famina: I. The A-Text* (Toronto, 1974), 64, line 7, and 117–18.

66 See *Aldhelmi Opera*, ed. Ehwald, p. 723, for references.

67 See *The Oldest English Texts*, ed. H. Sweet, EETS o.s. 83 (London, 1885), 102, gl. 1039 (Épinal Glossary), and 103, gl. 2052 (Corpus Glossary).

on 16 April 928 at Exeter;[68] the profusion of other Aldhelmian phrases in the same formula suggests that the draftsman of these charters, presumably someone attached to the king's household, had derived his knowledge of the word from the *De uirginitate*.[69] The adjective *triquadrus* is also found, in the context of a different formula, in a charter of King Athelstan dated 930; the charter in question is plainly spurious in its received form, but it was apparently based in part on genuine charters of the alliterative group issued in the 940s.[70] The phrase *Deo digne* is found three times in the Vulgate, and presumably has the same meaning here as there, that is, 'in a manner worthy of God'.[71] The verb *dogmatizo*, meaning 'to teach' or 'to propound a doctrine', had been used by St Augustine of Hippo; it does not seem to occur in the works of Aldhelm, though Aldhelm did use the nouns *dogmatista*, 'teacher', and *dogma*, '(divine) doctrine', from the same Greek root.[72] These words also occur in the alliterative charters: *dogmatizo* is used in the past tense (*dogmatizaui*) in a bishop's formula of attestation in S 544 (949); *dogma* occurs in the clause 'indicat dogmata dicens' incorporated in a proem common to S 556 and 557 (951); and *dogmatista* is used to describe Dunstan, abbot of Glastonbury, in the witness-list of S 633 (956). The conjunction *ast*, 'but', was much used by Aldhelm, and it too is used in the alliterative charters: in S 544 and 549 (949) it occurs in a formula introducing the boundary clause ('Ast sequitur terminatio'), and in S 633 (956) the conjunction is promoted to the status of a sub-king ('Ast regulus'), evidently as the result of a copyist's carelessness or ignorance.[73] Finally, the royal style applied to Athelstan ('Anglosæxna rex et rector') is closely related to the distinctive royal styles which occur in the alliterative charters: Edmund is styled 'rex et rector Angulsæxna' in S 479 (942);[74] and the collocation 'rex et rector' (which had been used in the style 'rex

68 S 399 and 400; see Keynes, *Diplomas*, p. 43 and n. 74.

69 See D. A. Bullough, 'The Educational Tradition in England from Alfred to Ælfric: Teaching *Utriusque Linguae*', *Settimane di studio del Centro italiano di studi sull'alto medioevo* 19 (1972), 453–94, at 469–70, and E. John, *Orbis Britanniae* (Leicester, 1966), pp. 49–50.

70 S 404 (*BCS* 667). The charter was preserved in the archives of Abingdon Abbey, and is a grant of an estate at Dumbleton in Gloucestershire to Abbot Cynath (of Evesham). Abingdon acquired the property in the early eleventh century (S 1488), and with it some earlier charters relating to the same estate; S 404 may have been concocted in connection with a dispute over Dumbleton in the late eleventh century (see *Chronicon Monasterii de Abingdon*, ed. Stevenson II, 35–6), on the basis of authentic alliterative charters in the Abingdon archives (e.g. S 544).

71 *TSD*, p. 58 and n. 2.

72 See *Aldhelmi Opera*, ed. Ehwald, p. 599, for references.

73 For *ast*, see R. E. Latham, *Dictionary of Medieval Latin from British Sources: Fascicule I A–B* (London, 1975), p. 146, and M. Lapidge, 'Three Latin Poems from Æthelwold's School at Winchester', *ASE* 1 (1972), 85–137, at 86–7.

74 The same style was probably employed in S 484 and 1606, but the texts of these charters were abbreviated by a later copyist; see *Charters of Burton Abbey*, ed. P. H. Sawyer, Anglo-Saxon Charters 2 (London, 1979), 11.

et rector totius huius Britanniae insulae' in charters of Athelstan dated 933 and 934)[75] occurs in S 520 (946) and in S 544 (949).[76] The most significant point here is not so much the use of 'Anglo-Saxons' in a royal style, for Alfred and Edward the Elder were both styled 'rex Angulsaxonum',[77] but rather the use of an Old English genitive plural (*Anglosæ̀xna*, or *Angulsæxna*) in what is properly a Latin context.[78]

The similarities between the inscription in the MacDurnan Gospels and the alliterative charters go beyond an acceptable coincidence, and should be capable of some rational explanation. It is difficult, indeed, to resist the idea that the person who drafted the inscription in the reign of Athelstan went on to draft some or all of the alliterative charters in the 940s and 950s, in which case it would be most natural to suppose that the inscription (as well as the gift of the book to Canterbury) dates from the closing years of Athelstan's reign, if only to bring it and the charters into a closer chronological relationship.[79] The charters themselves are often regarded as connected in some way with Cenwald, who may have begun his career as a royal chaplain,[80] and who was bishop of Worcester from 928 or 929 until 957 or 958;[81] he seems to have enjoyed a special relationship with King Athelstan, to judge from the fact that he was sent on an important mission to the continent in 929.[82] The case for associating the charters with Cenwald is compelling,[83] and certainly a better one cannot be made out for any other known person. Diplomatically, the alliterative charters have certain affinities with Mercian documents of the ninth century,[84] and Cenwald would presumably have become familiar with

75 S 420 and 427; neither charter is acceptable in its received form, but the royal styles in both probably reflect a genuine usage of Athelstan's reign.

76 Cf. S 548 and 550; see also Athelstan's style in the witness-list of S 404.

77 For Alfred's royal styles, see Keynes and Lapidge, *Alfred the Great*, pp. 38–9 and 227–8; for the continued employment of the style 'rex Angulsaxonum' in Edward's reign, see, e.g., S 362, 363, 368 and 369 (all from different archives).

78 When political circumstances allowed, the style 'rex Angulsæxna' was expanded (in other charters of the alliterative group) to cover rule over the Northumbrians, the 'pagans' and the 'Britons': see S 520, 549, 569, 572 and 633 (and cf. S 392 and 566).

79 Cf. Wood, 'King Æthelstan's Empire', pp. 257–8.

80 See E. E. Barker, 'Two Lost Documents of King Athelstan', *ASE* 6 (1977), 137–43, at 139 and 143.

81 M. A. O'Donovan, 'An Interim Revision of Episcopal Dates for the Province of Canterbury, 850–950: Part II', *ASE* 2 (1973), 91–113, at 113, and C. R. Hart, *The Early Charters of Northern England and the North Midlands* (Leicester, 1973), pp. 310–11.

82 See below, pp. 198–201.

83 See *Charters of Burton*, ed. Sawyer, pp. xlvii–xlix, and *EHD*, pp. 372–3.

84 In particular, the formulas wishing well to those who protect or increase the grant, and ill to those who do otherwise, seen in S 404, 472, 479 and 569, are related to similar formulas found in charters from the Worcester archives, e.g. S 179, 208, 210, 214, 1262, 1273 and 1278 (cf. S 76 and 154); the use of *pax* in several of these Worcester charters may be compared with formulas in S 404, 479, 548, 566 and 574.

the documents in the Worcester archives during the 930s. He is the only person who attests all of the alliterative charters with full witness-lists,[85] and significant elements of the style are used in a Worcester lease granted in his name in 957.[86] The distribution of the estates covered by the charters has a distinctly 'Mercian' flavour, for the great majority lie in the dioceses of Lichfield, Worcester and Dorchester.[87] It is important to emphasize, however, that the charters themselves seem to have been produced at meetings of the king's councillors held in various places throughout southern England;[88] whoever wrote them was presumably authorized by the king to do so on the occasion of the meeting, so we need not imagine that they were actually drawn up in an ecclesiastical scriptorium (for example, at Worcester). We might conclude that Cenwald (perhaps as a special favourite of the king) was invited by Athelstan to compose the inscription for the MacDurnan Gospels, sometime towards the end of the reign when the king wished to give the book to Canterbury, and that Cenwald was subsequently commissioned by Athelstan's immediate successors to compose charters on certain occasions for certain 'Mercian' estates or beneficiaries. It is an attractive hypothesis, but at the end of the day one incapable of proof.

## MANUSCRIPT GIVEN TO BATH ABBEY

### BL Cotton Claudius B. v

BL Cotton Claudius B. v is a copy of the Acts of the Council of Constantinople (680), written on the continent towards the end of the ninth century.[89] The first

85 S 392, 404, 479, 520, 544, 549, 550, 556, 557, 566, 569, 574 and 633; note that his name is usually spelt *Koenwald*, and that in S 544, 566, 569 and 633 he is described as *monachus*. A short text added in the tenth century on the last leaf of the manuscript of the Old English Pastoral Care sent to Worcester (Oxford, Bodleian Library, Hatton 20, 98v: facsimile, *The Pastoral Care*, ed. N. R. Ker, EEMF 6 (Copenhagen, 1956); see *ibid.* p. 24) concludes 'Koenwald monachus. Ælfric clericus hoc conposuit'. If this implies that 'Koenwald', presumably Cenwald, bishop of Worcester, played some part in the addition of this text, it provides further evidence for the association between him and the alliterative charters: for the words immediately before this ending are 'Fiat pax Christi nobiscum inperpetuum', which recall the formula 'Pax Christi nobiscum Amen' in S 566 and 574 (and cf. S 548).

86 S 1290 (*BCS* 993), in which his name is spelt *Koenwald*. Some of the features of the alliterative charters recur in later Worcester leases, e.g. S 1308, 1354, 1364 and 1370.

87 The only exceptions are S 472 and 473, which relate to estates in Wiltshire, in the diocese of Ramsbury; note, however, that these charters are in favour of Wulfric, who may be the same man as the beneficiary of S 520 and 550 (both in the alliterative group), and as such, perhaps, a Mercian thegn.

88 See Keynes, *Diplomas*, p. 82, n. 165.

89 Thompson and Warner, *Catalogue of Ancient Manuscripts*, p. 88. Rella, 'Continental Manuscripts', p. 111, gives the origin of this manuscript as Aachen, citing W. Koehler, *Die*

quire of the manuscript is now fols. 4–9: 4r was originally left blank, and the text begins with a long heading in capitals which extends from 4v to 5r. At some time in the tenth century an inscription, in Anglo-Saxon square minuscule, was entered in a space at the bottom of 5r (see pl. VI):

+ Hunc codicem Æthelt˹s˺anus rex tradidit Deo et alme Christi genetrici sanctisque Petro et Benedicto in Bathonie ciuitatis coenobio ob remunerationem suæ animæ. Et quisquis hos legerit caracteres, omnipotenti pro eo proque suis amicis fundat preces.[90]

It is difficult to judge on the basis of script alone whether the inscription is strictly contemporary with the reign of Athelstan, or whether it was written at a later date in the tenth century; but in either case there is no reason to doubt what the inscription reveals, that the manuscript came into the possession of King Athelstan and sooner or later was given by him to the abbey of Bath. It is often supposed that Athelstan had received the manuscript as a present from Otto I, at the time of Otto's marriage to his half-sister Edith in 929/30;[91] the possibility cannot be denied, but nor can one rule out the possibility that the manuscript had been brought to England some years earlier,[92] or indeed that it did not come into Athelstan's possession until the 930s. Accordingly, Athelstan could have given the manuscript to Bath at any time during his reign.[93]

The first part of the inscription ('Hunc codicem . . . suæ animæ') is of especial historical interest for the light it casts on the abbey of Bath in the first half of the tenth century. The abbey had originally been founded as a 'double monastery' towards the end of the seventh century, but by the eighth century it seems to have become a community for monks alone; it was then dedicated to

*karolingischen Miniaturen, II: Die Hofschule Karls des Grossen* (Berlin, 1958), pp. 47–8; but Koehler's attribution refers only to the miniature now pasted on to the last leaf of the manuscript, which has no original connection with Claudius B. v. See also W. Koehler, 'An Illustrated Evangelistary of the Ada School and its Model', *Jnl of the Warburg and Courtauld Institutes* 15 (1952), 48–66.

90 'King Athelstan gave this book to God and to the holy mother of Christ and to the saints Peter and Benedict in the monastery of the city of Bath, for the salvation of his soul. And may whoever reads these letters make prayers to the Almighty or him and for his friends.'

91 E.g. Thompson and Warner, *Catalogue of Ancient Manuscripts*, p. 88; Koehler, *Die karolingischen Miniaturen*, pp. 47–8; and Rella, 'Continental Manuscripts', p. 111.

92 Perhaps one should bear in mind, in this connection, that King Alfred appears to have been conscious of the activities of some of the early councils of the church; see Keynes and Lapidge, *Alfred the Great*, pp. 163–4.

93 On palaeographical grounds, the inscription might be placed nearer the end of the reign than the beginning. Note, incidentally, the upright **d** in *Benedicto*; but cf. E. Temple, *Anglo-Saxon Manuscripts 900–1066*, Survey of Manuscripts Illuminated in the Brit. Isles 2 (London, 1976), pls. 15, 17 and 18, for other examples in manuscripts written before or during Athelstan's reign.

St Peter, and belonged to – or was claimed by – the kings of Mercia.[94] Little is known of its status or fortunes in the ninth century, though it is quite likely that there was a religious community at Bath in the reign of Alfred, when the town was incorporated in the defensive network of burhs described in the *Burghal Hidage*.[95] The abbey was evidently in royal hands in 944, when King Edmund entrusted it as a place of refuge to a group of monks from Saint-Bertin (in Saint-Omer, Flanders):[96] these monks had chosen to leave their own monastery rather than submit to the regime imposed by the newly appointed abbot Gerhard of Brogne, so one imagines that in the later 940s Bath was served by a community basically opposed for whatever reasons to Gerhard's brand of reformed Benedictine monasticism. During the reign of Eadwig (955–9) the abbey was governed by a priest called Wulfgar and received several grants of land from the king;[97] its 'refoundation' as a Benedictine community probably took place under the influence of Dunstan in the early 960s.[98]

Against this background, it would seem likely that the abbey of Bath was in royal hands during the reign of Athelstan. According to one charter (S 414), dated 931, Athelstan gave land at Priston in Somerset and at Cold Ashton in Gloucestershire 'to Almighty God and to St Peter the Apostle and to the venerable community' at Bath; but the charter is undoubtedly spurious, so one could not rely on it alone as evidence of the community's existence at this time. There is another reference to King Athelstan's grant of Cold Ashton to Bath, in a charter running in the name of King Eadwig and representing the restoration of the land to the abbey after its recent appropriation;[99] but again it would be hazardous to place much faith in the charter in question. The inscription itself remains, therefore, the best evidence for the existence of a religious community at Bath in Athelstan's reign, and it reveals that the

94 See P. Sims-Williams, 'Continental Influence at Bath Monastery in the Seventh Century', *ASE* 4 (1975), 1–10, and S 1257 (*EHD*, no. 77). See also B. Cunliffe, 'Saxon Bath', *Anglo-Saxon Towns in Southern England*, ed. J. Haslam (Chichester, 1984), pp. 345–58.

95 Bath was on the border between Mercia and Wessex (see *Chronicle of Æthelweard*, ed. Campbell, p. 52), and it must have passed from one kingdom to the other as political circumstances changed. In 864 it was under Mercian control (S 210), but it was presumably under West Saxon control by the end of the ninth century; coins in the name of Edward the Elder were minted at Bath in the early tenth century (L. V. Grinsell, *The Bath Mint* (London, 1973), pp. 10–11).

96 Folcwin, *Gesta Abbatum S. Bertini Sithiensium*, ch. 107 (*EHD*, no. 26), ptd 'Gesta Abbatum S. Bertini Sithiensium', ed. O. Holder-Egger, MGH, Script. 13 (Hanover, 1881), 600–73, at 628–9.

97 S 610 and 643; cf. S 627, 661 and 664.

98 See *The Heads of Religious Houses: England and Wales 940–1216*, ed. D. Knowles *et al.* (Cambridge, 1972), pp. 27–8, and *Vita Dunstani*, ch. 34 (*Memorials of Saint Dunstan*, ed. W. Stubbs, Rolls Ser. (London, 1874), pp. 46–7).

99 S 664.

community enjoyed some degree of royal favour. Yet it specifies the gift of the manuscript as one 'to God and to the holy mother of Christ and to the saints Peter and Benedict in the monastery of the city of Bath'; and, as Robinson realized, it is odd that Benedict should be mentioned in such a context before the 'refoundation' of the community in the 960s.[100] So far as we can tell, the abbey was always dedicated in the Anglo-Saxon period to St Peter alone, so to that extent the reference to Benedict would be problematic at any time.[101] The most natural explanation, at least from a historical point of view, is that the inscription reflects conditions at Bath after its refoundation as a Benedictine community, in which case one would have to infer that it was written in or after the 960s; but it is not obvious why the community should have waited so long before recording the fact that they had received the manuscript from Athelstan, and besides, the other manuscripts with more clearly contemporary inscriptions must create a presumption that the inscription in Claudius B. v would have been made at the time of the gift. If we accept, on the other hand, that the inscription is contemporary, it would follow that Benedict was honoured at Bath in Athelstan's reign, whatever might have happened in the 940s and 950s; this might seem surprising, but on the basis of our knowledge of conditions in Athelstan's reign we should certainly not exclude the possibility that a group of people who had taken monastic vows gathered at Bath and observed there the Rule of St Benedict.[102]

The request for prayers in the second part of the inscription ('Et quisquis hos legerit caracteres, omnipotenti pro eo proque suis amicis fundat preces') recalls in a general way the ending of the inscription in Tiberius A. ii (see above, p. 149), and reminds us that the king's intention in making such gifts of precious manuscripts to religious communities was to secure their prayers and to ensure their support. The wording of the request in Claudius B. v (as in Tiberius A. ii) might have been devised especially for the purpose, but there is some possibility that it was modelled on an earlier inscription taken from another context (whether a single inscription or a collection). Bede, for example, is known to have compiled a *Liber epigrammatum*, and while the work itself is lost it has been suggested that this collection ended with the following epigram:

100 *TSD*, pp. 62–4.

101 Whenever the dedication is specified in Anglo-Saxon charters, it is to St Peter; the late-eleventh-century seal of Bath Abbey similarly specifies St Peter. For dedications to St Benedict, see F. Arnold-Forster, *Studies in Church Dedications, or England's Patron Saints*, 3 vols. (London, 1899) II, 8–10.

102 Ælfheah 'the Bald' (who became bishop of Winchester in 934) had apparently taken monastic vows by 925 (see S 394), and is known to have influenced Dunstan and Æthelwold at Athelstan's court; there may well have been others like him, and them. See also Hart, *Early Charters of Northern England*, p. 348.

Lector adesto uigil pagina queque canit.
Bede Dei famulus scripsi uersusque notaui.
Pro [quo] quisque legis obsecro funde preces.[103]

The last line of this epigram obviously bears comparison with the inscription in Claudius B. v,[104] though the sentiment is so commonplace that it would be hazardous to suggest that it was the direct source.[105] Another collection of epigrams was put together by (or for) Milred, bishop of Worcester (*c.* 743–75), drawing on various earlier collections, including Bede's *Liber epigrammatum*: this too has not survived complete, but a fragment (in Anglo-Saxon square minuscule) from what would appear to have been a mid-tenth-century copy of Milred's collection, now preserved in the library of the University of Illinois at Urbana, suggests that the collection might well have been known in Athelstan's reign.[106] It would be reasonable to conclude that a considerable quantity of epigrams, inscriptions and incidental verse might have been available in tenth-century England; and, while relatively little of this material actually survives, further search through similar material known to have circulated on the continent (and perhaps once in England) might bring to light other possible parallels for the Athelstan inscriptions.[107]

The later history of Claudius B. v is of some interest. It presumably remained at Bath throughout the Middle Ages,[108] for it was found there by John Leland in the sixteenth century. It is not mentioned in the short list of

103 See P. Sims-Williams, 'Milred of Worcester's Collection of Latin Epigrams and its Continental Counterparts', *ASE* 10 (1982), 21–38, at 38. See also M. Lapidge, 'Some Remnants of Bede's Lost *Liber Epigrammatum*', *EHR* 90 (1975), 798–820.

104 See also the inscription in BL Royal 1. A. XVIII, discussed below, pp. 165–70.

105 Compare, for example, the colophon in the MacRegol Gospels: Kenney, *Sources for the Early History of Ireland*, pp. 641–2 (no. 472).

106 See Sims-Williams, 'Milred of Worcester's Collection of Latin Epigrams', pp. 24–9. The Urbana manuscript was probably written in the 940s or 950s, so this point depends on the assumption that its exemplar was known in the immediately preceding period; the Urbana manuscript itself was apparently at Malmesbury in the Middle Ages, for William of Malmesbury seems to have used it in the twelfth century and the antiquary John Leland saw it there, and made extracts from it, in the sixteenth century. See, further, P. Sims-Williams, 'William of Malmesbury and La Silloge Epigrafica di Cambridge', *Archivum Historiae Pontificiae* 21 (1983), 9–33.

107 For various continental collections of such material, see Sims-Williams, 'Milred of Worcester's Collection of Latin Epigrams', pp. 28–38; references to analogous inscriptions entered in ninth- and tenth-century continental manuscripts are assembled in Schramm and Mütherich, *Denkmale*.

108 We may be thankful that it was not among the thirty-odd books removed from the library by Abbot Sæwold soon after the Norman Conquest, and given by him to the abbey of Saint-Vaast; see P. Grierson, 'Les Livres de l'Abbé Seiwold de Bath', *RB* 52 (1940), 96–116, and Lapidge, above, pp. 58–62.

books which he saw at Bath, recorded in his *Collectanea*,[109] but in his *Commentarii de scriptoribus Britannicis* he makes the following remark:

Paucis abhinc annis fui in *Badunensi* bibliotheca, ubi reperi aliquot non indoctos libros, venerandæ vetustatis thesauros, ab ipso *Ethelstano*, ut ex inscriptionibus apparuit, monachis dono datos; ex illis unum, captus cum antiquitate tum majestate operis (erat enim de *Synodis Pontificiis*) in palatinam bibliothecam illustrissimi regis *Henrici* octavi transtuli, at prius hoc hexastico inscriptum:

*Ethelstanus* erat nostræ pars maxima curæ,
Cujus nota mihi bibliotheca fuit.
Illo sublato, sexcentos amplius annos
Pulvere delitui squallidus atque situ:
Donec me pietas Magni revocavit ad auras
*Henrici*, digno restituitque loco.[110]

It would appear, therefore, that Athelstan had given several manuscripts to Bath (and that inscriptions were entered in each one); but Leland was particularly impressed by one 'de *Synodis Pontificiis*' (which must be Claudius B. v), decided to present it to King Henry VIII for the royal library, and himself composed the poem which he then wrote at the beginning of the manuscript. In fact, however, the poem does not occur in Claudius B. v, and one cannot prove that the manuscript ever reached King Henry's library;[111] so it remains uncertain what became of the manuscript after it was removed from Bath and before it was acquired by Sir Robert Cotton in the early seventeenth century.[112] As we shall see, a very similar (but not identical) poem was entered by Leland in another manuscript (BL Royal 1. A. XVIII), apparently given by Athelstan

109 *Joannis Lelandi Antiquarii De Rebus Britannicis Collectanea*, ed. T. Hearne, 2nd ed. (London, 1774) IV, 156–7.

110 *Commentarii de Scriptoribus Britannicis Auctore Joanne Lelando Londinate*, ed. A. Hall (Oxford, 1709), p. 160 (Oxford, Bodleian Library, Top. gen. c. 4, p. 122): 'A few years ago I was in the library at Bath, where I found several learned books – treasures of venerable age – which had been given to the monks by Athelstan himself, as appeared from inscriptions. I transferred one of them (attracted as much by the antiquity as by the splendour of the work, for it was 'de *Synodiis Pontificiis*') to the palace library of the illustrious King Henry VIII, having first entered this poem: "Athelstan was the principal agent of our preservation – his library was well-known to me. After his death, for six hundred years and more, I lay hidden, filthy in dust and mould, until the concern of great Henry recalled me back to the light of day and restored me to a worthy place."'

111 On the history of Henry's library, see G. F. Warner and J. P. Gilson, *Catalogue of Western Manuscripts in the Old Royal and King's Collections*, 4 vols. (London, 1921) I, xiv–xvi. Claudius B. v does not seem to occur in the inventory of Henry's library compiled in 1542, but it may not have been until that year that Leland visited Bath; see *The Itinerary of John Leland in or about the Years 1535–1543*, ed. L. Toulmin Smith, 5 vols. (London, 1907–10) I, 139–44, and cf. *ibid.* p. 107.

112 The manuscript is no. 183 in the Cotton catalogue of 1621 (BL Harley 6018, 86r).

to St Augustine's Abbey, Canterbury, and one might suppose that Leland had simply confused the two in his memory;[113] but it is conceivable that Leland wrote the poem on a separate leaf which he then added at the beginning of Claudius B. v, before presenting the manuscript to the king, and that this leaf was removed in the later sixteenth or early seventeenth century when the manuscript itself was transferred from the royal library into private hands.[114]

## MANUSCRIPT GIVEN TO ST AUGUSTINE'S, CANTERBURY

### BL Royal 1. A. XVIII

BL Royal 1. A. XVIII is a gospel-book, written on the continent, probably in Brittany, in the late ninth or early tenth century.[115] The first quire of the manuscript is a gathering of eight leaves (fols. 4–11), which contains the Eusebian canon tables, beginning on 4r.[116] This quire is preceded by three preliminary leaves: fol. 2 was probably inserted in the sixteenth century, but fols. 1 and 3 seem to have a more ancient association with the manuscript. The following inscription occurs on 3v (see pl. VII):

Hunc codicem ÆÐELSTAN rex deuota mente Dorobernensi tribuit ecclesie beato Augustino dicate et quisquis hoc legerit omnipotenti pro eo proque suis fundat preces.[117]

There has been some variety of opinion about the date of this inscription. For example, Thompson (1884) assigned it to the eleventh century, and was followed in this respect by Warner and Gilson (1921) and by Robinson

[113] Thompson and Warner, *Catalogue of Ancient Manuscripts*, p. 37; Warner and Gilson, *Catalogue of Western Manuscripts* I, 7; Grierson, 'Les Livres de l'Abbé Seiwold', p. 101, n. 5; and see, further, below, pp. 168–70.

[114] The preliminaries now consist of a single bifolium (fos. 2–3); the title 'Claudius B. 5' occurs on 2v, and the Cottonian table of contents occurs on 3r. Fol. 1 was a flyleaf, originally taken from BL Royal 13. D. I*; it is now rebound in the manuscript whence it came. There are other strays from the Old Royal Library in the Cotton collection; see, e.g., Ker, *Catalogue*, no. 344.

[115] Thompson and Warner, *Catalogue of Ancient Manuscripts*, p. 37; Warner and Gilson, *Catalogue of Western Manuscripts* I, 7; and Watson, *Catalogue of Dated and Datable Manuscripts* I, 148 (no. 853).

[116] The preliminary matter of the gospel-book is now bound at the end of the manuscript (fols. 193–9); the state of 199v suggests that these leaves have been in their present position for some time, though the absence of damage to the bottom corners of these leaves indicates (by comparison with the preceding leaves) that they have not always been in this position.

[117] 'With a devout mind King Athelstan gave this book to the church of Canterbury dedicated to St Augustine; and may whoever reads this make prayers to the Almighty for him and for his (friends).'

(1923);[118] but Kenney (1929) suggested the thirteenth century,[119] and Watson (1979) described the hand as apparently of the eleventh century but probably of the sixteenth century imitating a lost inscription.[120] The script is undeniably anomalous: the individual letter-forms are (by and large) those of Anglo-Saxon square minuscule of the tenth century, but the inscription has the appearance of having been written by one who lacked the fluency and confidence expected of an accomplished tenth-century scribe. The most reasonable inference is probably that the script is imitative; it cannot therefore be dated with any degree of confidence.

One should hesitate, however, before dismissing the inscription as a forgery, for there are certain palaeographical, textual and historical considerations which serve to complicate the issue. The leaf on which the inscription occurs has had a somewhat complex history.[121] The remnants of two drawings, one apparently the beaked head of an eagle looking left and the other an inclined human head, can just be detected immediately above the inscription; it is conceivable that they were trials for a group of the evangelists' symbols, but little more can be said about them.[122] The drawings were subsequently cleaned off, and the leaf was ruled in drypoint for 31 lines: the level at which the ruling stops, and the intervals between the lines, are comparable with the ruling in the main text of the gospel-book, but the ruling on 3v starts at the very top of the leaf and differs in certain other respects from that in the manuscript itself. It is difficult, therefore, to tell whether the leaf is an original part of the gospel-book, or whether it was added as a flyleaf at a later date. The words 'Diamate' and 'Umfridus me fecit' were written on 3r in large Gothic letters, possibly in the fourteenth century, and some later medieval pen-trials occur below the inscription on 3v; these features show that the leaf has existed since at least the medieval period, but of course they do not prove that it was always attached to this manuscript. The Athelstan inscription was entered after the ruling on 3v; unfortunately it does not appear to be possible to establish whether it is earlier or later than the drawings or the pen-trials. The whole of the leaf was then

118 Thompson and Warner, *Catalogue of Ancient Manuscripts*, p. 37; Warner and Gilson, *Catalogue of Western Manuscripts* I, 7; and *TSD*, p. 64.

119 Kenney, *Sources for the Early History of Ireland*, p. 656 (no. 504).

120 Watson, *Catalogue of Dated and Datable Manuscripts* I, 148 (no. 853).

121 I am grateful to Mr A. Parker (Senior Conservation Officer, Dept of Manuscripts, British Library) for valuable assistance when examining this leaf under a Video Spectral Comparator and microscope.

122 For a possibly analogous drawing, see Temple, *Anglo-Saxon Manuscripts*, pl. 28. The eagle's head might be compared with the figure on the Brandon plaque (see E. Okasha, 'A Supplement to *Hand-List of Anglo-Saxon Non-Runic Inscriptions*', *ASE* 11 (1983), 83–118, pl. I*a*), or with Alexander, *Insular Manuscripts*, pl. 314; the inclined human head is insufficiently distinct to make any comparison helpful.

stained in some way, and (not necessarily as part of the same process) the surface of the stain was scraped down, carefully avoiding the inscription, leaving the area of the inscription a darker brown than the rest. What all this means is a mystery.

There can be no doubt, on palaeographical and textual grounds, that there is some genuine basis to the inscription on 3v. The letter forms, and in particular the treatment of 'ÆĐELSTAN' in the first line – in capitals and with a distinctive form of 'L' (made up of two inclined strokes) – show that the scribe was following a tenth-century model. The king's name is treated in exactly the same way in Tiberius A. ii, 15v (see pl. III), and one might suppose, therefore, that this inscription was the direct source of the form in Royal 1. A. XVIII. The same treatment of proper names (in capitals, with the distinctive 'L') is found in original charters of the 940s, including (not surprisingly) some written by the scribe who wrote the inscription in Tiberius A. ii,[123] but it also occurs in charters written by another putatively 'royal' scribe;[124] so the possibility remains that the inscription in Royal 1. A. XVIII is modelled on a genuinely contemporary inscription other than that in Tiberius A. ii. So far as its text is concerned, the inscription in Royal 1. A. XVIII appears to be a conflation of the inscriptions in Claudius B. v (for 'Hunc codicem . . . rex . . . et quisquis hoc legerit omnipotenti pro eo proque suis fundat preces') and Tiberius A. ii (for 'ÆĐELSTAN . . . deuota mente dorobernensi tribuit ecclesie . . . dicate'), leaving 'beato Augustino' as the only part for which there is no direct parallel. One could infer that the person who wrote the inscription in Royal 1. A. XVIII had some reason for wishing to enhance the interest of this manuscript by associating it with Athelstan, and used Claudius B. v and Tiberius A. ii as models for the concoction of an analogous inscription for the St Augustine's book; it would follow that the inscription in Royal 1. A. XVIII was not forged until the middle of the sixteenth century or thereafter, since only then might the three manuscripts have been brought together.

It would be tempting to leave the inscription as a sixteenth-century forgery based on Claudius B. v and Tiberius A. ii, were it not for certain other factors. In the first place, it would be entirely appropriate that Athelstan should have come into the possession of a late-ninth- or early-tenth-century Breton manuscript. In the 920s Athelstan was in touch by letter with Radbod, prior of St Samson's of Dol,[125] continuing a relationship which had existed in the days of his father Edward the Elder and which may have originated during the reign of his grandfather Alfred the Great.[126] Furthermore, according to Breton

[123] S 552. [124] S 464 and 512.

[125] *GP*, pp. 399–400, and *Councils & Synods with Other Documents Relating to the English Church, I: A.D. 871–1204*, ed. D. Whitelock, M. Brett and C. N. L. Brooke (Oxford, 1981), pt 1, no. 9 (*EHD*, no. 228). [126] See Asser, *Vita Alfredi*, ch. 102.

tradition (represented by the 'Chronicle of Nantes'), Matuedoi, count of Poher, fled from Brittany 'for fear of the Danes' and sought refuge with a number of his followers in England; they were received by King Athelstan, who stood sponsor to Matuedoi's son Alan at his baptism and helped to bring Alan up; the refugees returned to Brittany a few years later, with Athelstan's support, and Alan 'Crooked Beard' proceeded to drive the Norsemen from the land.[127] There are several Breton gospel-books which are known or thought to have been brought to England in the tenth century,[128] and in view of Athelstan's relationship with both ecclesiastical and secular figures in Brittany it is possible that one or two of these books came as a gift to the king and were subsequently among those presented by him to religious houses in England.

A second factor to be borne in mind is that the antiquary John Leland, in the late 1530s or early 1540s, had cause to believe that Royal 1. A. XVIII was associated with King Athelstan. On 2v he entered the following inscription under his name:

Joannes Lelandus
Æthelstanus erat nostre pars maxima cure,
Cuius nota mihi bibliotheca fuit.
Illo sublato, sexcentos amplius annos
Pulvere delitui squalidus atque situ:
Nunc pietas sed me superas revocavit ad auras
Henrici, digno restituitque loco.

We saw above that Leland claimed in his *Commentarii* to have written a very similar poem in a manuscript 'de *Synodis Pontificiis*' which Athelstan had given to Bath, but that the poem is no longer to be found in the manuscript in question (Claudius B. v). Having composed this poem for insertion in one manuscript destined for Henry VIII's library, Leland might well have decided to enter it in another destined for the same place. By analogy with Claudius B. v, we could imagine that Leland found Royal 1. A. XVIII at St Augustine's, Canterbury,[129] and chose it for the royal library because he believed that it had

127 R. Merlet, *La Chronique de Nantes* (Paris, 1896), pp. 82–3 and 87–91 (*EHD*, no. 25). The Bretons arrived in England in 931 (Merlet, *Chronique*, p. 82, n. 4), and returned to Brittany in 936 (Lauer, *Flodoard*, p. 63; *EHD*, no. 24).

128 E.g. the Harkness Gospels (K. D. Hartzell, 'The Early Provenance of the Harkness Gospels', *Bull. of Research in the Humanities* 84 (1981), 85–97); the Leofric Gospels (*ibid.* p. 89, n. 6); the Bradfer-Lawrence Gospels (F. Wormald, *An Early Breton Gospel Book*, ed. J. Alexander, Roxburghe Club (Cambridge, 1977), p. 3); the Bodmin Gospels (*ibid.* p. 11); and BL Cotton Otho B. ix (below, p. 170). See also Gneuss, 'A Preliminary List', nos. 295, 532 and 688.

129 There is no reason to doubt the provenance of the manuscript; the names scratched in the fifteenth century on 8v (Thomas Lee, John Byrchynton and John Lynstryde) seem to be derived from places in Kent.

once belonged to King Athelstan; and we could imagine further that his reason for this belief was the occurrence in the manuscript of evidence that it was Athelstan who had given the manuscript to St Augustine's. It might be argued that Leland himself forged the inscription to 'corroborate' his story, using Claudius B. v and Tiberius A. ii as his models; or it might be argued that Leland made it all up, and that someone later in the sixteenth century forged the inscription (in the same way) to support Leland's claim that the manuscript had once belonged to Athelstan. But it is not clear why Leland, or anyone else for that matter, should have proceeded in such an elaborate way, or what he (or they) would have hoped to gain from the exercise; and in either case it would have been quite a coincidence if anyone in the sixteenth century had chosen to associate with King Athelstan a Breton manuscript of the right date, without good reason for doing so. It is most likely, therefore, that Leland found an inscription already in the manuscript; and it would follow that the inscription on 3v, though imitative, could not be based directly on those in Claudius B. v and Tiberius A. ii.

Under these circumstances, there seems to be only one way to account for the close textual relationship between the inscriptions in these three manuscripts. The inscription in Royal 1. A. XVIII could be a later copy of a genuinely tenth-century inscription in the same manuscript, made because the original was on a badly damaged or detached leaf; or it could be a copy of a genuine inscription in another St Augustine's book, which someone had cause to enter in Royal 1. A. XVIII. In either case, the copy would probably have been made at St Augustine's; and since it is well known that the imitation of Anglo-Saxon scripts was practised there in the Middle Ages, this need occasion no surprise.[130] The connection between the inscriptions in Royal 1. A. XVIII, Claudius B. v and Tiberius A. ii would therefore go back to the tenth century, and as such would be a matter of considerable importance: for the most natural inference would be that all three inscriptions, entered in manuscripts given to different religious houses, were written by men in close contact with each other, as variations on a common theme; and, since the inscription in Tiberius A. ii is demonstrably contemporary, and written by someone who can be identified as a royal scribe, it would follow further that the inscription in Claudius B. v and the hypothetically original inscription behind that in Royal 1. A. XVIII were also written by scribes in the service of the king.

The argument developed above arises from the need to explain how an inscription, which seems to be imitative, could be so closely related to the

130 See M. Hunter, 'The Facsimiles in Thomas Elmham's History of St Augustine's, Canterbury', *The Library* 5th ser. 28 (1973), 215–20.

inscriptions in two other manuscripts, when it seems to have existed before all three manuscripts could have been brought together, and when a straightforward act of forgery is anyway so difficult to accept; given the unknown variables, an infinite number of alternative explanations is available, so this argument is offered as a suggestion, not a solution. The later history of the manuscript is slightly more clear. If the inscription on 2v may be believed, the manuscript was presumably taken by Leland from St Augustine's and handed over to Henry VIII. As in the case of Claudius B. v, one cannot actually prove that it was in the royal library in the 1540s,[131] but if it was it must soon have been taken out, for by the end of the century it belonged to John, Lord Lumley: his name is written on the lower margin of 4r, and the manuscript is included in the catalogue of his books made in 1596.[132] Lumley's library was acquired by Prince Henry following Lumley's death in 1609, and was thereafter united with the Old Royal Library; [133] so in this way the Breton gospels came back into royal ownership.

## MANUSCRIPTS GIVEN TO ST CUTHBERT'S, CHESTER-LE-STREET

### BL Cotton Otho B. ix

BL Cotton Otho B. ix is a gospel-book written on the continent, probably in Brittany, in the late ninth or early tenth century.[134] It soon came into the possession of King Athelstan, who gave it to the community of St Cuthbert at Chester-le-Street, probably on the occasion of his expedition to the north in the summer of 934 (which culminated in the ravaging of Scotland).[135] The manuscript remained at Chester-le-Street for much of the tenth century, but in

131 See above, n. 111; Royal 1. A. XVIII does not seem to occur in the inventory of Henry's library compiled in 1542.

132 S. Jayne and F. R. Johnson, *The Lumley Library: the Catalogue of 1609* (London, 1956), p. 65 (no. 303): 'Evangelia quatuor, ex interpretatione et c, cum concordantiis, vetusta, data ab Athelstano rege, ecclesiae Dorovernensis, manusc.'

133 *Ibid.* pp. 13–20, and Warner and Gilson, *Catalogue of Western Manuscripts*, pp. xviii–xix.

134 R. A. B. Mynors, *Durham Cathedral Manuscripts to the End of the Twelfth Century* (Oxford, 1939), pp. 25–6 (no. 15), and Ker, *Catalogue*, no. 176. For its Breton origin, see J. Alexander, 'A Note on the Breton Gospel Books', Wormald, *An Early Breton Gospel Book*, ed. Alexander, pp. 13–28, at 13, n. 1, and F. Wormald, 'The Insular Script in Late Tenth Century English Latin MSS', *Comitato internazionale di scienze storiche: Atti del X Congresso internazionale, Roma 4–11 settembre 1955* (Rome, 1957), pp. 160–4, at 162–3.

135 For this expedition, see ASC 934 BCDE, 933 A. The belief that Athelstan visited St Cuthbert's community on this occasion depends on the *Historia de Sancto Cuthberto*, ch. 26 (*Symeonis Monachi Opera Omnia*, ed. T. Arnold, 2 vols., Rolls Ser. (London, 1882–5) I, 211); this work may originally have been compiled in the mid-tenth century (E. Craster, 'The Patrimony of St Cuthbert', *EHR* 69 (1954), 177–99), but various passages were interpolated and added in the eleventh century, of which the account of Athelstan's visit might be one.

the 990s the community of St Cuthbert left Chester-le-Street and found a new home at Durham;[136] so the manuscript was at Durham from the late tenth century, and presumably remained there until the sixteenth or early seventeenth century, when it was acquired by Sir Robert Cotton.[137] The manuscript was almost totally destroyed in the fire at Ashburnham House on 23 October 1731; twelve, or thirteen, leaves are said to have survived that disaster, but these were further damaged in a fire at the binder's premises on 10 July 1865, so all that now remain are twelve fragments, badly shrivelled and charred.[138] The original contents of the manuscript can, however, be reconstructed in some detail from accounts of it published before the fire of 1731, notably Thomas Smith's catalogue of the Cotton library (1696) and Humphrey Wanley's catalogue of Anglo-Saxon manuscripts (1705);[139] these sources may be supplemented by additions made in certain annotated copies of Smith's catalogue,[140] and by transcripts of particular items in the manuscript made by scholars active in the seventeenth and early eighteenth centuries.

The manuscript comprised 122 folios;[141] of the twelve surviving fragments, one (fol. 1) is the original opening leaf, two (fols. 2–3) are from the prelimi-

Statements to the same effect, in the *Historia regum*, ch. 83 (*Symeonis Monachi Opera Omnia*, ed. Arnold II, 93; *EHD*, no. 3, p. 278), in the *Historia Dunelmensis Ecclesiae*, ch. 18 (*Symeonis Monachi Opera Omnia*, ed. Arnold I, 75), and in the *Historia regum*, ch. 107 (*ibid.* II, 124), probably depend ultimately on the *Historia de S. Cuthberto*. Athelstan's name was entered in a prominent position in the *Liber uitae* of St Cuthbert's community (BL Cotton Domitian vii, 15r), probably – but not necessarily – in connection with a visit by the king to St Cuthbert's shrine; for a facsimile, see *Liber Vitae Ecclesiae Dunelmensis*, ed. A. H. Thompson, Surtees Soc. 136 (Durham, 1923).

136 See *The Relics of Saint Cuthbert*, ed. Battiscombe, pp. 36–8.

137 The manuscript was perhaps among the gospel-books listed in the Durham *Liber de reliquiis* (1383), ptd *Extracts from the Account Rolls of the Abbey of Durham* II, ed. J. T. Fowler, Surtees Soc. 100 (Durham, 1899), 425–40, at 432; for gospel-books in medieval library catalogues of Durham, see *Catalogi Veteres Librorum Ecclesiæ Cathedralis Dunelmi*, ed. B. Botfield, Surtees Soc. 7 (London, 1838), 16 and 91–2. The manuscript is no. 233 in the Cotton catalogue of 1621 (BL Harley 6018, 104r).

138 According to the 1732 report on the effects of the Cotton fire, 'a dozen pieces of leaves' survived (*Reports from Committees of the House of Commons* I [1773], 445–535, at 471); but Sir Frederic Madden (in his notes on the state of the Cotton manuscripts, compiled in 1866: BL Add. 62578) mentions thirteen leaves, including three with the letter of Eusebius, and then refers to the further damage sustained in 1865. For a reproduction of 7r (incorporating a decorated initial from the beginning of Mark's Gospel), see *The Golden Age of Anglo-Saxon Art 966–1066*, ed. J. Backhouse, D. Turner and L. Webster, British Museum exhibition catalogue (London, 1984), p. 25.

139 T. Smith, *Catalogus Librorum Manuscriptorum Bibliothecæ Cottonianæ* (Oxford, 1696), p. 70, and G. Hickes and H. Wanley, *Antiquæ Literaturæ Septentrionalis Libri Duo* (Oxford, 1705) II, 238.

140 The most useful of these for present purposes is Smith's own copy: Oxford, Bodleian Library, Smith 140. I am grateful to Richard Sharpe for sending me a transcript of Smith's annotations.

141 Keeper's Copy of Smith's catalogue in BL; also BL Add. 46911 (another annotated copy).

naries to the gospel-book, three (fols. 4–6) are from St Matthew's Gospel, five (fols. 7–11) are from St Mark's Gospel, and one (fol. 12) is from St John's Gospel. Fol. 1 may have been part of the first quire of the gospel-book itself, originally left blank, or a flyleaf, whether original or one added to the manuscript in the first half of the tenth century. A brief description of the contents of the manuscript was written on 1r, evidently by one of the Cottonian librarians in the seventeenth century.[142] The verso of fol. 1 received various additions concerning St Cuthbert in the tenth and eleventh centuries, and a certain amount of the text can still be read or reconstructed (see pl. VIII).[143] Lines 1–8 appear to be a prayer or hymn invoking the saint, written in Insular minuscule.[144] Lines 9–10, in the same hand, represent some form of colophon:

> Kł. Iuł. ƀdictus euernensicus pingere feci in
> honore sc̄i Cudbrechti episcubi.[145]

The most natural interpretation of these lines would seem to be that on the kalends of July (1 July) in some unspecified year Benedict *Euernensicus* (that is, the Irishman)[146] had the prayer written in the manuscript in honour of St Cuthbert the bishop.[147] To judge from the script, the prayer and the colophon were written in the first half of the tenth century, and it is possible that both were added to the manuscript on the occasion of its presentation to Chester-le-Street: Benedict the Irishman can perhaps be identified as the *Benedictus*

142 The text of the description is damaged by fire, but can be recovered from Durham, University Library, Mickleton and Spearman 36, p. 239; on this transcript, see below, n. 158.

143 Again, I am grateful to Mr A. Parker for his assistance with modern technology; reading the text by transmitted light proved rather more effective in this instance than the ultra-violet lamp or the Video Spectral Comparator.

144 It is difficult to reconstruct and construe the text, but it is hoped that publication of the plate will stimulate further study. Note the different spellings of Cuthbert's name: *Cudberectus* (line 1), *Cudbrecht* (line 4) and *Cudbercht* (line 7). Perhaps some reflection of the text may yet be found in later prayers or hymns composed at Chester-le-Street or Durham; see C. Hohler, 'The Durham Services in Honour of St Cuthbert', *The Relics of Saint Cuthbert*, ed. Battiscombe, pp. 155–91.

145 Much of the text is visible on pl. VIII; it is otherwise reconstructed from Wanley's description of the manuscript. Wanley supposed that the initial letter was **f**, in error for **k**; but compare the form of the standard abbreviation for Kalends in, e.g., the late-eleventh-century manuscript of the Annals of Inisfallen (Oxford, Bodleian Library, Rawlinson B. 503; facsimile, R. I. Best and E. Mac Neill, *The Annals of Inisfallen* (Dublin, 1933), e.g. pl. 12).

146 In Adomnán's *Vita Columbae*, *Euernia* is frequently used for 'Ireland', and *Euerniensis* is used for 'Irish'; see *Adomnan's Life of Columba*, ed. A. O. Anderson and M. O. Anderson (London, 1961), p. 30.

147 Robinson (*TSD*, p. 53) associated the colophon with the portrait of Athelstan and Cuthbert which preceded Matthew's Gospel (below, pp. 173–4); but 'pingere feci' need not refer to an act of painting, and in the manuscript the portrait would have been quite far apart from the colophon.

*episcopus* who attests a charter of Athelstan issued at (King's) Worthy in Hampshire on 21 June 931,[148] so we might reasonably expect to find him in the king's entourage at other times;[149] and if we may assume that the presentation was made in 934, it would be appropriate that it should have taken place around 1 July, since charters show that in 934 the king and his entourage were at Winchester on 28 May, at Nottingham on 7 June, and back in the south at Buckingham on 12 September,[150] making it quite likely that they were at Chester-le-Street, *en route* for Scotland, on 1 July. According to Smith, a text which he describes as 'lex omnium venientium ad festum S. Cuthberti' occurred at the beginning of the manuscript. Parts of this text can still be read on 1v, lines 11–14, written in small Caroline minuscule script apparently of the eleventh century; and the whole text can be reconstructed from a transcript made by James Mickleton in 1715.[151]

After this first leaf, the gospel-book itself began with the usual preliminaries: the letter of Jerome to Damasus (explaining the purpose of the new translation), Jerome's prologue (*Plures fuisse*), the letter of Eusebius to Carpianus (explaining the use of his canon tables), and then the Eusebian canons themselves. These preliminaries were apparently followed by a prologue and chapter-list for the Gospel of St Matthew. In the gospel-book in its original state these items were directly followed by a portrait of Matthew and the text of his Gospel, but it seems that in the tenth century an extra leaf was inserted immediately before the portrait.[152] On one side of this leaf was another portrait, of Athelstan presenting a book to St Cuthbert: Athelstan, on bended

148 S 413 (BCS 675). The episcopal witnesses comprise the two archbishops, and sixteen bishops (including those of all the southern dioceses, except Hereford and Sherborne): the first five represent the dioceses of Lichfield, Crediton, Worcester, Wells and Cornwall; these are followed by 'Benedictus episcopus'; the next five represent Dorchester, London, Ramsbury, Winchester and Selsey, followed by 'Cynsige episcopus' (? a suffragan of Ramsbury – S 1208) and 'Wulfhelm episcopus' (unidentified); the last three are Cyneferth of Rochester, Æscberht (? a suffragan of York – S 401), and Wigred of Chester-le-Street. Much remains to be done on the bishops who attest Athelstan's charters; but the evidence of this list suggests that Benedict was one of several suffragan bishops active in England at the time.

149 It must be admitted that Bishop Benedict does not occur in the witness-lists of the charters which were issued during the course of the expedition north in 934 (see next note); but this need not imply that he was not present.

150 S 425, 407 and 426.

151 'Hec est lex omnium uenientium ad festum S. Cuthberti. Septem diebus ante et post festum Sancti: omnes habebunt pacem ueniendo et redeundo et recta strata pergant, nec uagentur huc et illuc per uillas; et qui in pace ipsa pacem fregerit, emendet antequam de pace redeat'; ptd from Durham, University Library, Mickleton and Spearman 36, p. 239. I am most grateful to Professor Offler for drawing my attention to this transcript, and for his kindness in sending me a copy of it. In his annotated copy of his catalogue, Smith noted of this text: 'Characteres in ultimis lineis pene disparent. Sed lex illa in pagina post recensionem capitulorum S. Lucae reperitur plenius et planius.' See, further, below, p. 175 and n. 158.

152 For the position of this leaf, see Wanley's description of the manuscript.

knee, was shown crowned, offering the book to St Cuthbert with his right hand and holding a sceptre in his left hand; Cuthbert, seated in his church, was shown with a halo, giving the blessing with his right hand and holding a book in his left hand.[153] The following inscription, apparently written in display capitals, was placed above the portrait:

SCO̅ CVDBERHTO EPI̅S
EATHELSTAN ANGLO
RVM PIISIMVS REX
HOC EVVANGELIVM OFFE
RT[154]

It seems likely that this portrait and inscription represented the primary notice of Athelstan's gift of the gospel-book to St Cuthbert's: the portrait was evidently closely related to that of Athelstan and Cuthbert which serves as a frontispiece to Cambridge, Corpus Christi College 183 (see below, p. 180), and which is certainly contemporary; and in iconographical terms it probably stood in the same late antique tradition of presentation portraits transmitted through ninth-century Carolingian intermediaries.[155] At some later date, probably in the eleventh century, an Old English manumission (of ten men and women, for the soul of a certain 'Mældorð') was entered at about this point in the manuscript, probably on the verso of the leaf depicting Athelstan and Cuthbert;[156] the text of this document was fortunately transcribed by Cotton's

153 This reconstruction depends on descriptions by Smith ('Habetur quoque figura R. Æthelstani coronam in capite gestantis, cum libro in dextra, & sceptro in sinistra, & poplite flexo offerentis Evangelia S. Cuthberto, sedenti in Cathedra') and Wanley ('S. Cuthbertus Corona & Gloria caput redimitus, sedens, dextra benedicens, & sinistra volumen tenens: ante quem Æthelstanus Rex Diademate cinctus flexo poplite, dextra librum offert S. Cuthberto, sinistra sceptrum'); see also next note.

154 'Athelstan, the pious king of the English, gives this gospel-book to St Cuthbert, the bishop.' The text is reproduced from Wanley's description; one assumes that his use of capitals, and the layout, reflect the original. Richard James described the portrait and inscription as follows: 'huius [*sc.* Cuthbert] in principio sedentis in cathedra imago depingitur, cum imagine Æthelstani adgeniculantis et tradentis ei librum cum hac inscriptione "Sc̄o Cuðberhto episcopo Eathelstan Anglorum piissimus rex hoc evengelium offert"' (Oxford, Bodleian Library, James 18, p. 43).

155 See F. Wormald, 'The "Winchester School" before St Æthelwold', *England before the Conquest: Studies in Primary Sources presented to Dorothy Whitelock*, ed. P. Clemoes and K. Hughes (Cambridge, 1971), pp. 305–13, at 309; J. J. G. Alexander, 'The Benedictional of St Æthelwold and Anglo-Saxon Illumination of the Reform Period', *Tenth-Century Studies*, ed. Parsons, pp. 169–83, at 173; and Wood, 'King Æthelstan's Empire', pp. 268–9. See also D. Bullough, '"Imagines Regum" and their Significance in the Early Medieval West', *Studies in Memory of David Talbot Rice*, ed. G. Robertson and G. Henderson (Edinburgh, 1975), pp. 223–76.

156 Wanley states that it occurred at the bottom of the page preceding the Gospel of St Matthew; the Athelstan/Cuthbert portrait was perhaps on a recto, in which case the page in question would probably be the verso of the same leaf, otherwise blank.

librarian, Richard James, in about 1630, and has been printed from this transcript.[157]

After the portrait of Matthew and the text of his Gospel, the gospel-book continued with a prologue, chapter-list, portrait and Gospel of St Mark, followed by a prologue, chapter–list, portrait and Gospel of St Luke. There would seem to have been a blank space left after the chapter-list for Luke's Gospel, and in the twelfth century this was used for the insertion of an expanded version of the *Lex* of St Cuthbert, already seen in an earlier form on 1v; the expanded version is known from transcripts by Richard James (*c.* 1630), John Rowell (*c.* 1700) and James Mickleton (1715),[158] and has been printed from the first two (but not the third).[159]

Luke's Gospel was followed by a prologue, chapter-list, portrait and Gospel of St John. Again, there would seem to have been a blank space left after the chapter-list for John's Gospel, and this was used for the insertion (perhaps on separate occasions) of two Old English texts, presumably in the tenth or eleventh century.[160] The first, transcribed and printed by Wanley in 1705, was another record of King Athelstan's gift of the gospel-book to St Cuthbert's:

In nomine domini nostri Iesu Christi. Ic Æþelstan cyning selle þas boc into scō Cudberhte . 7 bebeode on Godes noman . 7 on þæs halgan weres . þæt hio næfre nan monn of þisse stowe · mid nanum facne ne reaflace ne afirre ne nane þara geofona þe ic to þisse stowe gedoo. Gif þonne hwelc monn to þæm dyrstig beo · þæt he þisses hwæt breoce oððe wende · beo he scyldig wiþ God 7 wiþ menn · 7 dæl neomende Iudases

157 H. H. E. Craster, 'Some Anglo-Saxon Records of the See of Durham', *AAe* 4th ser. 1 (1925), 189–98, at 190 (from Oxford, Bodleian Library, James 18, p. 43). Craster (*ibid.* p. 191, n. 3a) believed that Mældorth represented OE Mæthelthryth, a woman's name, but David Dumville advises me that it is more likely to represent Old Irish Mael Doraid.

158 Richard James's transcript is Oxford, Bodleian Library, James 18, pp. 43–4. John Rowell was registrar to the Dean and Chapter of Durham, *c.* 1694–1705; his original transcript is Durham, University Library, Mickleton and Spearman 10, p. 87, and he entered a copy in Durham, Dean and Chapter Muniments, Cart. II, 307v. James Mickleton (1688–1719) was a Durham lawyer and antiquary; he visited the Cotton library in 1715, where he first collated Rowell's original transcript against the manuscript (making a few corrections), and then took further notes about the manuscript, now Durham, University Library, Mickleton and Spearman 36, pp. 239–40 (consisting of a copy of the Cottonian table of contents, an extract from Smith's catalogue, a copy of the *Lex* of St Cuthbert (above, n. 151), and a copy of the expanded *Lex* which preceded Luke's Gospel).

159 *Historiæ Dunelmensis Scriptores Tres*, ed. J. Raine, Surtees Soc. 9 (London, 1839), ccccxxx–ccccxxxi (citing Rowell's transcripts), and E. Craster, 'The Peace of St Cuthbert', *JEH* 8 (1957), 93–5 (from James's transcript). Mickleton's text differs in certain respects from the others, so a new edition is needed.

160 Wanley states that the first of these texts was placed before St John's Gospel; but Smith (in an annotation to his copy of his catalogue) places it more specifically 'post recensionem capitulorum S. Joannis'. It is clear from Wanley's account that the second text occurred on the same page as the first.

hletes Scariothes, 7 on Domes dæge þæs egeslican cwides to geheranne 7 to onfone . discedite a me maledicti in ignem æternum et reliq.[161]

The chief interest of this inscription is that it was clearly written by someone who was familiar with the conventions of royal diplomas: it begins with a standard form of invocation, continues (after the disposition itself) with a prohibition clause, and ends with a sanction. We have already seen that two of the other inscriptions in manuscripts associated with Athelstan have close links with Latin diplomas: that in Tiberius A. ii (15v) employs a royal style current in the later 930s and was written by a scribe who is known also to have written royal diplomas in the 940s, and that in Lambeth 1370 anticipates the so-called 'alliterative' charters of the 940s and 950s. But if in these cases the diplomatic parallels were at least compatible with the assumption that the inscriptions themselves are genuine and contemporary, it has to be said in the case of this inscription in Otho B. ix that the parallels are easier to explain if one supposes that the inscription was written some time later in the tenth century. Prohibition clauses are more a feature of charters issued in the second half of the tenth century than of charters issued in the 930s,[162] and the wording of the sanction suggests a general familiarity with several different formulas current in the 940s and thereafter.[163] As we have seen, the primary inscription recording Athelstan's gift of the gospel-book to St Cuthbert's was probably that associated with the portrait placed in a prominent position before the portrait of St Matthew, so perhaps the Old English inscription inserted in a blank space after the chapter-list for the Gospel of St John should be regarded as a reiteration of the grant, added at a later date to strengthen its terms.[164]

161 Ptd (from Wanley) *Anglo-Saxon Charters*, ed. Robertson, p. 48 (no. 24), with translation, p. 49: 'In the name of our Lord Jesus Christ. I, King Athelstan, give this book to St Cuthbert's and enjoin in the name of God and of the holy saint, that no one remove it from this foundation by any fraud or robbery, or any of the gifts which I bestow on this foundation. If, however, anyone is so presumptuous as to violate or change this in any particular, he shall incur the wrath both of God and of men, and shall participate in the fate of Judas Iscariot, and on the Day of Judgement shall hear and receive the dread sentence, "Depart from me, ye accursed, into everlasting fire, etc.".' This inscription should be compared with that entered in the Stockholm Codex Aureus in the second half of the ninth century; see *SEHD*, no. 9 (*EHD*, no. 98).

162 Prohibition formulas occur in several charters of Athelstan, but the texts in question are not of good repute (e.g. S 386–9, 410, 424, 427, 434, 436 and 455); in genuine texts, they occur more frequently in the 940s and thereafter, and they are particularly characteristic of charters issued in the late tenth century.

163 That is to say, I cannot find any single formula which would account for the wording of the inscription in Otho B. ix; and in so far as it reflects awareness of expressions used in several different formulas current in the central decades of the tenth century, it is most natural to infer that it was composed after these formulas had been disseminated.

164 Robinson (*TSD*, p. 52) refers to the inscription as Athelstan's 'original dedication'.

1 Oxford, Bodleian Library, Rawlinson C. 697, 78v (see p. 144)

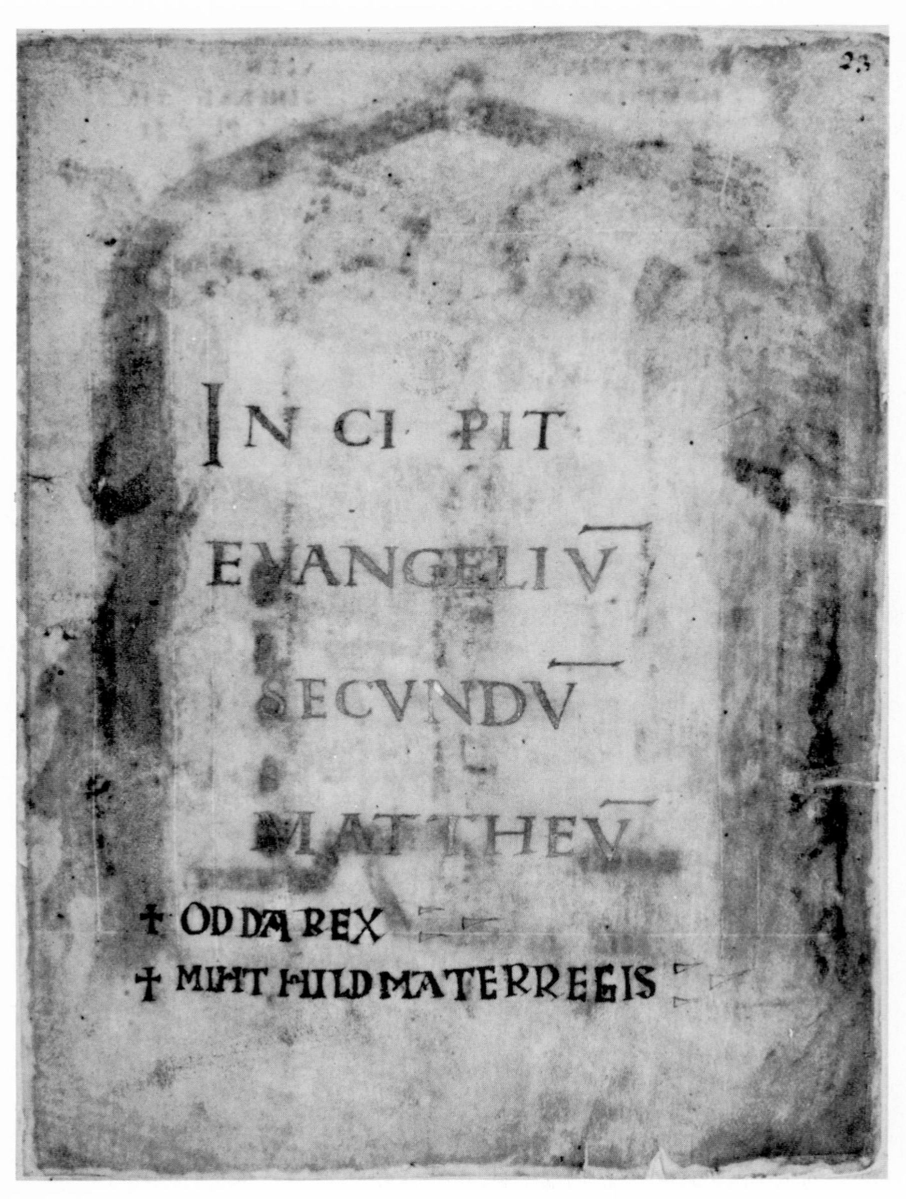
IN CI PIT
EVANGELIV
SECVNDV
MATTHEV
+ ODDA REX
+ MIHT HILD MATER REGIS

11 BL Cotton Tiberius A. ii, 24r (see pp. 147–9)

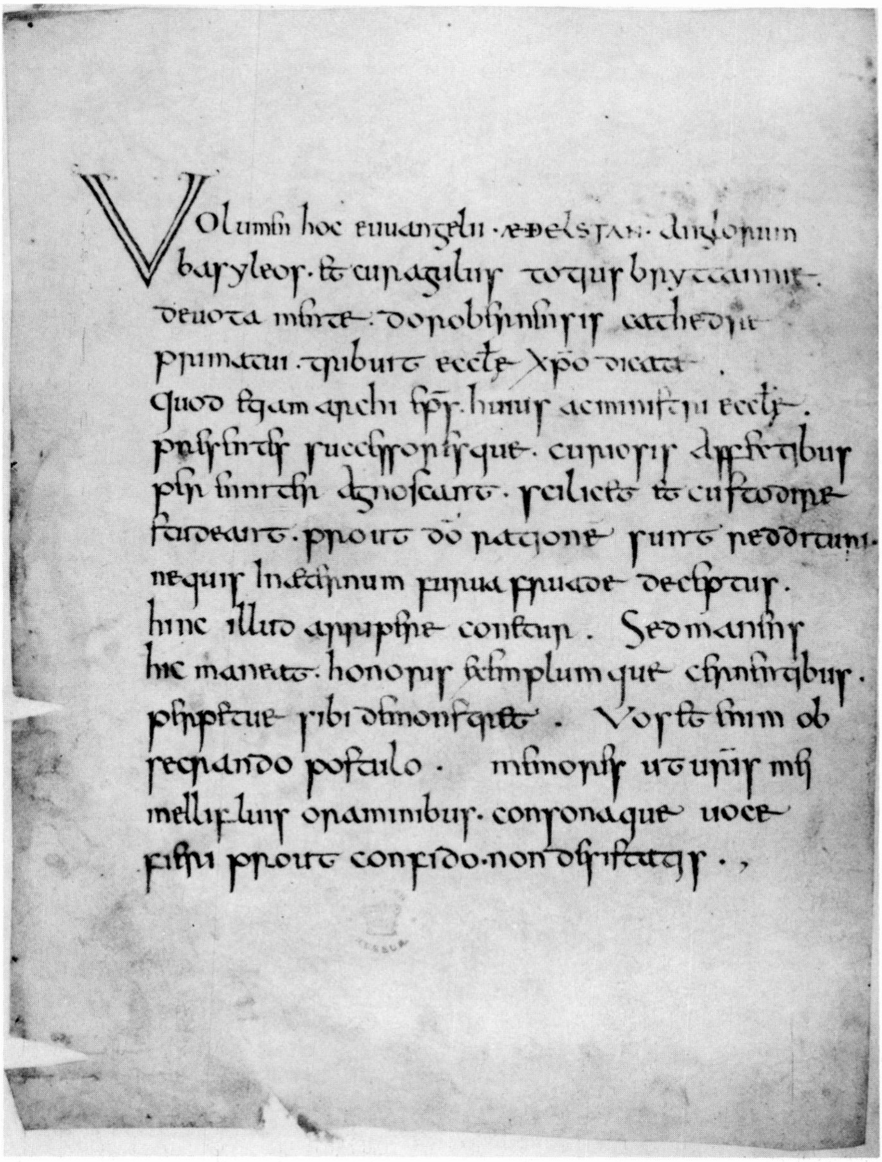

III BL Cotton Tiberius A. ii, 15v (see pp. 149–50)

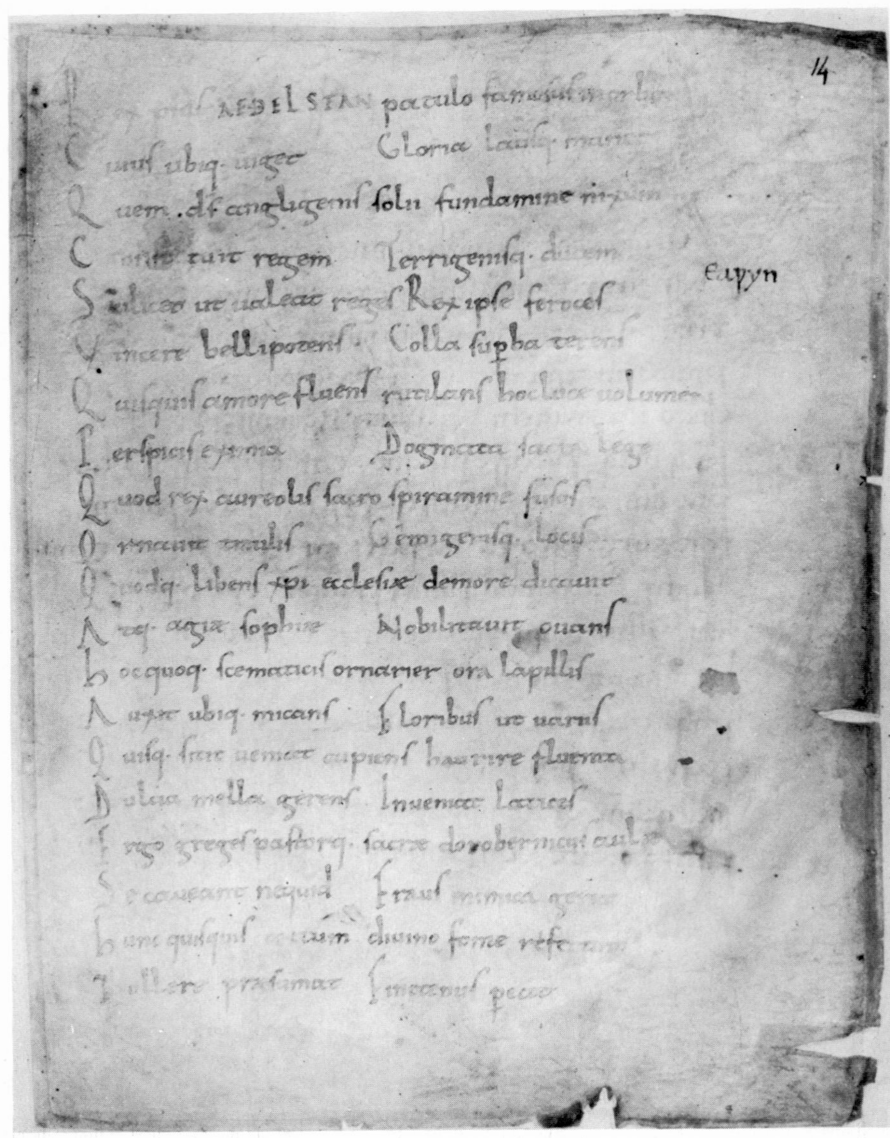

IV BL Cotton Tiberius A. ii, 15r (see pp. 150–1)

+ MÆIELBRIDVS·MAC
DVRNANI·ISTV·TEXTV
PER·TRIQVADRV·DO
DIGNE·DOGMATIZAT
AST·AETHELSTANVS
ANGLOSÆXNA·REX·ET
RECTOR·DORVERNENSI
METROPOLI·DAT·PÆVV

v London, Lambeth Palace Library, 1370, 3v (see pp. 153–9)

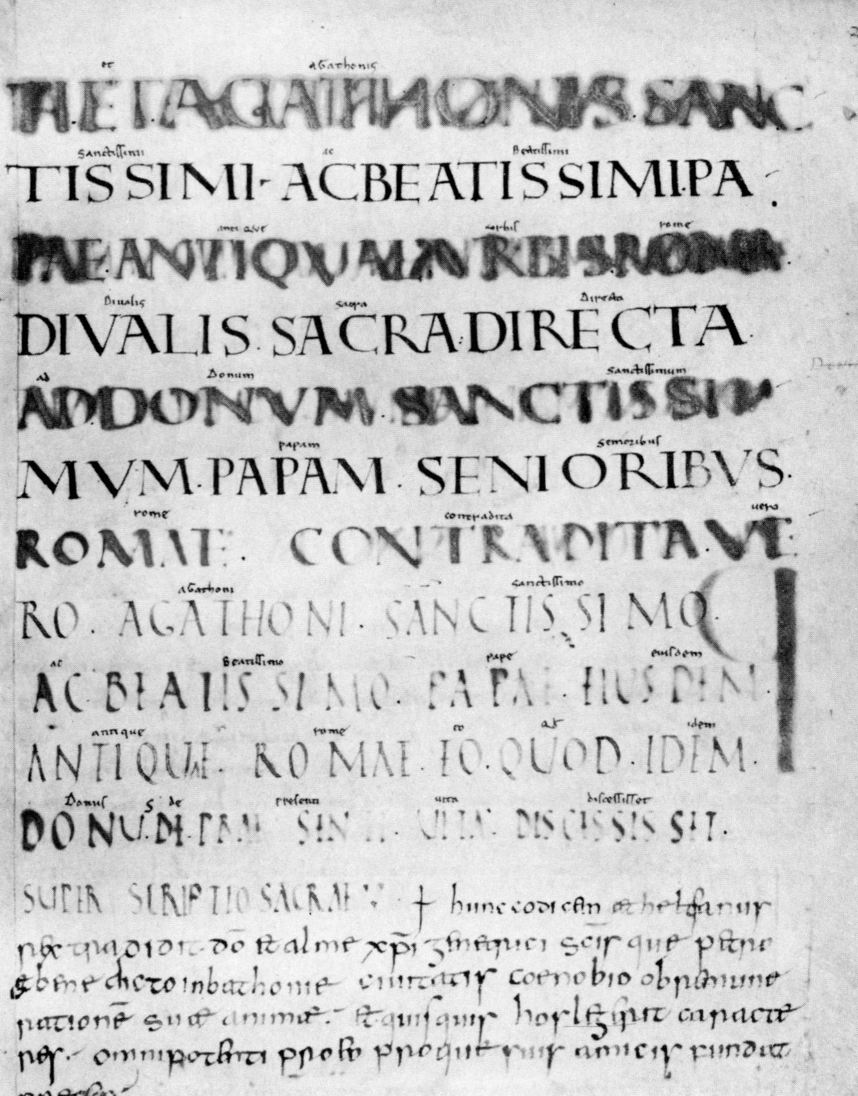

VI BL Cotton Claudius B. v, 5r (see pp. 160–3)

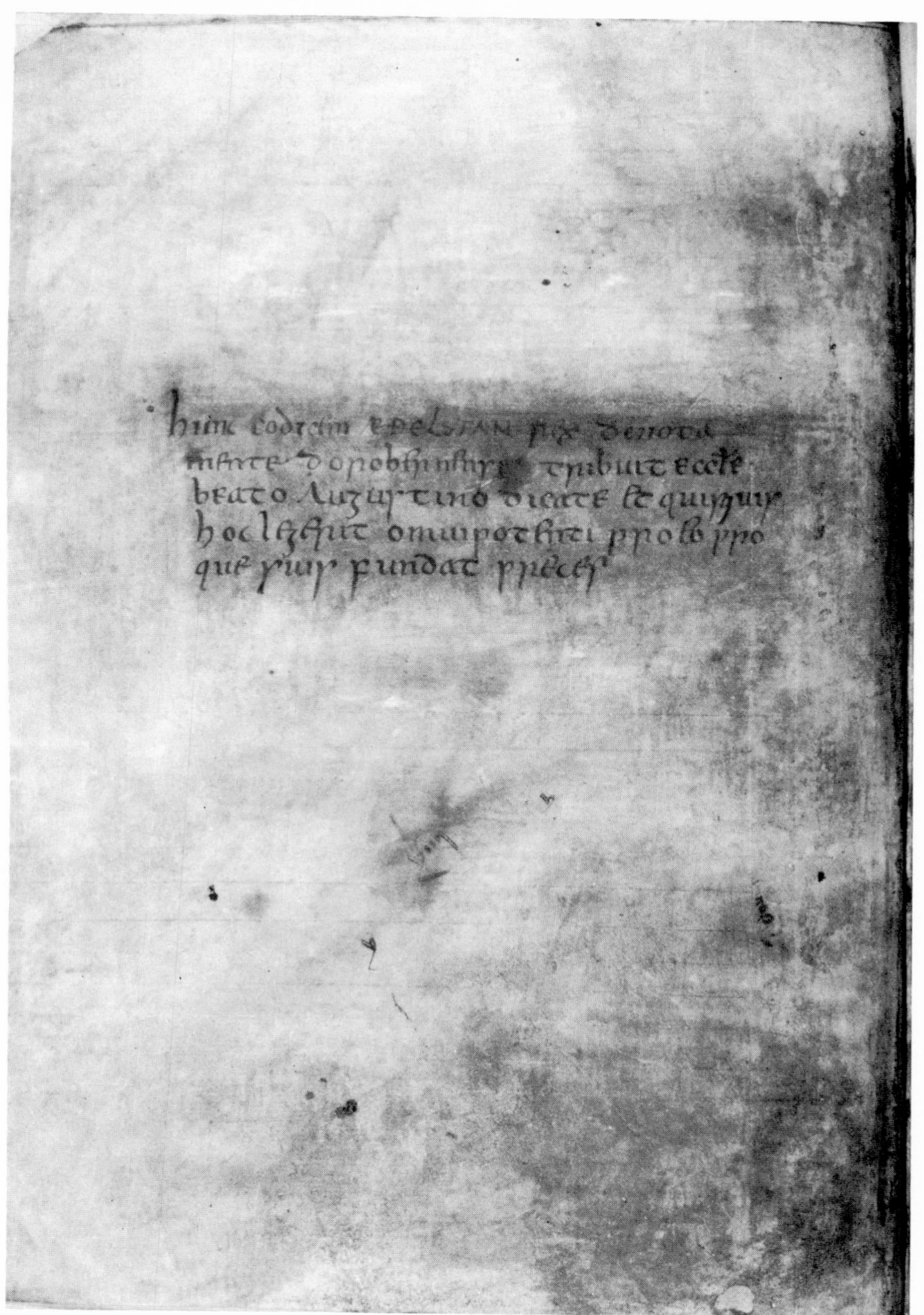
hunc codicem eðelstan rex deuota
mente [illegible] tribuit eccle
beato augustino dicate et quisquis
hoc legerit omnipotenti pro illo pro
que suis fundat preces

vii BL Royal 1. A. XVIII, 3v (see pp. 165–70)

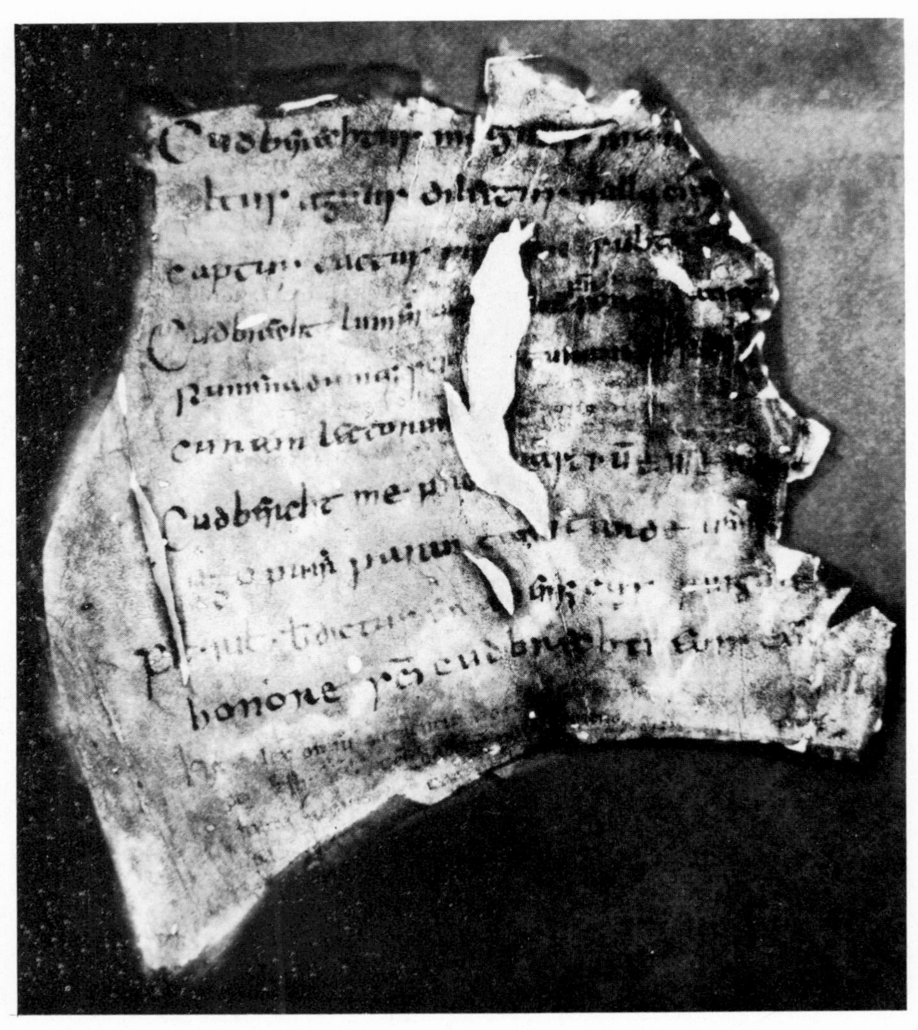

VIII BL Cotton Otho B. ix, IV (see pp. 172–3)
(photographed by transmitted light)

IX Cambridge, Corpus Christi College 183, IV (see p. 180)

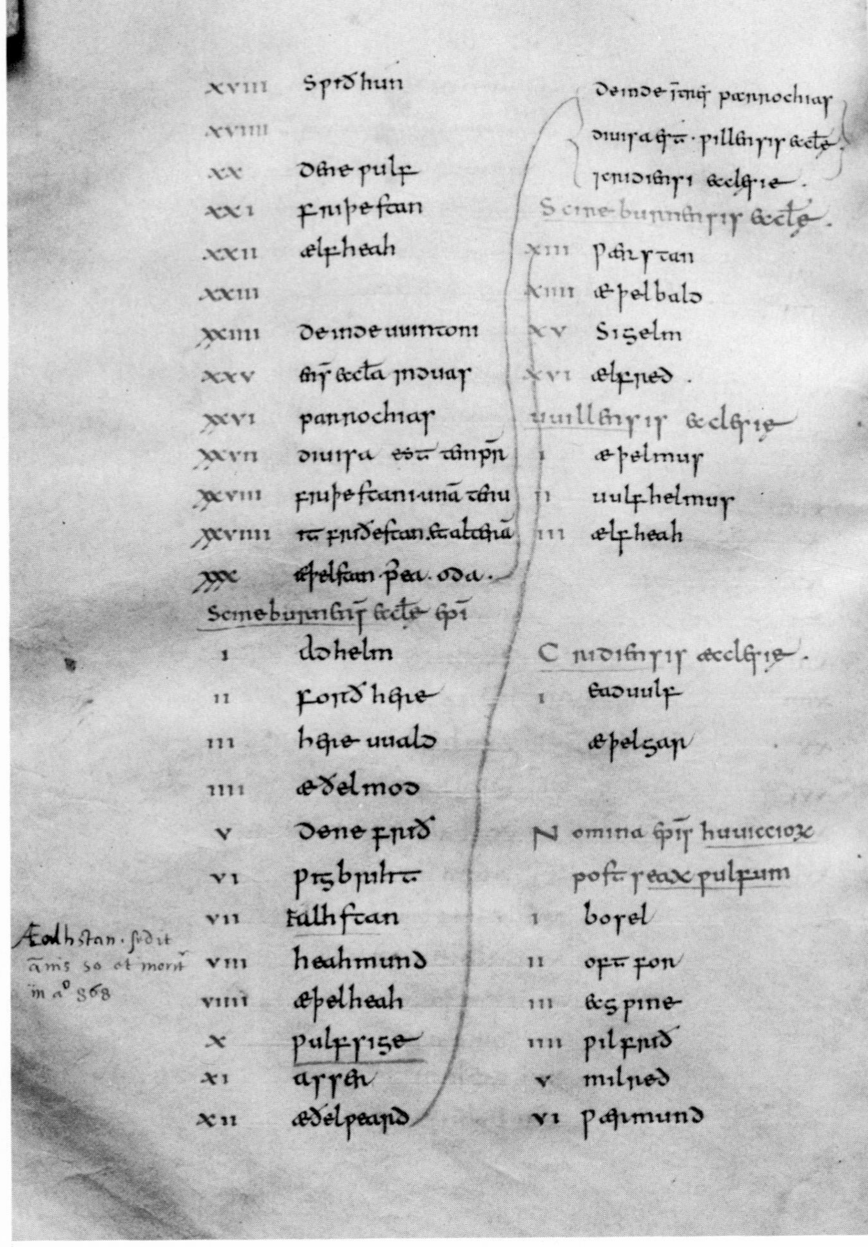

xviii Sigðhun
xviiii
xx Denepulf
xxi Friþestan
xxii ælfheah
xxiii
xxiiii Deinde uuintoni
xxv sunt secta in duas
xxvi pannochias
xxvii diuisa est tempore
xxviii Friþestani una tenu
xxviiii et Friðestan secunda
xxx Æþelstan et Oda.

Scireburnensis ecclesiae episcopi
i Aldhelm
ii Forðhere
iii Here uuald
iiii Æðelmod
v Denefrið
vi Wigberht
vii Ealhstan
viii Heahmund
viiii Æþelheah
x Wulfsige
xi Asser
xii Æðelpeard

Ealhstan sedit annis 50 et mort. in aº 868

Deinde sunt pannochias diuisa est in Willensis ecclesie et Sciraburnensis ecclesie.

Scireburnensis ecclesiae.
xiii Wærstan
xiiii Æþelbald
xv Sigelm
xvi Ælfred.

Uuillensis ecclesie
i Æþelmus
ii Wulfhelmus
iii Ælfheah

Cridiensis ecclesie.
i Eadulf
Æþelgar

Nomina episcoporum huuicciorum post Seaxwulfum
i Bosel
ii Oftfor
iii Ecgwine
iiii Wilfrið
v Milred
vi Wærmund

x Cambridge, Corpus Christi College 183, 62v (see pp. 183–4)

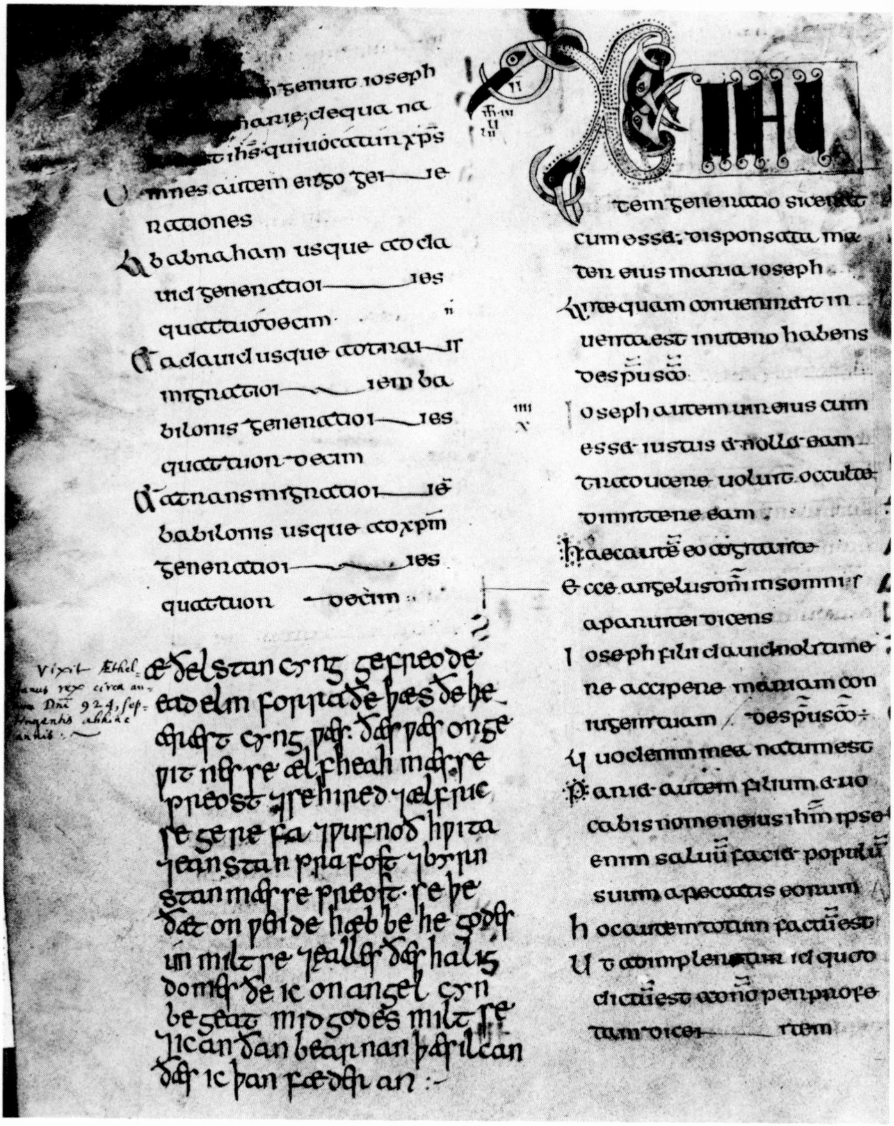

XI BL Royal I. B. VII, 15v (see pp. 185–6)

XII Coburg, Landesbibliothek, I, 168r (see pp. 189–93)

XIII St Gallen, Stiftsbibliothek, 915, p. 5 (see pp. 198–9)

xiv St Gallen, Stiftsarchiv, Cod. C 3 B 55, p. 77 (see p. 200)

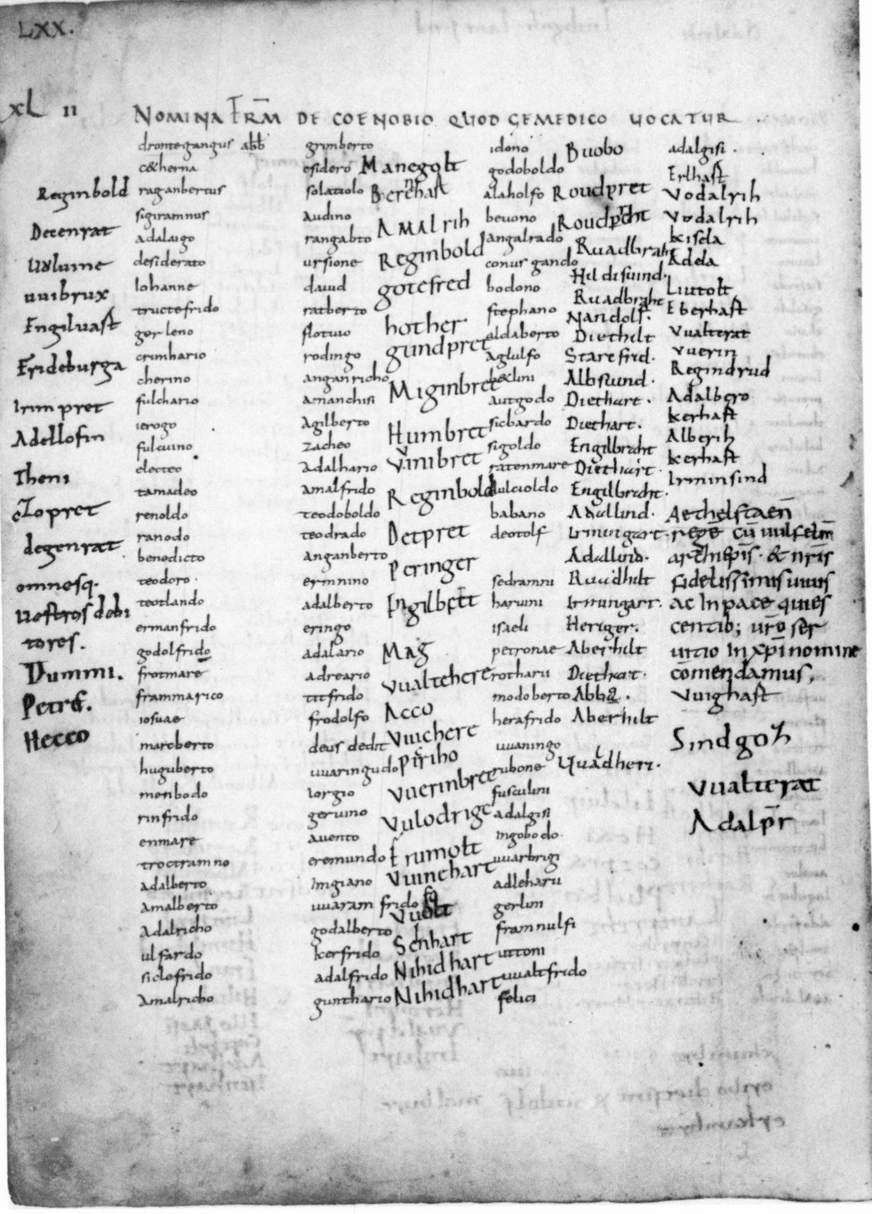
LXX.

xl ii NOMINA FR(AT)R(U)M DE COENOBIO QUOD GEMEDICO UOCATUR

Reginbold
Detenrat
Uuluuine
uuibrux
Engiluast
Fridiburga
Irminpret
Adellosin
Thens
Lopret
degenrat
omnesq.
nostros debitores.
Dummi.
Petrus.
Hecco

drotmeganguus abb
cetherna
raganbertus
sigiramnus
adalaigo
desiderato
Iohanne
tructefrido
gorleno
erimhario
cherino
fulchario
ierogo
fulcuino
electeo
tamadeo
renoldo
ranodo
benedicto
teodoro
teotlando
ermanfrido
godolfrido
frotmare
frammarico
iosuae
maroberto
huguberto
monbodo
rinfrido
enmare
trocteramno
adalberto
amalberto
adalricho
ulfardo
siclefrido
amalricho

grimberto
eisdero
solatiolo
audino
rangabrto
ursione
dauid
ratberto
flotuio
rodingo
anganricho
amanchisi
agilberto
zacheo
adalhario
amalfrido
teodoboldo
teodrado
anganberto
ermnino
adalberto
eringo
adalario
adreario
tetfrido
frodolfo
deus dedit
uuaringudo
lorgio
geruino
auento
eremundo
ingirano
uuaram
godalberto
kerfrido
adalfrido
gunthario

Manegolt
Berehast
Amalrih
Reginbold
gotefred
hother
gundpret
Miginbret
Humbret
Uuinbret
Reginbold
Detpret
Peringer
Engilbert
Mag
Uualtchere
Acco
Uuichere
Pfriho
Uuerinbret
Uulodrige
Frumolt
Uunnehart
frido
Uuolt
Senhart
Nihidhart
Nihidhart

idono
godoboldo
alaholfo
beuono
iangalrado
conur gando
bodono
stephano
aldaberto
agilulfo
hechini
autgodo
sicbardo
sigoldo
patenmare
uulcuoldo
babano
deotolf
sedramnu
haruini
isaeli
petronae
rotharu
modoberto
herafrido
uuaningo
rubone
fusculini
adalgisi
ingobodo
uuarbrigi
adleharu
gerlini
framnulfi
uttoni
uualtfrido
folici

Buobo
Roudpret
Roudpreht
Ruadbraht
Hel di suind
Ruadbrght
Nandolf
Diethilt
Starefrid
Albsuind
Diethart
Diethart
Engilbreht
Diethart
Engilbreht
Adallind
Irmingart
Adallind
Ruadhilt
Irmingart
Heriger
Aberhilt
Diethart
Abba
Aberhilt
Uuadheri

adalgisi
Erlhast
Uodalrih
Uodalrih
kisela
Adela
Liutolt
Eberhast
Uualtcrat
Uuerin
Regindrud
Adalbero
kerhast
Alberih
kerhast
Irminsind
Aethelstan rege cu(m) uulfelm(o) archiepis(copo) & n(ost)ris fidelissimis uuius ac in pace quiescentib(us) u(est)ro servitio in xpi nomine comendamus,
Uuighast
Sindgoz
Uualtcrat
Adalpr

XV Zürich, Zentralbibliothek, Rh. hist. 27, p. LXX (see p. 200)

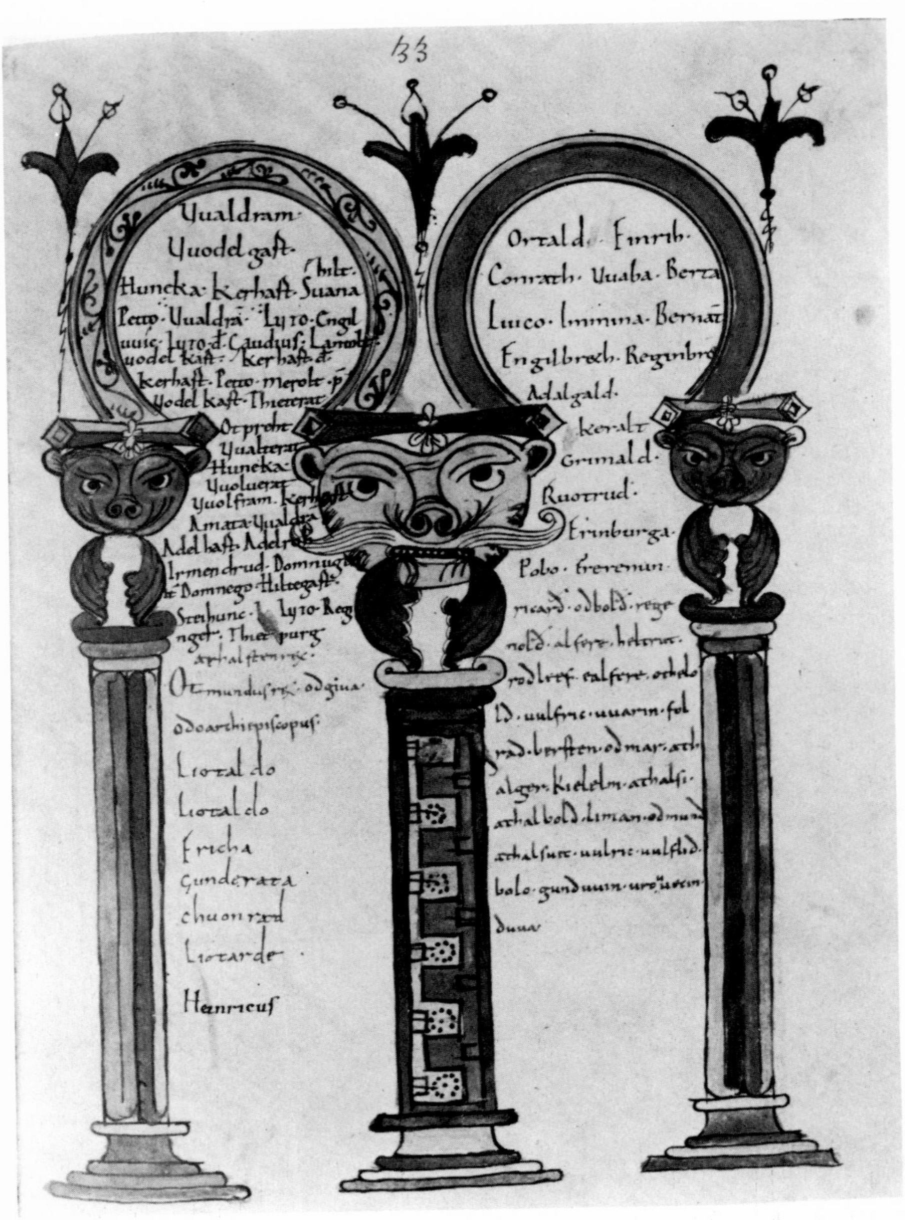

XVI St Gallen, Stiftsarchiv, Codex Fabariensis 1, p. 33 (see p. 201)

This Old English inscription was followed on the same page by another, described by Wanley as 'Nota Sax. de donis quæ (S. Cuthberto) contulit idem Rex Æthelstanus'.[165] Unfortunately, Wanley did not print the text; but it has long been recognized that a passage in the *Historia de S. Cuthberto* seems to have been based on a list of Athelstan's gifts to St Cuthbert's which was written in a gospel-book, presumably, therefore, the Old English list in Otho B. ix.[166] According to the *Historia*, Athelstan visited the shrine of St Cuthbert while *en route* for Scotland (a reference to his expedition in 934), and drew up a *testamentum* in which he recorded his gifts to the saint, and which he placed at Cuthbert's head.[167] The text of the document is then given in full, beginning as follows:

In nomine Domini nostri Iesu Christi. Ego Æþelstanus rex do sancto Cuthberto hunc textum euuangeliorum, .ii. casulas, et .i. albam, et .i. stolam, cum manipulo, et .i. cingulum . . .[168]

The list continues with a great variety of precious gifts, including 'a missal, two gospel-books ornamented with gold and silver, and a Life of St Cuthbert written in verse and prose'; so it would appear that Athelstan gave a total of five books to St Cuthbert's, three of which were copies of the gospels.[169] The list of gifts ends with a substantial estate at Wearmouth (with its several appendages) in Co. Durham,[170] and the document itself concludes with a sanction:

Hec omnia do sub Dei et sancti Cuthberti testimonio, ut siquis inde aliquid abstulerit, dampnetur in die iudicii cum Iuda traditore, et trudatur in ignem eternum, qui preparatus est diabolo et angelis eius.

It is naturally somewhat difficult to establish whether this Latin *testamentum* ever existed as a separate document placed in St Cuthbert's tomb, or whether it was composed by the compiler of the *Historia de S. Cuthberto* and should thus be regarded as no more than part of a good story; but the reference at the beginning to '*this* gospel-book' strongly suggests that the *testamentum* was directly based on information entered in a gospel-book, presumably Otho B. ix

165 See above, n. 160.

166 *TSD*, p. 52; *The Relics of Saint Cuthbert*, ed. Battiscombe, pp. 32–3.

167 *Symeonis Monachi Opera Omnia*, ed. Arnold I, 211; see above, n. 135. Athelstan's gifts were still to be seen at Durham in the early twelfth century (*Historia Dunelmensis Ecclesiae*, ch. 18: *ibid.* p. 75). See also Barker, 'Two Lost Documents', p. 142.

168 Ptd from Cambridge, University Library, Ff. 1. 27, pp. 201–2. The stole, maniple and girdle are presumably the embroideries found in the coffin of St Cuthbert in 1827; see *The Relics of Saint Cuthbert*, ed. Battiscombe, pp. 375–432, and below, n. 172.

169 For discussion of these books, see Lapidge, above, pp. 49–50. See also below, pp. 183–4.

170 Hart, *Early Charters of Northern England*, p. 118 (no. 120).

– which hardly encourages the view that it once had a separate existence in any form, let alone as a genuine record. We have already seen that the Old English inscription printed by Wanley, which referred to the gift of the gospel-book in particular, was probably a later-tenth-century addition to the manuscript; the Old English note on the king's gifts in general occurred on the same page (presumably underneath the inscription), and must have been either contemporary with it, or later still. If we assume that the Latin *testamentum* is a faithful translation of the Old English note, it would follow that both the inscription and the note were cast in the same semi-diplomatic form, beginning with an invocation and ending with a sanction; but it is perhaps more likely that the note was no more than a consolidated list of Athelstan's gifts (or supposed gifts) to St Cuthbert's, and that the Latin *testamentum* is a conflation of both the Old English records, taking its beginning and its end from the inscription and its central part from the note. This would have the effect of reducing from three to two the number of gospel-books given by Athelstan to St Cuthbert's, if the inscription and the note were intended to be taken separately. A more significant conclusion, however, arises from the suggestion that neither the *testamentum* nor the note is likely to have been a strictly contemporary record. There would no longer be any need to assume that all the gifts were handed over on a single occasion (in 934), for they could represent the fruits of Athelstan's generosity which had accumulated over a number of years. Otho B. ix could have been given in 934,[171] but the 'Life of St Cuthbert written in verse and prose' (of which more presently) could have been given on some later occasion. Moreover, the belief that all the items listed in the *testamentum* were given to St Cuthbert's by Athelstan himself would be undermined, since gifts received from others might well have been included in the list for good measure.[172]

After the prologue and chapter-list for John's Gospel, and the two inserted Old English inscriptions, Otho B. ix continued with a portrait of John and the text of his Gospel. The manuscript concluded with the capitulary-list, giving the readings appropriate for feast-days in each of the months of the year; but

171 The main reason for associating the gift of Otho B. ix with the (alleged) visit in 934 would be the dating of Benedict's inscription (above, p. 172) on '1 July', inasmuch as it fits well with the recorded progress of the expedition north; it should be noted, however, that Athelstan was at Eamont, Westmorland, on 12 July 927 (ASC 926 D).

172 Compare the list of relics given by King Athelstan to Exeter (see above, n. 7), which includes some (e.g. of King Edward the Martyr) which could not have had anything to do with him. It is conceivable, therefore, that the stole and maniple (commissioned by 'Ælfflæd' for Frithestan, bishop of Winchester (909–31)), and the 'girdle', were not in fact given to St Cuthbert's community by Athelstan himself; they may have been acquired at a later date, perhaps from one of Frithestan's successors as bishop of Winchester.

the details for July were missing in the late seventeenth century,[173] and may have been missing before. Various documents in Old English were entered on the last leaf. The first was a manumission, witnessed by St Cuthbert's community, of seven men, women and children by Alfred *lareow*, 'teacher', who can be identified as a member of the community at Durham in the first half of the eleventh century; the text of this document was transcribed by Richard James, and has been printed from his transcript.[174] The second document was a manumission of Dunecan, of P. his wife, and of their children with all their offspring, for Eadwulf and Mældord (presumably the 'Mældorð' whose manumission of ten persons was entered at an earlier point in the manuscript); but unfortunately the text of this manumission was neither printed by Wanley nor transcribed by James. The third document was a manumission by Eðered of his brother Earnon's daughter, witnessed by St Cuthbert's community; this was transcribed by James and has been printed from his transcript.[175] The Cottonian list of contents on 1r, and Smith's annotated copy of his 1696 catalogue, indicate that the manumissions on the last page of the manuscript were followed by a 'licentia nubendi a patruo nepti suae concessa' (that is, permission to marry granted by an uncle to his niece); Smith implies that this was in Old English, and had been transcribed by James,[176] and since Wanley does not mention such a text one has to assume that the reference is in fact a garbled allusion to the third manumission.

The above reconstruction of the contents of Otho B. ix is indeed a poor substitute for the original. Athelstan's gospel-book must take its place beside the other manuscripts in the Otho press, such as Otho A. x (the Chronicle of Æthelweard), Otho A. xii (Asser's Life of King Alfred) and Otho B. xi (the G manuscript of the Anglo-Saxon Chronicle), whose loss in the Cotton fire the historian has so much cause to regret. One can only hope that further light may yet be cast upon it: for example, by the identification of pictures which served as models for the portrait of Athelstan and Cuthbert; by tracing the influence of the portrait on other presentation scenes, or the influence of the Cuthbert prayers on later Durham services; or by the discovery of a transcription of the lost manumission or of the Old English note on King Athelstan's gifts.

173 This emerges from annotations in Smith's own copy of his catalogue

174 Craster, 'Some Anglo-Saxon Records', p. 190 (from Oxford, Bodleian Library, James 18, pp. 42–3).

175 *Ibid.* p. 191 (from Oxford, Bodleian Library, James 18, p. 43).

176 The last sentence of the description of Otho B. ix in Smith's catalogue reads 'In fine apponitur liber Homiliarum & vitarum, Saxonice'; in the annotated copy of his catalogue, Smith deleted 'liber . . . Saxonice' and added 'apponitur [in ultima pagina *deleted*] sunt et manumissionum antiquarum forma et licentia nubendi a Patruo nepti suae concessa. Saxonice, ut observat Jamesius.' The reference to 'liber Homiliarum & vitarum, Saxonice' properly belongs to the next entry in the catalogue, describing BL Cotton Otho B. x.

## Cambridge, Corpus Christi College 183

Cambridge, Corpus Christi College 183 is unique among the surviving manuscripts known to have been given by Athelstan to religious foundations, inasmuch as it is the only one wholly written in England during his reign.[177] Moreover, the manuscript would appear to have been commissioned especially for presentation by the king to Chester-le-Street, so it has important implications for the identification of a scriptorium which enjoyed royal patronage.

It is apparent from its physical structure that the manuscript was designed from the start as a volume intended for presentation by King Athelstan to St Cuthbert's community. The recto of the opening folio of the first quire (1r) was left blank, and the verso was used for the splendid picture of a king presenting a book to a saint (see pl. IX): the king, standing, is shown crowned, holding a book in both hands; and the saint, standing in front of his church, is shown with a halo, giving a blessing with his right hand and holding a book in his left hand. The composition is evidently quite closely related to the presentation scene in Otho B. ix (see above, pp. 173–4), and one imagines that both were made in the same centre and perhaps by the same artist; in Otho B. ix the figures were explicitly identified by an inscription, and while there is no such inscription in CCCC 183 there can be no doubt that the picture on 1v represents Athelstan presenting a book to St Cuthbert.[178]

The book was planned as a collection of texts celebrating the life of St Cuthbert. It starts opposite the presentation scene with Bede's prose *uita* (2r–56r), followed by extracts from the *Historia ecclesiastica gentis Anglorum* relating to St Cuthbert (56r–58r); after a blank leaf (58v) and some material of different nature (59r–69v), the collection continues with a list of difficult words in Bede's metrical *uita* (70rv), followed by the metrical *uita* itself (71r–92v) and a

177 See M. R. James, *A Descriptive Catalogue of the Manuscripts in the Library of Corpus Christi College, Cambridge*, 2 vols. (Cambridge, 1909–12) I, 426–41; Mynors, *Durham Cathedral Manuscripts*, p. 26 (no. 16); and D. N. Dumville, 'The Anglian Collection of Royal Genealogies and Regnal Lists', *ASE* 5 (1976), 23–50, at 25–6.

178 See Temple, *Anglo-Saxon Manuscripts*, pp. 37–8 (no. 6); the decoration around the presentation scene in CCCC 183 is closely related to that of the initial *P* on 6r, confirming that the portrait was from the beginning an integral part of the manuscript. CCCC 183 was certainly in Northumbria in the tenth century, and at Durham in the second half of the eleventh century; see Ker, *Catalogue*, pp. 64–5 (no. 42). It might be the 'Duæ vitæ Sancti Cuthberti' mentioned in a late-twelfth-century catalogue of Durham library (*Catalogi Veteres*, ed. Botfield, p. 3); but it cannot be either of the two manuscripts containing the lives of St Cuthbert mentioned in later medieval catalogues (*ibid.* pp. 29–30 and 107), since the entries in question specify the opening words of the second folio and these do not correspond to CCCC 183.

special liturgical office for the saint (92v–95v).[179] The material on 59r–69v is clearly an integral part of the original conception of the book. It comprises a list of popes, a list of the disciples of Christ, a collection of episcopal lists, and various regnal lists and royal genealogies, followed by a curious assemblage of miscellaneous information.[180] It is interesting, of course, that Athelstan and his advisers should have seen fit to prepare such a collection of material on Cuthbert for presentation to the saint's own community, and that they should have wished to include a special service for the saint apparently devised in Wessex.[181] The book would certainly demonstrate the honour in which St Cuthbert was held in the south, and by presenting it to St Cuthbert's community Athelstan might well have hoped to secure their goodwill and support, always useful in an area over which he had only recently extended his authority. By the same token, the decision to combine the Cuthbert material with a collection of episcopal and royal records may have been taken with some ulterior motive in mind: perhaps the purpose of the exercise was mainly educational, but it is conceivable that the king and his advisers hoped to remind the Northumbrian community of the essential unity of the Anglo-Saxon church, and to impress on them the ancient links which bound the various Anglo-Saxon kingdoms together (without going into details about their wars).

The papal and episcopal lists on 59r–64v afford the best evidence for dating the manuscript as a whole, and so for deciding on what occasion the king might have given it to Chester-le-Street.[182] The list of popes seems to have been based on information up-dated during the reign of Alfred,[183] for it extends to Hadrian III (884–5) and no further (though numbers were supplied in CCCC 183 for six successors). The episcopal lists for the Mercian dioceses (Worcester, Leicester, Lichfield, Hereford and Lindsey), for the North-

179 The collation of the manuscript is as follows: I⁸–VIII⁸ (fols. 1–64); IX⁸, 6 cancelled (fols. 65–71); X⁸ (fols. 72–9); XI⁸, 4 and 5 are singletons (fols. 80–7); XII⁸, plus 1 after 8 (fols. 88–96).

180 For a detailed description of this material, see James, *Descriptive Catalogue* I, 427–40.

181 See Hohler, 'The Durham Services', pp. 156–7. One would like to know whether the story of St Cuthbert appearing to King Alfred before the battle of Edington was current in Wessex in the early tenth century. The story is first attested as an eleventh-century interpolation in the *Historia de S. Cuthberto* (*Symeonis Monachi Opera Omnia*, ed. Arnold I, 204–6); but there is an allusion to it in that part of the *Historia regum* now attributed to Byrhtferth of Ramsey (*ibid.* II, 83 – if not itself an interpolation), and it is given in a slightly different form by William of Malmesbury (*GR* I, 125–6).

182 See J. A. Robinson, *The Saxon Bishops of Wells: a Historical Study in the Tenth Century*, Brit. Acad. Supplemental Papers 4 (London, 1918), 12–14, and R. I. Page, 'Anglo-Saxon Episcopal Lists', *Nottingham Med. Stud.* 9 (1965), 71–95 [pts 1 and 2], at 76, and 10 (1966), 2–24 [pt 3], at 8–12.

183 It may be significant, in this connection, that contacts between England and Rome seem to have been especially close during the 880s (to judge from entries in ASC).

umbrian dioceses (York, Hexham, Lindisfarne and Whithorn), for the East Anglian dioceses (Elmham and Dunwich), and for certain southern dioceses (Rochester, London and Selsey), do not extend beyond the middle of the ninth century (though again, in some cases, numbers were provided for successors). The lists for the archbishops of Canterbury and for the bishops of the dioceses of Wessex were doubtless derived in their earlier sections from the same source as the rest,[184] but unlike these others they extend to some point in the 930s. The last-named archbishop of Canterbury is Wulfhelm (926–41). The episcopal succession for Wessex in the first half of the tenth century was complicated by the reorganization of the ancient dioceses during the reign of Edward the Elder, when Winchester was divided in two (Winchester and Ramsbury) and Sherborne in three (Sherborne, Wells and Crediton);[185] the last-named bishops in the lists for each of these sees are Ælfheah (Winchester), Oda (Ramsbury), Alfred (Sherborne), Ælfheah (Wells) and Æthelgar (Crediton). The *terminus post quem* for the writing of the lists in CCCC 183 is thus determined by the inclusion of Ælfheah of Winchester and Æthelgar of Crediton: both seem to have succeeded their respective predecessors some time between June and December 934,[186] indicating that the manuscript was written between June 934 (at the very earliest) and October 939 (when King Athelstan died).[187]

This dating of the manuscript gives rise to a difficulty. According to the Latin *testamentum* incorporated in the *Historia de S. Cuthberto*, a 'Life of St Cuthbert in verse and prose' was included among the books given by Athelstan to St Cuthbert's on the occasion of his visit to Chester-le-Street *en route* for Scotland (in 934).[188] The book in question is evidently to be identified as CCCC 183, but if, on the evidence of the episcopal lists, the manuscript was

184 See Dumville, 'The Anglian Collection', pp. 41–2.

185 See Robinson, *Bishops of Wells*, pp. 7–28, and *EHD*, no. 229.

186 Ælfheah's predecessor Byrnstan attests S 425 (28 May 934) and 407 (7 June 934), and he died on 1 November 934 (ASC 933 A); Ælfheah is said to have succeeded to the bishopric in 935 (ASC 934 A, assuming that this annal, like that dated '933', is dislocated by one year). It seems, however, that Ælfheah was already acting as bishop before his formal installation (just as Byrnstan had himself been consecrated before his predecessor Frithestan's death), for he attests S 427 (16 December 934, assuming that the charter has a genuine base) and two other charters which might have been issued in 934 (S 429–30); in S 430 he is styled 'previsor in electione sua', so it does appear that he attested charters before his consecration. See, further, O'Donovan, 'Episcopal Lists: Pt II', pp. 111–12. Æthelgar's predecessor Eadwulf attests S 425 (28 May 934) and S 407 (7 June 934), and Æthelgar attests S 427 (16 December 934). See, further, M. A. O'Donovan, 'An Interim Revision of Episcopal Dates for the Province of Canterbury, 850–950: Part I', *ASE* 1 (1972), 23–44, at 36–7.

187 The list for the bishopric of Wells ends with Ælfheah (who attests charters in 937), and so stops short of his successor Wulfhelm, who seems to have become bishop in 937 or 938 (O'Donovan, 'Episcopal Dates: Pt II', p. 107); this might be taken to imply that the manuscript was written before 937 × 938, but it seems safer to rely on Athelstan's death as the *terminus ante quem*.

188 See above, p. 177.

not written before June 934, it is impossible to suppose that it was actually given to the community on that occasion: for the manuscript would have to have been finished by the time the journey north began, apparently in May.[189] It is worth noting, however, that the names of Ælfheah of Winchester and Æthelgar of Crediton, which establish the *terminus post quem* for the writing of the manuscript, both seem (at least on textual grounds) to be later additions (see pl. X): Ælfheah's name interrupts an otherwise natural progression from Frithestan to the statement about the division of the bishoprics in Frithestan's time, and Æthelgar's name follows that of his predecessor but without any number. If these two names are regarded as later additions, the *terminus post quem* for the writing of the manuscript would be determined by the inclusion of Alfred of Sherborne, who seems to have succeeded Sigehelm in 933;[190] so technically it would be conceivable that the manuscript was written in 933–4 and taken north in May 934, and that the names of Ælfheah and Æthelgar were added in June or July as last-minute up-dating when the manuscript was presented to Chester-le-Street. Fortunately, perhaps, this somewhat elaborate hypothesis does not receive much support from reference to the manuscript: the two names in question were obviously written by the main scribe (not in itself a fatal objection, since he could have travelled north with his bishop and the king); but so far as one can tell they were written at the same time (and with the same pen and ink) as the other names in the list. So it would probably be safest to conclude that the scribe of CCCC 183, writing between June 934 and October 939, was following an exemplar put together just a few years previously, and up-dated two of the lists from his own knowledge; consequently, the idea that CCCC 183 was given to St Cuthbert's in the summer of 934 must indeed be abandoned for good.

This conclusion gives further grounds for doubting the authority of the Latin *testamentum* in the *Historia de S. Cuthberto*: for the simplest explanation of the difficulty is that a general list of Athelstan's gifts to the community, which included a reference to 'a Life of St Cuthbert in verse and prose', has been conflated in the *testamentum* with a record of the gift of Otho B. ix, and thereby falsely linked to the supposed events of 934. And if we may abandon the *testamentum* as an authoritative record, we may also abandon the notion (which arose from the desire to reconcile the *testamentum* with the apparent date of CCCC 183) that the 'Life of St Cuthbert in verse and prose' was only promised to the community in 934, and that, once it had been written, it was actually delivered on a subsequent occasion.[191] There is, in fact, no evidence that

189 See above, p. 173.

190 Sigehelm attests S 418 (24 December 932), and Alfred attests S 425 (28 May 934). See, further, O'Donovan, 'Episcopal Dates: Pt II', pp. 105–6.

191 Robinson, *Bishops of Wells*, p. 13, and *TSD*, p. 54.

Athelstan ever returned to Chester-le-Street, though of course one cannot exclude the possibility that he did.[192] But a gift to a religious house would certainly not require a visit to that house,[193] so the options remain wide open: Athelstan could have given CCCC 183 to Chester-le-Street at any time between the latter part of 934 and the latter part of 939.

One would like to know where CCCC 183 was written, not least because identification of its origin would indicate to what scriptorium King Athelstan turned when commissioning a book intended for presentation to a religious house elsewhere. The main hand in CCCC 183 reappears in BL Royal 7. D. XXIV, pt ii, fols. 82–127 and 136–62, a manuscript of Aldhelm's prose *De uirginitate*;[194] but there is no independent evidence bearing on the origin of this manuscript, so the link does not assist in establishing the origin of CCCC 183. We must rely, therefore, on the episcopal lists. The fact that, apart from Canterbury, only the West Saxon sees are brought up to date, naturally points to a centre somewhere in Wessex. It is sometimes supposed that CCCC 183 was written at Winchester,[195] though not, it seems, for any particularly good reason. It is certainly difficult to sustain a belief in a Winchester origin after consideration of the episcopal list for the see. The scribe's information was remarkably defective (see pl. X): he omitted Swithhun's two immediate successors, Ealhferth and Tunberht, though he left a (single) blank space as if he were at least aware of the deficiency; and he also omitted Frithestan's successor Byrnstan, ending his list with Ælfheah.[196] One would expect a Winchester scribe to have known better, so one is forced to conclude that the scribe of CCCC 183 came from elsewhere, and probably from a house in the south-west.[197] Glastonbury must be a reasonable possibility; so too must

192 It is often supposed that Athelstan visited Chester-le-Street in 937, during the course of the *Brunanburh* campaign. The various options for the location of the battle-site currently include Bromborough (Cheshire), Bromswold (Northamptonshire–Huntingdonshire), Brinsworth (Yorkshire) and the Browney valley (west of Durham; see K. Harrison, 'A Note on the Battle of Brunanburh', *Durham Archaeol. Jnl* 1 (1984), 63–5); only the last would bring Athelstan into the vicinity of St Cuthbert's shrine, but one could hardly depend on this as evidence of a second visit.

193 We should bear in mind that King Alfred made gifts to churches in Wales, Cornwall, Gaul, Brittany, Northumbria and Ireland (Asser, *Vita Alfredi*, ch. 102), and that King Athelstan sent gifts to the monastery of Saint-Bertin (*EHD*, no. 26).

194 T. A. M. Bishop, 'An Early Example of the Square Minuscule', *Trans. of the Cambridge Bibliographical Soc.* 4 (1966), 246–52, at 247.

195 See, e.g., Parkes, 'Parker Manuscript', p. 163, n. 4, and 'A Fragment of an Early-Tenth-Century Anglo-Saxon Manuscript and its Significance', *ASE* 12 (1983), 129–40, at 137, n. 50; Temple, *Anglo-Saxon Manuscripts*, pp. 37–8; and R. Deshman, 'Anglo-Saxon Art after Alfred', *Art Bull.* 56 (1974), 176–200, at 195.

196 For the dates of these bishops, see O'Donovan, 'Episcopal Dates: Pt II', pp. 108–12.

197 See Robinson, *Bishops of Wells*, pp. 13–14, and D. N. Dumville, 'The Catalogue Texts', *An Eleventh-Century Anglo-Saxon Illustrated Miscellany: British Library Cotton Tiberius B. V*

Wells, where there is a parish church dedicated to St Cuthbert,[198] and where a fragment of a stone tombstone has recently been found which in its foliate ornament bears close comparison with the decoration around the borders of the presentation scene in CCCC 183.[199] Wherever CCCC 183 was written, it is important to remember that manuscripts of its quality could be produced in Athelstan's reign, at a time when the biographers of the monastic reformers of the later tenth century would have us believe that religion and learning were at a low ebb; and it is especially interesting to find that when the king wished to commission a manuscript he turned not to Winchester but to a house in the south-western heartland of his kingdom.

## OTHER MANUSCRIPTS ASSOCIATED WITH KING ATHELSTAN

### BL Royal 1. B. VII

BL Royal 1. B. VII is a gospel-book written in England, probably in Northumbria, in the first half of the eighth century.[200] Nothing appears to be known about its early history, but by the first half of the tenth century it must have been in the south of England, to judge from an Old English text entered in a blank space on 15v (see pl. XI):

Æðelstan cyng gefreode Eadelm forraðe þæs ðe he æræst cyng wæs . ðæs wæs on gewitnesse Ælfheah mæssepreost 7 se hired 7 Ælfric se gerefa 7 Wufnoð hwita 7 Eanstan prafost 7 Byrnstan mæssepreost . se þe ðæt onwende hæbbe he Godes unmiltse 7 ealles ðæs haligdomes ðe ic on Angelcyn begeat mid Godes miltse 7 ic an ðan bearnan þæs ilcan ðæs ic þan fæder an :[201]

*Part 1*, ed. P. McGurk, EEMF 21 (Copenhagen, 1983), 55–8. See also J. Higgitt, 'Glastonbury, Dunstan, Monasticism and Manuscripts', *Art Hist.* 2 (1979), 275–90, at 278.

198 See Robinson, *Bishop of Wells*, p. 14, and Arnold-Forster, *Church Dedications* II, 86–90. St Cuthbert's, Wells, is the largest parish church in Somerset; the present structure is Perpendicular, with elements dating back to the Norman period. Of course one cannot be sure whether the dedication of a presumed pre-Conquest predecessor was also to St Cuthbert.

199 See W. Rodwell, 'Wells: the Cathedral and City', *CA* 7 (1980–1), 38–44, at 41. The same style of decoration occurs elsewhere, e.g. on sculptured stones recently found in Gloucester; see C. M. Heighway, 'Excavations at Gloucester, Fifth Interim Report: St Oswald's Priory 1977–8', *AntJ* 60 (1980), 207–26, at 220–3.

200 *Codices Latini Antiquiores* II, ed. E. A. Lowe, 2nd ed. (Oxford, 1972), no. 213; Thompson and Warner, *Catalogue of Ancient Manuscripts*, pp. 19–20; Warner and Gilson, *Catalogue of Western Manuscripts* I, 10–11; Alexander, *Insular Manuscripts*, p. 48; and Ker, *Catalogue*, no. 246.

201 *SEHD*, no. 19; *EHD*, no. 140. 'King Athelstan freed Eadhelm very soon after he first became king. Ælfheah the mass-priest and the community [*or* household], Ælfric the reeve, Wulfnoth the White, Eanstan the provost, and Byrnstan the mass-priest were witnesses of this. He who averts this – may he have the disfavour of God and of all the relics which, by God's mercy, I have obtained in England. And I grant the children the same as I grant the father.'

The script is an early form of square minuscule, and there is no reason to believe that this is anything other than a genuine and contemporary document. It signifies, therefore, that King Athelstan freed a certain Eadhelm 'very soon after he first became king', and that the act was performed in the presence of Ælfheah the mass-priest and the *hired*, as well as Ælfric the reeve, Wulfnoth the White, Eanstan the provost and Byrnstan the mass-priest. The problem is how to account for the occurrence of this document in the manuscript.

It has been suggested that Royal 1. B. VII is the very book on which Athelstan swore his coronation oath in 925. This theory depends in the first instance on the supposition that the manuscript was at St Augustine's Abbey, Canterbury, in the early tenth century. It is then supposed that the community of St Augustine's lent the book to the archbishop of Canterbury, who used it for the administration of the coronation oath; whereupon Athelstan caused the manumission to be entered in the book, and expressed his gratitude for its loan by restoring an estate in Thanet to St Augustine's.[202]

The two suppositions on which the theory depends hardly constitute a strong foundation. In the first place, the only 'evidence' relating to the provenance of the manuscript is Wanley's statement that it appeared formerly to have belonged to Christ Church, Canterbury.[203] M. R. James, on the other hand, preferred to assign it to St Augustine's;[204] but even if its later medieval provenance was Canterbury, there could be no guarantee that it was already there by the beginning of Athelstan's reign. Secondly, it is rather difficult to accept the idea that the archbishop of Canterbury would have needed to borrow a suitable book from St Augustine's for the administration of the oath, or indeed that he would have been willing to use one of theirs in preference to one of his own.

The main structure of the argument is no stronger. The link between the manuscript and the coronation depends on the manumission, and in particular on the interpretation of its allusion to an occasion when Athelstan 'first became king' as a reference to the coronation itself.[205] It is far from clear, however, what was meant by this remark, for the circumstances of Athelstan's accession seem not to have been straightforward. Edward the Elder had taken

202 *TSD*, pp. 66–7; cf. Wood, 'King Æthelstan's Empire', p. 256.

203 See Hickes and Wanley, *Antiquæ Literaturæ Septentrionalis Libri Duo* II, 181: 'olim, ut videtur, Ecclesiæ Christi Salvatoris in Cantuaria'.

204 M. R. James, *The Ancient Libraries of Canterbury and Dover* (Cambridge, 1903), p. 532; no reason is given.

205 If *æræst cyng wæs* means, literally, '*first* became king', it would imply that a distinction was understood between that occasion and a later event in the process by which Athelstan came to power, and thus that the manumission was associated with the earlier event but drafted after the later one (or in anticipation of it); but the words could be translated, simply, 'became king', leaving it uncertain what stage in the process was intended.

control of Mercia during the course of his reign; and we may wonder whether, on his death (17 July 924), it was necessarily assumed that his composite kingdom would remain intact. Indeed, it seems that Edward's son Ælfweard was recognized as king by the West Saxons, and that the Mercians, for their part, chose Athelstan;[206] but this state of affairs did not last long (and is therefore glossed over in the Anglo-Saxon Chronicle),[207] for Ælfweard died on 1 August 924. The initial recognition of Ælfweard as king in Wessex might have reflected opposition in some quarters to Athelstan, and if so, Athelstan would have had to gain the support of those who had previously opted for his half-brother. It may, therefore, have been a while before his position was secure; certainly, it was not until 4 September 925 that he was actually consecrated king, at Kingston-upon-Thames in Surrey.[208] Against this background, the reference in the manumission might be to an event which took place before his coronation, either his recognition by the Mercians following Edward's death, or (and perhaps more likely) his recognition by all some time after Ælfweard's death; and since the regnal years in Athelstan's charters are often calculated from a date before his coronation, there can be no doubt that he did recognize an earlier 'beginning' to his reign.[209] It would be odd, therefore, that Athelstan should refer to his coronation as an occasion when he 'first became king'; and if this point is granted, there is no longer any reason to associate the manumission in Royal 1. B. VII with the coronation, and so no ground for regarding the manuscript itself as that on which the king had sworn his coronation oath.

The remaining plank in the theory is a document entered in three cartularies of St Augustine's Abbey, which records that Athelstan restored an estate at *Werburginland* in Thanet to St Augustine's on 4 September 925, in the first year

206 The belief that Ælfweard was recognized as king after his father's death depends on a remark in the *Liber uitae* of the New Minster Winchester (*Liber Vitae: Register and Martyrology of New Minster and Hyde Abbey Winchester*, ed. W. deG. Birch, Hampshire Record Soc. (London, 1892), p. 6), and on his inclusion in the version of the West Saxon regnal table entered in the *Textus Roffensis* (see D. N. Dumville, 'The West Saxon Genealogical Regnal List: Manuscripts and Texts' *Anglia* 103 (1985)), where he is allotted a reign of four weeks; see also *Two of the Saxon Chronicles Parallel*, ed. C. Plummer, 2 vols. (Oxford, 1892–9) II, 121. The belief that Athelstan began his reign as king of the Mercians depends on the statement in the Mercian Register that he was 'chosen by the Mercians as king' in 924.

207 The annal for 924 in the Mercian Register conflates the events of 924–6; compare the treatment of the events of 955–7 in ASC D.

208 S 394; Keynes, *Diplomas*, pp. 270–1. The date is confirmed by the reign-length of fourteen years, seven weeks and three days allotted to him in two versions of the West Saxon regnal table (see Dumville, 'Regnal List', forthcoming), representing the difference between 4 September 925 and 27 October 939.

209 E.g. the regnal year (10) in S 425 (28 May 934) is calculated from a point in 924; but the regnal year (3) in S 399–400 (16 April 928) is calculated from the coronation in 925.

of his reign, and on the day of his consecration.[210] Despite the unusual form of the document, there seems no reason to doubt that it is based on genuine information.[211] We may wonder, however, whether a grant made on the day of a king's coronation necessarily implies that the king was rewarding the beneficiary for services rendered in connection with the ceremony. Ceolwulf of Mercia granted land to the archbishop of Canterbury on the day of his coronation (17 September 822), and the charter records that he did so for love of God, out of respect for the archbishop, in gratitude for the consecration – and for the archbishop's 'acceptable money'.[212] But in another charter similarly issued on the occasion of a coronation, King Eadred is said to have 'constantly presented many gifts to many', and the charter in question records a grant of land to a layman.[213] It looks, in other words, as if a king might have been expected to be particularly generous at such a time,[214] so there is really no reason to attach special significance to Athelstan's grant to St Augustine's.

The theory that Royal 1. B. VII is the book on which Athelstan swore his coronation oath does not, therefore, have much to recommend it; so it remains to produce an alternative explanation of the connection between the manuscript and the king. It should perhaps be stressed that the manumission seems to be quite intimately associated with the king and those around him. Eadhelm was presumably one of the king's own slaves, and the manumission was performed in the wake of an event connected with Athelstan's accession. Moreover, it is quite possible that the witnesses had some connection with the royal household. Two can be identified with reasonable confidence: Ælfheah the mass-priest is probably he who became bishop of Wells in about 926, and Byrnstan the mass-priest he who became bishop of Winchester in 931;[215] both may have belonged to the king's household clergy before their promotion to the episcopal office. Under these circumstances, the *hired* mentioned in the manumission is perhaps more likely to be a reference to the royal household itself (or more particularly to its religious component), than to the community of some (unspecified) religious house; and it would seem appropriate that the terms of the manumission should be protected by invoking the king's own collection of relics, which would presumably have been in the custody of his clergy. We may wonder whether the king would have such an intimately

210 S 394 (*BCS* 641).

211 See Robinson, *Bishops of Wells*, pp. 30–3, and Lapidge, 'Some Latin Poems', p. 77, n. 74.

212 S 186 (*BCS* 370; *EHD*, no. 83).

213 S 520 (*BCS* 815; *EHD*, no. 105).

214 See also S 835 (Keynes, *Diplomas*, p. 238).

215 See Robinson, *Bishops of Wells*, pp. 32–3; Ælfheah also attests S 394, and is there joined by another Ælfheah, styled 'priest and monk', probably that Ælfheah ('the Bald') who succeeded Byrnstan as bishop of Winchester in 934 (see above, n. 186).

'royal' document entered in a manuscript belonging to an independent religious house. Of course it is possible,[216] but it seems more likely that the manumission was entered in Royal 1. B. VII because this manuscript belonged at the time to the king; in which case we could infer that the document was written by a scribe in his service.

## Coburg, Landesbibliothek 1

This manuscript, commonly known as the Gandersheim Gospels, was written at Metz in the middle of the ninth century (*c.* 860).[217] Its association with Athelstan depends on an inscription in Anglo-Saxon square minuscule near the bottom of the last leaf, 168r (see pl. XII):

+ eadgifu regina :-     æþelstan rex angulsaxonum
7 mercianorum :-

Certain observations need to be made before one may indulge in speculation about the significance of this inscription. In the first place, it looks as if the inscription is primarily associated with 'Queen Eadgifu': only her name is preceded by a cross, and from the position on the page she seems to take precedence over the king. Secondly, the inscription was presumably written by an Englishman, though the irregularity of letter-forms and spacing might

216 See D. Jenkins and M. E. Owen, 'The Welsh Marginalia in the Lichfield Gospels, Part I', *Cambridge Med. Celtic Stud.* 5 (1983), 37–66, at 62. The manumission in Royal 1. B. VII is one of the earliest of the Anglo-Saxon examples of the practice of inserting records in sacred books (usually gospel-books), which is attested throughout the tenth and eleventh centuries (but not, apparently, before; cf. Chaplais, 'Origin and Authenticity', pp. 33–5, and 'The Anglo-Saxon Chancery', pp. 58–60); the practice is attested in Wales as early as the ninth century (Jenkins and Owen, 'The Welsh Marginalia', pp. 56–61), so it is possible that it was introduced into England under Celtic influence (*ibid.* p. 65). For the English examples, see Ker, *Catalogue*, nos. 6, 22, 55, 126, 147, 176, 194, 237, 246 and 370 (from the tenth century), and nos. 20, 35, 42, 78, 119, 123, 131, 181, 185, 247, 274, 284, 291, 303, 315, 353, 364 and 402 (from the eleventh century); see also Temple, *Anglo-Saxon Manuscripts*, nos. 12, 68 and 75. For references to sacred books, now lost, which appear to have contained records, see H. H. E. Craster, 'The Red Book of Durham', *EHR* 40 (1925), 504–32, at 519–32 (a gospel-book at Durham); Scott, *Early History of Glastonbury*, pp. 118–19 (a gospel-book given by King Edmund to Glastonbury); and S 455 (a gospel-book at Muchelney). I am informed by Miss Susan Kelly that a book known as the *Textus S. Adriani*, which was preserved in the Middle Ages at St Augustine's, Canterbury, appears to have contained the texts of several documents relating to the abbey's endowment.

217 The manuscript is described, and its history discussed, by I. Hubay, *Die Handschriften der Landesbibliothek Coburg* (Coburg, 1962), pp. 9–16, and 'Zur Lebensgeschichte des Gandersheimer Evangeliars', *Jahrbuch der Coburger Landesstiftung* 1962, 93–8. See also Schramm and Mütherich, *Denkmale*, pp. 139–40 (no. 63).

suggest that the writer was not a professional or practised scribe.[218] Thirdly, the royal style accorded to Athelstan is anomalous. 'Rex Angulsaxonum' was a style introduced in Alfred's reign to signify his aspiration to kingship over an amalgamated English people, and it was also applied to Edward the Elder in the early tenth century.[219] It was probably intended to imply not only kingship of the West Saxons but authority over the Mercians as well, since it was apparently synonymous with 'rex Anglorum et Saxonum', and since in the later tenth century it was sometimes expanded to an all-embracing 'rex Angulsæxna et Norþhimbra imperator paganorum gubernator Brettonumque propugnator' (without explicit reference to the Mercians).[220] It follows that the style 'rex angulsaxonum 7 mercianorum' in the inscription in the Gandersheim Gospels was devised by someone who was not familiar with normal diplomatic usage,[221] but who was nevertheless aware that Athelstan's kingship represented an advance on that of his father and grandfather, in the sense that he had been formally 'chosen' by the Mercians as king at the outset of his reign.[222] One could argue further that the style is likely to reflect the situation between Athelstan's accession to Wessex and Mercia in 924/5, and the extension of his kingship over the Northumbrians in 927; but it would probably be dangerous to press this point too far.

The problem of interpretation immediately presented by this inscription is the identity of 'Queen Eadgifu'. The reference could be to Eadgifu, third wife of Edward the Elder and Athelstan's stepmother.[223] It would, however, be quite surprising to find her associated in this way with her stepson: there are no surviving Anglo-Saxon charters issued in the latter part of Edward's reign, so one cannot be sure of her status during her husband's lifetime, but it is significant that she does not occur in any of Athelstan's charters, suggesting that she may have remained in the background during her stepson's reign.[224] It is only during the reigns of her own sons, Edmund and Eadred, that she comes into prominence, frequently attesting their charters (normally styled 'regis mater') and evidently becoming a figure of considerable political influence.[225] Eadred made very generous provision for her in his will,[226] and it was possibly

218 On the other hand, it may be that the scribe was still perfecting his square minuscule, or that he had some difficulty in writing at the bottom of a leaf in a manuscript already bound.

219 See above, n. 77.

220 See above, n. 78.

221 The form *Mercianorum*, as opposed to *Merciorum*, is also unusual.

222 See above, p. 187.

223 William of Malmesbury, *GR* I, 136–7.

224 S 1211 (*SEHD*, no. 23) casts some light on Eadgifu's position at this time: while her husband was alive, she had withheld some title-deeds from a certain Goda, but after Edward's death Goda persuaded Athelstan to persuade her to relinquish all but one of them.

225 The career of Eadgifu is assessed by P. Stafford, 'The King's Wife in Wessex 800–1066', *Past and Present* 91 (1981), 3–27, at 5 and 25–6, and *Queens, Concubines and Dowagers: the King's Wife in the Early Middle Ages* (London, 1983), pp. 148–9. See also C. Hart, 'Two Queens of England', *Ampleforth Jnl* 82 (1977), 10–15 and 54, at 10–14.

226 S 1515 (*SEHD*, no. 21; *EHD*, no. 107).

out of resentment of her power that her grandson Eadwig deprived her of her status and property as soon as he came to the throne;[227] but she was restored to her former position by Eadwig's successor Edgar (another grandson),[228] and she died in or soon after 966.[229] On the other hand, the reference in the inscription could be to Eadgifu, daughter of Edward the Elder by his second wife Ælfflæd and thus Athelstan's half-sister. During her father's reign she was sent overseas to become the wife of Charles the Simple, king of the west Franks, but she returned to England after her husband's deposition in 923, bringing their child Louis (d'Outremer) with her.[230] She might well have continued to be styled 'queen' once back in England, and one presumes that she was on good terms with her half-brother; certainly it was with Athelstan's support that her son Louis was enabled to gain the west Frankish throne in 936, and Eadgifu returned to the continent with him.[231] A third possibility is that the reference is to Eadgifu, said to be the daughter of Edward the Elder by his third wife Eadgifu and thus another of Athelstan's half-sisters. According to William of Malmesbury, she married Louis, 'prince of the Aquitainians', who has been identified as Louis, brother of Rudolf II, king of upper Burgundy;[232] but nothing is known of her after her marriage.

227 S 1211 (*SEHD*, no. 23); *Vita Dunstani*, ch. 24 (*Memorials of Saint Dunstan*, ed. Stubbs, p. 36; and *EHD*, no. 234, p. 902).

228 *Vita Dunstani*, ch. 24 (see previous note); see also S 811 and 1211.

229 She attests the New Minster Winchester foundation charter (S 745) in 966; but she was probably dead by 967, when Edgar granted some of her property to Winflæd (S 754).

230 See *Chronicle of Æthelweard*, ed. Campbell, p. 2, and *GR* I, 116 and 136–7; on the date of the marriage, see Poole, 'Alpine Son-in-Law', p. 312. It is a reasonable assumption that Eadgifu accompanied her son back to England; see *Richer*, ed. Latouche I, 124.

231 For Louis's return, see Lauer, *Flodoard*, pp. 63–4 (*EHD*, no. 24), and *Richer*, ed. Latouche I, 128–32; Flodoard and Richer give details of Eadgifu's later activities in the Frankish kingdom.

232 This identification (made by Hlawitschka, above, n. 27) depends on the reasonable assumption that the information provided by William of Malmesbury is confused in detail. William distinguishes between *Edgiva* (Edward's daughter by his third wife Eadgifu: *GR* I, 137), who married Louis, *princeps Aquitanorum* (*ibid.* pp. 137 and 149), and *Aldgitha/Elfgiva* (Edward's daughter by his second wife Ælfflæd: *GR* I, 137), who was sent to Germany with her sister Edith and who married 'a certain duke [*dux*] near the Alps' (above, n. 27). William may not, however, have had any good authority for the name of Edith's sister, since the chronicler Æthelweard (his main source for these marriages) does not identify her; he may also have simply guessed the identity of her mother. Hrotsvitha of Gandersheim, on the other hand, knew Edith's sister as *Adiva* (? Eadgifu). It is possible, therefore, that the sister of Edith who married a 'duke' (or, according to Æthelweard, a 'king') near the Alps was called Eadgifu, and is the same person as the *Edgiva* who married Louis, *princeps Aquitanorum*. A 'duke' (or 'king') near the Alps might well be an upper Burgundian prince, and Louis, brother of Rudolf II, king of upper Burgundy, could be the one in question, if *princeps Aquitanorum* is regarded as an error for *princeps Alamannorum*. The older view, that Eadgifu's husband was Louis the Blind of Provence, is fraught with difficulty; see Poole, 'Alpine Son-in-Law', p. 312, n. 9.

One can interpret the inscription in a number of different ways, and it is not easy to choose between them. For example, it could have been written by an Englishman on the continent, visiting a royal court or a monastery: he might have been invited to enter in a gospel-book the names of those whom he particularly wished to be remembered in prayer, and for now irrecoverable reasons chose to specify Queen Eadgifu (either the king's stepmother or his half-sister: associating the former with Athelstan would not be politically sensitive in this context) and the king. One immediately thinks of Cenwald, bishop of Worcester, in this connection, since he is known to have visited Germany in 929;[233] but of course several other Englishmen are known to have gone abroad in Athelstan's reign (not to mention those whose visits went unrecorded), any one of whom might have suited the role just as well. An advantage of this hypothesis is that it allows the manuscript to remain in Germany, and requires only that the manuscript passed by some means from Metz (where it was written) to Gandersheim; it was at Gandersheim by the early eleventh century,[234] and may have been there for some time previously.[235] We could, on the other hand, proceed from the assumption that the Eadgifu named in the inscription is the wife of Charles the Simple. She might have acquired the manuscript from her husband, who could have inherited it from his grandfather Charles the Bald, who might in turn have received it as a present when he was crowned king of Lotharingia at Metz in 869.[236] On this hypothesis, it was perhaps Eadgifu who brought the manuscript to England, following her husband's deposition in 923, and who caused the inscription to be written in the manuscript (or conceivably she wrote it herself); the inscription could be a mark of ownership or reflect a desire to be remembered

233 See below, pp. 198–201. The inscription is associated with Cenwald by P. Chaplais, 'English Diplomatic Documents to the End of Edward III's Reign', *The Study of Medieval Records: Essays in Honour of Kathleen Major*, ed. D. A. Bullough and R. L. Storey (Oxford, 1971), pp. 22–56, at 23, n. 1, and by Wood, 'King Æthelstan's Empire', p. 257.

234 See Hubay, *Die Handschriften*, p. 9; the evidence is the list of lands belonging to Gandersheim entered (in the early eleventh century) on 168r (see pl. XII).

235 A Carolingian ivory of the Metz school (now in the Victoria and Albert Museum, London), depicting the crucifixion, is thought to have belonged to the original binding of the manuscript; see A. Goldschmidt, *Die Elfenbeinskulpturen aus der Zeit der karolingischen und sächsischen Kaiser VIII.–IX. Jahrhundert* I (Berlin, 1914), 49 (no. 88), and M. H. Longhurst, *Victoria and Albert Museum, Department of Architecture and Sculpture: Catalogue of Carvings in Ivory* I (London, 1927), 67–8. Another ivory, depicting the ascension, is still incorporated within the modern binding; see Goldschmidt, *Elfenbeinskulpturen*, p. 49 (no. 87), and references cited above, n. 217. The presence of a part of the original binding in England could be taken to suggest that the manuscript itself had once been in England, presumably in the tenth century (cf. Wood, 'King Æthelstan's Empire', pp. 260–1), but of course one could not discount the possibility that the ivory was detached at a later date and came to England separately.

236 See Hubay, *Die Handschriften*, pp. 11–12.

in prayer, and in either case she chose deferentially to link her name with that of her half-brother, the king. One might then suppose that Eadgifu herself took the manuscript back to the continent in 936, and that somehow it ended up at Gandersheim. A third hypothesis, which explains the inscription in terms of relations between Athelstan and the Saxon court, and which depends on an analogy with Tiberius A. ii, should also be considered. The manuscript might have been brought to England by Eadgifu, or it might have arrived in some other way. As part of a diplomatic exchange of gifts, perhaps on the occasion of Otto's marriage to Edith in 929/30, or when Otto was crowned in 936, Athelstan received Tiberius A. ii from the Saxon court and sooner or later caused the names of Otto and his mother Matilda to be entered in it as a way of recording the source of the gift, or as a way of honouring the donors and ensuring that they would be remembered in prayer;[237] in the same connection Athelstan presented the (Gandersheim) Gospels to Otto, but first had the names of Queen Eadgifu (by analogy, more likely his stepmother than his half-sister) and himself written on the last leaf, similarly to ensure that they would not be forgotten.[238] The main attraction of this hypothesis is that it provides the easiest occasion for the subsequent transfer of the manuscript to Gandersheim, since Otto might simply have given it to his niece Gerberga, abbess of Gandersheim in the latter part of the tenth century;[239] but one might think it odd that Athelstan should have given a German gospel-book to Otto (assuming, of course, that he would have been aware of its origin), or that his name should take second place to Eadgifu's, and besides, the prominence given to the inscriptions in Tiberius A. ii and the Gandersheim Gospels, in terms of their position and script, is hardly comparable. The second of these three hypotheses is perhaps to be preferred, though the preference could not be expressed with much conviction.

## BL Cotton Galba A. xviii

Of all the manuscripts which have some association with King Athelstan, BL Cotton Galba A. xviii is the only one customarily known by his name; it is

[237] See above, p. 149. For an example of the entering of a king's name (and the names of a few others) in a gospel-book, evidently for the purpose of remembering him (and them) in prayer, see BL Royal 1. D. IX, 42v (Ker, *Catalogue*, no. 247); the *Liber uitae* of Thorney (BL Add. 40000; *ibid.* no. 131) is a development of the same practice.

[238] The view that Tiberius A. ii and the Gandersheim Gospels were gift and counter-gift, exchanged between Otto and Athelstan in 929 (or 936), seems to have gained general currency: see, e.g., Hubay, *Die Handschriften*, p. 9; Chaplais, 'Diplomatic Documents', p. 23, n. 1; and Wood, 'King Æthelstan's Empire', pp. 259–60.

[239] See Hubay, *Die Handschriften*, p. 9.

ironic, therefore, that the claim of the so-called 'Athelstan Psalter' once to have belonged to the king is based on the slenderest of evidence. The core of the manuscript is a ninth-century continental psalter, augmented while still on the continent by a few supplementary leaves (containing prayers) added before the original flyleaf, and by the addition of more prayers in available space at the end.[240] The manuscript was evidently in England by the beginning of the tenth century, where it soon received further additions: a metrical calendar (with other computistical material) was placed at the front;[241] and at least five miniatures were specially prepared, and inserted at various points.[242] At a slightly later date, probably towards the middle of the tenth century, a collection of prayers, followed by a sequence of Greek texts, was added at the end.[243]

There is no contemporary evidence for the association between Galba A. xviii and King Athelstan. The metrical calendar added at the beginning of the manuscript includes obits of King Alfred (26 October) and his wife Ealhswith (3 December), which might suggest a link with the royal court; but it might alternatively suggest a link with any one of the minsters at Winchester (where – in the New Minster – both Alfred and his wife were buried), or indeed with some other place, since their memory was doubtless respected elsewhere.[244] Two features of the iconography of the added miniatures afford a very tenuous link with Athelstan. In the miniature on 2v Christ is shown with the symbols of the passion, including the lance (of Longinus), and in the miniature on 21r he is shown with the wound in his side exposed. Both features are said to be unusual at this date, and have been connected with Athelstan's acquisition in 926, from Hugh, duke of the Franks, of relics including the spear of Charlemagne (believed to have been Longinus's lance).[245] One should bear in mind,

240 See Thompson and Warner, *Catalogue of Ancient Manuscripts*, pp. 12–13, and Watson, *Catalogue of Dated and Datable Manuscripts* I, 102 (no. 532). Some obits of Carolingian rulers of the ninth century, associated in particular with Italy, were entered on the original flyleaf (28r).

241 The calendar (3r–14v) is ptd R. T. Hampson, *Medii Ævi Kalendarium*, 2 vols. (London, 1841) I, 397–420; see M. Lapidge, 'A Tenth-Century Metrical Calendar from Ramsey', *RB* 94 (1984), 326–69, at 342–8. The computistical material occupies 15r–20v; 18r and 19v are blank.

242 See Temple, *Anglo-Saxon Manuscripts*, pp. 36–7 (no. 5), and Deshman, 'Anglo-Saxon Art after Alfred', pp. 176–83; see also below, nn. 245–6 and 253.

243 The prayers occupy 178r–199v, and the Greek texts occupy 199v–200v.

244 Bishop, *Liturgica Historica*, pp. 253–6, argued that the calendar was the work of Irishmen who had visited the West Saxon court in the late ninth or early tenth century, and thus regarded it as a Winchester production; but the court was certainly not synonymous with Winchester.

245 For the relics, see William of Malmesbury, *GR* I, 150 (*EHD*, no. 8, pp. 308–9), and above, p. 143; the connection between the relics and the iconography of the miniatures is made by Alexander, 'The Benedictional of St Æthelwold', pp. 171–2. On the significance of the relics

however, that the miniatures seem (on art-historical grounds) to have been produced in connection with the metrical calendar, and that the calendar seems (on palaeographical grounds) not to have been written later than the first quarter of the tenth century;[246] moreover, the iconography of the miniatures might well have been a response to conventions in Carolingian manuscript illumination and ivory carving of the latter part of the ninth century.[247] It is possible, therefore, that the miniatures were painted before Athelstan received the lance, so it would be dangerous to make too much of the point. The case for associating the psalter with Athelstan, in so far as it turns on contemporary evidence, seems otherwise to depend on the origin of the miniatures and metrical calendar, and on the tenth-century provenance of the manuscript as a whole. It is usually supposed that the miniatures and calendar originated at Winchester,[248] and that (in some unspecified way) this supports the view that the psalter belonged to Athelstan; but the case for Winchester is not securely established, and even if it were it is not clear how or why it would help. It does seem likely, on the other hand, that the psalter was at Winchester in the later tenth and eleventh centuries, if only to judge from the apparent influence of the miniatures on the decoration of manuscripts known to have been produced there,[249] and from a poem, entered on a leaf now lost, which could be of Winchester interest.[250] But again, it is not clear how the later provenance of the

themselves, see L. H. Loomis, 'The Holy Relics of Charlemagne and King Athelstan: the Lances of Longinus and St Mauricius', *Speculum* 25 (1950), 437–56; and K. J. Leyser, 'The Tenth Century in Byzantine–Western Relationships', *Medieval Germany and its Neighbours 900–1250* (London, 1982), pp. 103–37, at 116–17, and *Rule and Conflict*, p. 88.

246 The miniatures are linked to the decorated initials in the calendar by style of decoration and pigments; the leaf with the first miniature (fol. 2) is apparently a singleton, inserted near the beginning of the first quire (now fols. 1–11), and that with the second (fol. 21) is a singleton added at the end of the second quire (now fols. 12–21). The Insular minuscule script of the calendar would most naturally be assigned to the ninth century, were it not for the obits of Alfred and Ealhswith; see D. N. Dumville, 'The *Anglo-Saxon Chronicle* and the Origins of English Square Minuscule Script' (forthcoming).

247 See, e.g., Longhurst, *Catalogue of Carvings in Ivory*, pp. 66–8, for two Metz ivories depicting the crucifixion and showing Longinus with the lance and Stephaton with the sponge; one is illustrated in P. Williamson, *An Introduction to Medieval Ivory Carvings* (London, 1982), p. 25, and the other is that mentioned above, n. 235.

248 See above, n. 244, and Deshman, 'Anglo-Saxon Art after Alfred', pp. 192–5. See also Parkes, 'Parker Manuscript', pp. 162–3, and 'A Fragment', p. 137, n. 50.

249 See Wormald, 'The "Winchester School" before St Æthelwold', pp. 308–9, and Alexander, 'The Benedictional of St Æthelwold', pp. 176–80.

250 See Smith, *Catalogus*, p. 62. The poem commemorates the gift of a cross by Bishop Stigand, and, since it is known that Stigand gave a cross to the Old Minster Winchester, the poem is often interpreted as evidence that the manuscript was at Winchester in the later eleventh century; but Stigand also gave crosses to several other churches (e.g. St Augustine's, Canterbury, Bury St Edmunds and Ely; see C. R. Dodwell, *Anglo-Saxon Art: a New Perspective* (Manchester, 1982), pp. 211–13).

psalter would affect the point at issue: the notion that because Athelstan gave manuscripts to other houses, he must also have given some to Winchester, is quite reasonable, but as applied specifically to Galba A. xviii it is purely wishful thinking.[251]

In the final analysis, therefore, the association of Galba A. xviii with Athelstan depends on whatever trust one is inclined to place in a sixteenth-century note written on 1r: 'psaltirium Regis Ethelstani Emptum per dompnum Thomam Rectorem de colbroke Wynton 1542 precium [ ]' – the price was originally given but subsequently erased. Thomas Dackomb, rector of St Peter Colebrook, Winchester, and a minor canon of Winchester Cathedral, accumulated a small collection of manuscripts in the middle of the sixteenth century, including several purchased from religious houses in Winchester.[252] He wrote similar notes on the first leaves of nearly all his manuscripts, without making extravagant claims for them, so one imagines that he had some reason for describing his psalter as Athelstan's. At best, his statement might have been based on an inscription entered on a leaf now lost;[253] at worst, he might have been taken in by some salesman's patter. One can only conclude that while there is nothing in the manuscript which is incompatible with the notion that it may have belonged to Athelstan, equally there is nothing which proves that it did.[254]

## CONCLUSIONS

On the strength of his activities as a collector of relics and books, King Athelstan has been described as 'the Pierpont Morgan of his age';[255] on the strength of his generosity in distributing the fruits of his labours, he might equally be described as the Isaac Wolfson of the tenth century. Perhaps the scale of his activities and the degree of his generosity were exceeded by those

[251] Cf. Bishop, *Liturgica Historica*, p. 141, n. 1.

[252] See A. G. Watson, 'A Sixteenth-Century Collector: Thomas Dackomb, 1496–*c.*1572', *The Library* 5th ser. 18 (1963), 204–17, esp. 212.

[253] It is plain that the manuscript has been mutilated. One of the miniatures added to the manuscript in the early tenth century (and placed opposite the beginning of Psalm 1) was removed, probably in the sixteenth century, and is now Oxford, Bodleian Library, Rawlinson B. 484, fol. 85; there was apparently another miniature opposite the beginning of Psalm 51, but this is now lost. The folio with the added poem (see above, n. 250) was to be found near the end of the manuscript in the late seventeenth century, but it too is lost.

[254] The manuscript belonged to Lord Lumley at the beginning of the seventeenth century (Jayne and Johnson, *Lumley Library*, p. 105 (no. 755)) and to Sir Robert Cotton by 1612 (as shown by his signature on 1r; it is no. 114 in the Cotton catalogue of 1621, BL Harley 6018, 60r); both regarded it as Athelstan's book, but perhaps only on the basis of Dackomb's note.

[255] Brooke, *The Saxon & Norman Kings*, p. 132.

who came after, and perhaps the range of his books did not match up to the contents of the palace libraries of Charlemagne, Louis the Pious and Charles the Bald;[256] but such comparisons do not detract from the significance of Athelstan's collection. Most of the books associated with him were written overseas, and their presence in England in the first half of the tenth century is symbolic of the varied ties that bound England and her neighbours together: the personal links between the West Saxon royal family and different ruling families on the continent played a large part, but were complemented by more informal relations between the West Saxon kings and religious houses outside their realms, by visits of foreigners to England, and by the travels of Englishmen abroad. It is important to remember that in the wide range of his contacts, with Francia, Germany, Brittany and Ireland (and other places besides), Athelstan was building on foundations laid by his predecessors Edward the Elder and Alfred the Great; so one should certainly not suppose that all of the manuscripts were imported during his reign.

The inscriptions which attest Athelstan's former ownership of some of the manuscripts discussed above are of considerable significance in their own right. Athelstan can hardly have been the only king to accumulate manuscripts, or the only one to give them away to religious houses; but inscriptions recording such activity are restricted to him alone, which suggests that they reflect a conscious desire on his part to be remembered for his munificence.[257] And if the initiative for making the inscriptions came from Athelstan himself, it seems reasonable to believe that the scribes who wrote them were (at the time) in the service of the king; the similarities between inscriptions in manuscripts given to different religious houses support this idea, while the connections of some with contemporary charters might reflect the other activities of the scribes.

The chief interest of Athelstan's books, however, springs from their

256 For the third, see R. McKitterick, 'Charles the Bald (823–877) and his Library: the Patronage of Learning', *EHR* 95 (1980), 28–47; for the first two, see *ibid.* p. 28, n. 6.

257 Other kings in the tenth century are known (or alleged) to have given books to religious houses (see, e.g., Scott, *Early History of Glastonbury*, pp. 118–19, for a gospel-book given by Edmund to Glastonbury, and *Liber Eliensis*, ed. E. O. Blake, Camden 3rd ser. 92 (London, 1962), 290–1, for a gospel-book given by Edgar to Ely); if it was the 'beneficiaries' who wrote the inscriptions recording such gifts, it is not obvious why they should have apparently restricted themselves to gifts received from Athelstan. The Athelstan inscriptions should be compared with those which Leofric, bishop of Exeter, caused to be entered in several of the books which he gave to his cathedral library: see Ker, *Catalogue*, nos. 20, 32, 84, 236, 291, 294, 296, 315 and 316, and M. Förster, 'The Donations of Leofric to Exeter', R. W. Chambers, M. Förster and R. Flower, *The Exeter Book of Old English Poetry* (Exeter, 1933), pp. 10–32, esp. 11, n. 3; see also Lapidge, above, pp. 64–9. For other inscriptions recording gifts of books to churches, see Ker, *Catalogue*, nos. 115 and 385; and for various references to traffic in books, see Dodwell, *Anglo-Saxon Art*, pp. 22, 95, 202–3 and 224.

relation to the king's patronage of religion and learning. They provide tangible support for the idea that Athelstan's court was a place where people of different backgrounds met and shared their knowledge. The environment provided by the king played a crucial part in the origins of the monastic reform movement in England, for those who had been moved to espouse the cause exerted an influence on others at court, Dunstan and Æthelwold among them. Moreover, the manuscripts imported into England in the first half of the tenth century doubtless contributed much to the development of Anglo-Saxon learning and art. Athelstan's books should serve finally to remind us that as a patron of the church he stands high in the line of succession from Alfred to Edgar. Athelstan may not have approached the distinction of his grandfather as a scholar, though he is said to have been a learned man; but at least it is clear that he was no less conscious than Alfred of the need to promote the interests of the men who intercede with God, and in this respect he provided an excellent example for Edgar to follow.

## APPENDIX

# The visit of Bishop Cenwald to Germany

The visit of Cenwald, bishop of Worcester, to Germany in the late autumn of 929 is one of the most striking examples of contact between England and the continent during the reign of King Athelstan. It affords a glimpse of one of the ways in which manuscripts written on the continent might have come into Athelstan's possession, and, more generally, it shows how knowledge of ecclesiastical developments on the continent was transmitted to England. The purpose of this Appendix, and of the accompanying plates, is to make the evidence relating to the visit more readily accessible.

The visit is not recorded in any English source; but an account of it was entered in a manuscript at the abbey of St Gallen (St Gallen, Stiftsbibliothek, 915, p. 5: see pl. XIII):[1]

> Anno ab incarnatione Domini dcccc xx viiii indictione ii Keonuuald uenerabilis episcopus, profectus ab Anglis, omnibus monasteriis per totam Germaniam, cum oblatione de argento non modica et in id ipsum a rege Anglorum eadem sibi tradita, uisitatis, in idibus Octob. uenit ad monasterium sancti Galli; quique gratissime a fratribus susceptus et eiusdem patroni nostri festiuitatem cum illis celebrando quatuor ibidem dies demoratus est. Secundo autem postquam monasterium ingressus est, hoc est

[1] For this manuscript, see A. T. Bruckner, *Scriptoria Medii Aevi Helvetica* III (Geneva, 1938), 122, and *Libri Confraternitatum Sancti Galli Augiensis Fabariensis*, ed. P. Piper, MGH, Libri confraternitatum (Berlin, 1884), p. 8; see also Bishop, *Liturgica Historica*, pp. 349–50.

in ipso depositionis sancti Galli die [16 October], basilicam intrauit et pecuniam copiosam secum attulit, de qua partem altario imposuit, partem etiam utilitati fratrum donauit. Post hec, eo in conuentum nostrum introducto, omnis congregatio concessit ei annonam unius fratris et eandem orationem quam pro quolibet de nostris, siue uiuente siue uita decedente, facere solemus pro illo facturam perpetualiter promisit. Hec sunt autem nomina que conscribi rogauit: Rex Anglorum Adalstean, Keonouuald episcopus, Uuighart, Kenuun, Conrat, Keonolaf, Uuundrud, Keondrud.[2]

To judge from this account, Cenwald had visited 'all the monasteries throughout Germany' before arriving at St Gallen on 15 October 929; and it seems that he had been entrusted by King Athelstan with quantities of silver, presumably for distribution among the various places that he visited. We may infer, therefore, that Cenwald's visit was sanctioned by the king; and since it was at precisely this time, in the autumn of 929, that Athelstan sent his two half-sisters, Edith and *Adiva*, to Germany, in response to Henry the Fowler's request for a bride for his son Otto,[3] we may well imagine that the primary purpose of Cenwald's visit was to accompany the two princesses to the Saxon court.[4] It is also conceivable that Cenwald had been instructed to acquire some relics for the king at the same time, and perhaps even books as well; while Cenwald doubtless took advantage of the occasion to familiarize himself with conditions in the German monasteries.[5]

[2] *Libri Confraternitatum*, ed. Piper, pp. 136–7; Robinson, *Bishops of Wells*, pp. 60–1; and *Councils & Synods*, ed. Whitelock *et al.* pt I, p. 42 (no. 10). 'In the year of the Lord's Incarnation 929, the second indiction, the venerable Bishop Cenwald, coming from the English, once he had visited all the monasteries throughout Germany (with a substantial offering of silver which had been entrusted to him by the king of the English for the purpose), came to the monastery of St Gallen on 15 October. He was received joyfully by the monks, and stayed there for four days in order to celebrate with them the feast of St Gall our patron. And on the second day after his arrival at the monastery, that is on the anniversary of the burial of St Gall [16 October], he entered the church, bringing an abundance of money with him, part of which he placed on the altar and part he donated for the use of the monks. After this, he was led into our monastery, and the whole community gave him the allowance of a monk, and promised to say on his behalf, in perpetuity, the same prayer as we are accustomed to say for anyone of our own, whether living or dead. And these are the names which he asked to be recorded: Athelstan, king of the English; Bishop Cenwald; Wigheard; Coenwynn; Coenred; Coenlaf; Wynthryth; Coenthryth.'

[3] See above, p. 148.

[4] See Robinson, *Bishops of Wells*, p. 41, n. 1, and Schmid, 'Die Thronfolge Ottos des Grossen', p. 116. Cenwald's visit to the more southerly monasteries of St Gallen and Reichenau may have been in connection with the marriage of *Adiva* to a Burgundian prince; see above, nn. 27 and 232.

[5] He may already have taken monastic vows; see Barker, 'Two Lost Documents', p. 139. His later profession of the monastic life is attested by those charters, dated between 949 and 956, in which he is styled *monachus* (see above, n. 85); in the early-twelfth-century Worcester chronicle, he is described as 'vir magnæ humilitatis et monasticæ professionis' (*Florentii Wigorniensis Monachi Chronicon ex Chronicis*, ed. B. Thorpe, 2 vols. (London, 1848–9) I, 137). See also D. Whitelock, *Some Anglo-Saxon Bishops of London*, Chambers Memorial Lecture 1974 (London, 1975), p. 20, for the suggestion that another purpose of Cenwald's visit to Germany in 929 may have been to recruit men for the English church.

The account in St Gallen, Stiftsbibliothek, 915 concludes with a list of eight people who at Cenwald's request were to be remembered in the community's prayers: King Athelstan, Cenwald himself, a certain 'Wighart' (OE Wigheard), and five others (OE Coenwynn, Coenred, Coenlaf, Wynthryth and Coenthryth), some of whom, if only to judge from their names, may have been relatives of Cenwald.[6] It was evidently on the same occasion that a much longer list of names was entered in the confraternity book of St Gallen (St Gallen, Stiftsarchiv, Cod. C 3 B 55, p. 77: see pl. XIV):[7]

> Adalsten rex, Uuolfhelmus archiepiscopus, Eluuinus episcopus, Eotkarus episcopus, Uuunisge episcopus, Sigihelm episcopus, Oda episcopus, Fridosten episcopus, Cunifrid episcopus, Kenod abba, Albrich abba, Cudret, Erdulf, Fridolef, Uuulfun, Ortgar, Osfred, Elfsie, Adaluierd, Eluuin, Adaluuin, Berectuuin, Uulfilt, Uuighart, Conrat, Kenuun, Uundrud, Keonuuad episcopus, Kenolaf, Keondrud, cum ceteris.[8]

Here the king is followed by Wulfhelm, archbishop of Canterbury, and seven bishops (all holding office in 929): Ælfwine of Lichfield, Edgar of Hereford, Winsige of Dorchester, Sigehelm of Sherborne, Oda of Ramsbury, Frithestan of Winchester and Cyneferth of Rochester. The two abbots are Cynath of Evesham and an unidentified Ælfric.[9] The twelve names which follow (OE Cuthred, Eardwulf, Frithuleaf, Wulfrun, Ordgar, Osferth, Ælfsige, Æthelweard, Ælfwine, Æthelwine, Berhtwine and Wulfhild) cannot be identified with certainty, but may have been men and women in Cenwald's party. The list concludes with the names which occur (after the king's) in the other St Gallen manuscript, including Wigheard and Bishop Cenwald, though they are given in a different order.

An entry in the confraternity book of Reichenau (Zürich, Zentralbibliothek, Rh. hist. 27, p. LXX: see pl. XV) is probably related to Cenwald's visit to the German monasteries in 929, if only to judge from the mention of Wigheard at the end:

> Aethelstaenum regem cum Uulfelmo archiepiscopo et nostris fidelissimis uiuis ac in pace quiescentibus uestro seruitio in Christi nomine commendamus. Uuighart.[10]

The entry is written in Caroline minuscule; it may have been dictated by Wigheard, but it seems unlikely that he was actually the scribe.[11]

6 *Councils & Synods*, ed. Whitelock *et al.*, pt 1, p. 41.

7 For this manuscript, see *Libri Confraternitatum*, ed. Piper, pp. 3–4.

8 *Ibid.* p. 100; Robinson, *Bishops of Wells*, p. 61; and *Councils & Synods*, ed. Whitelock *et al.*, pt 1, pp. 42–3 (no. 10).

9 For Cynath, see *TSD*, pp. 35–40; there are several subscriptions of an Abbot Ælfric in Athelstan's charters (e.g. S 412–13, 416, 418, 422 and 425).

10 *Libri Confraternitatum*, ed. Piper, p. 238; Robinson, *Bishops of Wells*, p. 61. For a description and complete facsimile of the manuscript, see J. Autenrieth, D. Geuenich and K. Schmid, *Das Verbrüderungsbuch der Abtei Reichenau. Einleitung, Register, Faksimile*, MGH, Libri memoriales et necrologia n.s. 1 (Hanover, 1979). 'In the name of Christ, we commend King Athelstan to your service, together with Archbishop Wulfhelm and our friends both living and resting in peace. Wigheard.'

11 Cf. *Libri Confraternitatum*, ed. Piper, p. 238 n.; but the script is not English, and it may be doubted that Wigheard would have written his name in a German form.

An entry in the confraternity book of Pfäfers (St Gallen, Stiftsarchiv, Cod. Fabariensis 1, p. 33: see pl. XVI) is sometimes linked to Cenwald's visit, but it must belong to a later date:

> Athalsten rex. Otmundus rex. Odgiua. Odo archiepiscopus.[12]

The reference to King Edmund (939–46) and Oda, archbishop of Canterbury (941–58), presumably implies that the entry belongs to the years between 941 and 946; and it looks as if Athelstan's name was inserted by the scribe as an afterthought. *Odgiua*, in this context, is most likely to refer to Eadgifu, mother of King Edmund.[13] The names opposite this entry, in the right-hand column, seem to have been written on the same occasion:

> Ricardus, Odboldus, Regenoldus, Alfere, Heltrut, Rodleef, Ealfere, Othelold, Uulfric, Uuarin, Folrad, Bersten, Odmar, Athalger, Kielelm, Athalsi, Athalbold, Liman, Odmund, Athalsuit, Uulric, Uulflid, Bolo, Gunduuin, Uro, Uuecin, Duua.[14]

Some of these names are German and some English, but none can be identified for certain. It is possible that these entries in the Pfäfers book are to be connected with Archbishop Oda, and that they reflect a visit by him and his retinue to the abbey;[15] he may have been going to (or coming from) Rome,[16] or he may have been visiting monasteries as Cenwald had done before him. Whatever the explanation, it is likely that such visits occurred more frequently than the surviving evidence suggests, and that the contacts established by Athelstan were maintained, and extended, by his successors.

12 *Ibid.* p. 363; Robinson, *Bishops of Wells*, p. 61. For an account of the manuscript, see A. T. Bruckner, *Scriptoria Medii Aevi Helvetica* I (Geneva, 1935), 86, and for a complete facsimile, see *Liber Viventium Fabariensis*, ed. A. Bruckner, H. R. Sennhauser and F. Perret (Basle, 1973).

13 If not, the reference may be to one or other of Athelstan's half-sisters, either Eadgifu, formerly wife of Charles the Simple, or Eadgifu, wife of a 'prince of the Aquitainians'; see above, pp. 190–1.

14 *Libri Confraternitatum*, ed. Piper, p. 363, and Robinson, *Bishops of Wells*, p. 61.

15 An entry in a book of confraternity does not necessarily imply a visit (cf. *EHD*, no. 228: Edward the Elder 'commended himself by letters to the confraternity of St Samson'), but the associated assortment of other names in this case seems to suggest one.

16 Bishop (*Liturgica Historica*, p. 355) and J. M. Clark (*The Abbey of St Gall as a Centre of Literature & Art* (Cambridge, 1926), p. 65) suggest that Oda was on his way to Rome to collect his pallium.

# II

# The Texts

## Texts, Sources and Interpretations

# Thoughts on Ephrem the Syrian in Anglo-Saxon England

PATRICK SIMS-WILLIAMS

Not all the Fathers of the Church are represented in Migne's Patrologia Graeca and Patrologia Latina. An important voice, represented by perhaps two to three thousand Greek manuscripts and some fifty pre-twelfth-century Latin manuscripts,[1] is that of 'Ephrem Syrus', whose Greek works have not been printed since the eighteenth century and whose Latin works were last printed in the sixteenth.[2] Not all these works were translated from the authentic Syriac writings of St Ephrem of Edessa (*ob.* 373), or even from Syriac, but a leavening of the genuine work of the saint is found in many of them. Readers of this volume presented to Peter Clemoes will already be aware, from the quite typical homily recently translated by Allen and Calder,[3] of the potential attraction for western medieval readers of 'Ephrem', who preaches asceticism, humility, the imminence of judgement, and the love of God in direct, powerfully rhetorical and sensuous language.

Was 'Ephrem' read in Anglo-Saxon England? In view of the number of manuscripts and library-catalogue entries on the continent it is likely enough that he was known here too, but only one pre-Conquest manuscript seems to survive: London, Lambeth Palace 204 (s. xi[1]), perhaps from Christ Church,

[1] D. Hemmerdinger-Iliadou, 'Vers une nouvelle édition de l'Éphrem grec', *Studia Patristica* 3 [= Texte und Untersuchungen 78] (1961), 72–80, esp. 72, and 'Éphrem grec – Éphrem latin', *Dictionnaire de spiritualité* IV (1960), cols. 800–19, esp. col. 818; A. Siegmund, *Die Überlieferung der griechischen christlichen Literatur in der lateinischen Kirche bis zum zwölften Jahrhundert* (Munich, 1949), pp. 67–71; and S. I. Mercati, 'Animadversiones in Roberti Valentini Dissertationem de Septem Sermonum Ephraem Versione Quadam Antiqua', *Bessarione* 36 (1920), 177–91, esp. 178–80. The indispensable guide to 'Ephrem' is M. Geerard, *Clavis Patrum Graecorum* II (Turnhout, 1974), 366–468.

[2] For the Greek texts, see *Sancti Ephraem Syri Opera Omnia quae exstant . . . Graece et Latine*, ed. J. S. Assemani, 3 vols. (Rome, 1732–46), hereafter cited as 'Assemani'. For the medieval Latin version (not to be confused with various fifteenth-century and later translations from the Greek), see below, n. 11. A work of Ephrem was known in Greek translation to Jerome, who admired it; see P. Courcelle, *Les Lettres grecques en occident de Macrobe à Cassiodore* (Paris, 1948), p. 109.

[3] M. J. B. Allen and D. G. Calder, *Sources and Analogues of Old English Poetry* (Cambridge and Totowa, NJ, 1976), pp. 86–93.

Canterbury, or from Ely.[4] This manuscript contains Gregory's *Dialogi* and a 'liber beati Efrem' (119v–129v) with the characteristic 'Ephremic' incipit 'Dolor me compellit . . .'. This *liber* is an incomplete version of a work variously entitled *Ammonitio*, *Monita*, *Institutio ad monachos*, and *De compunctione cordis* in Latin manuscripts, but known to modern scholarship as *Sermo asceticus*, from *Λόγος ᾿Ασκητικός*, the title given to the Greek original in Assemani's eighteenth-century edition.[5] The Greek text, which is extant in a number of recensions or reworkings, is partly based on extant hymns by Ephrem and on two Syriac sermons doubtfully attributed to him, but it also includes long stretches, unparalleled in Syriac, which cannot be authentic.[6] Like others of the Greek works ascribed to Ephrem, the *Sermo asceticus* seems to be a distillation of several different writers' teachings on the monastic life. It reads, nevertheless, like an urgent exhortation by Ephrem himself speaking in the first person, and this doubtless contributed to its popularity: translations were made into Coptic, Arabic, Ethiopic, Armenian, Georgian, Slavonic and Latin.[7] The Latin translation must have been made as early as the sixth century, for it is found already in Paris, BN lat. 12634, the (probably Italian) manuscript of the *Regula magistri* written in the late sixth or early seventh century.[8] Here it is entitled 'Ammonitio sancti Effrem ad monachos' in the incipit (77v) and 'Institutio sancti Efremis diaconi data [a]d monachos' in the explicit (142r). The Latin version is next attested in France, in a fragmentary seventh-century manuscript from Corbie now forming the flyleaves of BN lat. 10399 and Amiens, Bibliothèque Municipale, 12, and in quotations by Defensor of Ligugé in his *Liber scintillarum*.[9] From the eighth century onwards the *Sermo asceticus* is well attested as one of a group of six or seven *opuscula* attributed to Ephrem, all save one of which are similarly dependent on known Greek

[4] See H. Gneuss, 'A Preliminary List of Manuscripts written or owned in England up to 1100', *ASE* 9 (1981), 1–60, at 33 (no. 510). The pre-Conquest relevance of the two further manuscripts mentioned by T. H. Bestul ('Ephraim the Syrian and Old English Poetry', *Anglia* 99 (1981), 1–24, at 14) is very doubtful.

[5] Assemani I, 40–70. For variant versions in Assemani and elsewhere see the references given by D. Hemmerdinger-Iliadou, 'Les Doublets de l'édition de l'Éphrem grec par Assemani', *Orientalia Christiana Periodica* 24 (1958), 371–82, at 372, and 'Vers une nouvelle édition', pp. 74 and 79–80; and Geerard, *Clavis* II, 370–2 (no. 3909).

[6] I. Hausherr, *Penthos: La Doctrine de la componction dans l'Orient chrétien*, Orientalia Christiana Analecta 132 (Rome, 1944), 48, n. 35; Hemmerdinger-Iliadou, 'Éphrem grec – Éphrem latin', col. 802; and Geerard, *Clavis* II, 371. (The passages which I shall be discussing below are apparently not attested in Syriac.)

[7] *Ibid.* II, 372–3.

[8] For the date, see E. A. Lowe, *Codices Latini Antiquiores*, 11 vols. and suppl. (Oxford, 1934–72), Suppl., p. 55 (no. 646).

[9] *Ibid.* VI, no. 708; Hemmerdinger-Iliadou, 'Éphrem grec – Éphrem latin', cols. 816 and 819; J. Kirchmeyer and D. Hemmerdinger-Iliadou, 'Saint Éphrem et le "Liber Scintillarum"', *Recherches de science religieuse* 46 (1958), 545–50.

originals.[10] The immense popularity of these *opuscula* throughout the Middle Ages is demonstrated by the innumerable surviving manuscripts and by the fact that they were printed before 1493.[11]

In view of the popularity of 'Ephrem' on the continent, the lack of any Anglo-Saxon manuscript earlier than the eleventh century is surprising and perhaps fortuitous. Nevertheless, it is somewhat embarrassing that no quotations of 'Ephrem' by Anglo-Latin writers have been discovered, if one may leave aside as a special case the glosses attributed to Theodore of Tarsus, which may well refer to the Greek corpus.[12] Until recently one might have fallen back on the Ephremic borrowings by Old English poets, which have been widely accepted since the beginning of this century, but Thomas H. Bestul has now cast real doubt on the closeness and significance of the verbal parallels and thematic similarities alleged by earlier Old English scholars, concluding that 'there is little in favor of the view that Ephraim was a direct source for any Old English literary text'.[13] 'If scholars accept this as the final word', remarks a reviewer in the *Old English Newsletter*, Bestul 'will effectually have shut the door on this small corridor of research'.[14] The present paper is not intended to prise open that particular door (though it may be wondered whether it is only the relative inaccessibility of the Latin 'Ephrem' that has prevented students of late Old English prose from finding sources there). I wish instead to suggest that the question of Anglo-Saxon knowledge of 'Ephrem' may be approached by a different route: by closer scrutiny of the surviving Anglo-Latin texts and manuscripts. A number of genres might repay examination – a particularly promising area is the body of texts concerning death and judgement.[15] Here I

[10] Hemmerdinger-Iliadou, 'Éphrem grec – Éphrem latin', col. 816, and 'Vers une nouvelle édition', p. 74, and E. Dekkers and A. Gaar, *Clavis Patrum Latinorum*, 2nd ed. (Steenbrugge, 1961), p. 254 (no. 1143). Only the *De die iudicii et de resurrectione* is unattested in Greek (Geerard, *Clavis* II, 444: no. 4080); 'is extant' on p. 81 of my article cited in n. 18 below was a printer's error for 'is not extant' after I passed the proofs!

[11] *Libri Sancti Effrem* . . ., probably printed by Kilian Fischer (Piscator) at Freiburg im Breisgau. There is a copy in the British Library. I have used two editions in Cambridge University Library: *Sanctissimi Ephraem Syri Opuscula Omnia quae apud Latinos reperiri potuerunt* (Cologne, 1547), which seems to be based on Fischer's edition, and *Opuscula Quaedam Divina Beati Ephraem* (Dillingen, [1563]), which is independent. Cf. A. Wilmart, 'La Fausse Lettre latine de Macaire', *Revue d'ascétique et de mystique* 3 (1922), 411–19, at 414, n. 16. On the early printed versions, see also Mercati, 'Animadversiones', p. 180, and Hemmerdinger-Iliadou 'Éphrem grec – Éphrem latin', col. 816.

[12] B. Bischoff, *Mittelalterliche Studien*, 3 vols. (Stuttgart, 1966–81) I, 208. Apart from Theodore only Alcuin, *Officia per ferias*, is cited by J. D. A. Ogilvy, *Books Known to the English, 597–1066* (Cambridge, Mass., 1967), p. 135; but the attribution to Alcuin is false (see below, p. 211).

[13] 'Ephraim and Old English Poetry', p. 22.

[14] T. G. H[ahn], *OEN* 16.1 (1982), 53.

[15] In searching for parallels to the personified deeds which reproach the monk of Wenlock in the vision reported by Boniface (*Die Briefe des Heiligen Bonifatius und Lullus*, ed. M. Tangl, MGH, Epist. select. I (Berlin, 1916), 9–10 (*ep.* 10)), the nearest I discovered was in 'Ephrem', *De*

have chosen to make a start with the early English prayer-books, not so much because they are likely to be the most fruitful genre – for obviously they cannot prove acquaintance with works as opposed to extracts – as because the 'Ephremic' element in them has already been the subject of obscure and oracular comments by Edmund Bishop, which demand elucidation, since they continue to influence and mislead even careful scholars. This is an essay in rectification and amplification, which also attempts in passing to raise some points of method relevant to the investigation of the early Anglo-Saxon devotional tradition.

The early-ninth-century Book of Cerne (Cambridge, University Library, Ll. 1. 10) includes an *Oratio ad dominum sancti Effremis* (71v–72r), and other prayers are attributed to Ephrem in continental collections of prayers. Bestul dismisses the evidence of these attributions too briskly:

> A number of private devotional prayers are attributed to Ephraim in various collections throughout the early Middle Ages, and since they most certainly do not belong among Ephraim's genuine works they are better taken as a sign of his reputation for holiness than as evidence for authorship.[16]

Admittedly, a connection between the Syriac works of the saint of Edessa and these prayers cannot be established, but I shall show that in several cases they derive from the Graeco-Latin 'Ephremic' corpus, in particular from the above-mentioned *opuscula*, which Bestul himself ventures to treat as among the 'genuine' (as opposed to 'spurious') works of the saint.

An obvious starting-point for this investigation is the Book of Cerne *Oratio ad dominum* (Prayer 46) mentioned above, for this is the only prayer in the Anglo-Saxon prayer-books attributed to Ephrem. It follows a number of anonymous prayers with unhelpful titles such as *Oratio utilis*, but precedes an *Oratio ad dominum ab Alchfriðo anch*[*orita*] *compositum* [*sic*] (no. 47) and *Item alia*

*beatitudine animae*: 'Grandis timor est, fratres, in illa hora mortis et separationis animae a corpore. Assistent enim tunc ipse animae opera eius quae per diem noctemque bona et mala gessit. Angeli etiam festinant ac properant excludere eam a corpore. At illa audiens actus suos egredi pertimescit, quia peccatoris anima cum metu magno et timore horrendo separatur a corpore, et tremens ac iugiter deflens pergit ad aeternum iudicium. Ea ergo hora cum anima diuiditur a corpore, uidens uniuersa opera sua, dicit eis "Date mihi unius hore spatium, donec egrediar". Et respondent simul omnia opera eius et dicunt ei: "Tu nos egisti. Tua opera sumus. Tecum semper ibimus, tecumque pergemus ad deum." Sancta etenim anima cum separatur a corpore, non timet nec metuit; sed magis gaudens cum fiducia pergit ad deum, euecta officiis angelorum' (BL Harley 3060, fol. 129; on this manuscript, see below, p. 218). Cf. *Sanctissimi Ephraem Opuscula*, fols. 53b–54a; *Opuscula Quaedam*, fols. 11b–12a. The last sentence is missing from the Greek texts printed by Assemani I, 295, and III, 376. On this work, see Geerard, *Clavis* II, 386 (no. 3935).

16 'Ephraim and Old English Poetry', pp. 3–4. The Book of Cerne is ed. A. B. Kuypers, *The Prayer Book of Aedeluald the Bishop commonly called The Book of Cerne* (Cambridge, 1902). I have collated this with the manuscript. Prayer 46, on account of its Ephremic attribution, is reprinted by A. Hamman, *Patrologia Latina: Supplementum* (Paris, 1958–) IV, cols. 640–1.

*eiusdem* (no. 48). This Alchfrith can confidently be identified with the anchorite of the same name who wrote an extant letter, heavily indebted to Columbanus, to a certain Hyglac, *lector et presbiter*, doubtless the same person as the Hyglac, *presbiter atque lector*, who taught the early-ninth-century Northumbrian poet Æthilwulf.[17] This perhaps suggests a late-eighth-century, specifically English context (perhaps under Irish influence) for Prayer 46 and the surrounding prayers of the Book of Cerne. The suggestion is reinforced by the facts that Prayer 44 is also to be found in the (Insular) pseudo-Bedan *Collectanea*,[18] while nos. 38–43 (except no. 42, which is unique) recur in the slightly later English Book of Nunnaminster (London, BL Harley 2965, 19v–20r, 20v–21r, 21v–22r, 24r and 36v–37r).[19] Most of the prayers shared with the Book of Nunnaminster belong to a cycle of prayers on the life of Christ of which elements are also to be found in the slightly earlier English prayer-book, BL Royal 2. A. XX (s. viii²),[20] but not at all in the Carolingian and later continental collections, a fact which leads one to suppose that the cycle was a late-eighth- and early-ninth-century development which occurred after Alcuin's departure for the continent and consequently enjoyed a purely English popularity.

I have dwelt on the eighth-century English context of Prayer 46 in the hopes that it may shed some light on its origin, for despite the attribution to Ephrem it seems to be an original Latin composition, to judge at least by the use of rhyme:

> Deus excelsissime, deus misericordissime,
> susceptor animarum, salus infirmantium,
> qui es rerum conditor, uniuersorum creator . . .

The clue to the Ephremic attribution is to be found in Kuypers's appendix on 'Attributions of Prayers in the Book of Cerne' at the end of his edition. His main conclusion is negative, that 'little reliance can be placed upon the attributions found in these early prayer books', and on the *Oratio Effremis* he comments:

17 W. Levison, *England and the Continent in the Eighth Century* (Oxford, 1946), pp. 295–302; *Æthelwulf De Abbatibus*, ed. A. Campbell (Oxford, 1967), pp. xxvii–xxix; K. Hughes, 'Some Aspects of Irish Influence on Early English Private Prayer', *Studia Celtica* 5 (1970) 48–61, at 59; and Barré, *Prières anciennes de l'occident à la mère du Sauveur des origines à saint Anselme* (Paris, 1963), pp. 56 and 68–9.

18 PL 94, cols. 560–1. On this work, see P. Sims-Williams, 'Thought, Word and Deed: an Irish Triad', *Ériu* 29 (1978), 78–111, at 88; P. Kitson, 'Lapidary Traditions in Anglo-Saxon England: Part II, Bede's *Explanatio Apocalypsis* and Related Books', *ASE* 12 (1983), 73–123, at 100–1.

19 *An Ancient Manuscript of the Eighth or Ninth Century formerly belonging to St Mary's Abbey, or Nunnaminster, Winchester*, ed. W. deG. Birch, Hampshire Record Soc. (London and Winchester, 1889). Elements of Prayer 43 in the Book of Cerne recur in Prayer XVIII in the Bury Psalter; see below, n. 57.

20 BL Royal 2. A. XX, 29r–38v. The manuscript is ptd Kuypers, *Book of Cerne*, pp. 201–25. See also *ibid.* pp. xviii and xxvii–xxix, where 'Gelasian' influence on the cycle is noted.

No. 46, which I have not found elsewhere, is attributed to S. Ephrem, and it may be noted that the prayer which immediately precedes it, No. 45, which is unassigned in *Cerne* and the *Book of Nunnaminster*, is attributed to S. Ephrem in Alcuin's *Officia per Ferias* and in the *Fleury Prayer Book*.[21]

To these references may be added the Psalter of Odbert (Saint-Bertin, AD 999), where a version of Prayer 45 is entitled *Oratio sancti Effrem*.[22] The obvious conclusion to be drawn is surely not that the attribution of no. 46 in the Book of Cerne is mere fantasy but that it has been displaced from no. 45; perhaps 'Incipit oratio ad dominum sancti effremis' should be emended to 'Explicit oratio ad dominum sancti effremis'. Such misplacing of rubrics may explain many of the misattributions in the early medieval prayer-books (another instance involving 'Ephrem' will be noted in connection with the Tours prayer-book at Troyes; see below, p. 224). Not only mechanical errors are involved, however. Some attributions look as if they are based on mistaken guesses, due to similarities in style or content to the works of a Father of the Church. Or they may indicate place of origin rather than authorship; an *Oratio sancti Patricii* or *Oratio sancti Isidori* at least may be of Irish or Spanish origin.[23] Some of the prayers attributed to Augustine, Gregory, and so on, may be the work of namesakes of these Fathers.[24] But without doubt some of the attributions are based on the wildest guesswork. I suspect that the widespread attribution of Cerne Prayers 6 and 15 to St Jerome and St Gregory, which is faithfully reproduced in numerous copies,[25] may indicate an Irish origin; early Irish scholars inherited from the *filid* a conviction that their honour depended on seeming omniscient, and the fruits of this conviction may be seen in their

[21] *Ibid.* pp. 232–3. On these other texts, see below.

[22] V. Leroquais, *Les Psautiers manuscrits latins des bibliothèques publiques de France*, 2 vols. (Macon, 1940–1) I, 98: Boulogne-sur-Mer, Bibliothèque Municipale, 20, fol. 231.

[23] An 'Oratio Isidori pro omnibus Christianis', first found in the Fleury Prayer-Book and *Officia per ferias* (PL 101, cols. 556 and 1387–8) is based on an important prayer in the Spanish liturgy (*Le Liber Ordinum*, ed. M. Férotin (Paris, 1904), cols. 234–5 and 319, n. 1). I discuss the significance of this in an unpublished paper. Cf. Barré, *Prières anciennes*, p. 30 and n. 61.

[24] Cf. Paul Grosjean, 'Sur quelques exégètes irlandais du VIIe siècle', *Sacris Erudiri* 7 (1955), 67–98.

[25] For other copies of no. 6, see Sims-Williams, 'Thought, Word and Deed', p. 100 and n. 133. For other copies of no. 15, see Kuypers, *Cerne*, p. 232; A. Wilmart, 'Le Manuel de prières de saint Jean Gualbert', *RB* 48 (1936), 259–99, at 281 and n. 3; M. Frost, 'A Prayer Book from St Emmeran, Ratisbon', *JTS* 30 (1928–9), 32–45, at 33, 35 and 43–4; R. E. McNally, *Der irische Liber de Numeris* (Munich, 1957), pp. 13 and 27; PL 94, cols. 559–60 (pseudo-Bedan *Collectanea*); Pierre Salmon, *Analecta Liturgica*, Studi e testi 273 (Rome, 1974), 138, n. 50; *Die Glossen des Psalters von Mondsee*, ed. F. Unterkircher, Spicilegium Friburgense 20 (Freiburg, 1974), 513–14; Odilo Heiming, 'Ein benediktinisch–ambrosianisches Gebetbuch des frühen 11. Jahrhunderts (Brit. Mus. Egerton 3763)', *Archiv für Liturgiewissenschaft* 8.2 (1964), 325–435, at 411–12 (no. 25); T. H. Bestul, 'A Note on the Contents of the Anselm Manuscript, Bodleian Library, Laud Misc. 508', *Manuscripta* 21 (1977), 167–70, at 169 (item 4); and the further literature cited by these authorities.

obsession with 'names for the nameless' in the bible or the extraordinary lengths to which they went to attribute the anonymous hymns in the *Liber hymnorum*, to give only two examples.[26]

Prayer 45, the prayer before the one attributed to Ephrem in the Book of Cerne, is as follows (a lacuna due to homoeoteleuton is supplied in square brackets from the other copies; the italicized phrases will be discussed below):

*Item oratio*

Domine deus meus et saluator meus, quare me dereliquisti? Miserere mei deus, quoniam tu es *amator hominum* solus. Salua me peccatorem quia *tu es solus sine peccato.* Erue me de coeno iniquitatum mearum, ut non infigar in aeternum. Libera me ex ore inimici mei; ecce enim ut leo rugiens deuorare me cupit. Excita potentiam tuam et ueni ut saluum me facies. Corrusca corruscationes tuas et disperge uirtutem inimici. [71v] *Amator hominis, benignissime* deus, adiuro te per miserationes tuas, ne me cum edis a sinistris tuis statuas cum his qui te exacerbauerunt. Ne dicas mihi ['Nescio te', sed tribue mihi] propter magnam misericordiam tuam indesinenter cordis conpunctionem et fletum, et sanctifica me ut templum fiam gratiae tuae, per te christe iesu. Amen.

As noted by Kuypers, the above prayer may have had a place in the Book of Nunnaminster, for at the foot of 33v, just before a lost leaf, there is the opening of a *Sancta oratio*: 'Deus meus et saluator meus quare me dere [. . .]'. There is also an extract from it in Munich, Bayerische Staatsbibliothek, Clm. 14248 (St Emmeran, Regensburg, s. ix²), 165r: 'Amator hominum atque benignissime deus adiuro te per miserationes tuas ne me cum edis a sinistris statues.'[27] In content this prayer-book is closely related to the early English prayer-books and may be said to have been compiled under direct or indirect Anglo-Saxon (or at least Insular) influence. The same may be said of the early-ninth-century Fleury Prayer-Book (Orléans, Bibliothèque Municipale, 184), whose litany and script show it to have been written in south Germany, and the mid-ninth-century *Officia per ferias* (Paris, BN lat. 1153, fols. 1–98), which has no direct connection with Alcuin, but is a compilation made at Saint-Denis (witness the prominence given to St Denis in the litany at 79v and 80v).[28] In both

26 Cf. R. Flower, *The Irish Tradition* (Oxford, 1947), pp. 1–3; D. N. Dumville, 'Biblical Apocrypha and the Early Irish: a Preliminary Investigation', *Proc. of the R. Irish Acad.* 73 C (1973), 299–338, references at 315; and *The Irish Liber Hymnorum*, ed. J. H. Bernard and R. Atkinson, HBS 13–14 (London, 1898).

27 Frost, 'Prayer Book from St Emmeran', p. 36, and B. Bischoff, *Die südostdeutschen Schreibschulen und Bibliotheken der Karolingerzeit: I. Die bayerischen Diözesen*, 2nd ed. (Wiesbaden, 1960), p. 193.

28 On the Fleury Prayer-Book, see Bischoff, *Mittelalterliche Studien* III, 26, n. 107, and 101, and the earlier literature cited in Sims-Williams, 'Thought, Word and Deed', p. 100, n. 130. A date *c.* 820 × 830 has recently been given by D. A. Bullough, 'Alcuin and the Kingdom of Heaven: Liturgy, Theology, and the Carolingian Age', *Carolingian Essays: Andrew W. Mellon Lectures in Early Christian Studies*, ed. U.-R. Blumenthal (Washington, DC, 1983), pp. 1–69, at 13, n. 29, and 14. On the *Officia per ferias*, see Wilmart, 'Le Manuel', p. 263, n. 2; it and the Fleury Prayer-Book are ptd PL 101, cols. 510–612 and 1383–1416 respectively.

collections, which are often textually close, many prayers are attributed to the Fathers of the Church; the Fleury Prayer-Book calls them 'Orationes . . . quas beati patres . . . quotidie cantare solebant'. (Is this an attempt to emphasize the prayers' authority against the suspicion that they might include items of Irish origin?)[29] In the Fleury Prayer-Book our *Oratio sancti Ephrem diaconi* (Prayer 45 in the Book of Cerne) stands between an *Oratio beati Hieronymi presbiteri* (Prayer 6 in the Book of Cerne), probably of Insular origin, and an *Oratio beati Gregorii*, which is elsewhere anonymous.[30] In the *Officia per ferias* it follows an *Oratio sancti Isidori*, beginning: 'Succurre mihi, Deus meus, antequam mors ueniat, antequam mors me perimat, antequam tartarus rapiat, antequam flamma comburat, antequam tenebrae me inuoluant, antequam sine fine deficiam . . .'[31] This is welcome confirmation that not all attributions here are false, for it is an extract from Isidore's popular *Synonyma de lamentatione animae peccatricis*. Moreover, the next prayer but one in the Fleury book after *Oratio sancti Effrem diaconi* is another prayer with the same title (incipit 'Pone, domine, lacrimas meas in conspectu tuo . . .'), and this is an extract from the prayer *Obsecro te, saluator mundi* with which 'Ephrem' concludes the *Sermo asceticus*.[32]

For further light on Prayer 45 one naturally turns to Edmund Bishop's

[29] Cf. the contemporary problem of the Irish penitentials which circulated anonymously or under spurious patristic authority; see Allen J. Frantzen, *The Literature of Penance in Anglo-Saxon England* (New Brunswick, NJ, 1983), pp. 20, 92 and 98. I quote the Fleury Prayer-Book from PL 101, col. 1383; I have not been able to consult the manuscript.

[30] *Ibid.* cols. 1385–6. On the Jerome and Gregory prayers, see respectively Sims-Williams, 'Thought, Word and Deed', pp. 100–1, and Wilmart, 'Le Manuel', p. 291, n. 4.

[31] PL 101, cols. 605–6 (BN lat. 1153, 93v–94r; I failed to take the opportunity to check whether there is any relationship with the text of the *Synonyma* beginning at 99r). It is a very free version of the passage of the *Synonyma* beginning at PL 83, col. 841. See, further, below, p. 217 and n. 57.

[32] PL 101, col. 607 (BN lat. 1153, 95r). The word *meas* is an interlinear addition. In the title the saint's name here and in the prayer on 94r is 'Effr[ ]m', two letters having been erased in each case. That the *De compunctione cordis* (i.e. *Sermo asceticus*) was the source was stated by Mercati, 'Animadversiones', p. 181, without further references, but his observation has been forgotten in subsequent scholarship. For comparison I give the passage from the oldest manuscript (cf. also below, pp. 221–2), BN lat. 12634, 141r–142r: 'Pone, domine, lacr[im]as meas in conspectu tuo sicut in repromissione tua, ut reuertatur inimicus retrorsum et expauescens conturbetur, cum me uiderit in locum quem praeparauerunt miserationes tuae. Expectans autem me inimicus uidere in locum quem mihi propter delicta mea praeparauerat, uideat [me] in locum uitae et lucis aeternae, et conuersus in tenebras conturbetur, quia nequaquam uoluntas eius in me perfecta est. Ita benignissime, ita amator hominum deus, ita qui solus es sine peccato, effunde super me inmensam misericordiam tuam, et praesta mihi ut et ego, et hii qui diligunt te, regni tui efficiamur heredes, et tibi dantes gloriam tuam, adoremus bonitatem et dicamus pariter, qui digni fuerimus uidere instabilem [*sic*] pulchritudinem maiestatis tuae, dicamus "Gloria patri, qui fecit nos, et gloria filio, qui saluabit nos, et gloria sancto spiritui, qui renouabit nos in infinita saecula saeculorum."'

celebrated 'Liturgical Note' appended to Kuypers's edition of the Book of Cerne (pp. 234–83). The object of this 'Note' was

> to enquire whether the prayers contained in the *Book of Cerne* afford evidence of familiarity on the part of the writers with the Early Latin liturgical documents, and to ascertain with which particular books, or with which group or groups, of such books the writers may have been particularly conversant. (p. 234)

Bishop proceeds by gathering sixty-nine phrases from the Book of Cerne whose liturgical parallels seem particularly diagnostic, and concludes from them that the writers were less familiar with the Gallican sacramentaries than they were with the 'Roman' liturgy represented in the Gelasian Sacramentary, with the Spanish liturgy represented by the 'Mozarabic' *Missale mixtum* of 1500 or with Irish liturgical books similar to the Bobbio and Stowe Missals (p. 283). The whole discussion is girt about with expressions of caution, but nevertheless one pitfall is not wholly avoided: the apparent assumption that if a prayer contains a non-biblical phrase – or even sometimes a biblical phrase[33] – which can be paralleled in a liturgical book it is a liturgical reminiscence. In fact, while some of the sixty-nine items cited are clear liturgical quotations – for instance item 20, 'manus tuas sanctas ac uenerabiles' in Prayer 17 is an overt echo of 'accepit panem in sanctas ac uenerabiles manus suas' in the canon of the mass[34] – other items may be of non-liturgical origin and have passed independently into the traditions of public liturgy and private devotion from a third source. Item 12, for example, is the epithet *medicus* applied to Christ. Bishop finds that this is not employed in the Roman and Gallican liturgies but is common in the Bobbio and 'Mozarabic' Missals; and so it forms a striking element in his table

33 Item 15 is 'qui fecisti caelum, et terram, mare et omnia quae in eis sunt' (Acts IV.24), regarded as an Irish symptom in liturgy. See also H. M. Bannister, 'Some Recently Discovered Fragments of Irish Sacramentaries', *JTS* 5 (1904), 49–75, at 67; but cf. A. Wilmart, E. A. Lowe and H. A. Wilson, *The Bobbio Missal: Notes and Studies*, HBS 61 (London, 1924), 18, n. 5. The phrase is common enough in prayer-books, e.g. PL 101, cols. 469 and 600; Heiming, 'Ein benediktinisch–ambrosianisches Gebetbuch', p. 403 (no. 9); and cf. Adolph Frantz, *Die kirchlichen Benediktionen im Mittelalter*, 2 vols. (Freiburg im Breisgau, 1909) I, 408, 418 etc.

34 For parallel texts of the canon, see E. Bishop, *Liturgica Historica* (Oxford, 1918), pp. 84–5, and *Das irische Palimpsestsakramentar im Clm 14429 der Staatsbibliothek München*, ed. A. Dold and L. Eizenhöfer, Texte und Arbeiten 53–4 (Beuron, 1964), 15–18. On the introduction and significance of *ac uenerabiles*, see C. Mohrmann, *Études sur le latin des chrétiens*, 3 vols. (Rome, 1961–5) III, 232 and 235. Bede quotes a version with this wording; see G. G. Willis, *Further Essays in Early Roman Liturgy*, Alcuin Club Collections 50 (London, 1968), 221, n. 1. Its absence from the Irish sacramentary edited by Dold and Eizenhöfer, and from the 'Mozarabic' liturgy (Paul Séjourné, *Saint Isidore de Séville: Son rôle dans l'histoire du droit canonique* (Paris, 1929), p. 180) is noteworthy. See also the quotation in Royal 2. A. XX, 24v, and that at p. 226 below.

showing the affinities of the Book of Cerne prayers.[35] But is it necessarily a *liturgical* reminiscence? 'Physician' (*âsyâ*) is Ephrem's favourite title for Christ; might not *medicus* have reached our writers via the Latin 'Ephrem'?[36] Again, Augustine uses the epithet frequently,[37] and could easily have inspired both the writers of the Bobbio and 'Mozarabic' masses and the authors of the early English prayers. In fact a prayer in Royal 2. A. XX, 21v, which includes the words 'medicus es et eger sum', is taken directly from Augustine's *Confessiones*.[38] Here, then, Bishop errs in taking liturgical parallels to indicate liturgical sources.

Prayer 45 figures in the 'Liturgical Note' under item 13, 'tu es unus/solus sine peccato', words also found in Prayer 10, which is almost certainly an Irish composition, to judge by its content and its transmission elsewhere (moreover it is attributed to St Patrick in a ninth-century manuscript, which may be significant).[39] Bishop looks for a comparable phrase in the western liturgies and finds only 'solus sine peccati macula sacerdos/pontifex', in the 'Mozarabic' *Missale mixtum*, the Bobbio Missal and the Carolingian Supplement to the Gregorian Sacramentary, adding that 'on the supposition that *Bobiens.* is an Irish book, and that the compiler of the *Suppl. Greg.* was the Englishman Alcuin, the descent of these passages is easily to be conjectured' (presumably from Spain via Insular channels).[40] Be this as it may, the western liturgies, as

35 'Liturgical Note', in Kuypers, *Cerne*, pp. 246 and 276. See, further, *Le Liber Ordinum*, ed. Férotin, col. 779 (s.v. *medicus*); *Le Liber Mozarabicus Sacramentorum*, ed. M. Férotin (Paris, 1912), cols. 1057–8; G. Manz, *Ausdrucksformen der lateinischen Liturgiesprache bis ins elfte Jahrhundert*, Texte und Arbeiten, Beiheft 1 (Beuron, 1941), 291–3; and *Das irische Palimpsestsakramentar*, ed. Dold and Eizenhöfer, p. 157. For the oriental origin of the epithet, see U. Monneret de Villard, *Le leggende orientali sui Magi evangelici*, Studi e testi 163 (Rome, 1952), 91–8.

36 R. Murray, *Symbols of Church and Kingdom: a Study in Early Syriac Tradition* (Cambridge, 1975), pp. 199–203; see, e.g., *Opuscula Quaedam*, fols. 17–18 and 34b.

37 D. Lenfant, *Concordantiae Augustiniae*, 2 vols. (Paris, 1656–65), s.v. *medicamentum* etc.; J. Courtès, 'Saint Augustin et la médecine', *Augustinus Magister. Congrès international augustinien, Paris 1954: Communications*, 3 vols. (Paris, n.d.) I, 43–51; and R. Arbesmann, 'The Concept of "Christus Medicus" in St Augustine', *Traditio* 10 (1954), 1–28. For some early Insular references to medicine in relation to Christ or his pastors, see *Gildas*, ed. H. Williams, 2 vols. (London, 1899–1901) I, 178, n. 1; *Sancti Columbani Opera*, ed. G. S. M. Walker, Scriptores Latini Hiberniae 2 (Dublin, 1957), 120 and 172; *The Irish Penitentials*, ed. L. Bieler, Scriptores Latini Hiberniae 5 (Dublin, 1963), 46–7; *Aldhelmi Opera*, ed. R. Ehwald, MGH, Auct. antiq. 15 (Berlin, 1919), 235 and 484; and *The Earliest Life of Gregory the Great by an Anonymous Monk of Whitby*, ed. B. Colgrave (Lawrence, Kan., 1968), pp. 114 and 154, n. 92. See, further, Frantzen, *Literature of Penance*, pp. 30–1 (and n. 29), 65, 84–5, 87 and 89.

38 PL 32, col. 795 (x.28, § 39). This early borrowing is not noted by Pierre Courcelle in his survey 'Le "Sero te amavi" à travers les siècles', *Recherches sur les Confessions de saint Augustin*, 2nd ed. (Paris, 1968), pp. 464–78.

39 For these other versions of Prayer 10, see Sims-Williams, 'Thought, Word and Deed', p. 108, nn. 178–9. Cf. also Frantzen, *Literature of Penance*, p. 88.

40 'Liturgical Note', p. 247; cf. below, n. 51.

Bishop himself says, leave 'the precise words used in *Cerne* unaccounted for'.[41] Instead of looking outside the liturgy Bishop turns to eastern liturgies and notes that the epithet μόνος ἀναμάρτητος is applied to Christ in the Liturgy of St James, and that Jerome in his *Dialogus aduersus Pelagianos* (II.23), remarks on the daily use of this epithet, 'quod in lingua nostra dicitur, *qui solus es sine peccato*'.[42] Bishop observes moreover that the epithet φιλάνθρωπος (corresponding to *amator hominum* in Prayer 45, quoted above) occurs near it in the Liturgy of St James – though not as closely, at least in the extant texts, as Bishop's conflated quotation suggests.[43] Bishop concludes his note on item 13: 'The resemblance can hardly by any possibility be accidental; but by what road this passage of the Liturgy of Jerusalem found its way into England is a question that does not admit of a simple answer.' Once again, then, Bishop postulates a liturgical origin for two phrases, even though in this case both are unattested in western liturgy.[44] This is hardly satisfactory, for both Greek expressions are common in the works of the eastern Fathers.[45]

In the very influential conclusion to his 'Liturgical Note' Bishop returns to the Greek formulas of Prayer 45 and brings them into relation with 'Ephrem', within a *Spanish* context. The Irish and 'Gelasian' affinities of the Book of Cerne prayers are dealt with briefly – quite reasonably, since they are what might be expected in Anglo-Saxon England.[46] Bishop devotes most space to

41 *Ibid.* p. 247. (They may, however, have influenced the author of Prayer 10, who uses the word *sacerdos* in the preceding sentence but one.) Manz, *Ausdrucksformen*, pp. 436–7 (no. 870), quotes 'quia tu es inmortalis et sine peccato solus, Domine Deus noster' from the Leofric Missal (ed. F. E. Warren (Oxford, 1883), p. 8), but this is not strictly speaking liturgical, but rather an *apologia*, occurring also in the Fleury Prayer-Book (PL 101, col. 1408, where *solus* is part of a new sentence) and elsewhere; see F. Cabrol, 'Apologies', *Dictionnaire d'archéologie chrétienne et de liturgie* I, pt ii (1907), cols. 2595–8, nos. 59, 99, 154 and 164, and Levison, *England and the Continent*, p. 284. Cf. the private prayer *Tibi soli Domino peccaui, quia tu solus es sine peccato* (*Liber Precationum quas Carolus Calvus in unum colligi mandavit* [ed. F. Felicianus] (Ingolstadt, 1583), p. 117. Cf. *Precum Libelli Quattuor Aevi Karolini*, ed. A. Wilmart (Rome, 1940), p. 37, line 21). 42 PL 23, col. 587.

43 See *La Liturgie de saint Jacques*, ed. B.-Ch. Mercier, Patrologia Orientalis 26.2 (Paris, 1946), 220, line 17, and 222, line 1. Cf. G. Dix, *The Shape of the Liturgy* (London, [1945]), p. 195.

44 Manz, *Ausdrucksformen*, p. 63 (no. 41), cites no liturgical examples of *amator hominum*. In the early private prayer-books I have noticed examples (in addition to those noted elsewhere in this paper) in a prayer which first appears at Tours *c.* 804 (*Precum Libelli*, ed. Wilmart, p. 19; cf. PL 101, col. 604, and *Liber Precationum*, ed. Felicianus, p. 119 – the addition of *benignissime* in the PL (*Officia per ferias*) text suggests influence from 'Ephrem'), and in another in the mid-ninth-century Italian *Liber de psalmorum usu* (PL 101, col. 495; *Manuale Precum Sancti Joannis Gualberti*, ed. A. Salvini (Rome, 1933), p. 54; cf. Wilmart, 'Le Manuel', p. 286 (no. 52), and Salmon, *Analecta Liturgica*, p. 145 (no. 181)). The common phrase *amator animarum* is of course distinct.

45 *A Patristic Greek Lexicon*, ed. G. W. H. Lampe (Oxford, 1961), s.vv.

46 On England and the Gelasian Sacramentary, see Bullough, 'Alcuin and the Kingdom of Heaven', pp. 11–12, n. 26.

the 'Spanish symptoms', and a later essay under this title takes the matter still further.[47] His thinking was dominated by the then novel convictions that the seventh-century Visigothic church of Spain had a seminal rôle in the western church, for instance in the spread of eastern ideas, in the growth of religious intolerance, and in the development of the cult of the Virgin Mary,[48] and in particular that it exercised a *direct* influence[49] on the seventh-century Irish and English churches. Bishop adduces varied evidence, ranging from items of vocabulary in the Book of Cerne (such as *medicus*) to direct borrowings by Insular writers (such as Aldhelm's alleged use of Julian of Toledo,[50] which furnishes Bishop with a crucial *terminus ante quem* for Visigothic influence); among these he includes, somewhat boldly, Alcuin's use *in Francia* of Spanish burial services.[51] As far as the Book of Cerne is concerned, the interpretation of its 'Spanish symptoms' is bedevilled by the late date of the Spanish sources cited, and one is often left wondering whether the Spanish sources may not have been influenced by the Insular material, directly or indirectly through France,[52] rather than vice versa. Bishop's two most spectacular examples of textual (as opposed to lexical) influence from Spain are the appearance of parts of Prayer 19 (*Domine iesu christe, adoro te in crucem ascendentem*) in the Good Friday service in the 'Mozarabic' *Missale mixtum* of 1500 and of Prayer 49 (*Deus iustitiae, te deprecor*) in the eleventh-century Spanish *Liber ordinum*.[53] Yet it is

[47] 'Liturgical Note', pp. 277–80 and 282–3, and *Liturgica Historica*, pp. 165–210. Cf. H. Mayr-Harting, *The Coming of Christianity to Anglo-Saxon England* (London, 1972), pp. 127–8, 181–2, 185–7 and 199–200.

[48] Cf. N. Abercrombie, *The Life and Work of Edmund Bishop* (London, 1959), p. 362. See also p. 289.

[49] *Direct*, rather than via Gaul, because of the lack of Spanish/Irish material in the Gallican sacramentaries; see 'Liturgical Note', pp. 277–8, and *Liturgica Historica*, pp. 165 and 180–2. The picture has been changed somewhat by more recent discoveries, such as *Das Sakramentar im Schabcodex M 12 sup. der Biblioteca Ambrosiana*, ed. A. Dold, Texte und Arbeiten 43 (Beuron, 1952). Cf. L. Brou, 'Encore les "Spanish Symptoms" et leur contre-partie', *Hispania Sacra* 7 (1954), 467–85, esp. 475–6; J. N. Hillgarth, 'The East, Visigothic Spain and the Irish', *Studia Patristica* 4 [= Texte und Untersuchungen 79] (1961), 442–56, at 446, n. 5, and 453, and 'Visigothic Spain and Early Christian Ireland', *Proc. of the* R. *Irish Acad.* 62C (1962), 167–94, at 193–4 and n. 142. See also E. James, 'Ireland and Western Gaul in the Merovingian Period', *Ireland in Early Mediaeval Europe: Studies in Memory of Kathleen Hughes*, ed. D. Whitelock, R. McKitterick and D. Dumville (Cambridge, 1982), pp. 362–86.

[50] *Liturgica Historica*, pp. 169–70. But cf. V. Law, 'The Study of Latin Grammar in Eighth-Century Southumbria', *ASE* 12 (1983) 43–71, at 54–5.

[51] Bishop's view that Alcuin used Spanish material brought from England is accepted, e.g., by G. Rowell, *The Liturgy of Christian Burial*, Alcuin Club Collections 59 (London, 1977), 63–4, but the argumentation in *Liturgica Historica*, p. 168, is hardly cogent. In any case Alcuin's responsibility for the Supplement is now doubted; see Bullough, 'Alcuin and the Kingdom of Heaven', pp. 66–7.

[52] Cf. Brou, 'Encore les "Spanish Symptoms"'.

[53] Bishop, 'Liturgical Note', pp. 253–4, and *Liturgica Historica*, pp. 167 and 169. Although not in the *Liber Ordinum* or *Liber Mozarabicus Sacramentorum*, the Good Friday prayer has now turned up in *El Sacramentari, Ritual i Pontifical de Roda, Cod. 16 de l'arxiu de la Catedral de Lleida c. 1000*, ed. J. R. Barriga Planas (Barcelona, 1975), pp. 420–1.

possible, as Bishop's pupil André Wilmart supposes, that both these prayers, which were widely diffused on the continent in Carolingian and later times, are Insular compositions which found their way to Spain at a comparatively late date.[54] Bishop made surprisingly little use of the indubitably early Visigothic material which was available in his day, such as the seventh-century *Oracional Visigótico*.[55] He did incline to the view that Prayer 56 ('Sancta dei genetrix, semper uirgo . . .') was inspired by the seventh-century Spanish devotion to the Virgin manifested in the works of Ildefonsus of Toledo (*ob.* 667), but offered no close textual correspondences and admitted that the matter was subjective; the most recent authority on Marian prayers regards it as a probably English composition, hardly earlier than the mid-eighth century and perhaps contemporary with the prayers of Alchfrith the anchorite.[56] The whole subject of 'Spanish symptoms' in early England clearly needs to be re-examined in the light of the early Spanish material now available.

It is in the context of such questionable 'Spanish symptoms' that Bishop comes to the relationship of 'Ephrem' and Prayer 45 in the Book of Cerne. He makes three distinct points. The first can be dealt with briefly: that Prayer 50 (*Succurre mihi, domine, antequam moriar*), which is one of numerous adaptations of Isidore's *Synonyma*, as we have seen,[57] is also to be found printed among the Latin works of 'Ephrem'.[58] The implication is presumably meant to be that the works of 'Ephrem' and Isidore were transmitted together through Visigothic

54 A. Wilmart, 'Prières médiévales pour l'adoration de la Croix', *Ephemerides Liturgicae* 46 (1932), 22–65, at 25, n. 1, and 28, n. 2 (cf. similarly L. Gjerløw, *Adoratio Crucis* (Oslo, 1961), p. 19), and 'Le Manuel', p. 293, n. 2 (cf. further evidence in Sims-Williams, 'Thought, Word and Deed', pp. 101–3).

55 Ed. J. Vives (Barcelona, 1946); cf. Bishop, 'Liturgical Note', pp. 239–40.

56 Bishop, 'Liturgical Note', p. 280, n. 1; *Liturgica Historica*, pp. 174–8; similarly Mayr-Harting, *Coming of Christianity*, pp. 186–7 and 307, n. 56; but see Barré, *Prières anciennes*, pp. 66–8 and 70. On Ildefonsus, see Barré, pp. 30–4. Bishop's treatment in *Liturgica Historica*, pp. 176–8, of pseudo-Ildefonsus, *Sermo* IX (on which cf. now *Ambrosii Autperti Opera*, ed. R. Weber, 3 vols., CCSL, CM 27 and 27A–B (Turnhout, 1975–9) III, 888 and 1034) is justly criticized by B. Capelle, 'La Messe gallicane de l'assomption: Son Rayonnement, ses sources', *Miscellanea Liturgica in honorem L. Cuniberti Mohlberg*, 2 vols. (Rome, 1948–9) II, 33–59.

57 See above, p. 212. For other versions, see the references given in P. Sims-Williams, 'An Unpublished Seventh- or Eighth-Century Anglo-Latin Letter in Boulogne-sur-Mer MS 74 (82)', *MÆ* 48 (1979), 1–22, at 17–18, n. 31; to which add 'The Prayers of the Bury Psalter', ed. A. Wilmart, *Downside Rev.* 48 (1930), 198–216, nos. XV and XVIII (for the latter, see also Wilmart, 'Le Manuel', p. 281 (no. 23), and Heiming, 'Ein benediktinisch–ambrosianisches Gebetbuch', p. 404 (no. 10)), and Leroquais, *Psautiers* I, 98, and II, 121; and below, nn. 58 and 60.

58 Bishop, 'Liturgical Note', p. 278; Geerard, *Clavis* II, 447–8 (no. 4088). See also Assemani I, lxxxii (no. 31), and III, 578. The source cited is Vatican City, Biblioteca Apostolica Vaticana, lat. 517, which is a late medieval prayer-book (s. xiv/xv). The same selection from the *Synonyma* is found in Troyes, Bibliothèque Municipale, 1742 (on which see below, p. 220) as an *Oratio sancti Esidori* (*Precum Libelli*, ed. Wilmart, pp. 19–21), and anonymously in a thirteenth-century manuscript analysed by A. Wilmart, 'Un Livret de prières provenant de la chartreuse de Trisulti', *Ephemerides Liturgicae* 49 (1935), 28–45, at 40 (no. 15). Something very

channels, perhaps along the Syria–Spain–Ireland route so well trodden by modern scholars.[59] This is not the only possibility of course! The misattribution of *Succurre mihi* to Ephrem is no older than the eleventh century, so far as I know.[60] It may have arisen by mechanical error, through the prayer occurring beside 'Ephremic' prayers in earlier collections like the ninth-century *Officia per ferias* discussed above. Or medieval readers may quite understandably have associated the emotional, lyrical and biblical *stilus Isidorianus* of the *Synonyma*[61] with the not dissimilar voice of the Latin 'Ephrem'.

Bishop's second point is that the main contents of BL Harley 3060, which he dated 'saec. ix seemingly', but subsequently 'x?', are works by seventh-century Spanish writers, such as Julian and Ildefonsus of Toledo, and the *opuscula* of 'Ephrem'. He inferred that, 'though not written in Spain', Harley 3060 'appears from its contents . . . to descend from earlier Visigothic material'.[62] This is surely to go too far beyond the evidence. While it is not unlikely that the *opuscula* were known in seventh- and eighth-century Spain, as in France and Italy, the earliest direct evidence, so far as I know, is in a quotation by Elipandus of Toledo at the end of the eighth century.[63] In any case there still remains a gap to be bridged between Harley 3060 (or its exemplar or ancestor) and Anglo-Saxon England, for there is nothing to connect the manuscript itself with England before it came into the Harley collection from the library of Johann Georg Graevius (1632–1703).[64] Bishop attempts to bridge this gap by means of an anonymous prayer which follows the *Sermo asceticus* on 168v:

similar occurs in Alcuin's *De laude Dei* (on which see Bullough, 'Alcuin and the Kingdom of Heaven', p. 4, n. 10); see Radu Constantinescu, 'Alcuin et les "Libelli Precum" de l'époque carolingienne', *Revue de l'histoire de la spiritualité* 50 (1974), 17–56, at 30–1.

59 Bishop hints at such a line of transmission in *Liturgica Historica*, pp. 161–3 and 178, n. 3. In modern scholarship this 'Liturgical Trade Route: East to West' (to quote the title of a paper by J. H. Crehan, *Studies* 65 (1976), 87–99) is still busy, but there is a welcome tendency to consider other lines of communication between the east and Ireland; see, for example, J. Stevenson, 'Ascent through the Heavens, from Egypt to Ireland', *Cambridge Med. Celtic Stud.* 5 (1983), 21–35. Bestul ('Ephraim and Old English Poetry', pp. 8–9) rightly sees that the occurrence of 'Ephrem' and Isidore together in manuscripts is of little significance in view of Isidore's popularity. See also Mayr-Harting, *Coming of Christianity*, p. 127.

60 Paris, BN lat. 11550, fol. 315; Leroquais, *Psautiers* II, 108.

61 J. Fontaine, *Isidore de Séville et la culture classique dans l'Espagne wisigothique*, 2 vols. (Paris, 1959) II, 818–19, 'Théorie et pratique du style chez Isidore de Séville', *Vigiliae Christianae* 14 (1960), 65–101, at 71–8, and 'Isidore de Séville auteur "ascétique": Les Énigmes des *Synonyma*', *SM* 3rd ser. 6 (1965), 163–95.

62 'Liturgical Note', p. 278, and *Liturgica Historica*, p. 169. P. Salmon ('Livrets de prières de l'époque carolingienne', *RB* 86 (1976), 218–34) lists it at 227 as 's. XI–XII. *Patristica*, provient d'Allemagne', but Bullough now describes it as 'a ?French MS of s.X$^{2}$' ('Alcuin and the Kingdom of Heaven', p. 12, n. 28).

63 PL 96, col. 860; Hemmerdinger-Iliadou, 'Éphrem grec – Éphrem latin', col. 819.

64 A. C. Clark, 'The Library of J. G. Graevius', *Classical Rev.* 5 (1891), 365–72, at 370 (no. 17); C. E. Wright, *Fontes Harleiani* (London, 1972), pp. 168–9.

INCIPIT ORATIO DEO

Domine deus omnipotens qui in trinitate perfecta dominaris et regnas, *parce anime mee, parce factis meis, parce malis meis*, parce cogitationibus meis, *parce peccatis meis et criminibus. Visita infirmum, cura egrotum, sana languentem. Da cor quod te timeat, oculos qui te uideant, aures que*[65] *te audiant, sensum qui te intelligat*, mentem que[65] te diligat. Libera me, domine, de aduersariorum potestate ut non me permittas temptari super id quod possim sustinere. Eripe me, domine, de laqueo mortis et de delectatione carnali uel de temptatione mortali. Obsecro uos sancti apostoli omnes intercedite pro me. Tam martyres quam confessores intercedite pro me. Intercedite pro me nouem ordines angelorum *ut ad portum salutis* inlesus *merear peruenire*. Per Christum dominum nostrum.

As Bishop points out, the italicized phrases in the above prayer recur in one or more of the Book of Cerne prayers (20, 21, 24 and 49), while the invocations towards the end bear a slight (and, I would say, insignificant) resemblance to those in other prayers in the Book of Cerne and BL Royal 2. A. XX. He draws the conclusion that this *Oratio Deo* was the source drawn upon by the compilers of these prayers, working either in England or, as he later came to think possible in view of the appearance of Prayer 49 in the *Liber ordinum*, in Spain.[66] Three observations must be made here. First of all, there is nothing to associate the prayer with the name of Ephrem – Bishop does not make any such association explicitly, but understandably has been misunderstood as so doing. In the second place, nothing connects the *Oratio Deo* with the other contents of Harley 3060 or with Spain; it is one of three short items on the last two folios of the manuscript, as yet unidentified elsewhere, which are as likely to have been added as makeweights as to have been transmitted from an exemplar. The only other copies of the *Oratio Deo* known to me are from eleventh-century north French psalters: Cambrai, Bibliothèque Municipale, 54(55) (Saint-Amand, s. xi[1]), 13r, and Boulogne-sur-Mer, Bibliothèque Municipale, 20 (Saint-Bertin, AD 999), 229r.[67] These have no Spanish connection. Thirdly, it is at least as likely that the author of the *Oratio Deo* distilled his short prayer from versions of the Book of Cerne prayers, which were widely diffused on the continent by the ninth and tenth centuries,[68] as that the compilers of the Book of Cerne

65 The vowels are written over erasures.

66 'Liturgical Note', pp. 278–80, and *Liturgica Historica*, p. 169 and n. 2. On the *Liber Ordinum* text, see above, p. 216 and n. 53. Bullough ('Alcuin and the Kingdom of Heaven', p. 12 and n. 28) is mistaken in listing Prayers 21, 24, 49 and 50 as based on 'Efremic' texts.

67 Leroquais, *Psautiers* I, 98 and 118.

68 Other versions of Prayer 20: Wilmart, 'Le Manuel', p. 280, n. 4; Salmon, *Analecta Liturgica*, p. 143 (no. 152); *Precum Libelli*, ed. Wilmart, pp. 40–1; and Bestul, 'Note on the Contents of the Anselm Manuscript', p. 169 (item 11). Of Prayer 21: Sims-Williams, 'Thought, Word and Deed', p. 101, n. 139. Of Prayer 24: Salmon, *Analecta Liturgica*, pp. 152, 161 and 177 (nos. 250, 363 and 528; the text cited *ibid.* p. 138, no. 109, lacks the relevant passage: see *Venerabilis Josephi Mariae Thomasii Opera Omnia*, ed. J. Blanchinus [Bianchini] (Rome, 1741), pp. 538–9); Kuypers, *Cerne*, pp. xxxii–xxxiii; Wilmart, 'Le Manuel', p. 294, n. 3, and *Auteurs spirituels et*

prayers excerpted the *Oratio Deo* without incorporating it in its entirety. If one takes into account the continental texts of the Book of Cerne prayers it is not necessary to suppose that the author of the *Oratio Deo* consulted all four of the prayers enumerated above. Some version or congener of Prayer 20 would seem to have been used for the words '*ut . . . ad portum salutis* aeterne te duce *merear peruenire*',[69] but Prayers 21 and 24 (which look like derivatives of Prayer 49)[70] need only be cited because they respectively include the phrases *parce factis* and *parce peccatis*, which are absent from the Book of Cerne's and some other copies of Prayer 49.[71] Both are present, however, in the text of Prayer 49 in Troyes, Bibliothèque Municipale, 1742, pt i, 52v, written at Tours about the time of Alcuin's death (804):

Deus iustitiae . . . parce animae meae, parce malis meis, *parce factis meis* atque criminibus, *parce peccatis meis*. Uisita infirmum, cura aegrotum, sana languentem. Da cor quod te timeat, sensum qui te intellegat, oculos[72] qui te uideant . . .[73]

The Harley 3060 *Oratio Deo* may descend from a text of Prayer 49 similar[74] to that in the Troyes manuscript. One must conclude, rather negatively, that the *Oratio Deo* has no clear relevance to the question of Visigothic or 'Ephremic' elements in the Book of Cerne. On a more positive note, the above discussion has indicated the need for close textual comparison between the copies of prayers extant from several early medieval centres: since scribes did not copy prayers exactly but altered their exemplars very freely, such comparison would be sure to shed welcome light on the relations between those centres.

*textes dévots du moyen âge latin* (Paris, 1932), p. 574, n. 1; Heiming, 'Ein benediktinisch–ambrosianisches Gebetbuch', pp. 399 (no. 2), and 432; and *Die Glossen des Psalters von Mondsee*, ed. Unterkircher, pp. 514–15 (most of these versions of Prayer 24 break off or diverge before reaching the passage singled out by Bishop; it may be a composite prayer in the Book of Cerne). Of Prayer 49: Sims-Williams, 'Thought, Word and Deed', pp. 101–3.

69 No better parallel is cited by Manz, *Ausdrucksformen*, pp. 384–5.

70 On Prayer 21, see Sims-Williams, 'Thought, Word and Deed', p. 101, n. 139. On the apparently composite, secondary character of Prayer 24, see above, n. 68.

71 Including Royal 2. A. XX, 47v; the Fleury Prayer-Book and *Officia per ferias* have *peccatis* only (PL 101, cols. 598 and 1394), as does Heiming, 'Ein benediktinisch–ambrosianisches Gebetbuch', p. 407 (no. 16).

72 The Book of Cerne and the other texts listed in the preceding note add *cordis* here – evidently an addition, since it is not present in the apocryphal source, the *Acts of St John*; see Sims-Williams, 'Thought, Word and Deed', p. 103.

73 E. K. Rand, *Studies in the Script of Tours, I. A Survey of the Manuscripts of Tours*, 2 vols. (Cambridge, Mass., 1929) II, pl. LIV/3, and *Precum Libelli*, ed. Wilmart, p. 9. *Factis* and *peccatis* are similarly included in the *Liber ordinum*, ed. Férotin, col. 266, and in the various adaptations of Prayer 49 listed in Sims-Williams, 'Thought, Word and Deed', p. 103, n. 151.

74 But probably not identical, as the Troyes version and the other versions listed in the preceding note omit 'aures . . . audiant'; cf. Sims-Williams, 'Thought, Word and Deed', p. 103 and nn. 151–2.

Bishop's third and final point about the 'Ephremic' element in the Book of Cerne takes us still further away from Spain, but brings us closer to a non-liturgical explanation for the phrases *amator hominum* and *solus sine peccato* in Prayer 45. He proposes that the author of this prayer drew these expressions, and the adjective *benignissimus*, from the prayer *Obsecro te, saluator mundi* with which the *Sermo asceticus* concludes. For convenience, probably, Bishop referred to the text of the *Sermo asceticus* in Harley 3060,[75] and for convenience I print this below, though there is no reason to suppose that this text of the *Sermo* is more relevant to the Book of Cerne prayer than any other. The main text is from 167v–168v, and the variant readings are from 122v–124r, where the passage is given as a separate 'ORATIO DONNI EFFRE*M*', between the Spanish works and the 'Ephremic' *opuscula*.[76]

HARLEY 3060, 167v–168v

Obsecro te, saluator mundi,[1] Iesu Christe, respice in me et miserere mei, et libera me a multitudine iniquitatum mearum. Spreui enim omnia bona[2] que fecisti mecum a iuuentute mea. Me enim idiotam ac sine intellectum fecisti uas repletum[3] scientie,[4] et multiplicata est super me gratia tua, et satiauit[5] esuriem meam et refrigerauit sitim meam, et illuminauit obscuritatem meam, [6]et compescuit ab errore cogitationes meas,[6] repleuitque [7]scientiam meam.[7] Et nunc adoro te,[8] obsecro [9]te, procido tibi[9] ac supplico te[10] confitens infirmitatem[11] meam. Propter tuam [12]humanitatem sine fluctus[12] gratie tue et conserua mihi eam in thesaurum tuum,[13] ut[14] rursum mihi tribuas eam in illa die ne iterum irascaris mihi,[15] *amator hominum*. Non enim[16] [17]sustineo fluctus[17] inundationis eius. Ideo[18] obsecro te, proterue agens, eo quod supra modum multiplicata est super me. Lingua enim mea infirmata est, non occurrens[19] disserere eam. Obstupuit[20] [168r] autem[21] et mens mea non sustinens[22] multitudinem fluctuum eius. Imago et splendor benedicti patris, da mihi refrigerium [23]a fluctibus eius,[23] ut ignis enim cor meum renesque comburit.[24] Ibi autem[25] mihi eam tribue rursum et salua[26] in regno tuo, et ne memineris iniquitatum mearum, et[27] dona[28] mihi petitionem meam,[29] quia tu solus dator[30] uite mee es. Cooperi quoque iniquitates meas ab omnibus notis meis, et suscipe lacrimas meas. Adpropinquent[31] ad

75 'Liturgical Note', p. 279; in the footnotes he also refers to another BL manuscript, Royal 5. E. III, which is of no importance. Bishop notes that some passages in the Latin are not in the Greek text ptd Assemani I, 69–70; but see the fuller version at Assemani II, 373–7 (an incipit of yet another version of *Obsecro te* is given at III, 462). In the absence of a critical edition of the Greek text, which is known from manuscripts later than the Latin text (cf. Assemani II, xliv), this fuller version can be regarded as of equal authority. Kirchmeyer and Hemmerdinger-Iliadou ('Saint Éphrem et le "Liber Scintillarum"', p. 549) note that Defensor of Ligugé quotes a Latin version of the *Sermo asceticus* closer to the variant at Assemani II, 372BD, than that at I, 66F–67A. Latin texts of *Obsecro te* may also be found in *Sanctissimi Ephraem Syri Opuscula*, fol. 25, and in *Opuscula Quaedam*, fols. 82b–83a. See also above, n. 32.

76 The spelling *donni* is compatible with a tenth- or eleventh-century French origin for the manuscript (cf. above, n. 62); see, e.g., J. H. Hessels, 'Memoranda on Medieval Latin, No. 2: Irminon's Polyptychum', *TPS* 1899–1902, 471–552, at 529.

te fletus mei.[32] Memento etiam [33]lacrimarum mearum[33] quas produxi in conspectu sanctorum martyrum[34] tuorum, ut misericordiam inueniam in hora illa horribili, ut protegas me sub pennis gratie tue. Si autem uolueris facere mecum secundum iniquitates meas, heu mihi miserabili. *Amator hominum benignissime*, legio a te gregem porcorum absque lacrimis postulauit et dedisti ei. Ego autem [35]a te[35] cum fletu et gemitibus supplico [36]bonitatem tuam.[36] Libera me ab iniquitatibus meis et dona mihi [37]possessionem regni tui.[37] In me itaque peccatore demonstra ineffabilem misericordiam tuam, et fac me participem latronis illius qui per unum uerbum heres paradysi effectus est.[38] Illuc me introduc propter tuam benignitatem [39]et absconde me[39] in medio arborum,[40] et[41] uideam locum illum[42] ubi Adam[43] cum claritate epulabatur,[44] ubi ei[45] dictum est 'Adam, ubi es?', [46]ut orationem[46] et gloriam tibi offeram, quia exaudisti orationem meam et iniquitates meas despexisti.[47] Pone[48] lacrimas meas in conspectu tuo, sicut et[49] in promissione[50] tua, ut auertatur[51] inimicus[52] retrorsum et expauescens conturbetur, cum me uiderit in loco[53] quem preparauit [54]manus tue misericordie.[54] Expectans autem me inimicus uidere in loco quem mihi[55] preparauerat, uideat me in loco uite et conuersus in tenebras conturbetur, [168v] quia nequaquam uoluntas eius effecta est. *Ita benignissime, ita amator hominum, ita qui solus es sine peccato*, effunde super me [56]ineffabilem et[56] immensam misericordiam tuam, et presta[57] ut [58]ego et omnes[58] qui diligunt te regni tui efficiamur heredes, et uidentes gloriam tuam, adoremus bonitatem tuam et dicamus pariter, qui digni fuerimus uidere insatiabilem pulchritudinem [59]maiestatis tue:[59] 'Gloria patri, qui fecit nos, et gloria filio, qui saluauit nos, et gloria sancto spiritui, qui renouauit nos, per[60] infinita seculorum secula. [61]FINIT INSTITUTIO SANCTI EFFREM AD MONACHOS.[61]

Variants from 122v–124r:

[1]*adds* domine [2]*om.* [3]plenum [4]*adds* et sapientiae [5]sanauit [6–6]*om.* [7–7]sinus meos [8]et [9–9]quoque [10]*om.* [11]humilitatem [12–12]humilitatem sume fructum [13]*om.* [14]et [15]*om.* [16]*om.* [17–17]sustinens fletus [18]Ideoque [19]ualens [20]obstupui [21]*om.* [22]sustinet [23–23]affluentibus eam [24]comburet [25]enim [26]*adds* me [27]*adds* audebo postulare [28]da [29]*adds* et facito apud me mansionem cum benedicto patre tuo in die aduentus tui et da mihi petitionem meam [30]protector [31]et apropinquet [32]meus [33–33]lacrimas meas [34]*om.* [35–35]*om.* [36–36]bonitati tue [37]regnum tuum [38]*adds* in possessionem repromissionis [39–39]Abscondarque ibi [40]*adds* eius [41]ut [42]*om.* [43]*adds* occultatus est [44]et letitia [45]*om.* [46–46]adorationem [47]dispersisti [48]*adds* domine [49]*om.* [50]repromissione [51]reuertatur [52]*adds* meus [53]locum [54–54]miserationes tue [55]*adds* propter delicta mea [56–56]*om.* [57]da mihi [58–58]et ego et hi [59–59]tuam[60] in [61–61]AMHN

The italicized phrases correspond to *φιλάνθρωπε*, *φιλάνθρωπε ἀγαθέ*[77] and *ναὶ ἀγαθὲ, ναὶ φιλάνθρωπε, ναὶ ὁ μόνος ἀ[να]μάρτητος*[78] in the Greek. In concluding that the above prayer 'may have been the channel whereby the expressions occurring also in the Liturgy of S. James found their way into *Cerne*'[79] Bishop comes very near to the truth. But the truth of the matter is

[77] Assemani II, 375E and 376C; not at I, 69–70.

[78] *Ibid.* 376F; variant at I, 70B.

[79] 'Liturgical Note', p. 280.

simpler. Throughout the *Sermo asceticus* the epithets ὁ ἀγαθὸς Θεὸς καὶ φιλάνθρωπος, φιλάνθρωπος ἀγαθὸς, ὁ μόνος φιλάνθρωπος, and so on, are of frequent occurrence,[80] and Prayer 45 in the Book of Cerne is related to two of these other passages, rather than to the closing prayer *Obsecro te, saluator mundi.*

The second half of the *Sermo* contains a good deal of advice on prayer, and at one point 'Ephrem' illustrates how a penitent should pray.[81] Such pattern-prayers were an important source for the compilers of prayer-books,[82] and the Latin version of this one is the basis of the first part of Prayer 45 (down to the foot of 71r). For comparison I transcribe the text from the earliest manuscript, BN lat. 12634, 112v–113r (mentioned above); the variants are from Harley 3060, 157v–158r.[83]

Accede ergo ad eum inprobiter**[1]** et procidens ante eum ingemesce**[2]** et plorans dicito ei: 'Domine meus et saluator meus, quare me derelinquisti? Miserere mei quia tu es *amator hominum* solus et**[3]** salua me peccatorem quia tu**[4]** *solus sine peccato* es.**[5]** Extrahe me **[6]**de ceno**[6]** iniquitatum mearum ut non tibi**[7]** infigar in saecula saeculorum. Libera me ex**[8]** ore inimici mei; ecce enim ut leo rugit deuorare me cupiens. Excita potentiam tuam et ueni ut saluum me facias. [Corusca] coruscationes tuas et disperge uirtutem eius . . .'

**[1]**improbe **[2]**ingemiscens **[3]***om.* **[4]***adds* es **[5]***om.* **[6–6]**a facinore **[7]***om.* **[8]**de

The rest of Prayer 45 is also taken from a part of the *Sermo asceticus* unnoticed by Bishop. An earlier section of the work concludes with a prayer beginning 'φιλάνθρωπε, Ἀγαθὲ . . .'.[84] In the Latin version in BN lat. 12634, 104v–105r, this runs as follows (the variants are from Harley 3060, 154v–155r):

80 Assemani I, 56D, 64DF, 65BC and 68C; also the lacuna filled by Hemmerdinger-Iliadou, 'Vers une nouvelle édition', p. 80, and 'O what a Lover of man is this God!', in the Coptic version (*Coptic Martyrdoms etc. in the Dialect of Upper Egypt*, ed. and transl. E. A. Wallis Budge (London, 1914), p. 422) but not in Assemani I, 48F–49A.

81 Assemani I, 58A; cf. *Sanctissimi Ephraem Opuscula*, fol. 25, and *Opuscula Quaedam*, fol. 65a.

82 I. Hausherr, 'Comment priaient les pères', *Revue d'ascétique et mystique* 32 (1956), 33–58 and 284–97, esp. 292.

83 The word *corusca* is supplied from the Harley manuscript; in the BN manuscript it has been scratched out, presumably under suspicion of dittography. Conversely in BN lat. 1153, 94v (PL 101, col. 606) the scribe at first omitted the word and then supplied it in the margin.

84 Assemani I, 53EF, and III, 362B–E. Cf. *Sanctissimi Ephraem Opuscula*, fol. 20a; and the slightly shorter text in *Opuscula Quaedam*, fol. 59b. The Coptic version, 'The Askêtikon of Apa Ephraim', includes this part, and Budge's translation (*Coptic Martyrdoms*, p. 429) from a manuscript of *c.* 1000 may be quoted as a control: 'I adjure Thee, O God, by Thy loving-kindness, Thou Lover of mankind, Thou Good God, place Thou me not on Thy left hand, and cast me not away with the goats, who have provoked Thee to wrath. And say not unto me, "I know thee not." But because of Thy great mercy, make me, so long as I remain in the body, continue to weep by day and by night, and to groan over my sins, and do Thou prepare my heart to be a dwelling-place for Thy holy grace. Even though I am a wicked sinner I will not cease to knock at the door of Thy compassion. Even though I am careless I will not desert Thy path, O my God.'

*Amator hominum benignissime deus*,[1] adiuro te per miserationes tuas, ne me cum hedis ad[2] sinistris tuis[3] statuas cum his qui te exacerbauerunt. Ne dicas mihi 'Nescio te'. Sed[3] tribue mihi propter multam misericordiam tuam indesinenter cordis[3] compunctionem et fletum et humilia cor meum et sanctifica me[3] ut fiam templum gratiae tuae. Nam etsi peccator sum et impie gessi; tamen[3] ad ianuam tuam semper[4] pulso. [5]Et si[5] piger sum et incuriosus; adtamen[6] uiam tuam incedo.

[1]*om.* [2]a [3]*om.* [4]iugiter [5–5]etsi [6]tamen

It is now clear that the *Sermo asceticus* of 'Ephrem' was not just the intermediary by which the so-called 'liturgical' expressions *solus sine peccato* and *amator hominum* reached Prayer 45 in the Book of Cerne, but the direct source for the whole of this prayer, whose attribution in the continental manuscripts is therefore vindicated. It is impossible to say whether the excerpting was done in England – unfortunately the eleventh-century Anglo-Saxon text of the *Sermo asceticus* in London, Lambeth Palace Library, 204 breaks off with a doxology shortly before reaching the prayer *Amator hominum benignissime deus* – but this is quite possible; certainly there is no reason to think of Spain as a likely candidate.

This discovery encourages one to look for more extracts from 'Ephrem' in the Anglo-Saxon prayer-books. Harley 7653 (s. viii/ix, according to Lowe) includes an untitled prayer, partially adapted for use by a woman (*famula*), with the familiar 'Ephremic' phrase *solus sine peccato* (6v–7r):[85]

Deus altissime, deus misericordie, *qui solus sine peccato es*, tribue mihi peccatori [*sic*] fiduciam in illa hora propter multas miserationes tuas, ut ne tunc apareat, que nunc uelata est, impietas mea coram expectatoribus angelis et archangelis, patriarchis [7r] et prophetis, apostolis, iustis et sanctis. Sed salua me pia gratia et miseratione tua. Induc me in paradiso deliciarum tuarum cum omnibus perfectis. Suscipe orat[io]nem famule tue precibus omniu[m] sanctorum tuorum qui tibi a seculo placuerunt, quoniam tibi debetur omnis adoratio et gloria per omnia secula seculorum.

That this is extracted from a longer work is obvious from the failure to specify *illa hora*. The same text (with *peccatori*, but *serui tui* for *famule tue*) is also to be found in the already-discussed Tours prayer-book, Troyes 1742, pt i, fol. 60, and here it is the first of nine *Orationes sancti Effrem diaconi*.[86] (The heading *oratio eiusdem* given to the other eight is undoubtedly due to a mechanical error at

85 Harley 7653 was ptd Birch, *An Ancient Manuscript*, pp. 114–19, and, more fully, F. E. Warren, *The Antiphonary of Bangor*, 2 vols., HBS 4 and 10 (London, 1893–5) II, 83–6. The script is English; see Lowe, *Codices Latini Antiquiores* II, no. 204, who gives a facsimile of part of our prayer. The widespread belief that it is Irish (e.g. Kuypers, *Cerne*, p. xxiv) has led to overconfident statements about the Irish elements in all the early prayer-books.

86 Rand, *Survey of the Manuscripts of Tours* II, pl. LIV/1, and *Precum Libelli*, ed. Wilmart, pp. 14–17 (nos. 6–14).

some stage, since they are nowhere else ascribed to Ephrem.)[87] Later copies appear in the mid-ninth-century Italian collection known as the *Liber de psalmorum usu*, where it is entitled *Oratio sancti Effrem ad postulandum fontem lacrimarum*,[88] and in other continental prayer-books listed by André Wilmart.[89] Wilmart says that 'l'origine de la pièce paraît être insulaire'. On the contrary, it is taken from the conclusion of the *De poenitentia*, one of the 'Ephrem' *opuscula*, and the context there explains both the reference to *illa hora* and the *De psalmorum usu* title. I quote from BL Harley 3060, 135r:[90]

Quis dabit capiti meo aquam immensam et oculis meis fontem lacrimarum iugiter emanantem, donec tempus est suscipiendi lacrimas, ut plorem memetipsum die ac nocte obsecrans dominum, ne indignus inueniar in hora temporis eius, et ne audiam illam sententiam formidandam, 'Discede a me, operarius iniquitatis; nescio te quis sis'? Deus altissime, qui *solus sine peccato* es, tribue mihi peccatori gratiam in illa hora propter multas et innumeras miserationes tuas, et ne tunc appareat, que nunc uelata est, impietas mea coram exspectatoribus angelis et archangelis, prophetis, et apostolis, iustis et sanctis. Sed salua me impium gratia et miseratione tua, et induc me in paradysum delitiarum cum omnibus perfectis. Suscipe orationem serui tui, domine, precibus omnium sanctorum tuorum qui tibi a seculo placuerunt, quia tibi debetur omnis gloria et adoratio in secula seculorum. Amen. EXPLICIT LIBER TERTIUS.

The Greek original of the *De poenitentia* is one of a number of metrical works whose connection with any Syriac original is still uncertain.[91] Ironically, the 'Ephrem' leitmotiv which attracted our attention to the prayer, 'solus sine peccato', may be an error in translation, for the Greek texts printed by Assemani read ὁ μόνος ἀθάνατος or diverge still further.[92]

87 Nos. 7–14 recur as a set, anonymously, in a mid-ninth-century Tours prayer-book (BN lat. 13388) ptd *ibid.* pp. 139–41; in the Fleury Prayer-Book (PL 101, cols. 1399–1400); and in some other sources noted Barré, *Prières anciennes*, pp. 11–13, 52 and 73, and Bullough, 'Alcuin and the Kingdom of Heaven', p. 13, n. 29 – to these add Heiming, 'Ein benediktinisch–ambrosianisches Gebetbuch', pp. 410–11 (nos. 20–4); Wilmart, 'Le Manuel', pp. 276–9 and 283–6 (nos. 1–4, 9, 35, 44 and 49); 'Prayers of the Bury Psalter', ed. Wilmart, pp. 203–5 (nos. V–VII); and the Nonantola Psalter (Vatican City, Biblioteca Apostolica Vaticana, lat. 84, s. xi), ptd Bianchini, *Thomasii Opera*, p. 525 (cf. Salmon, *Analecta Liturgica*, p. 135, n. 23; see also *ibid.* pp. 151 and 167 (nos. 232–5 and 419–21)). Barré and Bullough suggest that this set of prayers was disseminated from Tours, but this is uncertain.

88 Wilmart, 'Le Manuel', p. 279, and Salmon, *Analecta Liturgica*, p. 143 (no. 147). See also the later Italian version at p. 178 (no. 547).

89 'Le Manuel', p. 279, n. 3; add the Psalter of Odbert, Boulogne-sur-Mer, Bibliothèque Municipale, 20, 229v (Saint-Bertin, AD 999), for which see Leroquais, *Psautiers* I, 98.

90 Cf. *Sanctissimi Ephraem Opuscula*, fols. 64b–65a, and *Opuscula Quaedam*, fols. 23b–24a.

91 Hemmerdinger-Iliadou, 'Éphrem grec – Éphrem latin', cols. 804–5, and Geerard, *Clavis* II, 376 (no. 3915).

92 Assemani I, 153, and III, 505. Consultation of the Slavonic and other versions might establish the original reading.

As in the case of the Book of Cerne prayer based on the *Sermo asceticus*, one cannot know whether the *Deus altissime* was extracted in England or came here from elsewhere as a separate prayer. (Indeed, it may have been extracted independently at more than one centre.) Yet even if the English in the early Anglo-Saxon period knew no more of 'Ephrem' than is contained in their surviving prayer-books, enough of this exotic voice came through in them to make an impact on those with ears to hear. And that there were some Anglo-Saxons with ears to hear is shown by one of the peculiarly English prayers on the life of Christ in BL Royal 2. A. XX, fol. 32:[93]

Karitatis auctor, cast[it]atis doctor, et *amator hominum, benignissime deus*, Christe, qui brachia tua extendisti crucis in ligno, ad me porrige manum misericordiae tuae. Timoris tui acumine ac tremoris, agnitionisque et dilectionis pectus meum perfora durissimum, qui sanctas et uenerabiles manus tuas in cruce perforare clauibus pertullisti; measque manus et pectus ab omnibus absolue uulneribus uitiorum, qui te tuasque permissisti manus innocentes cruci adfigere, domine mi, Iesu Christe.

This meditation on the crucifixion has not the depth of *The Dream of the Rood*, needless to say; nevertheless, it is worked out with great sensitivity. It will be noted that beside the subtle liturgical reminiscence, 'sanctas et uenerabiles manus', which brings the Last Supper to mind, there is also an apposite non-liturgical reminiscence: 'amator hominum, benignissime deus' from 'Ephrem'. Our pre-Conquest writer anticipates by many centuries the affective language of Anselm's *Oratio ad Christum cum mens uult eius amore feruere*; and Anselm, too, invokes Christ as 'amator hominum benignissime . . .'.[94]

[93] See above, p. 209. D. Bullough ('Alcuino e la tradizione culturale insulare', *Settimane di studio del Centro italiano di studi sull'alto medioevo* 20 (1972), 571–600, at 591) sees a connection (which I cannot see) between this unique prayer and one of the prayers in Troyes 1742, *Domine Iesu Christe, rex uirginum, integritatis amator* (*Precum Libelli*, ed. Wilmart, p. 16 (no. 11)), which he tentatively attributes to Alcuin ('Alcuin and the Kingdom of Heaven', pp. 14–15). The latter prayer is one of the set of eight prayers mentioned above, p. 224 and n. 87. If it was indeed by Alcuin, would the Tours scribe of Troyes 1742 have given Ephrem's name to it? For further copies of the prayer, see, besides n. 87 above and Bullough's notes, Wilmart, 'Le Manuel', p. 278 and n. 2; PL 138, col. 1318; *The Portiforium of Saint Wulstan*, ed. A. Hughes, 2 vols., HBS 89–90 (London, 1958–60) II, 2; and *The Missal of St Augustine's Abbey Canterbury*, ed. M. Rule (Cambridge, 1896), p. 4.

[94] *S. Anselmi Opera Omnia* III, ed. F. S. Schmitt (Edinburgh, 1946), 9. Two prayers attributed to Ephrem which have not been discussed above are an *Oratio sancti Effrem* in the *De psalmorum usu* (see Wilmart, 'Le Manuel', p. 292 and n. 4: 'texte inédit, sans autre appui'), and an *Oratio sancti Effrem diaconi de compunctione cordis* in BL Royal 5. A. VII, fols. 15–21 (s. xii$^{ex}$) and in Paris, Bibliothèque Mazarine, 1709 (1027) (s. xi), 33v; see Bestul, 'Ephraim and Old English Poetry', p. 4, n. 12. The incipit of the latter in Royal 5 A. VII is 'Sana me, domine, et sanabor, quia solus es patiens et misericors medicus'. It introduces a long extract from the *Sermo asceticus*, concluding with the prayer *Obsecro te, saluator mundi*. Salmon ('Livrets de prières', p. 227) mentions an 'Ephremic' prayer, which I have not seen, in Montpellier, Bibliothèque Universitaire (Médecine), 40 (s. viii/ix).

# On the library of the Old English martyrologist

J. E. CROSS

When Henri Quentin[1] discussed the sources for the notices in Bede's 'historical' or 'narrative' martyrology, which is reputedly the first of the genre, no one doubted his conclusion that Bede went directly to saints' legends and other works for the descriptive details. Some of my medievalist friends, however, who do not work on sources, are unwilling to grant a similar breadth of reading to the anonymous English composer of the ninth-century Old English Martyrology (hereafter OEM). They will accept, for example, a *uita* as an ultimate source but incline to think that, in our case, the martyrologist could have seen his brief notice in another intermediary text which had already made the summary. There are, however, procedures for source analysis which sift evidence and offer conclusions with reasons. An investigation of sources should include a comparison with the likely source in which correspondences of significant detail (names, numbers, images, echo of word and phrase) are noted; it should also include a comparison with all other possible sources[2] which may eventually be rejected – although, normally, it is too tedious to present the rejections in print. One notice in OEM may be considered briefly, that on Paul the Hermit (10 January),[3] to illustrate the normal method of investigation.

For Bede's martyrology, information was taken from Jerome's *Vita S. Pauli*,[4] chs. 4, 7 and 14, as Quentin said,[5] and no one has doubted. The

1 H. Quentin, *Les Martyrologes historiques du moyen âge: Étude sur la formation du martyrologe romain*, 2nd ed. (Paris, 1908).

2 As Ludwig Bieler once said to me with a typical smile, 'Comparison of sources is not only with what is, or what may be, but with what is not.'

3 *Das altenglische Martyrologium*, ed. G. Kotzor, 2 vols., Bayerische Akademie der Wissenschaften, Phil.–hist. Klasse, Abhandlungen n.s. 88 (Munich, 1981) II, 14, and *An Old English Martyrology*, ed. G. Herzfeld, EETS o.s. 116 (London, 1900), 16. All quotations of OEM in this paper are from Kotzor's edition, but general readers may consult Herzfeld's inaccurate edition, which includes an English translation. For brevity of annotation the designation of feast-day is presented in the text for each saint. This will serve in place of page-references in the two editions.

4 Jerome's *Vita S. Pauli* is listed *BHL*, no. 6596, and is ed. PL 23, cols. 17–28. For bibliography pertaining to martyrologies discussed below, see J. Dubois, *Les Martyrologes du moyen âge latin* (Turnhout, 1978).

5 Quentin, *Les Martyrologes*, p. 99.

unprinted Lyons martyrology (seen in manuscript) is exactly as Bede on Paul; Ado added only *apud Thebaidem* to Bede's words; Hrabanus Maurus copied Bede but added that Jerome wrote the *Vita S. Pauli*, that a raven fed Paul, and that the palm supplied clothing (from the *Vita S. Pauli*, chs. 10 and 12).[6] The details, however, in OEM correspond to those in the *Vita S. Pauli*, chs. 4, 7, 6, 17, 10, 14, 16 and 17 in that order, and an item is added from Aldhelm, *De uirginitate*.[7] Slight hints of Bede's influence may be Paul's age when he went into the desert, that is, precisely sixteen (whereas Jerome says 'circiter annorum sexdecim') and Paul's age at death, given precisely in Bede but assumed from Jerome. Probably our composer consulted Bede's text (see below) and then decided to write a fuller notice drawing on Aldhelm and the *Vita S. Pauli*, but one cannot doubt a reading of the *Vita* for some, if not all, of the information in OEM which corresponds to that Latin text. Obviously, source analysts deal in probabilities, as in every other kind of investigation in the humanities.

The noted and persistent habits of our composer aid the search for probability in what otherwise could be more doubtful cases. The original writer was a fluent reader of Latin, abstracting accurately if he composed in Latin, abstracting and translating accurately if he composed in Old English,[8] although a few errors in the present texts seem to derive from hasty reading of long saints' legends.[9] He was a good précis writer, who was concerned to

[6] Quentin (*ibid.* p. 123) discusses the Lyons martyrology as preserved in Paris, BN lat. 3879; the entry for Paul is on 69r. For Ado's martyrology on Paul, see PL 123, col. 213. For Hrabanus, see *Rabani Mauri Martyrologium*, ed. J. McCulloh, CCSL, CM 44 (Turnhout, 1979), 8.

[7] To illustrate Paul's solitude, OEM notes: 'there he never saw nor heard anything else than the roaring (*grymetung*) of lions and the howling (*gerar*) of wolves', information lacking in the *Vita S. Pauli*. In his prose *De uirginitate* (ch. 28), Aldhelm records that Paul in the wilderness scorned 'truculentos leonum fremitus', and in his *Carmen de uirginitate* (lines 790–1), Aldhelm says that lions and wolves were submissive to him. Aldhelm's works are consulted by the martyrologist (see below) and his statements here probably gave impetus for the Old English phrase. For Aldhelm's works, see *Aldhelmi Opera*, ed. R. Ehwald, MGH, Auct. antiq. 15 (Berlin, 1919), 265 (prose) and 386 (poem).

[8] For detailed illustration, see J. E. Cross, 'The Latinity of the Ninth-Century Old English Martyrologist', *Studies in Earlier Old English Prose*, ed. P. Szarmach (Binghamton, NY, forthcoming).

[9] For one case, see J. E. Cross, 'The *Passio S. Laurentii et aliorum*: Latin Manuscripts and the Old English Martyrology', *MS* 45 (1983), 200–13, at 210, where Irenaeus (26 August) is called a *cægbora*, 'key-bearer', in OEM, whereas in the best Latin manuscripts he is a *cloacarius*, 'sewer-man'. The martyrologist probably saw something like *clauacarius* (a man who deals with keys or locks), but the process of the story should have prompted him to this error. Another such case may be for Benedict of Nursia (21 March), where in OEM the path for the saint's soul was covered in '*white* covering(s)' but in the source, Gregory's *Dialogi* (II.37), merely with *palleis*, 'coverings' (see *Das altenglische Martyrologium*, ed. Kotzor II, 297),

transmit information, who often echoed snatches of speech verbatim,[10] and who reflected images[11] from sources in the overwhelming majority of cases which I have been able to identify. Again and again he was prepared to add detail from other than his main source for an individual notice,[12] and was, in my view, a ninth-century scholar concerned to present an informative and readable text from a variety of books available in his library.

For the present study the martyrology is regarded as the original composition, whether in Latin or Old English,[13] which can be reconstructed with good reason from the extant Old English texts. Sources noted below are regarded as direct sources unless stated otherwise.

All the editors of OEM have identified sources where they could. T. O. Cockayne noted that he had done what he could with 'what scant leisure permitted',[14] but his general knowledge is sometimes of value. George Herzfeld, however, considered the source material in relation to Latin texts in print, and a number of his findings still stand. Günter Kotzor limited his work on sources to the firm contacts since he has always known of my work with Latin manuscripts, particularly on those saints' lives which have not been presented in collated editions.[15] By, as it were, producing collated editions of such Latin texts, and sometimes by distinguishing new Latin versions of legends,[16] it has often been possible to demonstrate the actual Latin words which our composer saw, and to ascertain his methods of work.

perhaps a confusion with *palleo*, 'to grow pale'. Such errors are rare, and normally understandable.

10 More than sixty examples of direct speech are recorded in OEM. For some illustrations of the way the martyrologist either echoes or rewords speeches in Latin texts, see Cross, 'Latinity', *passim*, for eight examples, and especially the close echo of the words of the manuscript in the two speeches by the Tergemini (17 January) and their grandmother. See also J. E. Cross, 'Saints' Lives in Old English. Latin Manuscripts and Vernacular Accounts: *The Old English Martyrology*', *Peritia* 1 (1982), 38–62, for three examples, including especially the prayer of George (23 April) which is almost verbatim as in Graz, Universitätsbibliothek, 412, and its variant texts. Other examples may be found in discussions of individual notices, under my name, in recent numbers of *N&Q*.

11 For some discussion of images, see J. E. Cross, 'A Lost Life of Hilda of Whitby: the Evidence of the *Old English Martyrology*', *Acta* 6 (1979), 21–43, at 30–4.

12 See the illustrations discussed below.

13 Although earlier scholars assumed that the martyrology was first composed in Latin, the evidence is slight and debatable. See, on this, Cross, 'Latinity'. On the other hand I see no means, at present, of demonstrating that OEM was first composed in Old English.

14 T. O. Cockayne, *The Shrine* (London, 1864–70), p. 45.

15 For the editions of Herzfeld and Kotzor, see above, n. 3.

16 See, for example, J. E. Cross, 'A *Virgo* in the *Old English Martyrology*', *N&Q* 29 (1982), 102–6. For the publication of an unrecorded version, see J. E. Cross and C. J. Tuplin, 'An Unrecorded Variant of the *Passio S. Christinae* and the *Old English Martyrology*', *Traditio* 36 (1980), 161–236.

## BOOKS OR SOURCES NAMED IN THE OEM

### Bede, *Historia ecclesiastica gentis Anglorum*[17]

The naming of a book or source in the Middle Ages is not a guarantee that the work was directly consulted, but Bede's *Historia ecclesiastica* is so persistently named, and the words so largely and widely echoed (particularly for saints who have not, apparently, warranted full *uitae*) that its availability should not be doubted. The book is variously named as 'on Angelcynnes bocum' (Chad, 2 March; Germanus, 1 August; Æthelburg, 11 October; Cedd, 26 October; and Hygebald, 14 December); as 'on istoria Anglorum' (John of Beverley, 7 May); as 'on Ongelcynnes bocum, þæt is on istoria Anglorum' (the two Hewalds, 3 October) and as 'on Ongelcynnes steore þæt is on historia Anglorum' (Augustine of Canterbury, 26 May). Apart from minor information on occasions, the *Historia ecclesiastica* was the sole source for the above notices. It also provided all or some information in the sections on Furseus (16 January), Columba (9 June), Alban (22 June), Æthelthryth (23 June), Oswald (5 August), Aidan (31 August) and Hild of Whitby (17 November).

### Aldhelm, *De uirginitate* (prose and poem)

Once, in the notice for the three sisters, Agape, Chionia and Irene (3 April), the martyrologist says of them: 'þis syndon swiðe mære fæmnan on *De uirginitate*, þæt is "on fæmnena bocum".'[18] Earlier scholars noted some contacts with Aldhelm's poem,[19] but distinctive echoes indicate abstractions of information from the prose work as well. Aldhelm's two works are normally used as additional (not main) sources for individual sections. It is thus necessary for a demonstration of the clear and possible echoes of Aldhelm's works to prove the main source, together with information used from Aldhelm which is lacking in such a main source. Some sections have been analysed in such detail in print. These include contacts with the prose *De uirginitate* in the notices for John the Evangelist (27 December), Agnes (21 January), Christina (19 July), the Assumption of the Virgin (15 August), Cosmas and Damian (27 September), Antoninus of Apamea (as alternative, 2

[17] For a discussion of the notices which draw on Bede's *Historia ecclesiastica* and a consideration of Herzfeld's views, see J. E. Cross, 'A Lost Life of Hilda of Whitby', pp. 21–30. Kotzor (*Das altenglische Martyrologium*) has given full illustrations from Bede's *Historia* at the appropriate places.

[18] *Das altenglische Martyrologium*, ed. Kotzor, II, 49, and *An Old English Martyrology*, ed. Herzfeld, p. 52.

[19] See below, n. 21.

September) and Chrysanthus and Daria (28 November).[20] Contacts with the *Carmen de uirginitate* noted in print are for Agape, Chionia and Irene (3 April), Rufina and Secunda (10 July) and Lucy of Syracuse (13 December).[21] A few additions, unfortunately without full demonstration in print, are possible for the notices on Paul the Hermit (10 January, prose and poem), Athanasius of Alexandria (2 May, prose and poem) and Anatolia and Audax (10 July, poem).[22]

For the section on Gregory Nazianzen (19 March), Herzfeld[23] noted as source the *uita* doubtfully attributed to Rufinus and printed by Lipomanus. Kotzor[24] has traced this edition and agrees with Herzfeld. But Aldhelm included Gregory Nazianzen in his *De uirginitate* and used the same Rufinus *uita* as source.[25] Two small details (together with a persistent consultation of Aldhelm) which vary from the *uita* suggest a use of Aldhelm: namely, that the vision was *nihtlice*, whereas the Rufinus *uita* states, and Aldhelm omits, that Gregory was sitting and reading when he fell asleep;[26] and that the figures of *Sapientia* and *Castitas* were 'sisters', as only in Aldhelm's poem.[27] One could argue that the only detail which is not in Aldhelm's works is that the figures were *fægre fæmnan* precisely (cf. *decoras . . . feminas* of the Rufinus *uita*),

20 For demonstration, see, on John, J. E. Cross, 'The Apostles in the Old English Martyrology', *Mediaevalia* 5 (1979), 15–59, at 34–7; on Agnes, see Cross, 'A Lost Life of Hilda of Whitby', pp. 31–2; on Christina, see Cross and Tuplin, 'An Unrecorded Variant', p. 164; on the Assumption, see Cross, 'The Use of Patristic Homilies in the *Old English Martyrology*', *ASE* (forthcoming); on Cosmas and Damian, see Cross, 'Cosmas and Damian in the *Old English Martyrology*', *N&Q* 30 (1983), 15–18, at 16; on Antoninus, see Cross, 'Antoninus of Apamea and an Image in the *Old English Martyrology*', *N&Q* n.s. 31 (1984), 18–22, at 21; and on Chrysanthus and Daria, see *Das altenglische Martyrologium*, ed. Kotzor, II, 372.

21 Contact with Aldhelm's *Carmen de uirginitate* for Rufina was first noted by Cockayne, *The Shrine*, p. 103, and for Agape in *An Old English Martyrology*, ed. Herzfeld, p. 228. For Lucy, see a demonstration in Cross, 'Latinity'.

22 These contacts have not been demonstrated. But, on Paul, see above, n. 7; for Athanasius, echoes of phrase occur which differ from the ultimate source, Rufinus's translation of Eusebius, *Historia ecclesiastica* X (I).15; for Anatolia and Audax, echoes of word and phrase are present which are not in the main source, a text of the short *passio* (*BHL*, no. 418). For this last pair of saints Herzfeld (*An Old English Martyrology*, p. xxxix) chose the long *passio* (*BHL*, no. 417) printed in Acta Sanctorum.

23 *An Old English Martyrology*, ed. Herzfeld, p. xxxvii; the full reference is to A. Lipomanus, *Sanctorum Priscorum Patrum Vitae*, 8 vols. (Venice, 1551–60) I, 280–1.

24 *Das altenglische Martyrologium*, ed. Kotzor, II, 293.

25 *Aldhelmi Opera*, ed. Ehwald, p. 263, n. 1.

26 The Rufinus *uita* has 'uidit per soporem sedenti sibi et legenti duas decoras . . . feminas'; cf. Aldhelm, prose *De uirginitate*, 'pulchrae uisionis oromate somno sopitus clementer solatur' (*Aldhelmi Opera*, ed. Ehwald, p. 262), and *Carmen de uirginitate*, 'tempore nam quodam geminas per somnia cernens . . . puellas' (*ibid.* p. 383).

27 *Carmen de uirginitate*, lines 720–1: 'Ne . . . iuuenis . . . uultum contemne sororum' (*ibid.* p. 383).

although Aldhelm's *Carmen de uirginitate* (line 716) notes 'Virgineo uidit fulgentes flore puellas', and Aldhelm could thus have been the sole source for the whole notice.

That Gregory Nazianzen was a 'chaste bishop'[28] is emphasized in all three sources, but OEM also states of Babyllas (24 January): 'Đis wæs swiðe clæne biscop, ond his clænnes swiðe mære wæs',[29] although no attention is drawn to his chastity in the main source, the *passio* (*BHL*, no. 890), or indeed in Aldhelm's description. The statement was probably inspired simply by the inclusion of Babyllas in Aldhelm's *De uirginitate*.

## Adomnan, *De locis sanctis*[30]

The name of Adomnan's informant, Arculphus, is recorded on six occasions, three times in the notice for Ascension Day (5 May) and once each in the entries for *Solstitia* (24 June), George (23 April) and Jerome (30 September). Apart from the note of the feast-day, Adomnan's book is the complete source for the section on *Solstitia*, but offers details for the composite notices for Ascension, George and Jerome. The work also provides information for the entries on 'se sexta worolde dæg' (23 March), Annunciation/Crucifixion (25 March) and Resurrection (27 March). All the above identifications were made by Cockayne, but one other detail from Adomnan occurs in the section on Christ's birth (25 December), a fascinating composite notice.

## Gregory the Great, *Homiliae .xl. in euangelia*

The martyrologist introduces an anecdote about Processus and Martianus (2 July) with the words 'be þam sæde Sanctus Gregorius', and the story comes in detail from *Homilia* xxxii.7, as Herzfeld noted.[31] Gregory's homilies also provide detailed information and word for the entries for Emiliana (5 January: *Homilia* xxxviii.15) and for Cassius (June 29: *Homilia* xxxvii.9), and present most of the information in the entry on Felicitas (23 November: *Homilia*

28 The variant Old English manuscript (see *Das altenglische Martyrologium*, ed. Kotzor, II, 35) reads *halgan* in place of *clænan* (genitive), but context, source, and the *lectio difficilior* rule indicate that *clænan* was the original reading.

29 *Das altenglische Martyrologium*, ed. Kotzor II, 25, and *An Old English Martyrology*, ed. Herzfeld, p. 30.

30 For a more detailed demonstration of the information in this paragraph, see J. E. Cross, 'The Influence of Irish Texts and Traditions on the Old English Martyrology', *Proc. of the* R. *Irish Acad.* 81C (1981), 173–92, at 180–5.

31 *An Old English Martyrology*, ed. Herzfeld, p. xxxix.

iii.3).[32] It is possible that the martyrologist consulted these individual homilies of Gregory in a later homiliary, but only one of the four was used in the popular homiliaries of Alanus of Farfa and Paul the Deacon – for Felicitas, in Paul the Deacon (*Homilia* iii).[33] The martyrologist reveals a typically English veneration for Gregory, 'se us fulwiht onsænde',[34] in his notice for the pope, and, in my view, had available other individual works (see below, on the *Dialogi* and *Moralia in Iob*). I suggest that the *Homiliae* as a collection was available separately to our composer.

## *Scripture*

Analysis of sources should not overlook the obvious. The notice on Resurrection (27 March) records of Christ that 'æfter his æriste hine tyn siðum monnum ætywde, swa hit on his godspelle awriten is',[35] but the martyrologist is unlikely to have made the count, since it had been made by Augustine, *De consensu evangelistarum* (III.xxv.83) and the demonstration had also been presented within homiletic pieces and commentaries, within my knowledge in Vatican City, Biblioteca Apostolica Vaticana, Reg. lat. 49 (the so-named *Catechesis Celtica*), in Munich, Bayerische Staatsbibliothek, Clm. 14418 (s. ix) 4v–6r, and Clm. 6235 (s. ix$^{med}$ or ix$^{2}$), 66r, a manuscript apparently copied from an Insular exemplar.[36] The entry for Simon and Thaddeus (28 October) notes that Simon's mother is named 'on Cristes bocum Maria Cleophe', and Luke (18 October) is described as 'se wrat þone þriddan dæl Cristes boca',[37] neither of which statements necessitate an actual consultation of scripture.

It should not be doubted, however, that the martyrologist knew sections of

32 *Ibid.* p. xlii for Felicitas, and Cockayne, *The Shrine*, pp. 48 and 98 for Emiliana and Cassius.

33 See R. Grégoire, *Les Homéliaires du moyen âge*, Rerum Ecclesiasticarum Documenta, ser. maior 6 (Rome, 1966), 112 (Commune Sanctorum, no. 124).

34 The phrase is used twice, in the notice for Emiliana (5 January) and for Gregory himself (12 March).

35 *Das altenglische Martyrologium*, ed. Kotzor, II, 47, and *An Old English Martyrology*, ed. Herzfeld, p. 50.

36 For a full discussion of the notice on Resurrection, see Cross, 'Irish Texts', p. 184. For the reference to Clm. 14418, see Cross, 'Use of Patristic Homilies'. For a description of Clm. 6235 and comment on its place of origin, see B. Bischoff, 'Wendepunkte in der Geschichte der lateinischen Exegese im Frühmittelalter', in his *Mittelalterliche Studien*, 3 vols. (Stuttgart, 1966–81) I, 205–73, at 259. A translation of this article is ptd *Biblical Studies: the Medieval Irish Contribution*, ed. M. McNamara (Dublin, 1976), where the reference in question is found on p. 162.

37 On Simon, see *Das altenglische Martyrologium*, ed. Kotzor, II, 240, and *An Old English Martyrology*, ed. Herzfeld, p. 196. On Luke, see *Das altenglische Martyrologium*, ed. Kotzor, II, 230, and *An Old English Martyrology*, ed. Herzfeld, p. 186.

scripture. His notice on the Maccabees (1 August) echoed scriptural words from II Maccabees vii and ix, and none of the legendaries on these martyrs seen by me, although drawing on scripture, has comments from II Maccabees ix.[38] Many of the minor details in the descriptions, especially of scriptural people and notices of general church festivals, have details ultimately deriving from scripture, probably directly, although maybe from memory. We should note, however, that such phrases as 'halgan gewritu secgað' (3 May), 'gewrytu secgað' (21 December) and 'on gewritum' (22 June) do not refer to scripture.[39]

### The 'old' and the 'new' sacramentary

Thirteen saints are celebrated in OEM merely by a *mæsse-song* or a *mæsse*, eight of these recorded 'on ðæm ealdan sacramentorium, ðæt is on ðæm ealdan mæsse-bocum' (as for Priscus, 1 June), but normally designated as 'on ðæm mæssebocum' (as for Agapitus, 18 August) – but otherwise 'on ðæm (þam) ealdran (yldran) mæssebocum', three 'on þam niwran sacramentorium, þæt is on þam niwran bocum' – and two celebrated in general terms 'mid mæssesongum', presumably in both the old and the new books (Gordianus, 10 May, and the Octave of Peter and Paul, 6 July). Kotzor has produced a careful survey of scholars' attempts at identification of the two types of sacramentary, but the rarity of comparative material makes conclusions tentative.[40]

## OTHER TEXTS IDENTIFIABLE AS SOURCES OF THE OEM

### A calendar (or calendars)

The majority of feast-days or obits for saints are 'common', being found in other martyrologies or calendars of the same period or before, and obviously read by our martyrologist. When a thorough comparison is made with all the extant texts the differences may show up some rarity of choice of certain feast-days. Some saints, who are rarely or more locally recorded, appear to have an obit from the source of the descriptive material: for example, Emiliana (5 January) and Cassius (29 June) from Gregory's *Homiliae .xl. in euangelia* (see

38 For a fuller discussion of Maccabees, see Cross, 'Use of Patristic Homilies'.

39 The notice for 3 May is the Finding of the Cross, and the reference is to an *inuentio* account; for 21 December the reference is to accounts of the death of Thomas the apostle (see below); for 22 June the reference is to the name given to James as 'Iacobus Alphei'. On Thomas and James Alphaei, see Cross, 'The Apostles', pp. 21–3 and 29–31 respectively.

40 The complete set of references is given and the problems discussed in detail by Kotzor, *Das altenglische Martyrologium* I, 258–66.

above), Zoe (4 July) from a *Passio S. Sebastiani*[41] and Pope John (18 May) from the *Liber pontificalis*.[42] Some saints have obits which are not the same as those in 'continental' martyrologies but are as found in 'Insular' texts: for example, Barnabas (10 June)[43] as in the Martyrology of Oengus and the Metrical Calendar of York, and Christopher (28 April)[44] as in Oengus and Bede's Martyrology (Family II). A number of English and Irish saints, as could be expected, confirm the Englishness of the martyrology in choice of obit: for example, Furseus (16 January) as in the Martyrology of Oengus, Chad (2 March) as in the Calendar of Willibrord, Wilfrid (24 April) as in the Metrical Calendar of York.[45] For some obits I have not yet found parallels, but more work needs to be done on the calendar exhibited by OEM.

## A legendary and individual saints' legends

It is as certain as can be that the martyrologist consulted a legendary for various saints whose brief *uitae* or *passiones* bore those saints' names and who were the main figures in those legends, even if the particular legendary cannot be identified. Examples of such *uitae* which have been demonstrated as sources are: Columba of Sens (31 December), Mary Magdalen (22 July), Genesius of Rome (25 August), Genesius of Arles (24 October), Eusebius of Vercelli (1 August) and Justus of Beauvais (18 October).[46] It is also probable that some longer legends were seen in a legendary; among these are the *Passio S.*

41 The celebration of Zoe's day is not recorded in the Hieronymian martyrology or in 'Insular' martyrologies. Her day is 5 July in Florus of Lyons (see Quentin, *Les Martyrologes*, p. 432) and Ado (PL 123, col. 297). I have presented an argument in a completed but unpublished paper on 'The Use of a *Passio S. Sebastiani* in the *Old English Martyrology*'.

42 Pope John's obit (18 May) in OEM varies from the date chosen in known martyrologies, but corresponds to texts of the *Liber pontificalis* (an identifiable source; see below), cited by Quentin, *Les Martyrologes*, p. 104.

43 On the obit for Barnabas, see Cross, 'The Apostles', pp. 40–1.

44 For Christopher, see *The Martyrology of Oengus the Culdee*, ed. W. Stokes, HBS 29 (London, 1905), 109; on Bede, see Quentin, *Les Martyrologes*, p. 50.

45 For Furseus, see *The Martyrology of Oengus*, ed. Stokes, p. 36; the saint appears on this day in later English calendars. For Chad, see *The Calendar of Willibrord*, ed. H. A. Wilson, HBS 55 (London, 1918), 5; the day is, of course, given in Bede, *Historia ecclesiastica* IV.3. For Wilfrid, see A. Wilmart, 'Un Témoin anglo-saxon du calendrier métrique d'York', *RB* 46 (1934), 41–69, at 66, and Quentin, *Les Martyrologes*, p. 124.

46 For Columba, see J. E. Cross, 'Columba of Sens in the *Old English Martyrology*', *N&Q* 30 (1983), 195–8. For Mary Magdalen, see Cross, 'Mary Magdalen in the *Old English Martyrology*: the Earliest Extant "Narrat Josephus" Variant of her Legend', *Speculum* 53 (1978), 16–25. For the two saints named Genesius, see Cross, 'Genesius of Rome and Genesius of Arles', *N&Q* 31 (1984), 149–52. For Eusebius of Vercelli and Justus of Beauvais, see Cross, 'Two Saints in the *Old English Martyrology*', *NM* 78 (1977), 101–7.

*Laurentii*[47] (a source for nine notices), which was often broken up in legendaries under the names of subsidiary but important figures, and the *Passio S. Sebastiani*[48] (a source for five entries) which, in manuscripts ranging in date from the seventh century to the tenth, was not broken up but sometimes abbreviated by omissions. But leaving aside sources for entries which I think to be from separate books, and noting as only one *uita* or *passio* those which are the source for more than one entry, there are yet over a hundred separate legends used for information in the notices of OEM. If the martyrologist did not use more than one collection, this would surely have run to a number of volumes. No single manuscript which I have seen from the early medieval period includes all the legends which are used as sources for OEM.

There is also some evidence that the martyrologist on occasion consulted two versions of a legend. In the account for Thomas (21 December) OEM reports two ways in which the apostle is said to have been killed: by sword, as in the *Passio S. Thomae*, the main source for the entry, and by spears, ultimately from the separate pseudo-Abdias account, although probably directly from one or both of the two brief summaries of lives of Fathers, Isidore and pseudo-Isidore, *De ortu et obitu patrum* (on which, see below).[49] In the notice for Cosmas and Damian (27 September), however, the gift which caused distrust between the two doctors is named in this way: 'gewritu secgað þæt ðæt wære þreo ægero'.[50] Most probably the specification came from a different version of the legend from that used as a main source.[51]

The existence of 'mixed' versions of certain legends, however, prevents further progress along this line of argument. Such a 'mixed' version for the *Reuelatio S. Stephani* does exist and could have been used for the notice on 3 August, but there is no valid 'mixed' version for George (23 April) or Antonius of Apamea (2 September), where either 'mixed' versions or two versions were the sources for the respective entries.[52]

[47] See Cross, '*Passio S. Laurentii*', pp. 201–2 (on the manuscripts).

[48] The *Passio* was the source for Sebastian (20 January; note that in *An Old English Martyrology*, ed. Herzfeld, p. xxxvii, the source is wrongly given as Bede's Martyrology), Marcus and Marcellianus (18 June), Zoe (4 July), Tranquillinus (6 July) and Tiburtius (11 August). Rome, Vatican City, Biblioteca Apostolica Vaticana, lat. 5771 preserves an abbreviated text of the *Passio*.

[49] On Thomas's manner of death, see Cross, 'The Apostles', pp. 22–3.

[50] *Das altenglische Martyrologium*, ed. Kotzor, II, 221.

[51] See Cross, 'Cosmas and Damian'.

[52] On the *Revelatio* and George, see Cross, 'Saints' Lives in Old English', pp. 40–51. On Antoninus, see Cross, 'Antoninus', pp. 20–1.

## A homiliary and/or individual homilies

Leaving aside the use of Gregory's *Homiliae .xl. in euangelia* (see above), the following individual homilies were read:[53]

- i Augustine, *Sermo* cccix (PL 38, col. 1411) for Cyprian of Carthage (14 September)
- ii Fulgentius of Ruspe, *Sermo* vi (PL 65, col. 741) for Cyprian (probably)
- iii Caesarius of Arles, *Sermo* ccxvi for the Nativity of John the Baptist (24 June)
- iv Caesarius, *Sermo* ccvii for the Rogations before Ascension Day
- v Caesarius, *Sermo* ccviii for these same Rogations
- vi Petrus Chrysologus, *Sermo* xci (PL 52, col. 455) for the Nativity of John the Baptist (24 June)
- vii Petrus Chrysologus, *Sermo* clii (PL 52, col. 604) for the Holy Innocents (28 December)
- viii the anonymous sermon *Legimus in ecclesiasticis historiis* for All Saints' Day (1 November)
- ix a sermon similar to pseudo-Augustine *Sermo* clx (PL 39, col. 2059) for Christ's Descent to Hell (26 March)
- x pseudo-Maximus of Turin *Sermo* viii for Eusebius of Vercelli (1 August) (probably)
- xi sermons on Perpetua and Felicitas (7 March) (possibly)
- xii sermons on Epiphany for commonplace significations (possibly)
- xiii sermons on the Octave of Christ (1 January) for significations (possibly)

It is likely that the sermons for the general feasts were seen in a homiliary for the liturgical year. This is certainly the case with nos. iii, iv, v, vi, vii, viii, ix, xii and xiii, which are included in various homiliaries of the period, but it is less likely that nos. i, ii, x and xi for individual saints were to be found in such homiliaries.

One entry very probably indicates the use of a homiliary, namely the story of the miracle in the notice for Stephen (26 December) which was originally recorded by Augustine (*De civitate Dei* XXII.8), but is found in a version based on Augustine in Paul the Deacon's Homiliary.[54]

[53] For a discussion of the use of the sermons itemized in this section, see Cross, 'Use of Patristic Homilies'. See also Cross, 'Blickling Homily XIV and the Old English Martyrology on John the Baptist', *Anglia* 93 (1975), 145–60, at 154–6 (on nos. iii and vi), '*Legimus in Ecclesiasticis Historiis*: a Sermon for All Saints and its Use in Old English Prose', *Traditio* 33 (1977), 101–35, at 131–4 (on no. viii), 'Two Saints', pp. 101–3 (on no. x), and 'Irish Texts', pp. 190–1 (on no. xiii). For Perpetua and Felicitas (no. xi) there are items of information not contained in the various *passiones* (*BHL*, nos. 6633–6) which are, however, found in some sermons on the saints.

[54] For more detail, see Cross, 'Saints' Lives in Old English', p. 44.

Other works of Bede

(i) VITA S. CUTHBERTI (prose). Details, with verbal echo on many occasions, for notices on Cuthbert (20 March), Æthelwald (21 April) and Eadberht (6 May) are taken from the *Vita S. Cuthberti.* All three saints are also described in Bede's *Historia ecclesiastica*, but echo of phraseology indicates a consultation of the *Vita*; for example, on Æthelwald's death Bede notes, 'mansit autem idem uir Dei in insula Farne .xii. annis, ibidemque defunctus' (*HE* v.1), but the *Vita S. Cuthberti*, after noting Æthelwald's hermitage on Farne, says, 'at postquam ipse quoque expletis ibi duodecim continuis annis gaudium supernae beatitudinis intrauit' (ch. 46), which forms the basis for the detail in OEM: 'ond æfter þon þe he twelf gear ðær wunode, þa eode he on ðone gefean ðære ecean eadignesse'.[55] There are other reasons for suggesting that the *Vita S. Cuthberti* was seen separately. Information used in OEM comes from widely separated sections of the long *Vita*, and indicates a reading of the whole, certainly from ch. 7, on Cuthbert's heavenly food and association with angels, to ch. 46, the final chapter on Æthelwald's death. Similarly, ch. 4 alone provides the information that Aidan (31 August) saw Cuthbert's soul.[56] Details concerning Eadbert and Æthelwald in OEM are most probably derived from the *Vita*, since no separate biographies of these saintly men are known. Extant manuscript evidence[57] indicates that the *Vita* was normally associated in manuscript with other Cuthbert material or with other longer lives of a few, mostly English, saints. Only once, in Oxford, Bodleian Library, Fell 3 (Salisbury, s. xi/xii) does the *Vita* appear in company with many other saints' lives (thirty in all). What evidence is available suggests that Bede's *Vita S. Cuthberti* may have been read in a manuscript containing other works, but not in the legendary of the martyrologist's house.

(ii) HISTORIA ABBATUM. Echo of word and phrase in three entries, for Benedict Biscop of Wearmouth (12 January), Eostorwine (7 March) and

[55] For the citation from Bede's *Historia ecclesiastica*, see *Bede's Ecclesiastical History of the English People*, ed. B. Colgrave and R. A. B. Mynors (Oxford, 1969), p. 456; for that from the *Vita S. Cuthberti*, see B. Colgrave, *Two Lives of St Cuthbert* (Cambridge, 1940), p. 302; and for that from OEM, see *Das altenglische Martyrologium*, ed. Kotzor, II, 58, and *An Old English Martyrology*, ed. Herzfeld, p. 58. The notices are considered in detail in Kotzor (*ibid.* II, 294–5, 302 and 310–11). Kotzor (*ibid.* II, 295) also notes that the designation of one of the brothers as 'ðæs mynstres profoste' in the notice on Cuthbert is not found in the *Vita S. Cuthberti* itself, but Colgrave (*Two Lives*, p. 353) records marginal glosses in certain manuscripts to the effect that this man's name was Fridumund or Fridmund, and notes that a name Fridumund occurs under the list of abbots in the *Liber uitae* (of Durham and Lindisfarne). An abbot could earlier have been a 'profost' or 'prafost' (Latin *praepositus*), a second-in-command to an abbot.

[56] For an analysis of the notice on Aidan, see Cross, 'A Lost Life of Hilda of Whitby', pp. 27–8, and *Das altenglische Martyrologium*, ed. Kotzor, II, 344.

[57] On the manuscripts, see Colgrave, *Two Lives*, pp. 20–9.

Ceolfrith (25 September), indicate a reading of Bede's *Historia abbatum*[58] and just possibly, for one hint, a consultation of the anonymous *Vita S. Ceolfridi*.[59] Bede's work normally appears entire in the manuscripts noted by Plummer[60] and, as such, is unlikely to have been presented for an individual saint's day.

(iii) DE TEMPORUM RATIONE. As the editors of OEM have demonstrated,[61] *De temporum ratione* (hereafter *DTR*), chs. 12 (*De mensibus Romanorum*) and 15 (*De mensibus Anglorum*) provided the Latin and English names for the months, together with the explanations of the English names where they are given, for the brief introductions to the sequence of entries for each month in OEM.

Herzfeld also noted the *Chronica maiora* contained in *DTR* (ch. 66) as the source for the entries on Anastasius of Persia (22 January) and Augustine of Hippo (28 August).[62] These *Chronica* were certainly used, but some further discussion is now needed. Recently Carmela Franklin and Paul Meyvaert[63] have made a case that the 'lost' *Passio S. Anastasii* (which Bede says that he produced as revision of a bad Latin translation of the original Greek legend) is, in fact, the version designated *BHL*, no. 408. There are correspondences (and some differences)[64] between *BHL*, no. 408 and the account in the *Chronica maiora* of the saint, but, notably, *BHL*, no. 408 does not record the final resting-place for the relics, as do both OEM and the *Chronica*. At one minor point OEM agrees with *BHL*, no. 408 against the *Chronica*, that Heraclius was a *casere* (*BHL*, no. 408: *imperator*; *Chronica*: *princeps*), but, as Franklin and Meyvaert note, the *Chronica* differ from *BHL*, no. 408 in calling Chosdroe *rex* (*BHL*, no. 408: *imperator*), which is equivalent to *cining* in OEM. All the other information in the notice in OEM, save one item which is not in *BHL*, no. 408,[65] is found in the *Chronica*.

58 For detailed analyses of these sources, see *Das altenglische Martyrologium*, ed. Kotzor, II, 283, 291 and 355–6.

59 Kotzor (*ibid.* II, 356) notes that the location of Langres 'on Burgenda mægðe' in the entry for Ceolfrith is found only in the anonymous *Vita S. Ceolfridi*, but he is careful in his conclusions. There are hints elsewhere of the martyrologist's general geographical knowledge.

60 *Venerabilis Baedae Opera Historica*, ed. C. Plummer, 2 vols. (Oxford, 1896) I, cxxxii–cl.

61 *An Old English Martyrology*, ed. Herzfeld, p. xxxiv, and *Das altenglische Martyrologium*, ed. Kotzor, I, 268; illustrated in Kotzor's explanatory notes at relevant places in vol. II.

62 *An Old English Martyrology*, ed. Herzfeld, pp. xxxvii and xl. Kotzor (*Das altenglische Martyrologium* I, 268, n. 375) regards the use of the *Chronica maiora* as *möglich* and does not give equivalents at II, 287 and 342.

63 C. V. Franklin and P. J. Meyvaert, 'Has Bede's Version of the "Passio S. Anastasii" come down to us in BHL 408?', *AB* 100–2 (1982) [*Mélanges offerts à Baudouin de Gaiffier et François Halkin*], 373–400.

64 Franklin and Meyvaert, 'Bede's Version', pp. 394–5.

65 The item is the carrying round of the head in Rome. This is noted in the story of a miracle printed in *AB* 11 (1892), 233–41, from Milan, Biblioteca Ambrosiana, B 49 inf. (s. xii). The miracle is also preserved in Orléans, Bibliothèque Municipale, 342 (290) (s. xi), a manuscript

Similarly, concerning the entry in OEM for Augustine of Hippo (28 August), the *uita* by Possidius does not record the *translationes* of Augustine's body which are described in the *Chronica*, and, with some verbal echo of the Latin,[66] also in OEM.

Other hints of contact between the *Chronica maiora* – a work easily accessible – and OEM have and may be noted. I have suggested a possible recall of the Latin for a phrase in the notice on All Saints' (1 November),[67] and now suggest that the designated resting-places for Antony the Hermit (17 January) and for Perpetua and Felicitas (7 March) in OEM also came from the *Chronica*,[68] since neither is found in the respective *passiones*.

(iv) MARTYROLOGIUM. Within his summary-list of sources Herzfeld chose Bede's *Martyrologium* as source for twenty-one entries, normally brief notices, although he had expressed doubts about OEM's exact relationship to Bede's

noted by H. Gneuss as having been written or owned in England (see *ASE* 9 (1981), 55). From internal evidence the record of the miracle has been dated as eighth-century, and represents an up-dating of material in OEM.

66 Compare OEM (*Das altenglische Martyrologium*, ed. Kotzor, II, 191–2): 'Ac þa hergodon þa hæþnan Sarcinware on þa stowe [*sc.* Sardinia]. Đa forðon Leodbrond, Longbearda cyning, mid micle feo gebohte Agustinus lichoman, ond hine gelædde in Ticinan ða burh, ond hine þær gesette mid gelimplicre are', and the account in the *Chronica maiora*: 'Liuthbrandu audiens quod Sarraceni depopulata Sardinia etiam loca fedarent illa, ubi ossa sancti Augustini episcopi propter uastationem barbarorum olim translata et honorifice fuerant condita, misit et dato magno praetio accepit et transtulit ea in Ticinis ibique cum debito tanto patri honore recondidit' (*Chronica Minora saec. IV. V. VI. VII*, ed. T. Mommsen, MGH; Auct. antiq. 13 (Berlin, 1898), 321).

67 See Cross, '*Legimus in ecclesiasticis historiis*', p. 133.

68 The editors have noted only, but rightly, Athanasius, *Vita S. Antonii* in the Latin translation of Evagrius as source for the notice on Antony (see *Das altenglische Martyrologium*, ed. Kotzor, II, 285). Two Latin versions now known (see L. W. Barnard, 'The Date of S. Athanasius' *Vita Antonii*', *Vigiliae Christianae* 27 (1974), 168), but both agree (ch. 92) that, for Antony, 'nemo scit ubi est absconsum' except the two brothers who buried the saint's body (citation from *La Plus Ancienne Version latine de la vie de S. Antoine par S. Athanase*, ed. H. Hoppenbrouwers, Latinitas Christianorum Primaeva 14 (Nijmegen, 1960), 191. But OEM (*Das altenglische Martyrologium*, ed. Kotzor, II, 18) notes: 'his lichoma resteð on ðære miclan ceastre Alexandria', just as Bede records in the *Chronica maiora*: 'Corpus sancti Antoni monachi . . . Alexandriam defertur et in ecclesia beati baptistae Iohannis humatur' (*Chronica Minora*, ed. Mommsen, p. 307). For Perpetua and Felicitas, OEM (*ibid.* II, 29) notes 'ðara lichoma resteþ on Cartagine þære miclan ceastre on Affrica mægðe'; the martyrologies of Bede and Hrabanus Maurus record the saints as lying 'apud Carthaginem' (Quentin, *Les Martyrologes*, p. 88, and *Rabani Mauri Martyrologium*, ed. McCulloh, p. 26), as does Bede's *Chronica maiora*: 'apud Kartaginem Africae' (*Chronica Minora*, ed. Mommsen, p. 289). None of the *passiones* now ed. C. J. M. J. van Beek, *Passio Sanctarum Perpetuae et Felicitatis* (Nijmegen, 1936), note the burial-place, and other martyrologies locate the saints differently (e.g. 'in Mauritania, ciuitate Tuburbitanorum', as in the Hieronymian martyrology and Florus of Lyons (Quentin, *Les Martyrologes*, p. 274) and in Ado of Vienne (PL 123, col. 236)).

work.[69] Kotzor has now demonstrated that details in sixteen of these notices[70] are lacking in Bede's text, which thus, at least, cannot be a sole source for these. For the remaining five, as Kotzor noted,[71] it could be the source, although minor problems need attention for the entry on Januarius (19 September).[72] Yet none of these need be based on Bede, since Bede's own sources – the various individual *passiones* – could have provided the relevant details.

I think, however, that if Herzfeld had looked for less he might have found more. It is likely that our composer read Bede's work (reputedly the first and also an English narrative martyrology), since he knew other writings of Bede and could have used the earlier author's martyrology as a model. But some distinctive similarities of word and phrase indicate more conclusively a use of Bede's *Martyrologium* as an additional source within individual notices. For Felix of Nola (14 January) only Bede's *Martyrologium* of the available accounts has the detail of *cochleis*, for which OEM's 'sæscellum' is a fair rendering.[73] On Cassianus *Ludimagister* (13 August), two phrases[74] describing his tortures by

69 *An Old English Martyrology*, ed. Herzfeld, p. xxxiv.

70 *Das altenglische Martyrologium* I, 208–16: on Hilarius (13 January), Felix (14 January), Marcellus (16 January), Prisca (18 January), Sebastian (20 January), Emerentiana (23 January), the Finding of John's Head (27? February), Mark (25 April), Gordianus (10 May), Ferreolus and Ferrucius (16 June), the seven sons of Felicitas (10 July), Symphorosa and her sons (18 July), Donatus and Hilarinus (7 August), Cassianus (13 August), Andochius and Thyrsus (24 September) and Cyrilla (28 October). Detailed discussions of some of these notices have appeared in print. On Marcellus, see J. E. Cross, 'Popes of Rome in the Old English Martyrology', *Arca* 3 (1979), 191–211, at 191–3. On John's Head, see Cross, 'John the Baptist' pp. 158–60. On Mark, see Cross, 'Irish Texts', pp. 188–9. On Cyrilla, see Cross, '*Passio S. Laurentii*', p. 212. A comparison with the relevant section of Bede's *Martyrologium* for the other notices will confirm Kotzor's conclusions.

71 *Ibid.*: on Marius and his family (20 January), Macedonius, Patricia and Modesta (13 March), Calepodius (10 May), Januarius (19 September) and Fausta and Evilasius (20 September). For Calepodius there is merely a calendar-type entry. For Macedonius, Patricia and Modesta a manuscript folio has been lost and if the Englishman had written a narrative notice, Bede's *Martyrologium* with its calendar-type entry would not have been a sufficient source.

72 In the notice on Januarius, OEM designates both Festus and Desiderius *deaconas*, but in both Bede's *Martyrologium* and printed texts of the *passiones*, Desiderius is a *lector*, and OEM says that Januarius was martyred at Beneventum, not Puteolana as in Bede and the *passiones*. These may have been changes made for the sake of summary or errors of hasty reading. But I have not yet discovered the exact text of the *passio* which OEM used. Januarius goes with Sosius (23 September), for whom two details do not appear in printed texts. I have found one of these in a variant manuscript text and hope to find the other.

73 OEM in *Das altenglische Martyrologium*, ed. Kotzor, II, 16, and *An Old English Martyrology*, ed. Herzfeld, p. 18; Bede's *Martyrologium* in Quentin, *Les Martyrologes*, p. 107. Kotzor (*ibid.* II, 284) does not analyse this section, but corresponding details indicate also a reading of Bede's *Vita S. Felicis* as well as of other material.

74 OEM in *Das altenglische Martyrologium*, ed. Kotzor, II, 180, and *An Old English Martyrology*, ed. Herzfeld, p. 146; Bede in Quentin, *Les Martyrologes*, p. 68.

his pupils are nearer to Bede's words than to those of variant texts of the *passio*. Compare OEM ('hi hyne ofslogen mid heora writbredum') with Bede's *Martyrologium* ('alii cum tabulis et buxibus feriebant'); and also 'his þrowung wæs þe lengre ond þy heardre, þy þe hyra handa wæron unstrange hine to acwellanne', with Bede ('. . . quorum quanto infirmior erat manus, tanto grauiorem martyrii poenam, dilata morte, faciebat'). The names of the three boys martyred with Babyllas (24 January) – 'Urbanus, Prilidanus, Epolanus' – in OEM are not in the main source, the *passio* (*BHL*, no. 890), but in Bede, who records them in the genitive: 'Urbani, Pridilani et Epoloni'.[75] On the assumption that our writer consulted Bede as he clearly looked at Aldhelm, further confirmation may be found elsewhere.[76]

## *Anonymous works of Insular origin*

i *De ordine creaturarum*.[77] This book, once attributed to Isidore, draws material from the tract *De mirabilibus sacrae scripturae* (written in 655 by one 'Augustinus Hibernicus'), and, in turn, provided material for Bede, *De natura rerum* (written *c.* 700). It is available in early manuscripts, notably Basle, Universitäts bibliothek F. III. 15b (? Northumbria, s. viii[1]) and Paris, BN lat. 9561 (possibly English origin but certainly by an English scribe, s. viii[2]).[78] It was composed probably in England or Ireland. Corresponding detail and verbal echoes indicate that the work was used for the notices on the 2nd–6th Days of Creation (19–23 March).

ii Pseudo-Isidore, *De ortu et obitu patrum (patriarcharum)*.[79] The late R. E. McNally was preparing an edition of this *De ortu* which, he argued, was a 'sister-work of the Irish pseudo-Isidorian *Liber de numeris*', since both originated 'about the middle of the eighth century in south-east Germany, probably in the wide circle of the Irish bishop, Virgil of Salzburg', and since both works

[75] OEM in *Das altenglische Martyrologium*, ed. Kotzor, II, 25, and *An Old English Martyrology*, ed. Herzfeld, p. 30; Bede in Quentin, *Les Martyrologes*, p. 49, ultimately from Gregory of Tours, *Historia Francorum* I.30 (as noted in B. Mombritius, *Sanctuarium uel Vitae Sanctorum*, 2 vols., 2nd ed. (Paris, 1910) I, 627).

[76] See Cross, 'Latinity', on Lucy of Syracuse.

[77] For the information in this section, apart from notification of early manuscripts, see J. E. Cross, '*De Ordine Creaturarum Liber* in Old English Prose', *Anglia* 90 (1972), 132–40, at 133–8.

[78] For the Basle and Paris manuscripts, see now H. Gneuss, 'A Preliminary List of Manuscripts written or owned in England up to 1100', *ASE* 9 (1981), 1–60, at 49 (no. 785, Basle) and 56 (no. 894, Paris).

[79] For references to statements in this section and a more detailed argument about contacts, see Cross, 'Irish Texts', pp. 186–91.

demonstrate 'pronounced Irish symptoms of thought and expression'.[80] The earliest manuscript is Colmar, Bibliothèque Municipale, 39 (s. viii/ix). The work is used for details mainly in the composite notices for scriptural people, some of whom have no *uitae*. Such distinctive comments in pseudo-Isidore and in OEM, from among likely sources, include an extended 'etymology' for Thomas (21 December), an exactly equivalent lineage for Simon (28 October), the dating of a *translatio* for Andrew (30 November), the tradition of a curious intermittent *Assumptio* for John the Evangelist (27 December) as an extension of his commonly attested *Dormitio*, a phrase ('furtum laudabile') describing Mark's secret writing of his gospel from Peter's words (Mark, 25 April), detail in the notice for Luke (18 October), and the name of Jesus in the *tres linguae sacrae* within the entry for the Octave of Christ and St Mary (1 January). In my view, the total number of these debts confirms the supposition of direct dependence of OEM on *De ortu et obitu.*

## Isidore, *De ortu et obitu patrum*[81]

Pseudo-Isidore, *De ortu* (discussed above) was based on the authentic Isidorian text, so that the two tracts had material in common. Details common to both these Latin texts and to OEM, but distinctive to the three, confirm that either one or the other Latin text was consulted. Two details, however, not in pseudo-Isidore but in Isidore and in OEM suggest that the authentic Isidore was available. The details are: names of nations in Thomas's mission-field (21 December) and the mission-field for Andrew (30 November).

## *Liber pontificalis*

A recension of the *Liber pontificalis*[82] was the sole source for entries on seven popes of Rome: Anteros (3 January), Telesphor (6 January), Marcellus (16 January), Urbanus (25 May), Stephanus (2 August), Marcus (7 October) and Callistus (14 October). It provides some details in the notices for four more popes – Fabian (20 January), John (18 May), Sixtus (6 August) and Clement (23 November) – and also for one other saint, Pancratius (12 May).[83]

80 See R. E. McNally, '"Christus" in the pseudo-Isidorian *Liber de ortu et obitu patriarcharum*', *Traditio* 21 (1965), 167–83, at 168–9.

81 On the use of Isidore in OEM, see Cross, 'The Apostles', pp. 23 (Thomas) and 28 (Andrew).

82 On the use of the *Liber pontificalis* for popes, see Cross, 'Popes of Rome'.

83 The notice for Pancratius has not been fully considered in print, and cannot be discussed briefly here. The skein of significant details in OEM (names, numbers, distinctive state-

### *Verba seniorum* (*Vitae* or *Vitas patrum*)

What the title *Vitae* or *Vitas patrum* meant to the Anglo-Saxons who noted it[84] probably needs a more detailed discussion than can be presented here. For OEM, Constance Rosenthal claimed that nine notices derived from this work as 'secondary' source.[85] She, however, used the collection printed by Rosweyde and was conscious that the early editor may have incorporated too much.[86] It may be that the section now known as *Verba seniorum* circulated as a separate work in the ninth century when OEM was composed, as, in fact, is suggested by Columba Batlle's recent survey of manuscripts of the *Verba seniorum* under a variant title, *Adhortationes sanctorum patrum*.[87] Only two of eleven manuscripts written before AD 900 also contain some of the longer lives of desert saints included within Rosweyde's edition: namely, Brussels, Bibliothèque Royale, lat. 8216–18 (Hilarion, Malchus, Paul and Antony) and Rome, Biblioteca Vallicelliana, C 47 (Marina, at the end of the manuscript). At present, I am inclined to doubt that longer lives of desert saints used by OEM were found in a collection of Desert Father material.

But OEM has one detailed contact with the words in the *Verba seniorum*, the entry for Arsenius (19 July). Bede[88] had recorded an anecdote about Arsenius in his *Martyrologium*, but our independently minded composer rejected Bede's choice, and took two other reminiscences of the saint's piety. Herzfeld[89]

ments) indicate a use of *BHL*, no. 6421, but of a variant *text* of that printed in *Acta Sanctorum*, *Maii* III, 21, and of that preserved in the English manuscript now Oxford, Bodleian Library, Fell 4 and ptd A. E. Huisman, *Die Verehrung des heiligen Pancratius in West- und Mittel-europa* (Haarlem, 1938), pp. 16–18. Huizman regards *BHL*, no. 6421 as most nearly representing the original legend. This *passio* does not (nor does any other variant version listed in *BHL*) include any equivalent of the last statement found in OEM: 'ond his cirice getimbred oð þysne ondweardan dæg'. *Liber pontificalis* says that Pope Symmachus founded or rebuilt the church and that it was restored by Pope Honorius; see *Liber Pontificalis Pars Prior*, ed. T. Mommsen, MGH, Gesta Pontificum Romanorum I (Berlin, 1918), 124 and 172. Gregory the Great preached his *Homilia* xxvii 'in basilica sancti Pancratii martyris' (PL 76, col. 1204).

84 Wherever Ælfric names the work and abstracts an anecdote, the material comes from the *Verba seniorum* section of the vast and composite work that is called the *Vitae patrum* (the whole collection was first edited in the seventeenth century by Heribert Rosweyde, and is repr. PL 73–4).

85 C. L. Rosenthal, *The 'Vitae Patrum' in Old English Literature* (Philadelphia, Pa, 1936), pp. 55–7. She follows Herzfeld in assuming that the direct source of our extant martyrology is a Latin martyrology.

86 *Ibid*. p. 12.

87 C. M. Batlle, *Die 'Adhortationes Sanctorum Patrum' ('Verba Seniorum') im lateinischen Mittelalter* (Münster, 1971), pp. 17–22.

88 Quentin, *Les Martyrologes*, p. 99.

89 *An Old English Martyrology*, ed. Herzfeld, p. xl. Kotzor (*Das altenglische Martyrologium* II, 330) refers to general discussions about the saint.

referred to *Acta Sanctorum* for the first anecdote about sleep as a bad servant, but inaccurately, since the editors of the *Acta* here print a Greek text with a 'modern' Latin translation. Rosenthal,[90] however, noted two accounts of this story in Rosweyde's text, and the second of these presents the sequence of words which was used in OEM.

The second anecdote has not appeared in print despite J. G. Freire's edition collated from many manuscripts of the *Apophthegmata patrum* (or *Verba seniorum*).[91] Guy Philippart, however, reviewed Freire's book and noted 'une révision germanique du VIIIe s. sous forme d'anthologie: la recension courte',[92] extant in three manuscripts, of which I have seen the earliest, Stuttgart, Württembergische Landesbibliothek, Theol. fol. 303 (s. viii/ix).[93] This includes the first story on 10r and the unpublished second anecdote on 7r: 'Sanctae memoriae Theophilus archiepiscopus, cum moryturus esset, dixit: Beatus es, abba Arseni, quia semper hanc horam ante oculos habuisti.' OEM reads:[94] 'Cwæþ sum halig biscop, ða he wæs on sawlenga, be þeossum fæder: Arsenius, þu wære eadig, forþon ðu hæfdest a þas tid beforan þinum eagum.'

## Gregory, *Dialogi*

As an ultimate or direct source Gregory's *Dialogi* provided information for the notice on Benedict of Nursia (21 March) (specifically bk II, preface, II.3, II.4 and II.37) including some verbal echoes; and for Pope John (18 May), some information is taken from the *Dialogi* III.2(3) and, with clear verbal echo, from IV.30.[95] These contacts may appear too few to suggest that the martyrologist had not read Gregory on Benedict and John in some intermediary work, but Gregory's *Dialogi*, bk II was the fullest account of the founder of the Benedictine order, and Pope John does not appear to have been the subject of

90 Rosenthal, *The 'Vitae Patrum'*, p. 55 (the reference is to PL 73, col. 807). She notes (*ibid.* p. 56) verbal echoes of the narration at PL 73, col. 865.

91 J. G. Freire, *A versão Latina por Pascásio de Dume dos Apophthegmata Patrum*, 2 vols. (Coimbra, 1971).

92 G. Philippart, 'Vitae Patrum, trois travaux récents sur d'anciennes traductions latines', *AB* 92 (1974), 359.

93 On the Stuttgart manuscript, see E. A. Lowe, *Codices Latini Antiquiores* IX (Oxford, 1959), no. 1355. The anthology is also preserved in Lincoln, Cathedral Library, 222 (s. xii/xiii); the stories are found on 89r (the first) and 86v–87r (the second).

94 *Das altenglische Martyrologium*, ed. Kotzor, II, 155, and *An Old English Martyrology*, ed. Herzfeld, p. 124.

95 On Pope John, see Cross, 'Popes of Rome', p. 195. Kotzor (*Das altenglische Martyrologium* II, 296–7) illustrates the contacts with Gregory for Benedict.

biography in extant manuscripts. The *Dialogi* circulated in Anglo-Saxon England,[96] as is well known.

## Gregory, *Moralia in Iob*

Whether ultimately or directly, the martyrologist used sentences from Gregory's *Moralia in Iob* (III.7) for the Decollation of John the Baptist (29 August).[97] As I have argued, the martyrologist used a variety of sources for the four feasts of John in OEM, and all the notices appear to be free compositions using these varied sources. Such a man as John the Baptist would not have a *uita*.

## *Anglo-Latin saints' lives*

It is difficult to be certain that the longer Anglo-Latin *uitae* were seen separately, but information within OEM is taken from widely separated chapters of Eddius Stephanus, *Vita S. Wilfridi* (that is, from chs. 1, 56, 65, 66 and 68) for the notice on Wilfrid (24 April); and from Felix, *Vita S. Guthlaci* for Guthlac (11 April) in varied order (that is, chs. 50, 10, 4, 5, 7 and 29 respectively), and for Pega (9 January), a brief reference to a miracle in ch. 53, the final chapter.[98] In her thorough survey of Guthlac materials, Jane Roberts[99] suggested that 'it is more likely that the brief note [in OEM] on Guthlac stems directly from some litany, collect or other martyrology'. This could be, of course, but one should say that the martyrologist follows the same method here for these two Anglo-Latin *uitae* as when abstracting, for example, from Jerome, *Vita S. Pauli* for Paul the Hermit (see above) and from Athanasius, *Vita S. Antonii* for Antony (17 January; selections taken from chs. 2, 89, 14, 7, 5, 6, 8, 9, 11, 12, 40, 93, 91 and 92 respectively).[100] This is not to say that all of these longer lives could not have been included in legend collections.

96 On Latin manuscripts, see Gneuss, *ASE* 9 (1981), 1–60 (nos. 34, 208, 510, 667, 715 and 924) (not including manuscripts of Werferth's English translation). See also references to Gregory's *Dialogi* in the Anglo-Saxon booklists ptd Lapidge, above, p. 85.

97 See Cross, 'John the Baptist', pp. 156–7.

98 Kotzor has illustrated the contacts for Wilfrid (*Das altenglische Martyrologium* II, 303–4), Guthlac (*ibid.* II, 301) and Pega (*ibid.* II, 282).

99 Jane Roberts, 'An Inventory of Early Guthlac Materials', *MS* 32 (1970), 193–233, at 204.

100 The notice for Antony has not been discussed in print. Minor details indicate that the translation by Evagrius was the *passio* used.

## *Liturgical books*

It is certain that the composer of OEM had access to various liturgical books and may have used these, working possibly from memory, on some occasions. I note a few details which have parallels in Latin texts but, obviously, the martyrologist may not have seen the details exactly where they have been found. An epithet used to describe Euphemia (16 September), 'Ure fædras hi nemdon þa sigefæstan fæmnan', corresponds to the phrase *uirgo triumphatrix* found in texts of the Ambrosian Missal.[101] Words in the notice on Patrick (17 March), 'ða cyld clypodon ond cwædon: Cum, Sancte Patrice, ond gehæle us ec', are similar to lines from the Hymn of St Secundinus, preserved in the Antiphonary of Bangor and the Irish *Liber hymnorum*:

> Hibernenses omnes clamant ad te pueri,
> ueni, Sancte Patricii, saluos nos facere.[102]

A statement about Mary for her Assumption (15 August) has verbal echoes of the pseudo-Gregorian *Liber responsalis*; compare OEM, 'ond heo nu scineþ on þam heofonlican mægene betwyh þa þreatas haligra fæmnena, swa swa sunne scineþ on þisne middangeard. Englas þær blissiaþ, ond heahenglas þær wynsumiaþ, and ealle þa halgan þær gefeoþ in Sancta Marian', with pseudo-Gregory, 'O quam pulchra et speciosa est Maria, uirgo Dei, quae de mundo migrauit ad Christum; inter choros uirginum fulget sicut sol in uirtute coelesti. Gaudent angeli, exsultant archangeli in Maria uirgine.'[103] There appear to be no other echoes of missal, hymnal or antiphonary in OEM, yet such – if not exactly these – books must have been known, and other liturgical books may have provided detail for Pentecost (15 May) and for *Letania maior* (25 April).[104]

## *Other books*

Geographical or topographical details are sometimes recorded in OEM although not found in the main sources for the respective sections.[105] Also, one

101 See J. E. Cross, 'Euphemia and the Ambrosian Missal', *N&Q* 30 (1983), 18–22, for a detailed discussion of the notice.

102 See Cross, 'Irish Texts', pp. 173–6, for a detailed discussion of the notice.

103 Mary Clayton, 'The Cult of the Virgin Mary in Anglo-Saxon England, with Special Reference to the Vernacular Texts' (unpubl. D.Phil. dissertation, Oxford Univ., 1983), p. 161, first noted this parallel. For the citation from OEM, see *Das altenglische Martyrologium*, ed. Kotzor, II, 181, and *An Old English Martyrology*, ed. Herzfeld, p. 146. For pseudo-Gregory, see PL 78, col. 798.

104 See Cross, 'The Use of Patristic Homilies'.

105 I have not reached satisfactory conclusions about these.

anecdote is derived ultimately from Eusebius, *Historia ecclesiastica*, namely the story of Fabian's election as pope (20 January). But other such details found in this work[106] are also recorded in other Latin texts, and hence the *Historia ecclesiastica* may not be a direct source here. Similarly, the *Gospel of pseudo-Matthew*[107] was the sole source for the entry on the Nativity of Mary (8 September), but the tract also occurs in legendary collections, so it may not have been consulted as a separate work.

## *Lost literature*

The martyrologist's habitual care in abstracting from already identified sources with recognizable echo of word and detail suggests that the source has not been found in cases where significant detail in OEM has no Latin parallel as yet. A number of isolated details remain unidentified, suggesting that the exact variant *text* of a *version* of a saint's legend has not been, and may not be, seen. This may be so for the notice on Ambrose (5 April), where details in the anecdote about the general (*heretoga*) differ from those in the *Vita S. Ambrosii* by one Paulinus, although all the remaining information corresponds.[108] But considerable variations from extant Latin sources, on occasions, suggest that another *version* of a saint's legend existed for the martyrologist, but is not now extant. I have argued a case[109] for a 'lost' *uita* of Hild of Whitby, since her notice (17 November) includes distinctive details which are missing from, or at variance with, Bede's *Historia ecclesiastica*, the only account of her life known at present. The notice for Columba or Columcille (9 June) includes a miracle which is not recorded in the printed *uitae* of Columba, nor found among other Columban material.[110] The entry for Æthelwald (21 April) has an anecdote about the hermit which is not recorded in Bede's *Historia ecclesiastica* or in his *Vita S. Cuthberti*, but may have appeared in some other kind of record. There is no monk and hermit Mamilianus (15 September) in present records. Although the notice has similarities to episodes in the life of St Goar, as Kotzor has noted,[111] these similarities merely indicate another example of a certain kind of

106 See Cross, 'Popes of Rome', p. 193.

107 Kotzor (*Das altenglische Martyrologium* II, 348–9) has discussed this entry.

108 The notice has not been considered fully, but a comparison with Paulinus's *Vita S. Ambrosii* indicates that the story of the general does not correspond in detail. The martyrologist's normal methods of dealing with his identified sources indicate that he did not use the *Vita S. Ambrosii* as it is known at present.

109 See Cross, 'A Lost Life of Hilda of Whitby'.

110 For a presentation of the material, see Cross, 'Irish Texts', pp. 177–8. Máire Herbert of Cork has generously considered other Columban material for me, but without success.

111 *Das altenglische Martyrologium*, ed. Kotzor, II, 352.

story. I have tested possible corruptions of the name without success.

This small group of saints' lives, obviously, could well have been seen within a legendary rather than as separate works, but I have thought it important to reveal our few major failures (out of more than two hundred notices) for readers with different kinds of knowledge.

# The orientation system in the Old English Orosius: shifted or not?

MICHAEL KORHAMMER

When Ohthere told his lord, King Alfred, that he had sailed north along the coast of northern Norway and then, at the end of it, had turned east, and when the translator of the Old English Orosius placed the Baltic north of the south Danes and the north Danes 'be eastan him 7 be norþan'[1] – they certainly did not know what kind of stumbling-block they had left for historians and philologists a thousand years later. From humble beginnings[2] there eventually developed the full-grown theory of an Old Scandinavian shifted-orientation system[3] which moved all the cardinal points 45° clockwise (Old Scandinavian N = modern NE)[4] or even 60° clockwise.[5] Although this theory was rejected by C. A. E. Jessen, S. Lönborg and N. Beckmann,[6] by O. S. Reuter in his

1 All quotations of the Old English Orosius (hereafter Or.) are by page and line of *The Old English Orosius*, ed. J. Bately, EETS s.s. 6 (London, 1980). Here the reference is to 13/14–17.

2 'Truly, King Alfred deviates somewhat from the true situation of the countries of the world in his account of the nations in the east sea, seeing that he places the north somewhat too far towards the north-east. . .' (R. T. Hampson, 'An Essay on the Geography of King Alfred the Great', J. Bosworth, *A Literal English Translation of King Alfred's Anglo-Saxon Version of the Compendious History of the World by Orosius* (London, 1855), p. 35).

3 The idea of a shift was first discussed H. G. Porthan, 'Försök at uplysa Konung Ælfreds geographiska Beskrifning öfver den europeiska Norden', *Kongl. Vitterhets Historie och Antiquitets Academiens Handlingar* 6 (1800), 37–106, and R. K. Rask, 'Ottárs og Ulfstens korte Rejseberetninger med dansk Oversættelse, kritiske Anmerkninger og andre Oplysninger', *Det Skandinaviske Litteraturselskabs Skrifter* 11 (1815), 1–132. The subject was later taken up by, among others, the following authors: H. Schilling, *König Ælfreds angelsächsische Bearbeitung der Weltgeschichte des Orosius* (Halle, 1886); G. Storm, 'Om opdagelsen af "Nordkap" og veien til "det hvide hav"', *Det Norske Geografiske Selskabs Årbog* 5 (1893–4), 91–106; F. Nansen, *Nord i taakeheimen. Utforskningen av jordens nordlige strøk i tidlige tider* (Copenhagen, 1911); L. Weibull, 'De gamla nordbornas väderstrecksbegrepp', *Scandia* 1 (1928), 292–312; K. Malone, 'King Alfred's North: a Study in Mediaeval Geography', *Speculum* 5 (1930), 139–67; and R. Ekblom, 'Den forntida nordiska orienteringen och Wulfstans resa til Truso', *Fornvännen* 33 (1938), 49–68, 'Der Volksname *Osti* in Alfreds des Großen Orosius-Übersetzung', *SN* 13 (1940), 161–73, 'Alfred the Great as Geographer', *SN* 14 (1941–2), 115–44, and 'King Alfred, Ohthere and Wulfstan', *SN* 32 (1960), 3–13.

4 Nansen, *Nord i taakeheimen*, p. 131; Weibull, 'De gamla nordbornas väderstrecksbegrepp', p. 303; and Malone, 'King Alfred's North', p. 152.

5 Ekblom, in all his publications quoted above, n. 3.

6 Cf. Ekblom, 'Alfred the Great as Geographer', p. 125.

valuable *Germanische Himmelskunde*,[7] by A. Ellegård[8] in rather harsh and R. Derolez[9] in more lenient vein, it has apparently enjoyed great popularity, especially among Scandinavian scholars, and has continued to be quoted in publications concerned with the geography of the Old English Orosius.[10] The aim of the present paper is not to go into a detailed treatment of particular problems of geography in the Old English Orosius, but to assess the whole theory of a special Old Scandinavian orientation, thereby also analysing the usage and meaning of some Old English directional terms.

## THE 'OLD SCANDINAVIAN' SYSTEM OF ORIENTATION

The two main champions of a distinctive Old Scandinavian system of orientation are Malone and Ekblom. Malone's method is rather simple and might be called descriptive. Going through the geography of Or. he treats all the instances where the geographical information contained in Or. and the geographical facts are, in his opinion, at variance: whereas, for example, Or. 18/16–17 claims that the Alps are west of Istria, a look at the map shows that they are really north-west of that peninsula.[11] Malone comes to the conclusion that the author of the Old English Orosius uses two different systems of orientation, the 'classical' one (when he is correct according to modern standards) and the 'shifted system' (when his bearings show a steady 45° shift clockwise as compared to modern measurements). There is no regular and consistent distribution recognizable in the usage of the two systems: 'The shifted system is most prominent in his interpolations (= additions to the Latin Orosius: *Germania*, Ohthere's and Wulfstan's narrations), but is by no means confined to these.'[12] This would imply, however, that the translator of the Old English Orosius must sometimes have been so much under the influence of the shifted system that he even 'corrected' Orosius's geographical information (in the case of Asia Minor, for instance) – a not very likely idea on the whole. Malone does not attempt to find an explanation for the origin of the shift.

[7] O. S. Reuter, *Germanische Himmelskunde. Untersuchungen zur Geschichte des Geistes* (Munich, 1934), pp. 5–17.

[8] 'De gamla nordbornas väderstrecksuppfattning', *Lychnos* 1954–5, 1–20, and 'The Old Scandinavian System of Orientation', *SN* 32 (1960), 241–8.

[9] 'The Orientation System in the Old English Orosius', *England before the Conquest*, ed. P. Clemoes and K. Hughes (Cambridge, 1971), pp. 253–68.

[10] Cf. *Altenglisches Lesebuch: Prosa*, ed. J. Raith, 2nd ed. (Munich, 1958), pp. 66, 67, 68 and 73, and *Sweet's Anglo-Saxon Reader in Prose and Verse*, 15th ed., ed. D. Whitelock (Oxford, 1967), p. 229. Although the latest editor of Or. speaks out against the shift (*The Old English Orosius*, ed. Bately, pp. lxiii–lxvii), the often-quoted Ekblom seems to get off too lightly at her hands.

[11] 'King Alfred's North', p. 150.

[12] *Ibid.* p. 166.

Derolez was right in drawing attention to Malone's silent assumption that the bearings of the Old English Orosius could be treated 'as if Anglo-Saxons in the ninth century had access to maps that did not differ fundamentally from the products of modern cartography'.[13] However, when Derolez tried to prove that three of Malone's examples of clockwise shift were rather of a counter-clockwise kind[14] he was mistaken himself: if we for once follow Malone's argument that Or. 10/23–6 puts *Cilicia* and *Isauria* to the east of the Roman province Asia Minor (they are in fact SE),[15] then the shift is indeed clockwise; Or.'s 'wrong' east then coincides with our normal south-east: the whole wind-rose has been turned clockwise as compared to the normal compass card. The same consideration applies to Malone's remark about the *Pelorus*-corner of Sicily and the Straits of Messina:[16] Or.'s 'wrong' north means true north-east, and that constitutes a clockwise shift.[17] Derolez would have done better to counter Malone's implicit conclusion that the location of *Gallia Bellica* (= *Belgica*) as south of *Britannia* (Or. 19/12–13) displays a shift of 45° clockwise.[18] If we insist on a true south-easterly location of *Gallia Bellica*, the new north must be shifted to our astronomical NW (= counter-clockwise); with a clockwise shift *Gallia Bellica* would lie 'be eastan him'.

Ekblom's method is more systematic but also more complicated, and in fact I doubt whether all readers of his main article of 1941–2 have been able to grasp fully what he means. His arguments may be summed up under six headings:

1. Only the geography of central and northern Europe, where evidence independent of the Latin Orosius is available, is taken into account.
2. Ekblom correctly stresses the fact that the points of the compass given in Or. must not be interpreted as precise points (such as E = 90° or S = 180°) but as sectors[19] (a truth which Malone apparently took for granted). Since Ekblom assumes the author of the Old English Orosius to have used an eight-point compass system (Malone makes the same assumption silently), one sector comprises exactly 360° ÷ 8 = 45°, that means 22·5° on either side of each cardinal or half-cardinal point. As long as the data in Or. depart less than 22·5° clockwise from the actual bearings (as measured by Ekblom), the deviation is considered normal.
3. Ekblom constantly speaks of the Old Scandinavian orientation and its 60° clockwise deviation as if it were an established and undoubted fact – without adducing any kind of proof: 'I have dealt with this question earlier, concluding that the deviation

[13] 'The Orientation System', p. 256.
[14] *Ibid.* p. 257.
[15] 'King Alfred's North', p. 164.
[16] *Ibid.* p. 165.
[17] The best way to avoid errors when treating these kinds of shift is to place a ruler on a map and to make the north shift visible: when the ruler points SW–NE its top indicates shifted north and the shift is clockwise; with the ruler lying SE–NW the shift is counter-clockwise. Shifted east and west are at right angles to the ruler.
[18] 'King Alfred's North', pp. 143–4.
[19] 'Alfred the Great as Geographer', p. 123.

is in round numbers 60°';[20] in the accompanying footnote, where one might expect more details, Ekblom only cites Bjørnbo as another authority for the 60°, but has apparently forgotten to give a bibliographical reference to his own earlier work. So the inquisitive reader turns to Ekblom's article of 1938[21] – undeterred by the fact that the opus is written in Swedish – and becomes even more frustrated by the paucity of evidence or proof. As far as the reality of an Old Scandinavian orientation is concerned, Ekblom simply refers the reader to Weibull's article[22] (where he found most of his medieval sources for such an orientation anyway); from the Old English Orosius he cites nine examples; others come from Adam of Bremen, the *Knytlingasaga* and the 'Icelandic description of the earth'.[23] These twenty-three alleged 'wrong' bearings and courses (no pages or lines are given) are *per definitionem* considered Old Scandinavian simply by their being wrong clockwise. With Adam of Bremen there is the odd situation that according to Ekblom's theory he is supposed to have used three different systems of orientation:[24] our normal one, the 'Old Scandinavian' one, and finally, in the description of Sweden, one with four 'wrong' bearings anti-clockwise (which Ekblom interprets as a kind of hypercorrection under the influence of the Old Scandinavian system!). That Adam's average clockwise deviation (one might also call it 'amount of incorrectness'), at which Ekblom arrived by means of a map, is 60° has to be taken on trust; the bearings on the map which he offers[25] are hardly recognizable, nor are any individual figures of degrees given. This then, unbeknown to the reader of Ekblom's article of 1941–2, is the meagre background; it is the sum of the proof on which the author bases his further conclusions: 'Now as the mean deviation for Old Scandinavian bearings is about 60°, from what we have said above it is clear that every deviation clockwise above 30° may justly be due to Old Scandinavian orientation. If the deviation is less, it may be supposed that normal orientation was intended.'[26]

4. The sense of certitude and self-confidence that emanates from every page of Ekblom's main article stems from his claim that he has, exclusively in the *Germania* part of Or., found twenty-three examples[27] of Old Scandinavian orientation, that is, twenty-three cases of clockwise deviation greater than 30°. He maintains that there is not a single similar counter-clockwise deviation which might discredit his theory;[28] six examples with 'a considerable deviation' (from the normal system) are said to lie below the 30° margin and are thus not taken into consideration.[29] Apart from the fact that

[20] *Ibid.* p. 122.

[21] 'Den forntida nordiska orienteringen'.

[22] 'De gamla nordbornas väderstrecksbegrepp'.

[23] No bibliographical reference is given; see, however, Weibull, 'De gamla nordbornas väderstrecksbegrepp', pp. 299–303.

[24] 'Den forntida nordiska orienteringen', pp. 58–60. Ekblom ('Alfred the Great as Geographer', p. 123), like Weibull, explains this intermingling of systems by the influence of Christianity and continental civilization.

[25] 'Den forntida nordiska orienteringen', p. 57.

[26] 'Alfred the Great as Geographer', p. 123.

[27] The same number as above but only partially identical.

[28] 'Alfred the Great as Geographer', p. 125.

[29] 'Yet they should all have been given another bearing, since the deviations are all more than 22·5° from the centre of the octant concerned' (*ibid.* p. 124).

several of his twenty-three 'deviations'[30] are extremely debatable on account of the arrangement of his 'centres',[31] at least one other 'Old Scandinavian' bearing would have occurred in south-eastern Europe if Ekblom had not committed a philological error: east of 'Carendran londe' (Carinthia) Or. 13/7–8 places 'Pulgara land' and continues: '7 be eastan þæm is Creca land'. As *þæm* clearly refers to the Bulgars and not, as Ekblom claims, to Carinthia,[32] Greece is here thought to lie east of the Bulgars and that constitutes a clockwise deviation of considerably more than 30°. But here Ekblom's theory, which does not allow Old Scandinavian orientation thus far south, proved stronger than any philological scruples.

The twenty-three instances of Old Scandinavian orientation just mentioned are not summed up in a list but have to be gleaned individually from Ekblom's discussion and his two maps. In Ekblom's last article, however, which was published posthumously in 1960, a table (found among his papers) of 'values of the deviations' for these twenty-three bearings plus calculations is added in a footnote.[33] The method used here by the author becomes clear after some hard thinking: for each bearing he adduces the precise angle (ranging from −22° to +22°) by which the actual bearing on the map deviates from his postulated Old Scandinavian (half-)cardinal point; the columns of the minus and of the plus deviations are each added up and divided by the number of bearings. The results, namely the average deviations, are −7·5° and +7·3°, which apparently meant for Ekblom that they nearly cancelled each other out and he thus arrived at an average of 59·8° ('Let us call it 60°'). In fact the sums and averages do not all follow from the printed figures: my own calculations would come out at −10·3° and +5·4°, but that is beside the point.

5. How did Ekblom come by these extraordinarily precise bearings and figures?[34] By a very simple – and very unscientific – method. In order to measure the angles by which Or.'s bearings differ from the 'correct' ones, he drew lines on a map and connected the various nations and areas located by Or. in relation to each other ('To the south of the east Franks are the Swabians', Or. 12/25); but before he could do that he rather arbitrarily established 'centres' for these nations.[35] Thus he maintains that 'careful

[30] The number ought rather to be twenty as on Ekblom's map ('Alfred the Great as Geographer', p. 141) the bearings numbered 11–12 (the mouth of the Elbe and the Frisians, Or. 12/30) and 13–15 (the Angles, Sillende and 'sumne dæl Dene', Or. 12/31) are identical.

[31] For the idea of 'centres', see below, heading 5 and n. 35.

[32] 'Alfred the Great as Geographer', p. 122; cf. *The Old English Orosius*, ed. Bately, p. 172.

[33] 'King Alfred, Ohthere and Wulfstan', p. 5, n. 1. Ellegård ('The Old Scandinavian System', p. 241) wonders whether Ekblom really considered these notes ready for publication, a view I heartily endorse. Ellegård's error of expanding R. Ekblom to Rudolf Ekblom was repeated by Derolez ('The Orientation System', p. 258). Cf. Ekblom, 'King Alfred, Ohthere and Wulfstan', p. 13: '. . . the Vistula deprives the Elbing of its name, and Ellegård deprives me of mine. I am called Richard Ekblom.'

[34] '. . . previous methods have been far less minute than mine' ('Alfred the Great as Geographer', p. 129).

[35] See above, p. 00. The *Ostsæ*, which Or. 13/15–16 places to the north of the south Danes, has its 'centre' *c.* 50 km north of Zealand ('Alfred the Great as Geographer', no. 35 (p. 141)); the location of the south Danes in the northern part of the Jutland peninsula ('at about Silkeborg south of Viborg', *ibid.* p. 134) places them more northerly (in the normal sense) than the north

calculation has led me to believe that their [*sc.* the east Franks'] geographical centre must have lain east of Mount Spessart, by the town of Gemünden';[36] the Saxon centre is placed east of Verden;[37] and, most amusing of all, that of the still problematical *Osti* is located between Greifswalder Bodden, Peene and Schwinge, 'ungefähr 12 km südlich von Wusterhusen';[38] whereas according to W. Brüske the latter territory was submerged right up to the end of the twelfth century![39] Derolez is certainly justified in asking whether the idea of such centres 'can ever have entered the head of a ninth-century geographer'.[40] Incidentally, another example of curious reasoning is provided by Ekblom's statement that the bearing from Ohthere's second turning-point, Cape Orlov, to his probable goal, the mouth of the Varzuga river, is S 60° W:[41] what a surprise for the mariner to find that when he sailed *suðryhte* (Or. 14/16–17) his south course, interpreted in 'Old Scandinavian' terms, would take him across roughly 120 nautical miles of dry land!

6. Ekblom's Old Scandinavian bearings are restricted to the more northerly parts of *Germania*,[42] an improvement on Malone. However, contrary to expectation, these bearings do not stand apart but are sometimes intimately interwoven with normally orientated ones. While the five bearings by which Or. 12/29–13/2 places the mouth of the river Elbe, the land Angeln, the Obodrites (*Afdrede*), the Havolans (*Hæfeldan*) and the Siusles (*Sysyle*) in relation to the Old Saxons, are all interpreted as Old Scandinavian, the immediately following SE bearing to the Moravians (*Maroara*, Or. 13/2–3) is declared to be normal orientation.[43] Or.'s bearings from the Croats and Bornholm to the Sarmatians[44] count as normal usage; from the *Sweon*, however, the bearing is 'Old Scandinavian' (Or. 13/13, 24 and 26). According to Ekblom the south Danes have:

(a) the North Sea to their normal west (Or. 13/14);
(b) the *Ostsæ* to their Old Scandinavian north (13/15–16);
(c) the north Danes to their Old Scandinavian north-east (13/16);

Danes, whose centre Ekblom puts 'just north of Roskilde' (Zealand) although he says that they also lived in Skåne and up to central Halland/Sweden. Ohthere's words that south of *Sciringesheal* a big sea flows inland (Or. 16/9–10) are turned into the statement that the Skagerrak 'is thus thought to run north' ('Alfred the Great as Geographer', no. 59. (p. 140)). The Norwegians (*Norþmenn*, no. 55), who live west of the *Sweon* (Or. 13/27), are simply reduced to the Trondheim area, and the 'centre' of *Cwenland* (Or. 13/26) is placed in Finland, north-east of the Gulf of Bothnia, although Ohthere says clearly that the *Cwenas* sometimes harry the Norwegians and vice versa (Or. 15/34–5). The placing of the centres for the *Sermende* (Sarmatians) and the absolutely unknown *Mægþa land* (Or. 13/12–13) south of Lithuania is born of pure fantasy, or more correctly, of the desire to prove a point by any means; cf. Bately, *Orosius*, p. 174: 'As for the location of *Mægþa land* . . . speculation is valueless.'

36 'Alfred the Great as Geographer', p. 127.

37 *Ibid.* p. 130.

38 'Der Volksname *Osti*', p. 170.

39 Cf. *Orosius*, ed. Bately, p. 177.

40 'The Orientation System', p. 259.

41 'Alfred the Great as Geographer', p. 137.

42 Cf. the two maps, *ibid.* pp. 141 and 143.

43 For this and the following, see 'Alfred the Great as Geographer', pp. 130–6.

44 Cf. above, n. 35.

(d) the *Afdrede* to their Old Scandinavian east (13/17–18); and
(e) the mouth of the Elbe and some Saxons yet again to their normal south (13/18–19).

Finally, the bearing from the *Sweon* to 'þone sæs earm Osti' in the south (Or. 13/24–5) is considered normal orientation, while the following four bearings (13/26–8) to the Sarmatians, the *Cwenas*, the *Scridefinne* and the Norwegians receive the label 'Old Scandinavian'. And the reader, already perplexed by the constant intermingling of systems, asks himself why the northern orientation should have been used, five times out of six, with the Old Saxon centre as starting-point: Ekblom's conclusion is that '. . . these statements must have come from an informant under Scandinavian influence'.[45] And why is normal orientation used for all data about the island of Bornholm? It 'seems not to have been very closely connected with Scandinavia in Alfred's time; according to Wulfstan the Bornholmers had a king of their own'.[46] The reader's patience is here strained beyond its limits.

Is Ekblom's intermingling of two systems of orientation at all probable? If the Old Scandinavian system really existed, the author of Or. would surely have known about such a significant divergence and about its consequent interference with the normal system: without any explanation to the reader (and there is none) his geography would simply have become chaotic and that was certainly not his intention.

In summary it may be said that Ekblom's theory suffers from many serious shortcomings and is not very convincing, and this impression is corroborated by certain other features of his articles. Many of his very definite and self-assured statements may sound impressive at first but are not borne out by contemporary or later scholarship.[47] And the unfounded criticism he sometimes levels at other scholars not of his opinion[48] tends further to weaken his position and provokes yet more criticism.

45 'Alfred the Great as Geographer', p. 123. 46 *Ibid.* p. 124.

47 Cf. *Orosius*, ed. Bately, pp. 168–98 *passim*. See also below, p. 262, n. 70.

48 Nearly all the points in which Ekblom ('Alfred the Great as Geographer', pp. 122, 126, 128 and 130) finds fault with Malone or Reuter are unjustified. Malone's interpretation ('King Alfred's North', p. 153) of the relation between *Pulgara land* and Greece (see above, p. 255) is absolutely correct. Contrary to Ekblom's allegations Malone (*ibid.* pp. 151 and 153) does not in the least use Or.'s statements about the direction of the Rhine and about the location of the Vistula country and the Dalamintzians to support his own theory; his location of the *Surpe* (Or. 13/12) is probably correct and thus also his statement that the 'shift' is clockwise (*ibid.* p. 153). Reuter (*Germanische Himmelskunde*, p. 6) does not say that the general course of the Rhine is due NW but that the course with which it flows into the sea is 'in Wirklichkeit nordwestlich'. Ekblom's general attitude to the opinions of other scholars is well exemplified in his 'Alfred the Great as Geographer', pp. 128–9. Even King Alfred is not spared: his 'statement [that the *Ostsæ* lies north of the north Danes] is decidedly wrong' (*ibid.* p. 134), and his 'Behauptung, dass Bornholm nördlich von den *Osti* liege, muss ohne weiteres als irreführend bezeichnet werden' ('Der Volksname *Osti*', p. 171).

Leaving the Old English Orosius aside for the time being, let us turn to the general question of how probable it is that the inhabitants of old Norway and Sweden had their north where we have our north-east. Since the magnetic compass in its rudimentary form did not appear in Europe before the twelfth century (and then only in the Mediterranean), it is not even theoretically possible to propose a case of abnormal magnetic variation in Scandinavia. How convincing are the different solutions which have been brought forward to explain the supposed shift of orientation? Is it indeed likely that the Scandinavians should originally have established their cardinal direction north under the influence of the trend of the Norwegian coast[49] or of the course of the important navigation channel past the islands Smöla and Hitra towards the Trondheim Fjord;[50] or, alternatively, that they should have taken their cardinal east either (a) from the point on the horizon where the midwinter sun rises,[51] especially in the Trondheim district,[52] or (b) from the direction of the openings in northern cairn graves,[53] or (c) from the direction of the great rivers in north Sweden?[54] Before the advent of the magnetic compass ancient and medieval man had only the heavenly bodies to supply him with the cardinal directions. At night the Pole Star (although at that time not exactly in the pole of the sky but circling round it at a certain distance) indicated true north. During the day the position of the sun at noon, when it ceased to ascend and began to descend (= culminated), gave him due south, and the shadow it cast at this time indicated true north. In the Mediterranean the sunrise and sunset positions did not diverge too far from due east and west (*c.* 30° towards north and south) in the course of a year,[55] but in northern latitudes these positions altered very quickly, moving along the whole eastern and western horizons and only indicating true east and west, as everywhere in the world, at the time of the vernal and autumnal equinoxes. In northern countries the N–S meridian was therefore more important than in the Mediterranean because true east and west, at right angles to that line, were also derived from it (at least in a system of

[49] Suggested by Nansen, *Nord i taakeheimen*, p. 131.

[50] Cf. Ekblom, 'Den forntida nordiska orienteringen', p. 55, and 'Alfred the Great as Geographer', p. 125.

[51] Cf. Weibull, 'De gamla nordbornas väderstrecksbegrepp', pp. 310–11.

[52] Cf. Ekblom, 'Den forntida nordiska orienteringen', pp. 53–6, and 'Alfred the Great as Geographer', p. 125.

[53] Cf. Weibull, 'De gamla nordbornas väderstrecksbegrepp', pp. 308–12.

[54] Cf. Ekblom, 'King Alfred, Ohthere and Wulfstan', p. 3.

[55] Cf. E. G. R. Taylor, *The Haven-Finding Art: a History of Navigation from Odysseus to Captain Cook* (London, 1956), p. 7; her chapter 'Signs in the Sky' (pp. 3–20) is a good introduction to elementary astronomy.

normal orientation). Finally, north of the Arctic Circle, the summer midnight sun indicated true north when, after sinking towards the horizon, it did not set but began to ascend again.

Let us now presume that the ancient inhabitants of the Trondheim district, which has been named as the place of origin of the Old Scandinavian orientation,[56] were so grateful for the prospect of longer days and a new year and new life at the time of the midwinter sunrise that they adopted their cardinal east from the position of the midwinter sunrise (E 60°S = 60° south of east = 150° on the 360° compass scale) and derived the other cardinal points from it. These points (shifted 60° clockwise compared to normal orientation) could be remembered by the use of certain landmarks (mountain tops, trees or houses) and could be used quite normally. But what happened if someone from Trondheim left his familiar surroundings – something which seafarers, for instance, would have done habitually? Did he consult the sun in order to calculate due south and then add two-thirds of a quadrant to get his familiar south? Or subtract one third to arrive at shifted east?[57] Or did he, rather, sailing along the Atlantic coast of Norway, adopt the direction of this coast as his new N–S meridian (which would then embody a shift of only some 45° clockwise)? It is very probable that a Norse ship which, after leaving harbour, turned to port along the coast was said to be 'sailing south (along the land)' and 'sailing north' when it turned to starboard. This is the way that the Old Norse terms *land-suðr*, 'south-east', and *land-norðr*, 'north-east', must have come into existence, in opposition to *út-suðr*, 'south-west', and *út-norðr*, 'north-west'. But this by no means implies that a sailor, without former experience, would have been able to make out the general run of the coast, at every point of his journey, and thus to deduct his cardinal north and south from it: with the many islands, promontories, fjords – and no sea charts – the overall direction of the coast would often simply not have been discernible.

Can this uncertainty about the trend of the coast also have been the reason for Ohthere saying (Or. 14/7–13) that after travelling northward for six days the land turned *eastryhte* and that he then sailed east by the land – although the general trend of the Kola peninsula is SE? That is what A. L. Binns suggests;[58] he thinks that Ohthere 'could not know whether the general direction of the day's run had been NE or NW' and, as his alteration of course near the North Cape would be about 90°, 'to call it E would follow from the previously assumed N'. But Binns forgets that his explanation will only do if Ohthere

56 By Ekblom; see above, p. 258.

57 Ekblom's remark ('Den forntida nordiska orienteringen', p. 58, n. 20) that according to his own calculations the sun stood in the Old Scandinavian south at 16 o'clock would not have helped the Norseman very much either.

58 'Ohtheriana VI: Ohthere's Northern Voyage', *Eng. and Germanic Stud.* 7 (1961), 50–1.

sailed in bad visibility when observation of the sun was not possible. At what time of the year did Ohthere sail? Certainly not in the winter, during the time of the polar night. April[59] seems still too early because the ice in the Gorlo, the entrance to the White Sea, usually only breaks up in May.[60] So May or June seems more likely, and during this time the sun would also not set at the North Cape and along the coast of Lapland.[61] That means if the sun near the North Cape, where he altered course (probably at Nordkyn), was not obscured by clouds (the Pole Star, like the other stars, would not be visible because of the light of the polar night), Ohthere would need only one glance at the midnight sun to see exactly where true north was; the disc of the sun was then standing only a few degrees above the horizon and its lowest point (=N) was easy to define.[62] But if the sun was indeed not visible and Ohthere's orientation therefore not absolutely precise, this would also affect his statement about the wind before which he was subsequently sailing. The reading of the Cotton manuscript (Tiberius B. i) is here 'westanwindes oððe hwon norþan' (Or. 14/13), which – with its *oððe* – could thus express Ohthere's uncertainty about the true wind-direction. The Lauderdale manuscript (now BL Add. 47967), 'the earlier and in many ways the "better" of the two major manuscripts',[63] however, has the reading 'westanwindes 7 hwon norþan',[64] which is usually interpreted as NW or, better, WNW: in this case Ohthere had a very precise idea of the wind and consequently, contrary to Binns's view (see above), of the lie of the land as well. At the next stopping-place on Ohthere's journey there is no ambiguity: the wind for which he was waiting was from due north (*ryhtnorþanwindes*, Or. 14/15), and he then sailed 'suðryhte be lande'. As in the case of his former north and east courses, this south course has also been adduced as an example of a shifted-orientation system.[65] But to produce

59 Suggested Binns, *ibid.* p. 50.

60 At least in the modern period; cf. Admiralty, *White Sea Pilot* (London, 1946), p. 23. It should, however, not be forgotten that from about AD 900 to 1200 the climate in these northern latitudes was considerably milder than today: corn was grown in some parts of Greenland, oats and barley in Iceland, wheat in the Trondheim district. The Viking Greenlanders were able to bury their dead deep in soil that has since been permanently frozen; cf. H. H. Lamb, *Climate: Present, Past and Future*, 2 vols. (London, 1972–7) II, 6, 252–3 and 437–8.

61 At the North Cape the centre of the sun is constantly above the horizon between 12 May and 30 July, and Lapland has full daylight from 26 May to 18 July. Cf. Admiralty, *Norway Pilot, Part II*, 3rd ed. (London, 1905), p. 9, and *White Sea Pilot*, p. 63.

62 See also Reuter, *Germanische Himmelskunde*, pp. 13–15.

63 *Orosius*, ed. Bately, p. cxvii.

64 Cf. 'east 7 hwon suð' in a charter: '. . . of þam þorne east 7 hwon suð on ge rihte to þam wege to gafer bice', see W. deG. Birch, *Cartularium Saxonicum*, 3 vols. and index (London, 1885–99) (cited hereafter as *BCS* by number and line), 810/4, and similarly 830/4; the charters are listed P. H. Sawyer, *Anglo-Saxon Charters: an Annotated List and Bibliography*, R. Hist. Soc. Guides and Handbooks 8 (London, 1968) (hereafter S), 517 and 523 respectively.

65 See above, p. 256.

evidence for it is even more difficult here: wherever the stopping-place from which he went south was, on the last leg of his journey Ohthere had to steer 280° (W 10° N) to arrive at the Varzuga river, which today is generally accepted as his destination, and this course could by no means be called south any longer. Binns would have us believe that Ohthere did not detect the gradual curve of the south coast of the Kola peninsula and 'that his compass directions are to be taken much more with reference to an assumed trend of the coastline than to any quarter of the heavens'.[66] But the idea that he could not detect an eventual alteration of the course by roughly 100° would give a poor account of 'an extremely prudent and skilful mariner':[67] even if the sun was behind clouds all the time he would probably have perceived the changed course from the wind and the waves. The most simple explanation of the problem seems to me the following:

1. The information about wind and coastline refers to the time of departure from the stopping-place and immediately afterwards. We may not, for example, assume that the WNW wind kept on blowing for four days and the north wind for five. When Ohthere left Nordkyn he could, from Cape Sletnes, probably see no further than Cape Makkaur (NW of Vardö) and his direct course there was 122°, that is, 32° south of east. So his *eastryhte* is not altogether wrong, and as there was no dramatic change of his course within the next four days, there was nothing more to tell. Are we to expect a more precise course from somebody 'hugging the coast'? A similar limitation applies to his journey from the second stopping-place somewhere near or south of Svyatoy Nos: on his first leg to the Varzuga he was indeed sailing southwards.
2. The wind, blowing in a straight line, could be described quite precisely: that is, in terms of the eight-point system of orientation using also half-cardinal points (W, NW, N, NE etc.: cf. 'westanwindes 7 hwon norþan', 'ryhtnorþanwindes'). But the overall course of an unknown coastline which stretched for 300 nautical miles or which went on in a curve for 150 miles was, without even a primitive map, more difficult to describe – and probably that was of no major interest to Ohthere anyway: here the four-point system was sufficient. For Ohthere as a skipper the location of his final destination had been fixed precisely enough: he had kept the land to starboard all the time, it had taken him fifteen days' sailing, and the journey had finished at a *micel ea* beyond which the land for the first time looked well cultivated again. This method, a precise eight-point system used in connection with wind and weather, and less precise (and less correct) information concerning the land, corresponds very well to usages still current in modern Iceland.[68] And it means further that it is not possible to pin down Ohthere's second turning-place any more precisely: it might have been Svyatoy Nos or Mys Malyy Gorodetskiy or Mys Orlov. But the term *suðryhte* does not permit us to say more.

66 'Ohthere's Northern Voyage', p. 51. 67 *Ibid.* p. 43.

68 Cf. E. Haugen ('The Semantics of Icelandic Orientation', *Word* 13 (1957), 447–60), who summarizes two articles by Stefán Einarsson; see also *Orosius*, ed. Bately, p. 181, and Ellegård, 'The Old Scandinavian System', pp. 244–5.

If Ohthere really had such a precise notion of the wind ('due north') in unfamiliar surroundings, his orientation must have been based on information directly gained from the sun.[69] From this it follows that he and all other Scandinavian seafarers (navigating regularly to the Orkneys and Shetlands, Britain, Ireland, Iceland, Greenland and even 'Vinland') must have used our normal compass system: the idea of a shifted system which had to derive its points from the normal one, anyway, would be absurd.[70]

## THE COMPASS POINTS IN THE OLD ENGLISH OROSIUS

Coming back to the Old English Orosius as a whole, our next question will be: how many points of the compass did the author of the geographical section use? He does indeed speak of *eastnorþ* (12/28), *norþanwestan* (12/29), *eastsuþ* (13/2) and *norþaneastan* (13/10), and so Malone and Ekblom take an eight-point system for granted; in fact, it is the basis for Ekblom's 'strict method'. Yet, strangely enough, Malone was apparently not disturbed by the fact that, in all four examples of 'clockwise shift' which he adduces at one place,[71] Or. should make use of 'wrong' cardinal points (W, S, W and N) which we have to interpret as 'correct' half-cardinal points (NW, SW, NW and NE); on another page the same applies to nine out of ten examples.[72] This ratio is puzzling, for if an eight-point system was indeed used consistently, we should expect a more balanced proportion of cardinal and half-cardinal points. The solution to the problem is simple: a few hours' work gives us a statistical table (see below, Appendix, p. 269).

The evidence of the table given in the Appendix is clear. With a ratio of 260 cardinal points (properly balanced among each other) to twenty-six half-cardinal points there can be no question of Or. generally using an eight-point system of direction. In remote parts of the world like Africa, Asia and the Mediterranean, half-cardinal points hardly occur at all: here the author, having

[69] If he had named the wind from its 'feel' (cold and dry, for instance), which was the basis of the Mediterranean wind-direction system (Taylor, *The Haven-Finding Art*, pp. 14–15), he would most probably have left out the *ryht*, 'due'.

[70] Ekblom's remark ('Den forntida nordiska orienteringen', p. 58) that a shifted orientation would have presented no problem to seafaring and that a ship at sea was steered simply with the help of the Pole Star (keeping this star on the starboard side at right angles to the keel-line for Iceland, at 45° astern for Scotland etc.; the sun is only mentioned in a footnote) reveals his utter ignorance of navigation and seafaring. That the north wind, for which Ohthere was waiting on the coast of the Kola peninsula, was 'in those parts the most favourable wind for a sailing boat of the period' ('King Alfred, Ohthere and Wulfstan', p. 9) may sound deceptively learned and knowledgeable and is therefore quoted verbally in *Orosius*, ed. Bately, p. 183; yet it is most probably Ekblom's own invention.

[71] 'King Alfred's North', p. 150. [72] *Ibid.* p. 153.

less exact information, stayed on the safe side by employing only four directions.[73] Thus Janet Bately's emendation of the manuscript reading *suþan* 20/22 (Africa) into *be westansuþan* loses some of its probability even though Orosius's Latin text reads *ab africo*. For Europe there were more and better data available; yet the proportions are far from being balanced, and even if the problematical cases (see below, Appendix, n. 2) were added to the half-cardinal directions the overall picture would not change. So the Old English Orosius normally makes use of four points, each comprising a sector of roughly 90°; only where he had more precise information at his disposal did the author use rather smaller sectors. We might speak of a four(-to-eight)-point system of orientation.

This system may perhaps be compared to the kind of reasoning that underlies the Old English translations of Latin wind-names. While normally half-cardinal points are used for terms like *circius*, 'westnorþwind', or *boreus*, 'eastnorþwind',[74] there are also exceptions. Thus in one of the Cleopatra glossaries we find 'circius et boreus: twegen norðwindas'.[75] Similarly, in one of the Old English glossed psalters the sentence 'Et excitauit austrum de caelo, et induxit in uirtute sua affricum' (Psalm LXXVII.26) is glossed '7 he awehte suþerne wind of heofone 7 he lædde on mægene his suþerne wind'.[76] In the case of the Cleopatra glossary, two half-cardinal directions (NW and NE) were collated into a cardinal one (N). In the psalter gloss the (due) south wind *auster* and the south-west wind *africus* were subsumed under one direction, and this is also found in the psalter versions J, K and T;[77] other versions, however, distinguish between *superne* (*suþan*) and *westansuþan* (A and C) or *suþanwestan wind* (B, E and G). That the geographical description of the Old English Orosius is normally in a four-point system is only to be expected in the ninth century. Even today, with all our knowledge and modern means – globes, atlases, road-maps, satellite photographs – the man of the twentieth century usually still thinks in terms of north and south, east and west.[78] For most of us the sun rises in the east and sets in the west. The world is divided into the rich

73 Cf. Derolez about the Latin Orosius: 'For Africa and Asia a four-point system . . . was all he needed' ('The Orientation System', p. 261).

74 Cf. Derolez, *ibid.* pp. 261–3.

75 *The Latin–Old English Glossary in MS Cotton Cleopatra A.III*, ed. W. G. Stryker (unpubl. Ph.D dissertation, Stanford Univ., 1952), p. 127 (no. 634). See also T. Wright and R. Wülker, *Anglo-Saxon and Old English Vocabularies* I (London, 1884), 378/8.

76 *Der altenglische Regius-Psalter. Eine Interlinearversion in Hs. Royal 2.B.5 des Brit. Mus.*, Studien zur englischen Philologie 18 (Halle, 1904), 144 (=psalter version D).

77 For the system of sigla for the Old English psalter glosses, see C. and K. Sisam, *The Salisbury Psalter*, EETS o.s. 242 (London, 1959), ix–x. Psalter J has wrong *supefne* for *superne* = *austrum*; or was it an attempt to express the due south direction? F writes *supdæl*, I *norðerne wind* for *affricum* (and *suþaneasterne wind* for *austrum*).

78 Cf. Reuter, *Germanische Himmelskunde*, p. 7, and Derolez, 'The Orientation System', p. 259.

north and the under-developed south; the west is in a military clinch with the east; 'the young man goes west' and 'the east is red'.[79] And when central Europeans 'go south' for their holidays this designation can stretch from north Africa and Spain through Italy, Yugoslavia and Greece to Romania and Bulgaria.

## OLD ENGLISH TERMINOLOGY FOR DIRECTIONS

If the author of the Old English Orosius normally makes use of a four-point system of orientation, and if his cardinal points are usually to be taken as 90° sectors, what is then the precise meaning of terms like *norþryhte* or *eastryhte* employed in the narration of Ohthere's arctic voyage? Ohthere reportedly sailed *norþryhte* towards Nordkyn, then the land bent *eastryhte* and later *suþryhte*.[80] At this second bend he had to wait for a favourable wind, and when it came it was a *ryhtnorþanwind* (14/15) which no doubt means 'wind from due north' (cf. Norwegian *rettnord*, 'due north'; German *recht voraus*, 'straight ahead', *rechtweisender Kurs*, 'true course', and *rechtweisend Nord*, 'true north'). The obvious meaning of *ryht-* in this latter case (and at 12/27: 'ryhte be eastan') was – by most readers (and by all dictionaries of Old English: Bosworth–Toller, Sweet, Clark Hall) – transferred to the first-named *norþryhte*, so that Ohthere now 'wanted to know how far the land stretched due north' and 'sailed due north along the land',[81] and apparently this interpretation of his course along the Norwegian Atlantic coast was a principal source for the theory of a shifted-orientation system in Scandinavia. Although Reuter denied categorically that *norþryhte* can mean 'due north' and hinted at a difference between prefixed and suffixed *ryht(e)*,[82] Janet Bately, keeping to the tradition-

[79] Cf. 'Oh, East is East, and West is West, and never the twain shall meet' (Rudyard Kipling, *The Ballad of East and West*). Interestingly enough Ekblom originally made use of similar arguments ('Den forntida nordiska orienteringen', p. 52); later he did not come back to them, probably because he realized that they were detrimental to his theory.

[80] These forms are concentrated between 14/5 and 14/17. In the following description of Norway forms in *-weard* like *easteweard* (15/25) predominate: although the change of expression may have been brought about by the descriptive character of the passage it remains conspicuous. Was a second interpreter or secretary who took down the notes responsible?

[81] '"Till den enden . . . reste han rätt norrut längs landet' (Weibull, 'De gamla nordbornas väderstrecksbegrepp', p. 293); similarly Bosworth, *A Literal English Translation*, p. 16 (where the Rhine also flows 'right north into the arm of the ocean', p. 34); Malone, 'King Alfred's North', pp. 140 and 158; Whitelock, *Sweet's Anglo-Saxon Reader*, p. 363: Derolez, 'The Orientation System', p. 253; K. Crossley-Holland, *The Anglo-Saxon World* (Woodbridge, 1982), p. 61; and Raith, *Altenglisches Lesebuch*, p. 70 ('due south'). Ekblom ('Alfred the Great as Geographer', pp. 116–19) does not enter the discussion but translates *norþryhte* etc. as 'northward' etc.

[82] *Germanische Himmelskunde*, p. 6, n. 1.

ally accepted meaning but rejecting the idea of a shifted north, devotes half a page in her commentary to the problem of how *norþryhte* and the facts of Scandinavian geography can be reconciled: '. . . we cannot assume that this is the term that Ohthere himself used', and '. . . *norþryhte* is used quite inappropriately and surely must represent an original "north", subsequently modified by the note-taking scribe, the author of Or., or even a hypothetical interpreter, unaware that he was distorting Ohthere's information'.[83] Is it perhaps possible that *norþryhte* does indeed not mean 'due north' but simply 'in a northerly direction', and that Reuter was right after all?

The only way to answer this question seems again to use a statistical method. If the suffixed *-ryhte* really denotes a very exact direction it must necessarily occur much less frequently in Old English literature than other, more general, terms of cardinal directions used adverbially. While such statistical work would, until recently, have taken a considerable time, the task has been much facilitated by the admirable Toronto *Microfiche Concordance to Old English*,[84] whose value for all kinds of word-studies can hardly be overestimated. A rough count[85] in the *Concordance* of listings under *west* shows that in the prose literature by far the most frequent adverbial usage is made of the simple cardinal direction without any morpheme added (some 256 occurrences);[86] it is followed by *west(e)w(e)ard* (some 44 occurrences: the frequent adjectival usage is excluded) and *westrihte* (some 28 occurrences). The proportion of *-weard* and *-rihte* is similar in the case of two other cardinal directions, north (*c.* 44 as against 20) and south (*c.* 29 as against 25). The suffix *-rihte* is apparently preferred in the charters but in general *westweard* and *westrihte* seem to have been regarded as synonymous. The preference for *-rihte* in the charters may be due to individual partiality (it often occurs in clusters)[87] but there is probably also a slight semantic differentiation: *-rihte*, like *on (ge)rihte*, *riht* + *to* (*on*, *wiþ*)[88]

[83] *Orosius*, p. 181.

[84] R. L. Venezky and A. diPaolo Healy, *A Microfiche Concordance to Old English* (Toronto, 1980).

[85] 'Rough count' not only because of the possibility of human error, but also because of problems of orthography (*ryhte*, *richte*, *rigte*, *reht* etc.; the morphemes written as one word or two; *west* with *w* or *wynn*) and interpretation (*westwearde*, adverb or inflected adjective?).

[86] In compounds (= half-cardinal points) the noun *west* appears only about ten times (glosses to Latin wind-names excepted); this agrees with our results concerning the four-point system of orientation in Or. (see above, pp. 262–3).

[87] Cf. the boundaries in a Winchester charter (*BCS* 605/13–20 = S 1443): 'Ærest suðrichte fron ðan beo*d*ærn to Sc̄e Gregories cirican, ðonne from ðære suðwesthyrnan Sc̄e Gregories cirican XII geurda westrichte to ðære strete, ðonne richte norð XIII geurde to ðære norðstræte, ðonne eastrichte XLIII geurde ⁊ VI fet to ðære eaststrete, ðonne suðrichte XX geurde ⁊ VI fet to ðære suðstrete, ðonne westrichte be ðære suðstrete to ðæn lictune VII geurde ⁊ VI fet, ðonne richt norð V geurde. Ðonne is ðæs *y*mbganges ealles ðri*o* furlanges ⁊ ðreo metgeurda.' (*Select English Historical Documents of the Ninth and Tenth Centuries*, ed. F. E. Harmer (Cambridge, 1914), p. 28).

[88] 'þonan rihte on þone herepað' (*BCS* 767/7 = S 476); 'þæt swa norþ on ge rihte andlang þæs smalan weges to þone here page' (*BCS* 801/19 = S 496).

seems to emphasize the element of straightness towards a goal, which may be expected in the case of boundaries – in a few instances *rihte* is even strengthened by a preceding *sheaft*[89] – while *-weard* only gives more general directions. If *-rihte*, on the other hand, were to indicate true cardinal points, we should end up with an astonishingly large number of rectangular estates in Anglo-Saxon England!

While the fairly balanced distribution of directional terms ending in *-weard* and *-rihte*, together with their usage, makes it probable that they are to be taken as near synonyms with the meaning 'in a . . . direction' 'towards . . . (in a straight line)', the adverb *riht(e)* 'due . . .' before a cardinal point is comparatively rare. Apart from the three occurrences in Or. (9/15, 12/27 and 14/15) I have counted only eight other examples; all but the following two are found in charters:[90]

. . . his broðra twegen geseagon ænne weg fram his mynstre rihte east on ðone heofon.[91]

. . . gange mæden man to wylle þe rihte east yrne 7 gehlade ane cuppan fulle forð mid ðam streame.[92]

In both cases the use of the cardinal point ('due east') is easily understandable, for it is conditioned by the context of miracle or superstition: the way up to heaven is in the direction of the (ideal) sunrise, and that is where the salutary water also flows to.

The statistical evidence for the meaning 'in a northerly (etc.) direction' of *norþryhte* (etc.) is supported by the following three examples from the Old English Bede, also found by means of the *Microfiche Concordance*. First, a reference to the location of Rochester:

Seo (= Hrofesceastre) is from Cantwarena byrig on feower 7 twentigum mila *westrihte*.[93]

89 'þanon west sceft rihte ofer ðone mor on þone weg' (*BCS* 1103/8 = S 669); 'sceaft ryht on cuddan cnoll easte weardne' (*BCS* 1343/2 + 4, 8, 11 and 15 = S 405).

90 *BCS* 674/24 ('swa on ge rihte norð east ofer ge manan hylle') = S 412; *BCS* 779/4 = S 514; *BCS* 945/10 = S 587; *BCS* 605/15 and 19 ('richte norð' twice; text above, n. 87) = S 1443. S 830 is ed. J. B. Davidson, 'On some Anglo-Saxon Charters at Exeter', *JBAA* 39 (1883), 259–303 (no. 8, line 2).

91 *Das altenglische Martyrologium*, ed. G. Kotzor, 2 vols., Bayerische Akademie der Wissenschaften, Phil.-hist. Klasse, Abhandlungen n.s. 88 (Munich, 1981) I, 40, lines 9–11 (21 March).

92 *Anglo-Saxon Magic and Medicine*, ed. J. H. G. Grattan and C. Singer, Publ. of the Wellcome Hist. Medical Museum n.s. 3 (London, 1952), 196.

93 *The Old English Version of Bede's Ecclesiastical History of the English People*, ed. T. Miller, EETS o.s. 95–6 (London, 1890–1), 104/24. 'Distat autem a Doruuerni milibus passuum ferme XXIIII ad occidentem' (II.3; *Bede's Ecclesiastical History of the English People*, ed. B. Colgrave and R. A. B. Mynors (Oxford, 1969), p. 142).

The bearing from Canterbury to Rochester is 286° on the compass scale; it is thus 16° north of due west. Secondly, a reference to the 'hill of Wilfare':

. . . Wilfaresdun. Seo is tyn milum *westrihte* from Cetreht weorþige.[94]

X mila *westrihte*.[95]

The exact position of 'the hill of Wilfare' (near Catterick, North Yorkshire) is unknown. The Latin 'contra solstitialem occasum' of the *Historia ecclesiastica*, however, makes it clear that due west is certainly not meant: the adjective *solstitialis* is used for the summer solstice on 21 June (the winter solstice would be called *brumalis*), and at the end of the longest day of the year the sun, in the latitude of Yorkshire (54° N), sets in the north-west (the precise direction is 313°, that is W 43° N).[96] Thirdly, a reference to the location of Britain as seen from Ireland:

We witan heonan noht feor oðer ealond *eastrihte*, þæt we magon oft leohtum dagum geseon.[97]

It is most unlikely that the Irish (*Scotti*), when they wanted to get rid of the Picts recently landed 'on the northern shores' of Ireland, would tell them that the stretch of coast they could sometimes see lay 'due east'; furthermore, looking towards Britain from the narrowest channel, near Belfast, the direction is between NE and ENE.

## CONCLUSIONS

The combined weight of these examples and the relative frequency of *-rihte* puts an end to the traditional semantic equation of the adverb *rihte* and the suffix *-rihte*. While the former defines an exact cardinal point, the latter gives only the general direction and is thus etymologically comparable not with the above-mentioned German *recht-* but with German *Richtung*. If Ohthere 'wanted to know how far north, to what northern latitude the land stretched' and 'sailed northwards along the land', then the need for a shift of the compass

94 *The Old English Version*, ed. Miller, p. 194/18. '. . . Uilfaresdun, id est Mons Uilfari, et est a uico Cataractone X ferme milibus passuum contra solstitialem occasum secretus' (III.14; *Bede's Ecclesiastical History*, ed. Colgrave and Mynors, p. 256).

95 Gloss in BL Cotton Tiberius C. ii, fol. 73, on the text in n. 94. Cf. N. R. Ker, *Catalogue of Manuscripts containing Anglo-Saxon* (Oxford, 1957), p. 261.

96 Information from Dr Karl August Keil, Augsburg. In astronomical terms the azimuth is 133°.

97 *The Old English Version*, ed. Miller, p. 28/13. 'Novimus insulam esse aliam non procul a nostra contra ortum solis, quam saepe lucidioribus diebus de longe aspicere solemus' (I.1; *Bede's Ecclesiastical History*, ed. Colgrave and Mynors, p. 18).

points no longer exists. The shift-theory itself has, I hope, been proved methodically inconsistent, impracticable and historically improbable. Information concerning directions in the Old English Orosius is to be taken within the frame of a sector that can vary between *c.* 90° and 45°. If, interpreted in this sense, some directional data in the Old English Orosius still seem to conflict with modern notions of geography, then other reasons will have to be found, such as the possible influence of a *mappa mundi*, as Derolez suggested,[98] the dependence on itineraries as proposed by Ellegård,[99] or, in the last resort, simply the lack of adequate knowledge. The idea of a shifted-orientation system should, however, be rejected once and for all.

98 'The Orientation System', pp. 264–8.
99 'De gamla nordbornas väderstrecksuppfattning'.

## APPENDIX

## *Occurrence of the (half-)cardinal points in the Old English Orosius*

| | Norþ | Suþ | East | West | NW | NE | SW | SE | Ratio of cardinal to half-cardinal points |
|---|---|---|---|---|---|---|---|---|---|
| Introduction | 3 | 6 | 4 | 5 | 1 | — | 1 | — | 18:2 |
| Asia | 19 | 13 | 13 | 15 | — | 1 | — | 1 | 60:2 |
| *Germania* | 15 | 10 | 15 | 7 | 3 | 3 | — | 1 | 47:7[2] |
| Ohthere and Wulfstan | 14 | 6 | 7 | — | 2? | — | — | — | 26:2 |
| Southern Europe | 12 | 12 | 9 | 13 | 5 | 2 | 4 | 2 | 46:13[2] |
| Africa | 7 | 10[1] | 8 | 8 | — | — | —[1] | — | 33:0 |
| Mediterranean islands | 8 | 7 | 5 | 9 | — | — | — | — | 29:0[2] |
| Total | 78 | 64 | 61 | 57 | 11 | 6 | 5 | 4 | 260:26 |

NOTE: The table contains all terms of direction including compounds (second element *-dæl*, *-healf*, *-weard*, *-ryhte*, *-gemæro* etc.) but excluding names like *Eastfrancan*, *Suþdene* or *Westsæ*.

[1] Bately's emendation of MS *suþan* into *be westansuþan* has here not been accepted.

[2] Terms consisting of two cardinal points connected by *and* (like 'be suþan him 7 be eastan sindon Bægware,' 12/26) have been counted as two cardinal directions: *Germania*, 12/26 and 13/16; southern Europe, 18/32, 18/35 and 19/7; Mediterranean islands, 20/30; only Wulfstan's 'west 7 norþ on sæ' (16/36) appears under NW (but with misgivings).

In my opinion there must be some reason for Or.'s avoidance here of expressions like *norþanwestan* etc. In four cases a personal pronoun (*him*, *hyre*) separates the two directions, in another four cases the preposition *be* is repeated; at 19/7, 'hyre is be westan garsecg 7 be norðan', the noun comes in between. The context each time allows the interpretation that the nation or country in question was supposed to be situated in two or parts of two (90°-) sectors; at 20/30 this has the express backing of the Latin Orosius ('ab occasu et septentrione'). For different opinions, cf. Ekblom, 'Alfred the Great as Geographer', pp. 127–8; Derolez, 'The Orientation System', p. 263; and *Orosius*, ed. Bately, p. 167.

# Anglo-Saxons on the mind

M. R. GODDEN

Peter Clemoes's essay '*Mens absentia cogitans* in *The Seafarer* and *The Wanderer*'[1] drew attention to important similarities between the psychological theories of the patristic tradition and the way in which Anglo-Saxon poets present the workings of the mind. Further exploration has begun to show how rich a seam he has opened up, of interest for Old English prose as well as poetry. Anglo-Saxon writers have important and often novel things to say about the nature of the mind and soul, and their discussions touch significantly on a problem of continuing interest, the relationship of psychological ideas and linguistic expression. What follows is the product of some rather tentative researches on this subject.

Two distinct traditions of thought about the mind are evident among the Anglo-Saxons. There is, first of all, a classical tradition represented by Alcuin of York (writing in Latin and on the continent, but influential for Anglo-Saxon vernacular writers), King Alfred and Ælfric of Eynsham, who were consciously working in a line which went back through late antique writers such as St Augustine and Boethius to Plato, but developed that tradition in interesting and individual ways. In particular they show the gradual development of a unitary concept of the inner self, identifying the intellectual mind with the immortal soul and life-spirit. Secondly, there is a vernacular tradition more deeply rooted in the language, represented particularly by the poets but occasionally reflected even in the work of Alfred and Ælfric. It was a tradition which preserved the ancient distinction of soul and mind, while associating the mind at least as much with passion as with intellect.

## THE CLASSICAL TRADITION

### Alcuin

The psychological literature of the Christian Middle Ages is said to begin with

[1] '*Mens absentia cogitans* in *The Seafarer* and *The Wanderer*', *Medieval Literature and Civilization. Studies in Memory of G. N. Garmonsway*, ed. D. A. Pearsall and R. A. Waldron (London, 1969), pp. 62–77.

Alcuin's *De animae ratione*.[2] Alcuin draws heavily on earlier writers, including Augustine, Cassian and probably Lactantius, but develops his own distinctive views, which are of considerable interest quite apart from their influence on later Anglo-Saxon writers using the vernacular. As his title indicates, his concern is with the soul, but he understands the soul as primarily an intellectual faculty. He begins, it is true, by acknowledging the old Platonic division of the soul into three parts, the rational, irascible and concupiscible:

Triplex est enim animae, ut philosophi uolunt, natura: est in ea quaedam pars concupiscibilis, alia rationalis, tertia irascibilis. Duas enim habent harum partes nobiscum bestiae et animalia communes, id est, concupiscentiam et iram. Homo solus inter mortales ratione uiget, consilio ualet, intelligentia antecellit. Sed his duobus, id est, concupiscentiae et irae, ratio, quae mentis propria est, imperare debet.

Here Alcuin seems to accept the traditional view, passed down to him through Augustine, that the soul embraces intellect, passion and desire, and is partially shared with the animals. However, he goes on to say that the principal part of the soul is the mind (*mens*) and is soon equating the soul with the rational mind: 'Una est anima, quae mens dicitur', he says; the soul or mind (*anima uel animus*) is 'an intellectual, rational spirit'; the soul (*anima*) is 'the spirit of life, but not of that life which is in animals, lacking a rational mind'. After the initial obeisance to Plato, Alcuin takes the soul as more or less identical with the conscious, rational mind.

In equating the soul with the mind Alcuin is consciously differing from Augustine, who consistently distinguishes the two. For Augustine the mind is only the better part of the human soul, which also has lesser parts which are shared with the animals. The soul is for him more a life-spirit than an intellectual spirit. 'Not the soul, therefore, but that which excels in the soul is called mind', he says.[3] The deliberateness of Alcuin's change is clear enough if one watches him reworking Augustine on the triad of memory, will and understanding:

Haec igitur tria, memoria, intellegentia, uoluntas, quoniam non sunt tres uitae sed una uita, nec tres mentes sed una mens, consequenter utique nec tres substantiae sunt sed una substantia. Memoria quippe quod uita et mens et substantia dicitur ad se ipsam dicitur; quod uero memoria dicitur ad aliquid relatiue dicitur.

(Augustine, *De trinitate* X.11)

Una est enim *anima* quae mens dicitur una uita et una substantia, quae haec tria habet in se: sed haec tria non sunt tres uitae, sed una uita; nec tres mentes, sed una mens; nec tres

[2] PL 101, cols. 639–50. See K. Werner, *Der Entwickelungsgang der mittelalterlichen Psychologie von Alcuin bis Albertus Magnus*, Denkschriften der Kaiserlichen Akademie der Wissenschaften, Phil.-hist. Classe 25 (Vienna, 1876), 70.

[3] Augustine, *De trinitate* XV.7, ed. W. J. Mountain, CCSL 50 (Turnhout, 1968), 475.

substantiae sunt, sed una substantia. Quod uero *anima* uel mens, uel uita, uel substantia dicitur, ad seipsam dicitur; quod uero memoria uel intelligentia uel uoluntas dicitur, ad aliquid relatiue dicitur. (Alcuin, *De animae ratione*, ch. 6; my italics)

It is possible that Alcuin's awareness of the issue was strengthened by his reading of Lactantius, who devotes a chapter of his *De opificio Dei* to the question whether the soul and mind are the same thing and presents some arguments on both sides, without coming to a conclusion.[4] In making the equation Alcuin broadly sets the pattern for subsequent academic discussion down to Aquinas, although writers differ on the degree of identity; but as we shall see, the primitive and popular notion of a soul quite distinct from the mind and devoid of psychological powers continues in vernacular literature.

Alcuin's interest is particularly in the way that the soul's mental activity mirrors God, as a testimony to its spiritual nature and high status: the soul, he says, 'is ennobled with the image and likeness of the Creator in its principal part, which is called the *mens*'. The interrelationships of memory, understanding and will mirror the divine Trinity. The mind's ability to conjure up images of things both known and unknown mimics God's work as creator. Its ability to be mentally present in an instant at any point in the world or in time imitates the divine ability to be everywhere at all times.

What is striking about this view of the soul's mental powers is Alcuin's insistence that the soul's likeness to God resides in its engagement with the real material world. For Augustine the imagination is a dubious faculty, and the mind resembles God only in so far as it contemplates eternal truths rather than 'the handling of temporal things'; engagement with the senses belongs to an inferior part of the soul.[5] For Alcuin it is the mind's power to remember or imagine people and places that shows its God-like quality. Even dreaming is a reflection of the soul's high powers in Alcuin's view.[6] He emphasizes that the soul is invisible, bodiless, without weight or colour, but it is also, and properly, engaged with material reality and illusions of reality. There is for him no essential conflict in the soul between the activity of the rational mind and the realms of imagination and sensation. Similarly, the Platonic and Augustinian notion of a war within the soul between reason, desire and passion finds some reflection in Alcuin's account, but he primarily sees the latter powers as spiritual forces, designed for the needs of the soul rather than the body.

[4] *De opificio Dei*, ed. S. Brandt, CSEL 27 (Vienna, 1893), ch. 18. Alcuin mentions Lactantius among the authors available at York (see M. Lapidge, 'Surviving Booklists from Anglo-Saxon England', above, p. 46); but since Lactantius is named in a list of Christian–Latin poets, it is probable that the *Carmen de aue phoenice* rather than *De opificio Dei* is in question.

[5] See esp. *De trinitate* X.7, XI.5 and XII.7.

[6] That, at least, seems to be what is meant by his statement that the soul is not even at rest when a man is asleep. Alcuin is perhaps influenced by Lactantius (*De opificio Dei*, ch. 18) again here.

Vicious or irrational behaviour in man is not simply the victory of the lower elements of the soul over the reason, but reflects the free will of the conscious mind, to choose good or evil.

For Alcuin, then, there is a unitary inner self identified both with the conscious rational mind and the immortal life-spirit and God-like in its power, including (indeed especially) the creative and poetic powers of imagination and dream.

## Alfred

The influence of Alcuin's treatise first appears in England itself with King Alfred's translation of Boethius's treatise *De consolatione Philosophiae*.[7] In bk III, met. ix Boethius gives an account of the universe drawn mainly from Plato's *Timaeus*. It is quite the most difficult and challenging section of the whole work, and became a focal point in the commentaries of the tenth century.[8] In the course of the poem Boethius refers in passing to the threefold soul. Most commentators agree that he is talking about the World Soul (the three parts are Same, Other and Being according to modern commentators, and earth, sea and sky according to some ninth- and tenth-century commentators), though some early commentaries also mention the Platonic notion of the threefold human soul.[9] Alfred takes it as a reference to the human soul and gives an explanation which is clearly drawn from Alcuin's account (quoted above, p. 272):

> Forþi ic cwæð þæt sio sawul wære þreofeald, forþamþe uðwitan secgað þæt hio hæbbe þrio gecynd. An ðara gecynda is þæt heo bið wilnigende, oðer þæt hio bið irsiende, þridde þæt hio bið gesceadwis. Twa þara gecynda habbað netenu swa same swa men; oðer þara is wilnung, oðer is irsung. Ac se man ana hæfð gesceadwisnesse, nalles na oðrum gesceaft; forði he hæfð oferþungen ealle þa eorðlican gesceafta mid geðeahte and mid andgite. Forþam seo gesceadwisnes sceal wealdan ægðer ge þære wilnunga ge þæs yrres, forþamþe hio is synderlic cræft þære saule. (81/16–25)

It is possible that the passage reached Alfred via a commentary or gloss, but no such commentary has yet been found, and in any case Alcuin's work was certainly available in England at a later date. It seems likely, therefore, that Alfred knew the whole work. His treatment of the soul and mind in his

7 *King Alfred's Old English Version of Boethius 'De Consolatione Philosophiae'*, ed. W. J. Sedgefield (Oxford, 1899) (hereafter Sedgefield); subsequent references are to page and line-number of this edition.

8 J. Beaumont, 'The Latin Tradition of the *De Consolatione Philosophiae*', *Boethius: his Life, Thought and Influence*, ed. M. Gibson (Oxford, 1981), pp. 278–305.

9 See P. Courcelle, *La Consolation de Philosophie dans la tradition littéraire* (Paris, 1967), pp. 272 and 276–7.

translation of Boethius shows distinct similarities to Alcuin's ideas. Boethius himself is careful to keep mind and soul separate. He nearly always refers to the centre of human consciousness as the *mens* or *animus*, occasionally as the *cor*. Desire of good is naturally implanted in the mind, he says; passions assail the mind; the mind rises to heaven to contemplate God. If he speaks of the soul, *anima*, it is for special reasons, as when he is referring to the soul which exists before and after the life of the individual, or the soul which is common to animals as well as men.[10] The soul is for him both greater than the human mind or consciousness, as pre-existing it, and less, since it is also found in animals. He seems, indeed, to suggest that the soul becomes the mind, and thereby loses some of its powers, when it becomes imprisoned within the body. Alfred, however, frequently substitutes *sawl* for Boethius's *mens* or *cor* in reference to the inner self,[11] and seems to treat mind (*mod*) and soul (*sawl*) as very closely related concepts. Boethius's seed of truth in the heart becomes Alfred's seed of truth dwelling in the soul when the soul and body are joined.[12] The health of minds, *salus animorum*, becomes *sawla hælo*.[13] *Sawl* and *mod* are interchanged in this passage, for instance, from the end of bk II, pr. 7:

> Sio sawl færð swiðe friolice to hefonum, siððan hio ontiged bið, and of þæm carcerne þæs lichoman onlesed bið. Heo forsihð þonne eall ðas eorðlican þing, and fægnað þæs þæt hio mot brucan þæs heofonlican siððan hio bið abrogden from ðæm eorðlican. Þonne þæt mod him selfum gewita bið Godes willan. (45/27–32)

The first two sentences parallel Boethius's statement about the *mens*; the last is Alfred's addition. Alfred seems to have been content with Boethius's view of the conscious rational mind as the essential inner self but wanted to emphasize its identity with the soul or immortal life-spirit. The same equation is made in Alfred's Soliloquies, and particularly in his great affirmation towards the end of that work: 'Nu ic gehyre þæt min sawel is æcu and a lifað, and eall þæt min mod and min gescadwisnesse goodra crefta gegadrad, þæt mot þa simle habban, and ic gehere æac þæt min gewit is æce.'[14] Indeed, Alfred offers a proof that the individual *mod* has existed since Creation and will survive the body, and has his persona reply: 'Me ðincð nu þæt þu hæbbe genoh swetole gesæd þæt ælces mannes sawl nu si, and a beo, and a were syððan god ærest þone forman man gescop.'[15] (This notion of the pre-existence of souls was later to be

[10] Boethius, *De consolatione Philosophiae* III, pr. xi and V, pr. ii.

[11] These changes are noted K. Otten, *König Alfreds Boethius* (Tübingen, 1964), p. 173. See also H. Schelp, 'Der geistige Mensch im Wortschatz Alfreds des Grossen' (unpubl. dissertation, Göttingen Univ., 1956).

[12] Boethius, *De consolatione Philosophiae* III, met. xi; Sedgefield, p. 95/13–14.

[13] Boethius, *De consolatione Philosophiae* IV, pr. vi; Sedgefield, p. 132/14–15.

[14] *King Alfred's Version of St Augustine's Soliloquies*, ed. T. A. Carnicelli (Cambridge, Mass., 1969), p. 91/21–4.

[15] *Ibid.* p. 91/9–11.

challenged by Ælfric.) The close association of soul and rational mind is also reflected in the one significant change which Alfred makes to Alcuin's statement of the Platonic doctrine of the threefold soul: where Alcuin had said that *ratio* is the special property of the mind ('ratio quae mentis propria est'), Alfred calls reason the distinctive property of the *soul* ('hio is synderlic cræft þære saule'), thus bringing the statement into line with Alcuin's later point that the soul is a rational spirit.

Perhaps because he identifies mind and soul Alfred tends to personalize the mind, treating it as a kind of inner self or personality. He frequently substitutes *mod* for the 'I' or 'me' of Boethius, and indeed creates a personification *Mod* who takes the place of the 'I' of the Latin text in the dialogue with Philosophy:

Þa ic þa þis leoð, cwæð Boetius, geomriende asungen hæfde, þa com þær gan in to me heofencund Wisdom, and þæt min murnende mod mid his wordum gegrette, and þus cwæð . . . Ða eode se Wisdom near, cwæð Boetius, minum hreowsiendum geþohte, and hit swa niowul þa hwæthwega up arærde; adrigde þa mines modes eagan, and hit fran bliþum wordum hwæðer hit oncneowe his fostermodor. Mid þam þe ða þæt Mod wið his bewende, þa gecneow hit swiðe sweotele his agne modor. (8/15–9/1)

*Mod* can be used as the subject of verbs: 'ælc mod wilnað soðes godes to begitanne' (53/11). The same tendency to use *mod* rather than the first person pronoun is evident in Alfred's translation of Gregory's *Regula pastoralis*.

Like Alcuin, Alfred attributes a very high status to the mind. In this he follows Boethius, but he sometimes takes the argument further. In bk v Boethius distinguishes four levels of understanding: *sensus*, or the physical senses, which the lowest animals have; *imaginatio* (a limited ability to recognize and understand shapes and identities), which is found in higher animals; reason, which is found in men; and *intelligentia*, a direct perception of ultimate truth and forms, which is the divine understanding. Alfred follows him on *sensus*, which he calls 'andgit'; has doubts over *imaginatio*, which he renders 'rædels' (presumably meaning conjecture) but then drops from discussion; agrees in ascribing reason (*gesceadwisnes*) to men; but then attributes *intelligentia*, translated as 'gewis andgit', certain or direct understanding, to angels and wise men, not just to God. Intellectually, in his view, man can reach the level of the angels. Similarly, he elsewhere interjects a remark that only men and angels have reason: 'nis nan þe hæbbe friodom and gesceadwisnesse buton englum and monnum'.[16] What seems particularly to interest Alfred in the Platonic theory of the threefold soul is not its power to explain the interplay of intellect and passion in man, but its placing of man intellectually above the animals and

[16] Sedgefield, p. 140/30–1.

close to God and the angels. Trapped within the human body is an essentially rational inner self, called *mod* or *sawl*; it has existed since the beginning of time and will survive the body till the end of time. It is in supreme control of the self, and grief, ignorance and vice are attributes of the *mod*, not of some lesser part of the soul or the body:

Eala þæt hit is micel cræft þæs modes for þone lichoman. Be swilcum and be swylcum þu miht ongitan þæt se cræft þæs lichoman bið on þam mode, and þætte ælcum men ma deriað his modes unþeawas. Ðæs modes unþeawas tioð eallne þone lichoman to him, and þæs lichoman mettrumnes ne mæg þæt mod eallunga to him getion.

(116/29–34)

Only once in his translation of Boethius does Alfred use the word *gast*, 'spirit', and that instance is intriguing. Boethius says that some activities of the individual are the result of natural impulses rather than conscious volition, and he gives as one example drawing breath while we sleep: 'quod in somno spiritum ducimus nescientes' (III, pr. 11). Alfred takes *spiritum* in a different sense and speaks of our spirit wandering abroad while we sleep, without us wishing it or having power over it:

Swa eac ure gast bið swiðe wide farende urum unwillum and ures ungewealdes for his gecynde, nalles for his willan; þæt bið þonne we slapað. (93/6–9)

The reference is presumably to dreaming. Alcuin mentions dreaming as an activity of the soul and also uses journeying outside the body as an image of thought and imagination, but he is insistent that the soul does not actually leave the body except at death. Alfred seems to be referring to actual journeying, and his emphasis that it is not guided by our conscious volition or control makes it unlikely that he sees it as an activity of the mind or soul as these are understood by him. Hence the use of *gast* rather than *sawl*. Alfred seems to be reflecting the common folk-belief that in dreams and trances an inner spirit or soul (usually quite distinct from the conscious mind) leaves the body and wanders about in the world.[17] The remark is prompted by a misunderstanding of Boethius's Latin text, but Alfred would hardly have interpreted the text in this way if he had not been thoroughly familiar with the idea and given it some credence. What it suggests is a distinction between the *sawl*, which is identified with the conscious mind and the immortal life-spirit, and the *gast*, which represents a kind of alien subconscious. But it may be that Alfred is referring to two quite separate traditions without seeking to reconcile them.

[17] Cf. J. Bremmer, *The Early Greek Concept of the Soul* (Princeton, NJ, 1983), esp. Appendix Two, 'The Wandering Soul in Western European Folk Tradition'.

## Ælfric

Writing a century later Ælfric draws on both Alcuin and Alfred for his own main treatise on the nature of the mind. The text exists in three versions, probably all by Ælfric, although the interrelationships (on which see Appendix, below, pp. 296–8) are complex: a Latin version, found in a Boulogne manuscript of Latin texts all associated with Ælfric; an English version, occurring as the first item in Ælfric's Lives of Saints collection; and a later English version surviving only in a twelfth-century manuscript.[18] My discussion will deal mainly with the second of these, the most familiar and accessible. The first third of the text is on the nature of God and the ways in which he differs from man and the rest of creation; several passages are adapted from Alfred's translation of Boethius,[19] others show resemblances to discussions of the same themes elsewhere in Ælfric's work. The remainder of the text is on the nature of the soul and is mainly drawn from Alcuin's *De animae ratione*.[20]

Ælfric accepts Alcuin's belief in the primarily intellectual character of the soul, and takes over his discussion of the soul's comprehensive imaginative power, its supreme control within the individual, the likeness between the Trinity and the soul's own triad of memory, understanding and will, and the soul's manifestation under different names according to its different intellectual functions. However, he seems uncomfortable with Alcuin's tendency to use soul and mind as interchangeable terms. Alcuin's reference to the mind as the principal part of the soul is omitted, and in the discussion of memory, will and understanding, where Augustine had spoken of the mind only and Alcuin had referred to the mind and the soul as equivalents, Ælfric carefully specifies the soul only:

> An sawul is and an lif and an edwist, þe þas ðreo þing hæfð on hire, and þas ðreo ðing na synd na ðreo lif ac an, ne þreo edwiste ac an. Seo sawul oððe þæt lif oððe seo edwist synd gecwædene to hyre sylfra.
>
> (LS, no. i, lines 114–18; cf. above, p. 272, for Augustine and Alcuin)

Similarly, Alcuin's statement that the soul or mind (*anima uel animus*) is an intellectual, rational spirit becomes in Ælfric simply 'the soul is a rational

[18] The two English versions are in *Ælfric's Lives of Saints*, ed. W. W. Skeat, EETS o.s. 76, 82, 94 and 114 (London, 1881–1900) (hereafter LS), no. i, and *Twelfth-Century Homilies in MS Bodley 34*, ed. A. O. Belfour, EETS o.s. 137 (London, 1909), no. ix. The Latin version is found in Boulogne, Bibliothèque Municipale, 63. All three versions have recently been meticulously edited by T. H. Leinbaugh, 'Liturgical Homilies in Ælfric's Lives of Saints' (unpubl. Ph.D. dissertation, Harvard Univ., 1980). I am exceedingly grateful to Professor Leinbaugh for permission to use his dissertation.

[19] Ælfric's use of Alfred's translation was noted W. F. Bolton, 'The Alfredian Boethius in Ælfric's *Lives of Saints* I', *N&Q* 19 (1972), 406–7.

[20] The source was identified P. Clemoes, '*Mens absentia cogitans*'.

spirit' ('seo sawul is gesceadwis gast': LS, no. i, line 171). Ælfric had used Alcuin's passage on the memory, will and understanding in an earlier work and there too omitted the reference to mind.[21] The reason is not, I think, that he shares Augustine's view that the soul includes lesser elements as well as the mind, for he clearly sees the soul as an intellectual power and attributes to the soul what Augustine would ascribe to the mind. For the same reason it is not that he shares the more popular view of the soul as the treasure to be guarded by the mental faculties. The soul is distinctly the thinking power or agent in Ælfric's account. The point is perhaps rather that, while seeing a very close association between the soul and the mind, he prefers to think of the mind as the instrument or locus of the soul rather than an inner personalized spirit or self, as Alcuin and Alfred see it. Thus Alcuin says that a man pictures Rome in his mind, and he describes the process as the mind returning to the memory and the soul forming a figure or image; soul and mind seem to be, once again, variations on synonyms. Ælfric speaks of the soul creating the city in her thought ('on hire geþohte') and, again, creating in her mind ('on hire mode') whatever she hears spoken of.[22] The distinction perhaps arose from an attempt to impose clarity on an inherited nomenclature. Having identified the *sawl* as the intellectual faculty Ælfric was perhaps reluctant to treat *mod* as a mere synonym, though he acknowledges that it is the name by which we refer to the soul in its knowledge and understanding rôles.

Because the soul is, in Ælfric's view, the intellectual, rational self, its possession distinguishes man from the beasts and places him close to the angels. This is the theme of the first section of his treatise, before he begins to draw on Alcuin. Ælfric's particular interest here and elsewhere is not so much the soul's likeness to God as the theme of hierarchy; that is, the place which man's possession of mind and soul allots him in the chain of being. Thus he takes from Alfred the distinction between God, who has no beginning or end; angels and men, who have beginning but no end; and animals who have both beginning and end:

Wast þu þæt þreo ðing sindon on þis middangearde? An is hwilendlic, ðæt hæfð ægðer ge fruman ge ende; and nat ðeah nanwuht ðæs ðe hwilendlic is, nauðer ne his fruman ne his ende. Oðer ðing is ece, þæt hæfð fruman and næfð nænne ende; and wat hwonne hit onginð, and wat þæt hit næfre ne geendað; þæt sint englas and monna saula. Þridde ðing is ece buton ende and buton anginne; þæt is God.

(Alfred's Boethius, 147/25–148/3)

Ðreo þing synd on middanearde, an is hwilwendlic, þe hæfð ægðer ge ordfruman ge ende, þæt synd nytenu and ealle sawul-lease þing þe ongunnan þa þa hi god gesceop,

[21] *The Homilies of the Anglo-Saxon Church: the First Part, containing the Sermones Catholici or Homilies of Ælfric*, ed. B. Thorpe, 2 vols. (London, 1843–6) (hereafter CH I) I, 288.

[22] *LS*, no. i, lines 130–6.

and æft geændiað and to nahte gewurðaþ. Oðer þing is ece, swa þæt hit hæfð ordfruman and næfð nænne ende, þæt synd ænglas and manna saula, þe ongunnen ða þa hi god gesceop, ac hi ne geendiað næfre. Đridde þing is ece, swa þæt hit næfð naðor ne ordfruman ne ende, þæt is se ana ælmihtiga god. (LS, no. i, lines 25–32)

Similarly he takes Alfred's version of Boethius, bk v, met. v to show the separation of man from the animals, but develops it through his own successive recastings to emphasize man's intellectual place with respect to animals, angels and God.[23]

The opening of the discussion of the soul shows the same interest in hierarchy. All *catholici* agree that the soul is like God and created by him but not made of his nature. The philosophers say that the soul is threefold, partially resembling the beasts but greater than them:

Uþwytan sæcgað þæt þære sawle gecynd is ðryfeald. An dæl is on hire gewylnigendlic, oðer yrsigendlic, þrydde gesceadwislic. Twægen þissera dæla habbað deor and nytenu mid us, þæt is gewylnunge and yrre. Se man ana hæfð gescead and ræd and andgit. (LS, no. i, 96–100)

(Ælfric is here drawing on Alcuin by way of his own Latin adaptation, but verbal resemblances to Alfred's version of the same passage suggest that Ælfric may have recalled that version.)

The identification of the soul with the intellectual faculty and the concern with man's place in the chain of being are reflected in Ælfric's insistent denial that animals have souls. St Augustine identifies the soul with the life-spirit and naturally attributes souls to animals, and indeed to all living beings; it is the rational soul, alias the mind, that man alone possesses.[24] Alcuin generally avoids the question, but one sentence in his treatise suggests a rejection of Augustine's view: 'the soul is the spirit of life, but not of that life which is in animals, lacking a rational mind'.[25] Alfred seems prepared to follow Boethius in attributing souls to animals, though his mind was perhaps uncertain on the issue. His use of Alcuin's passage on the threefold soul does not necessarily imply that animals have souls, as Otten has suggested,[26] especially since Alfred changes the last clause so as to say that reason (the element not shared by animals) is the special property of the soul. He recasts Boethius's clearest reference to animals having souls,[27] but two adjacent passages do seem to imply that the possession of a soul extends beyond human beings:

[23] See below, p. 296. [24] Cf., e.g., *De ciuitate Dei* VII.29.

[25] *De animæ ratione*, ch. 12. [26] *König Alfreds Boethius*, p. 175.

[27] 'Nam ne in animalibus quidem manendi amor ex animae uoluntatibus, uerum ex naturae principiis uenit' (Boethius, *De consolatione Philosophiae* III, pr. xi); 'Hwæt, þa nytenu ðonne and eac þa oðra gesceafta ma wilniað þæs þe hi wilniað for gecynde ðonne for willan' (Sedgefield, p. 93/9–11).

Ælc wuht wolde bion hal and libban, þara þe me cwucu ðincð; bute ic nat be treowum and be wyrtum, and be swelcum gesceaftum swelce nane sawle nabbað. (91/8–11)

Ne þearft ðu no tweogan ymbe þæt þe þu ær tweodest, þæt is be þam gesceaftum þe nane sawle nabbað; ælc þara gesceafta þe sawle hæfð, ge eac þa þe nabbað, willniað simle to bionne. (93/24–7)

Ælfric, however, repeatedly rejects the view that animals have souls. He makes the point at least a dozen times in his various writings, always, so far as I can discover, as a personal interjection in the argument of any authority that he is following. One might note, for instance, his rendering of one of Alcuin's *Interrogationes*:

Inter omnia animantia terrae nullum rationale inueniebatur nisi ille solus.

Nan nyten næfde nan gescead ne sawle buton he ana.[28]

(The reference is to Adam.) He similarly recasts a passage from Gregory the Great which implies that animals have souls though plants do not:

Sunt herbae et arbusta: uiuunt quidem, sed non sentiunt. Viuunt dico, non per animam, sed per uiriditatem . . . [citing I Cor. xv.36] . . . Bruta uero animalia sunt, uiuunt, sentiunt, sed non discernunt. (PL 76, col. 1214)

Gærs and treowa lybbað butan felnysse; hi ne lybbað na ðurh sawle, ac ðurh heora grennysse. Nytenu lybbað and habbað felnysse, butan gesceade: hi nabbað nan gescead, forðan ðe hi sind sawullease. (CH I, p. 302)

The point is often linked by Ælfric with animals' lack of reason, as in these two passages, but also with their own mortality, as in this incidental exchange in a saint's legend:

Canis enim pro factis malis in ignem aeternum non mittetur, sed semel mortuus, et corpore simul moritur et flatu.

Hund is sawulleas and on helle ne ðrowað.[29]

The soul is essentially both rational and immortal, and cannot therefore be ascribed to animals. Ælfric's repeated insistence on the point suggests that he was consciously taking issue with others, perhaps his contemporaries, perhaps his patristic authorities, perhaps Alfred.

Alcuin's passing reference to the subject in *De animae ratione* seems unlikely to have been enough to explain Ælfric's confidence and insistence on the

[28] *Ælfric's Anglo-Saxon Version of Alcuini Interrogationes Sigewulfi in Genesin*, ed. G. E. MacLean (Halle, 1883), ch. 33.

[29] *Acta Sanctorum*, ed. J. Bolland *et al.*, *Maii*, I, 374; *Ælfric's Catholic Homilies: the Second Series, Text*, ed. M. Godden, EETS s.s. 5 (London, 1979) (cited hereafter as CH II), no. xviii, lines 75–6.

point. Another possible influence is Cassiodorus, ch. 3 of whose *De anima* begins with the words '*anima* is properly applied to man, not to animals, because their life is based on the blood'.[30] One of Ælfric's statements on the subject, in fact possibly his earliest, is quite close to this:

He ne sealde nanum nytene ne nanum fisce nane sawle; ac heora blod is heora lif, and swa hraðe swa hi beoð deade, swa beoð hi mid ealle geendode. (CH I, p. 16)

That Ælfric knew Cassiodorus's treatise is suggested by a very close parallel in his main discussion of the mind, interjected in a passage that is otherwise drawn from Alcuin:

Paruulis enim ratio crescit longa meditatione, non anima.
(Cassiodorus, *De anima*, ch. 7, lines 57–8)

Paruulis enim ratio crescit, non anima, et proficiendo ad uirtutem non maior fit, sed melior, nec corporalem recepit quantitatem.
(Ælfric, Boulogne text, ed. Leinbaugh)

Gescead wexð on cildrum na seo sawul, and seo sawul þihþ on mægenum and ne bið na mare þonne heo æt fruman wæs ac bið betere, ne heo ne underfehð lichomlice mycelnysse. (LS, no. i, lines 110–12)

The latter part of Ælfric's interpolated comment resembles not Cassiodorus but the latter's source, Augustine's *De quantitate animae*:

. . . proficiendo enim ad uirtutem peruenit . . . quidquid anima cum aetate proficit . . . non mihi uidetur fieri maior, sed melior. (PL 32, col. 1051)

But the first part is clearly from Cassiodorus rather than Augustine. Ælfric perhaps added the point as an answer to the problem raised by associating the soul with the intellect, which might be taken to suggest that the dimension or 'degree' of soul in an individual varies with his intellectual powers. This may be one reason why he seems to shun an actual identification of soul with mind.

One other text known to Ælfric makes a point of denying that animals have souls: namely, a passage entitled *De sabbato* in a work known as the *Excerptiones Egberti*:

Homines creat in animabus et corporibus, et animalia et bestias sine animabus; omnis anima hominis a Deo datur, et ipse renouat creaturas suas.[31]

The work shows many close parallels with Ælfric's pastoral letters, and the *De sabbato* passage is undoubtedly closely related to a passage in one of his homilies:

30 Cassiodorus, *De anima*, ed. J. W. Halporn, CCSL 96 (Turnhout, 1973), ch. 3. I owe this reference to Father Osmund Lewry.

31 Ptd *Ancient Laws and Institutes of England*, ed. B. Thorpe, 2 vols. (London, 1840) II, 97–127; the passage from *De sabbato* is found on p. 102.

Deus Creator omnium creauit hominem in sexta feria, et in sabbato requieuit ab operibus suis, et sanctificauit sabbatum propter futuram significationem passionis Christi, et quietis in sepulchro. Non ideo requieuit quia lassus esset, qui omnia sine labore fecit, cuius omnipotentia non potest lassari; et sic requieuit ab operibus suis, ut non alias creaturas quam antea fecerat postea fecisset. Non fecit alias creaturas postea, sed ipsas quas tunc fecit, omni anno usque in finem seculi facit. Homines creat in animabus et corporibus, et animalia et bestias sine animabus; omnis anima hominis a Deo datur, et ipse renouat creaturas suas, sicut Christus in Euuangelio ait: 'Pater meus usquemodo operatur, et ego operor.' . . . Et nos ipsi debemus esse spiritaliter sabbatum sabbatizantes, id est, uacantes ab operibus seruitutis, id est, peccatis.

On six dagum geworhte god ealle gesceafta . and geendode hi on ðam seofoðan . þæt is se sæternesdæg . þa gereste he hine . and ðone dæg gehalgode; Ne gereste he hine for ði þæt he werig wære . se ðe ealle ðing deð buton geswince . ac he geswac ða his weorces; He geswac ðæs dihtes ealra his weorca . ac he ne geswac na to gemenigfyldenne þæra gesceafta æftergengnyssa; God geswac ða his weorces . swa þæt he na ma gecynda siððan ne gesceop . ac swa ðeah he gemenigfylt dæghwomlice þa ylcan gecynd swa swa crist cwæð on his godspelle; Pater meus usque modo operatur . et ego operor; . . . Oðer restendæg is us eac toweard . . . gif we nu ðeowtlicera weorca . þæt sind synna geswicað; (CH II, no. xii, 274–84 and 308–11)

However, the status of the *Excerptiones* is unclear. It is a rather fluid and unstructured assembly of mainly ecclesiastical canons and biblical and patristic excerpts on the duties of the clergy and rules for the laity, varying considerably in order and content from one manuscript to another, and thought to have been compiled in late Anglo-Saxon England. The most recent editor[32] argues that the author was one Hucarius, a deacon of St German's in Cornwall, but the evidence is very slight. The *De sabbato* passage occurs in only one copy of the collection, in the eleventh-century Wulfstan manuscript, now London, BL Cotton Nero A. i, and it is so extraordinarily close in thought and expression to Ælfric's work (there are parallels with other homilies as well as the one quoted) that one must at least entertain the possibility that Ælfric himself wrote it; he may, indeed, have had a hand in compiling the whole collection. If the *De sabbato* passage is not by him it shows that someone else in Ælfric's time took an interest in the question of animals and souls, but it is hardly enough to have determined Ælfric's own views on the subject.

The topic is closely associated in Ælfric's thought with his views on the origin of the individual soul. Augustine discusses various different theories, including the possibility that the soul is derived from the parents, without coming to a conclusion.[33] Cassiodorus does likewise, referring back to

32 R. A. Aronstam, 'The Latin Canonical Tradition in Late Anglo-Saxon England: the *Excerptiones Egberti*' (unpubl. Ph.D dissertation, Columbia Univ., 1974).

33 *De libero arbitrio*, ed. W. M. Green, CCSL 29 (Turnhout, 1970), ch. 21 (pp. 309–12).

Augustine.[34] Alcuin, in his *De animae ratione*, offers only the general statement that the soul derives from God. Alfred, as we have seen, states firmly in his version of Augustine's *Soliloquia* that 'each man's soul has existed since the first man was created'.[35] I do not know where he found this idea. It is not from his main source (Augustine's *Soliloquia*) and the editors have suggested no parallels; the pre-existence of souls is taken for granted by Boethius, but there is nothing to match Alfred's proof. Ælfric sets his face firmly against such a view, insisting that the soul does not pre-exist the body but is shaped by God in an individual act of creation and implanted in the foetus:

Ælces mannes sawl bið þurh God gesceapen . . . Þæs mannes antimber bið of ðam fæder and of ðære meder, ac God gescypð þone lichaman of ðam antimbre, and asent on þone lichaman sawle. Ne bið seo sawl nahwar wunigende æror, ac God hi gescypð þærrihte, and beset on ðone lichaman, and læt hi habban agenne cyre.

(CH I, p. 292)

The point recurs repeatedly in his work, sometimes – as here – in opposition to the doctrine of the pre-existence of souls, sometimes in opposition to the theory (known as traducianism) that souls are derived from parents, sometimes specifying both, as in the following:

God gescipð ælce dæge edniwe sawle and on lichaman geliffæst, swa swa we leorniað on bocum, and þa sawla ne beoð nahwær gesceapene ær þan þe God hi asent to þam gesceapenan lichaman on heora moder innoþum, and hi swa men wurþað. Nu ge magon tocnawan þæt ure sawla ne cumað of fæder ne of meder, ac se heofenlica Fæder gescipð þone lichaman and hine geliffæst mid sawle.[36]

It even finds a place in his Latin *uita* of St Æthelwold, where the saint's mother feels the soul entering the unborn child while attending mass, and Ælfric notes that this is an argument against the traducianist view:

Iterum ipsa mater quadam die stans in aecclesia stipata ciuibus, causa sanctam missam audiendi, sensit uenisse animam pueri, quem gestabat in utero, et intrasse in eum, sicut postea ipse sanctus, qui nasciturus erat, iam episcopus, gaudendo nobis narrauit. Ex quo ostenditur eum electum Deo extitisse etiam antequam nasceretur, et animam hominis non a patre uel a matre uenire sed a solo creatore unicuique dari.[37]

None of Ælfric's discussions of the topic comes from the sources he was following; they are mainly successive reworkings of the same main points,

[34] *De anima*, ch. 9. [35] *Soliloquies*, ed. Carnicelli, p. 91/9–11.

[36] *Homilies of Ælfric: a Supplementary Collection*, ed. J. C. Pope, 2 vols., EETS o.s. 259–60 (London, 1967–8), no. ii, line 220.

[37] In *Three Lives of English Saints*, ed. M. Winterbottom (Toronto, 1972), p. 18 (ch. 3). The point also appears in Wulfstan's *Vita S. Athelwoldi* (ed. *ibid.* pp. 33–63, at 35–6), but it is so characteristic of Ælfric's thought as to amount to an argument for the priority of his version.

usually in the context of Creation. His assurance on the point is striking: when he remarks in his very first homily that 'some people wonder where the soul comes from, the father or the mother; I say, from neither . . .', he is, after all, referring not to the idle speculations of contemporaries but to the uncertainties of such authorities as Augustine and Cassiodorus as well as rejecting the certainties of Alfred. The 'as we read in books' (*swa swa we leorniað on bocum*) of the passage quoted above (p. 284) is provocatively vague; the source is in fact Ælfric's own Second Series homily no. xii, which is here, if anything, drawing on his first homily in the First Series and the passage *De sabbato*, which has just the brief but probably significant 'omnis anima hominis a Deo datur'. (The whole passage is reworked yet again in Ælfric's *Hexameron*.)

Both doctrines on which Ælfric takes such a firm stand have obvious connections with his views on the mind and the soul. The soul is not just a life-spirit but a rational and immortal spirit unique to man and created specifically by God for each individual, to endow him simultaneously with life and understanding. It is primarily an intellectual inner self, whose mental activity imitates God and distinguishes man from the beasts. The capacity for passion and lust is a reflection not of some lower part of the soul but of the free will, to choose good or evil, which is granted to the soul when it is created. Soul and mind are thus very closely associated, although as a matter of terminology Ælfric prefers, at least when being careful, to call the intellectual inner self *sawl*, reserving *mod* for the locus or instrument of the soul's thought.

## THE VERNACULAR TRADITION

What we have seen so far are ideas about the mind and soul articulated by writers who were building on the late antique intellectual tradition and familiar with the traditional Latin terminology. That other Anglo-Saxons held quite different notions of the soul is suggested by a passing remark in Ælfric's *De temporibus anni*, rejecting the theory that the soul is breath: 'Nis na seo orðung ðe we utblawað . and innateoð ure sawul . ac is seo lyft þe we on lybbað on ðisum deadlicum life.'[38] The remark is repeated in the two English versions of his homily on the soul,[39] but nothing in the context or sources of either work seems particularly to have prompted it. Its absence from the Latin version of the treatise suggests that the ambiguity of Latin *spiritus* is not at issue here. Presumably the primitive identification of soul with breath was current among Ælfric's readers or listeners.

38 *Ælfric's De temporibus anni*, ed. H. Henel, EETS o.s. 213 (London, 1942), 72.

39 LS, no. i, lines 214–16; Belfour, no. ix, p. 94/11–12.

Outside the classical tradition consciously followed by Alfred and Ælfric, views on the mind and soul are not developed in any detail or rigour by Anglo-Saxon writers, but there are often important implications in the way that they talk about the mind, thought and emotion, and in the terminology they use. The intimate relationship which exists between the psychological ideas developed by a particular culture and the language in which those ideas are expressed was emphasized by I. A. Richards in his *Mencius on the Mind*. More recently the anthropologist Rodney Needham has discussed the linguistic aspects of the concept of belief, and suggested that the psychological terms used by different cultures may describe quite different inner experiences:

> If the inner states hypothetically in question are universal, it is to be expected that any language will have responded to them. On the other hand, we have to contemplate the possibility that some other linguistic tradition will have established (not simply named) an inner state for which English makes no provision.[40]

This is clearly as true of the language of the Anglo-Saxons as of living languages. As an example one might take the way in which emotion is expressed in Anglo-Saxon. The Modern English use of 'feel', adapted from terms of sensory perception, does not seem to occur in Old English; there is no equivalent to *feeling* sad, angry, hostile, affectionate; the verbs *gefelan* and *gefredan* seem only to be used of physical sensation. On the other hand it is quite common to speak of 'taking' various mental states, such as anger or love, using the verb *niman*: 'nimð lufe to Gode', 'gif ure mod nimð gelustfullunge', 'nam micelne graman and andan', 'genam nið', 'nam oferhygd', 'naman ondan', 'niman geleafan', 'niman mod', 'genom wynne', 'genaman æfest' and 'niman ellen'. A few similar usages do survive in Modern English but seem to be either rather archaic, petrified phrases ('take courage') or used to suggest a rather wilful, often artificial, variety of emotion ('take delight', 'take offence', 'take umbrage'). The Old English examples do not seem to be similarly restricted in tone. There was presumably some rooted sense that passions, or feelings towards other people and things, did not just take hold of one from outside or inside but involved, at some level, an act of will. Such uses link with the prevalence of active, simplex verbs for psychological states where Modern English has to use a periphrastic form with an adjective: *modigian* 'to be proud', *yrsian*, 'to be angry', *murnan*, 'to be sad', *gladian*, 'to be happy'. Linguistically, at least, passions can resemble mental actions rather than mental states.

A different kind of example is the term *ingehyd*, as it is used by Ælfric. Literally it means inner thought or inner mind, but it translates both *scientia*

40 *Circumstantial Deliveries* (Berkeley and London, 1981), p. 59. See also the same author's *Belief, Language and Experience* (Chicago and London, 1972).

and *conscientia* in Latin and it is impossible to find a close equivalent for it in either Latin or Modern English. It very often means something like 'inner disposition', a quality of will, perhaps the direction of the will, but sometimes an aspect of love: 'let us love God with good *ingehyd*'; the church opens her *ingehyd* and secret thoughts to Christ; the ascetic life and *synderlic ingehyd*, 'solitary dedication'(?), of anchorites; St Martin retained inwardly the *muneclice ingehyd* ('monastic disposition'(?), but translating *uirtus*) while outwardly maintaining the rôle of a bishop; the sinful cleric perverts the *ingehyd* of his flock.[41] When it translates *conscientia* it seems to mean the inner mind or consciousness of innocence or guilt: 'our glory is the testimony of our *ingehyd*'; the righteous is afraid on the Day of Judgement, for although he has pleased God through *ingehyd*, the *ingehyd* (= *conscientia*) trembles there, frightened by the great terror of the general judgement.[42] When it translates *scientia* it means knowledge or understanding, but the only really informative context relates it to intuitive understanding rather than learned knowledge: St Matthew reports that the Holy Ghost at Pentecost gave the apostles *ingehyd* of all wisdom and all languages.[43] The term seems to cover both cognition and volition, as well as the inner self from which they proceed. Similar uses can be found in other Anglo-Saxon writers, and the freedom and confidence with which Ælfric uses the term suggests that it did represent a precise and meaningful concept.

The Anglo-Saxon terms for the mind itself present quite the most intriguing implications. The standard word in ordinary prose is *mod*, used to designate the locus or instrument of thought and imagination and, in Alfred at least, the intellectual faculty. In Anglo-Saxon generally, however, *mod* also carries the meaning 'courage' and 'pride', and its derivatives all point in the direction of these latter meanings: *modig*, 'brave', 'proud', *modignes* and *ofermod*, 'pride', 'arrogance', *modigian*, 'to be arrogant', *ormod*, 'devoid of spirit', 'hopeless'. These are quite different from the derivatives of the Latin and Modern English terms for the mind, such as 'mental', 'magnanimous', 'mindful', 'high-minded'. In so far as it refers to a power rather than a location or centre of consciousness, *mod* seems to convey to many Anglo-Saxon writers not so much the intellectual, rational faculty but something more like an inner passion or wilfulness, an intensification of the self that can be dangerous. Authors often in fact speak – especially in verse texts[44] – of the need to control or restrain the *mod*. *The Seafarer* and *Maxims I* speak in similar terms on this point:

[41] CH II, nos. xix, line 60, and xl, lines 194–5; CH I, p. 544; CH II, no. xxxiv, lines 119–20; and CH I, p. 514, respectively.

[42] CH II, no. xxxix, lines 68 and 171–4.

[43] CH II, no. xxxii, lines 102–3.

[44] Verse texts are quoted from *The Exeter Book*, ed. G. P. Krapp and E. V. K. Dobbie, ASPR 3 (Columbia and London, 1936).

Stieran mon sceal strongum mode, ond þæt on staþelum healdan.
(*The Seafarer*, line 109)

Styran sceal mon strongum mode. Storm oft holm gebringeþ.
(*Maxims I*, line 50)

A patient man is defined as one who has controlled his *mod*:

Sum gewealdenmod
þafað in geþylde. (*The Gifts of Men*, lines 70b–1a)

Restraining a murderous spirit seems to be what is meant by controlling the mind in *Beowulf*, lines 1150b–1a:

ne meahte wæfre mod
forhabban in hreþre.

A very similar point occurs in prose, when Ælfric remarks that anger causes a man to lose control of his *mod* and thus commit murder and other great crimes:

Se feorða leahtor is ira, þæt is on englisc weamodnyss, seo deð þæt se man nah his modes geweald, and macað manslihtas and mycele yfelu. (LS, no. xvi, line 286).

(The implication seems to be that it is the *mod* set free of restraint that initiates murder.) A more interesting example is Ælfric's presentation of *mod* as a slightly wilful, independent faculty, less rational than the self, in a discussion of temptation:

Deofol tiht us to yfele, ac we sceolon hit onscunian, and ne geniman nane lustfullunge to ðære tihtinge: gif þonne ure mod nimð gelustfullunge, þonne sceole we huru wiðstandan, þæt ðær ne beo nan geðafung to ðam yfelan weorce. Seo yfele tihting is of deofle; ðonne bið oft þæs mannes mod gebiged to ðære lustfullunge, hwilon eac aslit to ðære geðafunge; forðon þe we sind of synfullum flæsce acennede. (CH I, p. 176)

That such expressions reflect not simply two or three distinct referents of the same word but a genuine way of thinking about the mind is suggested by the appearance of similar statements using other words for the mind:

Hyge sceal gehealden, hond gewealden (*Maxims I*, line 121)

Heald hordlocan, hyge fæste bind (*Homiletic Fragment II*, line 3)

Þæt biþ in eorle indryhten þeaw,
þæt he his ferðlocan fæste binde,
healde his hordcofan, hycge swa he wille. (*The Wanderer*, lines 12–14)

Such expressions invite us to see a distinction between the conscious self and some other, inner power which we might legitimately gloss as 'mind' though it could also be translated in particular contexts as 'passion', 'temper', 'mood'.

As well as *mod*, Anglo-Saxon poetry uses for the concept 'mind' the poetic terms *hyge*, *sefa* and *ferð*, besides various compounds based on these elements. These seem to be used more or less interchangeably and are generally rendered in Modern English as 'heart', 'mind', 'spirit' or 'soul', according to context and the translator's sense of the poet's meaning. The kind of uncertainty this can create is indicated by Tolkien's comments on *Beowulf*, lines 1150b–1a ('ne meahte wæfre mod / forhabban in hreþre'); this might, Tolkien suggests, refer to Finn's soul and therefore his death, to be translated 'his soul was sped (*or rather*, he could not keep his soul from wandering)', or it might refer to the feelings of Hengest and his fellow-Danes, in which case it should be rendered 'the deep-stirred feelings could not be prisoned in their breast'.[45] Tolkien rules out the former on the grounds of narrative logic, but it could probably have been ruled out on linguistic grounds. Whatever case there might be for rendering *mod* as soul in the sense of inner self, it does not seem to be used in poetry for the spirit which leaves the body at death or survives death. *Sawl* is the word used for that in *Beowulf* and other Old English poetry, and indeed in prose, along with *gast*, while *mod* refers to thought and emotion. In fact *Beowulf* and most other Anglo-Saxon poems seem to preserve a distinction, comparable to that found in Homer,[46] between the *sawl* which is invoked with reference to death and the afterlife but has no psychological powers or activities, and the inner self or mind (*mod*, *hyge* etc.) which is responsible for thought and emotion.[47] As we have seen, Alfred and Ælfric, working consciously in a classical tradition of psychological theory, actively countered this distinction. Something very like it, however, seems to operate in the Anglo-Saxon dialogues of the body and the soul, both in prose and verse, where the soul after death attributes to the body all the acts and decisions made during life which have condemned the soul to its everlasting fate;[48] the soul in this view is the helpless victim (or beneficiary) of a separate mental faculty which is associated with the body. The same distinction is made, more explicitly, in the Early Middle English psychological allegory *Sawles Warde*[49] where the soul is God's precious treasure deposited in the house called Man, which is ruled and guarded by the mental faculty Wit. (The distinction, significantly, does not

45 J. R. R. Tolkien, *Finn and Hengest*, ed. A. Bliss (London, 1982), p. 140.

46 Cf. Bremmer, *The Early Greek Concept*, pp. 14ff.

47 One possible exception to this pattern is the poem *Guthlac A*, where *gast* is used of both the inner self which experiences grief and the departing soul, and where *mod* is used once (line 26) with a possible reference to the soul departing in death; but the interpretation of line 26 is very uncertain (see the most recent edition of the poem by J. Roberts, *The Guthlac Poems of the Exeter Book* (Oxford, 1979), pp. 127–8).

48 See the texts ptd R. Willard, 'The Address of the Soul to the Body', *PMLA* 50 (1935), 957–83.

49 Ed. most recently in *Early Middle English Verse and Prose*, ed. J. A. W. Bennett and G. V. Smithers, rev. ed. (Oxford, 1968), pp. 247–61.

operate in the Latin source,[50] where the house is *conscientia*, the master *animus* and the treasures to be guarded are the virtues; the soul or *anima* plays no part, presumably because it is deemed as comprehending *animus* rather than being distinct from it.) In such works the existence of the soul, like that of Homer's ψῦχή, only becomes evident under the threat or fact of death; it is quite different from the active mental faculty.

The classical and vernacular traditions differ on the locus of the mind. Plato had located the rational soul in the head, the irascible or spirited soul in the breast and the concupiscible soul in the abdomen; Cassiodorus devotes a chapter to the question of the location of the soul, and expresses a preference for the head.[51] Nothing is said on the question in Alcuin's treatise or Alfred's Boethius or Ælfric's homily, and the omission appears to be deliberate; Alfred in translating Boethius deletes every one of his source's references to the heart as seat of the soul or mind, substituting *mod* or *gewit* or *sawl*, and when Ælfric argues that 'head' in a particular biblical text stands for the mind he significantly does not use the argument that the mind is located in the head.[52] The point may be that all three authors closely associate the intellectual faculty, whether called mind or soul, with the life-spirit, which has to be seen as pervading all parts of the body – a point which both Alcuin and Ælfric make. Outside these texts, however, there is ample evidence that the mind is normally thought of as residing in the heart or thereabouts. The phrase 'thoughts of the heart' (*heortan geþohtas*) occurs in the *Maxims* and in *The Wife's Lament* as well as in *The Seafarer*. The *Maxims* also place the mind in the *breostum*, and *The Wanderer* places it in the *breostcofa*. There are frequent references too to the *hreþer* as the seat of the mind or place of thought and emotion: 'I can tell you more than you, *hygecræftig*, can comprehend with *mod* in your *hreþer*' (*The Order of the World*); 'let not anger overpower you in *hreþer*' (*Precepts*). *Hreþer* is glossed as 'bosom' or 'breast' in Bosworth–Toller, but uses seem to suggest something more like 'lungs' or the part of the body containing the lungs. Possibly, as Onians argues,[53] this goes back to a traditional association of the soul with breath (a view mentioned by Ælfric, as we have seen), though it is not clear that this association extended to the mental faculty as well as the life-spirit. In texts where Ælfric is not being rigorous he too refers to the heart and breast as the seat of thought and passion, just as Alfred in his Pastoral Care seems quite happy to adopt St Gregory's uses of *cor* and *pectus*, rendered as *heorte* and *breost*, for the locus of thought and feeling. Indeed, at one point in the Boethius,

50 'De Custodia Interioris Hominis', *Memorials of St Anselm*, ed. R. W. Southern and F. S. Schmitt (London, 1969), pp. 355–60.

51 *De anima*, ch. 10.

52 CH I, p. 612.

53 R. B. Onians, *The Origins of European Thought about the Body, the Mind, the Soul, the World, Time and Fate* (Cambridge, 1951).

where he is not following his sources closely, he introduces *heorte* as the place where man's inner self is locked up: fame 'opens the secrecy of a man's heart and penetrates the locks of another's heart'[54] (a rather cryptic extension of Boethius's point about speech).

As perhaps follows from its location in the heart, the mind is seen as both a faculty of thought and a faculty of feeling or emotion. It is common to think with the *mod* but also possible to love with it: 'ic for tæle ne mæg / ænigne moncynnes mode gelufian'.[55] In *Beowulf*, *mod* is used of wisdom ('on mode frod', 'mid modes snyttrum') and the idea of building Heorot came from Hrothgar's *mod*, but the word is also much used of grief and happiness ('murnende mod', 'modes myrhðe'). *The Wanderer* refers to the *mod* darkening with despair, and Ælfric too says that someone grew dark in *mode*, probably meaning angry.[56] *Hyge* is used similarly of both thought and emotion. This perhaps helps to explain the tendency to refer to emotion as a mental action: the same 'mind' is deemed to be responsible for both conscious decisions and 'feelings' of passion. It helps to explain, too, the concept of 'mind' as an unruly, wayward, passionate faculty.

Two poems in particular, *The Wanderer* and *The Seafarer*, show a rich and complex picture of the workings of the mind, and I should like finally to turn to these.

## '*The Wanderer*'

*The Wanderer* uses various apparently synonymous terms for the mind, *mod*, *hyge*, *modsefa* and *ferð*:

> Ne mæg werig *mod*   wyrde wiðstondan,
> ne seo hreo *hyge*   helpe gefremman.
> Forðon domgeorne   dreorigne oft
> in hyra breostcofan   bindað fæste;
> swa ic *modsefan* minne sceolde . . .   (15–19)
>
> Se þonne þisne wealsteal   wise geþohte
> ond þis deorce lif   deope geondþenceð,
> frod in *ferðe* . . .   (88–90a)
>
> Swa cwæð snottor on *mode* . . .   (111a)

The mind's location is the *breostcofa*, 'breast-coffer' (line 18), which is presumably what is referred to metaphorically as the *ferðloca* and *hordcofa* at lines 13–14a:

[54] Sedgefield, p. 28/14. Similarly, Alfred sometimes introduces *heorte* as the seat of the mind/soul when turning into verse his original prose translations of Boethius's metres.

[55] *Resignation*, 106b–7.

[56] LS, no. xxv, line 329.

. . . þæt he his ferðlocan fæste binde,
healde his hordcofan . . .

Similarly, thought is located in the *hreðer* at line 72a, grief in the heart (49b) and in the breast (113a). Rather strikingly, the 'mind'-words are associated almost exclusively with emotion rather than with thought. The mind is weary (*werig mod*, 15a; *werigne sefan*, 58b), troubled or turbulent (*hreo hyge*, 16a), caught up in care or anxiety (*modcearig*, 2b) and inclined to darken (59). The mind is the source of wisdom and the place of dream-fantasies (41–4), and it can create imaginary figures and illusions (50–5). Conscious thought and understanding, however, are attributed not to the mind but to the self: 'hycge swa he wille' (14b), 'gemon he selesecgas' (34a), 'se þonne þisne wealsteal wise geþohte' (88). The most striking sentence is the one at lines 58–60:

Forþon ic geþencan ne mæg geond þas woruld
for hwan modsefa min ne gesweorce,
þonne ic eorla lif eal geondþence . . .

The lines sharply distinguish between the mind or *modsefa* as agent of emotion and 'I' as subject or agent of thinking. Further than that, they suggest an astonishing dislocation between the self and the mind. Ever since Descartes the mind has been the one thing that has been an open book to the self. The poet here implies that the *mod* has its reasons for not darkening (that is, becoming black and bitter or black and gloomy) but they are unknown to the possessor of the mind, who can only think about the world and be aware that his mind has unaccountably remained undarkened; or perhaps he implies that the mind has a fortitude whose origins are not the conscious thought and understanding of the speaker. The *modsefa* seems to be an inner self or consciousness which the conscious self cannot penetrate. (One could of course render *modsefa* as something like 'disposition'; we are close perhaps to that semantic element of *mod* which enabled it to develop into ModE 'mood'. Yet the sum of all the other uses of *mod* and related words within this poem force us to think of it as a substance or entity rather than a quality belonging to the mind.) Something similar is suggested by lines 70–2:

Beorn sceal gebidan, þonne he beot spriceð,
oþþæt collenferð cunne gearwe
hwider hreþra gehygd hweorfan wille.

That is, the thought of the heart stems from an inner self with its own volition, which a man needs to learn to understand and anticipate, since it can, presumably, dictate his actions in spite of his conscious self. Indeed, the whole poem dwells on the separation of self and mind. It speaks of the obligation to keep the mind captive, to fetter it, and also of the compulsion to send it over the sea; uncontrolled, the mind hallucinates and fantasizes. Throughout the poem there is a recognition of two levels or centres of consciousness, one associated with awareness and perception and the other (for which the 'mind'-words are mainly used) associated with emotion and volition, memory and imagination. It is a distinction that perhaps lies behind the opening paradox of the poem, as the solitary wanderer goes on waiting for, and perhaps experiences, divine favour despite all the evidence presented to his conscious mind of the fixity of his fate. It is, intriguingly, the emotional, subconscious mind, with its refusal to darken, that ultimately carries the values of the poem.

## '*The Seafarer*'

*The Seafarer* similarly associates the 'mind'-words (*mod*, *ferð* and *hyge*) particularly with emotion and volition:

hungor innan slat
merewerges mod . . . (11b–12a)

ne ænig hleomæga
feasceaftig ferð frefran meahte . . . (25b–6)

Ne biþ him to hearpan hyge ne to hringþege,
ne to wife wyn ne to worulde hyht. (44–5)

There is again a dislocation of self from mind, with the latter functioning here as an intense inner will battering at the reluctant self:

Forþon cnyssað nu
heortan geþohtas, þæt ic hean streamas,
sealtyþa gelac sylf cunnige;
monað modes lust mæla gehwylce
ferð to feran, þæt ic feor heonan
elþeodigra eard gesece. (33b–8)

*Ic* seems here to be almost identified with the body rather than the mind, though perhaps it would be better to define it as that aspect of the self which controls the body's actions. The poem reverses the psychological situation of *The Wanderer*, with the mind no longer fettered by the self but escaping and assailing it, urging it to action:

Forþon nu min hyge hweorfeð ofer hreþerlocan,
min modsefa mid mereflode
ofer hwæles eþel hweorfeð wide,
eorþan sceatas, cymeð eft to me
gifre ond grædig, gielleð anfloga,
hweteð on hwælweg hreþer unwearnum
ofer holma gelagu. (58–64a)

As Peter Clemoes has shown,[57] there is a striking similarity between this picture of the mind travelling over land and sea and Alcuin's account of the mind/soul flying over lands and seas in the act of imagination. F. N. M. Diekstra has pointed to further parallels with Lactantius and Ambrose, who similarly describe the act of memory or imagination as a journey of the mind.[58] What *The Seafarer* seems to be offering, however, is an image of volition rather than imagination, calling the speaker to a journey; it develops the point already made at lines 33b–8 (quoted above) where the *modes lust* continually urges the seafarer to make the voyage to the land of strangers.

Like *The Wanderer*, then, the poem distinguishes two centres of consciousness: an inner, urgent, passionate personality and a more reluctant self which controls action.[59] (Neither is explicitly identified with the soul, which is mentioned specifically only at line 100, in a reference to death and judgement; indeed, lines 94–6 imply that thinking with the mind (*hyge*) is the work of the body.) Whether the 'mind'-words refer exclusively to the inner spirit is unclear in this poem. The clause at lines 36–7a, 'monað modes lust . . . ferð to feran', is rendered by Hamer 'the heartfelt wishes urge the spirit to venture' and by Bradley 'my mind's desire . . . urges the soul to set out'.[60] If the translators intend a distinction between 'heart' and 'spirit' or between 'mind' and 'soul', it is not one in any way suggested by OE *mod* and *ferð* as they are used in the poetry generally; if such a distinction is not supplied it does seem rather odd to say that the mind's desire urges the mind. As I. L. Gordon points out,[61] it is possible to take *ferð* as subject of *monað*, parallel with *modes lust*; there is something to be said for this, with an implied *me* as object, thus distinguishing between the *mod* or *ferð* which urges and the self which is urged. Lines 50–1a, 'ealle þa gemoniað modes fusne / sefan to siþe', are similar. Hamer takes *sefan* as object and translates 'all this urges forth the eager spirit', but Bradley takes it as a genitive, parallel to *modes*, and renders 'all these urge anyone eager of mind and of spirit', which would perhaps allow us to sustain the association of the 'mind'-words with the eager inner mind.[62] It is possible, then, to read into *The Seafarer* the same linguistic distinction between an inner self called *mod* or *hyge* or *ferð* or *sefa* and an outer, conscious self that seems to operate in *The Wanderer*;

57 Clemoes, '*Mens absentia cogitans*'.

58 F. N. M. Diekstra, '*The Seafarer* 58–66a: the Flight of the Exiled Soul to its Fatherland', *Neophilologus* 55 (1971), 433–46.

59 There are some similarities here to a Germanic conception of the spirit/soul reconstructed from mainly Norse evidence; see V. Salmon, '*The Wanderer* and *The Seafarer* and the Old English Conception of the Soul', *MLR* 55 (1960), 1–10.

60 R. Hamer, *A Choice of Anglo-Saxon Verse* (London, 1970), p. 189, and S. A. J. Bradley, *Anglo-Saxon Poetry* (London, 1982), p. 333.

61 *The Seafarer*, ed. I. L. Gordon (London, 1960), p. 38.

62 Hamer, *A Choice*, p. 189, and Bradley, *Anglo-Saxon Poetry*, p. 333.

but it may be that the poet used the 'mind'-words rather casually for both levels of consciousness.

The rôle of the *mod* in *The Seafarer* is incitement to a journey which is associated with the divine will and the joys of the Lord. Yet it is difficult to know what to make of lines 108–9:

> Meotod him þæt mod gestaþelað, forþon he in his meahte gelyfeð.
> Stieran mon sceal strongum mode, ond þæt on staþelum healdan.

The notion of God stabilizing the *mod*, and of man's duty to control or restrain his strong *mod* and keep it in its place (if that is how line 109 should be construed), suggests the idea of the dangerous, rebellious inner force which the semantic field of *mod* and frequent references in other poems point to. This is not inconsistent with the earlier view of the mind's passionate, urgent quality, but it *is* inconsistent with the value placed on the *mod*'s promptings earlier in the poem. The poet seems to have drifted into a proverbial, prudential way of talking about the *mod* which neglects the fact that its passion is for things divine.

## CONCLUSIONS

Anglo-Saxon views on the mind are varied and subtle. For Alcuin, Alfred and Ælfric, the mind is very closely identified with the soul, which is simultaneously the spirit of life, the immortal self and the intellectual faculty. Passion and desire are seen as conscious choices of the rational soul, proceeding from the exercise of free will or from ignorance. The emphasis is on a unitary inner self. For Alfred this inner self is a pre-existent soul-and-mind, temporarily trapped in the body; for Ælfric it is more specifically linked to the individual, for whom it is created by God after conception. In Ælfric's view this soul/mind sets man firmly apart from the beasts, whereas Alfred seems prepared to find it in at least the higher animals. The poets, perhaps here reflecting tendencies in normal Anglo-Saxon usage, are more inclined to associate the 'mind' with emotion and a kind of passionate volition and self-assertion, and to distinguish it from the conscious self. It seems to be closely associated with mood and individual personality, a kind of mixture of id and ego in opposition to a super-ego. The poets generally distinguish it from the soul or spirit which leaves the body in death and survives in another world. The resulting sense of multiple personality is powerfully expressed in the urgent passionate tensions of *The Seafarer*.

APPENDIX

# Note on the relationship of LS, no. i, Belfour, no. ix and the Boulogne Latin version

These are three versions of the same basic text, cast in the form of a homily for Christ's Nativity. For the first part of the text, on the nature of God, Ælfric draws partly on Alfred's Boethius, and the successive recastings of *De consolatione Philosophiae*, bk v, met. v show clearly the relative order of the three versions and their relationship to each other:

Boethius, *De consolatione Philosophiae* v, met. v

Quam uariis terras animalia permeant figuris!
Namque alia extento sunt corpore pulueremque uerrunt
Continuumque trahunt ui pectoris incitata sulcum,
Sunt quibus alarum leuitas uaga uerberetque uentos
Et liquido longi spatia aetheris enatet uolatu,
Haec pressisse solo uestigia gressibusque gaudent
Vel uirides campos transmittere uel subire siluas.
Quae uariis uideas licet omnia discrepare formis,
Prona tamen facies hebetes ualet ingrauare sensus.
Unica gens hominum celsum leuat altius cacumen
Atque leuis recto stat corpore despicitque terras.
Haec nisi terrenus male desipis, admonet figura,
Qui recto caelum uultu petis exserisque frontem,
In sublime feras animum quoque, ne grauata pessum
Inferior sidat mens corpore celsius leuato.

Alfred's Boethius

Hwæt, þu miht ongitan þæt manig wyht is mistlice ferende geond eorþan, and sint swiðe ungelices hiwes, and ungelice farað. Sume licgað mid eallon lichoman on eorþan, and swa smuhende farað þæt him nauþer ne fet ne fiðeras ne fultumað; and sume bið twiofete, sume fiowerfete, sume fleogende, and ealle þeah bioð ofdune healde wið þære eorðan, and þider willniað, oððe þæs þe hi lyst oððe þæs þe hi beþurfon. Ac se mann ana gæþ uprihte; þæt tacnað þæt he sceal ma þencan up þonne nyðer, þi læs þæt mod sie nioðoror þonne ðe lichoma. (Sedgefield, p. 147/2–10)

Ælfric, Lives of Saints

Ða gesceafta þe þæs an scyppend gesceop synden mænig-fealde, and mislices hiwes, and ungelice farað. Sume sindon ungesewenlice gastas butan lichoman, swa swa synd ænglas on heofonum. Sume syndan creopende on eorðan mid eallum lichoman, swa swa wurmas doð. Sume gað on twam fotum, sume on feower fotum. Sume fleoð mid fyðerum, sume on flodum swimmað, and hi ealle swa-þæh alotene beoð to þære eorðan weard, and þider wilniað oððe þæs þe him lyst oððe þæs þe hi beþurfon, ac se man ana gæð uprihte; þæt getacnað þæt he sceall ma þæncan upp þonne nyðer, þelæs þe þæt mod sy neoðer þonne se lichoma, and he sceal smeagen embe þæt æce lif þe he to gesceapen wæs swiðor þonne embe þa eorðlican þing, swa swa his wæstm him gebicnað. (LS, no. i, lines 49–61)

### The Boulogne text

Creaturae uero quas unus Creator creauit multiplices sunt et uariae figurae, et non uno modo uiuunt; ex quibus quaedam sunt incorporalia et inuisibilia, ut angeli in caelo nullo terreno cibo utentes. Alia namque corporalia sunt, ratione carentia, et toto corpore in terra reptantia sicut uermes. Quaedam uero ambulant duobus pedibus, quedam quattuor; quaedam pennis uolant in aere; quaedam etiam natatilia sunt ut pissces in mari, et in amne uagantia, quae sine aquis uiuere nequeunt, et nos in aquis suffocamus. Omnia tamen ad terram inclinantur, de qua alimenta sumunt, et quicquid desiderant uel indigent. Sed homo solus recta statura ambulat, qui ad imaginem Dei creatus est et proprio incessu significat quod debet plus de celestibus meditari quam de terrenis, plus de eternis quam de infimis, ne forte mens eius fiat inferior corpore. (ed. Leinbaugh)

### The Belfour homily

Nu beoð þa gesceaftæ þe þe an Scyppend iscop mislice heowes and monifealdes cyndes; and heo alle ne libbæð na on ane wisæ. Summe heo beoð unlichamlice and eac unsegenlice swa beoð englæs; heo nabbæð nænne lichame, and heo libbæð on heofene, swiðe bliþful on Godes isihðe, and heo eorðlice mætes næfre ne brucæð. Summe heo beoð lichamlice, and unsceadwise, and mid alle lichame on eorþe creopaþ; þæt is, all wyrmcyn, swa swa eow fulcuð is. Summe gað on twam fotum; summe beoð feowerfote. Summe swimmæð on flode; summe fleoð geont þas lyft. Þa fixas nabbæþ nan lif buton wætere; ne we ne magon libban noht longe on watere. Ealle heo beoþ alytene and lybbæþ bi þare eorþan, ac þe mon ane hæfð uprihtne geong, for þam þe he is isceapen to his Scyppendes anlicnesse. He is on sawle liffæst mid gesceadwisnesse, and his geong bitacnæð, þenne he uprihtes gæð, þæt he sceal smeagen embe God and embe þa heofenlice þing swiðor þenne embe ða eorðlice þing, swiðor embe þa ecan þonne embe þa ateoriendlice, forþi læs ðe his mod beo bineoðan his lichame.

(Belfour, no. ix, pp. 82/29–84/11)

Alfred is clearly paraphrasing Boethius's Latin text here, and there is no need to posit any further source or influence for him. Ælfric adapts and expands that paraphrase in LS, no. i, while retaining many close verbal parallels that attest the directness of the debt; the Boulogne Latin text, resembling LS, no. i, rather than Alfred's version, but expanding the references to angels and fish which Ælfric had added in recasting Alfred, must be a translation and expansion of the LS, no. i passage; Belfour, no. ix very closely resembles the Latin version of Boulogne rather than LS, no. i, and the complete absence of significant verbal similarities between the two Old English versions suggests that Belfour, no. ix is a retranslation of the Boulogne Latin text, not an intermediary between LS, no. i, and Boulogne. Thus both textual development and verbal parallels indicate the order: Boethius (Latin) – Alfred's Boethius (Old English) – LS, no. i (Old English) – Boulogne text (Latin) – Belfour, no. ix (Old English). This relationship holds for the whole of the first part of the homily: LS, no i gives every sign of being the original version, with the Boulogne text being an expansion and translation of it into Latin and Belfour, no. ix certainly very like Boulogne and probably a retranslation of it.

A quite different relationship must be posited for the remainder of the homily. The ultimate source here is Alcuin's *De animae ratione*, and the very close verbal agreement between Alcuin's wording and the Boulogne Latin text of the homily shows that no English version could have intervened between them; the Boulogne text must be an adaptation and abridgement of Alcuin's treatise. The LS, no. i English version, closely resembling the Boulogne text but showing some further slight adaptation and small additions, and revealing no independent use of Alcuin's treatise, must be an adapted translation of the Boulogne text. Belfour, no. ix, incorporating the changes made by LS, no. i and showing many verbal parallels with it, must be based on LS, no. i itself. Thus for this second and longer part of the homily, the relationship is: Alcuin (Latin) – Boulogne text (Latin) – LS, no. i (Old English) – Belfour, no. ix (Old English). Whatever explanation one offers for this complex set of relationships, it seems clear that the Boulogne Latin text, being partly based on LS, no. i, as well as serving as source for both LS, no. i and Belfour, no. ix, must have been written by Ælfric, like the two Old English texts. I would suppose that at some early stage Ælfric made a Latin abridgement and adaptation of Alcuin's treatise, probably in the knowledge that he would not be able to obtain access to the treatise at a later date. (In the same way, he made excerpts from Julian of Toledo's *Prognosticon futuri saeculi*, preserved in the same Boulogne manuscript.) Subsequently, I take it, Ælfric used this précis as the basis of LS, no. i, prefaced with new material which was partly his own and partly drawn from Alfred's Boethius. When he later was called on to produce a Latin version of LS, no. i (perhaps for a different readership; Ælfric also produced parallel Latin and English versions of his pastoral letters), he naturally used his original Latin adaptation of Alcuin for the second part rather than retranslating that part of LS, no. i. When he needed to provide a new English version of the homily some considerable time later, he naturally used the Boulogne Latin version as basis for the first part, knowing that it included the improvements which he had made since issuing LS, no. i, but used the LS, no. i version for the rest, knowing that it represented his further thoughts, and perhaps also that it was already adapted for a vernacular readership.

# The homilies of the Blickling manuscript

D. G. SCRAGG

In a review of Rudolph Willard's facsimile edition of *The Blickling Homilies* in the series Early English Manuscripts in Facsimile, Peter Clemoes,[1] in characteristically mild but firm tones, pointed out a number of limitations in Willard's introduction, in particular that it failed to address itself to questions of the compilation of the set of homilies in the book and of their circulation. He offered some suggestions on how such questions should be answered, but, necessarily within the scope of a review, these were no more than pointers for a fuller study. This paper seeks to explore just two of these aspects of the Blickling manuscript (now Princeton University Library, W. H. Scheide Collection 71, henceforth referred to as B): its physical make-up and the degree and nature of its overlap in content with other manuscripts. Its findings should be considered preparatory to the fuller linguistic examination of the texts which will follow from the preparation of a new edition.[2]

## THE PHYSICAL MAKE-UP OF THE MANUSCRIPT

B is incomplete as preserved; as presently constituted it consists of nineteen quires.[3] Three of them, quires 10, 15 and 16, are signed at the foot of the verso of the final leaf with the letters P, U and X respectively. If P is here, as it is usually, the fifteenth letter of the Anglo-Saxon alphabet, five quires have been lost before what is now quire 10. A lacuna in the text shows that one of them is lost between the surviving quires 9 and 10. It is generally assumed that the

[1] *MÆ* 31 (1962), 60–3, reviewing EEMF 10 (Copenhagen, 1960).

[2] A new edition is in course of preparation by R. L. Collins of the University of Rochester, to replace *The Blickling Homilies*, ed. R. Morris, EETS o.s. 58, 63 and 73 (London, 1874–80), repr. in one vol. (1967) and referred to henceforth as Morris. A linguistic analysis of B may be attempted more profitably when all surviving copies of the Blickling Homilies are edited in conjunction with their Latin sources. The standard early linguistic study is A. K. Hardy, *Die Sprache der 'Blickling Homilien'* (Leipzig, 1899).

[3] Cf. the collations in N. R. Ker, *Catalogue of Manuscripts containing Anglo-Saxon* (Oxford, 1957), pp. 451–5; Willard, *Blickling Homilies*, pp. 24–5; R. L Collins, *Anglo-Saxon Vernacular Manuscripts in America* (New York, 1976), p. 52; and that offered below, p. 302.

others were lost from the beginning (quire 1 opens in mid-sentence and Willard[4] reports traces of what he took to be a signature E at the end of the first gathering) but it should be observed that there are a number of points in the manuscript at which there is coincidence of the end of a quire and the end of an item, where quires might have been lost.[5]

The present quire 1 is a regular eight-leaf gathering, containing the conclusion of Homily no. i, the text ending part-way down $1^6$ verso (6v). The words in the last five lines of the homily are widely spaced, perhaps because the scribe had no immediate expectation of copying another item. It is possible that the homily was copied page for page from the exemplar, since on $1^3$ recto and $1^4$ recto (3r and 4r) the text of the last line or two overruns the margin, while on $1^6$ recto (6r) there is space left after the final word[6] for the first word overleaf, *halgan*. The wide spacing at the end of Homily no. i and the lack of any comparable sign of page for page copying of Homily no. ii suggest that the two items may not have been copied consecutively from a single source, but there is no firm evidence to prove it. Homily no. ii, which follows Homily no. i on $1^6$ verso (6v) without a break, completes quire 1 and is concluded in quire 2, where it is followed, again without a break, by Homily no. iii. Quire 2 is described by Willard[7] as a six-leaf gathering (three bifolia) with an added leaf (singleton) at the beginning. Since scribes do not normally begin quires with what would be a very vulnerable singleton, we might presume that this was a quire of eight (four bifolia) originally, the final leaf of which was removed or lost.[8] Marcia A. Dalbey[9] has argued convincingly that there is a hiatus in the text caused by the loss of this leaf. Thus the first two quires of B as it now survives were originally eights, the normal size of gathering for the period. However, quire 3 is not an eight but a six which is almost filled by the latter part of Homily no. iii, the writing being spaced out at the end and the last six lines of $3^6$ verso (21v) remaining blank. Homily no. iv begins the next quire. It would appear that quire 3 was specially constructed to take the remainder of the text of Homily no. iii and only that. What was intended to follow was presumably already written, otherwise it would have been started on the remaining blank lines of $3^6$.

4 *Blickling Homilies*, p. 25.

5 See below. The reader may find it helpful to read the next few paragraphs in conjunction with fig. 1 (p. 304).

6 The space is filled with a long extension to the tongue of final *e*.

7 *Blickling Homilies*, p. 24.

8 Aside from the question of vulnerability, it is unlikely that a scribe would spend time preparing a half-sheet at the beginning of a quire. Faced with material for seven leaves (three sheets and a half), he would have placed the half-sheet between folded full-sheets as in quire 10; cf. Ker, *Catalogue*, p. xxiv.

9 'A Textual Crux in the Third Blickling Homily', *ELN* 5 (1968), 241–3.

Homily no. iv is the only item on quires 4 and 5, and this is not accidental. Though quire 4 is a regular eight, 5 is a bifolium only. In the last two lines of quire 5 the writing is cramped and overruns the margins, clearly to ensure that the text was completed on the page. This suggests that either there was no expectation of continuing with another item after Homily no. iv, or, more likely, the next item was already written. With hindsight, it appears odd that the scribe did not properly assess the length of his copying task before beginning Homily no. iv and construct a ten-leaf quire for it (as he was to do in quire 7), since this would have obviated the need to use a vulnerable single bifolium between full quires. The explanation may be that the item was originally copied for a different purpose: the writing space is wider than usual in quire 4,[10] and though Willard[11] refers to quire 5 as a bifolium, its two leaves were not conjugate but were singletons which had become accidentally separated in the manuscript as it survived to modern times.[12] Willard gives no reason for his assertion that they constitute a bifolium, and it may simply be a natural assumption. But if we see them not as a conjugate bifolium but as two singletons, it is possible that they were the beginning of a fuller quire, the rest of which was cut off when they were added to the present homiliary. Alternatively, quire 4 may originally have been part of another manuscript, the end of the item it contains being recopied when the decision was made to add it to the Blickling set.

Homilies nos. v and vi apparently formed a single copying task, the one running on from the other, the two filling quires 6 (an eight: fols. 32–9) and 7 (a ten: fols. 40–9). At the end of quire 7 four lines remain blank, which suggests that the next item was already prepared. Homily no. vii is the only item in quire 8, which Willard[13] describes as an eight (four bifolia) with an added singleton at the beginning. Again it seems likely that the quire was a ten (five bifolia), the last leaf of which was deliberately removed because it was blank, the homily ending on the verso of the last surviving leaf, with much space wasted in the final lines of writing and a blank line and a half at the end. We cannot be sure that the lost leaf was blank, however, as the following quire (9) has lost its

10 The writing space varies from page to page but, except for a few pages in quire 1, it is always under 100 mm outside quire 4 and 105 mm or above in that quire. Also, only in quires 1, 4 and 5 do some pages have 22 lines, all other quires having uniformly 21.

11 *Blickling Homilies*, p. 24.

12 References to the manuscript in published works are complicated because the pages were reordered in the rebinding of 1955 (*Blickling Homilies*, ed. Willard, p. 21) and because Morris published his pp. 237–8 (now fol. 31) as a fragmentary Homily no. xvi instead of a part of Homily no. iv. I refer to the folio numbers of the manuscript as it now exists and as it is represented in the facsimile. To convert Morris's and Ker's page numbers to the present folio numbers, divide by two and, between fols. 31 and 119, add one. Morris Homilies nos. xvii–xix are here nos. xvi–xviii.

13 *Blickling Homilies*, p. 24.

outer bifolium and the next item (Homily no. viii) thus begins imperfectly.

With quire 9 begins a block of (originally) nine quires, the second of which is now lost. These quires are much more uniform than those they follow. Six of the nine were eights, though two of them, 9 and 12, have suffered loss of leaves and there is consequent loss of text.[14] Quire 10 has nine leaves, four bifolia with an added singleton after 5 (fol. 70)[15] and quire 11 is a six. Why there should have been these departures is not clear, though they seem not to have been suggested by textual needs. Quire 16 is described by Willard[16] as four bifolia preceded by a singleton, but again this is almost certainly a ten with the last leaf removed. The writing in the last five lines of the final surviving leaf (fol. 119) is widely spread, as the scribe attempted to fill out the leaf with the conclusion of his item (Homily no. xv). The next item, beginning a fresh quire, is by a different scribe (see below) and was clearly written independently. Homily no. xv is a very long piece, which the scribe was half-way through copying when he ended the previous quire, 15. In constructing a ten-leaf quire, he apparently knew both that this item was to be the last of his task (otherwise why not make an eight and run over into another quire?) and that he needed for it more than his regular eight. Had he expected to use only nine leaves, he would probably have inserted a half-sheet between full sheets as he had done in quire 10. As it happened, he hardly had sufficient material to fill nine of his ten leaves, as the ever more widely spaced writing so conspicuous on $16^{7}$ verso – $16^{9}$ verso (117v–119v) shows. Having managed to fill $16^{9}$ he removed $16^{10}$, and hence the later quire signature (X) appears at the foot of $16^{9}$. Of the three final quires of the volume, containing Homilies nos. xvi–xviii, two are uniform eights, and so possibly was the third though only four leaves of it now remain.[17]

To summarize the foregoing, I propose the following new collation of B: $1^{8}$, $2^{8}$ wants 8 (after fol. 15), $3^{6}$, $4^{8}$, $5^{2}$ (perhaps two singletons), $6^{8}$, $7^{10}$, $8^{10}$ wants 10 (probably blank), $9^{8}$ wants 1 and 8 (after fols. 58 and 64), $10^{8}$ + 1 leaf after 5 (fol. 70), $11^{6}$, $12^{8}$ wants 7 (after fol. 85), $13–15^{8}$, $16^{10}$ wants 10 (probably blank), $17–18^{8}$, $19^{8}$ wants 1 (before fol. 136), 6, 7 and 8 (after fol. 139).

Two scribes worked on B.[18] Scribe 1 wrote all of quires 1–7 (Homilies nos.

14 That the lost quire was an eight is suggested by the amount of text lost. If the two surviving pages of Homily no. ix are representative, and if the homily in B was the same as that surviving in other manuscripts (as seems likely; see below, p. 305), material for nine manuscript leaves has been lost, one from quire 9 and eight more.

15 Ker's description of quire 10 as a ten lacking its opening leaf (*Catalogue*, p. 454) is a mistake resulting from a miscalculation of the leaves lost between surviving quires 9 and 10.

16 *Blickling Homilies*, p. 24.

17 Ker, *Catalogue*, p. 454, assumes that the very fragmentary quire 19 was an eight. Willard (*Blickling Homilies*, ed. Willard, p. 25) states that it was a six, but gives no reason for adducing that from the surviving four singletons.

18 Cf. Ker, *Catalogue*, pp. 454–5; Willard, *Blickling Homilies*, pp. 26–38; and Collins, *Manuscripts in America*, pp. 52–3.

i–vi) and is the principal scribe in quires 8–15. Scribe 2 wrote the incipit to Homily no. vii at the beginning of quire 8, interrupted the writing in quires 10, 12 and 15, and was solely responsible for quires 17–19. His intervention in quires 10, 12 and 15 is not easily explained.[19] Not only did he write the beginning of Homilies nos. x and xv but he returned to both at later stages, and he also wrote the conclusion of Homilies nos. xii and xiv and intervened in xiii.

We may divide the quires of B and the homilies they contain into three distinct blocks. In block **a** we have a set of homilies (nos. i–vii) ordered to follow the church year to Easter. Homily no. i is apparently an Annunciation homily and Homily no. ii is for Quinquagesima. Although the Annunciation is traditionally celebrated on 25 March, after Quinquagesima, this order of homilies for those days is not unknown elsewhere in Old English.[20] Then follow items for the first, third and fifth Sundays in Lent (Homilies nos. iii–v), Palm Sunday (no. vi) and Easter Day (no. vii). In this block the homiliary is an original compilation, at least three breaks in the copying of items being discernible. Homily no. iv almost certainly was written before Homily no. iii, and Homily no. v probably before Homily no. iv. Homily no. vii was written independently of Homily no. vi and probably also of Homily no. viii. In block **b** are Homilies nos. viii–xv, which continue the Temporale of nos. ii–vii with general pieces suitable for the post-Easter period (nos. viii–x),[21] ending with the Ascension (no. xi) and Pentecost (no. xii), and then move into a Sanctorale. The quires, and therefore the items, in this block appear to have been written consecutively, but this need not mean that the block is taken from a single source. The intervention of scribe 2, particularly in his writing of the opening of Homilies nos. x and xv and the conclusion of Homilies nos. xii and xiv,[22] may have been to ensure that scribe 1 followed a preconceived selection from a variety of sources. Finally, block **c** consists of Homilies nos. xvi–xviii continuing the Sanctorale, all three in hand 2. The divisions may be summarized in a table (see fig. 1).

If Homily no. iv was written independently of nos. iii and v, and Homily no. vii independently of nos. vi and viii, and if there was (as seems likely) a time-lag between the writing of Homilies nos. i and ii, then block **a** must have been pieced together, perhaps over a period of time, from a number of sources. The dislocation of items even suggests that the sources were not together in one

[19] Cf. *Blickling Homilies*, ed. Willard, p. 27.

[20] This is also the order followed in the Worcester manuscript, now Oxford, Bodleian Library, Hatton 114 (Ker, *Catalogue*, p. 394, items 40 and 41).

[21] Willard (*Blickling Homilies*, ed. Willard, p. 38) suggests that Homilies nos. viii–x are for Rogationtide.

[22] Writing the conclusion of an item might be to ensure that a more mechanical scribe did not continue copying the next piece in that source.

| Block | Quire | Folios | Items | Scribes |
|---|---|---|---|---|
| a | 1 | 1–8 | i–iii | 1 |
| | 2 | 9–15 | | |
| | 3 | 16–21 | | |
| | 4 | 22–9 | iv | |
| | 5 | 30–1 | | |
| | 6 | 32–9 | v–vi | |
| | 7 | 40–9 | | |
| | 8 | 50–8 | vii | 2 (incipit only) and 1 |
| b | 9 | 59–64 | viii–xv | 1 |
| | [lost quire] | | | |
| | 10 | 65–73 | | 2 and 1 |
| | 11 | 74–9 | | 1 |
| | 12 | 80–6 | | 1 and 2 |
| | 13 | 87–94 | | 1 |
| | 14 | 95–102 | | 1 |
| | 15 | 103–10 | | 1 and 2 |
| | 16 | 111–19 | | 1 |
| c | 17 | 120–7 | xvi–xviii | 2 |
| | 18 | 128–35 | | |
| | 19 | 136–9 | | |

FIG. 1 The relationship of quires and items in the Blickling manuscript (B)

centre so that their organization could be decided ahead of copying, and our opportunity for determining where the scribes were working may therefore be that much diminished. However, in blocks **b** and **c** it appears that the scribes (or their master, if scribe 2 is not he) had the order of items in mind. Hence it is likely that even if Homilies nos. viii–xviii were not copied from a single source, the archetypes of each of them were together in one centre. For some indication of where that centre might have been, we must look at copies of the items in B in other manuscripts.

## THE RELATIONSHIP OF B WITH OTHER MANUSCRIPTS

Few manuscripts have significant overlap of content with B. A few lines of the conclusion of Blickling no. v appear at the end of the composite Napier no. xxix in O,[23] but even in this short extract there are verbal differences. Another

[23] The sigla used in this discussion (besides B) are:
- A Vercelli, Biblioteca Capitolare, CXVII
- C Oxford, Bodleian Library, Junius 85 + 86
- E Oxford, Bodleian Library, Bodley 340 + 342
- F Cambridge, Corpus Christi College 198

item in O (Cameron B.3.2.28) in part parallels Blickling no. vii, but only because each draws independently on the same Latin source.[24] O offers no firm evidence on which to localize B.

Blickling no. ix is a homily found in complete or adapted form in seven other versions,[25] but in B the greater part of it has been lost. There remain only the contents of two and a half leaves at the beginning and the last clause of the explicit. Nevertheless some textual affinities can be shown. Versions of the whole of Blickling no. ix survive in AKN; the text of KN, with the extant parts of B, was printed by Napier in his collection of homilies attributed to Wulfstan (Napier no. xlix); in A the piece is Vercelli no. x. Part of the same homily (including the conclusion) is variously used in items in CIJ and in another item in K, in all of which we may compare the text with the surviving explicit in B. Collation of the full text in ABKN shows that A is from an independent line of transmission: it has a unique introductory paragraph and numerous verbal differences that mark it off from BKN. Where substantive differences occur within BKN, B generally has readings in common with N, while K frequently has what is probably the earlier reading found also in A: for example, in a heavily rhetorical passage, the Virgin is called *wuldor* in AK but, more

I Oxford, Bodleian Library, Bodley 343
J London, BL Cotton Faustina A. ix
K Cambridge, Corpus Christi College 302
N Cambridge, Corpus Christi College 419 and 421
O Oxford, Bodleian Library, Junius 121 and Hatton 113 and 114.

The overlap of content in these manuscripts and their relationships are discussed further in my 'The Corpus of Vernacular Homilies and Prose Saints' Lives before Ælfric', *ASE* 8 (1979), 223–77. For references to individual homilies other than those in B, I employ the following abbreviations: Assmann = *Angelsächsische Homilien und Heiligenleben*, ed. B. Assmann, Bibliothek der angelsächsischen Prosa 3 (Kassel, 1889), repr. with supplementary introduction by P. Clemoes (Darmstadt, 1964); CH I = the forthcoming edition of the First Series of Ælfric's Catholic Homilies by P. Clemoes; CH II = *Ælfric's Catholic Homilies: the Second Series, Text*, ed. M. Godden, EETS s.s. 5 (London, 1979); Cameron = A. Cameron, 'A List of Old English Texts', *A Plan for the Dictionary of Old English*, ed. R. Frank and A. Cameron (Toronto, 1973); Fadda = *Nuove omelie anglosassoni della rinascenza benedettina*, ed. A. M. L. Fadda, Filologia germanica testi e studi 1 (Florence, 1977); LS = *Ælfric's Lives of Saints*, ed. W. W. Skeat, EETS o.s. 76, 82, 94 and 114 (London, 1881–1900); Napier = *Wulfstan: Sammlung der ihm zugeschriebenen Homilien*, ed. A. S. Napier (Berlin, 1883), repr. with a bibliographical suppl. by K. Ostheeren (Dublin and Zürich, 1967); Pope = *Homilies of Ælfric: a Supplementary Collection*, ed. J. C. Pope, EETS o.s. 259–60 (London, 1967–8); and Vercelli = *Vercelli Homilies IX–XXIII*, ed. P. E. Szarmach (Toronto, 1981).

24 See Y. L. Downs, 'An Edition of an Old English Easter Day Homily on the Harrowing of Hell' (unpubl. M.A. dissertation, Manchester Univ., 1980).

25 I ignore the few sentences found in Napier no. xxx in O, which do not correspond to any part of the text surviving in B. I have shown in my 'Napier's "Wulfstan" Homily XXX: its Sources, its Relationship to the Vercelli Book and its Style', *ASE* 6 (1977), 197–211, that these are taken from a text identical with that in A.

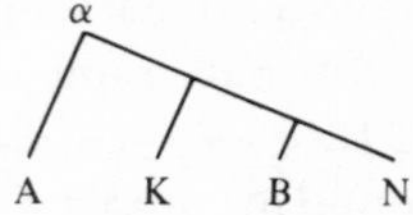


FIG. 2 The relationship of copies of Blickling no. ix

prosaically, *cwen* in BN.[26] The relationship is shown diagrammatically in fig. 2. Frequent copying and progressive modernization of this apparently popular homily has, however, produced idiosyncratic readings in all versions (showing that no one is dependent on another), and occasionally these produce patterns which appear to contradict the one shown in the stemma. The most difficult of these is the reading BK *mægsibbe* (K:-*y*-), a word expressing Christ's kinship with man, AN *mægensybbe* (N: -*i*-), 'powerful love (?)'.[27] I suspect that here we have an example of two scribes independently making the same alteration of a rare compound (*mægsibbe*) to one in which the first element parallels that in words commonly associated with the deity (e.g. *mægenþrym*), in other words, a case of popular etymology. This need not disturb the stemma.

The overlap with CIJK in the final sentence of the homily is hardly substantial enough to show relationships, particularly since scribes alter concluding formulas so freely. However, it is probably significant that I (together with A) has Christ ruling in heaven 'mid eallum his halgum' (i.e. his saints), where all other texts treat the last word as an adjective and add *sawlum*. The latter is a somewhat surprising departure from a conventional formula. It is possible that it is original, with AI 'normalizing' the phrase, but AI elsewhere suggest access to better copy,[28] and the probability is that we have here an alteration common to all but these two manuscripts. Hence B is not to be linked with I. The fragment of the homily preserved in C is too brief for its precise textual affinities to be shown.[29] This leaves only the shortened homily in JK (Napier 257/9–end). Although this piece has not been published (Cameron lists it independently as B.3.2.7), my own collation of it with copies of the full Blickling no. ix shows that it follows the distinctive readings of N,[30] and therefore it, like N, may be linked with B. This may be useful to a consideration of the textual links of B, for though B and N do not overlap

[26] Napier no. xlix is this homily printed from N (Napier's A) with variants from B and K (his B and D); *wuldor*: *cwen* occurs at 251/8 (references are to page and line of the edition). For other substantive differences between BN and K, see Napier 250/17; 251/2, 13, 14 and 19; and 252/2, 6 and 11. [27] Napier 252/9.

[28] Cf. J. E. Cross, '"Ubi Sunt" Passages in Old English – Sources and Relationships', *Vetenskaps-Societeten i Lund, Årsbok 1956*, 26–44, at 31–2.

[29] Cf. P. E. Szarmach, 'MS. Junius 85 f. 2r and Napier 49', *ELN* 14 (1977), 241–6.

[30] See my discussion in 'The Corpus of Vernacular Homilies', p. 230, n. 7.

outside Blickling no. ix, B does have other overlap of content with J and with that part of K which is closely related to J.

J is a late copy of an expanded Ælfrician Temporale.[31] The additions include the shortened version of Blickling no. ix just referred to, an abridged version of Blickling no. vi, and a composite homily (Assmann no. xiv) which is made up almost entirely of selections from Blickling no. viii, a homily in C (Fadda no. i) and Vercelli no. xv. K is a more selective copy of the Temporale, having most of the additions found in J (but not Blickling no. vi) and with extra pieces which include the full version of Blickling no. ix discussed above. Textually J and K are very close where they overlap; in considering the links between their ancestor and B, it will be simplest to refer only to J. The adaptation and selection of material mean that the parts of Blickling nos. vi and viii in J are not close to the original homilies as represented by B. But whoever compiled the set in J had access to copies of three homilies in B, however great the distance between them textually, and it is perhaps not without significance that these three are Blickling nos. vi, viii and ix when it has been shown above that Blickling no. vii was copied into B independently of nos. vi and viii. It is possible that the three items were available in a single source both to the scribe of B and to whoever adapted them into the forms now found in J, though in view of the distance between B and J textually and chronologically it would be unsafe to try to take the hypothesis any further.[32]

The relationship of B and C is more difficult to determine. Potentially, C is an important witness to the development of B. In its seven items it has four points of overlap: it contains copies of Blickling nos. iv, ix and xvii, and it has a copy of the piece (Fadda no. i) from which the compiler of Assmann no. xiv took an extract, to follow his conflation of Blickling no. viii. C would be a useful manuscript with which to link B, since much is known about its background: its scribes use south-eastern spellings regularly,[33] its single Ælfric piece is drawn from the copy sent to Archbishop Sigeric,[34] and there is a good case to be made for identifying it with an entry in a fifteenth-century catalogue of St Augustine's, Canterbury.[35] However, nothing can be deduced from

[31] See *Homilies of Ælfric*, ed. Pope, pp. 48–52, and *Ælfric: the Second Series*, ed. Godden, pp. xlvii–l.

[32] It ought to be possible to test the hypothesis by linguistic means, but results from my own partial survey proved inconclusive. Homily no. vii stands out in having three examples of the uncommon forms *þeossa*, *þeossum* (only Homilies nos. ii and xii have other examples in B, one in each), but this merely adds support to the suggestion of the textual independence of no. vii from its neighbours, and does not show any link between nos. vi and viii.

[33] Cf. *The Old English Vision of St Paul*, ed. A. diPaolo Healey (Cambridge, Mass., 1978), pp. 31–8.

[34] Cf. *Ælfric: the Second Series*, ed. Godden, pp. lix–lx.

[35] Cf. *The Old English Vision of St Paul*, ed. Healey, pp. 16–18.

Assmann no. xiv about the relationship of B and C, except that homilies which found their separate way into B and C (and also A) existed also in copies which were together in a single centre, for someone to make a composite piece from them. Furthermore, Blickling no. ix is fragmentary in both B and C, and all that can be said confidently is that the text of both appears not to be from the line of transmission exemplified in A. Three versions of Blickling no. xvii survive, in B, C and A. Again it is clear that the text in A is from a different line of transmission from that in B and C, such differences as exist between the latter being relatively slight and explicable as the result of scribal error in either or both texts.[36] In contrast, in Blickling no. iv, which survives only in B and C, there are many textual differences, the result of systematic minor verbal change in B where C remains faithful to the Latin source.[37] For example, in B the exhortation not to avoid payment of tithes, which is a principal theme of the piece, is frequently couched in the first person plural, where in C the homilist follows the Latin in using the second person. A single sentence will illustrate:[38]

| | | | |
|---|---|---|---|
| B | 7 gif we þæt nu ne doþ,<br>þonne wyrce we us myccle<br>synne on þon. | C | 7 gif ge þæs alatigeað,<br>þonne wyrceað ge eow<br>synne on þon. |

If the relationship of B and C in Blickling no. i is different from that in their copies of Blickling no. xvii, it cannot be assumed that the appearance of both homilies in the two manuscripts is more than coincidence,[39] and, without more concrete evidence, this must be the case with the other points of overlap also. C does not help to determine anything about the sources of B.

Two other manuscripts, A and F, have significant overlap with B. The first of these, the Vercelli Book, is often associated with B in histories of Old English literature as the most important witnesses to the homiletic tradition before Ælfric and Wulfstan. There are three points of overlap: Blickling no. ix corresponds to Vercelli no. x and Blickling no. xvii to Vercelli no. xviii, while both contain copies of homilies drawn upon by the compiler of Assmann no. xiv.[40] As has been observed, the latter connection is tenuous. In Blickling no. ix, as has already been shown, the text in B is quite independent of that in A. In

[36] See A. S. Napier, 'Notes on the Blickling Homilies', *MP* 1 (1903), 303–8.

[37] See R. Willard, 'The Blickling-Junius Tithing Homily and Caesarius of Arles', *Philologica: the Malone Anniversary Studies*, ed. T. A. Kirby and H. B. Woolf (Baltimore, 1949), pp. 65–78.

[38] Cf. Morris, 41/6 (references to specific readings in B are to page and line of Morris's edition).

[39] It is possible that the scribe of B introduced these changes in copying Blickling no. iv, to make the piece fit into his set, and that such changes were not necessary in the copying of Blickling no. xvii (which was, in any case, entered into B by a different scribe). Thus it could be argued that the two items were in the same source, and that B and C are more closely related than I have suggested, but it seems to me that the evidence is against such an assumption.

[40] It is noticeable too that a number of items in these two manuscripts draw independently upon the same Latin sources, but this stresses their lack of overlap rather than links them.

Blickling no. xvii, whereas B and C are textually close, A is again drawing upon a distinct line of transmission.[41] One of the few firm statements that can be made about the history of B is that its scribes did not have access to any of the sources used in the compilation of A.

Finally we turn to F, which has copies of Blickling no. xiii and Blickling no. xviii, and another item which is an Ælfric Lenten sermon, *De penitentia* (originally published as an appendix to *Catholic Homilies*[42]), coupled with part of Blickling no. x. It is significant that the make-up of B suggests that these three items were available in one centre to the scribes of B.[43] We need to determine if that centre might be the one in which the scribes of F worked a generation later, and for that it is necessary to introduce a long digression on the compilation of F.

## THE COMPILATION OF F AND ITS RELATIONSHIP WITH B

F is a large manuscript on which many scribes worked over a number of years. Ker[44] divides it into three parts: I, an incomplete copy of a basically Ælfrician homiliary from Canterbury which, as Kenneth Sisam[45] has shown, is represented complete in E; II, additions to that homiliary, mostly again from the work of Ælfric, but also including the three items found in B; III, later additions which are of no relevance to this study. The construction of part I may be seen in tabular form in fig. 3.

| Block | Quires | Folios | Items | Scribe |
|---|---|---|---|---|
| **a** | 1–3 (eights) | iii and 1–23 | 1–4 | 1 |
| **b** | 4–11 (eights) | 24–87 | 4–12 | 2 |
| **c** | 12–18 (eights) and 19 (six) | 88–149 | 12–22 | 3 |
| **d** | 21–4 (eights) and 25 (ten) | 160–201 | 23–7 | 2 |
| **e** | 26–7 (eights) | 202–17 | 27–32 | 3 |
| **f** | 32–6 (eights) | 248–87 | 33–43 (part) | 4 |

FIG. 3 The construction of Cambridge, Corpus Christi College 198 (F) part I

41 This is made clear in Napier, 'Notes on the Blickling Homilies'.

42 *The Sermones Catholici or Homilies of Ælfric*, ed. B. Thorpe, Ælfric Soc., 2 vols. (London, 1844–6) II, 602–8. See also the discussion by K. Sisam, 'MSS. Bodley 340 and 342: Ælfric's *Catholic Homilies*' in his *Studies in the History of Old English Literature* (Oxford, 1953), pp. 148–98, at 166–8, and by P. A. M. Clemoes, 'The Chronology of Ælfric's Works', *The Anglo-Saxons: Studies . . . presented to Bruce Dickins*, ed. P. Clemoes (London, 1959), pp. 212–47, esp. 221 and n. 2.

43 See above, p. 304.

44 *Catalogue*, pp. 76–82.

45 *Studies*, pp. 150–6.

It contains in blocks **a** to **e** the first half of the Canterbury homiliary complete[46] (homilies for Sundays and feast-days following the order of the church year from Christmas to 3 May) and in block **f** eleven homilies from later in the series (Ascension Day to the end of June). It is copied by four scribes, at least two of them writing in tandem, for block **d** was begun before block **c** was finished, which is why scribe 3 ended his block **c** with a smaller quire than usual, and similarly scribe 2 had to adjust his final quire of block **d** to a ten because scribe 3 had already begun block **e**. Scribe 1 also wrote a table of contents covering items 1–32.

In part II we have modification and development of the set by a number of new scribes designated by Ker scribes 5 to 8, although his scribe 7 may in fact be two.[47] Though the work of scribes of the two parts is never found within a single quire, their writing is judged nearly contemporary,[48] and there are two links between them: scribe 5 inserted one quire between blocks **c** and **d** (though his items are not in the table of contents) and he added four more quires between **e** and **f**; scribe 8 began a new block of quires after block **f** by completing the item that was incomplete at the end of that block. Since his text is from the same source as that copied by scribe 4[49] it would appear that he was copying from a quire containing Canterbury set items that originally followed block **f** but was now to be discarded. After completing that one item, he added others from a different source. The construction of part II is summarized in fig. 4.

The work of scribe 5 is self-contained. He added homilies to the Canterbury set and perhaps rubricated the items of that set, though Ker also states that he may have added the titles to items 54 and 55,[50] respectively by scribes 7 and 6, which would then provide a link between him and them. In $\mathbf{g}^{\mathrm{i}}$ are two extra Lenten homilies (CH II, nos. viii and xiii) inserted at an appropriate place in the set on a single enlarged quire, the last three lines of which remain blank. The conclusion that the quire was made for its present position is inescapable. Presumably block $\mathbf{g}^{\mathrm{ii}}$, containing two additional Easter homilies (CH II, nos. xv and xvi) and three for the common of saints (CH II, nos. xxxvii–xxxix), was similarly made to fit here. The work of scribe 6 and his helpers is likewise self-contained: three blocks, $\mathbf{j}^{\mathrm{i-iii}}$, perhaps once contiguous but now interrupted by the later work of part III, containing five items suitable for reading on saints'

46 Except for E, item 8 (Vercelli no. ix), which is replaced in F and related manuscripts with an Ælfric item.

47 Ker (*Catalogue*, p. 82) identifies the work of scribe 7a, and adds the possibility that the last few pages of my block $\mathbf{g}^{\mathrm{ii}}$ (see fig. 4) may be by yet another hand.

48 Ker, *Catalogue*, p. 82.

49 Private communication from Peter Clemoes. For obvious reasons I was not able to explain at the time the use to which I would put the information.

50 *Catalogue*, p. 82.

| Block | Quires | Folios | Items | Scribes |
|---|---|---|---|---|
| **g**[i] | 20 (ten) | 150–9 | 44–5 | 5 |
| **g**[ii] | 28–30 (eights) and 31 (six + 1 leaf after 4, wants 7) | 218–47 | 46–51 | 5 |
| **h** | 37–41 (eights) | 288–327 | conclusion of 43 and 58–63 | 8, with later additions (part III) |
| **j**[i] | 42–5 (eights) (45[8] verso is blank) | 328–59 | 52–4 | 6 and, for item 54, 7 |
| **j**[ii] | 46 (eight, wants 8, probably blank) | 360–6 | 55 | 6 and, for most of 366v, 7a |
| **j**[iii] | 49 (eight) | 378–85 | 56–7 | 6 |
| **k** | 50 (ten, wants 10) | 386–94 | 64 and another partial item, now erased | 8 |

FIG. 4 The construction of Cambridge, Corpus Christi College 198 (F) part II

days in the correct order from 1 August to 11 November: LS, no. xxv, CH I, no. xxix, Blickling no. xiii, CH I, no. xxxiv and CH II, no. xxxiv. The blank spaces between the blocks show that these items were assembled here for the first time. The work of scribe 8 is rather more confused. It is in two blocks, **h** and **k**. In the first, after recopying the conclusion of an item of the Canterbury set, the scribe added six pieces: CH II, no. xvii, LS, no. xv, LS, no. v, CH I, no. xi, the composite *De penitentia* + Blickling no. x and Pope no. iv. In block **k** all that now survives is Blickling no. xviii, but this was once followed by the beginning of *De uirginitate* (probably scrapped by Parker because it was incomplete[51]). The latter is a collection of excerpts from Ælfric, probably not compiled by him.[52] Block **h** ended with a quire which was written on the first two leaves only, so we should probably see scribe 8's work as incomplete.

Sisam's discussion of F part I ends with the words 'here the Corpus manuscript loses its orderly character',[53] but this does not mean that the collection in part II is wholly disorderly. Blocks **g**[i] and [ii] are scribe 5's augmentation of the Canterbury set, deliberate and logical. Block **h** by scribe 8 begins with the conclusion of an item of the Canterbury set which, at this point, contains a number of items from Catholic Homilies First and Second Series on the apostles Peter and Paul. Block **h** continues with Ælfric pieces on two more apostles (James and Mark), adds another saint's life (Sebastian, feast-day 20 January), and then turns to three items for Lent. This is the least

[51] *Ibid.* p. 81. [52] See *Homilies of Ælfric*, ed. Pope, p. 802. [53] *Studies*, p. 155.

organized part of the manuscript, though, as is observed above, it is probably unfinished. Blocks **j**$^{i-iii}$ have saints' lives from later in the year, and these are followed by the Blickling piece for St Andrew (block **k**) in its proper place chronologically. The items of the Canterbury set excluded in the rearrangement effected by the part II scribes may be illuminating too. Between blocks **e** and **f** of part I are omitted nine items found in the comparable collection in E (mainly items for the Rogation period). After block **f**, the items presumably discarded in F covered Sundays from the post-Pentecost period to Advent (as well as some general items). These are replaced in F by (for the most part) saints' lives.[54] The aim of scribes 6 to 8 seems to have been to end the Temporale sequence soon after Pentecost and then to concentrate in the latter part of the year on a Sanctorale.

The detailed arrangement of F part II is unique to this manuscript and is original. It draws on a wide range of Ælfric material, but some of its items are not 'authorized' by Ælfric (*De uirginitate* and the composite of *De penitentia* + Blickling no. x). Two, *De penitentia* and CH II, no. xxxiv, were dropped from later recensions of the Second Series when Ælfric incorporated their contents into the Lives of Saints, so they must derive here from relatively early copies. Malcolm Godden[55] reports of the Second Series items in block **g** that, although they are of a 'somewhat more advanced' version than that of the first recension, they do not show the changes of Ælfric's second recension. The one item outside the Catholic Homilies and the Lives is Pope no. iv, but this has been shown to have been composed before the Lives.[56] It would seem that, although the compilers of F part II were writing well into the eleventh century, they had available to them only material known to have existed before the end of the tenth.

Pope's comment on the last item of block **h** in F, that it 'stands almost entirely apart'[57] textually, may be said of all items in part II except those shared with B.[58] This makes more difficult the task of identifying the place of origin of the manuscript. Two areas must be considered. There is clear association of

[54] Block **f** itself parallels a part of E except that one item (E, item 47 – fourth Sunday after Pentecost) is omitted. The items that remain are for Ascension Day, Pentecost, the second and third Sundays after Pentecost, John the Baptist, St Peter and St Paul.

[55] *Ælfric: the Second Series*, p. xxx.

[56] See Clemoes, 'Chronology', p. 221 (where the piece is referred to as 'Müller'), and *Homilies of Ælfric*, ed. Pope, pp. 21–2.

[57] *Homilies of Ælfric*, p. 262.

[58] The F copy of LS, no. xv shares a number of readings with the twelfth-century manuscript Cambridge, University Library, Ii. 1. 33. The relationship between the two is worthy of further investigation. Though the original collection of items in the latter appears to have no textual associations beyond that with F, there are a number of additions, some of which are drawn from sources used by the scribes of F part I (see *Ælfric: the Second Series*, ed. Godden, pp. xliv–xlv).

part I with south-eastern (Canterbury or Rochester) manuscripts, though both Sisam and Pope hesitate about assigning F to that area.[59] The description of the manuscript given above suggests a dislocation between the work of scribes 1 to 4 and that of 5 to 8 consonant with the movement of the manuscript from one centre to another, and the likelihood is that part II was not made in the centre which produced part I. F as a whole is annotated by the 'tremulous' scribe of Worcester, and Ker notes some spellings in part III that he believes indicate a western origin for that section.[60] Godden goes so far as to suggest that the block **g** homilies may 'derive from a copy of the [Second] Series sent to Worcester' at 'the beginning of the known relationship between Ælfric and Wulfstan',[61] though Pope had earlier argued against a Worcester origin on the grounds that 'its numerous hands are not of the Worcester type'[62] and Worcester scribes 'had access to a greater range of Ælfric's work'.[63] Though a Worcester origin cannot be excluded, the weight of present evidence indicates that part II was written elsewhere.

The importance of all this may be seen when we examine the closeness of the relationship of F and B. The copies of Blickling homilies in F were entered by scribes 7 and 8. Although there is no certain link between them, the likelihood is that they were working in the same scriptorium. There they had available copies of Blickling nos. xiii and xviii (and arguably a full text of Blickling no. x too). The textual relationship of B and F is the same in each homily: F (the later manuscript) is not dependent upon B but is so close to it that we must assume that they have a common ancestor lying no great distance behind them. The relationship is closest in Blickling no. xiii, for F scribe 7 is a mechanical and unthinking copyist. Some unusual spellings (e.g. *góod* 'good', *culufre*, 'dove'[64]) appear in both manuscripts, as do simple errors (e.g. *geongweardode* for *ge-ondweardode*, 'answered', *earan* for *earman*, *deoflum* for *deoflu*).[65] The two manuscripts also have upper-case letters, often of a distinctive shape, at the same points of the text,[66] and have other palaeographic details in common.[67]

59 Sisam, *Studies*, p. 155, n. 4, and *Homilies of Ælfric*, ed. Pope, p. 180.

60 *Catalogue*, p. 82. It is doubtful if the late-eleventh-century entry of part of an Office of St Guthlac at the end of F (see Ker, *Catalogue*, p. 81) can help place the manuscript; the saint appears to have been widely popular (see *Cynewulf's 'Elene'*, ed. P. O. E. Gradon (London, 1958), p. 4).

61 *Ælfric: the Second Series*, pp. xciii–xciv.

62 *Homilies of Ælfric*, ed. Pope, p. 180.

63 *Ibid.* p. 22.

64 Morris 139/29 and 157/12.

65 Morris 157/9, 159/9 and 159/13. Mechanical errors (such as the omission or unwarranted appearance of the *m*-abbreviation) would be unlikely to survive unaltered during a long transmission history. It is possible that the graphs *g* and *d* were in some way confused or confusable in the source; both manuscripts have *mægenes* for *mægdenes* (Morris 159/4) and F has *d* corrected to *g* more than once. Morris silently printed *geondweardode* but omitted the word from the glossary.

66 E.g. those in the margin of B, 88v and F, 353r.

67 E.g. in Latin *æt* for &, Morris 141/7.

But F, despite a high proportion of mechanical errors (especially the omission of letters and short words) preserves some better readings which show access to a text behind B rather than to B itself.[68] The case of Blickling no. xiii is slightly different, since it is copied into F by scribe 8, who appears throughout his work to be writing with less slavish dependence upon his sources.[69] It is therefore not surprising that we do not find examples of mechanical errors common to the two manuscripts. There are, nevertheless, other signs of a close textual relationship between the two: occasional rare forms (for example, nominative plural *discipulos*[70]) and aspects of manuscript presentation.[71] Again, F has some true readings, however, where B has homoeoteleuton.[72] The relationship of Blickling no. x in the two manuscripts is more complex, perhaps because in F we have not a simple copy but a text adapted slightly to fit into a composite structure.[73] All that can be said with confidence is that again F

[68] E.g. F has the correct *stengum* against B *strengþum* (Morris 151/1). In view of the very limited understanding of Latin shown by the scribe of F, better readings in Latin quotations are perhaps more telling: *In exitu Israel de Egipto* (B: *Il exitu Israhel ex Egypto*) (Morris 149/22), and *do*, 'I give' (B *da*) (Morris 157/27).

[69] E.g. there is some modification of the second half of the Canterbury set homily (F, item 43) with which he began his block **h**. Throughout his work we find occasional inserted words and phrases to 'clarify' the text (cf. in Pope no. iv, lines 39, 142, 147 and 198, and the omission of 'unnecessary' words in lines 144, 145, 241 and 274, text cited by Pope as E). He also makes silly errors, simplifies repeated short words (*hi*, *swa*), writes *u* for *y* and vice versa, and confuses vowels in a word-final position in all the items he copies.

[70] Morris 235/19. The appearance of the Latin accusative plural inflection *-os* in the loan-word *discipul* is rare in Old English but it is a none the less clearly established form. It seems to have been adopted at an early period as the generic plural form, to be used in both subject and object positions and also after the preposition *be* (normally + dative in Old English). Other recorded instances are: (1) Vercelli no. i (*Die Vercelli-Homilien*, ed. M. Förster, Bibliothek der angelsächsischen Prosa 12 (Hamburg, 1932), repr. (Darmstadt, 1964), p. 9, line 77) 'be his discipulos' in MS A with four later manuscripts reading *þegnum*; (2) Blickling no. xvii/Vercelli no. xviii (Morris 225/13) *discipulos* accusative plural in B, but anglicized in C to *discipulas* and replaced in A by *þegnas*; (3) the same (Morris 227/11) *discipulos* nominative plural in B, *discipulo* in C, passage lacking in A. A further example of *discipulo* nominative plural (probably for *-os*) appears in another item in C (Fadda no. i, line 117). F is thus the only eleventh-century manuscript to retain the *-os* form. (Morris in his glossary draws attention to a similar confusion of the Latin nominative inflection in this homily, *discipuli* appearing twice as nominative plural and twice as accusative plural. Again F preserves all examples.)

[71] Note the closeness of presentation of the conclusion: both manuscripts have *AMEN* spread across the final line with the punctuation mark ;. In no other piece in F does scribe 8 conclude an item in this way.

[72] In printing Blickling no. xviii (his no. xix), Morris used F to piece out the text in B at 237/9–10, and he should have done so also at 235/18 (as the facing translation shows), where the text should read 'Ða se morgen geworden wæs [þa se haliga Andreas licgende wæs] beforan Mermedonia'.

[73] Cf. Morris 115/13–15, where F has a different reading from the incomprehensible one in B which has clearly suffered in transmission. There are also, however, a great many differences which involve pairs of words, phrases or even clauses reversed. I suspect that here the compiler of the piece in F is copying Blickling no. x with some freedom.

helps reveal a mechanical error in B.[74]

Proving relationships between manuscripts is notoriously difficult, but it is apparent that we have in F a manuscript which is very much closer to B than is any other that has been discussed. Despite some problems that remain, the evidence points to scribes of F part II having had available to them an Old English source or sources very like that or those used by the scribes of B. If any further light is to be shed on the origin of B, it is most likely to come from F.

## THE PLACE OF B IN THE HOMILETIC TRADITION

The manuscripts here referred to as A and B, the Vercelli Book and the Blickling Homilies, are our two principal witnesses to the state of homiletic writing in English before the work of Ælfric appeared. Comparison between them can illuminate each, and perhaps also the vernacular homiletic tradition as a whole. I have argued that B is an original collection, put together, perhaps over a period of time, from a number of sources. In this it is like A,[75] but there the similarity ends. In A the collection appears to be haphazard; any principle of arrangement by which it was compiled still eludes us. The scribe seems to have copied his items in blocks from his sources without any overall plan. In B, as is shown above, the scribes took care to put together a book which followed a preconceived design, following the chronology of the church year, and they perhaps took individual items from different sources, rather than blocks of items. Much less is known, however, about the popularity and distribution of the items in B than about those in A. Whereas a great many of the homilies in A can be traced to the south-east, about whose textual traditions we have relatively full information, few of those in B can be associated, by their appearance in other copies, with a particular centre. B obviously represents a very different textual tradition from that of A, even in the items that they share, and though it has some overlap with other south-eastern manuscripts of the eleventh century or later (C, JK and N) the parallel passages are not close enough to suggest dependence on the same sources. It is probably safe to conclude that B is not of south-eastern origin.

74 At Morris 113/23, the bones of a dead man exhort a living friend: 'gemyne þis 7 ongyt þe sylfne, þæt þu eart nu þæt ic wæs io' (B), which not only reads better as *gemune me* . . . (F) but seems in this form closer to the probable source: 'adtende ad me, et agnosce te . . . Quod tu us, ego fui.' For the Latin text and its relations with the Old English, see J. E. Cross, '*The Dry Bones Speak* – a Theme in Some Old English Homilies', *JEGP* 56 (1957), 434–9. Cross does not consider this particular crux, presumably because he did not have the text of F. It seems to me to strengthen the case he makes for the Latin he cites as the source for this part of the Old English homily.

75 See my 'The Compilation of the Vercelli Book', *ASE* 2 (1973), 189–207, and *The Vercelli Book*, ed. C. Sisam, EEMF 19 (Copenhagen, 1976), 37–44.

If the homilies in B represent a different pre-Ælfrician tradition from those in A, it would be satisfying to be able to identify its area of origin. We are fortunate to have in F a book which, despite the limitations in its overlap, is very close to B. For though no detailed work on the language of F part II has appeared, the possibility of localizing it on the basis of the spellings favoured by its scribes is very much greater than is the case with B, because of its later date.[76] This is one direction that future research can take. It should be noted that F is perhaps even closer to B than the limited overlap of content discussed in this paper suggests. Like B, it is an original compilation, drawing upon a number of sources. Its arrangement is similar to that of B. The latter is a Temporale running from some point before Lent to Pentecost, followed by a Sanctorale. F, when it was adapted by the addition of the part II items, became basically a Temporale from Christmas to the third Sunday after Pentecost, followed by a Sanctorale (albeit an interrupted one). Although this pattern is an obvious one,[77] its appearance in both manuscripts is a possible further pointer to their production in the same centre. And that centre may have been an isolated one, for just as B has no clear link with any other set of anonymous homilies, so F part II cannot be associated with any other surviving Ælfric collection. The language of B leads us to believe that its origin was Mercian,[78] and, as with F part II, a Worcester origin cannot be excluded, though there is no evidence to support it.[79] The possibility of a Mercian origin of F part II now needs to be investigated, though it may have to be admitted finally that even if B and F part II were produced in the same centre, it is one that we otherwise know nothing about.[80]

76 Ker (*Catalogue*, pp. xv–xviii) lists more than three times as many manuscripts contemporary with F parts I and II as with B.

77 The same pattern is found in other manuscripts, notably perhaps in O from Worcester.

78 The conclusion of R. J. Menner ('The Anglian Vocabulary of the Blickling Homilies', *Philologica*, ed. Kirby and Woolf, pp. 56–64) is that the homilies 'were originally written in Mercia or by Mercians'.

79 Menner (and others referred to in his paper) discusses a possible East Mercian origin for the homilies, but this does not preclude their being copied in the west. Two links between B and the Worcester MS O in terms of the ordering of items have been noted above; see pp. 303, n. 20, and 316, n. 77.

80 I am grateful to the British Academy for a research award that enabled me to visit Princeton in 1984, and to Mr Scheide and his librarian Mrs Mina Bryan for allowing me access there to the Blickling manuscript.

# The liturgical background of the Old English Advent lyrics: a reappraisal

SUSAN RANKIN

That the group of lyrics occupying most of the first surviving gathering of the Exeter Book of Old English poetry[1] was inspired in part by the great 'O' antiphons of Advent has long been recognized. Not only in their subject-matter but also in the structure and rhetoric of individual poems – all begin *Eala* and thus mirror the Latin invocative 'O' – they reflect their poet's close knowledge of these antiphons.[2] As a group, the lyrics develop two themes predominant in the Latin liturgy of the Advent season: the expectancy of Christians, awaiting the coming of the Messiah, and their great need of a Saviour:

Nu þu sylfa cum
heofones heahcyning. Bring us hælo lif. (Lyric 6, lines 20b–1)[3]
Veni ad saluandum nos Domine Deus noster. (*O Emmanuel*)

[1] Exeter, Cathedral Library, 3501, fols. 8–14. Formerly a gathering of eight, the first leaf is now lost: the present lyric 1 begins imperfectly and probably was preceded by three others; see J. C. Pope, 'Palaeography and Poetry: some Solved and Unsolved Problems of the Exeter Book', *Medieval Scribes, Manuscripts and Libraries: Essays presented to N. R. Ker*, ed. M. B. Parkes and A. G. Watson (London, 1978), pp. 25–65, esp. 30–2. The series ends on 14r and is followed directly by Cynewulf's poem on the Ascension (*Christ II*). The present fols. 1–7 were not originally part of the Exeter Book; see N. R. Ker, *Catalogue of Manuscripts containing Anglo-Saxon* (Oxford, 1957), p. 153. The manuscript, written probably in the second half of the tenth century, was presented to Exeter Cathedral by Bishop Leofric; for facsimile and commentary, see *The Exeter Book of Old English Poetry*, ed. R. W. Chambers, M. Förster and R. Flower (London, 1933).

[2] The principal studies of the relationship between the Advent lyrics and their liturgical background are *The Christ of Cynewulf*, ed. A. S. Cook (Boston, Mass., 1900), repr. with introduction by J. C. Pope (Hamden, Conn., 1964); E. Burgert, *The Dependence of Part I of Cynewulf's Christ upon the Antiphonary* (Washington, DC, 1921); *The Advent Lyrics of the Exeter Book*, ed. J. J. Campbell (Princeton, NJ, 1959) with further bibliography; and R. B. Burlin, *The Old English Advent: a Typological Commentary* (New Haven, Conn., 1968). For a summary of bibliography, with English translations of suggested Latin sources, see *Sources and Analogues of Old English Poetry*, trans. M. J. B. Allen and D. G. Calder (Cambridge, 1976), pp. 70–7.

[3] *Advent Lyrics*, ed. Campbell, p. 57; he translates: 'Now come yourself, High King of Heaven. Bring the life of salvation to us.'

More widely still, the lyrics show their author to have been thoroughly steeped in Christian thought and learning:[4] obviously he was a member of a Christian community, quite possibly a monk.

The following discussion will be concerned with the relationship between the lyrics and the Latin liturgy. Since the lyrics were edited and studied as a group by Campbell and by Burlin,[5] much new work on medieval liturgies, in particular the publication of several medieval antiphoners by R.-J. Hesbert,[6] has allowed clarification of several problems. First, I shall attempt to define more closely than previous scholars could the liturgical tradition from which the Old English poet derived his repertory of 'O' antiphons; secondly, I shall examine the particular make-up of the poet's repertory, as known from his lyrics, and the sequence in which he arranged his poems.[7]

## THE LITURGICAL BACKGROUND

When discussing the antiphon texts on which the Advent lyrics were based, earlier scholars have referred to the *Liber responsorialis* of St Gregory,[8] clearly believing it to possess some degree of authority. In fact, no such book exists; that is, no book of Office or mass chants known to have been sanctioned by Pope Gregory I survives – indeed, it is unclear what relationship the earliest extant chant-books (of the late eighth and ninth centuries) bear to the work of St Gregory the Great.[9] The source of previous scholars' assumptions about Gregory's alleged chant-book was clearly the Compiègne Antiphoner, now

4 See esp. Burlin, *Typological Commentary*.

5 See above, n. 2, and the works there cited.

6 *Corpus Antiphonalium Officii*, ed. R.-J. Hesbert, 6 vols. (Rome, 1963–79) (henceforth cited as *CAO*)

7 In the Exeter Book, lyrics 4, 7, 9 and 11 each have a large initial E and begin on a new line, whereas the others (except 1, which begins acephalously) each simply follow the end of the previous lyric, and have a small initial E. I have not been able to discover any reason, either in the content of the lyrics, or in the physical features of the manuscript, for this variable presentation. In the absence of any clear indication to the contrary I assume the order in the Exeter Book was the author's own.

8 See, e.g., *Advent Lyrics*, ed. Campbell, pp. 6–8, and Burlin, *Typological Commentary,* pp. 40–1.

9 Most of the earliest chant-books originate in Frankish territory, and record the so-called 'Gregorian' repertory, now recognized as a combination of Roman and Frankish elements. The earliest Roman chant-books date from the eleventh century, and include a repertory both related to and distinct from that of the Gregorian books. Much controversy surrounds the relationship between these two musical and liturgical traditions. For an explanation of the facts and various hypotheses, see H. Hucke, 'Gregorian and Old-Roman Chant', *The New Grove Dictionary of Music and Musicians*, ed. S. Sadie, 20 vols. (London, Washington, DC, and Hong Kong, 1980) VII, 693–7. For an illuminating survey of the wider questions raised by the various repertories of western chant, their relationship to pre-ninth-century (unnotated) musical repertories and to the work of Pope Gregory I, see H. Hucke, 'Towards a New Historical View of Gregorian Chant', *Jnl of the Amer. Musicological Soc.* 33 (1980), 437–67.

Paris, BN lat. 17436, thought to have been prepared in north-east France for Charles the Bald in the mid-ninth century.[10] This book was first edited in 1705, and later reproduced in Patrologia Latina, as one of Gregory's works.[11] Whilst this is indeed the earliest surviving complete antiphoner (although unnotated),[12] there is good reason to suppose that, as a Roman–Frankish chant-book, it does not at all reflect Roman usage at the time of Pope Gregory, or contemporary English usage.[13] Specifically in the matter of 'O' antiphons, the Compiègne Antiphoner includes only eight, whereas a collection of liturgical texts assembled by Alcuin at York *c.* 790 in his *De laude Dei* included ten.[14] Nevertheless, from the time of Augustine's arrival in Britain as Gregory's envoy in 597, until at least the mid-eighth century, the strongest influence on English liturgical practice came direct from Rome, and it is at this point that any study of English chant traditions must begin.

Almost all of what we know of English chant in the early Middle Ages depends on the record of contemporary witnesses, principally Bede.[15] The earliest extant English chant-books date from the late tenth century,[16] and as

[10] L. Brou, 'L'Antiphonaire de Compiègne', *Etudes grégoriennes* 4 (1961), 20–3. The manuscript is ed. *CAO* 1 (*Manuscripti "Cursus Romanus"*).

[11] *Sancti Gregorii Papae I: Opera Omnia*, 4 vols. (Paris, 1705) IV, 733–878, and PL 78, cols. 725–850.

[12] It includes chants of both the mass and the Office, an early practice maintained in later Ambrosian and Mozarabic books, but largely abandoned in Gregorian books produced after the Carolingian reforms of the late eighth and early ninth centuries. For a summary history of early antiphoners, see K. Gamber, *Codices Liturgici Latini Antiquiores*, 2nd ed., 2 vols. (Freiburg, 1968) II, 492–526. Unless otherwise noted, I shall use the term 'antiphoner' in its later sense, to mean a book of chants for the Office.

[13] See above, n. 9. The Compiègne Antiphoner may not directly correspond to the use of any particular church, as much as to the personal taste of Charles the Bald; see Brou, 'Compiègne'.

[14] The inclusion of 'O' antiphons in *De laude Dei* was first noted by R. Constantinescu, 'Alcuin et les "Libelli Precum" de l'époque carolingienne', *Revue d'histoire de la spiritualité* 50 (1974), 17–56; this study includes an edition of all the liturgical texts in the collection. For other important discussion, see D. A. Bullough, 'Alcuin and the Kingdom of Heaven: Liturgy, Theology and the Carolingian Age', *Carolingian Essays*, ed. U.-R. Blumenthal (Washington, DC, 1983), pp. 1–69, esp. 4–14. The connection between Advent lyric 7 and the text *O Ioseph* found in *De laude Dei* is independently noticed here and in *Sources and Analogues*, trans. Allen and Calder (attributing the discovery to T. D. Hill). I understand that Professor Bullough is currently preparing a new edition of the *De laude Dei*.

[15] For the fullest accounts of early English chant traditions, see *Le Codex F.160 de la Bibliothèque de la Cathédrale de Worcester, Antiphonaire monastique (XIIIe siècle)*, Paléographie musicale 12 (Tournai, 1922), 27–8 and 99–110, and D. Knowles, *The Monastic Order in England* (Cambridge, 1949), pp. 545–60.

[16] For lists of early English chant-books, see A. Holschneider, *Die Organa von Winchester* (Hildesheim, 1968), p. 82; S. Corbin, *Die Neumen* (Cologne, 1977), p. 3.134–6; S. Rankin, 'Neumatic Notations in Anglo-Saxon England', *Musicologie médiévale: Notations–Séquences* (Paris, forthcoming); and H. Gneuss, 'Liturgical Books in Anglo-Saxon England and their Old English Terminology', above, pp. 91–141, at 116–18.

such show the influence of northern French and Lotharingian churches, with which the Benedictine reformers had most contact.[17] It is therefore impossible to establish exactly what repertory of mass and Office chants was in use in centres such as Canterbury and York during the seventh, eighth, ninth and earlier tenth centuries. However, in spite of Pope Gregory's reply to a request from Augustine for help in liturgical matters, in which the pope shows he has no particular desire to impose Roman liturgical practice in England,[18] it must be assumed that contemporary Roman usage was the basis of what Augustine and his companions taught at Canterbury.

In contrast to the many problems encountered by Charlemagne when two centuries later he attempted to impose Roman liturgical and musical practice throughout his Frankish empire,[19] we do not hear from Bede of any native resistance to the new chant in seventh-century England. That at least one part of the ecclesiastical community not only accepted, but indeed was eager to learn, the Roman chant is demonstrated by the invitations extended to cantors to come from Rome to Britain, and from Canterbury to northern England. Bede reports how, in 633, James the Deacon, who had accompanied Paulinus, archbishop of York, from Rome 'etiam magister ecclesiasticae cantionis iuxta morem Romanorum siue Cantuariorum multis coepit existere'.[20] Later he describes Eddius Stephanus, also from Kent, as 'primusque . . . cantandi magister Nordanhymbrorum ecclesiis', with the exception of James.[21] In the early years of the eighth century, Acca, bishop of Hexham, brought Maban 'cantatorem quoque egregium' north; here, the detail of Bede's account is of considerable interest:

. . . Maban, qui a successoribus discipulorum beati papae Gregorii in Cantia fuerat cantandi sonos edoctus, ad se suosque instituendos accersiit, ac per annos xii tenuit,

17 Knowles, *Monastic Order*, pp. 552–4.

18 Although Gregory's authorship of the *Libellus responsionum* as quoted by Bede and several other eighth-century sources has been questioned, P. Meyvaert argues convincingly for its authenticity; see his 'Diversity within Unity, a Gregorian Theme', *Heythrop Jnl* 4 (1963), 141–62, and 'Bede's Text of the *Libellus Responsionum* of Gregory the Great to Augustine of Canterbury', *England before the Conquest*, ed. P. Clemoes and K. Hughes (Cambridge, 1971), pp. 15–33.

19 For a general account of the Carolingian liturgical reforms, see C. Vogel, 'La Réforme liturgique sous Charlemagne', *Karl der Grosse, Lebenswerk und Nachleben*, ed. W. Braunfels, B. Bischoff *et al.*, 4 vols. (Düsseldorf, 1965) II (*Das geistige Leben*), 217–32, with further bibliography. See also D. A. Bullough, 'Roman Books and Carolingian *Renovatio*', *Renaissance and Renewal in Christian History*, ed. D. Baker (Oxford, 1977), pp. 23–50. For a brief survey with particular reference to chant and chant-books, see W. Apel, *Gregorian Chant* (Bloomington, Ind., 1958), pp. 79–83.

20 *Bede's Ecclesiastical History of the English People*, ed. B. Colgrave and R. A. B. Mynors (Oxford, 1969), pp. 206–7 (II. 20), with this translation: 'he also began to instruct many in singing, after the manner of Rome and the Kentish people'.

21 *Ibid.* pp. 334–5 (IV. 2).

quatinus et quae illi non nouerant carmina ecclesiastica doceret, et ea quae quondam cognita longo usu uel neglegentia inueterare coeperant, huius doctrina priscum renouarentur in statum.[22]

But either the English were slow to learn, or simply found it difficult to retain a new and strange musical repertory by memory, for they often sought help from Rome. During 679/80, at the invitation of Benedict Biscop, John, precentor of St Peter's and abbot of the monastery of St Martin, came to the newly established monastery of Wearmouth to teach the cantors of that house 'ordinem uidelicet ritumque canendi ac legendi uiua uoce'.[23] As elsewhere, Bede defines John's mission precisely: he was to teach the monks 'cursum canendi annuum, *sicut ad sanctum Petrum Romae agebatur*' (my italics).[24] A decree of the Council of *Clofeshoh*, which met in 747, might be understood to imply either a certain desperation in the face of diverse practices, or a wish for conformity with Roman practice for its own sake: 'in baptismi officio, in missarum celebratione, in cantilenae modo celebrantur, iuxta exemplar uidelicet quod scriptum de Romana habemus ecclesia'.[25] Meanwhile, the author of the sixteenth *interrogatio* in Egbert's *Dialogi*,[26] mentioning antiphoners and missals of St Gregory brought to England by Augustine (books of which we have not previously heard), seems to imply that English liturgical practice was, by the mid-eighth century, on a surer footing than in the days of Benedict Biscop: 'quod non solum nostra testantur antiphonaria, sed et ipsa quae cum missalibus suis conspeximus apud apostolorum Petri et Pauli limina'.[27]

This last remark, which, for whatever reasons, seeks to authenticate English practice by identifying it with Rome both historically and in the present (at the

[22] *Ibid.* pp. 530–1 (v. 20): 'he [Acca] invited a famous singer named Maban, who had been instructed in methods of singing by the successors of the disciples of St Gregory in Kent, to teach him and his people; he kept him for twelve years teaching them such church music as they did not know, while the music which they once knew and which had begun to deteriorate by long use or neglect was restored to its original form'.

[23] *Ibid.* pp. 388–9 (IV. 18): 'the order and manner of singing and reading aloud'. The intimate association between singing and reading aloud (and, analogously, between early musical notations and systems of punctuation) has been discussed by L. Treitler, 'Reading and Singing: on the Genesis of Occidental Music Writing', *Early Music Hist.* 4 (forthcoming). M. Parkes ('Punctuation or Pause and Effect', *Medieval Eloquence*, ed. J. J. Murphy (Berkeley, Calif., 1978), pp. 127–42) explains how punctuation could be used to show a singer or reader how to recite the written text.

[24] *Bede's Ecclesiastical History*, ed. Colgrave and Mynors, pp. 388–9 (IV. 18).

[25] *Councils and Ecclesiastical Documents relating to Great Britain and Ireland*, ed. A. W. Haddan and W. Stubbs, 3 vols. (Oxford, 1869–73), III, 367.

[26] Bullough ('Roman Books', pp. 30–1) questions the attribution of the *Dialogi* to Egbert, and suggests his successor as archbishop of York, Ælberht, as the more likely author.

[27] *Councils*, ed. Haddan and Stubbs, pp. 411–12.

time), appears very difficult to accept at face value. Comparison of the hundred or so liturgical texts assembled by Alcuin in his *De laude Dei* (under the heading *De antiphonario*) with chant repertories from other European regions suggests that Gregory's directions to gather together the best of Roman, English, Frankish and other liturgical material[28] had, generally speaking, been followed in England, if not invariably: Alcuin's collection includes texts of demonstrably Roman, Gallican and possibly Hispanic provenance,[29] and many which have no concordances elsewhere and may represent native English compositions just as well as an older layer, now lost, of Roman chant.[30] Moreover, visiting Wearmouth a century or so earlier, the Roman archchanter John, according to Bede, had written down *while he was there* all that was necessary for the celebration of feast-days throughout the year;[31] his book was still in the monastery in Bede's lifetime, and many copies of it had been made for use elsewhere.[32] It seems possible (perhaps likely) that, since the book was not itself brought from Rome, John incorporated some native English practices, particularly material for local English feasts.

It is important to realize that neither the Romans nor the English had any means of notating music at this time;[33] the insistence on 'as it is written in the Roman books' has to be understood in reference to texts, and/or their liturgical order, or perhaps with even less definition. The continuous need for cantors from Rome, or Canterbury, can be explained by the foreign nature of the Roman chant. It was not a native musical repertory: if it was to take root in people's memories, to be passed from one generation to the next, in short to become part of oral tradition, more time and teaching were required than were available to the English,[34] although, as the major Roman establishment,

[28] See above, n. 18. The relevant passage from the *Libellus responsionum* is discussed and translated by Bullough, 'Roman Books', p. 25.

[29] Bullough, 'Alcuin', pp. 5–8, and, less reliably, Constantinescu, 'Alcuin', pp. 38–54.

[30] A preliminary attempt to trace the texts in other (mainly later) books has identified only half of them, including the 'O' antiphons, various antiphons for Christmas Vespers and Epiphany, and Rogation antiphons. Identification is rendered more difficult by the fragmentary nature of the texts; some are in fact parts, but not necessarily the first, of longer texts recorded elsewhere. Many of Constantinescu's sources for these texts have proved unverifiable.

[31] *Bede's Ecclesiastical History*, ed. Colgrave and Mynors, pp. 388–9 (IV.18).

[32] *Ibid.*

[33] See Hucke, 'Towards a New Historical View', p. 446, on Roman notation, and Rankin, 'Neumatic Notations', on English notations.

[34] Important studies of the processes of oral traditions in music, particularly during the early medieval period, and of the change-over from oral to written traditions in ecclesiastical chant, have been made by L. Treitler in a series of papers, of which the most recent are 'Transmission and the Study of Music History', *International Musicological Society: Report of the Twelfth Congress, Berkeley 1977* (Basle and London, 1981), pp. 202–11, and 'Oral, Written and Literate Process in the Transmission of Medieval Music', *Speculum* 56 (1981), 471–91 (with

Canterbury appears to have retained the tradition better than other centres. Before the invention of stave notation in the early eleventh century, it took ten years to train a cantor, according to Guido of Arezzo;[35] and this cantor is assumed to be living in a place where he had heard the chant since birth. In effect, John the Archchanter was able to stay only a year or so at Wearmouth; the book which he left and which was known to Bede might have contained lists or full texts of chants, but not musical notation. That Maban stayed twelve years at Hexham, teaching not just new but also old music 'which had begun to deteriorate by long use', makes perfect sense when it is understood that music itself was not notated but memorized.

It was in the face of a similar problem, though on a grander scale, that various systems of musical notation were developed in the Frankish empire in the ninth century.[36] There are very few references to ecclesiastical music in England in the ninth and tenth centuries, but what there are show that the old problems persisted: King Alfred brought the cantor (*cantator*) Grimbald from Saint-Bertin,[37] and sixty years later, during his abbacy at Abingdon, Æthelwold sent to Corbie for monks to teach his own the proper singing of the chant.[38] It was probably only at this time, with the impetus provided by the great monastic revival, that conditions in England were favourable to the establishment of musical notation as an indigenous practice and recognized means of communicating and recording the chant repertory.[39] Moreover, English ecclesiastics not only learned about notation from northern France,

earlier bibliography), and by H. Hucke in 'Der Übergang von mündlicher zu schriftlicher Musiküberlieferung im Mittelalter', *International Musicological Society: Report of the Twelfth Congress*, pp. 180–91.

35 In the letter to Brother Michael, Guido explains that, using his new system of notation, he needs only one year instead of ten to form a cantor; see 'Epistola Guidonis Michaeli Monacho de Ignoto Cantu', *Scriptores Ecclesiastici de Musica Sacra*, ed. M. Gerbert, 4 vols. (Saint-Blaise, 1784) II, 43b. The letter was written *c.* 1032; see *Hucbald, Guido, and John on Music: Three Medieval Treatises*, trans. W. Babb, ed. with introductions C. V. Palisca, index of chants A. E. Planchart (New Haven and London, 1978), p. 51.

36 The earliest dated examples of musical notation occur in sources of the anonymous *Musica enchiriadis* and the *Musica disciplina* of Aurelian of Réome dated after 840; ninth-century examples of notation fall into two distinct categories, differentiated by the types and functions of the books in which they appear – broadly speaking, theoretical and practical (ecclesiastical chant) sources. Modern views of musical notation have recently been extensively revised by L. Treitler; see 'The Early History of Music Writing in the West', *Jnl of the Amer. Musicological Soc.* 35 (1982), 237–79, and 'Reading and Singing'.

37 See *Life of King Alfred*, ed. W. H. Stevenson (Oxford, 1904), repr. with suppl. by D. Whitelock (Oxford, 1959), p. 63 (ch. 78).

38 Knowles, *Monastic Order*, pp. 551–2.

39 For a discussion of the ways in which some early English notations worked as a record of the chant repertory, see S. Rankin, 'From Memory to Record: Exeter Musical Notations of the Mid-Eleventh Century', *ASE* 13 (1984), 97–111.

they also looked there for help in liturgical matters in general, for with the relatively newly gained knowledge of Roman chant in Francia there was, on the face of it, no longer any need to send to Rome for help.

Apart from a few statements that a particular chant was sung on a particular occasion – for instance, *O rex gloriose* by Bede on his death-bed[40] – no specific information about the chants actually sung in English churches during these four centuries is conveyed. For knowledge of the Office chant repertory in pre-Conquest England, we are dependent on only three substantial sources. The section *De antiphonario* in Alcuin's *De laude Dei* is the earliest of these. This collection may represent York use of the late eighth century, since it was compiled there *c.* 790. However, even after allowance has been made for its origin as a devotional selection rather than as a compendium of liturgical practice, *De antiphonario* remains far removed from any other recorded English or European chant repertories; without a more thorough study than is at present available, little more can be said of it.[41] More than 250 years separates the *De laude Dei* florilegium from the other two important sources, the two books known as the Leofric and Wulfstan Collectars; both include large though incomplete repertories of Office antiphons and responsories, alongside collects and readings for the daily Office. Although no thorough study of its chant repertory has been made, the Leofric Collectar, written at Exeter Cathedral *c.* 1070,[42] is known to show the influence of Leofric's early education in Lotharingia.[43] The Wulfstan Collectar, written for use at Worcester *c.* 1065–6, has strong affinities with at least one Winchester book.[44] Both Worcester and Winchester had been major centres of the English monastic revival – inspired by the Cluniac and Lotharingian reforms – under their bishops Oswald (Worcester, 961–92) and Æthelwold (Winchester, 963–84).

Continental antiphoners or other sources of information about Office

[40] *Bede's Ecclesiastical History*, ed. Colgrave and Mynors, p. 582, in the letter of Cuthbert the Deacon *de obitu Bedae*. The antiphon in question is ed. *CAO* III (*Inuitatoria et Antiphonae*), no. 4079. All the *CAO* sources have *glorie* rather than *gloriose*. Modelled on the Advent 'O's, this antiphon was sung to the *Magnificat* on Ascension Day. Its melody was based on that of the Advent 'O's, but adapted fairly freely.

[41] See above, nn. 14 and 30.

[42] The book is one of those presented to Exeter Cathedral by Bishop Leofric before his death in 1072. On the basis of a study of its script, it has been suggested that it was written towards the end of the period 1050–72; see E. M. Drage, 'Bishop Leofric and the Exeter Cathedral Chapter 1050–1072: a Reassessment of the Manuscript Evidence' (unpubl. D. Phil. dissertation, Oxford Univ., 1978).

[43] *The Leofric Collectar*, ed. E. S. Dewick and W. H. Frere, 2 vols., HBS 45 and 56 (London, 1914–21) II, esp. xxiv–xxxiv.

[44] *Ibid.*, which refers to this book as the Wulstan Collectar. It is itself edited under the title *The Portiforium of St Wulstan*, ed. A. Hughes, 2 vols., HBS 89–90 (London, 1958–60), where the link with Winchester books is mentioned briefly (II, vi).

chants, including 'O' antiphons, are not much more numerous before the year 1000, comprising only Amalarius of Metz's *De ordine antiphonarii* and the Compiègne Antiphoner mentioned above.[45] The *De ordine*, completed by Amalarius as his last work in 837, was intended to accompany an antiphoner compiled by him in response to the Carolingian move towards conformity with Roman practice, after he had consulted a Roman antiphoner deposited at Corbie.[46] But, although the *De ordine* is a most informative document, its influence, as well as that of the lost antiphoner which it accompanied, should not be overestimated. It is known only in a late printed copy, no medieval manuscript copy having survived[47] – a situation which implies a much smaller circulation than that of the ever-popular *De officiis ecclesiasticis*.[48] Besides, it is not known for which church Amalarius intended his new antiphoner, if indeed it had a definite liturgical destination; certainly his order of chants is not found in any manuscript tradition of antiphoners.[49] However, clearer information about what was actually sung in various European centres is available in a comparatively large number of books written after the millennium. These include an antiphoner written *c.* 1000 at St Gallen by the monk Hartker, edited

45 *Amalarii Episcopi Opera Liturgica Omnia*, ed. J. M. Hanssens, 3 vols. (Rome, 1950) III, 13–224. Unfortunately one of the earliest documents (s. viii[ex]) which list mass and Office chants includes those for the four Sundays of Advent but not for the ferias, and consequently omits all mention of 'O' antiphons. For an edition of the list with facsimiles, see J. Froger, 'Le Fragment de Lucques (fin du VIIIe siècle)', *Études grégoriennes* 18 (1979), 145–53. In another ninth-century work on the antiphoner, the *De antiphonario*, Agobard of Lyon attempted to remove all non-scriptural texts from the liturgy; see *Agobardi Lugdunensis Opera Omnia*, ed. L. van Acker, CCSL, CM 52 (Turnhout, 1981), 335–51. Agobard does not mention 'O' antiphons, however.

46 *Ibid.* pp. 13–15. Amalarius found that the Corbie exemplar of a Roman antiphoner differed from that with which he was familiar in Metz not only in its liturgical order but also in the antiphons and responsories included.

47 *Ibid.* I, 200.

48 *Ibid.* I, 120–31, where fifty-nine medieval sources of the *De officiis* (named *Liber officialis* here) are listed.

49 R. Evans, 'Amalarius of Metz and the Singing of the Carolingian Offices' (unpubl. Ph.D. dissertation, City Univ. of New York, 1977), argues, first, that Amalarius's antiphoner never actually existed in tangible collected form (rather, when Amalarius mentioned 'our antiphoner' he indicated 'that complex of antiphons and responsories that Amalarius and his community were using at the time, and for which he gives his rationale [in the *De ordine antiphonarii*]'); and, secondly, that the proximity of Amalarius's writing of a study of the antiphoner (836–7), and his fall from favour (838), would have allowed little time for his ideas on Office liturgy to assert themselves. Evans compares the choice and order of chants implied in the *De ordine antiphonarii* with those in Vatican City, Archivio di San Pietro, B 79 (Old Roman; see below, n. 54), Hartker's Antiphoner (St Gallen 391, see below, Appendix I) and a Metz Tonary (*Der karolingischer Tonar von Metz*, ed. W. Lipphardt (Münster, 1965)). Unfortunately, Evans's conclusions following this comparison relate more to the way in which Amalarius used his sources than to his influence on later chant traditions.

in *CAO* along with the Compiègne Antiphoner, and ten others of Italian, Spanish, French and German origins.

For the purposes of comparing 'O' antiphon repertories, I have examined a large number of continental and English books, some of which will not be cited here, either because they simply did not contain 'O' antiphons, or because their repertory and order of presentation was exactly that of another earlier and geographically close source already cited. The books which I have selected for comparison can be categorized as follows:

A. Early Engish Office-books (pre-Conquest);
B. Amalarius's *De ordine antiphonarii*;
C. Gregorian Office-books edited in *CAO*;
D. Office-books of the Ambrosian and Old Roman liturgies;
E. Other Gregorian Office-books (including later English).[50]

Appendix I (below, pp. 338–9) lists the 'O' antiphon repertories in each source under consideration; the items are numbered according to the order of the antiphons in the source concerned. Library shelf-marks, together with details of date and origin in each case, are given in the notes accompanying Appendix I.

## THE OLD ENGLISH ADVENT LYRICS

Previous research has cited Latin antiphon texts beginning 'O', to which eleven out of the twelve surviving Old English lyrics are related; only lyric 11, *Eala seo wlitige*, lacks a generally accepted solution, although *O beata et benedicta et gloriosa trinitas* (first suggested by Cook, but rejected by Campbell and Burlin) still appears the most satisfactory suggestion.[51] Including the recently

[50] The Mozarabic chant-books do not have the 'O' antiphons; see *Oracional visigótico*, ed. J. Vives, Monumenta Hispaniae Sacra, serie liturgica 1 (Barcelona, 1946), and M. Randell, *An Index to the Chant of the Mozarabic Rite* (Princeton, NJ, 1973).

[51] *Cynewulf*, ed. Cook, p. 108; *Advent Lyrics*, ed. Campbell, pp. 31 and 99; and Burlin, *Typological Commentary*, pp. 162–3. Campbell objected to *O beata* on the grounds that lyric 11 'is not basically a poem about the Trinity'. But, if the poet needed an antiphon beginning 'O' and could find none in the Christmas liturgy (see below, my discussion of lyric 11), why should he not choose a Trinity antiphon? Burlin offered a hypothetical reconstruction of an antiphon combining elements which form the foundation for the whole lyric. Given the special position of this lyric in the series (again see my discussion below) and its own peculiar nature, there seems no need to seek all this material in one single antiphon. *O beata* is the first antiphon of Lauds in the Office of the Trinity probably composed by Stephen of Liège in the early tenth century. Of the five Lauds antiphons, the first four go in similar-texted pairs, and all begin 'O'; all five are concerned with praise and form a likely background to lyric 11:
(1) O beata et benedicta et gloriosa Trinitas, Pater, et Filius, et Spiritus Sanctus.℣. Tibi laus, tibi gloria, tibi gratiarum actio.

cited antiphons to which lyrics 7 and 10 are related[52] (the former antiphon found uniquely in *De laude Dei*), the antiphons are:

| | | |
|---|---|---|
| 1 | O rex gentium[53] | *CAO*, no. 4078 |
| 2 | O clauis Dauid | *CAO*, no. 4010 |
| 3 | O Ierusalem | *CAO*, no. 4034 |
| 4 | O uirgo uirginum | *CAO*, no. 4091 |
| 5 | O oriens | *CAO*, no. 4050 |
| 6 | O Emmanuel | *CAO*, no. 4025 |
| 7 | O Ioseph | not recorded in *CAO* |
| 8 | O rex pacifice | *CAO*, no. 4080 |
| 9 | O mundi Domina | *CAO*, no. 4048 |
| 10 | O celorum Domine | *CAO*, no. 4012 |
| 12 | O admirabile commercium | *CAO*, no. 3985 |

Only nos. 1–10 are actually great Advent antiphons. No. 12, *O admirabile commercium*, appears as the first antiphon of Lauds on the octave of Christmas (1 January) in both Roman and Frankish books.[54] It must belong to a very old layer of chant, since it is universally recorded by all early antiphoners which have the appropriate part of the liturgical year, as well as by the *De laude Dei* selection.[55] Both musically and textually, *O admirabile commercium* is quite

(2) O uera, summa, sempiterna Trinitas, Pater, et Filius, et Spiritus Sanctus.℣. Tibi laus, tibi gloria, tibi gratiarum actio.

(5) Te iure laudant, te adorant, te glorificant omnes creature tue, O beata Trinitas.℣. Tibi laus, tibi gloria, tibi gratiarum actio.

(These texts are cited from R. Jonsson, *Historia: Études sur la genèse des offices versifiés* (Stockholm, 1968), p. 224). This series of antiphons is itself directly based on the Invocation to the Holy Trinity of Alcuin: PL 101, cols. 54–6. Alcuin's hymn could well have been known by the Old English poet. Lyric 11 can be divided into three parts: lines 1–7, probably based on an 'O' antiphon; lines 8–25, concentrating on angels; and lines 26–38, based on the *Sanctus* and *Benedictus* of the mass, and rightfully sung by angels; see *Advent Lyrics*, ed. Campbell, pp. 33 and 91, and Burlin, *Typological Commentary*, pp. 163–5. Given the poet's intention to write a poem 'on the general subject of praise' (*Advent Lyrics*, ed. Campbell, p. 32), and the way in which the Trinitarian texts all lead in a similar direction, they would have suggested themselves to him naturally.

52 Bullough, 'Alcuin', p. 7, and S. Tugwell, 'Advent Lyrics 348–77 (Lyric No. X)', *MÆ* 39 (1970), 34.

53 In the *Vita S. Dunstani*, written *c.* 1000, Dunstan is said to have heard the following antiphon in a vision: 'O rex gentium, dominator omnium propter sedem maiestatis tuae, da nobis indulgentiam, rex Christe peccatorum, alleluia'; see *Memorials of Saint Dunstan*, ed. W. Stubbs, Rolls Ser. (London, 1874), p. 41. This text is not attested in any of the sources edited in *CAO*, however.

54 *CAO* I (*Manuscripti "Cursus Romanus"*), 60–1, and II (*Manuscripti "Cursus Monasticus"*), 94–5 and *Josephi Mariae Thomasii Opera Omnia IV*, ed. A. F. Vezzosi (Rome, 1749), p. 46; pp. 1–170 include an edition of the Old Roman Antiphoner preserved in Vatican City, Archivio di San Pietro, B 79.

55 Its use appears to have been unaffected by the diversity of practice as regards the Feast of the Circumcision, observed in Spain and Gaul since the mid-sixth century, but not adopted at Rome until the mid-eleventh century.

distinct from the Advent 'O's, and can be linked with them only by virtue of its opening invocation, 'O'.

The great 'O' Advent antiphons belong to a special class of Office antiphons, those sung to the gospel canticles of Lauds (*Benedictus*) and Vespers (*Magnificat*) rather than to psalms.[56] The manner of performance of canticle antiphons was, however, analogous to that of other Office antiphons: antiphon–canticle or psalm–antiphon. And, as was the case in other groups of Office antiphons, the great 'O's all use the same melody, adapting it to suit the particular phrase and stress structure of an individual text. This second mode melody was not itself used for any antiphon outside the Advent series, and thus became a distinguishing mark of the group and provided a musical basis for later textual imitations. That, additionally, the great 'O' antiphons were considered a special group within the larger context of *Benedictus* and *Magnificat* antiphons is clear from the manner of their presentation in the medieval sources. Introductory rubrics often included the adjective *maiores*;[57] more significantly, in the majority of books, the 'O' antiphons were notated or otherwise recorded together as a series, rather than each individual antiphon being recorded with the liturgy of the day on which it was actually sung (in the manner of other canticle antiphons).

'O' antiphons are already numerous in the earliest sources which mention them: Alcuin collects ten,[58] Amalarius eight;[59] in later sources it is not uncommon to find a series of twelve, or, as in one case, thirteen.[60] Seven of these antiphons, beginning *O sapientia*, *O Adonay*, *O radix*, *O clauis*, *O oriens*, *O rex gentium* and *O Emmanuel*, always appear without exception in any series. As they form a distinct and coherent stylistic group, it has been generally assumed (as first implied by Amalarius) that they were composed by one person.[61] The

56 See M. Huglo, 'Antiphon', *The New Grove* I, 478. The 'O' antiphons were usually sung to the *Magnificat*, but were occasionally linked with the *Benedictus*, e.g. in the Old Roman Antiphoner, *Thomasii Opera Omnia*, ed. Vezzosi, p. 27. Burlin (*Typological Commentary*, pp. 42–3) mentions the 'relegation' of 'certain additional 'O's to the service "ad crucem"', in the Antiphonary of Hartker. I can find no basis for his suggestion: Hartker merely has the rubric IN PROXIMA EBDOMADA NATALIS DOMINI (*CAO* II (*Manuscripti "Cursus Monasticus"*), 56).

57 E.g. in the Compiègne Antiphoner; see 'Antiphonae maiores in euangelio': *CAO* I (*Manuscripti "Cursus Romanus"*), 28.

58 Constantinescu, 'Alcuin', pp. 40–1. I print Alcuin's 'O' antiphon texts in Appendix II (below, p. 340), newly transcribed from one of the manuscript sources.

59 *Amalarii Episcopi Opera*, ed. Hanssens III, 44–9.

60 *CAO* I (*Manuscripti "Cursus Romanus"*) 28–31, and II (*Manuscripti "Cursus Monasticus"*), 55–7.

61 *Amalarii Episcopi Opera*, ed. Hanssens III, 44. For the best short study of the 'O' antiphons, including details of their biblical sources, see M. Huglo, 'O Antiphons', *The New Catholic Encyclopedia*, 17 vols. (Washington, DC, 1967–79) X, 587–8. See also P. Guéranger, 'Les Grandes Antiennes', *RB* 2 (1885–6), 512–16; H. Thurston, 'The Great Antiphons, Heralds of

seven antiphons in question are all addressed to the Messiah, and share a common text structure: an opening invocation, followed by two or three amplifying phrases, and finally an appeal beginning *ueni*. Within this structure there is some variation of phrase length, and in the number of short phrases – in all cases except one there are six:

> O radix Iesse   qui stas in signum populorum
> super quem continebunt reges os suum   quem gentes deprecabuntur
> ueni ad liberandum nos   iam noli tardare.
> O oriens   splendor lucis eterne
> et sol iustitiae
> ueni et illumina sedentes in tenebris   et umbra mortis.

The melody shared by all these texts also has six phrases (*O oriens* omits the fourth), and recitations within each phrase can be expanded or contracted as necessary:

Christmas', *The Month* 106 (1905), 616–31; and C. Callewaert, 'De groote Adventsantifonen O', *Sacris Erudiri: Fragmenta Liturgica Collecta*, ed. the monks of St Peter's, Aldenburg (Steenbrugge, 1940), pp. 405–18.

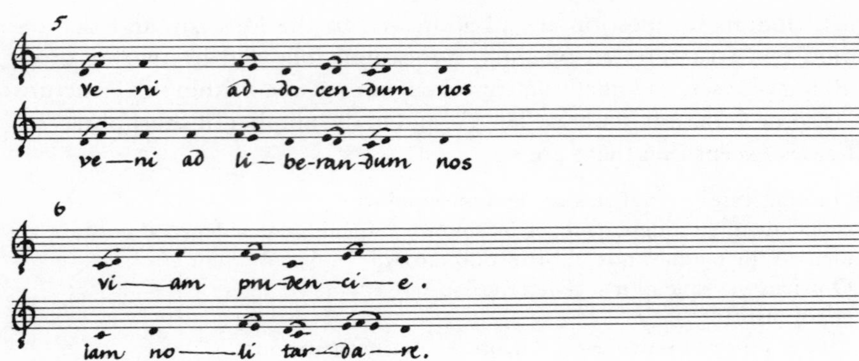


FIG. 5 The melody for the six-phrase 'O' antiphons (from Paris, BN lat. 17296)

An interesting musical characteristic is the pairing of the opening phrase with that beginning *ueni*, thus providing musical reinforcement for the appeal *ueni*, and articulating the whole structure:

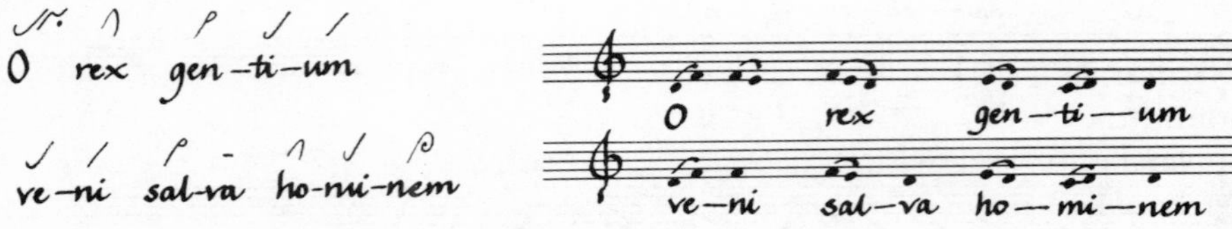


FIG. 6 The pairing of melodic phrases in 'O' antiphons, as recorded in a staved version (Paris, BN lat. 17296) and a neumed version (St Gallen, Stiftsbibliothek, 391)

None of the other Advent 'O' antiphons transmitted in early sources reproduces the text pattern of the central seven in all its significant characteristics; only one (*O celorum Domine*) includes an appeal beginning *ueni*, and again only one (*O rex pacifice*) is addressed to the Messiah. *O uirgo uirginum* is rather longer than any other, and includes two questions:

O uirgo uirginum   quomodo fiet istud
quia nec primum similem uisa est   nec habere sequentem?
Filiae Ierusalem quid me admiramini?   Diuina est mysterium hoc quod cernitis.

Three others, *O Gabriel*, *O mundi Domina* and *O Ierusalem*, conform only to the six-phrase dimensions of the central seven. A musical reflection of the change of text pattern is the loss of melodic identity between the opening and fifth (*ueni*) phrases, where these have no especial sense relation:

FIG. 7 The loss of melodic identity between opening and fifth phrases, as recorded in a staved version (Paris, BN lat. 17296) and a neumed version (St Gallen, Stiftsbibliothek, 391)

However, the pairing is preserved in *O uirgo uirginum*, where the fifth phrase begins *Filiae Ierusalem*:

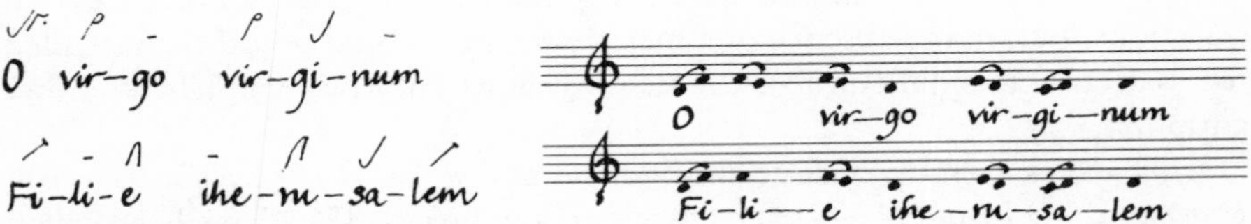


FIG. 8 The pairing of melodic phrases in *O uirgo uirginum*, as illustrated in a staved version (Paris, BN lat. 17296) and a neumed version (St Gallen, Stiftsbibliothek, 391)

Although the stylistic coherence of the central seven antiphons is beyond doubt, they are found transmitted alone, without additional 'O' antiphons, only in books of the later Middle Ages, such as those of the Cistercian order.[62] Without exception in the early books, *O uirgo uirginum* accompanies the first seven. These eight form the limit of the repertory known to Amalarius, and also that of the Compiègne Antiphoner and Wulfstan Collectar from Worcester. With the addition of *O Thoma*, composed for the feast of St Thomas the Apostle on 21 December, this comprises the repertory of 'O' antiphons known in many places affected by the Carolingian reforms (Saint-Denis and later French books) and by the later Cluniac reform (Saint-Maur, Lucca and Lewes), and found in books of the later medieval English rites (Sarum, Exeter and Hereford). *O Thoma* certainly appears to be a Frankish rather than a Roman composition, being conspicuously absent from Roman and Ambrosian books; its absence from both Alcuin's and Amalarius's collections and from the Compiègne and Hartker Antiphoners, but its invariable inclusion in eleventh-century Frankish and English sources, could imply a date of composition

62 From the time of their foundation in 1098, the Cistercians made several attempts to restore the 'true Gregorian chant', eliminating all material thought to have been later additions to the original *Ordo*, and rewriting the melodies to conform to what they imagined to be Gregorian melodic principles. In general they simplified and, in consequence, reduced the musical repertory.

anywhere in the ninth century or the tenth. Of all the other 'imitation' 'O' antiphons transmitted singly, and known only in confined areas, there are no more than two to which the Old English lyrics are related. First, *O celorum* is noted in *CAO* as appearing in the Ivrea Antiphoner only, but it is found also in a later book from the region of Campania, south of Rome.[63] Further research is needed to establish whether it really belonged to an individual Ivrea repertory and was diffused from there (and, if so, at what date), or whether it was more widely known in Italy at an early date. Secondly, *O Ioseph*, which is known only from the *De laude Dei* and as a source for the Old English lyrics, may have been a native English composition, although, of course, it might have an Italian ancestry even more obscure than that of *O celorum*. Like *O uirgo* it includes two questions, but, in the absence of a melody – which could reveal the intended text pattern – it is difficult to estimate to what extent it was modelled on that antiphon.

This leaves a group of four antiphons – *O Gabriel*, *O rex pacifice*, *O mundi Domina* and *O Ierusalem* – often transmitted as a group. They have been called 'monastic 'O's', perhaps because of their earliest appearance all together in Hartker's Antiphoner, but actually they appear in equal prevalence in both monastic and secular sources. In fact, their transmission pattern is not so much monastic as regional, for, apart from the English books, they are only found in books of southern German, Swiss and north Italian origin from, for example, St Gallen, Rheinau, Bamberg, Ivrea, Monza and Salzburg. In the English, the Old Roman and a few other Italian sources, members of this group of four are sometimes found not *en bloc* but individually or in pairs. Both *De laude Dei* and the twelfth-century Roman Antiphoner have only *O Ierusalem*; the Leofric Collectar has *O Gabriel* and *O mundi Domina*, whilst the Verona Antiphoner has *O rex pacifice* and *O Ierusalem*, and an eleventh-century Brescia breviary has *O mundi Domina* only. To what extent these isolated appearances might be due to lack of transmission of the others (because they had all been separately composed and transmitted), or to deliberate selection based on liturgical needs or personal wishes, is unclear. It is certain, however, that none of the four belonged to the standard west Frankish repertory, and that Alcuin knew *O Ierusalem* through the intermediary of an imported south German/Swiss or north Italian source. Since this antiphon, on the evidence of Alcuin's knowledge of it, was composed before 790, it is possible that all four were composed and available *in toto* by that date. As to the central seven and *O uirgo*, it goes without saying that they belonged to some of the oldest layers of Roman chant,

63 Oxford, Bodleian Library, Canonici liturg. 339, 93v–94r. This book comprises a choir breviary (noted in parts) and votive missal, compiled during the early and late fourteenth century. Its exact origin is unknown.

and probably were known in England from the time of Augustine's arrival in 597, or from the time of their composition, if this was later.[64]

Much more can now be said about the Old English poet's selection of 'O' antiphons.[65] Of the basic group of seven + *O uirgo*, the extant lyrics use only five, omitting the first three, *O sapientia*, *O Adonay* and *O radix*. Since this omission is not matched in any recorded liturgical repertory, it seems improbable that these three antiphons were not known to the Old English poet. On these grounds I would agree with Burgert, Burlin and Pope that these three antiphons are likely to have been paraphrased in three now lost lyrics opening the series.[66] The lyrics also use three of the group of four antiphons associated with south German/Swiss and north Italian repertories: *O rex pacifice*, *O mundi Domina* and *O Ierusalem*. Since *De laude Dei* has only one of these, the Wulfstan Collectar none and the Leofric Collectar also only one, the lyrics do not match up with any other extant English sources. Including as it does also *O celorum* and *O Ioseph*, the poet's repertory of 'O' antiphons is in fact unique, and is no more closely related to the *De laude Dei* group than to south German/Swiss and north Italian repertories. Moreover, probably no fewer than fifteen 'O' antiphons were known to the poet, a number unmatched anywhere else. Either the poet had access to at least two sources which included different repertories of 'O' antiphons, or his source included all the 'O's which could be collected together, whether they were liturgically required or not. Obviously his source was not the *De laude Dei* itself;[67] but both his sources and Alcuin's evidently had some common ancestry in books imported into England, probably north

[64] They date from before 735, if the report that Bede dying sang *O rex gloriose* is correct (see above, n. 40). On the basis of a textual link between *O sapientia* and Boethius's *De consolatione Philosophiae*, Cabaniss has suggested that they were known and used as early as the beginning of the sixth century; see J. A. Cabaniss, 'A Note on the Date of the Great Advent Antiphons', *Speculum* 22 (1947), 440–2. But, of course, such a link really provides only a *terminus a quo* for their composition.

[65] In spite of the poet's extensive liturgical knowledge – undoubtedly he must have been familiar with the 'O' antiphon melodies – the structure of his Old English poems is quite independent of these melodies: he used only the 'O' antiphon texts as a basis for his lyrics.

[66] See above, n. 1, and the works cited above, n. 2.

[67] That Alcuin's *De laude Dei* was not one of his sources is clear from the fact that the closing lines of *O radix* and *O Emmanuel* as preserved in *De laude Dei* differ from those of other sources:

| | |
|---|---|
| *O radix* | *CAO*: ueni ad liberandum nos iam noli tardare |
| | Alcuin: ueni ad saluandum nos Domine Deus noster |
| *O Emmanuel* | *CAO*: ueni ad saluandum nos Domine Deus noster |
| | Alcuin: ueni ad saluandum nos iam noli tardare. |

Such a confusion might be the result of scribal error long after the compilation of the *De laude Dei*, but the possibility exists that the lines were already interchanged in early sources. No lyric based on *O radix* survives; lyric 6 corresponds more closely to the usual version of *O Emmanuel* than to that in *De laude Dei*.

Italian in origin. We can infer that probably this large repertory of 'O' antiphons was available in England by the late eighth century at the latest, for, once the English liturgies came under Frankish rather than direct Roman influence, the repertory of 'O' antiphons appears to have contracted. Thus, while no exact *termini post quem* or *ante quem* for the composition of the Old English lyrics can be deduced from this evidence, it is at least likely that the poems were composed well before the mid-tenth century, when the great Benedictine revival introduced a new wave of Frankish liturgical influence.

One other question remains: what determined the order of the Advent lyrics, as recorded (for us, imperfectly at the beginning) in the Exeter Book? The liturgical sources of 'O' antiphons mostly show a standard pattern, beginning with *O sapientia* and continuing through the basic series of seven to *O uirgo uirginum* as the eighth, as in the Compiègne Antiphoner, and both the Leofric and the Wulfstan Collectars. Alcuin placed *O rex gentium* (usually sixth) before *O clauis* (usually fourth), but otherwise his order accords with the majority of other sources. Amalarius consciously rejected the usual order, inventing his own, based on the sevenfold gifts of the Holy Spirit.[68] For the antiphons outside the basic group various sources share patterns, while others have unique orders; in general the extra 'O's follow the basic group of eight. Remarkably, the order of the first ten surviving Old English lyrics – those which match with Advent 'O' antiphons – has no parallel in the liturgical sources.

Something which has not previously been recognized, however, is the manner in which, as a cycle, the twelve surviving lyrics follow the pattern of a part of the liturgical year. In lyric 11, *Eala seo wlitige*, described by Campbell as the lyric 'which reaches the highest point of emotional intensity',[69] clearly the long-awaited Advent has transpired:

þa mid ryhte sculon reordberende
earme eorðware, ealle mægene
hergan healice, nu us hælend god
wærfæst onwrah þæt we hine witan moton. (Lyric 11, lines 4–7)[70]

Besides this direct clue, there are several ways in which this lyric develops liturgical themes of Christmas rather than Advent. The protagonists include not just God and man, but also hosts of angels, who are singing:

68 *Amalarii Episcopi Opera*, ed. Hanssens III, 44–9.

69 *Advent Lyrics*, ed. Campbell, p. 10. Cook (*Cynewulf*, ed. Cook, p. 113) sees the final lyric (rather than lyric 11) as 'a sort of climax'.

70 *Ibid.* pp. 74–5; he translates:
poor earth-bound men with all their might
should praise highly now that the faithful Saviour
has revealed God to us that we may know Him.

Forþon hy, dædhwæte, dome geswiðde,
þæt soðfæste seraphinnes cynn,
uppe mid englum a bremende,
unaþreotendum þrymmum singað
ful healice hludan stefne,
fægre feor ond neah. (Lyric 11, lines 8–13a)[71]

Given the Advent context created by the preceding lyrics, this cannot fail to bring to mind the scene described in Luke II.8–14 and portraying angels singing to frightened shepherds *Gloria in excelsis Deo!* In the Latin liturgy, this thread of the Christmas story was introduced in the first Office of Christmas Day, at Matins, and developed further in the Office of Lauds in the antiphon series *Quem uidistis*, *Genuit puerpera*, *Angelus ad pastores*, *Facta est cum angelo*, *Pastores dicite* or *Paruulus filius*, and the *Benedictus* antiphon *Gloria in excelsis Deo.*[72] Another link between lyric 11 and the Christmas liturgy is the emphasis on praise of God. Short parts of lyrics 1–10 are devoted to straightforward praise, but none is so overwhelmingly dominated by it; the last thirteen lines of lyric 11, which the poet has put into the mouth of the angels, speak most eloquently:

Halig eart þu, halig, heahengla brego,
soð sigores frea, simle þu bist halig,
dryhtna dryhten! A þin dom wunað
eorðlic mid ældum in ælce tid
wide geweorðad. Þu eart weoroda god,
forþon þu gefyldest foldan ond rodoras,
wigendra hleo, wuldres þines,
helm alwihta. Sie þe in heannessum
ece hælo, ond in eorþan lof,
beorht mid beornum. Þu gebletsad leofa,
þe in dryhtnes noman dugeþum cwome
heanum to hroþre. Þe in heahþum sie
a butan ende ece herenis. (Lyric 11, lines 26–38)[73]

71 *Ibid.*

Indeed they, the eager ones confirmed in glory,
the righteous race of seraphim
ever celebrating above among angels,
sing with unwearied strength,
exaltedly with loud voices,
beautifully far and near.

72 *CAO* I (*Manuscripti "Cursus Romanus"*), 34–7, and II (*Manuscripti "Cursus Monasticus"*), 64–7.

73 *Advent Lyrics*, ed. Campbell, pp. 74–5:

Holy art thou, holy, Prince of Archangels,
true Lord of Victory, ever art thou holy,
God of Gods. Always thy praise endures

Such free and intense expression can be understood only as the fervent response of the Christian community to that event for which they had waited and prayed throughout Advent – the birth of Christ.

In the last lyric, the liturgical pattern is carried on: the underlying antiphon, *O admirabile commercium*, celebrates the Virgin Birth (referred to in the past tense), and was sung a week after Christmas. The poet's choice of Latin text is interesting, for that reference to change in human life brought about by divine intervention, 'Eala hwæt, þæt is wræclic wrixl in wera life',[74] is one of the most characteristic features of the Christian festivals of Christmas and Easter. More significantly, *O admirabile commercium* remains close to the spirit of Christmas itself, and is not concerned with other events commemorated during this period, such as the Slaying of the Innocents (feast on 28 December), the Circumcision (1 January) or the coming Epiphany (6 January). Finally, this last lyric closes with words which imitate a familiar liturgical formula: 'siþþan eardað ealne widan feorh wunað butan ende. Amen.'[75]

## CONCLUSIONS

Whilst the internal order of the first ten surviving Old English lyrics does not have a liturgical precedent, there is a clear liturgical basis for the overall pattern. And it is not just in their arrangement, moving to Christmas and beyond, that the lyrics are liturgically inspired. As a cycle, they have a rhythm corresponding to that part of the liturgical year which they follow: a long period of waiting (lyrics 1–10), a short time of intense emotional reaction at Christmas (lyric 11), and, afterwards, a time for comprehension of the Christmas events, before the feast of the Epiphany (lyric 12). Through this liturgical examination, it has become apparent that, far from writing a group of lyrics based on those Advent antiphons known by his community, the poet made deliberate choices and selections. By choosing antiphons characteristic

on earth among men in every epoch
widely honoured. Thou art the God of Hosts
since thou hast filled heaven and earth
with thy great glory, Protector of warriors,
Shield of all beings. To thee be in the highest
eternal glory and on earth praise,
bright among men. Live thou blessed
who in the name of the Lord came to men,
a solace to the lowly. To thee on high
be everlasting praise world without end.

74 *Ibid.* pp. 76–7: 'O what a marvellous change in the life of men.'

75 *Ibid.*: 'where he thereafter lives blessed, dwells eternally, world without end. Amen.'

of different liturgical periods, and by amplifying their points of contact with the Christmas story, he gave a flow and integrity to the whole cycle. In range and in spirit, more essentially than has been previously realized, these 'Advent' lyrics can indeed be said to have been founded in Roman liturgical texts and practices.

# Manuscript Sources of ‘O’ Antiphons

| *‘O’ antiphons* | *CAO* no. | Advent lyrics | De laude Dei | Amalarius | LC/Exeter | WC/Worcester | H/St Gallen | R/Rheinau | D/Saint-Denis | F/Saint-Maur | S/Silos | L/Benevento | C/Compiègne | G/Gallican | B/Bamberg | E/Ivrea | M/Monza | V/Verona | Ambrosian | Old Roman | Sarum | Gloucester | Coldingham | Lewes | Brescia | Lucca | Sondrio | Milan | Saint-Martial | Mont-Renaud | Besançon | Freising | Salzburg | Würzburg |
|---|---|---|---|---|---|---|---|---|---|---|---|---|---|---|---|---|---|---|---|---|---|---|---|---|---|---|---|---|---|---|---|---|---|---|
| O sapientia | 4081 | | 1 | 1 | 1 | 1 | 1 | 1 | 1 | 1 | 1 | 1 | 1 | 1 | 1 | 1 | 1 | 1 | 6 | 1 | 1 | 1 | 1 | 1 | 1 | 1 | 1 | 1 | 1 | 1 | 1 | 1 | 1 | 1 |
| O Adonay | 3988 | | 2 | 6 | 2 | 2 | 2 | 2 | 2 | 2 | 2 | 2 | 2 | 2 | 2 | 2 | 2 | 2 | 7 | 2 | 2 | 2 | 2 | 2 | 2 | 2 | 2 | 2 | 2 | 2 | 2 | 2 | 2 | 2 |
| O radix | 4075 | | 3 | 4 | 3 | 3 | 3 | 3 | 3 | 3 | 3 | 3 | 3 | 3 | 3 | 3 | 3 | 3 | 1 | 3 | 3 | 3 | 3 | 3 | 3 | 3 | 3 | 3 | 3 | 3 | 3 | 3 | 3 | 3 |
| O clauis | 4010 | 2 | 5 | 2 | 4 | 4 | 4 | 4 | 4 | 4 | 4 | 4 | 4 | 4 | 4 | 4 | 4 | 4 | 2 | 4 | 4 | 4 | 4 | 4 | 4 | 4 | 4 | 4 | 4 | 4 | 4 | 4 | 4 | 4 |
| O oriens | 4050 | 5 | 6 | 5 | 5 | 5 | 5 | 5 | 5 | 7 | 5 | 5 | 5 | 5 | 5 | 5 | 5 | 5 | 3 | 5 | 5 | 5 | 6 | 7 | 5 | 7 | 12 | 5 | 5 | 5 | 5 | 5 | 5 | 5 |
| O rex gentium | 4078 | 1 | 4 | 7 | 6 | 6 | 6 | 6 | 6 | 5 | 6 | | 6 | 6 | 6 | 6 | 6 | 6 | 4 | 6 | 6 | 6 | 7 | 5 | 6 | 5 | 5 | 6 | 6 | 6 | 6 | 6 | 6 | 6 |
| O Emmanuel | 4025 | 6 | 7 | 3 | 7 | 7 | 7 | 8 | 7 | 6 | 7 | | 7 | 7 | 7 | 7 | 9 | 7 | 5 | 7 | 7 | 7 | 8 | 6 | 7 | 6 | 6 | 7 | 7 | 7 | 7 | 8 | 8 | 8 |
| O uirgo | 4091 | 4 | 8 | 8 | 8 | 8 | 8 | 11 | 8 | 8 | 8 | | 8 | 8 | 8 | 8 | 8 | 8 | 8 | 8 | 8 | | 9 | 8 | 8 | 8 | 10 | 8 | 8 | 8 | | 11 | 11 | 11 |
| O Gabriel | 4028 | | | | 12 | | 9 | 9 | | | | | | | 9 | 9 | 7 | | | | | | | | | | 8 | 9 | | | | 9 | 9 | 9 |
| O rex pacifice | 4080 | 8 | | | | | 10 | 7 | | | | | | | 10 | 10 | 11 | 10 | | | | | | | | | 7 | | | | | 7 | 7 | 7 |
| O mundi Domina | 4048 | 9 | | | 11 | | 11 | 12 | | | | | | | 12 | 11 | 12 | | | | | | | | | | 11 | | | | | 12 | 12 | 12 |
| O Ierusalem | 4034 | 3 | | | | | 12 | 10 | | | | | | | 11 | 12 | 13 | 11 | | 9 | | | | | | | 9 | | | | | 10 | 10 | 10 |
| O Thoma | 4083 | | | | 9 | | | √ | 9 | √ | 9 | √ | | 10 | √ | √ | 10 | 12 | | | 9 | 8 | 5 | | | | | | | | | | | |
| O celorum | 4012 | 10 | | | | | | | | | | | | | | 13 | | | | | | | | | | | | | | | | | | |
| O celes | 4011 | | | | | | | | | | | | | | | | | 9 | | | | | | | | | | | | | | | | |
| O summe | 4082 | | | | | | | | | | | | | 9 | | | | | | | | | | | | | | | | | | | | |
| O rex iustitiae | — | | | | 10 | | | | | | | | | | | | | | | | | | | | | | | | | | | | | |
| O Ioseph | — | 7 | | | | | | | | | | | | | | | | | | | | | | | | | | | | | | | | |

√ denotes appearance of *O Thoma* in the book, but separately from the series of Advent ‘O’s. Series 1 2 3 4 5 6 7 8 9 (such as Sarum) and 1 2 3 4 6 7 8 9 5 (such as Coldingham) are effectively similar. In the first *O Thoma* is mentioned at the end of the series simply because it was a late addition, whereas in the second it has been inserted at the correct point, to be sung on 21 December.

# NOTES

## A. ENGLISH SOURCES

*De laude Dei* — Bamberg, Staatsbibliothek, Misc. Patr. 17 (B. II. 10) (s. x$^{ex}$), 133v–61v.
Escorial, Real Biblioteca, b IV 17 (southern France, s. ix$^{med}$), fols. 93–108; see Bullough, 'Alcuin', pp. 4–5.

*LC/Exeter* — London, BL Harley 2961 (Exeter, *c.* 1070); see above, n. 42.

*WC/Worcester* — Cambridge, Corpus Christi College 391 (Worcester, *c.* 1065); see above, n. 44.

## B. *Amalarius, De ordine antiphonarii*; see above, n. 45.

## C. CAO SOURCES

*H/St Gallen* — St Gallen, Stiftsbibliothek, 391 (St Gallen, s. x/xi).

*R/Rheinau* — Zürich, Zentralbibliothek, Rheinau 28 (Rheinau, s. xiii).

*D/Saint-Denis* — Paris, BN lat. 17296 (Saint-Denis, s. xii).

*F/Saint-Maur* — Paris, BN lat. 12584 (Saint-Maur-des-Fossés, s. xi/xii).

*S/Silos* — London, BL Add. 30850 (Silos, s. xi).

*L/Benevento* — Benevento, Cathedral Library, V. 21 (Benevento, s. xii$^{ex}$).

*C/Compiègne* — Paris, BN lat. 17436 (north-east France, *c.* 860–77); see above, nn. 10 and 13.

*G/Gallican* — Durham, Cathedral Library, B. III. 11 (northern France, s. xi).

*B/Bamberg* — Bamberg, Staatsbibliothek, lit. 23 (Bamberg, s. xii$^{ex}$).

*E/Ivrea* — Ivrea, Cathedral Library, 106 (Ivrea, s. xi).

*M/Monza* — Monza, Cathedral Library, c. 12. 75 (Monza, s. xi).

*V/Verona* — Verona, Cathedral Library, 98 (Verona, s. xi).

## D. AMBROSIAN AND OLD ROMAN BOOKS

*Ambrosian* — London, BL Add. 34209 (Milan, s. xii); *Antiphonarium Ambrosianum du Musée Britannique (XIIe siècle), Codex Additional 34209*, 2 vols., Paléographie musicale 5–6 (Solesmes, 1896–1900).

*Old Roman* — London, BL Add. 29988 (Rome (? for the Lateran Basilica), s. xii).

## E. OTHER GREGORIAN (INCLUDING ENGLISH) BOOKS

*Sarum* — Salisbury, Cathedral Library, 152 (Salisbury, s. xv); partial facsimile in *Antiphonale Sarisburiense*, ed. W. H. Frere, Plainsong and Med. Music Soc. (London, 1901–24). Exeter and Hereford have the same series; see *Ordinale Exoniense*, ed. J. N. Dalton and G. H. Doble, 4 vols., HBS 37, 38, 63 and 79 (London, 1909–40), and *The Hereford Breviary*, ed. W. H. Frere and L. E. G. Brown, 3 vols., HBS 26, 40 and 46 (London, 1904–15).

*Gloucester* — Oxford, Jesus College 10 (St Peter's, Gloucester, s. xii).

*Coldingham* — London, BL Harley 4664 (Coldingham (mainly Durham use), s. xiii$^{ex}$).

*Lewes* — Cambridge, Fitzwilliam Museum 369 (Lewes Priory, Sussex (Cluniac), s. xiii); the same series is found in Oxford, University College 101 (Priory of St John, Pontefract (Cluniac), s. xiii$^{ex}$).

*Brescia* — Oxford, Bodleian Library, Canonici liturg. 366 (Cathedral of Our Lady's Assumption, Brescia, s. xi/xii).

*Lucca* — Lucca, Cathedral Library, 601; *Antiphonaire monastique, XIIe siècle. Codex 601 de la Bibliothèque capitulaire de Lucques*, Paléographie musicale 9–10 (Tournai, 1909).

*Sondrio* — Oxford, Bodleian Library, Canonici liturg. 202 (St Peter's, Sondrio, s. xii/xiii).

*Milan* — Oxford, Bodleian Library, Lat. liturg. c. 1. (? Milan, s. xiii$^{in}$).

*Saint-Martial* — Paris, BN lat. 1085 (Saint-Martial de Limoges, s. x).

*Mont Renaud* — Private collection, Paris; *Le Manuscrit de Mont-Renaud, Xe siècle: Graduel et antiphonaire de Noyon*, Paléographie musicale 16 (Solesmes, 1955).

*Besançon* — Oxford, Bodleian Library, Lat. liturg. f. 1 (Cistercian, diocese of Besançon, s. xiii).

*Freising* — Oxford, Bodleian Library, Lat. liturg. b. 7, fols. 21–4 (fragments) (Scheyern, diocese of Freising, s. xi/xii).

*Salzburg* — Vienna, Nationalbibliothek, 2700 (St Peter's Salzburg, s. xii); *Das Antiphonar von St Peter*, ed. F. Unterkircher and O. Demus (Graz, 1974).

*Würzburg* — Oxford, Bodleian Library, Canonici liturg. 297 (diocese of Würzburg, s. xii).

APPENDIX II

# 'O' Antiphons from Alcuin's *De Laude Dei*

Bamberg, Staatsbibliothek, Misc. Patr. 17 (B. II. 10), 149r–v

[149r]
O sapientia quae ex ore altissimi prodisti,
adtingens a fine usque ad finem fortiter suauiter disponensque omnia:
ueni ad docendum nos uiam prudentiae.

O Adonay et dux domus Israel,
qui Moysi in flammae ignis rubo apparuisti et ei in Sina legem dedisti:
ueni ad redimendum nos in brachio extento.

O radix Iesse qui stas in signum populorum,
super quem continebunt reges os suum, quem gentes deprecabuntur:
ueni ad saluandum nos, Domine Deus noster.

[149v]
O rex gentium et desideratus earum,
lapisque angularis qui facis utraque unum:
ueni salua hominem, quem de limo formasti.

O clauis Dauid et sceptrum domus Israel,
qui aperis et nemo claudit, claudis et nemo aperit:
ueni et educ uinctos de domo carceris, sedentes in tenebris et umbra mortis.

O oriens, splendor lucis aeternae et sol iustitiae:
ueni et inlumina sedentes in tenebris et umbra mortis.

O Emmanuel, rex et legifer noster,
expectatio gentium et saluator earum:
ueni ad saluandum nos; iam noli tardare.

O uirgo uirginum, quomodo fiet istud, quia nec prima te similis uisa es
nec habebis sequentem? Filiae Hierusalem, quid me admiramini?
Diuinum est misterium hoc quod cernitis.

O H<i>erusalem, ciuitas Dei summi,
leua in circuitu oculos tuos et uide Dominum Deum tuum:
ecce iam ueniet soluere te a uinculo.

O Iosep<h>, quomodo credidisti quod antea expauisti?
Quid enim? In ea natum est de Spiritu Sancto ē [*sic*]
quem Gabrihel annuncians Christum esse uenturum.

# The Office in late Anglo-Saxon monasticism

M. McC. GATCH

This paper has two purposes. The first is to stress that the ordering of the liturgical life of monks and nuns was a central objective (indeed, the primary purpose) of the late Anglo-Saxon monastic reform and to outline some of the materials for study of the Divine Office that are available as scholarly resources for modern students who seek to study the literary influence of the tenth-century monastic reform. The second is to demonstrate, by means of an examination of the homiletical and instructional writings based on the Old Testament by Abbot Ælfric, that knowledge of the liturgy is germane to understanding the purposes for which this set of vernacular texts was written and the principles by which materials were selected for explication or paraphrase. The latter is an exploration that can only be undertaken in the light of Peter Clemoes's indispensable studies of the canon and chronology of the work of the man who proudly styled himself 'munuc ond mæssepreost' as well as 'alumnus Æthelwoldi'.

## MATERIALS FOR THE STUDY OF THE OFFICE

It is perhaps inevitable that most students of the tenth-century reform or revival of monasticism in England have treated the movement as a political phenomenon.[1] It was, of course, inevitably a political phenomenon, if only because it was initiated and carried out by the king, Edgar, and his well-born ecclesiastical officers, the archbishop of Canterbury and the bishops of Winchester and Worcester. The reformers intended not so much to liberate the monasteries in England from lay domination, and thereby to free the monks to live under a truly monastic rule, as to restore monastic observance in a country where it had all but disappeared until recent years when men like the three reforming bishops had been drawn to the continental example of a

[1] Amongst the basic accounts, D. Knowles's (*The Monastic Order in England*, 2nd ed. (Cambridge, 1963), pp. 31–56) and F. M. Stenton's (*Anglo-Saxon England*, 3rd ed. (London, 1971), pp. 433–69) remain fundamental for all subsequent study.

reinvigorated monasticism. This aim, like that of the continental reformers, would also have political and economic repercussions and results. Edgar's support of the reform was, of course, epitomized by the production of the *Regularis concordia* at an ecclesiastical council held at Winchester – a council perhaps held in conjunction with his magnificent coronation in 973, some fourteen years after he had ascended the throne of the kings of the West Saxons.[2]

The *Regularis concordia* itself, however, is less concerned with the political ramifications of the reform than with the internal lives of the monasteries in Edgar's realm and with the quality and integrity of life in the monasteries that the reform was intended to assure. Eric John remarked, provocatively, in a recent account of the reform:

> Historians have tended to see the problem of early tenth-century monasticism in twelfth-century terms. Almost all monasteries, by that time, were communities of bachelor clergymen sharing a common way of life laid down in certain documents, i.e. *Rules*... In the tenth century [as opposed to the twelfth] the reformers had to cope with an over-successful integration of the religious life into that of the secular world of kindred groups.[3]

John argues that the Anglo-Saxon reformers under Edgar were breaking up the 'integration of the religious life' with the 'secular world of kindred groups'. That is, they were disrupting the social bonds of loyalty within the family group which, on the continent, had led to the domination of monasteries by lay proprietors or even to the private ownership of churches (*Eigenkirchen*).[4] The reformers were moving towards the regularization of monastic life (which would include, among other things, stricter enforcement of celibacy) by establishing new standards and expectations of accountability for monastic communities. They were also – and this would have far-reaching effects for the constitution of the English church in the later Middle Ages – bringing into the monastic purview institutions conventionally managed elsewhere in the church by secular clergy. For rather than impose a canonical life upon secular clergy or cathedral canons by some such means as the

[2] See Symons, '*Regularis Concordia*: History and Derivation', *Tenth-Century Studies*, ed. D. Parsons (London and Chichester, 1975), pp. 37–59, esp. p. 42.

[3] 'The Age of Edgar', *The Anglo-Saxons*, ed. J. Campbell (Oxford, 1982), pp. 160–89, at 182.

[4] Nineteenth- and twentieth-century study of European monastic reform (especially of the 'Cluniac' movement) tended until the most recent decades to stress the political perspective: the reformers, on this view, aimed at freeing monasticism from control by local, lay lords. For a recent review of this literature, see B. H. Rosenwein, *Rhinoceros Bound: Cluny in the Tenth Century* (Philadelphia, Pa, 1982), esp. ch. 1. Eric John's account (above, n. 3) of the reform is very much influenced by this earlier tradition.

imposition of the Rule of Chrodegang,[5] the English in the late tenth century were reforming the major cathedrals as monasteries[6] and making monks the occupants of sees, some of which remained monastic foundations (an English peculiarity) until the reign of Henry VIII.

Yet these political ramifications of the reform, important though they were and whether or not they were foremost in the minds of the reformers, would not have been the matters that had immediate impact upon the lives of the *monachi sanctimonialesque*[7] for whose guidance and governance (according to the title in London, BL Cotton Tiberius A. iii) the *Regularis concordia* was composed and promulgated. For ordinary nuns and monks in their day-to-day life the body of the *Concordia* would have been far more important than its proem, which discusses the social and political sanctions (and ramifications) of the document and of the ecclesiastical council at which it was adopted. Far from being overtly or intentionally political, however, the chapters of the *Concordia* are concerned exclusively with the spiritual or liturgical life of the men and women who lived in the monasteries, that is, with the performance of the Divine Office. They begin in ch. 1 with the admonition that every act, including rising in the morning, should begin with blessing (that is, signing oneself with the cross and invoking the Trinity), and end in ch. 12 with

[5] Chrodegang's Rule was instituted at Exeter in 1050 by Bishop Leofric, who had been a secular clerk in the royal household before his consecration; see F. Barlow, *The English Church 1000–1066*, 2nd ed. (London, 1979), pp. 84 and 213–15, and *Leofric of Exeter*, ed. F. Barlow *et al.* (Exeter, 1972), p. 10. Leofric's bilingual copy of Chrodegang survives as Cambridge, Corpus Christi College 191 (see N. R. Ker, *Catalogue of Manuscripts containing Anglo-Saxon* (Oxford, 1957), no. 46); it is ed. A. S. Napier, *The Old English Version of the Enlarged Rule of Chrodegang together with the Latin Original: an Old English Version of the 'Capitula of Theodulf' together with the Latin Original. An Interlinear Old English Rendering of the Epitome of Benedict of Aniane*, EETS o.s. 150 (London, 1916). On the place of Chrodegang's *Regula* in the history of the Office, see P. Salmon, *L'Office Divin: Histoire de la formation du bréviaire*, Lex Orandi 27 (Paris, 1959), 27–34 (trans. Sr David Mary as *The Breviary through the Ages* (Collegeville, Minn., 1962), pp. 8–11). Barlow (*English Church*, p. 283) associates Ælfric with the regularization or canonization of the lives of secular clergy by attributing to him Fehr's 'Anhang III', which, however, is *not* by Ælfric (*Die Hirtenbriefe Ælfrics in altenglischer und lateinischer Fassung*, ed. B. Fehr, Bibliothek der angelsächsischen Prosa 9 (Hamburg, 1914), repr. with Suppl. to the Introduction by P. Clemoes (Darmstadt, 1966), pp. 234–49 (see Clemoes's remarks on the attribution at p. cxlvi). The introduction of canons' rules seems to be associated with bishops born or trained in Lotharingia who were appointed to English sees in the mid-eleventh century.

[6] D. H. Farmer, 'The Progress of the Monastic Revival', *Tenth-Century Studies*, ed. Parsons, pp. 10–19, at 19. See also Knowles, *Monastic Order*, pp. 65 and 129–34, and K. Edwards, *The English Secular Cathedrals in the Middle Ages: a Constitutional Study with Special Reference to the Fourteenth Century*, 2nd ed. (Manchester, 1967), pp. 10–11.

[7] *Regularis Concordia*, ed. T. Symons (London, 1953), p. 1.

directions for ceremonies to be observed at the death of a member of the community.

All this is said not simply to iterate the obvious but to suggest that it is surprising that so little has been done either to examine the daily life of the English religious who were governed by the *Regularis concordia* adopted by monastics and bishops at Winchester in the 970s or to relate the annual cursus of the Office to the cultural history of pre-Conquest England. The very title *Regularis concordia* implies an agreement or concord concerning the observance of the monastic life in the English realm, the resolution of conflicting uses or customs.[8] Perhaps the neglect of the liturgical contents of the *Concordia* is best to be explained by the very great difficulty of the history of the Divine Office as a subject for scholarly examination. The Divine Office is the daily round of 'non-sacramental services to be celebrated or recited at intervals during the day (and night)'.[9] Its history is confusing and daunting, especially before the thirteenth century, when under Franciscan leadership the liturgical use of the papal court chapel came to be widely adopted as the normative form of the Office.[10] Space does not allow even a summary of that history before the 970s. Suffice it to say that what by the tenth century seemed the most integral or basic elements of the Office were in fact only venerable accretions. With the rise of monasticism in the fourth century, the daily prayers of the early church had become fused with the monastic devotional practice of recitation of the

8 The term had traditional roots, however, and with the noun in the plural (*concordiae*) was used to refer to the 'Rules of the Desert Fathers' (see S. J. P. van Dijk and J. Hazelton Walker, *The Origins of the Modern Roman Liturgy: the Liturgy of the Papal Court and the Franciscan Order in the Thirteenth Century* (London and Westminster, Md, 1960), p. 19) and by Benedict of Aniane for a collection of *regulae* (*Regularis Concordia*, ed. Symons, p. 1, n. 1).

9 *The Study of Liturgy*, ed. C. Jones, G. Wainwright and E. Yarnold (London, 1978), p. 352. I am indebted to essays on the Divine Office in this volume by G. J. Cuming, W. Jardine Grisbroke and J. D. Crichton. For bibliography, see *ibid.* pp. 350–2, and R. W. Pfaff, *Medieval Latin Liturgy: a Select Bibliography*, Toronto Med. Bibliographies 9 (Toronto, 1982), *passim* (but note esp. Anglo-Saxon materials at pp. 84–7). Among the works often cited on the history of the Office, P. Batiffol's *Histoire du bréviaire romain* (Paris, 1911) is less highly regarded than the other standard history: S. Bäumer, *Histoire du bréviaire*, trans. R. Biron (Paris, 1905), to which the great English liturgical scholar Edmund Bishop made significant contributions. The most important recent studies are by P. Salmon, *L'Office divin* (cited above, n. 5) and *L'Office divin au moyen âge: Histoire de la formation du Bréviaire du IXe au XVIe siècle*, Lex Orandi 43 (Paris, 1967). A helpful work on the early history of the Office is P. F. Bradshaw, *Daily Prayer in the Early Church: a Study of the Origin and Early Development of the Divine Office*, Alcuin Club Collections 63 (London, 1981). For the history of the breviary in medieval England, see J. B. L. Tolhurst, *The Monastic Breviary of Hyde Abbey* VI (*Introduction to the English Monastic Breviaries*), HBS 80 (London, 1942). Also useful for reference are A. Hughes, *Medieval Manuscripts for Mass and Office: a Guide to their Organization and Terminology* (Toronto, 1982), and K. Gamber, *Codices Liturgici Latini Antiquiores*, 2nd ed. (Freiburg, 1968), esp. pp. 576–614.

10 See van Dijk and Walker, *Origins*.

psalter, with the coincidental result that the 'dominance of monasticism' had tended to separate the laity from the daily prayers.[11] And, somewhat later, scriptural readings were added, particularly to the Night Office, where the ideal came to be an annual reading of almost the entire canon of scripture as well as of narrative materials on the saints and exegetical materials from the Fathers. This significant and time-consuming elaboration of the Offices made them even more remote from the laity and created a burden that was difficult even for the monastic communities to sustain, and it led to the development of such devices for mitigating the burden of the readings as continuation of the reading outside the Office proper or abbreviation of the lections.[12] Dom Pierre Salmon, one of the most helpful of recent students of the history of the Office, has criticized the tendency of historians of the Office or the breviary to treat it

> almost exclusively from the standpoint of quantitative additions, without much concern with the modes of celebration. The historians have above all sought to find out when the different Hours with their component elements were introduced and became universal. They have been content with entering these acquisitions to the credit of the Office, as if its perfection were thought to increase by reason of these additions.[13]

In fact, the emergence of the breviary may be regarded as a later side-effect of the reform movements among which the tenth-century English reform is numbered. After the eleventh-century effort to universalize these reforms – or to introduce them into, and give them the sanction of, the Roman church – breviaries came into existence as volumes containing complete Offices in the order of the liturgical year or (for saints) of the calendar, replacing the small library of books that was required for the recitation of the Office in the earlier period. The twelfth-century choir breviary was in the first instance a device to aid normalization of the form of the Office as widely as possible throughout the church.[14] Later, there was a strong movement to regularize the lives of all the clergy and to make the regular recitation of the Office a requirement, even if the cleric in question were not able to participate in the recitation of the Office in the choir of his church. Under Franciscan influence in the thirteenth century, the breviary became a portable text for the full Office, the biblical and patristic readings in which were severely abbreviated; and it served both the tendency to regularize the lives of all clergy and the tendency to make recitation of the Office a devotional duty even when one could not be present in the choir.

For the period before the emergence of the breviary it often seems difficult

[11] Bradshaw, *Daily Prayer*, p. 123.

[12] Salmon, *Breviary through the Ages*, trans. Sr David Mary, ch. 4.

[13] *Ibid.* p. 40.

[14] Salmon, *Office Divin au moyen âge*, p. 85.

to gain a clear idea of what constituted the Office. Indeed, it is seemingly quite impossible to have any certainty about details of the observance of the Office in England before the Council of Winchester. But for the period from 970 to the Conquest material is reasonably abundant, if hardly complete. C. E. Hohler has spoken of the existence of 'some rather scrappy material for the Office' and noted (quite accurately) that no attempt has been made to list the materials for the liturgy of this period.[15] As a first step towards meeting this desideratum, I propose here to survey briefly the major materials presently available in print for the history of the Office from the reform to the Conquest. At the same time, an inventory of surviving Anglo-Saxon manuscript materials for the Office has been compiled and discussed by Helmut Gneuss, and is found elsewhere in this volume.[16]

One of the difficulties of the study of the Office in the period before synoptic breviaries were available is that a considerable collection of books was required for its liturgical performance. Salmon reports that as many as ten volumes are often in question.[17] Yet even these volumes of materials for the Office vary from time to time and from place to place. I know of no complete set of books for the Office from a given place or time anywhere in Europe in the early Middle Ages. The closest to a complete set may be the materials from Leofric's Exeter, a secular (or non-monastic) church.[18] Indeed, since liturgical manuscripts were seldom preserved after they had become obsolete, one should not be surprised at the paucity of the evidence. There are several lists of the liturgical books the clergy needed to have, but the inconsistencies of these lists – even of the three by Ælfric, two of them in Latin – raise as many questions as they solve.[19] Thus one might say that not only do we lack a complete set of the books used in any early medieval church for the performance of the Office, but we do not even have an agreed list of what those volumes would have been.

Obviously the core of the monastic liturgical observances is set out in the Rule itself, and at least from the time of the Council of Winchester the Rule observed by English monks was that of St Benedict. Study of the *Regula S. Benedicti* (as it was known in England) is greatly facilitated by the recent work

15 'Some Service-Books of the Later Saxon Church', *Tenth-Century Studies*, ed. Parsons, pp. 60–83, at 62, and pp. 219–20, n. 10.

16 'Liturgical Books in Anglo-Saxon England and their Old English Terminology', above, pp. 91–141, at 110–27.

17 *Office Divin au moyen âge*, pp. 30–1. See also van Dijk and Walker, *Origins*, pp. 28–9.

18 See the list ptd Michael Lapidge, 'Surviving Booklists from Anglo-Saxon England', above pp. 33–89, at 64–9 (no. X).

19 See my *Preaching and Theology in Anglo-Saxon England: Ælfric and Wulfstan* (Toronto, 1977), pp. 42–4.

of Mechthild Gretsch.[20] A copy of the Rule that in the early years of the eleventh century was at the monastery re-established by Æthelwold at Abingdon has recently been edited from Cambridge, Corpus Christi College 57.[21] For the secular clergy, especially in cathedral *familiae*, the eighth-century *Regula canonicorum* of Chrodegang of Metz was (as stated above) known and translated in Anglo-Saxon England. It was imposed on a number of English cathedrals in the decades just before the Conquest to 'regularize' the lives of secular *familiae* of clergy.[22]

Observance of the Benedictine Rule was hardly static, however, and even more important for our knowledge of the liturgical practices of English monastics are the specific customs under which they observed the Rule. Documents outlining such customs, sometimes called *ordines*, are more usually referred to as 'customaries' or *consuetudines*. Several survive from the continent from our period, many of them accessible either in the series Consuetudines Monasticae edited by Bruno Albers[23] or in the Corpus Consuetudinum Monasticarum edited by Kassius Hallinger.[24] Only two monastic customaries for England survive or are known to have been in existence before Lanfranc's Monastic Constitutions for Canterbury.[25] The first is, of course, the *Regularis concordia*, to which reference has already been made and which is readily available in the scholarly edition of Abbot Thomas Symons.[26]

20 *Die Regula Sancti Benedicti in England und ihre altenglische Übersetzung*, Texte und Untersuchungen zur englischen Philologie 2 (Munich, 1973), and 'Æthelwold's Translation of the *Regula Sancti Benedicti* and its Latin Exemplar', *ASE* 3 (1974), 125–51.

21 *The Rule of St Benedict: the Abingdon Copy*, ed. J. Chamberlin (Toronto, 1982). It would have been interesting to have had an edition of the complete manuscript (described by Chamberlin at p. 9), for it is consciously a reform document and contains materials by and related to Benedict of Aniane which were central to the rise of the monastic reform on the continent in the ninth century. The earliest extant copy of the Benedictine Rule, a manuscript of Anglo-Saxon origin, now Oxford, Bodleian Library, Hatton 48, has been published in facsimile as EEMF 15 (Copenhagen, 1968), ed. D. H. Farmer.

22 See above, n. 5. On observance of the *Regula canonicorum* at other English cathedrals in the mid-eleventh century, see Barlow, *Leofric*, p. 20, and Edwards, *English Secular Cathedrals*, pp. 8–12.

23 *Consuetudines Monasticae*, 5 vols. (Stuttgart and Monte Cassino, 1900–12).

24 Ten volumes of the Corpus Consuetudinum Monasticarum (cited hereafter as CCM) have appeared so far (Siegburg, 1963– ). As G. Constable points out, the *consuetudines* are 'far from the static monuments to tradition they are sometimes depicted, and they show signs of adaptation and revision'; see 'Monastic Legislation at Cluny in the Eleventh and Twelfth Centuries', *Proceedings of the Fourth International Congress of Medieval Canon Law, Toronto, 21–25 August 1972*, Monumenta Iuris Canonici, ser. C 5 (Vatican City, 1976), 151–61, at 154.

25 *Lanfranc's Monastic Constitutions*, ed. D. Knowles (London, 1951), repr. with customary materials from Lanfranc's Norman abbey at Bec, CCM 3–4 (Siegburg, 1967). For the Anglo-Saxon materials, see also Gneuss, above, p. 136.

26 Symons's conclusions about the sources of the *Regularis concordia* may need some revision after the recently discovered description of the customs of Fleury (written shortly after 1010 by a monk who had sojourned there during the abbacy of Abbo) has been published. This

The second English monastic *consuetudo* is Ælfric's Customary for Eynsham, which has commonly been called the 'Letter to the monks of Eynsham'.[27] This document, which I am presently editing, has been unduly neglected; and it may be worthwhile briefly to discuss its character and importance. The Eynsham Customary falls into three parts. The first is a letter to the 'egneshamnensibus fratribus' (p. 174), who have only recently been established as a community by Æþelmær and need instruction in the proper observance of the Rule. This Ælfric will provide, drawing on the consuetudinary promulgated by his master 'sanctus aðelwoldus uuintoniensis episcopus cum coepiscopis et abbatibus tempore EADGARI felicissimi regis anglorum' (p. 175). To this he will add some interpretative materials from Amalarius.[28] The second section of the Eynsham Customary, the body of the work, is the *consuetudo* proper, based

document has been identified by Dom Anselme Davril, 'Un Coutumier de Fleury du début du XIe siècle', *RB* 76 (1966), 351–4, and 'Un Moine de Fleury aux environs de l'an mil: Thierry, dit d'Amorbach', *Études ligériennes d'histoire et d'archéologie médiévales*, ed. R. Louis (Auxerre, 1975), pp. 97–104. Davril's edition of some thirteenth-century Fleury customaries has appeared as CCM 9 (Siegburg, 1976), but the promised edition of Thierry (scheduled to appear as CCM 7) has not yet been issued. In the meantime Dom Lin Donnat has argued that there are close connections between Thierry's recollection of Fleury customs and the *Regularis concordia* ('Recherches sur l'influence de Fleury au Xe siècle', *Études ligériennes*, ed. Louis, pp. 165–74). He argues, furthermore, that there is a far greater correspondence than has hitherto been recognized between Fleury's customs and those of Ghent and the German reformed houses (and also that there is very little resemblance between those of Fleury and Cluny). Thus one must be cautious in thinking of Fleury and Ghent as 'the two great foreign schools of monasticism' (Knowles, *Monastic Order*, p. 42) if one thereby implies some conflict or disunity between the two; hence the tendency to associate Fleury with Cluny must be abandoned. It will be necessary to study closely the text of Thierry – which is incomplete and (unlike the *Regularis concordia*) surveys the daily activities of the monasteries rather than the liturgical cursus for the year – before one can fully accept Donnat's conclusion that Fleury was a major source not only for Anglo-Saxon but also for German reformed monasticism.

27 'Excerpta ex institutionibus monasticis Æthelwoldi episcopi Wintoniensis compilata in usum fratrum Egneshamnensium per Ælfricum abbatem', Appendix VII, *Compotus Rolls of the Obedientiaries of St Swithun's Priory, Winchester*, ed. G. W. Kitchin, Hampshire Record Soc. (London and Winchester, 1892), pp. 173–98. Pending the publication of my own edition, I quote the text ptd *Compotus Rolls*. See also my 'Old English Literature and the Liturgy: Problems and Potential', *ASE* 6 (1977), 237–47, esp. 241–2.

28 Ælfric identifies himself here as *abbas* in a way that leads C. E. Hohler to question whether he was abbot at Eynsham; see 'Some Service Books', *Tenth-Century Studies*, ed. Parsons, p. 73. This passage is the sole authority by which Ælfric has been designated abbot of Eynsham, and Hohler is correct that it is not unequivocal. Perhaps, however, it is significant that Ælfric uses the same word *degens* to describe his association with Eynsham ('uideo uobiscum degens', p. 174) and with Æthelwold ('in scola eius degens multis annis', p. 175). Similarly, at the end of the final section of the document, Ælfric asks the monks to undertake in loyal obedience to himself observances more rigorous than the letter of the Rule requires ('obedientes mihi', p. 196). Perhaps the conventional language with which Ælfric established his authority to interpret the fine points of monastic observance to the Eynsham community has misled Hohler.

largely on *Regularis concordia* but with some additions from Amalarius of Metz, the hymnal and other liturgical sources. The ending of this section is clearly marked in the manuscript with an uncial rubric, 'finiunt consuetudines' (p. 194). The interest of this main portion of the Eynsham Customary is three fold. First, it is an abbreviation of the *Regularis concordia* by a faithful disciple of Æthelwold which witnesses monastic practice in a small community of fairly modest resources. Secondly, it gives evidence of simplication of some of the more elaborate (and famous) rites of the *Regularis concordia* and a lessening of the emphasis on royal patronage of monasticism in the earlier document. Finally, it gives glimpses of Ælfric's interpretation of the meaning of the Office, which is based on a special edition (the early *Retractiones* I) of Amalarius, which seems to have been the version chiefly known in pre-Conquest England. In the final section (pp. 194–6) Ælfric adds further details of monastic observance, dealing most notably with the lectionary and the *responsiones* for the Night Office, at the request of the Eynsham fraternity ('quia rogastis fratres', p. 194). This part of the document, until very recently the least discussed in the secondary literature, is perhaps the most important, for it supplements the *Concordia* and is in some respects a unique witness to English monastic usage in the first years of the eleventh century. I shall return in the latter part of this paper to this portion of the Eynsham Customary.

The rules and customaries are only general authorities for the monastic liturgy, however. For specific evidence we need the actual liturgical books. In some areas we have at least a sampling of evidence. The collectar, for example, was a book that gathered together the prayers (collects) for the Office. The collectar was often combined with the capitulary, a collection of short lessons (*capitula*) which were also read at the Offices by the chief liturgical officer present. Two important collectars with capitularies exist from the late Anglo-Saxon period, and both have been well edited: the so-called 'Leofric Collectar' (now London, BL Harley 2961) from the secular cathedral at Exeter in the mid-eleventh century,[29] and the so-called 'Portiforium of St Wulfstan' (now Cambridge, Corpus Christi College 391) from the monastic cathedral of Worcester immediately after the Conquest.[30] These collectars, both later than the time of Ælfric, preserve the so-called 'New Hymnal' and Cambridge, Corpus Christi College 391 preserves the monastic canticles (that is, chants from Old Testament texts used in the Night Office on Sundays and feasts). The hymnal and the canticles are available in recent scholarly editions by Helmut

[29] *The Leofric Collectar*, ed. E. S. Dewick and W. H. Frere, 2 vols., HBS 45–6 (London, 1914–21). Another secular English collectar is Durham, Cathedral Library, A. IV. 19, ed. U. Lindelöf, *Rituale Ecclesiae Dunhelmensis: the Durham Collectar*, Surtees Soc. 140 (London, 1927); a facsimile is *The Durham Ritual*, ed. T. J. Brown *et al.*, EEMF 16 (Copenhagen, 1969).

[30] *The Portiforium of Saint Wulstan*, ed. A. Hughes, 2 vols., HBS 89–90 (London, 1958–60).

Gneuss and Michael Korhammer.[31] The two collectars are also rich in antiphons and responds for the Offices. Evidence such as this can be used in consultation with the rich materials collected by R.-J. Hesbert in his monumental (if confusing and historically misdirected to the search for an Ur-Antiphonary) *Corpus Antiphonalium Officii*.[32] It should be stressed that, although both the Leofric and the Wulfstan Collectars contain much of the material that would be needed for a full breviary, they were intended for the use of 'the principal person present at any of the Day Hours' who is 'to say the Chapter and Collect'. For convenience, other materials were added, 'serving to give the user a more or less full reminder of other parts of the service, for which other persons were responsible'.[33] In other words, psalter, hymnal and calendar were added for further convenience. Yet technically these books are not considered breviaries.

Although much is known about the distribution of the psalter in the Offices,[34] less is known than we should wish about the biblical lections, narrative materials concerning the saints, and exegetical or homiletic

31 H. Gneuss, *Hymnar und Hymnen im englischen Mittelalter*, Buchreihe der Anglia 12 (Tübingen, 1968); M. Korhammer, *Die monastischen Cantica im Mittelalter*, Texte und Untersuchungen zur englischen Philologie 6 (Munich, 1976). Gneuss prints an edition of the Latin *Expositio hymnorum* and its accompanying Old English translation from two manuscripts of the Winchester tradition, now London, BL Cotton Julius A. vi and Vespasian D. xii. More recently the hymns of a manuscript in the Canterbury tradition, London, BL Add. 37517 (the 'Bosworth Psalter', on which see also M. Korhammer, 'The Origin of the Bosworth Psalter', *ASE* 2 (1973), 173–87), have been ed. G. R. Wieland, *The Canterbury Hymnal* (Toronto, 1982). The great resource for hymn studies is, of course, *Analecta Hymnica Medii Aevi*, ed. G. M. Dreves and C. Blume, 55 vols. (Leipzig, 1866–1922), with 3 vols. of indices (Berne, 1978). The term 'hymn' is reserved in the Middle Ages for non-biblical verse sung in the Offices.

32 Ed. in 6 vols., Rerum Ecclesiasticarum Documenta, ser. maior 7–12 (Rome, 1963–79). Hesbert has also studied the English antiphonary tradition (but of the post-Conquest period) on two occasions; see 'Les Antiphonaires monastiques insulaires', *RB* 92 (1982), 358–75, and 'The Sarum Antiphoner – its Sources and Influence', *Jnl of the Plainsong and Med. Music Soc.* 3 (1980), 49–55.

33 *Leofric Collectar*, ed. Dewick and Frere II, xix–xx. Salmon coins the useful term 'collectaires enrichis' for such manuscripts, carefully explaining why 'bréviaires' should be reserved for later developments (*L'Office divin*, pp. 18 and 53–60). On liturgical calendars, see *English Kalendars before A.D. 1100*, ed. F. Wormald, HBS 72 (London, 1934). Reference needs also to be made here to the tropers (collections, that is, of musical and textual elaborations, usually for the mass but sometimes for the Office); on them, see *The Winchester Troper*, ed. W. H. Frere, HBS 8 (London, 1894), and A. E. Planchart, *The Repertory of Tropes at Winchester*, 2 vols. (Princeton, NJ, 1977).

34 Hughes, *Medieval Manuscripts for Mass and Office*, p. 50–2, has useful tables for monastic and secular uses. Obviously, such general presentations should, if possible, be verified by reference to documents close in time and place to one's specific study. On the general principles organizing scriptural readings in liturgy with useful outline of the Offices, see S. J. P. van Dijk, 'The Bible in Liturgical Use', *The Cambridge History of the Bible*, ed. G. W. H. Lampe, 2 vols. (Cambridge, 1969) II, 220–52 and 520–1.

materials that were included in the Nocturns of the Night Office. Cyril L. Smetana has shown that study of the printed homiliaries can be fruitful for our understanding of Ælfric's sources, but future students of Ælfric will need to study the English homiliary manuscripts to learn even more about the resources available to this Anglo-Saxon sermon-writer and his treatment of them.[35] Patrick H. Zettel has recently shown that much of the material in Ælfric's Lives of Saints is based upon Latin hagiographical sources that were collected (and sometimes combined) in an English manuscript family of legendaries, which provided readings for the Nocturns on saints' days.[36] It is likely that we shall learn more about Old English sermons and hagiographic writings from study of the liturgical manuscripts through which they were transmitted to the vernacular writers. The Old English Martyrology has been under intensive study in recent years,[37] but it is a document that antedates the reform; by contrast, little has been written about the Latin martyrologies used in English monasteries between the time of the *Regularis concordia* and the Conquest.

There is a substantial body of material relating to the Office in Old English translation. One thinks of the translations of the Rule, of the hymns and canticles, and of documents like the so-called 'Old English Benedictine Office'.[38] Such texts raise many and fascinating questions – questions about the literacy of the clergy and about the relation of the laity to the Night Office and other parts of the liturgy one would think were attended only by clergy and

[35] 'Ælfric and the Early Medieval Homiliary', *Traditio* 15 (1959), 163–204, and 'Ælfric and the Homiliary of Haymo of Halberstadt', *Traditio* 17 (1961), 457–69. Smetana essayed a survey of the English manuscripts of the most important homiliary in 'Paul the Deacon's Patristic Anthology', *The Old English Homily and its Backgrounds*, ed. P. E. Szarmach and B. F. Huppé (Albany, NY, 1978), pp. 75–97. Since the publication of Smetana's studies and my *Preaching and Theology*, a major resource for study of Latin homiliaries has appeared: see R. Grégoire, *Homéliaires liturgiques médiévaux: Analyse de manuscrits*, Biblioteca degli 'Studi Medievali' 12 (Spoleto, 1980); but note that Grégoire does not at any point discuss manuscripts of Anglo-Saxon origin or provenance.

[36] 'Saints' Lives in Old English: Latin Manuscripts and Vernacular Accounts: Ælfric', *Peritia* 1 (1982), 17–37.

[37] There is a new edition by G. Kotzor, *Das altenglische Martyrologium*, 2 vols., Bayerische Akademie der Wissenschaften, Phil.-hist. Klasse, Abhandlungen n.s. 88 (Munich, 1981). J. E. Cross has recently published a lengthy series of articles on the sources of the Old English Martyrology, of which a recent example is 'Saints' Lives in Old English: Latin Manuscripts and Vernacular Accounts. The Old English Martyrology', *Peritia* 1 (1982) 38–62. On the martyrology tradition in general, see J. Dubois, *Les Martyrologes du moyen âge latin*, Typologie des sources du moyen âge occidental 26 (Turnhout, 1978), which does not, however, discuss Anglo-Saxon materials. In England, the martyrology was evidently read at the Capitular Office, not at one of the hours; see *Regularis Concordia*, ed. Symons, p. 17, and discussion by Gneuss, 'Liturgical Manuscripts', above, p. 128.

[38] J. M. Ure, *The Benedictine Office* (Edinburgh, 1957).

regulars. It is my personal hope that, as our knowledge of the surviving liturgical manuscripts increases, more scholars will seek to investigate and explain both the abundant evidence and the enormous lacunae that exist in the record of the late Anglo-Saxon monastic liturgy.

The preceding observations are very cursory, but it is hoped they give some sense of the problems and the promise of the study of the monastic Office as it was performed in England between the time of the reform and the Conquest. An attempt has been made to introduce the bibliography of printed sources for such study and to suggest some areas where work is needed. Next it is proposed to examine how, in one instance, study of the liturgical evidence may be useful to scholars interested primarily in Old English literature.

## THE EYNSHAM CUSTOMARY, THE NIGHT OFFICE AND ÆLFRIC'S WRITINGS ON THE OLD TESTAMENT

The final section of Ælfric's Eynsham Customary has largely been ignored both by students of the English writings of Ælfric and by liturgical scholars. It is an outline, with several supplementary notes, of the lectionary for the Night Office (that is, the Nocturns of what is now called Matins). In a brief discussion of Ælfric's work published in 1975, J. R. Hall has shown that Ælfric's lectionary descends from what was the source of the almost universal system of scriptural reading for the Night Office, the *Ordo Romanus* XIIIA.[39] Ælfric (or his source for this part of the Customary) interpolated into the list of readings sparse but valuable indications of the series of *responsiones* which were to be sung in association with the lections of the Nocturn; Hall in turn has used this series to reconstruct the kind of antiphonary in use in the reformed Anglo-Saxon monasteries. Ælfric gives a richer list of the *responsiones* than the only other eleventh-century manuscript of the *ordo* that combines information about lections and *responsiones*, however, so his text is unique and little can at present be said about the nature of his source or sources.[40]

In light of his summary of the lectionary, it is possible to develop a clearer understanding of the rationale of Ælfric's sermons, reading-pieces and translations of the Old Testament and of his principles for selecting materials for presentation at given seasons. In this regard, as in so many others, it was Ælfric's hope to make the riches of monastic devotional life available to a

39 'Some Liturgical Notes on Ælfric's *Letter to the Monks at Eynsham*', *Downside Rev.* 93 (1975), 297–303. For *Ordo* XIIIA, see M. Andrieu, *Les Ordines Romani du haut moyen âge*, 5 vols. (Louvain, 1931–61) II, 469–88.

40 *Ibid.* p. 298. The eleventh-century manuscript in question is Douai, Bibliothèque Municipale, 857.

wider public, the audience of his other vernacular writings.[41] The complexly structured Nocturns of the Night Office were the chief locus in the monastic liturgy of readings from scripture.[42] On Sundays and major feasts, the Night Office had three Nocturns, each having (*inter alia*) four lessons preceded by the recitation of six psalms with antiphons (or three canticles in the third Nocturn) and interspersed with *responsiones* and other matter. The lessons of the first two Nocturns (unless it was a saint's day) were scriptural; those for the third were the gospel incipit and homilies upon the gospel.[43] On winter weekdays and lesser feasts, there were only two Nocturns, of which only the first had three readings. On summer weekdays (the night being short) there was but one lesson – although Ælfric asked the Eynsham community to eschew this mitigation of liturgical rigour (p. 196). It should be recalled once again here that Ælfric's chief source for his *Sermones catholici* on the Sunday gospels was the homiliary, which provided the readings for the third Nocturn on Sundays and feasts.

*Ordo Romanus* XIIIA,[44] upon which the lectionary outline in the Eynsham Customary is based, emanates from the Lateran, probably in the first half of the eighth century. It differs from the earlier *Ordo* XIV in (among other ways) beginning the cycle on Septuagesima Sunday rather than Quinquagesima. The notion was that the whole of the canon of scipture was to be read in the Night Office in the course of the year. This implies, in brief, the following scheme:

Septuagesima through the fourth week in Lent:
: the Heptateuch (i.e. the Pentateuch plus Joshua and Judges, perhaps also Ruth)

Passion Sunday to the eve of Easter:
: Jeremiah (including the Lamentations)

Easter to the Octave of Pentecost:
: Acts, the canonical epistles, Apocalypse

There follow what were commonly called the 'summer histories':

Octave of Pentecost to the beginning of August:
: the four books of Kings (I–II Samuel, I–II Kings), Chronicles (Paralipomena)

41 On the problem of audience, see my *Preaching and Theology*, pp. 25–59.

42 On this structure, see Hughes, *Medieval Manuscripts for Mass and Office*, pp. 53–66, and Tolhurst, *Monastic Breviary* VI, 180–95. Both Hughes and Tolhurst use terminology that became customary after Ælfric's time: the Night Office is called Matins and the first of the little hours (Matins or *Laudes Matutinales* in England in the tenth century) is called Lauds.

43 Note, however, that only on the extra Sundays after Epiphany and the summer Sundays were the lessons in the first *and* second Nocturn scriptural; the normal arrangement was first Nocturn, scripture; second Nocturn, sermon; third Nocturn, homily; see Hughes, *Medieval Manuscripts for Mass and Office*, p. 16.

44 See Andrieu, *Les Ordines Romani* II, 481–8.

from the first Sunday in August:

the Solomon (Wisdom) books

from the first Sunday of September:

Job, Tobit, Judith, Esther, I–II Esdras (i.e. Ezra and Nehemiah – there is some question whether III–IV Esdras were included because of lurking doubts about their canonicity)

from the first Sunday of October:

Maccabees

Finally there was a series of prophetic and Pauline readings:

from the first Sunday of November:

Ezekiel, Daniel, the twelve minor prophets

from the first Sunday in Advent:

Isaiah

Three saints' days following Christmas (St Stephen, St John the Evangelist and Holy Innocents) and the Epiphany (6 January) have specified lections, as do their octaves and Epiphany.

From the Sunday after the Octave of Epiphany to Septuagesima:

the Pauline Epistles

The psalms and the gospels were, of course, otherwise covered in the course of the year.

As Hall observes,[45] there are several deviations from this system in Ælfric's list, which is found in the third part of the Eynsham Customary (CCCC 265, pp. 57–63). In pre-Lent and Lent he alludes only to Genesis (Septuagesima – III$^{a}$ Quadragesima) and Exodus (Media or IV$^{a}$ Quadragesima). Ælfric is more precise about Eastertide than is the *Ordo Romanus* XIIIA: the canonical epistles belong to Easter week, the Apocalypse is read from the second Sunday after Easter to the Ascension, and Acts from the Ascension to Pentecost. Ælfric is also more precise here and in his sermon *In octauis Pentecosten* (Pope, no. xi) on the observance of the week of the Sunday after Pentecost as an octave of the Trinity; thus he delays the beginning of the sequential readings of Kings to the second Sunday after Pentecost. He gives greater detail than *Ordo* XIIIA about the disposition of the September readings. Like other monastic writers, he mentions that on saints' days the course of scriptural reading may be interrupt-

45 'Liturgical Notes', pp. 299–301. As Hall notes, Cambridge, Corpus Christi College 190, a Worcester manuscript connected with the Wulfstan commonplace collection, contains on pp. 212–13 a copy of *Ordo* XIIIA – not mentioned by Andrieu – which 'lacks the distinguishing characteristics of Ælfric's list. Another outline of lections, which runs, however, from Christmas, is found in an Anglo-Saxon copy of the Romano-German Pontifical: Cambridge, Corpus Christi College 163, pp. 1–149 (on this manuscript, see M. Lapidge, 'The Origin of CCCC 163', *Trans. of the Cambridge Bibliographical Soc.* 8 (1981), 18–28); the *ordo* is Andrieu's *Ordo* L (ptd *Les Ordines Romani* v); see also *Le Pontifical romano-germanique du dixième siècle*, ed. C. Vogel and R. Elze, 3 vols., Studi e testi 226–7 and 269 (Rome, 1963–72).

ed by the inclusion of appropriate *uitae*, *passiones*, and *sermones*. These deviations from the system of *Ordo* XIIIA betray the fact that processes of accretion were already undermining the custom of reading the whole canon of scripture in the Offices each year. The devotion of mid-Lent Sunday to Exodus is symptomatic, and was already widespread. The Sarum Breviary, the evidence for which is quite late, attempts to keep something of the continuous readings from Kings, but all that remains is somewhat more than half of I Kings (I Samuel)[46] – and it is clear that, given saints' days, not all of that would often get read. We do know, however, from some of the earlier choir breviaries, that an effort was made to keep up the course of readings, although what could actually be read in the Offices themselves was restricted.[47]

Ælfric himself testifies in the Eynsham Customary that he participated in the usual compromise between the ideal of reading the full bible annually and the practical limitations on what could be fitted into the horarium. One read, for example, Genesis from Septuagesima to mid-Lent, and Exodus in the week of mid-Lent; but the whole Pentateuch (let alone the Heptateuch plus Ruth) could not be accommodated. The rest had to be read in the refectory: 'Et sciendum quod tota bibliotheca debet legi in circulo anni in ecclesia, sed quia nos pigri serui sumus et segnes legimus in refectorio quicquid de ea in ecclesia omittimus' (p. 196).[48] In other words, Ælfric followed approximately the system prescribed in *Ordo* XIIIA, but the system was modified in accordance with practical necessity. A point that will be seen to be important may be noted in passing here: although the laity might have been present to hear the readings of the Nocturns in church (a possibility that seems to me unlikely in the normal course of events), the readings were quite removed from lay persons when taken to the refectory. It should also be noted that in some respects Ælfric's standard was more rigorous than the norm. On weekdays in summer, because of the shortness of the night, most monasteries (following the Rule itself) reduced the lections in the Nocturns from three to one. But Ælfric specifically

46 *Breviarium ad Usum insignis Ecclesiae Sarum*, ed. F. Procter and C. Wordsworth, 3 vols. (Cambridge 1879–86; repr. Farnborough, 1970).

47 Useful indications of customary practice in the twelfth century can be had by reference to published descriptions of early breviaries: e.g. *Le Bréviaire de Ripoll, Paris B. N. Lat. 742: Étude sur sa composition et ses textes inédits*, ed. J. Lemarier, Scripta et Documenta 14 (Montserrat, 1965), and I. Mueller, 'Lektionar und Homiliar im hochmittelalterlichen Brevier von Disentis (Cod. Sangall. 403)', *Archiv für Liturgiewissenschaft* 11 (1969), 77–162.

48 'And let it be known that the whole Bible ought to be read in the course of a year in church; but, because we are indolent and sluggish servants, we read in refectory whatever we omit in church.' *Bibliotheca* is also used in Ælfric's Letter to Sigeweard (entitled 'On the Old and New Testament', *The Old English Heptateuch, Ælfric's Treatise on the Old and New Testament and his Preface to Genesis*, ed. S. J. Crawford, EETS o.s. 160 (London, 1922), repr. with additional material by N. R. Ker (London, 1969), pp. 15–75), line 443, to signify the entire canon of scripture.

thanked his monks at Eynsham, 'ut tres lectiones cum totidem responsoriis tota estate ad nocturnas sicut hieme iam preteritis annis tenuimus, quod nolumus uita comite deserere ferialibus noctibus' (p. 196).[49]

With these considerations concerning Ælfric's Old Testament lectionary for the Night Office in the background, we may turn to the question of the influence of the lectionary (or system of readings for the Night Office's Nocturn) on Ælfric's selection of materials from the Old Testament for presentation, usually to a lay audience, in sermons, translations or paraphrases.[50] For the purposes of this review, the entire canon of Ælfric's writings[51] has been examined. Because their purpose and sources are rather different, however, a number of summaries of material related to the Old Testament, which have been shown to belong to the genre of catechetical *narratio*, have been excluded from consideration here.[52] It will be useful to consider the Old Testament materials in three groups, roughly in the order of their composition as established by Peter Clemoes.

Ælfric's earliest Old Testament adaptations were sermons. Of these, the earliest are items included in the Second Series of *Sermones catholici* when it was issued, in 992 or 995:[53] no. xii, two *sententiae* for mid-Lent Sunday, and no. xxx,

49 '. . . that we maintained three lections with as many responsories the whole summer at Nocturns as in winter in past years; we do not wish to abandon this practice on ferial nights as long as we live.'

50 I anticipated this issue and hazarded tentative conclusions in *Preaching and Theology*, p. 203, n. 53.

51 The definitive studies of the canon are P. A. M. Clemoes, 'The Chronology of Ælfric's Works', *The Anglo-Saxons: Studies . . . presented to Bruce Dickins*, ed. P. Clemoes (London, 1959), pp. 212–47, and the introduction by J. C. Pope to his edition of the *Homilies of Ælfric: a Supplementary Collection*, EETS o.s. 259–60 (London, 1967–8), esp. 136–50. The minor differences between Clemoes and Pope do not affect my argument.

52 See V. Day, 'The Influence of the Catechetical *Narratio* on Old English and some other Medieval Literature', *ASE* 3 (1974), 51–61. The material excluded is *De Initio Creaturae* (*The Homilies of the Anglo-Saxon Church: the Sermones Catholici or Homilies of Ælfric*, 2 vols. (London, 1844–6; repr. New York, 1971) I, 8–29); Letter to Sigeweard (as cited above, n. 48); Letter to Wulfgeat (*Angelsächsische Homilien und Heiligenleben*, ed. B. Assmann, Bibliothek der angelsächsischen Prosa 3 (Kassel, 1889), repr. with introduction by P. Clemoes (Darmstadt, 1964), no. i); Hexameron (*Exameron Anglice or the Old English Hexameron*, ed. S. J. Crawford, Bibliothek der angelsächsischen Prosa 10 (Hamburg, 1921), repr. (Darmstadt, 1968)); and two unpublished pieces related to Hexameron from London, BL Cotton Otho C. i: 'De creatore et creatura' and 'De sex ætatibus huius seculi' (on which see Clemoes, 'Chronology', pp. 218 and 241–2, and Pope, *Homilies*, pp. 86–7 and 143). In discussing Hexameron, Day (p. 57) does not adequately emphasize the fact that hexaemeral narration was, especially for the ancient Greek Fathers, the beginning of catechetical instruction, as Augustine stresses in the passages quoted by Day (pp. 51–2) by stating that the narration is to begin with creation (expounding at length on cosmology and such other matters as the fall of the angels).

53 Clemoes ('Chronology', p. 224) and Pope (*Homilies*, p. 146) both accept the date 992, proposed K. Sisam, *Studies in the History of Old English Literature* (Oxford, 1953), pp. 157–60.

for the first Sunday in September. The Sunday sermons of the First Series, it will be recalled, are almost all on the gospel pericopes for the day. Most of them were, as Smetana showed, adapted from materials collected in the monastic homiliary for the Night Office.[54] In the Second Series, Ælfric expanded the range of liturgical days covered, but he felt it incumbent on him to produce alternative sermons for certain major Sundays. Thus, for Easter, he offered three choices: a sermon on the mass and expository pieces on the gospel pericopes for Monday and Wednesday of Easter week. He noted in the last that not all the people would be present to hear the Wednesday pericope, so it was appropriate to discuss it on Easter itself. As Malcolm Godden has convincingly argued, the Second Series is less prescriptive than the First: the preacher or reader is given materials and helpful notes to use more or less as he will in devising alternatives to the sermons of the First Series.[55] Mid-Lent or the fourth Sunday of Quadragesima seems also to have been provided with alternative sermons – the first on the exodus and the giving of the Law to Moses, the second on Joshua. Because only one late manuscript for the first of these items contains a homiletic doxology or closing for the first sermon, however, it may also have been Ælfric's intention that both be read.[56] Ælfric had expounded the gospel pericope for this Sunday in the First Series, and there were no other pericopes associated with the day.[57] For the Second Series, he turned his attention to two books of the Old Testament closely connected with mid-Lent in the Night Office ('æt Godes ðenungum'), Exodus and Joshua, evincing a characteristic hesitancy about exposing the laity to the mysteries of the Old Testament, which is marked by *deopan digelnysse*, 'deep obscurity'.[58] Ælfric's summary lectionary referred only to Exodus.[59] But many

But M. Godden has since made a case for 995 in his introduction to *Ælfric's Catholic Homilies, the Second Series: Text*, EETS s.s. 5 (London, 1979), xci. (I cite this edition hereafter for the Second Series as CH II, by item and line numbers; on the advisability of retaining Ælfric's title rather than the inaccurate and misleading (albeit ubiquitous) Catholic Homilies, see *Preaching and Theology*, pp. 50–1. Thorpe's edition of the First Series is similarly cited, but by pages rather than lines.)

54 See above, n. 35. The exceptions are CH I, nos. xxii (Pentecost, based on the Acts) and xxxix (I in Advent, based on Romans XIII), both exegetical and related to the readings and themes of the days.

55 'The Development of Ælfric's Second Series of *Catholic Homilies*', *ES* 54 (1973), 209–16.

56 See Godden's apparatus and note on CH II, no. xii, line 373.

57 The set of homilies for Fridays in Lent (Pope, *Homilies*, nos. ii–iii and v–vi) may later have helped fill a need for more sermon materials in the Lenten season.

58 CH II, no. xii, quoting lines 1 and 6.

59 Grégoire, *Homéliaires liturgiques*, p. 91, records that at least some versions of the Homiliary of Paul the Deacon had a sermon, attributed to St John Chrysostom 'de Moyse' for III Quadragesima (completing a series supplementary to sermons on the gospels which started with creation on Septuagesima and proceeded to the fall, Abraham and Isaac, Jacob and Esau and Joseph on subsequent Sundays).

collections of *responsiones* for the Night Office contain not only responsories and versicles related to readings from Exodus, but also 'Responsoria de Josue',[60] which would explain Ælfric's offering of alternative sermons on Moses and Joshua or of a single sermon composed of *sententiae* on both Moses and his successor.

The first of the passages for mid-Lent, after a summary of the events that brought Israel into Egypt, treats the ten plagues, the exodus through the Red Sea and the giving of the Law; and it offers typological and tropological explanations of these events. Ælfric's focus is upon the Law (as the rubric of one manuscript, *De lege Dei*, indicates). But there is also reason to suppose that the selection of materials was influenced by the readings of the Office and reflects the themes underlined in the week's set of *responsiones* for the first and second Nocturns, which touch on approximately the episodes of the exodus and on the giving of the Decalogue that Ælfric summarizes and explains in his sermon.[61] At any rate, the exodus section of the mid-Lent sermon fits closely the description of the day's theme in the Eynsham Customary: 'Media uero quadragesimae legimus exodum, et canimus "Locutus est Dominus ad Moysen"' (p. 194). The second passage for mid-Lent (*Secunda Sententia de hoc ipso* or *Secundus Sermo de Iosue et de pugnis eius*) deals with Joshua and the settlement and is again heavily typological and tropological.[62] In the latter instance Ælfric may well be providing edificatory material based on what the monks read in this liturgical season, not in church but in the refectory; for the principle of reading the Heptateuch must still have been observed. And reference to the *responsiones* for the fourth Sunday of Lent is again helpful in explaining the offering of an alternative or supplementary sermon on Joshua and in suggesting motifs from the Office that are reflected in Ælfric's summary of Joshua.[63] Ælfric's sermon is less closely related thematically and verbally to the Joshua *responsiones* than was the sermon on Moses to the exodus responsories, but at least the responsories demonstrate that the principle of covering the Heptateuch *in toto* had left some traces in the Sunday Offices.

Ælfric assigned yet another sermon to mid-Lent Sunday. It is printed as no. xiii in the Lives of Saints[64] and circulated a few years after the promulgation of

60 See Hesbert, *Corpus Antiphonalium Officii* I, 150–3 ('Cursus Romanus') and II, 274–7 ('Cursus Monasticus').

61 *Ibid.* II, 274–5. The full texts of the *responsiones* and their versicles are given alphabetically in vol. IV. At I, 150ff. the incipits from secular antiphonaries ('Cursus Romanus') are given; these do not contain material that is not in the monastic cursus of vol. II but reflect the secular tradition of three lections and responds in each Nocturn rather than four.

62 CH II, no. xii, lines 374–582.

63 Hesbert, as cited in n. 61. The Joshua responds seem to have occurred more often in secular than in monastic antiphonaries inventoried by Hesbert.

64 *Ælfric's Lives of Saints*, ed. W. W. Skeat, EETS o. s. 76, 82, 94 and 114 (London, 1881–1900; repr. London, 1966).

the Second Series. The text is a passage of Exodus (XVII. 8–13) in which the raising of Moses's hands in prayer enables Joshua to defeat the army of Amalek. Like the alternative sermons in the Second Series for the same Sunday, it is rich in spiritual interpretation; and (again similarly) it shows Ælfric once more turning at mid-Lent to biblical materials read at that season in the Night Office. A sermon from the period 1002 × 1005,[65] *De populo Israhel*, treats Exodus XXXII and Numbers XI, XIII, XIV, XVI and XXI. At the outset, it refers to the first of the mid-Lent sermons in *Sermones catholici* II and summarizes its contents. In *De populo* Ælfric proposes to resume the history of Israel; and, as Professor Pope remarks, the sermon takes up the history from the point at which it was left off in the former piece and 'concentrates on seven occasions when the people murmured or actively rebelled against God and Moses and incurred God's wrath'.[66] The entire mid-Lent group of Ælfric's sermons, which has been very cursorily reviewed here, grew, one supposes, from an effort to appropriate material from the monks' cursus of readings in the Night Office or the refectory for public teaching. The first item from the Second Series is close to the matters actually touched on in the *responsiones* for the third week of Lent; this narrative was extended with the *De populo Israhel*. In the meantime, sermons had also been prepared on the battle against Amalek and – in this instance again related to *responsiones* for mid-Lent – on Joshua. All this material is in sermon form.

Also in the form of a sermon is another selection in the Second Series of *Sermones catholici* which is securely tied to the cursus of readings in the Office: the Job sermon (no. XXX) which bears the rubric 'Dominica I in mense Septembri quando legitur Iob'. It need hardly be reiterated that the locus of this reading of Job was not the mass, where it is usually assumed Ælfric's sermons were read,[67] but the Nocturns. As was the case with the first piece on the exodus, the Old English beginning also makes explicit reference to the readings of Nocturns: 'Mine gebroðra. We rædað nu æt godes ðenungum be ðan eadigan were Iob'.[68] The first sentences of the piece seem almost to be addressed to clerical users of this preachers' source book, *mine gebroðra*; and Ælfric points out that, if Job is difficult for clerks, it is the more so for the illiterate. Thus great care is needed to interpret it to the laity.

The four mid-Lent pieces and the Job are the only adaptations of the Old Testament by Ælfric which are properly called sermons. The material treated in the mid-Lent pieces, it seems to me, continued throughout his career to attract his attention, not only because it was read in the Office in the season but

65 Pope, *Homilies*, no. XX. 66 *Ibid.* p. 638.

67 See my *Preaching and Theology*, p. 53.

68 CH II, no. XXX, lines 1–2 ('My brothers, we are now reading in the Divine Office about the blessed man, Job').

also because, with its emphasis on the People and the Law, it was peculiarly appropriate to the penitential and didactic or catechetical aspects of the Lenten season. Perhaps it is significant that, as he catalogues his Old Testament adaptations in the Letter to Sigeweard, Ælfric seems not to mention the mid-Lent sermons, although he alludes to translations about Moses and Joshua.[69] This is probably because the pieces are not translations but, strictly speaking, sermons. Job, also a sermon, may be regarded as a false start. Ælfric thought it might be possible to adapt the 'summer histories' of the lectionary for the Nocturns to purposes of general instruction. He states that he thought the problem a difficult one because of the complexity of the material and the problems of proper interpretation. For whatever reason, he apparently did not continue to adapt material from the Office lectionary in sermons for the Temporale.

To the second classification of Ælfric's Old Testament materials belong his Genesis translation and his translations from other parts of the historical books that survive as parts of an Old English Hexateuch.[70] Ælfric tells Æthelweard in the Preface that he translated Genesis 'to Isaace' in order to supply what was wanting in a translation of Genesis Æthelweard already had 'fram Isaace . . . oþ ende'.[71] In the Old English (composite) Hexateuch, most of Genesis I–XXII is by Ælfric. (The whole of Ælfric's translation of I–XXIV may well be preserved in Cambridge, University Library, Ii. 1. 33, a twelfth-century copy.) In addition, the compiler of the Hexateuch drew on Ælfric for Numbers XIII–end and Joshua (largely); he was also influenced by Ælfrician summaries in the latter part of Deuteronomy and the first chapter of Joshua. Genesis, which is equipped with a prefatory letter to Ælfric's patron, Ealdorman Æthelweard, must be treated separately. In the preface Ælfric states his reservations about translating Genesis. (I pass over here the difficulties raised by his comment at the end that he does not intend thereafter to translate Latin (biblical?) books into English.) Without adequate interpretation, many details of the book (the sexual mores of the patriarchs both before and under the Old Law, for example) are capable of misconstruction. The issue which must concern us here is why Æthelweard wanted Genesis in English. The answer I suggest can only be proved circumstantially, but it seems quite certainly correct: Æthelweard and his son Æthelmær were apparently pious churchmen

[69] See Crawford, *Heptateuch*, pp. 15–51, at lines 381–2 (Moses, perhaps referring to the text preserved as Numbers XIII–end in *Heptateuch*, pp. 315–31), 405–9 (Joshua 'awende . . . Æþelwearde ealdormen': i.e. *Heptateuch*, pp. 377–400).

[70] On Ælfric's contribution to the Hexateuch translation, see the discussion by P. Clemoes in *The Old English Illustrated Hexateuch*, ed. C. R. Dodwell and P. Clemoes, EEMF 18 (Copenhagen, 1974), 42–53, esp. 43–8.

[71] *Heptateuch*, ed. Crawford, pp. 76–80, lines 5–6.

who, like St Gerald of Aurillac, attempted to follow something like the monastic devotions and sought from Ælfric – in the case of the Lives of Saints – materials related to the monastic observance: 'þas boc be þæra halgena ðrowunga and life . . . þe mynster-menn mid heora þenungum him wurðiað'.[72] Æthelweard had a special copy of the *Sermones catholici* which supplied a substantial amount of reading in the vernacular for the Night Office on Sunday; the father and son also had the Lives of Saints for readings peculiar to the monastic Office. Their Genesis filled a similar need for the pre-Lenten and Lenten period. The full Hexateuch – if indeed they possessed it – would later fill this need in an ampler way, even though Ælfric would probably have thought it too ample for the laity in general.[73]

Finally, there remain several biblical adaptations by Ælfric, none of which is equipped with the kind of introductory comments customary for pieces he regarded as sermons for public reading. Thus they are properly classified by Peter Clemoes as 'non-liturgical narrative pieces' or as 'reading pieces'. It may be added that they are for private edification or devotions on the monastic model, as had been Æthelweard's Genesis. Ælfric applies several terms to these reading or narrative pieces in the Letter to Sigeweard: book, translation (*awendan*) – but never *cwide*, which he reserved for the only true sermon, Job. The writings in question range in date from the Lives of Saints group (*c.* 995) to the beginning of his abbacy in 1005 in roughly the following order: Kings and Maccabees;[74] parts of Joshua, Numbers and Judges, all incorporated by the compiler into the Heptateuch; and Esther and Judith.[75] One may note, first, that Ælfric limits himself severely to the historical books. In fact, save the rounding out of the materials for Lent from the Heptateuch, he was in the later stages rounding out a reasonably complete set of readings on the summer histories of the Office lectionaries. Ever concerned to avoid areas where the *digolnes*, 'secrecy', 'mystery', 'obscurity', was capable of misleading simpler folk, he did not attempt apocalyptic prophecy or wisdom.[76] In Kings (in both the piece issued with Lives of Saints and the summaries in the letters), he can be

[72] *Lives of Saints*, ed. Skeat, p. 4 ('this book concerning the sufferings (i.e. the *passiones*) and lives of the saints whom monks in their Offices honour amongst themselves'). On the piety of Æthelweard and Æthelmær, who was the founder of Eynsham, see my *Preaching and Theology*, p. 49. To the bibliography on Gerald of Aurillac, whom I suggested as a continental model for this sort of lay piety, may now be added Rosenwein, *Rhinoceros Bound*, pp. 73–83.

[73] It is also conceivable that the compiler of the Heptateuch, who retained Ælfric's Genesis preface, had in mind the needs of monolingual monastic novices or schoolboys and of secular clergy on whom the canonical obligation of participating in the Office was being imposed.

[74] *Lives of Saints*, ed. Skeat, nos. xvii and xxv. On the chronology, see Clemoes, 'Chronology', pp. 224–5.

[75] *Homilien*, ed. Assmann, nos. xiii–xix.

[76] The book of Job was regarded as an *historia* in the Middle Ages, although we would now class it amongst the Wisdom writings.

seen taking great care to avoid incidents such as David's relationship with Bathsheba or the Absalom episode, which might undermine the king's special place as author of the psalter and model of piety and kingship. If he presents an account of the evil of Ahab and Jezebel, it is against the background of the fulminations of Elijah. In presenting Judith, he suggests her tropological applicability to the lives of nuns in the piece itself; and in the Sigeweard letter he says she is an example 'þæt ge eower eard mid wæpnum beweriæn wið onwinnende here'.[77] At the end of Maccabees he adds a little piece on the three orders of society ('oratores, laboratores, bellatores'), largely to disabuse those who might argue that the religious, whose life is devoted to spiritual combat, should take up arms after the example of Judas Maccabaeus and his sons.[78]

It has been the argument of the second section of this essay that Ælfric's writings on the Old Testament ought to be understood – against the background of the outline of the Office lectionary in the Eynsham Customary – as an adaptation of materials from the monastic devotional life to the devotional life of laymen and non-monastic clergy. Since the Office lectionary included no less than the whole of the scriptural canon, and since Ælfric limited himself to the historical books, it might be objected that the case is insubstantial. There are, however, considerations that seem to me quite conclusively to mitigate such doubts. The first is that the earliest of these adaptations in the Second Series are homiletic in form and refer explicitly to the liturgical setting of the lections in the Offices. Ælfric seems, however, soon to have given up the notion of systematically adapting the Old Testament histories to public instruction of the laity – if, indeed, he ever entertained the idea. But – and this is the second consideration – he continued to produce material from the Old Testament in a context that can most clearly be understood as related to monastic custom. For Æthelweard, he translated the first half of Genesis as a supplement to other materials (sermons and hagiographic matter) which the ealdorman had related to the readings of the Night Office. Later, he produced further works which round out an almost complete set of summaries of the readings of the Office histories for Lent and the summer. Thus, just as his unprecedentedly full set of sermons on the Sunday gospels comes from the monastic homiliary for the Night Office, so too did his unprecedentedly full set of adaptations of the Old Testament. And so it is that an understanding of the Office, especially one based on Ælfric's own Eynsham Customary, offers us a key to the rationale for his major division of Ælfric's corpus and relates it securely to the rationale of his sermon-writing as well.

77 'That you should defend your land by force against hostile armies' (*Heptateuch*, ed. Crawford, p. 48, lines 778–80).

78 *Lives of Saints*, ed. Skeat II, 120–4.

# *The Judgement of the Damned* (from Cambridge, Corpus Christi College 201 and other manuscripts), and the definition of Old English verse

E. G. STANLEY

It is a paradoxically pleasing feature of the Anglo-Saxons, as seen from our side of the great gulf of time that separates us from them, that not a few of them, homilists and writers of annals, laws and charters among them, would have had reason to utter the converse of M. Jourdain's all too obvious truth: 'Par ma foy, il y a de quarante ans que je dis de la *Poésie*, sans que j'en sçeusse rien.' But much depends on how we define their verse. That problem of definition is not new, and has manifested itself in two related scholarly activities. First, to establish what demarcates verse from prose. Secondly, having made our collections of Old English poetry, to identify in the prose those passages which are close to passages of verse as we find it in our collections of Old English poetry.[1] There is a third activity, not new either, which identifies in the extant prose passages of verse not recognized as such in our collections of Old English poetry.

This paper, in honour of Peter Clemoes, falls within the third activity, but leads on inevitably to the first activity, defining the requirements of Old English verse to provide a basis for regarding as verse a piece of what looks rather like a piece of homiletic prose. In doing so I follow in the footsteps of Max Förster.[2]

[1] Esp. The Anglo-Saxon Poetic Records (ASPR), ed. G. P. Krapp and E. V. K. Dobbie, 6 vols. (New York and London, 1931–53); but the *Bibliothek der angelsächsischen Poesie*, ed. R. P. Wül(c)ker (and B. Assmann), 3 vols. (Kassel, 1883–98), remains useful, not least on account of some special features, including for *Judgement Day II* (*ibid.* II. 2, 250–72) the printing in parallel of related passages from the prose homily, from Oxford, Bodleian Library, Hatton 113, fols. 66–73. This homily is ed. A. (S.) Napier, *Wulfstan, Sammlung der ihm zugeschriebenen Homilien* (Berlin, 1883), repr. with a valuable bibliographical appendix by K. Ostheeren (Berlin, Zürich and Dublin, 1966), pp. 134–43.

[2] M. Förster produced two editions of the homily I discuss in this paper, the first in 'Der Vercelli-Codex CXVII nebst Abdruck einiger altenglischen Homilien der Handschrift', *Festschrift für Lorenz Morsbach*, ed. F. Holthausen and H. Spies, Studien zur englischen Philologie 50 (Halle, 1913), 21–179, at 87–95 (also ptd separately (Halle, 1913), where the homily is found on pp. 71–9), and the second in *Die Vercelli-Homilien*, Bibliothek der angelsächsischen Prosa 12 (Hamburg, 1932; repr. Darmstadt, 1964), 44–53. Förster discusses the 'metrische Form' in 'Der Vercelli-Codex', pp. 65–6 (pp. 49–50 of the separate printing).

I publish below (pp. 370–9) the text of the homily from Cambridge, Corpus Christi College 201 (C), pp. 78–80, previously available only in Napier's collation (printed in the apparatus to his edition).[3] Napier edited the text from London, BL Cotton Cleopatra B. xiii (N); and he gave variants also from Oxford, Bodleian Library, Hatton 114 (H) and Cambridge, Corpus Christi College 419 (B). A version, widely divergent, is extant twice (with variants) in the Vercelli Book (Vercelli, Biblioteca Capitolare, CXVII), Homilies II ($V^1$) and XXI ($V^2$), both of them edited.[4] N. R. Ker gives a good account of the manuscripts, and Celia Sisam's introduction to the facsimile edition of the Vercelli Book provides further information.[5] I also publish (below, pp. 382–5) the unemended texts of the poetic-seeming part of the homily from C, with variant readings from NHB, and parallel with it the corresponding part from $V^1$, with variant readings from $V^2$ (ignoring minor differences).

Förster's introduction to his edition of 1913 contains the first discussion of the nature of the rhythmical passages in $V^1$, which in his two editions he sets out as if they were verse:

Interessant ist, und wohl noch nicht beachtet, daß ein Teil der Predigt . . . metrische Form besitzt, was wahrscheinlich so zu erklären ist, daß der Homilet, wie es nachweisbar mit dem altenglischen Gedichte *Be domes dæge* [*Judgement Day II* in ASPR] bei Wulfstan (ed. Napier, S. 136 Z. 25 bis S. 140 Z. 2) geschehen ist, ein Stück aus einem fertig vorliegenden Gedichte in seine Predigt aufnahm. Aber auch sonst zeigt die Predigt eine dichterisch gehobene Sprache.[6]

Förster's parallel – between *Judgement Day II* and Napier's 'Wulfstan' Homily XXIX – is close not merely in connecting a rhythmical passage from a pseudo-Wulfstan homily with a poem, but also in subject-matter and especially in transmission; for the manuscript in which 'Wulfstan' XXIX is extant is Oxford, Bodleian Library, Hatton 113, which originally formed one collection with Hatton 114,[7] that is, our H. Verse passages embedded in prose also occur elsewhere in C, and it is of some interest that verse in C (though in a different part of the manuscript from that containing 'Wulfstan' XL, edited here) is used in a prose homily in H, and the poems immediately following *Judgement Day II*

3 Napier did not make use of the Vercelli Book for his edition of this homily, his XL (*Wulfstan*, pp. 182–90).

4 Förster's editions (as cited above, n. 2) include variants from Vercelli Homily XXI in his collation. It has been ed. P. E. Szarmach, *Vercelli Homilies IX–XXIII*, Toronto OE Ser. 5 (Toronto, 1981), 83–90.

5 N. R. Ker, *Catalogue of Manuscripts containing Anglo-Saxon* (Oxford, 1957), nos. 49 (C), 144 (N), 331 (H), 68 (B) and 394 (Vercelli), and *The Vercelli Book*, ed. C. Sisam, EEMF 19 (Copenhagen, 1976).

6 'Der Vercelli-Codex', p. 66 (p. 50 of separate printing). The relationship of verse to prose in *Judgement Day II* and 'Wulfstan' XXIX, had been discussed incidentally by H. Löhe in his edition, *Be Dōmes Dæge*, Bonner Beiträge zur Anglistik 22 (Bonn, 1907), 47–52.

7 See Ker, *Catalogue*, no. 331.

in C – that is, (ASPR's) *An Exhortation to Christian Living*, *A Summons to Prayer* and *The Lord's Prayer II*[8] – are used in 'Wulfstan' XXIX and XXX, both from Hatton 113.[9] What exactly the relationship is of the related pieces in prose and verse I do not know. In the case of *Judgement Day II* and the related passage in 'Wulfstan' XXIX (not, of course, the whole of the homily), it seems possible that the verse and the prose were produced by one author,[10] but that is less likely for other passages in 'Wulfstan' XXIX and XXX related to versified material.

It is probably significant that the principal subject-matter of these passages is the Day of Judgement; and I think that that must mean, as Otto Funke thought,[11] that the use of marked rhythm was felt to be appropriate for this, the most awesome of all Christian subjects. The use of marked rhythm in Old English prose is not, however, confined to homilies on Judgement Day; the 'Prose Phoenix' includes short passages from the poem *The Phoenix*.[12]

Förster also suggests that the homily extant in CNHB and V[1] and V[2] shows 'eine dichterisch gehobene Sprache' even in the parts not set out by him as verse in his editions of V[1]. Förster's description, 'poetically elevated diction', is subjective and vague. It could refer to the frequent exhortative *(ea)la hwæt*; or to the use of rhythm often in combination with alliteration in single half-lines. Examples of such rhythmical stringing together of parallel phrases occur in a passage like:

La hwæt, þon þam firenfullum þincað þæt nanwiht ne sy
þæs hates ne þæs cealdes
ne þæs heardes ne þæs hnesces
ne þæs wraðes ne þæs wynsumes
ne þæs eaðes ne þæs earfoðes
ne þæs leofes ne þæs laðes
þæt hi þonne mæge fram ures Drihtenes lufan ascadan . . .[13]

8 'Wulfstan' XL is article 37 in Ker's account of his no. 49; it comes in what Ker (*Catalogue*, p. 83) calls Part B of the manuscript. The first three poems are Ker's article 2(*a–c*), in his Part A; *The Lord's Prayer II* is Ker's article 57(*a*), again in his Part B, because it is in the main hand.

9 See L. Whitbread, '"Wulfstan" Homilies XXIX, XXX and Some Related Texts', *Anglia* 81 (1963), 347–64.

10 Cf. E. G. Stanley, 'Studies in the Prosaic Vocabulary of Old English Verse', *NM* 72 (1971), 385–418, at 389–90.

11 O. Funke 'Studien zur alliterierenden und rhythmisierenden Prosa in der älteren altenglischen Homiletik', *Anglia* 80 (1960), 9–36; he discusses our homily in §18 at 33–6. For the relationship of subject-matter to use of rhythmical prose, see *ibid.* pp. 16, 20–1 and 28; rhythmical prose is especially common in 'Mahn- und Drohpredigten', of which homilies on Judgement Day form a striking sub-group.

12 See A. S. Cook, *The Old English Elene, Phoenix, and Physiologus* (New Haven and London, 1919), pp. 128–31.

13 C, pp. 78/38–79/1 (see below, p. 372). In references to the text of the homily in C, I use throughout the manuscript pagination and manuscript line numbers, which are given in the margin of the following edition (though for line numbering only every fifth is given).

Except for the first pair of genitives (*hates* and *cealdes*) the homilist is joining pairs alliteratively. Occasional alliterative pairs include the following: '7 wepað 7 waniað' (C, p. 78/13) with which we may compare *Christ*, line 992, 'wepað wanende'; '7 eal forsingod mancyn þonne forswelgeð seo firenlust' (C, p. 78/16); 'In þam dæge beoð blawende þa byman' (V¹, line 14); '7 sæ sencte' (V¹, line 16); 'to smeagen*ne* 7 to sorgienne' (N, p. 185/6–7);[14] '7 fram wlite 7 fram wuldre heofona rices' (C, p. 79/7); '7 earmlice adisgode 7 adwealde' (C, p. 79/9); 'deaðberende deofol' (C, p. 79/10); '7 þæs willan ne wyrcan' (C, p. 79/12); '7 his þam saran suslum' (V¹, line 42). Or Förster may have been referring to the very occasional use of phrases familiar to us from verse but not necessarily consisting of any words belonging exclusively to verse, of which the best example is

7 þonne sona bið þam lichaman     laðlic leger gired.[15]

Of course, it does not scan and has double alliteration in what might be regarded as the second half-line. It does, however, come in a run of phrases many of which are joined into alliterative long lines. Except that the figure, 'preparing a hateful couch', is found in verse (in *Beowulf*, line 2436, 'morþorbed stred', and in *Andreas*, line 1092, 'hildbedd styred' (to quote the unemended reading of the manuscript) – for which see the notes in the editions), this line in the prose homily is not significantly different from other occasional alliterative combinations in the homily which a little resemble alliterative combinations into poetic long lines. Examples from the homily in C and in V¹ include the following:

bið swiðe egeslic 7 andryslic     eallum gesceaftum (V¹, line 2)
þone blodgemængedan middaneard     7 þæt mancyn þe nu is (C, p. 78/9–10)
goldes 7 seolfres     7 godwebbes (V¹, line 5)
swiðe egeslicu     7 ondryslicu (V¹, line 10)

It is possible, by juggling with the variants in the six manuscripts, to improve the 'scansion' of some of these lines, but where we are dealing with occasional alliterative ornaments rather than more regular alliterative discourse (as later in the homily) it seems to me a vain pursuit.

More interesting is the occurrence in the homily, and especially in the rhythmical passages in it, of rare compounds, some *hapax legomena*: thus ***wohgeorn*** (C, p. 78/18) and ***wyrmslite*** (C, p. 80/7),. besides slightly less rare ***wælslitende*** (C, p. 80/2–3; see also Napier 'Wulfstan' XLVI, p. 241/12); and

References to V¹ are given as the line numbering in Förster's edition of 1932 (cited above, n. 2). References to N are given as page and line numbers in Napier's edition (cited above, n. 1).

14 C, p. 79/4 has *to scamigenne*, N *to smeagende*, to be emended to *to smeagenne* as in HB – see the note on C, p. 79/4 (below, p. 372).

15 C, p. 80/1 (see below, p. 376). N reads:

'7 þonne sona þam lichaman bið     laðlic legerbed gegyrwed.

*swiltcwalu* (C, p. 80/9; there are also four occurrences in verse, twice in *Andreas* and once each in *Guthlac A* and *The Phoenix*, and compare *deaþcwalu* once each in *Elene* and *Beowulf*). The rhythmical structure of V[1], lines 78–105 (cf. C, p. 79/39–42.) was not sufficient to lead Förster to arrange the passage in print as if it were verse, as he did lines 47–72, and as I have done below (pp. 374–6) for a slightly longer passage (including the lines corresponding to Förster's lines 47–72). In extending the area of text for that arrangement I run into the problem of how to set out the rhythmical units and pairs of units into half-lines and long lines and how to treat the not always very close variants. For many lines the arrangement is far from certain; the dividing line between what looks more like prose than verse or verse than prose is far from sharp. Funke's discussion is good here:

Our study concerns itself in the main with the following questions: the occurrence of alliteration in pairs of words and groups of words; the occurrence of two-stress groups with and also without alliteration; the possibility of concatenating such groups into longer structures; the emergence of four-stress long lines to form looser or stricter alliterative verse lines. As regards alliteration in pairs or groups of words we must often consider if we are dealing with deliberate or accidental alliteration; in this connection we shall probably also have to consider the attitude elsewhere of the homilist to the use of alliteration. Similarly in the case of concatenation of two-stress and four-stress groups certainty cannot always be achieved because they are embedded in unrhythmical contexts.[16]

Funke's discussion does not concern itself with diction, till he comes to our Vercelli homily: 'As regards rhythm, this homily is an exception among the homilies considered by me in that the Old English native poetic alliterative mode in long lines breaks through in the *Diktion* of the homily in one lengthy passage, so that the surmise has been expressed that the homilist has inserted into this homily passages of an Old English alliterative poem not otherwise known to us.'[17] Funke's wording is not quite clear to me. When he uses the

16 'Studien', p. 10: 'Unsere Untersuchung kreist im wesentlichen um folgende Fragen: das Auftreten der Alliteration in Wortpaaren und Wortgruppen; das Erscheinen von zweihebigen Gruppen mit und auch ohne Alliteration; die mögliche Reihung solcher Gruppen zu längeren Gebilden; das Hervortreten von vierhebigen Langzeilen zu loseren oder strengeren Stabreimen. Was die Alliteration in Wortpaaren und Wortgruppen betrifft, wird man des öfteren zu überlegen haben, ob es sich um beabsichtigte oder zufällige Alliteration handelt; hiebei wird wohl die sonstige Haltung des Homileten zum Alliterationsgebrauch zu berücksichtigen sein. Auch über die Reihenbildung zweihebiger und vierhebiger Gruppen ist nicht immer eindeutig zu entscheiden, weil in unrhythmische Umgebung eingebettet.'

17 *Ibid.* p. 34: 'In rhythmischer Beziehung nimmt diese Predigt unter allen von mir untersuchten Homilien dadurch eine Ausnahmestellung ein, daß in ihrer Diktion in einer längeren Stelle der ae. nationale, poetische Stabreim in Langzeilen durchbricht, so daß man die Vermutung ausgesprochen hat, der ae. Homilet habe in diese Predigt Teile eines uns sonst nicht bekannten ae. stabenden Gedichtes aufgenommen.'

word *Diktion* he appears to mean 'style of discourse', that is, he is referring only to alliterative pairing of half-lines into long lines. He appears not to be referring to 'poetic diction', that is, to the use of words confined to Old English verse. Yet in the part of the homily referred to by Funke and set out as verse by Förster we do find some few poetic words. This is the element in the passage that differentiates it from rhythmical and alliterative prose. To be verse it must contain some items recognizable by us as from the language of Old English poetry; we may then go on if we wish, and allege that the author too recognized, and intentionally used, these items as a sign that his discourse here is poetical.

Naturally, for our text we can hardly expect words expressing heroic concepts. We are not dealing with a poem like *The Dream of the Rood*. We might expect rather words of the type *wuldorfæder*, 'Father of Glory', 'God', with which Cædmon led the way in *Cædmon's Hymn*. Lines 8 (C, p. 79/17) and 28 (C, p. 79/29) are essential here, and if my reasoning in the notes is accepted (see below, pp. 386 and 389), *elwihta* and perhaps an underlying **rodorwaldend* may have to be used as evidence. However, such reinstated poetic diction cannot be regarded as conclusive evidence. Nevertheless I assume that the passage (to which I give the title 'The Judgement of the Damned') is verse. How far should I go to make it metrically better than what has come down to us? In a restored text I might go further in metrical tinkering – even transposing half-lines[18] – than would be legitimate for a straightforward edition; my purpose, however, is to suggest only in the notes the underlying metrical structure, and the possibility of an original consistency which is not a feature of the extant versions: the edited text itself I leave, therefore, unemended.

The clearest examples of poetic diction in our homily are, however, not to be found in the passage printed as if it were verse by Förster and discussed as specially significant by Funke. The *hapax legomena* and the figure of 'preparing a hateful couch' come together at C, p. 80/1, near the beginning of a passage (C, p. 80/1–16) less easily arranged as verse than C, p. 79/15–35. In the text of the homily edited from C, I have included (and set out in rhythmical units like half-lines and lines) this passage too (below, p. 376). The arrangement involves many uncertainties, but the vocabulary has more certain poeticisms than any other part of the homily.

Comparing the extant verse texts, *The Judgement Day II* and sporadically *An Exhortation to Christian Living, A Summons to Prayer* and *The Lord's Prayer II*, with their related prose homilies ('Wulfstan' XXIX and XXX) reinforces any reluctance one may feel about an editorial process of metrical improvement. In

18 See the notes on lines 10 (C, p. 79/18) and 14 (C, p. 79/21), below, p. 387.

*Judgement Day II* some lines are incomplete, some lack alliteration, in some rhyme takes the place of alliteration;[19] these features are well discussed by E. V. K. Dobbie in the introduction to his edition.[20] Incomplete lines (ASPR gives lines 100, 104, 121, 270, and also 276 and 289 for which there is no parallel prose)[21] are not to be mended by reference to the prose. In view of such irregularities it is worth noting that the poems in C only rarely have double alliteration in the second half-line. *Judgement Day II*, line 152, has no alliteration in the first half-line, and so is not strictly relevant; line 222 has probably more deepseated trouble – the manuscript reads 'ne þara wera worn wihte', and nothing in the prose text corresponds to the line which has been variously and always violently emended. Double alliteration seems to occur twice in *Exhortation*, lines 72 and 74 (both involving *swiðe*); line 74 is difficult, and in his note Dobbie says of it that 'it may be that the text is otherwise corrupt at this point'; neither line has a parallel in the prose.

The following edition of the C-text of Napier's 'Wulfstan' XL, is made for one purpose only, to clarify the rhythm of the rhythmical parts which I print as if they were verse lines. The punctuation of the manuscripts marks off the strongly apparent rhythms by pointing, which is lighter in the non-rhythmical parts of the homily in all the manuscripts. They do not, however, use pointing sufficiently consistently for me to feel that it should be reproduced in the edited text. Instead I use modern punctuation and capitalization. Manuscript abbreviations are expanded silently. In view of the existing editions of $V^1$ and $V^2$ and especially of N with variants from H and B (as well as our C), I do not provide a full apparatus. The line numbers are those of the lines in the manuscript; a solidus is used for the end of each fifth manuscript line, regardless of whether I set it out as prose or verse, and the number in the margin refers to the manuscript lines. I give a translation. The notes deal only with textual matters, and since the rhythmical parts of the homily are at the centre of this study I annotate them (below, pp. 386–90) more heavily than the rest.

The end of the homily, from C, p. 80/16 onwards, is a compilation making use of genuine Wulfstan material. It is rhythmical in the manner of Wulfstan. In his appendix to the reprint of Napier's *Wulfstan*, K. Ostheeren gives references to discussions of this aspect of the homily.[22]

19 See the note on line 21 (below, p. 388) and the discussion by Kluge referred to there.

20 ASPR 6, lxxi–lxxii.

21 Cf. also *Exhortation*, lines 39, 46 and perhaps either 66 or 67, and *The Lord's Prayer II*, line 6; *Summons*, lines 3–4 are not merely incomplete, but require some emendation to give sense.

22 See above, n. 1.

[p. 78]

**L**eofan men, Ælmihti God us singallice manað 7 lærað þurh his þa halgan bec þæt we soð 7 riht don her on worlde on urum life gif we willað heofona rice begitan æfter þisse worlde 7 geborgene beon / on ðam egeslican dæge þæs micclan domes. Ðæs dæges weorc bið egesful eallum gesceaftum, **s**wa se apostol cwæð, 'In quo omnis creatura congemescit.' **O**n þam dæge heofon 7 eorðe cwaciað 7 heofað 7 sæ 7 ealle þa þe on him sindon. 7 on ðam dæge þa hleoðrigendan ligas forglendriað þone blodgemængedan middaneard, 7 þæt mancyn / þe nu is on idelum gilpe 7 on sinlustum 7 in ðam wohgestreon*um* goldes 7 seolfres beswicen, 7 þæs him naht ne ondrædað, ac him orsorh lætað. 7 on ðam dæge þæt earme mancyn 7 þæt synfulle ofer him silfum heofað 7 wepað 7 waniað þæt hi þonne swiðe forhtigað forðam ðe hig ær nolden heora sinna betan. 7 on þam dæge on ðam firenan wilme / sæ forhwirfeð 7 eorðe mid hyre dunum 7 heofonas mid hire tunglum, 7 eal forṣingod mancyn þonne forswelgeð seo firenlust heora ærran gewyrhta, 7 unrihtwise deman, 7 gerefan, 7 ealle þa wohgeornan worldrican mid heora golde 7 seolfre 7 godwebbum 7 eallum ungestreonum þonne forwurðað. **A**nd on ðam / dæge singað þa bíman on ðam feower scea*t*um middaneardes. 7 þonne ealle men arisað of deaðe, 7 swa hwæt mancynnes swa eorðe ær forswealh oððe fir forbærnde 7 sæ besæncte 7 wilde deor frætan 7 fugelas tobæran eal þi dæge ariseð. **O**n ðam dæge ure Drihten cymð mid his þam micclan mægenþrymme mid þam / .ix. endebirdnessum heofonwara. þæt bið mærlic 7 wundorlic mægenþrym. **A**nd þonne bið he þam synfullum swiðe wrað æteowed, 7 þam soðfæstum he bið bliðe gesewen. **A**nd þonne þa Iudeas magon swutollice geseon þone þe hi ær ahengon 7 acwealdon. **A**nd se soðfæsta Dema demeð anra gehwilcum æfter his gewirhtum, / swa swa we leorniað on halgum gewritum, '***R***_eddet Deus unicuique secundum opera sua_.' **Ð**æt is on ure geþeode, 'He forgilt þonne anra gehwilcum æfter his agenum gewirhtum.' **O**n ðam dæge bið ures Drihtenes ansyn, swa we ær sædon, reþe 7 egesful þam synfullum gesewen; 7 he bið bliðe 7 milde þam soðfæstum æteowed, þæt is

**78/6–7** Cf. Romans VIII.22: 'scimus enim quod omnis creatura ingemescit [v.l. *congemescit*] et parturit usque adhuc'.

**8** *ligas* (supported by V[1]) against v.l. *ligettas*.

**10** *sinlustum* with *i* for *y* (as also, for example, *sinna* 78/14 and *sinfullan* 79/35); wordplay *sin-*, 'continual', 'immense', with *sin(n)* for *synn*, 'sin', though not impossible, is therefore unlikely. MS *wohgestreones* an error only in C.

**18** *wohgeorn*: only here.

**19** *ungestreon*: only here.

**20** MS *sceaftum*: only in C; NHB *sceatum*, V[1] *sceattum*.

**23** As has often been pointed out, in C unstressed *-on* and *-an* (and the vowels of other endings) are used as if interchangeably; thus *frætan* and *bæran* for *fræton* and *bæron*.

**25** *endebirdnessum*: corr. from *-nesse*.

**30–1** Cf. II Timothy IV.14 'reddat [v.l. *reddet*] ei Dominus secundum opera eius'.

Dearly beloved, Almighty God continually admonishes and teaches us through his holy books that we act truthfully and righteously here in the world in our life if we wish to attain the kingdom of heaven after this world and be saved on the terrible day of this great judgement. The travail of that day will be fearful to all creatures, as the Apostle said, 'In which all creation groans.' On that day heaven and earth tremble and wail, and the sea and all that are thereon. And on that day the resounding flames consume the blood-drenched earth and that race of man which now is in vainglory and in sinful lusts and led astray in that ill-gotten treasure of gold and silver, and have no fear of it, but behave as if unconcerned. And on that day that poor and sinful race of man laments and weeps and moans over themselves that they then are very much afraid because they had not wanted to make amends for their sins. And on that day in that fiery surge the sea changes utterly and the earth with its mountains and the heavens with their stars, and the evil lust of their former deeds devours sinful mankind, and unjust judges and reeves, and all the wrong-loving, worldly rich, with their gold and silver and fine cloth and all false treasures, perish then. And on that day the trumpets resound in the four corners of the earth. And then all men arise from death, and whatsoever of mankind the earth had swallowed up or fire consumed and the sea drowned and savage beasts devoured and birds carried off, they all arise that day. On that day our Lord comes with his great and glorious might with the nine orders of those who dwell in heaven. That is a glorious and wonderful might. And then he will be revealed very angry to the sinful, and to the righteous he will appear very kind. And then the Jews can see clearly him whom they had hanged and slain. And the righteous Judge will judge each one according to his deserts, as we learn in Holy Scripture, 'God will reward each according to his works'. That is in our language, 'He rewards then every one according to his own deserts.' On that day our Lord's countenance will appear, as we have said, fierce and terrible to the sinful; and he will be revealed kind and mild to the righteous,

þam þe hi*m* / *to in* ðære swiðran healfe þonne beoð gelædde. Ða firenfullan witodlice hig beoð þonne on dæg on þare winstran healfe gehwirfede, 7 he þonne rædlice to heom cwið, 'Farað ge awirgedan on þæt ece fir þe wæs deofl*e* gegearwod 7 his gegængum eallum.' **L**a hwæt, þon þam firenfullum þinceð þæy nanwiht ne sy

þæs hates    ne þæs / cealdes
ne þæs heardes    ne þæs hnesces
ne þæs wraðes    ne þæs wynsumes
ne þæs eaðes    ne þæs earfoðes
[p. 79] ne þæs leofes /    ne þæs laðes

þæt hi þonne mæge fram ures Drihtenes lufan ascadan gif hi þonne þæs gewealdan mihton; 7 þa ungesæligan yrmingas nellað nu þæt geþencan ne his willan wurcan nu hi eaðe magon. **E**ala hwæt, þæt is ofer eal gemet

to scamigenne    7 to sorgienne /
7 on micelre care    to cweðanne
þæt þa earman synfullan    sculan þonne sare
aswæman    fram ansene
ures Drihtenes    7 ealra haligra
7 fram wlite    7 fram wuldre

heofona rices, 7 þanon gewitan in ða ecan tintregu helle wites. **L**a hwæt, manna mod sindon aþystrode

7 earmlice adisgode    7 adwealde

þæt hi ǽfre / sculon læton þæt deaðberende deofol mid ungemættre costnunge hi to ðam gedwell*e*, þæt hi swa micle sinne fremman swa hi nu doð 7 þæs willan ne wyrcan þe hi of éorðan lame geworhte 7 mid his gaste
[*Pr* 1] geliffæste 7 him ece lif begeat. La, hwæt þence we þæt we us ne ondrædað þone toweardan dæg þæs / micclan domes?

**35–6** MS *hig in to.*
**38** MS *deoflum.*
**39** *þon* with perhaps an erasure above *n* (from *þon̄* for *þonne*?).
**79/1–2** V[1], lines 24–6, has the sinful man as singular; some sense can be made of the C reading (cf. Bosworth–Toller, s.v. *wealdan* (thus N where C has *gewealdan*) V. (a), the subject of *mæge* is *nanwiht* 78/39): nothing, however good or bad, could cut them off from the love of our Lord, if they were in control of their destiny; but the conditional clause seems redundant or illogical.
**4** *scamigenne*: only in C; the other manuscripts have *smeagenne* (N *smeagende*), which is perhaps to be preferred.
**7** *aswæman* seems to have the sense 'pine, grieve', not 'roam'; see J. Roberts, *The Guthlac Poems* (Oxford, 1979), p. 182, note on line 1352; cf. *OED*, s.v. *Sweam* v.
**10** *læton* with *-on* for *-an*.
**10–11** The construction is mixed, confusing *þæt hi . . . sculon lætan deaðberende deofol . . . hi to ðam gedwellan, þæt* . . ., 'that they must suffer the mortiferous devil to seduce them to this, that', with *þæt hi . . . sculon lætan þæt deaðberende deofol . . . hi to ðam gedwell*e, *þæt* . . ., 'that they must suffer that the mortiferous devil seduce them to this, that'; the latter is easier syntax, and a stage of subj. sg. with *-en* for *-e* may underlie *-an* of *gedwellan* in the extant manuscripts.
**13–35** See below, pp. 386–90, for fuller notes.

that is to those who will be led towards him then on the right side. The sinful, truly they will be transferred on the day then to the left side, and he then says to them designedly, 'Go, you accursed ones, into that eternal fire which was prepared for the devil and all his companions.' Behold, then it seems to the sinful that there is nothing

so hot nor so cold
nor so hard nor so soft
nor so angry nor so gracious
nor so easy nor so difficult
nor so dear nor so hateful

that it can then cut them off from the love of our Lord if they could then be in control of the matter, and the unhappy wretches do not now wish to consider that nor to do his will now that they easily can. Alas, that is immeasurably a cause

to feel shame and sorrow for
and it is to be uttered in great grief
that the poor sinners must then grievously
pine away from the presence
of our Lord and of all saints
and from the splendour and from the glory

of the kingdom of heaven, and from there go into the eternal torments of the punishment of hell. Behold, the minds of men are darkened

and miserably turned to folly and error

that they must forever suffer that the mortiferous devil with immeasurable temptation seduce them that they sin so greatly as they do now and do not do the will of him who made them from clay of earth and with his spirit gave them life and gained eternal life for them. Lo, what are we thinking that we do not fear the imminent day of that great judgement?

[1] **Se** is yrmða dæg    7 ealra earfoða dæg.
[*Pr* 2] On ðam dæge us bið æteowed
[7] seo geopnung heofona    7 engla þrym
7 *el*wihtna rire    7 eorðan forwyrd,
treowleasra gewinn    7 tungla gefeal,
[10] þunorrade hlinn    7 se þistra storm,
þara lyfta léoma    7 þara liggetta gebrastl,
þara granigiendran / gesceaft    7 þara gasta gefeoht,
þa grymman gesihðe    7 þa godcundan miht,
se hata scur    7 helwara ream,
[15] þara beorga geberst    7 þara bimena sang,
se brada bryne ofer eal world    7 se bitera dæg,
se miccla cwealm    7 þara manna mán,
seo sare sorh    7 þara sawla gedal,
[20] se sara sið    7 se sorh/fulla dæg,
þæt brade beala    7 se birnenda grund,
þæt bitere wite    7 se blodiga stream,
feonda firhto    7 se firena ren,
[25] hæþenra granung    7 reafera wanung,
heofonwara fulmægn    7 heora hlafordes þrym,
þæt ongrislice gemot    7 seo egesfulle fird,
se reða waldend    7 se rihta dom,
ure firena edwit    7 þara / feonda gestal,
[30] þa blacan andwlitan    7 þæt bifigende wered,
se forhta cyrm    7 þara folca wop,
þara feonda grimnes
7 se hlude heof,
[35] þæt sarige mancyn    7 se synniga heap,
**s**eo granigende neowelnes    7 seo forglændrede hell,
þara wyrma ongrype
7 þara sorhhwita mæst,
se niðfulla here /
[40] 7 se teonfulla dæg.

[*Pr*3] **O**n þam dæge us bið eal þillic egsa æteowed and þa sinfullan woldon þonne gewiscan georne gif hi mihton þæt hi næfre acænnede ne wurdon fram fæder ne fram meder; 7 him þæt þonne wære leofre þonne eal middaneard to æhte geseald. **L**a hwæt, we nu ungesælige sind þæt we us bett / ne warniað 7 þæt we ne ondrædað us þe swiðor þe we dæghwamlice geseoð for urum eagum ure þa nihstan feallan 7 swiltan;/

**36** *gewiscan* corr. from *geswican*.
**40** *þe swiðor* with *i* intercalated after *þe* to indicate alternative form *þi*.
**41–2** *7 swiltan* like a catchword below *feallan 7*.

That is a day of miseries and a day of all hardships.
On that day will be revealed to us:
the opening of the heavens and the glory of the angels
and the fall of aliened creatures and the destruction of the earth,
the strife of the faithless and the fall of stars,
the roar of thunderstrokes and the dark storm,
the gleam of those currents of air and the crackle of lightnings,
the condition of those groaning ones and the battle of the souls,
the terrible sights and the divine powers,
the hot shower and the jubilation of the denizens of hell,
the bursting open of the grave-mounds and the song of the trumpets,
the broad fire throughout the world and the bitter day,
that great death and the moan of the men,
the sad sorrow and the parting of the souls,
that sad time and the mournful day,
that ample destruction and the burning abyss,
the bitter torment and the stream of blood,
the terror of devils and the fiery rain,
the groaning of the heathen and the lamentation of the spoliators,
the full power of the dwellers in heaven and the glory of their Lord,
the terrible assembly and the awesome host,
the stern Almighty and the just judgement,
our disgrace for sins and the accusation of the fiends,
the pale faces and the trembling host,
the fearful noise and the weeping of nations,
the ferocity of the fiends,
and the loud lamentation,
sorrowful humanity and the sinful multitude,
the groaning abyss and hell consumed utterly,
the seizing of the serpents
and the greatest of grievous torments,
the malicious army
and that day of distress.

On that day all such terror will be revealed to us and the sinful would then eagerly desire if they could that they had never been born of father and mother; and they would rather have that then when all the world (is) handed over as chattels. Alas, we are now wretched that we do not take better heed of ourselves and that we do not fear the more that we see daily before our eyes how our neighbours fall and perish;

[p. 80] 7 þonne sona bið þam lichaman laðlic leger gired
7 in ðare cealdan moldaṇ gebrosnoð
7 þæt lic þar to fulnesse gewurðeð
7 þam wælslitendum wyrmum wurðeð to æte.
þonne bið sorhlic sar
7 earmlic gedal lices 7 sawle.
**A**nd gif þonne seo sawle huru slidan sceal /
in ðam ece hellewitu
mid þam wérian 7 þam awirgedan gaste
7 þar þonne mid deoflum drohtnoð habban
on morðe 7 on mane,
on susle 7 on sáre,
on wean 7 on wyrmslitum,
betweonan deadum 7 deoflum,
on bryne 7 on biternesse,
on bealuwe 7 on bradum líge,
on yrmðum 7 on earfoðum,
on swiltcwale / 7 on sarum sorgum,
in *f*yrenum bryne 7 on fulnesse,
**o**n toða gristbitum 7 on tintregum,
in angmodnessa earmra sawla
**o**n cile 7 on wanunge,
**o**n hungre 7 on þurste,
**o**n hæte 7 on earfoðnesse,
**o**n neowlum attre 7 on écere forwirde,
**o**n arleasnesse
7 on mistlicum wita cynne,
**o**n muðe 7 on / fædme
þæs deadberendan dracan
se is deofol nemned.

Eala, leofan men, uton warnian us 7 georne beorgan wið þone egsan, 7 uton geornlice yfeles geswican 7 þurh Godes fultum to góde gedón þone dæl þe we don magon. **U**ton mán 7 morð æghwar forbugan 7 ealle fracoddæda swiðe ascunian. / **A**nd utan don swa ic lære: **u**tan God lufian inweardre heortan eallum mode 7 eallum mægne 7 Godes lage healdan. **A**nd uton gecnawan hu lǽne 7 hu lyðre þis lif is on to getruwianne, 7 hu oft hit wurð raþost forloren 7 forlæten þonne hit wære leofost gehealdon. **Ð**eos world is sorh/ful 7 fram dæge to dæge a swa leng swa wirse, forðam þe heo is on ofstum 7 hit nealæcð þam ende. **A**nd þi heo wære wurðe þæt hi ænig man

**80/1** *leger* has the support of V[1] and V[2] (which have *gegyrwed* and (like other manuscripts) *gegyred*), but other manuscripts have *legerbed*.
**5** *werian* could be either 'weary' or 'cursed'; 'weary' is more likely because of *awirgedan*, too close in sense and form to the alternative interpretation.
**11** MS *syrenum*.
**19** *m* of *mán* damaged.

and then at once a hateful couch will be prepared for the body
and it decays in the cold earth
and there the body decomposes
and becomes food for carrion-rending worms.
Then there will be grievous sorrow
and the miserable separation of body and soul.
And if then the soul must indeed fall
in everlasting torments of hell
with the weary and accursed spirit
and there then lead life with devils
in murder and in evil,
in torment and in sorrow,
in woe and in the gnawing of worms,
among the dead and the devils,
in fire and in bitterness,
in ruin and in broad flame,
in miseries and in hardships,
in death-throes and in grievous sorrows,
in fiery burning and in corruption,
in gnashing of teeth and in tortures,
in distress of mind of wretched souls,
in cold and in lamentation,
in hunger and in thirst,
in heat and in affliction,
in the venom of the pit and in eternal perdition,
in impiety
and in divers kinds of punishments,
in the mouth and in the embrace
of that mortiferous dragon
that is named devil.

Alas, dearly beloved, let us take heed and eagerly guard against that terror, and let us zealously leave off evil and through God's help turn to good the part we can do. Let us turn away from evil and murder everywhere and shun all crimes strenuously. And let us do as I teach: let us love God deep in our heart with all our mind and all our strength and keep God's law. And let us recognize how fleeting and how vile this life is to trust in, and how often it is lost soonest and given over when it might have been held most dear. This world is full of sorrow and from day to day at all times the longer the worse, because it is in haste and the end draws near. And therefore the world would

˹ne˺ lufode ealles to swiðe. **A**c lufian we þone hihstan cyningc 7 þæt uplice [rice], **a**nd ondrædan we us symle þone toweardan dom þe we ealle to sculan. **O**n þam dom ure / Drihten silf eowað us sona his blodigan sidan and his þirlan hánda 7 þa silfan rode þe he on ahangen wæs; **a**nd wile þonne æt us gewitan hu we him þæt geleanodan. **W**el þam þonne þe Gode ær wel gecwemdan swa swa hi scoldan. **H**i þonne siððan eac ece edlean þurh Godes gife þananforð habbað betweoh englum 7 heah/englum a to worlde on heofonan rice þar næfre leofe ne gedælað ne laðe ne gemetað, ac ðar halige heapas simle wuniað on wlite 7 on wuldre 7 on winsumnesse. **Đ**ar bið mærð 7 mirhð 7 ece blis mid Gode silfum 7 mid his halgum in ealra worlda world a buton ende. Amen.

**28** *uplice rice*: in C *rice* is om.
**33** *-cwemdan* with *-an* for *-on*, corr. from *-en*(?), *scoldan* with *-an* for *-on*.

be excellent if anyone did not love it altogether too much. But let us love the highest King and that realm above, and let us fear at all times the Judgement to come which we all must come to. In that Judgement our Lord himself will show us at once his bloody sides and his pierced hands and the very Cross which he was hanged upon; and he wishes then to know from us how we repaid him for that. Well will it be then with those who had pleased God well as they ought. They then thereafter will have their eternal reward too through God's grace for ever and ever among angels and archangels world without end in the kingdom of heaven where friends never part and foes never meet, but there the holy hosts dwell forever in splendour and in glory and in joyousness. There will be honour and joy and everlasting happiness in the presence of God himself and of his saints for ever and always world without end. Amen.

It would clearly have been possible to set out other parts of the homily as if they were verse. Rhythmical phrases occur several times, but they are not close to the rhythms of C, p. 79/16–35, which is at the centre of this study. Such word-pairs as the opening 'manað 7 læerað', or, with a touch of alliteration, 'heofað 7 wepað 7 waniað' (C, p. 78/13), and more clearly perhaps C, p. 78/16–19, are typical of other kinds of rhythm:

7 eal forsingod mancyn     þonne forswelgeð seo firenlust
heora ærran gewyrhta,
7 unrihtwise deman     7 gerefan
7 ealle þa wohgeornan     worldrican
mid heora golde 7 seolfre     7 godwebbum.

The end of the homily (C, p. 80/16–39) with its many echoes of Wulfstan, and similarities with 'Wulfstan' XLII (with which our homily shares many phrases, including even the opening of the most nearly metrical part, 'Se is yrmða dæg 7 ealra earfoða dæg', see Napier, p. 202, lines 18–19), could certainly be printed as Angus McIntosh printed rather more regular, genuine Wulfstan material.[23]

[23] The opening of the homily is Wulfstan's too; see D. Bethurum, *The Homilies of Wulfstan* (Oxford, 1957), p. 42; cf. K. Jost, *Wulfstanstudien*, Swiss Stud. in Eng. 23 (Berne, 1950), 217–18, and S. R. Levin, 'On the Authenticity of Five "Wulfstan" Homilies', *JEGP* 60 (1961), 452–4. A. McIntosh prints several Wulfstanian pieces in 'Wulfstan's Prose', *PBA*, 35 (1949),

Even what I have set out as if it were verse (thus C, pp. 78/40–79/1, 79/4–7 and 78/9), and especially the passage with a few words that may belong to verse rather than prose (that is C, p. 80/1–15), are not very like true verse at all; even some parts of what seems to me nearest to verse stray from metrical similarity with verse, as the end of the long passage does (C, p. 79/32–5). Nevertheless I think that Förster was right to speak of this part as possessing *metrische Form*.

In the pages that follow I produce an unemended text for this more strictly metrical part of the homily, to which I give the title 'The Judgement of the Damned'. All the manuscripts have been used, and in the Notes (below, pp. 386–90) I indicate how one might achieve better scansion than is found in any manuscript, and what better wording may underlie that in C or, in some cases, in any of the extant manuscripts.[24]

## DIGRESSION: AN INSTANCE OF SIMILAR AFFECTIVE RHYTHMS IN LATER ENGLISH

Before we get to the edited, newly won poetic text, *The Judgement of the Damned*, a short digression may be permissible. The history of English prose rhythms remains to be written. R. W. Chambers made a start in his celebrated 'On the Continuity of English Prose from Alfred to More and his School'.[25] Ian A. Gordon began his book, *The Movement of English Prose*,[26] with a first part in the title of which he echoes Chambers's title. Gordon's book continues the history from the Renaissance to the novels of the twentieth century; but in that short book there is not really room to trace examples in later literature of rhythmical features first to be seen in the prose of the Anglo-Saxons. A. J. Bliss has sought to lead the struggling student of Old English verse to feel that it is not a verse-form as 'alien and incomprehensible' as it appears, by pointing to frequent correspondences between it and the pentameters of later verse.[27]

109–42, especially 'Wulfstan' 1 (Napier, *Wulfstan*, p. 5, lines 7–end) and the *Sermo Lupi ad Anglos* (ed. D. Whitelock, 3rd ed. (London, 1963), lines 55–67). It is to be noted that McIntosh uses, as far as possible, the pointing of the manuscripts to help find the stress patterns; but the pointing is not always where one might expect it to be, and not infrequently in genuine Wulfstan texts after a run of very clear phrases conforming to the pattern discussed, less clear phrases occur with unhelpful manuscript pointing.

24 For the arrangement of the text, see above, p. 364.

25 An extract from the Introduction to Nicholas Harpsfield's *Life of Sir Thomas More*, ed. E. V. Hitchcock and R. W. Chambers, EETS o.s. 186 (London, 1931), ptd separately, EETS o.s. 191A (London, 1932).

26 I. A. Gordon, *The Movement of English Prose* (London, 1966).

27 'An Appreciation of Old English Metre', *English and Medieval Studies Presented to J. R. R. Tolkien on the Occasion of his Seventieth Birthday*, ed. N. Davis and C. L. Wrenn (London, 1962), pp. 27–40.

Marjorie Daunt has shown that there is some similarity between Old English verse rhythms and some rhythms found in living speech today,[28] and her views have been accepted by many. That too is thought to bridge the gulf between the alien ancient and the familiar modern.

I wish to draw attention to a modern parallel to the homiletic rhythmical discourse of the Anglo-Saxons presented and discussed in this paper, not to make the ancient material seem more relevant to us, but to show that by similar means we still achieve similar effects. Towards the end of the fourth act of *The Way of the World* Lady Wishfort rises to the deceptive situation by employing a variety of rhetorical skills as she addresses Waitwell disguised as Sir Rowland in the hope of winning him to matrimony. One of her speeches runs thus:

O Sir *Rowland*, the hours that he has dy'd away at my Feet, the Tears that he has shed, the Oaths that he has sworn, the Palpitations that he has felt, the Trances, and the Tremblings, the Ardors and the Ecstasies, the Kneelings and the Riseings, the Heart-heavings, and the hand-Gripings, the Pangs and the Pathetick Regards of his protesting Eyes! Oh no memory can Register.[29]

An ear attuned to the rhythms of the Old English homily will soon help towards an arrangement of these modern prose rhythms comparable with those used for rhythmical Old English discourse. There is no lack of alliteration, though it is not in regular use. Some lines may be seen as 'long lines' composed of two halves, the second often beginning with *and*. Thus:

O Sir *Rowland*,<br>
the hours that he has dy'd away at my Feet,<br>
the Tears that he has shed,<br>
the Oaths that he has sworn,<br>
the Palpitations that he has felt,<br>
the Trances, and the Tremblings,<br>
the Ardors and the Ecstasies,<br>
the Kneelings and the Riseings,<br>
the Heart-heavings, and the hand-Gripings,<br>
the Pangs and the Pathetick Regards<br>
of his protesting Eyes!<br>
Oh no memory can Register.

And now we can go back to our Old English text.

28 'Old English Verse and English Speech Rhythm', *Transactions of the Philological Society* (1946), 56–72; repr. *Essential Articles for the Study of Old English Poetry*, ed. J. B. Bessinger and S. J. Kahrl (Hamden, Conn., 1968), pp. 289–304.

29 First edition (London, 1700), p. 66; in eighteenth-century and later editions of Congreve's play, the speech comes in Act IV, scene xii. In H. Davis's edition, *The Complete Plays of William Congreve* (Chicago and London, 1967), which follows the edition of 1700, the speech is at p. 458, lines 511–17

E. G. Stanley

## THE JUDGEMENT OF THE DAMNED

### from C

[*Pr* 1] La, hwæt þence we þæt we us ne ondrædað þone toweardan [79/13]
dæg þæs / micclan domes: [15]
1 **S**e is yrmða dæg    7 ealra earfoða dæg.

[*Pr* 2] on ðam dæge us bið æteowed
7 7 seo geopnung heofona    7 engla þrym
7 ealwihtna rire    7 eorðan forwyrd,
treowleasra gewinn    7 tungla gefeal,
10 þunorrada hlinn    7 se þistra storm,
þara lyfta leóma    7 þara liggetta gebrastl,
þara granigendran / gesceaft    7 þara gasta gefeoht, [20]
þa grymman gesihðe    7 þa godcundan miht,
se hata scúr    7 helwara ream,
15 þara beorga geberst    7 þara bimena sang,
se brada bryne ofer ealworld    7 se bitera dæg,
se miccla cwealm    7 þara manna mán,
18 seo sare sorh    7 þara sawla gedal,

20 se sara sið    7 se sorh/fulla dæg, [25]

22 þæt brade beala    7 se birnenda grund,

*Variant readings from* NHB

*Pr* 1 B **L**a, C us *er. after* we,
B miclan
1 NH Se B **S**e, N yrmðæ, N and B 7
*Pr* 2 N In (*above* In *in diff. ink*: on), H In, B **I**n, N byð
7 NHB geopenung (N *fin.* g *corr.*, H i *above* ge-), N heofena ríces, B 7 H coros *above* þrym
8 B 7, NH helwihta B hellwihta, NHB hryre (H ruina *above* hryre), B 7, H damnatio *above* forwyrd
9 H certamen *above* gewinn, B gewin, B 7, H planet' *above* tungla, NHB gefeall
10 NH Ðunorrada, NHB hlynn, B 7, NHB þeostra þrosm (H caos *above* þrosm)
11 NH Ðæra B **Ð**ara, B 7, HN þæra, NB lígetta H ligeta, NHB blǽst
12 NHB þa graniendan, B 7, NH þæra
13 B **Ð**a, NHB grimman, N gesyhð HB gesihð, B 7
14 B 7 hellwara, NHB hréam
15 N þæra B **Ð**ara, N beorha, N i *above 2nd* e *of geberst*, H i *above* ge-, B 7, N þǽra, NHB býmena
16 NHB ealle woruld, B **A**nd
17 NHB micla, B 7 NH þæra, H malum *above* mán
18 B *om.* seo sare sorh, B 7, NH þæra, H i *above* ge-
20 B 7
22 B **Ð**æt, NHB bealo, B 7 NH byrnenda B beornenda

## THE JUDGEMENT OF THE DAMNED

### from V[1]

[10r20] [*Pr* 1] La hwæt, we us ne ondrædaþ þone toweardan ege domes dæges:
se is yrmþa dæg    7 earfoða dæg
7 unrotnesse dæg
7 cirmes dæg
7 wanunge dæg
7 sares dæg    7 sorges dæg
7 se þystra dæg.
[*Pr* 2] On þam dæge us bið æteowed /
[10v1] se opena heofon    7 engla þrym
7 eallwihtna hryre    7 eorþan forwyrht,
treowleasra gewinn    7 tungla gefeall,
þunorrada cýrm    7 se þystra storm,
7 þæra liga blæstm
7 graniendra gesceaft    7 þæra gasta gefeoht
[5] 7 sio grimme / gesyhð    7 þa godcundan miht
7 se hata scúr    7 hellwarena dream
7 þara bymena sang
7 se brada bryne    7 se bitera dæg
[V[2] 7 se micla cwyld    7 þara manna dream]
[V[2] 7 seo sarie sorh]    7 þara sawla gedal
7 se deað-berenda draca    7 deofla forwyrd

7 se nearwa seaþ    7 se swearta deaþ
7 se byrnenda grund

*Variant readings from* V[2]
*Pr* 1 Eala hwæt . . . þæs domes
1 Se ys yrmðe . . . earfoðnessa
3 cyrmes
5 sorge
*Pr* 2 On ˹ðam˺ dæge us byð ætywed
7 se ˹ge˺sewena
8 forwyrd
11 þara liga gebrasl
12 7 þa grangendan gesceafta, þara
13 seo, mihta
14 hat˹a˺
18 þa˹ra˺
19 dead-berenda

þæt bitere wite 7 se blodiga stream,
feonda firhto 7 se firena ren,
hæþenra granung 7 reafera wanung,
Heofonwara fulmægn 7 heora hlafordes þrym,
þæt ongrislice gemot 7 seo egesfulle fird,
se reða waldend 7 se rihta dom,
ure firena edwit 7 þara / feonda gestal,
þa blacan andwlitan 7 þæt bifigende wered,
se forhta cyrm 7 þara folca wop,

þara feonda grimnes
7 se hluda heof,
þæt sarige mancyn 7 se synniga heap,
**S**eo granigende neowelnes 7 seo forglændrede hell,
þara wyrma ongrype
7 þara sorhhwita mæst,
se niðfulla here /
7 se teonfulla dæg.

[*Pr* 3] **O**n þam dæge us bið eal þillic egsa æteowed.

23 B 7
24 NHB fyrhto, B 7, NHB fýrena, H regn
25 B reafena
26 N heofon-, B **H**eofon-, H Heofonwaru, NHB fulmægen, B 7
27 B ongryslice, H i *above* ge-, N and, B 7, H horribilis *above* egesfulle. NHB fyrd (H e *above* y)
28 NB wealdend, B 7
29 B **V**re, N fýrene H synna B fyrena, B 7, NB þæra, H i *above* ge-
30 N *faint* (*erased?*) i *above* i *of* andwlítan, H wlita *with* vultum *above it*. B 7, NH bifiende, H excercitum *above* wered
31 N cearm, H strepitus *above* cyrm, B 7, N þæra, N f *of* folca *damaged*
33 NH þæra B **Ð**ara *new para.*
34 B 7, B a *of* hluda *from downstroke of* (*prob.*) e, B heaf
35 NH mancynn, B 7, N syngia, H caterua *above* heap
36 NH seo B Seo, *washed out from* **S**eo, NHB graniende, N neowelnys H abissus *above* neowelnes B s *of* -nes *damaged*, B 7, N forglendreˊdeˋ H forgleddrede, B forglendredˊeˋ *with 2nd* d *squeezed in*
37 N þæra B **Ð**ara *new para.*, N i *above* y *of* óngrype, H ongripa B ongripe
38 B 7, N þæra, N sorhwihta HB sorhwita
39 B **S**e
40 B 7
*Pr* 3 NH On *without rubric*, N byð, NH eall NHB þyllic, HB egesa (H terribilia tempestas *above* egesa)

7 se blodiga stream
7 mycel fionda / fyrhto    7 se fyrena rén.
7 hæðenra granung    7 hira heriga fyll,
heofonwarena mengo    7 hiora hlafordes miht
7 þæt mycle gemot
7 sio reðe rod    7 se rihta dóm
7 þara feonda gestal
7 þa blácan 7wlitan    7 bifiendan word
7 þara folca wóp
32 ond se scamienda here

36 7 sio forglendrede / hell
37 7 þara wyrma gryre.

[*Pr*3] 7 þonne bið us æghwylc þyllic egesa æteowed.

24 and seo mycle fyrhto þara feonda
25 V² *om. 1st* 7, hyra
26 menigeo, hyra
27 mycele
28 seo
30 andwlitan 7 þa
32 7
36 seo byrnende
*Pr* 3 On þam dæge us byð ælc þylic egesa ætywed

## NOTES

Pr[ose] 1: $V^1$ and $V^2$ can be taken as with **La hwæt** (*Eala hwæt*) a compound exclamation, but the explicit question in CNHB, 'Why do we not fear?', has more life in it than the assertion, 'Alas, we do not fear.'

1b **ealra** gives double alliteration in the second half-line; $V^1$ is metrically best, and better than the $V^2$ half-line, *7 earfoðnessa dæg*.

2–4, 6 and 32 in $V^1$ and $V^2$, 33–4 and 37 in $V^1$ and $V^2$ and (differently) in CNHB, and 38–40 in CNHB are single half-lines. Such single half-lines are found in the homily outside this 'metrical' part.

5 **7 sares dæg**: Förster commenting on line 25a, where $V^1$ has 7 but $V^2$ (and CNHB) omits it, suggests that the copulative is perhaps to be om. throughout, as in all the manuscript readings of 26a. In C the only case of initial *7* in a line consisting, in my arrangement, of two half-lines joined by alliteration is 8a, where *7* is supported by all the manuscripts. The central ideas of line 5 are found also in line 18a and (though not in $V^1$ and $V^2$) in line 20 (and cf. lines 35 and 38). The repetitiousness of the metrical part of the homily makes any statement that a half-line may have been added too subjective to be useful. Metrically *sares dæg* would, of course, be short without initial *7*. The form **sorges** ($V^1$) is, according to Förster's note, possible in late Old English; but the only other example given in R. L. Venezky and A. diP. Healey, *A Microfiche Concordance to Old English* (Toronto, 1980), is *sorges 7 . . . sares* in the twelfth-century manuscript of Alfred's *Boethius* only (ed. W. J. Sedgefield, *King Alfred's Old English Version of Boethius* (Oxford, 1899), p. 16, line 18), and Sievers's reference must be to that (see K. Brunner, *Altenglische Grammatik nach der angelsächsischen Grammatik von Eduard Sievers* (Tübingen, 1965), §252, Anm. 2), but it is possible that there are other occurrences emended away by the editors.

8 **ealwihtna**: vocalic alliteration is required, so that *hel(l)wihta* of NHB is unlikely; C and $V^1$ and $V^2$ have *eal(l)wihtna*, but not all creation falls. The assumption of confusion of *æl-, eal-*, 'all', with *el-*, 'alien', underlying the readings provides the best explanation of the variants, and 'aliened creatures' are those damned on Judgement Day. The word occurs elsewhere only at *Beowulf*, line 1500, *ælwihta eard*. At *Andreas*, line 118, God is described as *helm ælwihta*, 'protector of all creatures', and similarly *helm* (or *cyning*) *eallwihta* at *Genesis A*, lines 113 and 978, and *Andreas*, line 1603. Both words are confined to verse. **forwyrd**: the variant *forwyrht*, in $V^1$ alone, was defended by Förster in 1932, though in his edition of 1913 he was inclined to emend to *forwyrd* of the other manuscripts, which is certainly a possible reading, with the sense as in the gloss in H 'damnatio' or perhaps simply 'destruction'. Förster regards the two words as synonymous, and *forwyrd* as 'prosaisch'. In verse *forwyrht* occurs only at *Christ*, line 1094, in the compound *manforwyrhtu* regarded by I. Gollancz and A. S. Cook in their editions as acc. pl. with *mān-* as first element, i.e. 'sins, crimes'. The exact meaning does not emerge from this context, Christ was hanged on the cross:

fore moncynnes    manforwyrhtu,
þær he leoflice    lifes ceapode,

'on account of the evil *forwyrhtu* of mankind, where he lovingly chaffered life', i.e. perhaps 'gave life for life', for *ceapian* can mean either 'to purchase' or 'to sell' and Christ did both. The sense of *forwyrht* may be 'misdeed', a sense supported in the Egbertian penitential material: *7 butan forwyrhtum*, 'et sine malefactis' (B. Thorpe, *Ancient Laws and Institutes of England* (London, 1840), octavo edn, II, 238–9, line 11 (folio edn, p. 392, lines 42–3); see Bosworth–Toller, *Supplement*, s.v. *forwyrht*, and cf. *MED*, s.v. *forwurht*, which gives Transitional English *forwurhtæ*.) The verb, OE *forwyrcan*, ME *forwirchen*, has the senses 'ruin, destroy; do wrong; forfeit' (see Bosworth–Toller and *Supplement, MED*, and cf. *OED*, s.v. *Forwork*; cf. further S. Feist, *Vergleichendes Wörterbuch der gotischen Sprache*

(Leiden, 1939), s.v. *fra-waúrhts*; Grimm, *Deutsches Wörterbuch*, s.v. *verwirken*; and E. Wessén, 'Om den äldsta kristna terminologien i de germanska fornspråken', *Arkiv för nordisk Filologi* 44 (1928), 106); from the evidence of the verb it seems that the noun *forwyrht* is not synonymous with *forwyrd*, but means 'forfeiture' in the several senses, some now obsolete, recorded *OED*, s.v. *Forfeiture*. Though *forwyrht* is a rarer noun than *forwyrd*, there is no reason for regarding it as a *lectio difficilior* in the unique reading in $V^1$; in any case, that concept has to be applied with great caution to vernacular material.

10 **storm** C, $V^1$ and $V^2$: NHB *þrosm* fits the context well ('dark smoke' is better than 'dark storm'), though such collocations as *se swearta storm* (*Metres of Boethius* 4.22) and, less close, *on digylnysse stormys*, 'in abscondito tempestatis' (Cambridge Psalter 80:8), make one hesitate before suggesting that *storm* should be regarded as a substitution to avoid double alliteration in a second half-line, a metrical flaw which could be the result of transposition in the archetype

se þistra þrosm    7 þunorrada hlinn

(where 7 introduced into the second half-line Type E constitutes an undesirable anacrusis). Probably it is best to leave the original order; when F. Klaeber reviewed Förster's edition of 1913 (in *JEGP* 18 (1919), 479) he said apropos of line 14 in NHB –

se hata scur    7 helwara hream –

'The double alliteration of the second half-line in this metrical passage will hardly be considered a serious obstacle.'

11b **gebras(t)l** C and $V^2$, **blæst(m)** NHB and $V^1$: there is no deciding between these readings, and the affinity here between C and $V^1$ need mean no more than that in each an original *gebras(t)l* has been replaced independently by a word not very different in general appearance. At a literal level, both crackling and a current of air attend lightning, but also fire ($V^1$ and $V^2$). The various senses specifically suited to lightning and explosions (including *OED*, s.v. *Blast* sb., 5) do not go back to Old English.

12a **þara** (only in C) seems better than nom. pl. *þa graniendan gesceaft(a)* (variously spelt), and gen. pl. is supported by $V^1$ *graniendra*; the *-an* of *granigendran* in C as a gen. pl. weak is not unparalleled in late Old English (cf. Brunner, *Altenglische Grammatik*, §276, Anm. 5), but I have found no parallel for gen. pl. *-endran* (cf. *ibid.* §286), and should be inclined to emend to the form in $V^1$ if editorial regularization of late Old English confusion of endings were more easily justified except on the grounds that the evidence should be brought into conformity with the grammar supposedly derived from it.

13 **gesihð** HB and *gesyhð* N and $V^1$ $V^2$ may have been regarded as assonating with *miht*; C's dissyllabic pl. *gesihðe* is perhaps in assonance with a dissyllabic form such as $V^2$ *mihta* pl., but if satisfactory scansion were looked for in this text endingless forms would be preferable.

14b **ream** C is presumably to some extent the result of a wish to avoid double alliteration in the second half-line. Klaeber (*JEGP* 18 (1919), 479), followed by Förster in his edition of 1932 and by Szarmach in his edition of $V^2$ (cited above, p. 364, n. 4), held that *dream* of $V^1$ and $V^2$ is less apt than *hream*. It is difficult to see why. Quite apart from the double alliteration in the second half-line (though that could be explained as the result of transposition of the two halves, i.e. the original might have read

helwara hream    7 se hata scur

with better scansion), there is every reason for thinking that the inhabitants of hell will have cause for merry din on Judgement Day. See also below, note on 17b, with *dream* $V^2$ as a variant – perhaps, as has been suggested, anticipated here in $V^2$ and even $V^1$ where 17 does not occur. (Cf. the following note, *ad finem*.)

16a **ofer ealworld** C, *ofer ealle woruld* NHB expands the metrically sufficient line *7 se brada bryne* of V[1] and V[2] (with redundant *7*: see above, note on line 5), perhaps to bring it more into accord with the length of other lines in this text. Repetition of words and ideas is common in this passage, so that the repetition of *brad* at 22a or *biter* at 23a and especially C, p. 80/8–9 *on bryne 7 on biternesse, on bealuwe 7 on bradum lige*, outside this passage in the homily, will cause no surprise to readers. The omission of some of the repetition in V[1] and V[2] – where the readings at lines 22 and 23 do not include the first half-lines, and the reading in V[1] corresponding to C, p. 80/2–3 (see Förster, *Die Vercelli-Homilien*, p. 51, lines 90–1), has, after *on* (MS *7*) *bryne 7 on biternesse*, nothing to correspond to *on bealuwe 7 on bradum lige* (and so also V[2]) – is not significant either. The C-reading *ealworld* is to be regarded as a compound, and appears to be a *hapax legomenon* here in English; though such compounds are easily found in Germanic languages, thus Modern Danish *alverden* (cf. Modern German *Weltall*, based on *All*, 'universe'; and hence ModE *world-all* q.v. in *OED* Supplement (1933)). The compound may have been formed from *ealle woruld* to reduce the half-line in length. C is elsewhere concerned, or so it may seem, to improve the prosody; thus at line 14b, where *hream* gives double alliteration in a second half-line which C's *ream* avoids (see above, note on line 14b).

17b **mán** comes at a place where noise seems appropriate, more so than moral condemnation of *mān*, 'sin, evil, guilt', so that I am inclined to look for an Old English antecedent of ModE *moan*, such as is suggested in *OED*, s.v. *Moan* sb. (note), and that in spite of the gloss 'malum' in H. If that interpretation of *mán* here is right it seems to be the only occurrence, and the word must have had a limited currency. That would account for the reading *dream* in V[2], repeated from 14b, perhaps because *mán*, 'moan', was unfamiliar to the scribe, or more probably because he understood it as 'moan' but thought to avoid confusion by substituting *dream*.

18a–23 In view of the omission in B of 18a, the similarity of 18a to elements of 20 and the similarity of 20 to 5, it may well be that the extant readings and omissions are the result of confusion at an early stage.

19a **deaðberende**: cf. the two other uses in this homily (C, pp. 79/10 and 80/15).

21 **seaþ** V[1] (*seað* V[2]): 'pit' in rhyme with *deaþ* (*deað* V[2]). For a related assonance, cf. *Laȝamon: Brut I*, ed. G. L. Brook and R. F. Leslie EETS o.s. 250 (London, 1963), p. 22 (line 423): 'inne deope seaðen: setten þa deade' – and cf. line 25 (and note, below). In Old English late verse lines with rhyme do not always observe the normal rules of alliteration; sometimes (as in line 25) there is no alliteration at all; see F. Kluge, 'Zur geschichte des reimes im altgermanischen', *BGDSL* 9 (1884), 422–50, esp. 434–6 (but the whole article contains relevant material), and E. V. K. Dobbie on *Judgement Day II*, ASPR 6, lxxi–lxxii. The weaker line *se sara sið* may be the result of an attempt to improve the alliteration. **se swearta deaþ** is unrelated to ModE 'The Black Death', on which see *OED*, s.v. *Death* 8.b.

22–3 See above, note on line 16a.

24a This half-line, though of course metrically sufficient as a Type A line, is shorter than any other in these verses. V[1] expands it and V[2] goes even further. Cf. above, note on line 16a.

25 A non-alliterative, rhyming line; cf. above, note on line 21. In the context the sense of the reading in V[1] and V[2] is not impossible: *7 hira heriga fyll*, 'and the downfall of their armies'. It could be the original line replaced by a familiar rhyming collocation, for which cf. the *Microfiche Concordance*, s.v. *granung* (10 ×), *granunga* (2 ×) and *granunge* (2 ×), but only here forming a rhyming unit longer than just of the two words joined by 'and'; for Middle English uses, see *MED*, s.v. *grōninge*, and cf. *OED*, s.v. *Woning*.

26 V[1] and V[2] have cross-alliteration; perhaps CNHB **ful-** was not in the original, and **þrym** may have replaced **miht** (both words have been used before, lines 7b and 13b).

27a **ongrislice** is required by the vocalic alliteration (cf. Förster's note, both 1913 and 1932), if, as seems likely, line 27b goes back to the original; in any case *myc(e)le* (V[1] and V[2]) seems feeble.

27b **fird**, perhaps in contradistinction to **here** (see lines 32a V¹ and esp. 39, and cf. line 25b in V¹ and V²), seems to refer to the heavenly host rather than to the devil's army (cf. *MED*, s.v. *fĕ̄rd(e)* n. (2), 4 (a); and see *Christ and Satan*, line 468, where *fyrd* is used of those released by Christ at the Harrowing).

28a **se reða waldend** CH (NB *wealdend*). On the spelling *waldend*, see E. G. Stanley, 'Spellings of the *Waldend* Group', *Studies in Language, Literature, and Culture of the Middle Ages and Later*, ed. E. B. Atwood and A. A. Hill (Austin, Tex., 1969), pp. 28–69; cf. A. Lutz, *Die Version G der angelsächsischen Chronik*, Texte und Untersuchungen zur englischen Philologie 11 (Munich, 1981), clxxxii–clxxxiii, who believes that the spellings are distinguished according to the 'Textsorte' in which the word occurs, *waldend* for verse, *wealdend* for prose; if that were so, and if CNHB go back to a single archetype (as I believe) it would be difficult to explain why two scribes (or their common intermediary) should have chosen to depart from a significant spelling in their exemplar, whichever it may have been in this borderland between verse and prose. The reading in V¹ and V² has double alliteration, *sio ređe rod*. The epithet is unparalleled in Old English verse or prose as far as I can find in the *Microfiche Concordance*, which has not even sorrowful or joyful with reference to the cross – holy, glorious, precious, golden, divine, radiant, great, high, heavy, true, all occur and it might be possible to argue for confusion of *ređe* with *reade* (cf. *Christ*, line 1101), but 'fierce' with reference to the cross presupposes a high degree of personification before the transference of the epithet could be undertaken. I suspect that something like *se reða rodorwaldend* underlies the extant readings; though the metre is not ideal, an expanded Type D line with dissyllabic anacrusis, but then the metre of this text is very far from ideal. The compound **rodorwaldend* is not found; *rodera waldend* is common.

30b **word** V¹ and V² is best explained as from a form of *weorod*, presumably *worod* (though that spelling is rare). Szarmach emends to *werod* following a suggestion in Förster's edition of 1913, no longer favoured by him in 1932. Though such a use is not recorded in Old English, *bifian* could presumably be used of the voice, and therefore perhaps of words – 'and trembling words' – unless *7 bifiendra word*, 'and the words of the trembling ones', were thought better. The reading of CNHB causes no difficulty, however, and though feeble may seem preferable; it has the support of the gloss in H.

32a **se scamienda here** V¹ and V² fits the context well: 'the shameful army' to be interpreted either, and better, as 'the army – cause of our shame' or as 'the army feeling a sense of shame'. Förster toys with the possibility of emending to *sariga* to bring the line nearer to 35a CNHB, but the attempt to reconcile CNHB with V¹ and V² for lines 31–40 is futile seeing that the divergence is so great.

36b **forglændrede** with *æ* in C for more usual *e*; cf. A. Campbell, *Old English Grammar* (Oxford, 1959, latest revision 1983), §193(*d*). The word seems to have caused trouble. The reading in H, *forgliddrede*, is a different word; see OE *gliddrian*, 'totter, slither', esp. in L. Goossens, *The Old English Glosses of MS. Brussels, Royal Library, 1650 (Aldhelm's De Laudibus Virginitatis)* (Brussels, 1974), no. 3989, and cf. *MED*, s.v. *gliteren*, esp. sense 3 first quotation unrelated to the sense 'glitter', evolved in Middle English. The verb *forglendrian* occurs in our homily also at C, p. 78/9 (*forbærnaþ* in V¹, Förster line 3) and in B the variant given by Napier, *Wulfstan*, p. 183/13, *forglendrede* instead of *forbærnde* C, p. 78/22 (so also V¹, Förster line 16). Förster (1913 and also 1932) – and similarly, for other occurrences, Bosworth–Toller, *Supplement*, s.v. *forglendrad*) suggests that at line 36b the reading should perhaps be *forglendrende*, i.e. 'devouring' rather than 'devoured'. But the reading of the manuscripts is not impossible: *forglændrede* may mean 'consumed utterly (by fire)' corresponding to the variant in B 'tottering to utter destruction'. Altering the text to *forglendrende* would, however, help to explain the feeble variant in V², *byrnende*.

37 **ongrype** (variously spelt) is *hapax legomenon*. It may mean 'attack, assault' as the cognates in the Germanic languages do; thus Bosworth–Toller, s.v. *ongripe*. The sense 'seizure' might, however, be closer to the senses of the related verbs and nouns, and would fit better here

too: the serpents are seizing the damned. The reading *gryre*, 'terror', of V¹ and V² is a feeble substitution of a more familiar word.

38 **sorhhwita**: gen. pl. for *sorhwita* (the best form only in HB; N has *sorhwihta*, 'of sorrowful creatures', which may be either an error or a feeble substitution; and C has *-hwita*, perhaps with southern inverted spelling of *hw* for *w*). Both *sorhwita* and *sorhwihta* are compounds not recorded elsewhere in Old English.

Pr[ose] 3. It is noteworthy that the closing prose sentence of this metrical piece echoes the wording of Prose 2, which opens it, as if to emphasize both the form of the passage and the sense of the verse lines which are in amplification of what will be manifested to sinners on Judgement Day.

## CONCLUSIONS

Our homily is from the borderland of verse and prose, and where exactly the boundary is to be drawn is not certain. To sum up, a few points may be isolated from the evidence of this text.

1. Cambridge, Corpus Christi College 201 has verse texts, *The Judgement Day II, An Exhortation to Christian Living, A Summons to Prayer* and *The Lord's Prayer II*, related to homilies in rhythmical prose, especially 'Wulfstan' XXIX and XXX. For 'Wulfstan' XL, which is related to Vercelli II (and again XXI), we may assume (with Förster) a similar relationship to an Old English poem no longer extant, but presumably similar in versification to the poems in this manuscript, which contains one of the versions of the homily.
2. Old English admonitory and comminatory homilies, pre-eminently those on the theme of Judgement Day, often have some alliteration, used either ornamentally as if for special emphasis, or structurally as part of rhythmical discourse.
3. It is not always easy to make 'long lines' out of word-pairs even when they alliterate; for example, C, pp. 78/41–79/1:

   ne þæs leofes    ne þæs laðes.

   There are some cases of linking by rhyme or assonance, for example, lines 21 (V¹, line 60), 25 (C, p. 79/27) and perhaps 13 (C, p. 79/21). Different rhythmical organization is found elsewhere in the homily, for example, C, p. 78/16–19, or the Wulfstanian end (C, p. 80/16–39).
4. Very occasionally a phrase known to us from verse occurs in our homily; thus 'bið þam lichaman laðlic leger(bed) (ge)gired' (cf. C, p. 80/1), but even that line does not scan like exact verse (except after much emendation).
5. As we have it, the 'metrical' part of the homily admits double alliteration in the second half-line, though this irregularity can easily be emended away; see the notes on lines 10 and 14b.
6. Not infrequently alliterative combinations occur in the homily which a little resemble such combinations in verse, though no close parallels are, in fact, to be found, and though the scansion would not be regular.

7. There are several *hapax legomena* in the homily, and one or two words are found outside our homily only in verse. Significant items of poetic diction may be added by emendation to the transmitted, genuine evidence; for example, *elwihta* (see above, note on line 8), and **rodorwaldend* (see above, note on line 28a).
8. The spellings *waldend* or *wealdend* (see above, note on line 28) do not in the form in which they occur in these manuscripts provide a safe base for conclusions, either on the subject of what the Anglo-Saxons themselves may have thought was the nature of this homily, whether verse or prose, or on the subject of what significance, if any, the spelling *waldend* may have had in late West Saxon.
9. In spite of much uncertainty, taking all the points of evidence together, some part of the homily does seem more nearly 'metrical', and some of the items of poetic diction occur in that part; but poetic diction is found in other passages of rhythmical discourse.
10. The existence in Old English of this borderland between verse and prose may be relevant to similar manifestations in continental Germanic dialects, and elsewhere[30] I have addressed myself to some of the issues raised.[31]

[30] 'Alliterative Ornament and Alliterative Rhythmical Discourse in Old High German and Old Frisian compared with Similar Manifestations in Old English', *BGDSL* 106 (1984), 184–217, esp. 207–11.

[31] I wish to express my thanks to the Master and Fellows of Corpus Christi College and the Librarian, Professor Raymond Page, for making me feel welcome whenever I came to consult the manuscripts in the Parker Library.

# Beowulf and the judgement of the righteous

STANLEY B. GREENFIELD

When Beowulf utters his last words on earth, the poet comments,

him of hræðre gewat
sawol secean soðfæstra dom.[1] (2819b–20)

Despite some critical attempts to find these lines ambiguous, they seem to state unequivocally that the hero's soul has found salvation.[2] Wiglaf seems equally certain that his lord's soul will find its just reward:

Sie sio bær gearo
ædre geæfned, þonne we ut cymen,
ond þonne geferian frean userne,
leofne mannan, þær he longe sceal
on ðæs Waldendes wære geþolian. (3105b–9)

Though Beowulf's other followers, riding about the barrow that is their lord's monument to time, give no testimony as to their belief in his eternal resting-place, they praise him ('as is fitting') in terms of impeccable moral qualities, some of which (in particular the assertion that he is 'manna mildust ond mon(ðw)ærust') are used elsewhere in Old English to describe Christ and saintly men.[3] Towards the end of the first part of the poem, the narrating voice had praised Beowulf's generosity, loyalty to his lord and companions, and restraint in using the 'ample gift' (*ginfæstan gife*) of his strength (2166b–83a). As he lies dying, the hero himself echoes these remarks, feeling that the *Waldend fira* will not be able to reckon him among those unrighteous who sought treacherous quarrels, were false to their oaths or murdered their kinsmen (2737–43). Unfortunately for critical consensus, neither the poet nor any of his characters says that Beowulf had *not* been proud, avaricious or imprudent; and

1 All quotations are from *Beowulf and the Fight at Finnsburg*, ed. F. Klaeber, 3rd ed. (Boston, Mass., 1950).

2 See, e.g., E. G. Stanley, 'Hæþenra Hyht in *Beowulf*', *Studies in Old English Literature in Honor of Arthur G. Brodeur*, ed. S. B. Greenfield (Eugene, Oreg., 1963), pp. 142–3, for a denial of Beowulf's salvation. See J. D. Niles, *Beowulf: the Poem and its Tradition* (Cambridge, Mass., 1983), p. 297, n. 11, for citations to the contrary.

3 See M. P. Richards, 'A Reexamination of *Beowulf* ll. 3180–3182', *ELN* 10 (1973), 163–7.

a sizeable number of recent critics, writing about the poet's monument to time, have, in relation to the dragon episode, laid those very charges to his hero's account. Others, in turn, have not been slow in rising to Beowulf's defence, even to seeing him in his last fight as a Christ figure. Interestingly enough, both critics who read the poem literally and those who read it allegorically or exegetically have included both detractors and defenders of Beowulf.[4]

Not uncoincidentally, there are disparate critical views of the Christian poet's attitude towards his poem's pagan heroic world. Some see the poet condemning that world because it necessarily lacks Christ's redeeming grace; some suggest that it is flawed purely as a socio-economic system, where the underpinnings of gift-giving are wars and social instability. Such views find poet and poem stressing the limits of heroism and the heroic world. On the other hand, some critics find the poet celebrating the heroic values of loyalty, courage and generosity, values consistent with his own Christian ethos.[5]

A few critics have been less moralistic. Shippey, for example, concludes that 'what the poet has done is to create a universe which is lifelike, consistent, a model for emulation, and one seen through a film of antique nostalgia; but which remains at the same time a world the poet and all his contemporaries could properly thank God they did not live in'.[6] (One may be forgiven for wondering, in light of the second half of that sentence, for whom that universe is 'a model for emulation'.) Chickering feels that the poet is asking his audience both to admire and to reject the heroic ideal.[7] Chase suggests that the poet's 'attitude towards heroic culture . . . is neither romantic idealizing nor puritan rejection, but a delicate balance of empathy and detachment'.[8] I am not sure that such contrarieties or balance can coexist comfortably in a work of art, or at least that we can accept them simultaneously. On the other hand, I am not quite ready to accept the 'heretical' view tentatively advanced by Douglas Short, that 'the poet may not have totally harmonized the various aspects of the dragon episode'.[9] Nor am I at all ready to accept what Tripp calls 'subtractive rectifications' of the text of this episode so as to remove inconsistencies and

[4] For a summary of bibliography on these positions, see D. D. Short, '*Beowulf* and Modern Critical Tradition', *A Fair Day in the Affections: Literary Essays in Honor of Robert B. White, Jr*, ed. J. D. Durant and M. T. Hester (Raleigh, NC, 1980), pp. 1–22, esp. 9–14.

[5] For the first of these views, see, e.g., R. W. Hanning, '*Beowulf* as Heroic History', *Medievalia et Humanistica* n.s. 5 (1974), 77–102; for the second, see H. Berger, Jr, and H. M. Leicester, Jr, 'Social Structure as Doom: the Limits of Heroism in *Beowulf*', *Old English Studies in Honor of John C. Pope*, ed. R. B. Burlin and E. B. Irving, Jr (Toronto, 1974), pp. 37–79; and for the third, see Niles, *Beowulf*, pp. 235–47.

[6] T. A. Shippey, *Beowulf* (London, 1978), p. 44.

[7] H. D. Chickering, Jr, *Beowulf: a Dual-Language Edition* (Garden City, NY, 1977), pp. 26–7.

[8] C. Chase, 'Saints' Lives, Royal Lives, and the Date of *Beowulf*', *The Dating of Beowulf*, ed. C. Chase (Toronto, 1981), pp. 161–71, at 161–2.

[9] Short, '*Beowulf* and Modern Critical Tradition', p. 11.

allow Beowulf to emerge 'as the ideal king he is'.[10] Perhaps there is still room to explore this dominant critical controversy of recent years; and I should like to take this opportunity to offer *ofer hronrade* some comments on it – both theoretical and substantive – as part of the *gombe* which this volume pays to Peter Clemoes.

For there to exist such critical disarray in our perceptions of the poem's *gestalt* and the poet's attitude towards hero and heroic world, there must be what Norman Rabkin, in commenting on a similar state of affairs in Shakespeare studies, calls 'centers of energy and turbulence' in the work which we reduce from our several perspectives into 'coded elements of [different] thematic formula[s]'.[11] Of course we recognize that *others'* perceived thematic designs in *Beowulf* are 'either generalized to the point of superficiality, or . . . [are] too narrow to accommodate large segments of the poem'.[12] That our *own* formulations may be far from the proper heat and centre of the poet's or the poem's design is, understandably but regrettably, less apparent to us.

It is not difficult to single out three such volatile centres that have produced negative perceptions of the hero. First, there is Hrothgar's sermon: why should he give this cautionary speech to Beowulf at the height of the young hero's triumph over the kin of Cain, if it is not to be a touchstone by which to judge (adversely) Beowulf's behaviour in the later part of the poem? Secondly, as if to justify Hrothgar's admonition, we find Beowulf's 'prideful' and 'avaricious' speech of lines 2518b–37, in which he asserts that the battle against the dragon is his responsibility alone, and that he will either win the gold or die in the attempt. And third comes Wiglaf's speech of lines 3077–109, in which Beowulf's young kinsman says that now the Geats must suffer *anes willan*, 'for the sake of one', that despite all their advice to shun the dragon their lord *heold on heahgesceap*: here Beowulf's imprudence or obstinacy is made manifest by his own liegeman, a view seemingly reinforced by the messenger's prophecy that Franks and Frisians, or Swedes, will swoop down upon the Geats once the word spreads that their lord is dead.

It is less easy to find *in the text itself* such centres as suggest that the poet is at all antipathetic to the ethical or social values of the heroic world he depicts. The poet is a Christian, true, and he specifically condemns the heathen practice of praying to the *gastbona* for help, a practice which (as he says) assigns one's soul to the fire's embrace. But this custom is mentioned and condemned only once, in lines 175–88; is it enough to sustain the weight of 3182 lines? Though the Geats (as well as the Danes) were historically heathens – and Beowulf is a

10 R. P. Tripp, Jr, *More About the Fight with the Dragon: Beowulf 2208b–3182, Commentary, Edition, and Translation* (Lanham, Md, 1983), p. ix.

11 N. Rabkin, *Shakespeare and the Problem of Meaning* (Chicago, Ill., 1981), p. 25.

12 Short, '*Beowulf* and Modern Critical Tradition', p. 9.

Geat – *they* are in no way so stigmatized. The argument that the poem's heroic world and its protagonist are flawed because they lack Christ's redeeming grace is really one *ex silentio*. Even the Christian excursus makes no mention of Christ's redemptive power, or of Christ for that matter. The God who governs human and seasonal *edwenden* in the *geardagum* of the narrative setting still rules such change, the 'authenticating voice' reiterates, in the poet's own time.[13] The argument that there is a fatal contradiction at the heart of heroic society, in that a hero–king, who behaves (as he must) with pride and action rather than with discretion and *mensura*, is a liability to his people, ultimately has to admit that 'abstract comments on pride in a king are to be found, not in *Beowulf*, but in early medieval works on kingship'[14] – again an appeal outside the text. The rather different argument that the hero–king who is so good in his rôle usurps the capacity for action from his warriors (hence Beowulf's desertion by his retainers), and thus suggests the limits of heroic society, depends on an assumed causal relationship *never made in the poem* between two facts.[15] And so forth.

On the other hand, John D. Niles, by closely examining Wiglaf's speech about the cowardice of the retainers, has recently made anew a case for the poet's approval of the heroic ethos. His conclusion is worth quoting:

> If the society portrayed in *Beowulf* is weak, its weakness can be ascribed to the too-frequent failure of people to live by the ethics that, when put into practice, hold society together. The fatal contradiction developed through the narrative of *Beowulf* is nothing inherent in heroic society, feudal society, capitalist or Marxist society, or any other social system. It is lodged within the recalcitrant breasts of human beings who in times of crisis find themselves unable to live up to the ideals to which their lips give assent. The poem does not criticize the hero for being unlike the Geats. It criticizes all of us for not being more like the hero.[16]

If by this time I seem to suggest that I believe the Christian poet looked with kindly eye on his heroic world and saw its ethical and social values (even if not its religious ones) as consonant and coextensive with his own, that is so. If I also give the impression that I perceive King Beowulf as flawed by pride, avarice or imprudence, that is *not* so. My view is that the poet has presented both the hero and his world with more *humanitas* than *Christianitas*; that to make us feel *lacrimae rerum* in his hero's death, he has humanized the 'marvellous' (or monstrous) Beowulf by making him fallible *in judgement* (his only flaw) and historicized his world so that we, the audience, are better able to

13 See my essay 'The Authenticating Voice in *Beowulf*', *ASE* 5 (1976), 51–62, at 55–7.

14 J. Leyerle, 'Beowulf the Hero and the King', *MÆ* 34 (1965), 89–102, at 98.

15 Berger and Leicester, 'Social Structure', pp. 64–5.

16 Niles, *Beowulf*, p. 247.

empathize with the tragic situation, to suffer with Wiglaf and the Geats, even as we stand in awe of the hero who held to his high fate.[17]

As to the poet's attitude towards the heroic ethos, there can be no doubt that he finds loyalty among kin and retainers highly praiseworthy. Consider, for example, the 'voice's' gnomic wisdom in lines 2600b–1 and 2708b–9a: 'sibb æfre ne mæg / wiht onwendan þam ðe wel þenceð' and 'swylc sceolde secg wesan, / þegn æt ðearfe!'. The heroic ideal of generosity or gift-giving and the value of treasure have, on the other hand, been much disputed. I have had my say elsewhere about the place of gold in the scheme of *Beowulf*: that the poet praises the giving, faults the hoarding.[18] There I observed that 'the contention of critics who would interpret the gold as a temptation to sin and an invitation to spiritual damnation . . . rest[s] . . . on presumed parallels between *Beowulf* and exegetical commentary, based on the assumption of a tacit understanding between poet and audience as to how to listen to or read poetry'[19] – that is, it too is an argument not based on the text. In that essay, however, I conceded that the gnomic passage of lines 2764b–6 was something of a stumbling block for my interpretation:

Sinc eaðe mæg,
gold on grund(e) gumcynnes gehwone
oferhigian, hyde se ðe wylle.

I could only suggest then that they did not have the same explicit Christian pointing of lines 100–2 of *The Seafarer* and, more tentatively, that they could be omitted (as a possible interpolation) without disturbing at all the metrical contour of the lines in which they are embedded. Now I think there is a better idea.

All the other gnomic or semi-gnomic passages in the second part of the poem (nine made by the 'voice' and two by Wiglaf, as I see them)[20] arise from and are 'natural' concomitants of the action that has been or is being described:

17 On Beowulf's 'marvellous' or monstrous nature, see my essay 'A Touch of the Monstrous in the Hero, or Beowulf Re-Marvellized', *ES* 63 (1982), 294–300, and Niles, *Beowulf*, pp. 3–30. Obviously I am disagreeing with Niles, however, when he says (p. 29): 'In the end, the audience . . . cannot really identify itself with Beowulf the man . . . We know too little of his everyday humanity, his normal human feelings and weaknesses, to be able to see him as an extension of ourselves.'

18 S. B. Greenfield, '"Gifstol" and Goldhoard in *Beowulf*', *Old English Studies in Honor of John C. Pope*, ed. Burlin and Irving, pp. 107–17.

19 *Ibid.* p. 115.

20 The nine by the 'voice' are lines 2275b–7, 2291–3a, 2514b, 2590b–1, 2600–1, 2708b–9a, 2858–9, 3062b–5 and 3174b–7; the two by Wiglaf are lines 2890b–1 and 3077–8. Some of these are discussed T. A. Shippey, 'Maxims in Old English Narrative: Literary Art or Traditional Wisdom?', *Oral Tradition, Literary Tradition: a Symposium*, ed. H. Bekker-Nielsen *et al.* (Odense, 1977), pp. 28–46.

they blend that action into universal traditional truth. The usual translation of this passage, with *oferhigian* as 'tempt' or 'overpower' and *hyde* as either 'hide' or 'heed', is quite at odds with the action being described: Wiglaf is viewing the treasure hoard at the command of Beowulf, and is in no way being tempted or overpowered by it, now or later. In line with the other gnomic comments, these words should be universalizing the exposure of the treasure. Peter Clemoes has astutely observed that Anglo-Saxon art, as well as *Beowulf*, 'shows insight into inner forces', and as one example in the poem he cites lines 864b–5:

hleapan leton,
on geflit faran fealwe mearas.

'The men', he comments, 'allowed their steeds to exert their natural tendency, identified as a certain kind of movement (*hleapan*) and as movement in competition (*on geflit faran*).'[21] With these considerations in mind, I think Niles's translation of the gnomic passage quoted above has much to recommend it:

Given the context of the passage, I take *oferhigian* rather in the sense of "outsmart." The treasure is just about to be brought out into the light, despite the efforts of a previous tribe of men to keep it hidden in the earth forever. *Hydan* means "hide," as it should. The lines amount to no more than a brief aside concerning the futility of burying riches: "Treasure, gold in the ground, can easily outsmart anyone, no matter who hides it!" This is essentially the reading of Bosworth and Toller, s.v. "*oferhigian*."[22]

This reading makes the passage consistent in kind and context with other such passages, reveals the inner force of treasure (compare below my comment on *lifað*, of the treasure, in 3167b), and reinforces the anti-hoarding theme of Hrothgar's sermon and of elsewhere in the poem.

That the poet has no quarrel with the heroic ideal of revenge may also be debatable. Yet we know the ideal or practice was not interdicted in Anglo-Saxon Christian England, and was even in some cases encouraged.[23] The *Beowulf* poet clearly approves of God's revenge on Cain's descendants in lines 111–14 and on the giants who 'behaved badly' in lines 1688–93. In human feuds he seems to distinguish between rightful actions and *unrihte* ones. Hygelac's Frisian raid was evidently one of the latter:

syþðan he for wlenco wean ahsode,
fæhðe to Frysum. (1206–7a)

[21] P. Clemoes, 'Action in *Beowulf* and our Perception of it', *Old English Poetry: Essays on Style*, ed. D. G. Calder (Berkeley, Calif., 1979), pp. 147–68, at 155.

[22] Niles, *Beowulf*, p. 299, n. 6.

[23] See D. Whitelock, *The Beginnings of English Society* (Harmondsworth, 1952), pp. 31–3.

But Beowulf's revenge on Onela for the Swedish king's killing of Heardred seems to have the poet's tacit approbation, to judge from the tone of lines 2391–6 (and, additionally, from 2390b, 'þæt wæs god cyning', if that verse refers to Beowulf rather than to Onela). Surely the poet does not fault Beowulf's revenge on Grendel and Grendel's mother; nor does he, I think, fault the hero's revenge on the dragon when he simply states: 'him ðæs guðcyning, / Wedera þioden wræce leornode' (2335b–6).

A further adverse judgement on the poem's heroic world is embodied in the concept of 'social guilt': feuds and violence are inevitable in a society where gifts must be obtained from someone in order to be given to others as rewards. Thus leaders, especially kings, need to perform deeds of derring-do for the acquisition of material treasures, but in so doing they make bad kings, exposing themselves to death and leaving their people leaderless. A subtle argument, drawn (as Shippey observes) 'from comparative considerations of Beowulf, Hrothgar, Hygelac', and encouraged by the 'interlace' structure of the poem. We

> think that the poet is demonstrating the inadequacy of heroic society; that he sees this the more forcibly for being a Christian; and that his rejection of overt finger-pointing first gives [us] the pleasure of ironic perception, and second shows [us] the glittering insidiousness of heroism, the way it perverts even the best of intentions. This whole approach offers evidently attractive baits, propounding an interesting sociological thesis, rejecting the cult of violence, and making it possible to give the poet immense credit for conscious artistry.[24]

But as with the exegetical critics' approach, this view finds no confirmation in the text: it rests on *our* sense of the poet's perspective, on unproven and unprovable ironies that may well be more modern than medieval.

In turning from consideration of the perspective on the heroic ethos in *Beowulf* to the view of the hero himself, we find, I think, equally tenuous rationales for negative *gestalten*. A brief examination of a short passage in what has been called 'the most influential [essay] in expressing the pejorative view of the hero and heroic society'[25] may not be amiss, for the ways of argument therein can tell us something more about the difficulties of evidential practices and about the questionability of adverse judgements of the hero. This analysis will lead into my own (I hope not so tenuous) arguments for a Beowulf who, in the dragon episode, may be fallible in judgement but is otherwise unexceptionable.

Discussing this episode, Leyerle says that Beowulf 'undertakes precipitant

[24] Shippey, *Beowulf*, pp. 37–8.

[25] Short '*Beowulf* and Modern Critical Tradition', p. 10; the essay is Leyerle's (cited above, n. 14).

action . . . the last of the foolhardy deeds attributed to him by Wiglaf'.[26] The passage in question is the following:

hlaford us
þis ellenweorc ana aðohte
to gefremmane, folces hyrde,
forðam he manna mæst mærða gefremede,
dæda dollicra. (2642b–6a)

Why is Beowulf's undertaking called *foolhardy*, we may ask? Why, indeed, is it the *last* of such deeds? There has been no suggestion of a series of foolhardy deeds in the poem. Beowulf's only action that qualifies for this epithet is his swimming match with Breca, which he admits was a foolish, youthful undertaking. Leyerle seems to have seized on the word *dollicra* in the passage he quotes (though he does not say so), since *dollice* in other contexts means something like that. But *dæda dollicra* is in variation with *mærða*, which in turn goes back to *ellenweorc* – and these terms are anything but pejorative. Whatever the normal meaning of *dollice*, it must have a favourable sense in this series; and we can find support for Klaeber's suggested gloss 'audacious, daring' (more consonant with the tenor of Wiglaf's speech) in the term *dolsceaða* (479a) used by Hrothgar when he says of Grendel's reign of terror 'God eaþe mæg / þone dolsceaða dæda getwæfan!' – hardly 'foolhardy-ravager'. The fact that *dol-* and *dæd* are in alliterative coupling in both lines suggests that the force of formulaic composition may be more powerful than 'normal' word-meaning. The pressure of the hermeneutic circle, I suspect, led Leyerle to the use of this rather dubious bit of evidence.[27]

So too in Leyerle's next paragraph:

[Beowulf] disdains the use of an adequate force against the dragon:

Oferhogode ða hringa fengel,
þæt he ðone widflogan weorode gesohte,
sidan herge. (2345–7a)

The verb *oferhogode* echoes Hrothgar's words *oferhygda dæl* (1740) and *oferhyda ne gym* (1760).

In this argument verbal echo from *within* the poem is used to suggest that, indeed, Beowulf is exemplifying precisely that pride and disdain against which

26 Leyerle, 'Beowulf the Hero', p. 95.

27 I would add that I find no evidence at all in Hrothgar's sermon for Leyerle's contention that the king's speech 'is, in part, a caution against *headlong* action' ('Beowulf the Hero', p. 97; my italics). The only possible referent for Leyerle's remark is Heremod's killing of his table companions; but this action is hardly on the same level as fighting a dragon to revenge one's people and gain treasure for them.

Hrothgar had warned the young hero. But if we look at what Hrothgar is actually saying, we find that the *oferhygd* he cautions against, in both lines 1740 and 1760, is connected with greed, with hoarding, with failure of generosity in gift-giving, and *not* with scorning to have help in battle. In fact, the poet goes on to point out, in the first historical digression of the second part of the poem, that Beowulf has plenty of past credentials to support his decision to move against the dragon:

forðon he ær fela
nearo neðende niða gedigde,
hildehlemma . . . (2349b–51a)

This passage, incidentally, would seem to disprove the arguments of the many critics who think that King Beowulf's fifty years of keeping the peace (2732a–6a) means he engaged in *no* human battle clashes.[28]

Lines 1760b–1a might, I suppose, be taken, by changing Klaeber's punctuation, with the verses that follow, 'Nu is þines blæd / ane hwile'; and many critics have also seemed to think that old King Beowulf, like the aged Hrothgar, suffered a decline in his *fortitudo*. But, whereas the Danish king is explicitly characterized in 1886b–7a as one whom old age has deprived of the joys of strength, no such observation is made about Beowulf. We should notice that he still has that *mægen* that overtaxes any sword (2682b–7) – it is surely not a failure in human strength that causes Nægling to break (2680b)! Once again we should recognize that Hrothgar's cautionary comments do not really apply to the Beowulf of the second part of the poem, except for his final generalization about mortality: 'semninga bið, / þæt þec, dryhtguma, deað oferswyðeð' (1767b–7).[29]

Thus far I have tried to indicate that Hrothgar's sermon is no touchstone for a negatively portrayed Beowulf of later days. Let me consider now more briefly the two other 'centers of energy and turbulence' I mentioned earlier.

Beowulf's speech in which he declares he will fight the dragon alone and gain the gold (2518b–37) is the first of these. Since I have considered this previously, I shall only refer the reader to that discussion.[30] The second 'centre' is a combination of Wiglaf's speech in lines 3077–109 with his messenger's preceding harangue in lines 2900–3027. In reviewing this locus,

[28] Cf. lines 2391–6. Note that Beowulf had survived many battle clashes *since* he had cleansed Hrothgar's hall (2351b–4a). This is clearly not a reference to further monster battles. Lines 2391–6 refer specifically to Beowulf's military support of Eadgils against Onela. Niles is the latest to overlook such evidence; see his *Beowulf*, pp. 252 and 304, n. 5, for bibliographic references to others of like mind.

[29] Beowulf's *oferhygd* is often compared to that of Byrhtnoth in *The Battle of Maldon* and that of Roland; but neither of the latter destroys his enemy by his self-sacrifice.

[30] '"Gifstol" and Goldhoard' (cited above, n. 18).

we had best include *all* the speeches, in order, after Beowulf dies and his soul seeks *soðfæstra dom*. When the cowards creep out of the woods and approach Wiglaf, he looks at the *unleofe*, comments that Beowulf threw away the war-gear he had equipped them with, and says further that they shall henceforth forgo

sincþego ond swyrdgifu,
eall eðelwyn eowrum cynne,
. . .
. . . syððan æðelingas
feorran gefricgean fleam eowerne,
domleasan dæd. Deað bið sella . . . (2884–5 and 2888b–90)

Then Wiglaf orders his messenger to announce the sad news to the waiting Geats; in his speech the messenger twice states that a time of war and revenge is inevitable once Franks and Frisians on the one hand and Swedes on the other learn of Beowulf's death. Some lines later, after the poet has told about the curse on the gold, Wiglaf again speaks (3077–109) and this time seems to accuse Beowulf of obstinacy in seeking the dragon, of not listening to all their advice for him to leave the dragon alone. From the inconsistencies in these accounts, a critic can select the evidence for either a positive or a negative view of the hero's actions – and so critics have done. Can *all* the evidence, including the difficult curse on the gold, be accounted for in a unified pattern?

That evidence, it seems to me, leads to an emphasis on fate and the interlacing threads that comprise human and societal doom and *dom*, 'glory': the retainers' cowardice that leads to their lord's death, the fact of their lord's death (one would hardly expect the messenger, who must be one of the cowards, to stress his and his comrades' failure to live up to their oaths of allegiance),[31] a force beyond human comprehension (the curse), and a hero's (proper) refusal to abide by his counsellors' (timid) advice to sidestep the dragon's challenge. Wiglaf sums all this up, it should be noted, not by blaming Beowulf for violating kingly *mensura* but, in a tight stylistic 'envelope' that emphasizes the combination of human will and 'determinism' in Beowulf's fate, he says:

*Heold* on heahgesceap; hord ys gesceawod,
grimme gegangen; wæs þæt gifeðe to swið,
þe þone [þeodcyning] þyder *ontyhte*. (3084–6; my italics)

We may recall young Beowulf's recognition of a similar juxtaposition of human and superhuman in his account of the Breca match, when a sea monster drew him to the depths:

[31] Still, the messenger echoes Wiglaf's comment about no more treasure-giving by indicating that *all* the hard-won treasure will be buried with Beowulf (3010b–17).

hwæþre me gyfeðe wearþ,
þæt ic aglæcan orde geræhte,
hildebille; heaþoræs fornam
mihtig meredeor þurh mine hand. (555b–8)

And the poet's own comment with regard to Beowulf's success in his fight with Grendel's mother:

ond halig God
geweold wigsigor; witig Drihten,
rodera Rædend hit on ryht gesced
yðelice, syþðan he eft astod. (1553b–5)

What the *Beowulf* poet thereby achieves in his poem is a miracle of the highest tragic art, wherein man's fate is balanced between his own human will and the power of forces beyond his control. We do not draw practical moral lessons about human behaviour from *Oedipus* or *King Lear*; nor should we scan *Beowulf* either as a mirror for princes or a reverse mirror-image of unkingly or sinful action.

That the hoard *grimme gegangen* is reburied in the earth,

þær hit nu gen lifað
eldrum swa unnyt, swa hi(t æro)r wæs, (3167b–8)

is something of a small centre of energy and turbulence for interpretation too. The poet does not explicitly say why it is reburied, but the fact that it *will* be given back to earth is first mentioned by the messenger in lines 3010b–17, after he has finished saying that the reasons he has just adduced (old feuds) will lead to resumption of 'sio fæhðo ond se feondscipe', and advised the Geats to hurry to see their dead lord, 'þe us beagas geaf' (3009b). The most likely inferences to be drawn from this juxtaposition are, first, that Beowulf deserves the hoard as a measure of his greatness, and, secondly, that the Geats (by their cowardice and dim prospects for the future) are unworthy of it. I do not recall anyone's having commented on the poet's use of the word *lifað* in 3167b, a strange word applied to gold, and one rendered by most translators, including myself, as 'remains' or the like. Perhaps the verb is being used in ironic contrast to the dead Beowulf and the soon-to-perish Geats? Perhaps the whole clause suggests that gold has a life of its own: it will reveal itself to those who fight for it (see the gnomic passage considered above) or to those who have God's grace (the thief; lines 3054b–7), but it will live, useless to those who have not the fortitude in *mod* and *mægen* to subjugate *its* life to their own will. Whatever the case, one sure effect of the comment is to make Beowulf's dying remark that he is glad to have won the gold for his people (2794–8) seem impercipient indeed; and *this* irony leads me to the final argument of this paper: that whatever negative impulse throbs through the dragon episode results from the humanization of the hero.

The terms of disapprobation which critics have applied to King Beowulf's behaviour in the dragon fight are all judgemental: proud, avaricious, obstinate, imprudent, rash etc. My term 'fallible (in understanding or perception of events)' carries no such connotations. What I am suggesting is that the hero, who by his very nature has something of the monstrous or marvellous in him,[32] is here made more human, so that the audience will react to his death more feelingly. Not a decline in his *fortitudo*, as I have argued above, but in his *sapientia*: not in what he does, but in what he perceives. And with this humanization the Geatish world he now moves in becomes more historicized than the Danish one of his exploits against the Grendel-kin.

My first remarks will be on the historicization. Attempts to link the Cain-descended monsters of the first part of the poem with the dragon, to see the *wyrm* or *draca* as a satanic figure that is somehow the progeny of Cain, or to see the dragon's feud in the perspective of the scriptural 'Great Feud' between God and his enemies, will not bear close scrutiny.[33] For all the beast's pyrotechnics, the dragon's world, if we can call the setting and action in the latter part of the poem by that term, has no suggestions such as 'Godes yrre bær' (711b – of Grendel), or of a wondrous light shining like heaven's candle (1570–2a – after Beowulf defeats Grendel's mother). To say that the poet had 'no need for further scriptural reference after the two kinfolk of Cain have been destroyed'[34] is begging the question, an admission that there is no textual evidence for the position being argued; but when the same critic continues with 'we have had Hrothgar's warning that calamity continues to come unexpected upon mankind: strife is *always* renewed', we can agree with what precedes the colon, but find no evidence that Hrothgar says what follows it (and we note that the following sentence of additional 'evidence' points outside the text to the 'Exeter Book maximist'). When we read further that 'the advent of another adversary of mankind is inevitable', we may note that although Grendel is called *feond mancynnes* and *mancynnes feond* (164a and 1276a) and *Godes andsaca(n)* (786b and 1682b), the dragon has a rather different set of terms for his designation: *eald uhtsceaða* (2271a), *ðeodsceaða* (2278a and 2688a), *guðsceaða* (2318a), *gearo guðfreca* (2414a), *mansceaða* (2514b) and *attorsceaða* (2839a). The dragon wears his adversarial nature with at least an epithetical difference.

32 See above, n. 17.

33 On the former, see, e.g., my review of D. Williams, *Cain and Beowulf: a Study in Secular Allegory* (Toronto, 1982) in *MP* 81 (1983), 191–4. The 'Great Feud' perspective has been advanced by M. Osborn, 'The Great Feud: Scriptural History and Strife in *Beowulf*', *PMLA* 93 (1978), 973–81.

34 Osborn, 'The Great Feud', p. 979.

The human feuds in the latter part of the poem are likewise more down-to-earth, more historical than legendary. I have explored elsewhere the force and place of 'history' in providing an epic sense of destiny in this part of the poem,[35] and shall not repeat myself here. This historical world is appropriate for, and lends credence to, Beowulf's humanity.

Beowulf's fallibility is exhibited most obviously in the discrepancy I have already touched on. That discrepancy cannot simply be an inconsistency of the kind Niles cogently argues for as 'the truncated motif' of the 'barbaric style' in which the poem is composed[36] – and Niles does not suggest it is such. It *must* be meant to indicate that the dying Beowulf no longer has the perspicacity he had when he told Hygelac about Freawaru's proposed marriage to Ingeld: he cannot see that his retainers' cowardice will render the treasure useless to his people. This failure is not surprising, perhaps, in view of the fact that Beowulf has always, by virtue of his marvellous abilities, acted alone. Whether his men draw their swords and hack futilely at a charmed-skin Grendel, or wait helplessly by the mere's edge, or flee precipitously into the woods, Beowulf has never counted on them. Even in human battles he seems to have been 'ana on orde' (2498b). No wonder, then, that he says the battle against the dragon is his responsibility alone, and that he cannot now understand the impact of his followers' treachery upon the Geats' future. There is irony here no doubt, but hardly of a judgemental kind. Rather, by Beowulf's fallible understanding we are made to feel the pathos of his self-sacrifice for a nation that cannot profit thereby.

But Beowulf has also misjudged with respect to the 'measure' of the battle, for the man who is his kinsman and retainer *does* help him defeat the foe 'ofer min gemet', as he says (2879a). The very notion that Beowulf *can* be helped this time further humanizes him. That the dragon is a more 'natural' phenomenon than the Grendel-kin, *un*associated with Cain or the Great Feud, is consonant with Wiglaf's being able to help, and creates an irony in that this time, when his followers *could* have helped the hero, they flee. The dying king misjudges again when he believes that Wiglaf can look after his people's needs: both Wiglaf's and his messenger's speeches point up that miscalculation. He who when young had the wisdom to suggest tactfully that Hrothgar's son Hrethric, if he were a worthy heir apparent, might go abroad while a threat to his succession existed (1836–9), now cannot perceive that no ordinary mortal, even one who has fought beyond his measure, is qualified to keep old enemies at bay in the face of the Geat's manifest weakness. How like in (fallible) judgement to us all the epic hero has become, despite his still imposing stature!

[35] S. B. Greenfield, 'Geatish History: Poetic Art and Epic Quality in *Beowulf*', *Neophilologus* 47 (1963), 211–17.

[36] Niles, *Beowulf*, pp. 167–76.

This falling-off in Beowulf's 'situational' grasp is revealed at the very start of the dragon episode when the hero, seeing his *gifstol* razed, thinks he may have offended God 'ofer ealde riht' (2330a). The audience, however, knows that his perception of the situation is wrong, that the monster has been loosed because of the cup's theft; and of course Beowulf later learns 'hwanan sio fæhð aras' (2403b). Though Beowulf has the wisdom to recognize that he will need an iron shield as protection against the dragon's flames, he seems unaware that the bone of the beast's skull is less vulnerable to penetration than its softer underbelly; whereas, for all his inexperience, Wiglaf has the shrewdness to strike lower down.

I shall mention but one further piece of evidence which suggests that old Beowulf but slenderly knows the score. In accounting for his life, in summing up his record as king, he says, among other things:

Ic on earde bad
mælgesceafta, heold min tela,
ne sohte searoniðas, ne me swor fela
aða on unriht. (2736b–9a)

Three hundred and more lines later, the poet comments that Beowulf, like other mortals, did not know how his death would come about:

þa he biorges weard
sohte searoniðas. (3066b–7a)

The formulaic repetition is startling. Is this just a case of non-significant formularity, or is the poet suggesting a further limit on his hero's percipience? Beowulf is obviously referring to *human* relations in giving his righteous reckoning, but the poet seems to indicate that his seeking out of the dragon was also a *searonið*, and the cause of his *worulde gedal*. I realize that this evidence can be interpreted otherwise to support the arguments of those who would see Beowulf as acting improperly in seeking out the dragon; but it, too, is a centre of energy and turbulence that should not be discounted or overlooked.

The reading I have proposed on the controversy over the hero and his world has tried to encompass the most relevant evidence on both sides, and to avoid the pitfalls of the hermeneutic circle (as much as possible) in argumentation. I am not that sanguine about my success on both scores. But I believe my reading is as plausible as any. One can comprehend a Beowulf whose actions in the latter part of the poem reveal him to be a peerless hero still – and action, as Peter Clemoes has observed, defines the agent in this poem[37] – even as his sapiential vulnerability in his final confrontation demarvellizes (rather than

[37] Clemoes, 'Action in *Beowulf*', esp. pp. 155–60.

indicts) him. The poet has forthrightly placed his hero's soul among those seeking the judgement of the righteous, but has not suggested that the audience judge him self-righteously. Rather, I believe, by revealing a weakness in the aged Beowulf he has somewhat humanized his hero's nature, making him easier of empathetic access to an audience's sensibilities. He helps thus awaken in the reader or listener 'a poignancy, a pathos . . . [which] springs from epic's presentation of man's accomplishments against the background of his mortality, from the implication the hero's fall entails for his people, from a sense of futility in the splendid achievement, a resignation and despair in the face of the limits of life'.[38] The Christian poet, indeed, sees, and aesthetically achieves, a continuity between the *geardagas* of the poem's heroic world and the *windagas* (1062) of his own time.[39] *Life* has its limits, not heroism or the heroic world: this, I think, might have been his answer to Alcuin's abiding question, 'Quid Hinieldus cum Christo?'.[40]

[38] S. B. Greenfield, 'Beowulf and Epic Tragedy', *Studies in Old English Literature in Honor of Arthur G. Brodeur*, ed. Greenfield, p. 104.

[39] Cf. above, n. 13.

[40] I should like to express my appreciation to Daniel G. Calder and Thelma N. Greenfield for their most helpful comments in the shaping of this paper.

# Linguistic evidence as a guide to the authorship of Old English verse: a reappraisal, with special reference to *Beowulf*

JANET BATELY

Over the last fifty years scholars have reached a number of important conclusions about the authorship of certain Old English poems. The unity of the Cynewulf canon has seemingly been confirmed: *Christ* has been divided into three separate poems and *Guthlac* and *Genesis* each into two. *The Wanderer* and *The Seafarer* are now seen to be single poetic entities, by poets with similar subject-matter but very different techniques.[1] Only in the case of *Beowulf* does there appear to be room still for controversy and uncertainty. The unity, and indeed the manner of transmission, of *Beowulf* as we have it have long been matters of interest to modern scholars. The integrity of the poem has been questioned in a number of ways, with some critics seeking to identify 'interpolations' (usually passages with a Christian reference) and others attempting major surgery. Thus, for instance, Ettmüller marked off in his translation a large number of lines added by what he termed 'clerical editors';[2] Müllenhoff explained the form and length of the poem by dividing it up into a core of four short lays and postulating contributions by at least six authors and interpolators;[3] Schücking presented a reasoned case for separate authorship of the third of these sections, which he called 'Beowulf's Homecoming', as a piece specially composed by a poet–editor to join two originally separate poems, *Beowulf* as we have it being a work of composite authorship.[4] Magoun, on the other hand, took the poem to be made up of three distinct folk-poems,

1 See J. Roberts, 'The Exeter Book: *Swa is lar 7 ar to spowendre spræce gelæded*', *Dutch Quarterly Rev. of Anglo-Amer. Letters* 11 (1981–4), 302–19, and *The Guthlac Poems of the Exeter Book* (Oxford, 1979); *The Wanderer*, ed. T. P. Dunning and A. J. Bliss (London, 1969); *Genesis A*, ed. A. N. Doane (Madison, Wisc., 1978); also S. Butler, 'The Cynewulf Question Revived', *NM* 83 (1982), 15–23. Quotations are from ASPR and from *Beowulf and the Fight at Finnsburg*, ed. F. Klaeber, 3rd ed. (Boston, Mass., 1950). For full details of occurrences, see *A Concordance to the Anglo-Saxon Poetic Records*, ed. J. B. Bessinger (Ithaca, NY, 1978).

2 L. Etmüller, *Beowulf* (Zürich, 1840).

3 K. Müllenhoff, *Beowulf* (Berlin, 1889).

4 L. Schücking, *Beowulfs Rückkehr* (Halle, 1905).

brought together through the industry of an anthologizing scribe,[5] while Sisam described the poem as we have it as a serial in three instalments which 'seems to have been built up to meet the demand for another story about the hero who destroyed Grendel', with the 'Return' appearing to be 'an extension of the two older stories of Grendel and Grendel's Mother made by the poet who gave *Beowulf* substantially the form in which it has survived'.[6]

Most recently the theory of a composite poem has been revived by Kevin Kiernan, who not only wishes to put the composition of *Beowulf* in the reign of Cnut, but sees the stories of the fights against Grendel and his mother on the one hand and against the dragon on the other as originally constituting two separate works, with a transition (Beowulf's Homecoming) composed specially to link them at a time when the Beowulf manuscript was being copied: 'Beowulf is a late fusion of two originally separate poems first accomplished, and therefore preserved, in the extant MS.' What we have in the Nowell Codex is 'an unfinished draft of a late collaboration', the stories of the fights in Denmark and the land of the Geats being by different but contemporary poets. And in Kiernan's view the second poet is apparently the second scribe of the manuscript, who 'increased, and continued to polish, an Anglo-Saxon treasure during the reign of a Danish Scylding lord'.[7] Kiernan divides the poem into three parts: lines 1–1887, 1888–2199 and 2200–3182.[8]

I do not wish to involve myself here in the controversy provoked either by Kiernan's palaeographical arguments,[9] or by his suggestion that the subject-

[5] F. P. Magoun, 'Beowulf B: a Folk-Poem on Beowulf's Death', *Early English and Norse Studies*, ed. A. Brown and P. Foote (London, 1963), pp. 127–40.

[6] K. Sisam, *The Structure of Beowulf* (Oxford, 1965), pp. 4, 5 and 50. Sisam (p. 5) sees the Grendel's mother sequal as older than the dragon fight.

[7] K. S. Kiernan, *Beowulf and the Beowulf Manuscript* (New Brunswick, NJ, 1981), pp. 272 and 278. Kiernan (p. 50) claims that 'a literate, 11th century Mercian poet' alone could have brought about the particular mixture of forms in *Beowulf*.

[8] I refer to these sections as parts 1, 2 and 3. Kiernan sees fol. 179 as a palimpsest, and the text from lines 2207 to 2231 as the result of redrafting by the second scribe some years after the rest of the poem was copied. The numerous corrections he assumes (p. 10) to be on the authority of the exemplar and therefore necessarily right. However, for similar care by a scribe who was not also the author, see *Genesis A*, ed. Doane, p. 14.

[9] I would, however, make one observation. Even if fol. 179 is a palimpsest with a new text inserted (and I am not convinced by Kiernan's arguments), this does not necessarily mean that 'there is no credible reason for the palimpsest other than revision' (p. 11) and that the extant text must be substantially different from the hypothetical erased one. Erasure and new entry are not unique to *Beowulf*. They are found, for instance, in the Anglo-Saxon Chronicle MS A, 13v (s.a. 860), with 'new' material in a different hand but belonging to the original text, and again on 6v of the same manuscript, where the version entered by the scribe has been erased and replaced by a slightly different version from another manuscript tradition; while David Dumville suggests that in order to make a satisfactory join between his own work and that of scribe 1, scribe 2 recopied 16v–17v after he had written fols. 18–25v, throwing away

matter precludes composition before the time of Cnut[10] – though on linguistic grounds I would argue that in the light of our present knowledge a date after AD 1000 seems improbable.[11] For example, both scribes occasionally use spellings that are not only typically early West Saxon (being normally absent from texts known to have been composed after *c.* 960) but are regularly removed from copies of ninth-century works made in the latter part of the Anglo-Saxon period.[12] Thus, *ie*-spellings corresponding to early West Saxon *ī̆e* are found 1 × in hand 1 and 2 × in hand 2 in *hiera, niehst-*, and *-giest-*.[13] To these must be added *ie* for West Saxon *ea* in *siexbennum* and *ie* for West Saxon *ēo* in *sie*, both in hand 2.[14] *ie* for *i* + *e* appears 59 × in *hie* (48 × in hand 1, 11 × in hand 2), beside the late West Saxon spellings *hy* 10 × (4 + 6), *hi* 9 × (3 + 6) and *hig* 3 × (3 + 0). *Beowulf* also has the verb form *sie* 3 × (2 + 1), beside the late West Saxon spellings *sy* 3 × (1 + 2) and *sig* 1 × (1 + 0).[15]

*Ie* as a graph representing the diphthong *ī̆e* seems to have had a relatively short existence in Old English, being limited in both space and time. Thus, not only is the diphthong confined to West Saxon dialects, it has already been monophthongized and replaced by *i-* or *y*-spellings, becoming used interchangeably with them, in late-ninth- and early-tenth-century manuscript copies.[16] I have not yet found it in any prose text known to have been

the first two folios of his own original stint. For partly erased substandard script with non-standard spelling, see the Anglo-Saxon Chronicle, MS A, 23v, lines 12–15. See, further, J. Bately, *The Anglo-Saxon Chronicle, MS A*, The Anglo-Saxon Chronicle: a Collaborative Edition [general editors D. Dumville and S. Keynes] 3 (Cambridge, 1985), Introduction.

10 In the light of our present knowledge even the late ninth century cannot be ruled out.

11 I agree with Kiernan, *Beowulf and the Beowulf Manuscript*, pp. 28–9, that the mixture of spellings does not necessarily mean a long history of textual transmission. See also A. Cameron, A. C. Amos, G. Waite *et al.*, 'A Reconsideration of the Language of Beowulf', *The Dating of Beowulf*, ed. C. Chase (Toronto, 1981), p. 37.

12 Scribe 1 is responsible for lines 1–1939, scribe 2 for lines 1949–end. I am again unconvinced by Kiernan's arguments (p. 243) for the spelling of 179r as indicating that this passage was written later than the rest of the poem.

13 *hiera* line 1164, Mercian *heara*, *hira*, *heora*, late West Saxon *hira*, *hyra*, *heora*; *niehst-* line 2511, Mercial *ne(h)st*, *next*, late West Saxon *nehst*, *nyhst*; and *-giest-* line 2560, poetic *gæst*, Mercian *gest*, late West Saxon *gyst*. See A. Campbell, *Old English Grammar* (Oxford, 1959), §§154.4, 188, 193(c), 200.4, 300–1, 674 n. 4, and 703. *Hyra* is found 8 ×, *heora* 4 ×, *hiora* and *hira* each 3 ×, *nystan* 1 ×.

14 *Siex-* for West Saxon *seax* is probably the result of confusion of it in its Anglian or late West Saxon form *sex* with the numeral 'six'; see Campbell, *Old English Grammar*, §§223 and 312. However, a possible very late (Kentish?) spelling *ie* for *æ*, as in texts such as the Canterbury Psalter and the *Visio Pauli* cannot be ruled out; see K. Sisam, *Studies in the History of Old English Literature* (Oxford, 1953), p. 43, n. 1, and *The Old English Vision of St Paul*, ed. A. diPaolo Healey (Cambridge, Mass., 1978), pp. 31–2. *Sie* for *sio* is found also in the Cotton Otho B. ii text of the Pastoral Care; see *The Pastoral Care, edited from British Museum MS Cotton Otho B. ii*, by I. Carlson, 2 vols. (Stockholm, 1975–8) I, 58–9.

15 See Campbell, *Old English Grammar*, §§703, 768 and 237(3). See also the spelling *hie* for expected *hio* in line 2019.

16 See Campbell, *Old English Grammar*, §300.

composed after 950.[17] Thus, in MS A of the Anglo-Saxon Chronicle, hands 1 and 2 used *ie* more frequently than *i* or *y*. Hand 2's last entry (made, probably, *c.* 930), is dated 920. However, in subsequent parts of the manuscript, written by later hands, the graph occurs only 1 ×, with *gieta* in hand 3 (*s.a.* 937, copied *c.* 950). In other copies of the Chronicle *y*- and *i*-spellings are the norm, even in the annals before 937.[18] A similar situation obtains in the Old English Orosius, where the early-tenth-century Lauderdale manuscript (BL, Add. 47967) frequently uses the graph *ie*, but the early-eleventh-century Cotton manuscript (BL, Cotton Tiberius B. i) has it only occasionally.[19] In the Boethius, *ie*-spellings are found with some frequency in both the mid-tenth-century MS B and the early-twelfth-century MS C; however, in the Soliloquies, which have survived only in a copy from the second quarter of the twelfth century, *ie*-spellings are only occasionally found, *y* being the preferred spelling.[20] We may compare the Otho manuscript (BL, Cotton Otho B. ii) of the Pastoral Care, where early West Saxon *ie* is normally replaced by *i*, though traces of the interchange of *ie* and *i* for original *i* found in the older manuscripts still survive.[21] Ælfric and Wulfstan, by contrast, appear only to have used *i*- and *y*-spellings. In verse *ie*-spellings are rare, though the graph *gie* occurs in some numbers in the Exeter Book and *Genesis A* and *B*; otherwise *ie* is mainly confined to *Genesis A* and *B* and *Solomon and Saturn*, with only occasional instances elsewhere.[22]

Less conclusive are *ie*-spellings corresponding to OE *i* + *e*, which contracted to diphthong *īe* in early West Saxon and subsequently shared its history, but apparently remained dissyllabic in non-West Saxon, being represented by *ie* in both Northumbrian and Mercian texts of the tenth century. At least two of the instances of the subjunctive singular *sie*, *sig*, *sy* in *Beowulf* are in positions in the line which indicate contraction typical of West Saxon, three are dissyllabic and

17 *ie* is found occasionally elsewhere in the *Beowulf* manuscript: in the Letter of Alexander (17 ×) and in the Wonders of the East (*hiera*, 1 ×), both copied by *Beowulf* scribe 1. It never occurs in *Judith*, the work of scribe 2. There are no instances of *ie* reported in P. Gradon, 'Studies in Late West-Saxon Labialization and Delabialization', *English and Medieval Studies presented to J. R. R. Tolkien*, ed. N. Davis and C. L. Wrenn (London, 1962), pp. 63–76.

18 for *ie*-, *y*- and *i*-spellings in the Anglo-Saxon Chronicle, MS A, see *The Anglo-Saxon Chronicle, MS A*, ed. Bately, Introduction. For MS B, see *The Anglo-Saxon Chronicle, MS B*, ed. S. Taylor, The Anglo-Saxon Chronicle: a Collaborative Edition 4 (Cambridge, 1983), lxxxv. MS C has *hiera s.a.* 755, *cierdon s.a.* 823 and *Frieðestan s.a.* 910; D has *Iercingafeld*- 2 × *s.a.* 915.

19 See *The Old English Orosius*, ed. J. Bately, EETS s.s. 6 (Oxford, 1980), xlii, li, liii, liv and lv.

20 See *King Alfred's version of St Augustine's Soliloquies* ed. T. A. Carnicelli (Cambridge, Mass., 1969), pp. 4–6.

21 See *The Pastoral Care*, ed. Carlson, pp. 45 and 47. The first scribe often has *i* corrected into an *ie*, which Carlson sees as most likely the spelling of the prototype.

22 For Wulfstan's usage, see *The Homilies of Wulfstan*, ed. D. Bethurum (Oxford, 1957). In the Junius manuscript, *Genesis*, *Exodus* and *Daniel* are written in a single hand, yet *ie*-spellings are frequent in *Genesis A* and *B*, while *Exodus* and *Daniel* each have one only.

two ambiguous metrically.[23] Both *hie*- and *sie*-spellings are normal in early West Saxon manuscripts. They are relatively infrequent in late copies of Alfredian texts and are seemingly absent from at least the best manuscripts of Ælfric and Wulfstan. In the prose texts of the *Beowulf* manuscript, copied by the first scribe of *Beowulf*, the distribution of forms varies from text to text, apparently reflecting the usage of the exemplars.[24] However, although in the Chronicle MS A the spelling *hie* occurs only sporadically except in hands 1 and 2, both of which prefer it to *hi*, it is found 2 × in hand 3 and 1 × in hand 5 in the entry for 1001, beside *hi* 3 ×, *hy* 11 × in this section. MS B has a preponderance of *hie*-spellings (199 × beside *hi* 7 ×), last using the form *s.a.* 974; MS C by contrast uses *hie* only 40 × up to annal 894, with *hi* as its norm.[25] In the verse too *hi*-spellings greatly outnumber *hie* and *hy*, but this is due to the very high numbers of examples in the Paris Psalter (349 ×) and the *Metres of Boethius* (114 ×, *hie* 1 ×). The scribes of the Vercelli Book and Junius manuscript use almost exclusively *hie* (121 × and 206 × respectively, beside *hi* 1 × and 6 ×, *hig* 0 and 1 ×) *Hy* is mainly confined to the Exeter Book (144 ×, beside *hi* 96 ×, *hie* only 4 ×). *Judith*, copied by scribe 2 of *Beowulf*, normally has *hie* (19 ×, *hi* 9 ×). The distribution of *sie*, *si*, *sy* and *sig* again varies according to the manuscript, with *sie* preferred in Vercelli (15: *si* 1 ×) and *sy* in the Exeter Book (38: *sie* 7 ×).[26] It is thus the proportions of *hie*- and *sie*-spellings in *Beowulf* to *hi*, *hy*, *sy*, and *sig* that must be taken into consideration in any argument about dating, not their appearance alone.

Also to be reckoned with in any discussion of the date of composition of *Beowulf* are the spellings *ryht* and *meaht*-. *Ryht* (line 1555) is a typical early West Saxon spelling. It is found 7 × in MS A of the Anglo-Saxon Chronicle, hand 1, beside *riht*, 2 × in hand 5 and 4 × in post-Conquest hands.[27] In the Lauderdale

[23] See Cameron and Amos, 'A Reconsideration', p. 45.

[24] The Wonders of the East have *hi*, *hy* some 60 ×, never *hie*, the Letter of Alexander *hie* 137 ×, beside *hi* 3 ×, while in the Life of St Christopher *hie* accounts for some half of the occurrences. *Sie* is found in the Letter of Alexander 1 ×, and in the Benedictine Rule 9 ×.

[25] Taylor (*The Anglo-Saxon Chronicle, MS B*, ed. Taylor, p. lxxxv) gives the figures for MS B as *hie* 199 ×, *hi* 7 × (between annals 878 and 905); C has *hi* 155 ×, but not before annal 652, beside *hie* 40 × and *hy* 4 ×. What pronunciation was current in the Mercian and Northumbrian dialects of very late Old English is not certain. The Mercian Rushworth 1 has mainly *hiæ* (92 ×), but also *hie* 64 ×, *hi* 3 × and *hy* 1 ×. *Sie* is common in Rushworth 1, as in the other Anglian glosses of the period.

[26] *Hi* occurs 641 ×, *hie* 444 ×, and *hy* 177 ×. Of the 177 instances of *hy*, 144 are in the Exeter Book, none in the Junius or Vercelli manuscripts. Only one of the six examples of *hi* in Junius is in the hand of the main scribe, the rest occurring in other hands, in *Christ and Satan*. The *Metres of Boethius* have *hy* 5 ×, the Paris Psalter 4 ×, and *Beowulf* itself 10 ×. In the Exeter Book the largest number of occurrences are in *Christ III* (26 ×) and *Guthlac A* (42 ×). *Elene* and *The Fates of the Apostles* have *hie* only, *Juliana* and *Christ II* both *hi* and *hy*.

[27] See Campbell, *Old English Grammar*, §§305 and 308. The last instance in hand 1 occurs *s.a.* 824. The word does not occur at all in the sections written by scribes 2, 3 and 4. Other manuscripts of the Anglo-Saxon Chronicle have only *riht*.

manuscript of the Orosius the spelling *ryht* is the norm, and *y*-spellings still persist alongside usual late West Saxon *i* in Cotton.[28] The Pastoral Care manuscript Cotton Otho B. ii still has *ryht* alongside *riht*. However, although the majority of instances of *ryht* recorded in the Toronto concordance are from Alfredian and poetic texts,[29] there are a few examples in tenth-century prose texts, notably charters (the latest of which is dated 931 × 939), the Laws of Athelstan (924–39) and the Benedictine Rule (*c.* 970), while I have found single instances in the printed texts of the Treaty of Edward and Guthrum and the Institutes of Polity, both attributed to Archbishop Wulfstan, and two in Ælfric, Catholic Homilies I.[30]

Similarly of significance, but to be interpreted with care, is the evidence provided by the distribution of the verb-forms *meaht-*, *meht-*. In *Beowulf* the verbal stem *meaht-* occurs 34 × (19 × in hand 1, 15 × in hand 2), beside *miht-* 20 × (14:6), and *meht-* 4 × (4:0).[31] We may compare the Lauderdale Orosius with *mehte* 164 ×, beside *meahte* 2 × (in the account of Ohthere's voyages) and *mæht-* 4 ×. The Cotton manuscript by contrast has *meaht-* 5 × in hand 1, 3 × in hand 3, beside normal *miht-*, *myht-* and occasional *meht-*.[32] *Meaht-* is the normal spelling in the earliest manuscripts of the Pastoral Care, but is never found in Cotton Otho B ii.[33] In MS A of the Anglo-Saxon Chronicle, hand 2 has *meht-* 17 ×, *meaht-* 1 ×,[34] and *meaht-* spellings also occur sporadically in MSS C and D. A few of these instances of *meaht-* are in the annals for the 890s and early 900s and correspond to forms with *mehte* in MS A; however, others are in the section 992–1011 and provide the only evidence in printed texts for the survival of this form in late Old English. *Mehte* is very rarely found in prose texts other than those of the Alfredian period. Indeed apart from a few instances in undated texts, notably the Blickling Homilies (2 ×), the Wonders of the East (1 ×), the Letter of Alexander (3 ×), and certain psalter glosses,[35] the only occurrences in works later than the Alfredian period are single instances in a charter dated 899 × 924, in Wulfstan's Homilies and the *Gerefa* (each 1 ×), and in the Laws of Edward and Æthelred II. In verse the form *mehte*

[28] See *The Old English Orosius*, ed. Bately, p. xlii.

[29] For details of occurrences I am greatly indebted to A. diPaolo Healey and R. L. Venezky, *A Microfiche Concordance to Old English* (Toronto, 1980) In verse the spelling *ryht* is found only 68 ×, mostly in the Exeter Book (and there mainly in *Christ I*, *II* and *III* and *Guthlac A* and *B*. It never occurs in the Junius manuscript. However, it is also found in *Elene* 2 ×, *Juliana* 3 × and *Andreas* 2 ×. In prose it is found in a number of charters, but none dated after 902.

[30] In CH I, 26/8 and 254/22, from the forthcoming edition by Clemoes.

[31] Between lines 1082 and 1877.

[32] See *The Old English Orosius*, ed. Bately, pp. xli, li, liii and liv.

[33] See *The Pastoral Care*, ed. Carlson, pp. 43 and 63.

[34] See *The Anglo-Saxon Chronicle, MS A*, ed. Bately, Introduction.

[35] The Wonders of the East has *mehte* 1 ×, the Letter of Alexander 3 ×, beside normal *meaht-*.

is confined to the four instances in *Beowulf* and to two others in *Andreas*; *meahte-* spellings are found more widely, though never in proportions comparable with those of *Beowulf*. Indeed only in the Exeter Book, in the Cynewulf canon and in *Genesis A* and *B* are they the norm, elsewhere *miht-* being the preferred spelling.[36] It may be significant that the exceptional late occurrences of *ryht* and the exceptional late occurrences of *meaht-* and *meht-* are never found together in one and the same demonstrably late text.

Any date of composition for *Beowulf* in or after the late tenth century can surely only be acceptable if some evidence is produced that typically 'early' spellings such as these[37] were current in scriptoria of the period, not merely taken over from older exemplars, and that a scribe of that period giving 'standard' spellings to non-West Saxon forms would have reason to consider *ie* as falling into that category. And this will necessitate an exhaustive study of all surviving manuscripts of the time. Such a study is not possible within the scope of this present essay, nor is the detailed survey of linguistic evidence necessary to evaluate the various theories of multiple authorship put forward for the poem. However, I should like here to combine some general comments on the special problems involved in an investigation of multiple authorship in the context of Old English verse, with a detailed exploration of one small area of linguistic usage, not only setting the three major sections of *Beowulf* one against the other but comparing distribution patterns in these sections and in the poem as a whole with those of the Cynewulf canon and with the other works whose unity has been challenged, that is, *Christ I*, *II* and *III*, *Guthlac A* and *B*, and *Genesis A* and *B*, with reference where appropriate to usage in the rest of the corpus.

The determination of authorship of an Old English work is not a simple matter, whatever the nature of the work involved, and the question of multiple authorship is the most difficult of all to resolve.[38] However, the different kinds pose different problems, calling for different solutions. Thus, a prose writer starts with his own spoken language as his primary linguistic base. A poet, by contrast, begins with an established corpus of words and collocations deemed by tradition as appropriate for verse, a very high proportion of which are

36 *Genesis A* and *B* have *meaht-* 53 ×, *miht-* 6 ×, the Cynewulf canon *meaht-* 23 ×, *miht-* 1 ×.

37 Other features of interest are the spellings *a* + *l* + consonant, *o* + nasal (typical of early West Saxon as well as of Mercian) and *cyning*, never *cyng* (*cing*), a form found rarely in Alfredian texts, though frequently in all parts of the Chronicle MS A and in later prose works.

38 See, e.g., the suggestion that the Benedictine Office was adapted by Wulfstan from a lost Old English text by Ælfric (*The Benedictine Office*, ed. J. Ure (Edinburgh, 1957)), refuted by P. Clemoes, *Anglia* 78 (1960), 265–83. See also *The Old English Orosius*, ed. Bately, pp. lxxv–lxxxi; J. Bately, 'King Alfred and the OE Translation of Orosius', *Anglia* 88 (1970), 433–60, and 'The Compilation of the Anglo-Saxon Chronicle, 60 B.C. to A.D. 890: Vocabulary as Evidence', *PBA* 64 (1978) (also issued separately), esp. 95–6.

absent from the author's spoken language, some possibly being typical of another dialect area.[39] A prose writer may, like a speaker, have his own personal preferences where choice of lexis is involved.[40] A poet is moved in his choice by wider considerations of metre and alliteration and by the need to set up 'an expectation of the congruous and complementary, expressed through recurrent collocations' which is built into the poetic system of Old English.[41] And in this context it should be noted that any minor variation used by a poet would be liable to removal in the course of transmission by reciter or scribe.[42] As for major variations from the poetic norm, given the smallness of the poetic corpus that has come down to us, it is often difficult to distinguish between a rare 'set pattern', coincidental duplication and a personal mannerism.[43] Since the use of alliteration is fundamental to the verse form, so choice of a stress-bearing lexical item (that is, generally speaking, a noun or adjective, less frequently other parts of speech) is determined to a very great degree by considerations of sound. Moreover, word order may also be adapted to suit special requirements. Subject-matter may likewise play a major rôle in determining which particular word or phrase is selected, or where an apparently distinctive form is employed. Thus, for instance, the dialect word *rec* is found only in part 3, but only there does the poet refer to the concept 'smoke'. The dialect word *scua* on the other hand is confined to part 1, but the West Saxon alternative, *sc(e)adu*, is also only found in this part of the poem.[44]

Where there is a wide range of words available to the poet the different sections of *Beowulf* sometimes not only have different preferences but make different choices – as in the case, for instance, of 'lord', 'ruler'. Thus, although *cyning* with its compounds *guþcyning* and *þeodcyning*, is found in all three parts, as

39 See, e.g., Sisam's comments on the *Metres of Beothius*, *Studies*, p. 297.

40 See, e.g., *Homilies of Ælfric, a Supplementary Collection*, ed. J. C. Pope, 2 vols., EETS o.s. 259–60 (London, 1967–8), 99–103; H. Gneuss, 'The Origin of Standard Old English and Æthelwold's School at Winchester', *ASE* 1 (1972), 63–83, at 76–8; and Bately, 'Lexical Evidence for the Authorship of the Prose Psalms in the Paris Psalter', *ASE* 10 (1982), 69–95.

41 R. Quirk, 'Poetic Language and Old English Metre', *Early English and Norse Studies*, ed. Brown and Foote, p. 153.

42 See, e.g., *The Battle of Brunanburh*, with variants such as *gefylled* and *afylled*, *ageted* and *forgrunden* and *oð* and *þæt*.

43 For instance, Magoun ('*Beowulf B*', pp. 134ff.) has drawn attention to the fact that half-lines of the type *uhthlemm þone*, found 6 × in *Beowulf*, are restricted to lines 2007, 2334, 2588, 2959, 2969 and 3081 of the final story (Kiernan's parts 2 and 3). However, they are also unique to that poem, and therefore can have a number of explanations, including that put forward by Campbell, that they might well derive from an older lay which became known to the poet as he was writing; see A. Campbell, 'The Use in "Beowulf" of Earlier Heroic Verse', *England before the Conquest*, ed. P. Clemoes and K. Hughes (Cambridge, 1971), p. 286.

44 For so-called dialect words in *Beowulf*, see, e.g., Cameron and Amos, 'A Reconsideration', pp. 73–5. In other poems *scua* and *sc(e)adu* similarly occur side by side; see e.g., *Exodus* and *Andreas*. *Wisdom* and *snyttru* are found in *Andreas* and *Elene* as well as in *Beowulf*.

are *dryhten*, *fengel*, *mondryhten*, *þeoden* and *wigendra hleo*, the forms *ealdor*, *eþelweard*, *Frea*, *freodryhten*, *-gifa*, *goldwine*, *hlaford* and *winedryhten* occur in parts 1 and 3 only, *brego*, *brytta*, *eorla hleo* and *wine* in parts 1 and 2. Unique to part 1 is *þengel* and to part 3 *b(e)aldor*.[45] In certain cases it is possible to demonstrate the appropriateness to context of the poet's selection, but modern ignorance as to the precise force of individual terms makes it difficult to react other than personally and subjectively to the choice in the majority of contexts. However, reference to other poetical works whose unity is not questioned shows that different distribution patterns do not necessarily mean different authorship. Thus, for instance, *Judith*, like *Beowulf*, employs a range of words to describe a king. Before his decapitation, Holofernes is described by ten different expressions denoting his position of authority, with *baldor*, *brego*, *dryhten*, *ealdor*, *ræswa*, *folctoga*, *goldwine*, *hearra*, *sinces brytta*[46] and *þeoden*. He is also described simply as *se rica*. In the section dealing with his decapitation Holofernes's rank is never referred to : he is described merely, but significantly, as a man. In the final section, by contrast, eight words denoting Holofernes's position are used, but only four of these – *baldor*, *brego*, *ræswa* and *þeoden* – are found also in the first section. The poet's change of usage is determined partly by shifts in his attitude to Holofernes, partly by demands of metre and alliteration, partly perhaps by whim. Similarly, *Elene* and *Juliana* both use *b(e)aldor*, *cyning*, *dryhten*, *frea*, *hlaford* and *þeoden*, but confined to *Elene* are *beaggifa*, *brytta*, *burgagend*, *goldwine* and *latteow*.

Even where differences in subject-matter or emphasis are not obviously involved, absence from one section of words used in another is not of itself necessarily significant. Thus, *nænig* is confined to parts 1 and 2 of *Beowulf*, where it occurs 7 × and 1 × respectively and *nan* is found only in part 1, where it occurs 2 ×. Neither is found in part 3. However, a similar restricted distribution pattern may be cited from *Judith*, where *nænig* is found 1 × in the first section and *nan* 3 × in the first and third sections only. *Christ I* has *nænig* 2 × and *nan* 2 ×. We may compare *Andreas*, *Guthlac B* and *Elene*, which have *nænig* only (4 ×, 4 × and 1 × respectively), and *Genesis A* and *Juliana* each with a single instance of *nan*.

If we turn from nouns, pronouns and adjectives to verbs and adverbs, we find that these less frequently contribute to alliterative patterns and are less frequently distinctively poetic. They should thus, in theory, allow more freedom for individual choice and so be more likely to reflect a writer's personal style. However, here too there are special considerations, notably those of metre. Thus, in the prose corpus, choice between *faran*, *feran* and the

45 *Þengel* is otherwise found only in *Exodus* (1 ×); *fengel* is unique to *Beowulf*.
46 Beside *morðres brytta* in the middle section.

'mixed' verb *faran*, *ferde*, on the one hand, and these forms and other variants such as *leoran*, *gangan* and *gan* on the other, can be a pointer to date, dialect and authorship.[47] However, this is not true of the verse, where, for instance, choice between *faran* and *feran* and *for* and *ferde* is often determined by the need for a long as opposed to a short syllable or one syllable rather than two. Thus, in *Beowulf* the verb *faran* is found 11 × (4:2:5), *feran* 8 × (7:0:1), with the difference in frequency resulting from a preference for past tense. *for(on)* (5 ×) over *ferdon* (2 ×). Most of the instances of *feran*, *ferdon* are in part 1, with one in part 3 and none in part 2.[48]

However, not only are these figures statistically non-significant, but similar fluctuations of usage can be cited from texts whose unity or common authorship is unquestioned. Thus, *Elene* has both *faran* and *feran* with a preference for *faran* (5:1), *Christ II* has *feran* only (2 ×), while *Juliana* has equal numbers of *faran* and *feran* (1:1). *Genesis A* on the other hand prefers *feran* (10:7), in this contrasting with *Genesis B*, which has only *faran*.[49] Similarly, just as *Beowulf* uses both *gan*, *eode* and *gangan*, *gang*, with a preference for the former, *Genesis A* has *gan*: *eode* more frequently than *gangan*. As for the non-West Saxon form *leoran*, this is never found in *Beowulf*, and occurs only 3 × elsewhere in the poetic corpus.

Similarly inconclusive are the distribution patterns of *gen* and *gena*. The former is recorded 45 × in verse, the latter 13 ×. In *Beowulf*, *gena* is confined to part 3 where it occurs 2 ×; *gen* is found 11 × with two instances in part 1, three in part 2 and six in part 3. We may compare *Genesis A*, *Guthlac A* and *Andreas* with both *g(i)en* and *g(i)ena*, *Elene*, *Juliana* and *Genesis B* with *g(i)en* only and *Guthlac B* with a single instance of *gena*.[50]

More likely to be productive is an examination of sentence words, which, not taking the stress, do not need to conform to alliterative patterns. Such an examination was undertaken by Schücking in his *Beowulfs Rückkehr*, one of his findings being that in Beowulf's Homecoming there are several syntactical usages that are unique in the poem: notably the conjunction *þy læs* (line 1981, elsewhere *þæt ne*), *ac* used as an interrogative particle (line 1990, normally 'but' in all parts) and the only certain case of *forþam*, rather than *forþan* or *forþon* as the conjunction 'because, since' (line 1957). However, not only is *þy læs* comparatively rare as a conjunction in Old English poetry, but it is frequently

47 See *The Homilies of Ælfric*, ed. Pope, p. 101; and Bately, 'Compilation', pp. 110, 111 and 127, and 'Prose Psalms', p. 88. A quick survey of 'key' words in prose shows the prose test to be non-applicable to at least the major verse texts.

48 Also *gefaran* 1 ×, *geferan* 2 ×.

49 Cf. *gefaran* (*Genesis A* 2 ×, *Genesis B* 1 ×); *geferan* (*Juliana* 2 ×, *Genesis A* and *B* each 1 ×).

50 Cf. *worn fela* (lines 530 and 1783), beside *worna fela*, lines 2003 and 2542, neither collocation found elsewhere in the poetic corpus.

found only once each in long poems other than *Beowulf*, and occurs only 6 × in the Cynewulf canon.[51] *Ac* used as an interrogative particle has an even more limited distribution in verse,[52] while the spellings *forþam*, *forþan* and *forþon* not infrequently interchange in copies of prose texts.[53]

Significantly, the evidence which Schücking produces for separate authorship is taken by Chambers to be inconclusive: 'To me, the fact that so careful and elaborate a study of the story of Beowulf's Return fails to betray any satisfactory evidence of separate authorship, is a confirmation of the verdict of "not proven" against the "dividers".' However, Chambers sees Schücking's approach as 'the right one'.[54] As my own contribution to the ongoing discussion I would submit a study of a slightly different kind, and investigate the handling in the different parts of the poem of clauses introduced by the conjunction 'after'.

*Beowulf* uses seven conjunction of time, *þa*, *þenden*, *þonne*, *ær*, *ærþon*, *oþþæt (oþþe)* and *siþþan*, all but one of which also function as adverbs, one – *ær* – as a preposition in a series which includes *oþ* and *æfter*. *Þa* is the most frequent, followed by *siþþan* 56 ×, *oþþæt* 34 × (including *oþþe* 1 ×), *þonne* 33 ×, *þenden* 12 × and *ær* 9 ×.[55] The same range is found in the rest of the poetic corpus,[56] with the addition of *oþ* as a conjunction and of *þa hwile (þe)*, which is found 9 × altogether in *The Battle of Maldon* and a handful of minor poems. However, the use of these forms varies from text to text and author to author, partly in response to differing attitudes to time, partly because of different narrative methods. Thus, for instance, *ær*-clauses are less frequent than *siþþan*-clauses in *Beowulf*, occurring 8 ×, with *ær þon* 1 ×, beside *siþþan* 56 ×. *Ær* adverb, however, is more frequent than *siþþan* adverb, occurring 52 × and 21 × respectively. *Elene* agrees with *Beowulf* in this, with *ær* adverb 22 ×, *siþþan* 16 × and *ær* conjunction 6 ×, *siþþan* 12 ×. Similarly, in *Juliana* the figures are *ær* adverb 15 ×, *siþþan* 3 ×, but *siþþan* conjunction and *ær*, *ærþon* are of equal

51 E.g. 1 × in *Genesis A* and *B* and *Daniel*, beside *Christ II* 3 ×, *Juliana* 2 ×, *Elene* 1 ×.

52 See F. Wenisch, *Spezifisch anglisches Wortgut in den nordhumbrischen Interlinearglossierungen des Lukasevangeliums* (Heidelberg, 1979), pp. 96–100, and, for the suggestion that this *ac* is a conjunction, B. Mitchell, 'Old English *ac* as an Interrogative Particle', *NM* 78 (1977), 98–100.

53 *Forþam* is found 18 × in verse, beside *forþon* 306 × and *forþan* 58 ×. For interchange of *forþan* and *forþon*, see *The Old English Orosius*, ed. Bately, pp. 14/15 and 139/16.

54 E. W. Chambers, *Beowulf: an Introduction*, 3rd ed. (Cambridge, 1959), pp. 117–20. For the importance of 'sentence-words' as an indication of authorship of prose works, see E. Liggins, 'The Authorship of the Old English Orosius', *Anglia* 78 (1970), 289–322.

55 For these and other temporal conjunctions, see Cameron and Amos, 'A Reconsideration', p. 66. It should be noted that the preposition *oþ* is found only in part 3, where it occurs 3 ×. I follow Bessinger in taking *siþþan* (lines 470 and 2064) to be adverbial.

56 I exclude the verse psalms of the Paris Psalter from the following survey in view of the close structural links between this version and the Latin psalms.

frequency (4:3:1); while *Christ II* has only adverbial *ær* (6 ×) and conjunction *siþþan* (4 ×). Again *siþþan* conjunction occurs more frequently than *oþþæt*, *oþþe* (56:34) in *Beowulf*, as in the Cynewulf canon (15:3) and *Exodus* (10:5); but in *Genesis A* and *Daniel* the reverse is true, with *oþþæt*, *oþþe* preferred to *siþþan* (38:22 and 18:13 respectively).

Similar fluctuations are found in the frequency of use of *siþþan* adverb and *æfter*. However, *siþþan* is by far the commoner of the two forms in the corpus as a whole, exceptions to the rule being due to particularly low numbers of instances of *siþþan*, as opposed to a relative increase in the frequency of *æfter*. Thus, for instance, there are equal numbers of *siþþan* and *æfter* in Exodus (2:2), *Daniel* (2:2), *Fates* (1:1) and *The Seafarer* (1:1), while *Christ II* has *æfter* 1 ×, *siþþan* adverb never. In *Beowulf*, however, *siþþan* adverb is preferred to *æfter*, as it is also in *Juliana*, *Andreas*, *Genesis A* and B and *Guthlac A* and B, while it is the only adverb form of 'afterwards' in *Elene*, *Phoenix*, *Judith* and *Christ I* and *III*.[57] Indeed, *æfter* adverb in any sense is very rare in the poetic corpus, the largest numbers of instances in any text apart from the Paris Psalter being found in *Genesis A* and *Andreas* (each 6 ×) and *Beowulf* and *Genesis B* (each 4 ×).[58] As regards the common collocations of *siþþan* adverb, *Beowulf* stands apart with *a siþþan* (a collocation otherwise found only 1 × in verse, in the Paris Psalter) used twice, in parts 1 and 3,[59] beside *siþþan a* in *Andreas* (2 ×), *Christ and Satan*, *Guthlac B*, *Phoenix* and the *Metres of Boethius*. The collocation *ær ne siþþan* (part 1 1 ×) is unique to *Beowulf* and *Christ I*, the normal collocation being of *ær* and *siþ*, as, for instance, in *Beowulf* part 3 *ær ond sið*, *Guthlac A* and *Christ III ær oððe sið*, *Guthlac B ær ne sið*, with the Cynewulf canon using *ær ne sið*, *ær ond sið*, *ær oþþe sið*, *sið ond ær* and *sið oððe ær*. We may compare *Guthlac A ær oþþe æfter*. The range of choices in these other texts shows that the difference in usage between parts 1 and 3 of *Beowulf* is not of itself necessarily significant.

The frequency of conjunction *siþþan* similarly varies from text to text. It is most common in *Beowulf*, where it occurs 56 × in 3182 lines with no marked difference in this distribution between the three parts. The text with the next greatest numbers is *Genesis A*, with twenty-two instances in 2319 lines. However, in its proportion of *siþþan* constructions per 100 lines of text, *Beowulf* (as parts 1 and 3 within it) is comparable only to *Exodus* and *Daniel* amongst the

57 In *Beowulf* the distribution of *siþþan* and *æfter* is Part 1, 9:3; Part 2, 6:1, Part 3, 6:1. Cf. *Andreas*, 8:6; *Genesis A*, 33:6. Usage in the Cynewulf canon is *Juliana*, 3:1, *Elene*, 16:0, *Christ II*, 0:1, *Fates*, 1:1.

58 *æfter* is more often used as a postposition than as a pure adverb; see, e.g., *Genesis A*, line 1143, *Beowulf*, line 2816. See also the constructions *æfter þon*, *æfter þissum* etc., not included in the discussion here. Never found are *æfter þæm þe*, *æfter þon þe* etc.

59 Cf. *a forð siþþan* (*Metres of Boethius* and Paris Psalter each 1 ×; *awa siþþan* (Paris Psalter 1 ×).

longer poems.[60] All three parts of *Beowulf* show a preference for *siþþan* conjunction over *siþþan* adverb, this time a preference shared by fewer than half of the other longer poetic texts.[61] The majority of verse texts, like the prose, use *siþþan* conjunction relatively rarely. In this connection it is interesting to note the marked differences between the three poems once known collectively as *Christ*, with *Christ I* using only *siþþan* adverb (7 ×) and *Christ III* having a preference for the adverb (4:1), but *Christ II* using only the conjunction (4 ×). Similarly, *Guthlac A* prefers the conjunction to the adverb (7:5) and *Guthlac B* the adverb to the conjunction (10:5).

It is, however, not only the frequency of occurrence of *siþþan* conjunction that is of potential significance to studies of authorship, but also the way in which it is used. And here the verse usage differs interestingly from the prose. In prose, the subordinate clause introduced by *siþþan* frequently opens a sentence. In the Old English Orosius, for example, the normal position of the *siþþan*-clause is in first place, where it occurs 17 ×, with ten instances in second place, following the main clause, and one instance intercalated in the main clause. Usually the substance of the *siþþan*-clause has already been given, and this clause is a repetition, serving to put its main clause in a 'historical' perspective. Thus, for instance, 90/21–3: 'He Alexandres wisan besceawade, swa he hit hine eft ham bebead on anum brede awriten; 7 siþþan hit awriten wæs, he hit oferworhte mid weaxe.' Occasionally, however, it does not merely repeat an existing link in a narrative chain, it replaces it. Thus, for instance, the chain *a*) Antigones seized Alexander's family; $b^1$) Cassander discovered this; $b^2$) after he discovered this, *c*) he joined other leaders against him, with a pattern $ab^1b^2c$, is reduced to a pattern $ab^2c$: 'Antigones to þæm fæstenne for þær Alexandres laf wæs 7 his sunu 7 hie þær begeat . . . Siþþan Cassander þæt geascade, þa geþoftade he wið Ptholomeus' (Or. 80/30–81/2). This telescoping of $b^1$ and $b^2$ is never found in sentences where the subordinate clause follows its principal. Correlation occurs 8 ×; more common is the pattern *siþþan . . . þonne*. We may compare the usage in the works of King Alfred, where about half the uncorrelated *siþþan*-clauses follow their principal.[62]

In the verse excluding *Beowulf*, by contrast, the normal position of the subordinate clause is after the main clause, though occasionally it is

[60] *Beowulf*, 1 per 56·8 lines; *Exodus* 1 per 59; and *Daniel*, 1 per 58. We may compare *Genesis A*, with 1 per 105·4; *Elene*, 1 per 110; *Juliana*, 1 per 182·7; and *Christ II*, 1 per 107.

[61] *Beowulf*, 56:21; *Andreas*, 14:8; *Daniel*, 13:2; *Exodus*, 10:2; *Guthlac A*, 7:5; *Juliana*, 4:3; *Judith*, 4:1; *Fates*, 3:1. For the opposite, see, e.g., *Genesis A*, 22:33; *Elene*, 12:16; *Guthlac B*, 5:10; *Genesis B*, 3:6; *Metres of Boethius*, 2:31; *Christ III*, 1:4.

[62] See Liggins, 'Authorship', pp. 296–8. Ælfric uses *siþþan*-clauses surprisingly rarely. For a survey of prose usage, see A. Adams, *The Syntax of the Temporal Clause in Old English Prose* (New York, 1907).

intercalated, with material belonging to the main clause both preceding and following it. Indeed only seven works have the subordinate clause in initial position in the sentence, with single instances in *Christ II*, *Elene*, *Daniel* and *Judith*, and two instances each in *Andreas*, *Genesis A* and the *Metres of Boethius*. In the majority of these instances the verb in the *siþþan*-clause is in the present tense and the reference normally to an event in the future. Of the exceptions all but two could be repunctuated, putting the subordinate clause in second position to the preceding clause.[63] Intercalation, either within a main clause or between a main clause and its object, occurs 14 × in seven works, *Elene* (1 ×), *Christ II* (1 ×), *Genesis A* (2 ×), and *Guthlac B* (2 ×), also *Exodus* (4 ×), *Daniel* (3 ×) and *The Wife's Lament* (1 ×).[64] Correlation is a feature only of *Daniel* and *Andreas* (each 1 ×),[65] though the use of clusters of forms, with two *siþþan*-clauses or *siþþan* adverb and conjunction in very close proximity, is a feature of *Genesis A*, *Elene* and *Juliana*, as well as of *Daniel*, *Soul and Body I* and *II*, *Solomon and Saturn*, *The Husband's Message*, *Exodus* and *Andreas*.[66] A combination of all three features is thus found only in *Daniel*, though two of the three occur in *Elene* and *Guthlac A*. Extension, that is the following of a *siþþan*-clause by a co-ordinate clause or by appositional material, is relatively frequent.

In *Beowulf* there are no sure instances of the *siþþan*-clause in head position.[67] Intercalation occurs 6 ×, all in that part of the poem which precedes the account of the dragon fight, but including the 'bridging passage' which joins Beowulf's Homecoming to the dragon episode;[68] clustering is found in four places, one in part 1, one in part 2, and two in part 3, with correlation occurring twice, in parts 2 and 3.[69] Extension is very commonly employed, throughout the poem. Apart from the limited distribution of intercalation, therefore (and it will be noted that of the poems attributed to Cynewulf only two have this

63 Capable of repunctuation are *Elene*, line 913, *Judith*, line 189, and *Andreas*, lines 1223 and 1337. In *Daniel*, line 661 a *siþþan*-clause occurs in head position, but in correlation with a following adverb; in *Christ II*, line 629 no narrative sequence is involved. The other instances are *Genesis A*, lines 1824 and 2854, and *Metres of Boethius* 24/25 and 29/31.

64 *Elene*, line 1050, *Christ II*, line 445, *Genesis A*, lines 2249 and 2677, *Guthlac B*, lines 935 and 1239, *Exodus*, lines 64, 132, 316 and 503, *Daniel*, lines 109, 459 and 759 and *The Wife's Lament*, line 3.

65 *Daniel*, lines 661–4, and *Andreas*, lines 1379–81.

66 *Genesis A*, lines 1136/8 and 2696/2698, *Elene*, lines 502/504/507, *Juliana*, lines 606/609, *Daniel*, lines 454/455/456/459 and 659/661/664, *Exodus*, lines 499/503, *The Husband's Message*, lines 22/24, *Solomon and Saturn*, lines 323/325, *Soul and Body*, lines 20/22 and *Andreas*, lines 1674/1678. In *Guthlac B*, lines 984/985/988 and 1040/1043 there are clusters of adverbs, also in *Elene*, lines 481/483 and 636/639 and in *Phoenix*, lines 577/579.

67 Line 2072 can be taken as concluding the previous sentence.

68 *Beowulf*, part 1, lines 115, 656; part 2, lines 2012, 2051 and 2124; part 3, line 2201.

69 *Beowulf*, part 1, lines 1198/1204/1206; part 2, lines 1947/1949/1951; part 3, lines 2351/2356 and 2911/2914; and *Beowulf* 2071/2072 and 2201/2207.

feature), there appears to be little difference in usage between the three parts of *Beowulf*. However, it is from an analysis of content rather than of position that the most interesting findings emerge.[70]

Since *siþþan* is a temporal conjunction, the primary function of the clauses which it introduces is to set the main clause in a context in time, whether in the sense 'after' or the sense 'since the time that'.[71] However, in the poems other than *Beowulf* the reference is very rarely to time of day or time of year. In single references in *The Phoenix*, *Genesis A* and *The Battle of Brunanburh* the coming of dawn or morning is described in terms of the appearance of the sun, while in *Judith* it is God's action in sending forth light that defines the time of the action in the main clause.[72] Time of year is even more rarely expressed through a *siþþan*-clause, the one instance that I have noted being an oblique one:

Heht nu sylfa þe
lustum læran þæt þu lagu drefde,
siþþan þu gehryde on hliþes oran
galan geomorne geac on bearwe. (*The Husband's Message* 20b–3)

*Siþþan*-clauses relating to 'historical' time outside the limits of a poem's narrative are only slightly less rare and serve mainly for amplification. *Phoenix*, lines 129–31 and *Juliana*, lines 497–500, for instance, refer to Creation, *Maxims*, lines 192–3 to the murder of Abel, while in *Daniel*, lines 4–7 a *siþþan*-clause is used to set the story of the attack by Nebuchadnezzar on the Jews in Jerusalem in the context of Moses and the exodus from Egypt. These references are by definition non-essential to the story-line. Similarly non-essential is a slightly larger group of *siþþan*-clauses relating to stages not in the world's time but in the individual's, or referring back to an earlier event in an individual's life that is not part of the main narrative of the poem. For instance, in *The Wife's Lament* the speaker refers to her growing up, in an intercalated *siþþan*-clause:

Ic þæt secgan mæg,
hwæt ic yrmþa gebad, siþþan ic up weox,
niwes oþþe ealdes, no ma þonne nu.[73] (2–4)

The largest group of *siþþan*-clauses, however, relates to 'historical' time within the limits of the poem's narrative line. These clauses normally refer to an event already mentioned in the narrative and are placed after the main clause,

70 In the following survey I exclude references to future events referred to in dialogue; also, except where otherwise stated, to the Paris Psalter.

71 The sense 'seeing that' is first recorded by *OED* from the Lambeth and Trinity Homilies.

72 *Phoenix*, lines 117–19, *Genesis A*, line 2439, *Brunanburh*, lines 13–16 and *Judith*, line 189.

73 In *The Wanderer*, on the other hand, although the death of friends and kinsmen is also outside the narrative line as conceived by the speaker, it is a piece of information which is of key importance to an understanding of the poem as a whole.

forming a pattern in the narrative $ab^1cb^2$. As in the prose, $b^2$ can be widely separated from $b^1$; thus, *Genesis A*, lines 1417–19,

For famig scip L and C
nihta under roderum, siððan nægledbord,
fær seleste, flod up ahof,

where the subordinate clause picks up a reference in line 1388, or as in *Guthlac A*, where there are repeated references to the saint's move to the wilderness. In these instances the $b^2$ clauses serve mainly as amplification. Sometimes $b^2$ is in close proximity to *a* and *c*, not infrequently containing a variation on $b^1$ and including related but slightly different material, as in *Andreas*:

Hærn eft onwand,
aryða geblond. Egesa gestilde,
widfæðme wæg. Wædu swæðorodon,
seoðþan hie ongeton þæt ðe god hæfde
wære bewunden, se ðe wuldres blæd
gestaðolade strangum mihtum.[74] (531–6)

And, as in prose, $b^1$ is sometimes dispensable, being implicit in the context. So, for instance, in *Juliana* we are told that the ruler summoned Juliana's father (*a*) and they spoke together (*c*). That the father obeyed the command and came to meet the ruler ($b^1$) does not need to be spelled out in prose or in verse. However, the poet includes an allusion to this stage in a $b^2$ clause, with 'they met' reduced to the selective detail 'they leaned their spears together':

het ða gefetigan ferend snelle,
hreoh ond hygeblind, haligre fæder,
recene to rune. Reord up astag
siþþan hy togædre garas hlændon,
hildeþremman. (60–4)

Similarly, in *Genesis A*, line 1236, a $b^2$ clause is used to produce an envelope pattern, rounding off a section dealing with the life history of Lamech, which has *siþþan* adverb or conjunction no fewer than three times:

Sunu æfter heold,
Lamech leodgeard, lange siððan
woruld bryttade. Wintra hæfde
twa and hundteontig þa seo tid gewearð
þæt se eorl ongan æðele cennan,
sunu and dohtor. Siððan lifde
fif and hundnigontig, frea moniges breac

74 Similarly *Daniel*, line 109 and *The Dream of the Rood*, lines 71–2.

wintra under wolcnum, werodes aldor,
and V hund eac; heold þæt folc teala,
bearna strynde, him byras wocan
eaforan and idesa. He þone yldestan
Noæ nemde, se niððum ær
land bryttade siððan Lamech gewat. (1224–36)

Here again the immediate sequence of events is dealt with by elements *a* and *c*, with *c* following logically upon *a*, while $b^2$ spells out an intervening stage which is dispensable. However, occasionally *b* is an 'essential' ingredient in a narrative sequence, with *c* representing a 'non-essential' personal (often emotional) reaction to it, and in this case too $b^1$ is sometimes omitted. Authorial preference plays a significant rôle here. The majority of instances have a main clause denoting pleasure, terror or unhappiness resulting from the event expressed through the subordinate clause, and are confined to a handful of texts – *Andreas*, *Elene*, *Juliana*, *Judith* and *Exodus*. Some form part of a sequence 'he spoke: they were sad/happy when they heard what he said', or 'they travelled: they rejoiced when they arrived'. Thus, in *Elene*, lines 237–51 we are told that Elene set sail and that

Wigan wæron bliðe,
collenferhðe, cwen siðes gefeah,
syþþan to hyðe hringedstefnan
ofer lagofæsten geliden hæfdon
on Creca land. Ceolas leton
æt sæfearoðe sande bewrecen . . .[75]

A variation of this, with new information, occurs in *Andreas*. When the saint journeys to the beach, we are told:

Se beorn wæs on hyhte,
syðþan he on waruðe widfæðme scip
modig gemette. (239–41)

Effect followed by cause in other $acb^2$ contexts, including a disruption of the narrative sequence in order to provide comment on it, is found only in *Andreas*, *Elene* and *Exodus*. Usually the stage in the narrative expressed by the *siþþan*-clause is either predictable from the preceding material or foreshadowed by it, as, for instance, in the sequence 'he spoke; they took action when they heard the speech', found in *Elene*, lines 998–1002 and 1006–16.[76]

[75] Similarly, *Elene*, line 57, *Juliana*, line 609, *Andreas*, lines 43, 455 and 893, *Judith*, line 160, *Exodus*, line 155, *Guthlac A*, line 723 and *Guthlac B*, line 1049; also ('they became wiser') *Andreas*, line 1677. Cf. *Andreas*, line 1223, with the *siþþan*-clause in first position unless repunctuated.

[76] So also *Andreas*, line 1223, repunctuated.

Sometimes, however, the *siþþan*-clause follows a comment on the action, as in *Elene*, lines 225–30, where we are told that the *eorla mengu* hastened to the shore, and that

Ða wæs orcnæwe idese siðfæt,
siððan wæges helm werode gesohte,

while in *Judith* the account of the approach of the Assyrians is interrupted by a reference to the insults the Israelites had experienced at their hands and the revenge subsequently taken:

Him þæt hearde wearð
æt ðam æscplega eallum forgolden
Assyrium, syððan Ebreas
under guðfanum gegan hæfden
to ðam fyrdwicum.[77] (216–20)

We may compare *Exodus*, with an intercalated clause providing information that is new but not essential to the narrative line:

. . . Fyrdwic aras
Bræddon æfter beorgum, siððan byme sang,
flotan feldhusum.[78] (129–33)

However, on one occasion both *c* and $b^2$ are essential components of the narrative sequence, with *c* the result of the event described in $b^2$, and depending upon it. In this instance the relationship between *a*, *b* and *c* is such that the postponement of *b* in some form until after *c* is abnormal and as a result has considerable dramatic force. Thus, in *The Dream of the Rood* what is really the central event in the poem, the death of Christ, is announced in a *siþþan*-clause, in a manner which relegates it to second place to the cross's experiences:

Bysmeredon hie unc butu ætgædere. Eall ic wæs mid blode bestemed
begoten of þæs guman sidan, siððan he hæfde his gast onsended. (48–9)

*Siþþan*-clauses in *Beowulf* fall into groups similar to those outlined above. However, there are a number of striking differences of distribution and usage between the poem and the rest of the corpus. First of all, *siþþan*-clauses are used to denote time of day no fewer than ten times, compared with a total of four in the rest of the verse. Five of these are either intercalated or followed by a co-ordinate or subordinate clause. Thus, for instance:

[77] See also *Elene*, line 1036 and *Phoenix*, line 224, where the poet is focusing on the loss and return of life, with the destruction and resurrection of the body in secondary position; and cf. *Andreas*, line 1075, with material foreshadowed in line 999.

[78] Also *Elene*, lines 116, 502 and 1050.

Gewat ða neosian, syþðan niht becom,
hean huses (115–16)

and

Wyrd ne cuþon,
geosceaft grimme, swa hit agangen wearð
eorlum manegum, syþðan æfen cwom,
ond him Hroþgar gewat to hofe sinum.[79] (1233–6)

All these clauses occur in parts 1 and 2 of the poem. However, the absence of this type from part 3 need not be an indication of a change of authorship. Only in the Grendel story does the alternation of night and day play a structural rôle,[80] while in the dragon episode the emphasis is on completion of an action or an event *before* the change from night to day, with the dragon returning to its lair 'ær dæges hwile' (line 2320) and the beleaguered Geats at Ravenswood being rescued at break of day, 'somod ærdæge' (line 2942), the *siþþan*-clause that follows immediately afterwards serving a very different function in the poem's patterning.

Again as in the rest of the poetic corpus, a number of *siþþan*-clauses set the main clause in the 'historical time' of the poem or in the life-span of one of its characters, without being essential to the narrative line. Thus, for instance, relating to points in the individual's life, we have the intercalated clause of line 656:

Næfre ic ænegum men ær alyfde,
siþðan ic hond ond rond hebban mihte,
ðryþærn Dena buton þe nu ða,

and, relating to 'historical' time within the poem's span, lines 2351–2, with their following co-ordinate clause:

he ær fela
nearo neðende niða gedigde,
hildehlemma, syððan he Hroðgares,
sigoreadig secg, sele fælsode,
ond æt guðe forgrap Grendeles mægum
laðan cynnes.[81] (2349b–54a)

However, by contrast to the usage in other poems, a large proportion of these *siþþan*-clauses, while not actually playing a part in the basic narrative line, contribute significantly to the body of information contained in the poem, often by sketching in one of those passages that in the past have been labelled as 'digressions'. Thus, *siþþan*-clauses in lines 886, 901 and 1689 introduce

[79] See also lines 413, 604, 648, 1077, 1784, 2072, 2103 and 2124.

[80] Usually marked also by a reference to Hrothgar seeking his bed. [81] See also line 1235.

accounts of the killing of a dragon by Sigemund, the decline of Heremod and the destruction of the giants. A cluster of *siþþan*-clauses (lines 1197–1207) introduces allusions to Hama and the necklace of the Brosings and to Hygelac's last expedition. This expedition is referred to again through the agency of a *siþþan*-clause in line 2914, while accounts of God's feud with Cain are similarly twice introduced by *siþþan*-clauses, in lines 106 and 1261. An important sub-group involves a 'flashback' in the course of the telling of a story. Thus, after Finn's death is announced, the poet spends six lines describing the events leading up to this, while at the very beginning of the poem a similar technique allows the poet to have the success of the Danes and of the Scylding dynasty as his main theme, and to fill in details of Scyld's mysterious arrival and childhood.[82]

Once again this usage, which is unique to *Beowulf*, extends to more than one section of the poem, being found in the accounts of the fights against Grendel, Grendel's mother and the dragon.

If we turn to the other main use of *siþþan*-clauses, that is as part of the narrative sequences *ab*¹*cb*² or *acb*², we yet again find that *Beowulf* differs in its usage from the rest of the corpus and that all three parts share these unique features. Thus, beside instances of *ab*¹*cb*², where *b*² is straightforward variation on *b*¹ – as in

[Hreðel] Godes leoht geceas;
eaferum læfde, swa deð eadig mon,
lond 7 leodbyrig, þa he of life gewat.
þa wæs synn ond sacu Sweona ond Geata,
ofer wid wæter wroht gemæne,
herenið hearda, syððan Hreðel swealt,
oððe him Ongenðeowes eaferan wæran
frome fyrdhwate . . .[83] (2469b–76a) –

we find instances where *b*² contains material of substance not found in *b*¹ (a feature not found in the other poems), as for instance the name of the dead father in the account of Ingeld's marriage:

Meaht ðe, min wine, mece gecnawan,
þone þin fæder to gefeohte bær
under heregriman hindeman siðe,
dyre iren, þær hyne Dene slogon,
wealdon wælstowe, syððan Wiðergyld læg,
æfter hæleþa hryre, hwate Scyldingas?[84] (2047–52)

[82] Lines 1148–9 and 6–7. See also lines 1945–51 and 2435–40.

[83] See also lines 1472 and 2388.

[84] See also lines 2501–2.

In all these cases the basic information given in the subordinate clause has already been provided and $b^2$ serves mainly as amplification. However, as in the rest of the corpus, $b^1$ in certain positions can be omitted and $b^2$, though following its principal, then takes over $b^1$'s rôle as the link in the sequence of events. And as in a handful of other poems, the principal, *c*, can describe an emotional response or reaction to the event described in $b^2$ or be a comment on it. Thus, for instance, in lines 129–33, after a reference to Grendel's fighting strength being made plain, Hrothgar is said to suffer *þegnsorge*,

> syðþan hie þæs laðan    last sceawedon,
> wergan gastes,

while in lines 1306–9 he is described as *on hreon mode*,

> syðþan he aldorþegn    unlyfigendne,
> þone deorestan    deadne wisse.[85]

However, in *Beowulf* these $b^2$ clauses are not only more frequent in occurrence but also sometimes contain material totally unpredictable from the context. Thus, for instance, beside a reference to the arrival of Grendel's mother at Heorot, followed by a comment on what happened when she burst into the hall (*acb*$^2$), an event not previously signalled but obviously inevitable –

> Com þa to Heorote,    ðær Hring-Dene
> geond þæt sæld swæfun,    þa þær sona wearð
> edhwyrft eorlum,    siþðan inne fealh
> Grendles modor    (1279–82) –

we find a reference to the expedition by Beowulf to the mere, followed by a comment on the people's reaction to the discovery of Æschere's head (also *acb*$^2$, but with $b^2$ conveying a new piece of information that is all the more startling because of its subordinate position):

> . . . he færinga    fyrgenbeamas
> ofer harne stan    hleonian funde,
> wynleasne wudu;    wæter under stod
> dreorig ond gedrefed.    Denum eallum wæs,
> winum Scyldinga,    weorce on mode
> to geþolianne,    ðegne monegum,
> oncyð eorla gehwæm,    syðþan Æscheres
> on þam holmclife    hafelan metton.    (1414–21)

As Irving comments, this is 'a sentence constructed rhetorically to convey the maximum shock, by the delayed naming of the object found'.[86]

[85] See lines 834, 982, 1775 and 2630.

[86] E. B. Irving, *A Reading of Beowulf* (New Haven, Conn., 1968), p. 79. See also *Beowulf*, ed. Klaeber, p. lvii.

Similarly in part 3, after a graphic description of how the Geats were besieged and threatened by Ongentheow, being promised death in the morning, we are told:

Frofor eft gelamp
sarigmodum somod ærdæge,
syððan hie Hygelaces horn ond byman,
gealdor ongeaton, þa se goda com
leoda dugoðe on last faran, (2941b–5)

an emotional response dramatized by the very word order.[87] This relegation of an important and 'unpredictable' stage in the narrative to a subordinate clause is found also after other kinds of head-clause, and these are not infrequently significant links in the narrative chain, of a type which, as we have seen, occurs elsewhere only in *The Dream of the Rood*. Thus, for instance, in lines 721–2 the result of Grendel's thrust at the door of Heorot is described before the action itself – letting the audience become aware of events in the order in which they would have been perceived by the Danes in the hall:

Duru sona onarn
fyrbendum fæst, syþðan he hire folmum æthran.

Likewise, the result of Beowulf's blow directed at Grendel's dead body is seen before it is described:

Hra wide sprong,
syþðan he æfter deaðe drepe þrowade,
heorosweng heardne, ond hine þa heafde becearf, (1588–90);

while, at the tense moment when Beowulf has fallen to the ground and it seems that he is about to be killed by Grendel's mother, we are told that

halig God
geweold wigsigor: witig Drihten,
rodera Rædend, hit on ryht gesced
yðelice, syþðan he eft astod (1553–6)

the syntax contributing to the poet's general narrative technique in this section of the poem, whereby the audience is kept guessing until the very last minute as to who will be victorious in the contest. This technique is repeated in line 2092.[88]

Similarly in part 3 the order *acb*², with disruption of narrative order, is displayed in the account of Hygelac's unexpected rescue of the Geats:

[87] See Irving, *A Reading*, p. 188.

[88] See also line 2092. If *Andreas*, line 1337 were repunctuated, it would show a similar treatment.

Þa wæs æht boden
Sweona leodum, segn Higelaces
freoðowong þone forð ofereodon,
syððan Hreðlingas to hagan þrungon. (2957b–60)

Finally in lines 1970–80 the poet leaps from a description of the preparations for Beowulf's arrival at Hygelac's court to a picture of him seated in the hall beside his king, a passage which the most recent prose rendering translates in the order $ab^2c$.[89]

Proof of single authorship for *Beowulf* as we have it cannot be founded on a limited analysis of selected linguistic details. However, a study of the handling of *siþþan* not only provides no evidence against the theory that one man was responsible for all three parts, it demonstrates the truth of Peter Clemoes's words, that although to many *Beowulf* seems like 'a sleeping monster, they would prefer not to disturb . . . the poem remains a primary force to be reckoned with'.[90]

89 See also lines 2201–3 with intercalation.

90 P. Clemoes, 'Style as a Criterion for Dating the Composition of *Beowulf*', *The Dating of Beowulf*, ed. Chase, p. 173.

# Index of Manuscripts

# Index of Old English Words

Only words whose form, meaning or use have been discussed in some detail have been included. All variant spellings and dialectal forms have been recorded.

# General Index

# General index

# General index